Civilising Criminal Justice

An International Restorative Agenda for Penal Reform

Edited by

David Cornwell

John Blad

and

Martin Wright

Civilising Criminal Justice
An International Restorative Agenda for Penal Reform
Edited by David Cornwell, John Blad and Martin Wright

ISBN 978-1-904380-04-7 (Paperback)
ISBN 978-1-908162–51-9 (Adobe E-book)
ISBN 978-1-908162-52-6 (Kindle/Epub E-book)

Cover design © 2013 Waterside Press. Design by www.gibgob.com

Cataloguing-In-Publication Data A record can be obtained from the British Library.

e-book *Civilising Criminal Justice* is available as an ebook and also to subscribers of Myilibrary, Dawsonera, Ebrary and Ebscohost.

Printed by CPI Group (UK) Ltd, Croydon, CR0 4YY.

Main UK distributor Gardners Books, 1 Whittle Drive, Eastbourne, East Sussex, BN23 6QH. Tel: +44 (0)1323 521777; sales@gardners.com; www.gardners.com

USA and Canada distributor Ingram Book Company, One Ingram Blvd, La Vergne, TN 37086, USA. (800) 937–8000, crders@ingrambook.com, ipage.ingrambook.com

Australia distributor Ingram Book Company, see ipage.ingramcontent.com

Published 2013 by
Waterside Press Ltd.
Sherfield Gables
Sherfield-on-Loddon
Hook, Hampshire
United Kingdom RG27 0JG

Telephone +44(0)1256 882250
E-mail enquiries@watersidepress.co.uk
Online catalogue WatersidePress.co.uk

Civilising Criminal Justice

An International Restorative Agenda for Penal Reform

Edited by David Cornwell, John Blad and Martin Wright

With a Foreword by John Braithwaite

❊ WATERSIDE PRESS

Table of Contents

Part 1: Civilising Procedure   47

3   **Retribution and/or Restoration? The Purpose of our Justice System
    through the Lens of Judges and Prosecutors**   115
    Borbála Fellegi

4   **Crime and Justice: A Shift in Perspective**   151
    Louis Blom-Cooper

5   **Civilising Civil Justice**   171
    Ann Skelton

6 **Seriousness: A Disproportionate Construction and Application?** 187
Christine Piper and Susan Easton

Part 2: Civilising Theory

7 **Civilisation of Criminal Justice: Restorative Justice Amongst other Strategies** 209
John Blad

Foreword

Many of the authors in this collection are people I have admired for their depth of character for a long time. I like to think they are attracted to this topic because there is also a depth of character, resolve combined with humility about capacity for error, to restorative justice as a movement for the transformation of society. The editors of this volume have done a wonderful job in assembling a distinguished and thoughtful group of writers on the past and future of restorative justice.

Some of the most civilising gems of restorative justice practice and writing do not use the expression restorative justice. A good example is Robert Baruch Bush and Joseph Folger's 1994 book, *The Promise of Mediation: Responding to Conflict through Empowerment and Recognition*. I like to read this work as a micro-theory of how to advance the civilisational virtues of what Lode Walgrave in this volume conceives as republican values. Empowerment and recognition are the key micro-foundations for building a democratic civilisation in Bush and Folger. Empowerment gives citizens voice in a democracy; it transforms them from being weak and alienated to becoming strong and contributing. Recognition means acknowledgement and empathy for the struggles of others. A brilliant micro-insight is that it is recognition that helps us move from being self-absorbed to being 'responsive'. At this micro-level, being responsive means being attentive and open to others so citizens can become part of the project of transforming relationships. Responsiveness means for Bush and Folger being attentive and open to others, prepared to see their point of view and responding to their good faith with trust.

Those who have read Shadd Maruna's great book, *Making Good: How Ex-Convicts Reform and Rebuild their Lives*, will see some common threads with all of this, though Bush and Folger contribute their helpful language of empowerment, recognition, responsiveness. Responsiveness born of recognition and strength born of empowerment are mutually reinforcing, enabling 'compassionate strength'. Relationships can be transformed on a foundation of compassionate strength from being destructive and demonising to constructive, connecting and humanising. We can conceive of connecting with one another's humanity as the micro-foundation in civility of a democratic republic. Conversely, alienation and demonisation are the micro-foundations of totalitarianism and authoritarianism. One civilising way of seeing restorative justice is as a method and a value frame for promoting the exit from alienation to compassionately strong citizenship. The path is via recognition and empowerment.

Civilising criminal justice is a great theme, but a tall order. Of all the great institutions passed down to western civilisation by the Enlightenment, none has been a greater failure than the criminal justice system. As Fred McElrea's chapter explains, one reason is that it has been less adaptive than other institutions, less responsive to transformations to the environment in which it operates. The practice of medicine of a century ago would be unrecognisable to a doctor training in the 21st century. As recently as a century ago, an encounter with a doctor was just as likely to leave a patient worse as better off. Medicine has been evidence-based in a way law has not. Encounters with the courts and prisons not only accelerate rather than decelerate criminal careers in a large proportion of cases, they also usually leave victims and affected family members feeling more damaged as a result of either the process or the outcome of the trial, or both. Restorative justice is of course not the only reform that would grow were our law to become more responsive and evidence-based.

When one reflects on a chapter such as Ann Skelton's in this book, one has to ask oneself how the institutionalised stupidity of British law could have run so deep that it learned nothing from centuries of colonialism in Africa, New Zealand and beyond. Of course some credit must be given to post-colonial South African, New Zealand or Canadian law to have drawn some quite potent lessons from indigenous law in recent decades. But was there anything one can identify in metropolitan British law that was learnt from the indigenous legal traditions of its colonies during the colonial era? Again, British medicine did learn a lot from indigenous medicine; British law did not. It was not a learning tradition. One reason is that the practice of law was a state-sanctioned cartel to a degree that the practice of health care was not. Some contestation to medicine came from competing professions such as pharmacy, physiotherapy, psychology and from 'traditional medicine' imported by immigrants that included technologies such as massage, meditation and acupuncture. Much of the western learning from indigenous medicine was actually mediated by the research of private pharmaceutical corporations running randomised controlled trials with indigenous therapies.

To be fair, British law since the mid-1990s has begun to learn from ubuntu, from mana, from healing circles, if not in the language of their creators. It is thanks to the assertiveness of British characters communicating in very British ways, such as Martin Wright and Sir Charles Pollard, that these lessons were put to good use in Britain during the past two decades. Likewise, one might say that The Netherlands has learnt more from the restorative communications of a John Blad than from the insights of generations of scholars of adat traditions from Indonesia. In my view there is also a great deal that western law could learn from Sharia law such as its much stronger commitment to the right of victims to forgive, with the state waiving punishment. Scratch the average westerner and you find underneath a person for whom learning from the superior wisdom of Sharia law on some issue is quite a strange or offensive idea. Even allowing Sharia law the space to operate in their society for Muslims who choose to believe in it is something westerners approach with profound reluctance or disdain. In some respects reluctance is justified, of course, because there are specific ways that Sharia law is a threat to rights even more dangerous than western law. Westerners are people who believe in the civilisational superiority of western law, deeply. Fictional narratives of the glorious contest between defence and prosecution to discover the truth are promulgated by the western media in collaboration with a legal profession who like to promote this fictional distortion of the production-line injustice system they in fact administer. Again there are exceptional media products that show the way the law puts the poor in prison and white bankers in the House of Lords, but these are not the standard fare.

So it does fall to social movement politics to offer an alternative narrative, to show new paths that pick up the evidence of superior ways of doing justice from other cultures, while preserving strengths of western law that the evidence shows to be real. None of this is to deny that many of those strengths of western law, like the idea of various separations of powers, and limits on abuse of power, are profound. Moreover, this volume shows through its contributions from some exceptionally distinguished western lawyers, that reformers from within western law can be exceptional in their wisdom.

Lode Walgrave points out in his chapter that 'Civilising Criminal Justice' to some could mean abolishing criminal law and replacing it with civil law, to others it could mean bringing greater civility to criminal justice. Elements of both options get some sophisticated attention in the scholarship of this volume. Robust critique of restorative interpretations of civility also provide some of the high points of the book.

It is early days in the grafting of restorative justice into western justice. Many mistakes have been made. Many more are yet to be discovered by probing research designs. Recent criminological re-framings of the limits and the effectiveness of Peelian policing, that has been with us for almost 200 years, are instructive. These re-framings have transcended the nihilism of just a couple of decades ago that investment in policing was irrelevant to crime control. Now we know that smart policing that is evidence-based can make a major contribution to crime prevention; dumb policing can waste taxpayers' money and even make crime worse.

It will take many decades of better science than we have now to know what is smart and dumb restorative justice, what is smart judicial justice and dumb judicial injustice (and prosecutorial injustice). This is because evidence-based policing (like correctional rehabilitation) is a big step ahead of evidence-based adjudication. The great thing about the leadership of David Cornwell, John Blad and Martin Wright in putting this collection together is that it makes some wonderful strides in refining an agenda of contests to be explored in that future empirical and normative work. This volume is a fine start to a project of civilising criminal justice that will challenge our grandchildren and theirs.

John Braithwaite
Australian National University
June 2013

Contributors

Dr Per Andersen (Norway) has been General Director of the National Mediation Service of Norway since 2004. It is a nationwide service with about 90 staff members, 650 mediators, and 22 local offices, besides the central office. From 1991 to 2004 he held positions in various Ministries, including Assistant Director General, Ministry of Justice and the Police. He has made presentations at conferences in Albania, Italy, Latvia, Scotland and Spain, hosted delegations to Norway from European and Far Eastern countries, and led projects in Albania and Latvia supported by the Norwegian Ministry of Foreign Affairs and the Mediation Service.

Professor John R Blad (The Netherlands) is Associate Professor of Criminal Law at Erasmus University, Rotterdam, founder of the Dutch Forum for Restorative Justice, and editor of the Dutch/Flemish *Journal for Restorative Justice* (*Tijdschrift voor Herstelrecht*). He is a co-editor of this work, and has published widely in the fields of criminal law and restorative justice. His PhD was awarded in 1996 on the work of Louk Hulsman: 'Abolitionisme als Strafrechtstheorie', Deventer: Gouda Quint. In 2011 he co-edited and reviewed, with René van Swaaningen, a re-print of Hulsman's most important articles in: *De Ontmaskering van het Strafrechtelijk Discours*, Den Haag: Boom Juridische Uitgevers. In 2012, he co-edited with Janny Dierx and others *Mediation in Criminal Matters* (*Mediation in Strafzaken*), Den Haag: SDU.

Sir Louis Blom-Cooper QC (United Kingdom) taught criminology and penology at Bedford College, University of London (1961–1981), and as a barrister practised in both criminal and civil cases. He was Chair of the Mental Health Act Commission (1987–1994), and Judge in the Court of Appeal of Jersey and of Guernsey (1988–1996). A former Chair of the Press Council (UK), he was also the first Independent Commissioner for the Holding Centres in Northern Ireland. He was also Chair (and later Vice-President) of the Howard League for Penal Reform, and of Victim Support, and has published many books on criminology and penology, including *Fine Lines* *and Distinctions: Murder, Manslaughter and the Taking of Human Life* (2011, Waterside Press) (with the late Terence Morris).

Jean-Pierre Bonafé-Schmitt (France) is a researcher in the sociology of law at the *Groupe d'Etude de Médiation, Centre Max Weber* (CNRS-University Lyon II). He also teaches mediation and conflict resolution in several universities. He founded the Master of Mediation at the University of Lyon II. He is also a founder of the *Boutiques de Droit* in Greater Lyons and the *Association Médiation de Lyon* (AMELY). He was a co-founder of the *Réseau des Médiateurs Associés*, and the *Centre d'Etude et de Formation des Médiateurs Associés*. He was vice-president of the INAVEM (*Institut National d'Aide aux Victimes et de la Médiation*) and other organizations. His books include *La Médiation: Une Justice Douce* (2002, Syros-alternative); *La Médiation Scolaire par les Élèves* (2000, Editions ESF); and *La Médiation Pénale en France et aux Etats-Unis* (2010, Editions REDS/Lextenso).

Dr David J Cornwell (United Kingdom) is a consultant criminologist and author, and a former prison governor and tutor at HM Prison Service College, Wakefield, UK. He has wide experience of custodial corrections in both the public and private sectors as a practitioner in the UK and at Bloemfontein in the Republic of South Africa. He is the author of a trilogy of books on restorative justice: *Criminal Punishment and Restorative Justice* (2006), *Doing Justice Better* (2007), and *The Penal Crisis and the Clapham Omnibus* (2009) all published by Waterside Press, and of numerous journal articles and conference papers. David Cornwell has undertaken consultancy assignments under the auspices of the Council of Europe in Poland (Themis Plan), and visited prisons in a number of European countries.

Dr Susan Easton (United Kingdom) is Reader in Law at Brunel Law School, a barrister and editor of the *International Journal of Discrimination and the Law*, published by Sage, and Director of the Criminal Justice Research Centre. Her books include: *Sentencing and Punishment: The Quest for Justice* (2012, OUP, 3rd edn.); *Prisoners' Rights: Principles and Practice* (2010, Routledge); *The Case for the Right to Silence* (1998, Ashgate); and *The Problem of Pornography: Regulation and the Right to Free Speech* (1994, Routledge). She has previously lectured at the Universities of Sussex and Sheffield. Susan Easton has a particular research interest in prisoners' rights, including voting rights, and the experience of imprisonment.

Professor Christine Piper (United Kingdom) is Professor of Law in the Law School of Brunel University. Her research and teaching interests are focused on family and child law and policy, sentencing and youth justice. Her books include: *Investing in Children: Policy, Law and Practice in Context* (2008, Willan Publishing/Routledge); *Sentencing and Punishment: The Quest for Justice* (with S. Easton, 2012, OUP, 3rd edn.); *How the Law Thinks about Children* (with M King, 1990, 1995, Ashgate); and *The Responsible Parent* (1993, Harvester Wheatsheaf/Simon & Schuster). She is an Associate Director of the Brunel Law School's Criminal Justice Research Centre and Family Law Research Group, and a member of the editorial board of *Child and Family Law Quarterly*. Christine Piper's current research interests include issues in youth justice.

Dr Borbála Fellegi (Hungary) PhD (ELTE), MA (ELTE), MPhil (Cantab) is the founder and Executive Director of the Foresee Research Group, and in that capacity is the leader of several national and international restorative justice-related research and action projects. Previously, she was a researcher for the European Forum for Restorative Justice and a consultant for the Council of Europe, the UNDOC, the National Crime Prevention Board, and the Office of Justice in Hungary. Among other publications, she is the author of *Towards Restoration and Peace* (2009, Napvilag), one of the first comprehensive studies of the implementation of restorative justice in Hungary.

Professor Serge Gutwirth (Belgium) is a Professor of Human Rights, Legal Theory, Comparative Law and Legal Research at the Faculty of Law and Criminology of the *Vrije Universiteit Brussel* (VUB), He holds a ten-year research fellowship in the framework of the VUB-Research contingent for his project 'Sciences and the Democratic Constitutional State: A Mutual Transformation Process'. Serge Gutwirth founded and still chairs the VUB-Research group Law Science Technology and Society. He publishes widely in Dutch, French and English and participates in interdisciplinary research projects. Serge Gutwirth is particularly interested in technical legal issues raised by technology (particularly in the field of data protection and privacy) and in more generic issues related to the articulation of law, sciences, technologies and societies.

Professor Paul De Hert (Belgium) holds the chair of 'Criminal Law', 'International and European Criminal Law' and 'Historical Introduction to Eight Major Constitutional Systems' at the *Vrije Universiteit Brussel* (VUB). In the past he has held the chair of 'Human Rights', 'Legal Theory' and 'Constitutional Criminal Law'. He is Director of the VUB-Research group on human rights (HUMR), Director of the Department of Interdisciplinary Studies of Law (Metajuridics) and a core member of the research group Law Science Technology and Society (LSTS). He also teaches the course 'Privacy and data protection' in the Institute of Law and Technology at Tilburg University. Paul De Hert is a board member of several Belgian, Dutch and (other) international scientific journals.

Dr Tapio Lappi-Seppälä (Finland) is the Director of the National Research Institute of Legal Policy and a member of the Finnish Academy of Sciences. Alongside his current position he has been acting as a part-time Professor in Criminology and Sociology of Law at the University of Helsinki. His long career as a senior legislative adviser in criminal law in the Ministry of Justice, includes memberships and chairmanships of several law reform committees. He has participated in international co-operation in criminal justice issues in the Scandinavian Research Council for Criminology, Council of Europe, in the International Penal and Penitentiary Foundation (Vice President 2005–2009), and in the European Society of Criminology (Member of the Board 2008–2010). Tapio Lappi-Seppälä's publications include several books, research-reports and articles on criminology, penal policy, sentencing and the system of sanctions.

Judge F W M (Fred) McElrea MA (New Zealand), LLB (Otago) LLM (Lond.) Dip Crim (Cantab) retired from full-time work as a judge after more than 20 years on the Bench, but still works part-time as a District Court Judge, Auckland District Court, New Zealand. He is Deputy Chair of Development Board, Restorative Justice Centre of Aotearoa/New Zealand, AUT University, Auckland, New Zealand.

Dr Federico Reggio (Italy) holds a PhD in Philosophy of Law, Method and Legal Traditions at the University of Padua, where he works as Senior Research Fellow (Department of Private Law and Jurisprudence). His research fields include restorative justice and theories of punishment, mediation, conflict resolution, legal methodology and argumentation. He is a member of the Verona Bar Association, as well as a professional civil mediator (2009-) and a trainer of civil mediators in Italy. In 2008, with a scholarship from the Verona University School of Law, he undertook research on 'Restorative Justice: Theoretical Foundations and Practical Applications', at the Centre for Justice and Peacebuilding, Eastern Mennonite University (Harrisonburg, Virginia, USA). Federico Reggio has written numerous articles and his book *Giustizia Dialogica: Luci e Ombre della Restorative Justice* (Milan: FrancoAngeli, 2010) was one of the winners of the competition for works by young scholars in the Italian Society of Philosophy of Law (2012).

Dr Ann Skelton (Republic of South Africa) is Director of the Centre for Child Law at the University of Pretoria, South Africa. Her doctoral thesis examined restorative justice with specific reference to children in the criminal justice system. She has published in South Africa and internationally on restorative justice including 'RJ as a Framework for Juvenile Justice Reform' (2002), *British Journal of Criminology*, vol.42, Issue 3, pp.496–513. She was also a member of the editorial committee of the *UN Handbook on Restorative Justice*, and (with Buyi Mbambo) a contributor to Lode Walgrave's notable work *Repositioning Restorative Justice* (Willan, 2003).

Dr Claire Spivakovsky (Australia) is a Lecturer in Criminology at Monash University, Australia. She has worked in the academic, community and government sectors conducting research into issues of social exclusion and disadvantage. Her first book, *Racialized Correctional Governance: The Mutual Constructions of Race and Criminal Justice*, was published in Ashgate's Advances in Criminology Series in early-2013.

Professor Thomas Trenczek (Germany) is Professor of Law at the University of Applied Sciences, Jena, an accredited mediator/trainer, and Director of *Die Waage* Dispute Resolution Centre in Hanover, Germany. He holds both German state law degrees, a PhD in law as well as an MA is Social Sciences. Since 1986, he has worked in the fields of dispute resolution, mediation and restorative justice, and is the author of several books, book chapters and conference/journal articles including *Law in Mediation* (2006), *Victim-Offender-Mediation and Restorative Justice in Europe* (2005), *Conflict Management in Civil Society* (2005) and *Mediation in Germany* (2003).

Professor Bas van Stokkom (The Netherlands) is a philosopher and sociologist. He has been a co-worker of the Centre for Ethics, Faculty of Philosophy, Radboud University Nijmegen, The Netherlands. He is Assistant Professor at the Criminological Institute, Radboud University, and Lecturer at the Faculty of Social Sciences, Free University, Amsterdam. His research concentrates on the fields of freedom of speech, deliberative democracy, restorative justice, and punishment ethics. Bas van Stokkom is secretary of the Dutch-Flemish journal *Tijdschrift voor Herstelrecht* (*Journal of Restorative Justice*) and co-editor of the studies *Images of Restorative Justice Theory* (2008), *Reflections on Reassurance Policing in the Low Countries* (2008), and *Public Forgiveness in Post-Conflict Contexts* (2011).

Professor Dr Lode Walgrave (Belgium) is Emeritus Professor in Criminology at the KU Leuven University in Belgium. He is a founding member and Chair of the International Network for Research on Restorative Justice and of the International Association for Criminology of Youth. He has researched in the field of restorative justice extensively. It was through his initiative that the Belgian government introduced restorative justice in the reformed Belgian Youth Justice Act from 2006 after a trial period by means of an action research project. He has contributed chapters to most of the recent international readers on restorative justice. His most recent book is *Restorative Justice: Self-Interest and Responsible Citizenship* (2008). In 2008, Lode Walgrave received the European Criminology Award.

Dr Martin Wright (United Kingdom) is a Senior Research Fellow at the Faculty of Health and Life Sciences at De Montfort University, Leicester, UK. He is a former Librarian of the Institute of Criminology, University of Cambridge, Director of the Howard League for Penal Reform, and Policy Officer for Victim Support. He was also a founder member of the European Forum for Restorative Justice, and of the (British) Restorative Justice Council. He is a volunteer mediator in Lambeth, South London, and with the CALM Mediation Service in West London. Martin Wright has been a prominent writer on restorative justice since the early 1990s, is an honorary fellow of the Institute of Conflict Resolution, Sofia, and holds a Diploma from the Polish Centre for Mediation. In 2012, he received the European Forum's European Restorative Justice Award. His books include *Making Good: Prisons, Punishment and Beyond* (reprinted 2008), and *Restoring Respect for Justice* (2nd edn. 2008). He was also co-editor of *Images of Restorative Justice Theory* (2007), and co-author of *Rebuilding Community Connections: Mediation and Restorative Justice in Europe* (Council of Europe, 2004).

The Author of the Foreword

John Braithwaite is a Distinguished Professor at the Australian National University, author of ground-breaking works on restorative justice and recipient of various awards including, in 2005, the Emile Durkheim Prize of the International Society of Criminology, for his lifetime contributions to that subject.

Editorial Preface

The Journey of this Book

This work has its origins in our belief that in the present era increasing numbers of academics, practitioners, and even some politicians are coming round to the reluctant conclusion that many criminal justice systems are simply 'not fit for purpose', and that 'more of the same' will not make them so. More specifically, that the machinery of criminal justice has expanded and intruded into the everyday lives of citizens to the point of becoming over-complex and also increasingly repressive. If this machinery needs to be re-designed, there may be much merit in returning to a considerably wider use of civil justice processes as a means of restoring justice to its principal stakeholders — offenders, victims of harm, and communities.

Civilising Criminal Justice has survived a protracted period of preparation, delayed beyond its originally projected publication date due to a number of technical and other exigencies which need not distract the reader. Persistence has been rewarded, and the resulting volume is rich in its wealth of insights into the shortcomings of contemporary criminal justice systems and its prescriptions for 'doing justice better' in the future.

As an editorial team we are deeply grateful for the patience and forbearance of the international group of authors who have contributed their time and considerable experiences to participation in this work. The challenging nature and thought-provoking content of their essays is both wide-ranging and intellectually stimulating, though also a chilling reminder of the extent to which justice 'systems' worldwide fall short of meeting the reasonable expectations of their stakeholders.

We have had to accommodate inevitable differences in authorship style, presentation, linguistic usage and translation in the process of compilation, but have attempted as far as possible to preserve the essential nature of the contributions as submitted by each of the authors. The diversity of the approaches towards 'civilising' criminal justice has, not surprisingly, caused much heart-searching in arriving at the most appropriate and logical grouping of chapters within the three parts of this volume.

Part I with its title 'Civilising Procedure' deals predominantly with structural issues relating to the delivery of justice, both historically and in its contemporary needs for renewal and improvement. Contributors to this part include David Cornwell (United Kingdom), Judge F. W. M. (Fred) McElrea (New Zealand), Borbála Fellegi (Hungary), Sir Louis Blom-Cooper QC (United Kingdom), Ann Skelton (Republic of South Africa), and Christine Piper and Susan Easton (United Kingdom).

Part II is devoted to 'Civilising Theory' within justice in a range of different contexts both civil and criminal. Within this part will be found essays by John Blad (The Netherlands), Serge Gutwirth and Paul De Hert (Belgium), Bas van Stokkom (The Netherlands), Federico Reggio (Italy) and Lode Walgrave (Belgium).

Part III places the focus of attention on 'Civilising Practice' with particular emphasis on the delivery of justice to offenders, victims and communities, and in the wider context of social institutions. It includes chapters by Martin Wright (United Kingdom), Thomas Trenczek (Germany), Jean-Pierre Bonafé-Schmitt (France), Claire Spivakovsky (Australia), Per Andersen (Norway), and Tapio Lappi-Seppälä (Finland). The latter two contributions in particular indicate vividly how significant change can be, and has been, achieved where there is a will to do so.

In the final section of the work we provide a short concluding commentary highlighting the principal issues arising from the three parts described above. We are hopeful that those who read this volume will be, as we have been, impressed by the positive and constructive approach that the contributing authors have brought to their deliberations on 'civilising' justice. That we perceive restorative justice as having a major part to play in such an important process will be self-evident: how this can be achieved by enabling restorative practices to take their place in the mainstream of justice delivery remains a challenge to which, we believe, this work fully responds.

In addition to the contributing authors, we would wish to mention and warmly thank a number of friends and colleagues for their assistance and encouragement during the compilation of this work. In particular we have had invaluable help from Helen Curtis, Jen Cowan, Robert Shaw, Joke Rademakers-Pesch and Sheila Guyot-Sutherland all of whom, in different ways have contributed immensely to the finalisation of this work. We also acknowledge with gratitude the support and encouragement of Bryan Gibson and the staff of Waterside Press, and thank them for their patience and perseverance in the course of this journey.

Introduction

The full title of this book — *Civilising Criminal Justice: An International Restorative Agenda for Penal Reform* — suggests that a number of different questions and issues may be implied from its original conception. Among these are questions about why criminal justice should be 'civilised', and, indeed, what is meant by 'civilising'? Why is an international agenda necessary? And further still, what is the nature of the penal reform considered desirable or essential, and how could it be brought about?

As the commissioning editors for this work, a criminal lawyer, a university research fellow and a former correctional practitioner, we found the debates arising from the questions both challenging and sometimes also almost confrontational. In the course of reading and assembling the much valued contributions of those whose chapters appear in this work, it became strikingly evident that we were far from alone in our differently internalised perceptions of the procedural, theoretical and practical issues implicit in the above questions. Moreover, we suspect that this 'uncertainty' remains deeply embedded in the situation in which restorative justice finds itself in relation to criminal justice 'systems' and practices throughout our contemporary world.

There are many and varied references within this book that suggest a broadening of civil justice processes to include matters of civil conflict and harm that presently lie within the domain of criminal justice. Indeed, it is within the fast-expanding area of mediation that there appears to be considerable potential for resolving disputes and inter-personal incidents presently classified as criminal offences to the satisfaction of all the parties concerned. It may be the case that different structures beyond the present confines of either civil or criminal justice may prove to be the best placed to foster reconciliation, reparation and restoration within the community setting rather than in the formal procedures of the courts.

Civil law, with its lesser standard of proof, may also be an adequate response to the investigation, adjudication and resolution of many less serious incidents of wrongdoing with less delay and cost than are common in criminal courts. Civil court procedures, with their less formal and ritualistic traditions, language and customary behaviours, might additionally prove more beneficial and less intimidating to witnesses and victims of offences — particularly those of a 'domestic' nature, or committed within a community setting.

Proponents of the restorative justice 'agenda' as a means towards the reform and improvement of criminal justice delivery within many established and emerging democracies worldwide have many different starting points in what promises to be a long journey towards the realisation of their goals and ambitions. Indeed, ever since the early and somewhat tentative expressions of restorative philosophy by Albert Eglash, Howard Zehr and others, such principles and desirable practices as could be identified with clarity quickly acquired a 'contextual coating' that became relevant to the differing situations in which restorative practices seemed to be appropriate and acceptable.

National identities, cultures and traditions heavily shape political and social attitudes towards justice processes whether these are civil or criminal in nature. The adversarial Anglo-Saxon and the inquisitorial Roman traditions exemplify essential differences of approach both within and beyond national boundaries. It is small wonder, then, that the explicitly critical questioning of the *status quo* inherent in the emergent restorative justice prescriptions for 'better justice' should be greeted with other than an (at the least) equivocal response.

These difficulties notwithstanding, restorative justice and its related practices have established at least a foothold within the criminological *psyche* of many nations as the chapters of this volume record. However tentative this foothold may be, and however admirable the prescriptions, restorative justice still faces the difficulty of convincing its sceptics that it is no 'new-fangled', primarily anti-retributive, 'soft on crime' agenda for reform: rather, that it seeks to do a number of things that 'traditional justice' leaves largely undone. Restorative justice requires that offenders take responsibility for their offence(s), offer apology to those offended against, and, where possible and appropriate, make reparation to victims of crime either directly or indirectly. Traditional justice makes no such demands.

Clearly a fully restorative response cannot be used in all cases. Where the accused denies involvement in the crime, a court process will be required to determine guilt or innocence. The offender's lack of remorse does not necessarily rule out a restorative process, because it can produce a change of attitude, but a judgement has to be made as to whether a meeting (or indirect contact through 'shuttle diplomacy') risks harming either participant. Where the offender is not found or the victim does not wish to take part, partially restorative measures such as support for victims and programmes for victim awareness will be required. Some sanction will be needed if the offender does not complete the reparation he or she has undertaken (provided that he or she was given a fair opportunity to do so): and for the minority where there is a substantial risk of serious re-offending, limitation or deprivation of liberty becomes inevitable. But it should be focused on reparation to the victim or the community, protection of the public and eventual reintegration of the offender, and not on punishment for its own sake.

One of the important threads that runs through this volume is the suggestion that it may be advantageous to re-examine the classification of certain (and mainly less serious) offences presently defined as crimes with a view to dealing with them as 'civil wrongs' requiring a lesser standard of proof than the 'beyond reasonable doubt' requirements of criminal law. If such a revisionary course were to be pursued, much time and expense could be saved in the criminal courts with the added possibility (and advantage) of resolving such cases through the use of restorative practices to the satisfaction of all parties to such wrongdoing—states, victims, offender and communities.

As the contributions to this work also clearly show, the *naissance* of restorative and reparative practices in different countries over the past two decades has resulted in a many-faceted situation in different stages of development and acceptance. The 'handed-down' traditions of justice administration are deep-rooted within many democracies, widely grounded in a somewhat fundamentalist legacy of retributivism which has a particular resonance for politicians, the mass media, and for the more affluent and influential sectors of societies. The latter in particular, perceiving offending as predominantly the wilfully deviant and antisocial product of fecklessness and 'normlessness', consider it more appropriate to demand punishment rather than correction as the primary response to crime.

Restorative justice, while acknowledging the need for sanctions as a response to illegal and harmful behaviour, seeks to reverse these deep-seated attitudes in a constructive manner that encourages pro-social behaviour and an awareness of the harm done to victims and to communities. It requires and facilitates offenders to 'put wrongs right' by accepting responsibility for the harm done, making apology for it, and by making reparation to those harmed. Where there is a willingness on the part of offenders to undertake such actions, restorative processes become the means by which they become enabled, empowered and encouraged to do so. Such a response is entirely different from that of punitive justice which makes no such demands.

This is, we venture to suggest, the core element of 'civilising justice', although as this volume shows, there are many different approaches evident in attempting to achieve this vision of 'better justice'. Viewed even more broadly, restorative practices have actual and potential applications more widespread than the relatively confined space of criminal justice. 'Civilising justice' also implies a wider *social* agenda to repair harm and resolve disputes in a variety of 'every day' situations in schools, employment, community relations, policing, and it might also be suggested, even in government and politics.

In pursuing these aims, restorative practices have had, and continue to have, to 'swim against the tide' of traditional responses to social problems. It is largely for this reason that progress in many modern democracies towards achievement of a restorative vision has been piecemeal and tentative. The core values of 'restorativism' do not sit comfortably alongside 'tough on crime' political agendas, strident media demands for ever more punitive responses to criminal activity, and the clamour of increasingly affluent populations for 'protection' from the depredations of those who opt to indulge in law-breaking behaviour — for whatever reasons.

And yet responses to illegal and antisocial behaviour remain widely ambivalent and frequently disproportionate. The 'misdemeanours' of those who manipulate and defraud economies of vast sums or wilfully invade personal privacy frequently evade justice beyond an extent of public censure, whereas the comparatively lesser 'crimes' of thieves and robbers, sexual deviants and the predatory call for public protection through ever-increasing use and duration of prison custody. Difficult as it may be to make sanctions reasonably proportionate to the seriousness of crime, justice remains ill-served by the evident imbalances in severity that impact most heavily upon the already most socially disadvantaged members of many contemporary societies.

'Civilising' criminal justice is also about repairing and reducing these and other forms of social harm and inequality as many of the chapters in this volume evidence from different perspectives. In so doing, the authors demonstrate many ways in which restorative principles and practices can 'make a difference' to the quality and security of the lives of citizens, those harmed by wrongdoing, and those who offend. This leaves the reader with the inevitable and uncomfortable question of what can practically be done to promote such reform and change?

Significant change requires a considerable measure of social consensus, tolerance, and a genuine willingness to seek the common good. It requires a move away from entrenched attitudes, pre-dispositions and traditional responses, and abandonment of populist prejudices in the interests of social cohesion and inclusiveness rather than of exclusiveness. Punishment is essentially exclusive: correction is potentially inclusive, and this is the essential difference that 'civilising' justice can achieve. Two particular chapters to be found in the concluding part of this volume, by Per Andersen (*Chapter 16*) and Tapio Lappi-Seppälä (*Chapter 17*), provide outstanding examples of how social consensus, once reached, can transform justice.

However, Howard Zehr, frequently referred to as the 'grandfather' of restorative justice, likened viewing its relationship with 'traditional' justice to a process of *'changing lenses'*, or of adopting a new focus for crime and justice (Zehr, 1990 and 1995). Even though at the outset he tended to view the retributive and restorative concepts of justice as 'polar opposites' to a marked extent, he later modified this view — following Conrad Brunk (2001: 31–56) — towards acceptance of the fact that the two are not entirely mutually exclusive (Zehr, 2002: 58–9). Within this volume the reader may perceive a similar perspective in what we have termed the 'civilising' process. And herein may be seen an evident dichotomy that proponents of restorative justice need to resolve if its prescriptions are to have the necessary credibility to enter the mainstream of criminal justice administration.

Proponents of restorative justice may be seen to fall into two distinct categories. The first of these categories includes those who perceive it as an *augmenting* agenda *within* criminal justice for dealing more effectively and humanely with certain types of offender who are genuinely amenable to its requirements (as stated previously) and wish to make amends for their wrongdoing. The second category of proponents includes those who see restorative justice as a *replacement* agenda that will, ultimately, overtake traditional criminal justice as the preferred means of dealing with all types of offender and offences. The implications of both of these approaches are evident within this work. The former agenda is essentially that of a pragmatic acceptance that lasting change is best attempted incrementally and by persuasion: the latter perceives the need for a more radical reform philosophy grounded in new ethical principles that will ultimately prove socially more beneficial once tested and implemented.

Either way, however, the change envisaged seeks to promote 'better criminal justice' than that widely encountered in many contemporary democracies. It implies facing many challenges, not the least of which is that dealing 'justly' with both the remorseful and the remorseless, the penitent and the impenitent offender. In its wider context, the restorative ethic perceives disputing parties as 'stakeholders' in a potential mediation process designed to reduce or limit harm and collateral damage, and promote social cohesion. Whether these ambitions will lead to making justice more 'civilised' the reader must decide.

Overview of the Chapters

In *Chapter 1,* Dr David Cornwell sets the scene for *Part I* with an historical account of the development of criminal justice philosophies and policies in England and Wales during the post-World War II decades of the 20th-century and into the present millennium. He also identifies a number of 'mythical' constructs and discourses that have critically affected this process of development, and the political influences that have contributed to the continuing penal crisis that has beset the criminal justice system for the past two decades in particular. He traces the emergence of a Ministry of Justice from 2007, but questions whether this will achieve much in making criminal justice more 'systematic', or, rather, merely replace one monolithic structure with another.

Cornwell reflects that the risk-averse political climate fuelled by media clamouring for increased public protection has generated a more widespread use of penal custody and an increase in its duration on the basis of predictive incapacitation. Worse, even, is the escalation in the use of indeterminate sentencing with the implementation of the provisions within the Criminal Justice Act 2003 for sentencing to imprisonment for public protection (IPP), and wider use of life sentences for offences other than murder. He also argues for a form of 'bifurcation' in sentencing that would enable offenders willing to accept responsibility for their crimes and make apology and reparation to victims for the harm caused, to be dealt with according to restorative justice principles. However, for the unrepentant and incorrigible offender, and those whose offences are heinous, it is accepted that 'traditional' justice becomes an inevitable outcome. The latter should, notwithstanding, be sentenced in strict proportion to the seriousness of their current offences without the 'aggravating' effect of considering previous offences for which they have been punished already.

Finally, Cornwell addresses the issue of mercy in the sentencing of repentant offenders as a 'civilising' aspect of criminal justice and the avoidance of unnecessary collateral damage to those dependent on them or who would assist them in their eventual restoration to law-abiding citizenship. He also reflects upon what are termed 'Anglo-Saxon' attitudes — principally of retribution and revenge, and an uncritical belief in the efficacy of deterrence and the reliability of predictive assessment — as inhibiting factors in delivery of 'better justice'. He concludes that the restorative ethic has a future, but that this will much depend upon dismantling myths and changing attitudes and pre-dispositions that presently impede delivery of more 'civilised' justice.

In *Chapter 2*, Judge Fred McElrea, drawing extensively on the research work of Professor John H. Langbein at Yale University, USA (Langbein, 2003), traces the history of the adversary trial model from the 'altercation trial' of the 16th-century and 17th-century to the evolution of the 'adversary' system of the 18th- century and beyond to the present day. He then contrasts this adversarial mode with that of restorative processes in 12 specific aspects of trial procedure, illustrated with historical references and commentary.

McElrea analyses the ways in which restorative principles and practices could have a 'leavening' effect on the operation of an adversarial system that is deeply embedded in the Anglo-Saxon tradition of justice and altogether unlikely to see its demise within the foreseeable future. It is this entrenchment within legal structures, the legal profession and judiciaries, McElrea concludes, that consigns restorative processes to the margins of criminal justice, even though there may be encouraging signs that legislators are increasingly amenable to change.

This chapter reflects on the shortcomings and questionable practices of the adversary system that actually inhibit and impede progress in reform of trial processes and procedures. He recommends the wider development and implementation of restorative practices *alongside* rather than in place of 'traditional' justice, and that only when these have distanced themselves and become established as 'default' positions will restorative justice thrive and prosper.

In *Chapter 3*, Dr Borbála Fellegi describes the outcomes of a research study conducted with Hungarian judges and prosecutors in relation to their attitudes towards restorative justice, particularly in relation to victim-offender mediation (VOM) which in 2007 was pending implementation into Hungarian criminal law. Given that judges and prosecutors would effectively pursue the role of gatekeepers in relation to that development, the response towards it became important to assess before these officials could acquire empirical experience of VOM in its practical applications.

The research ascertained the general views of, and attitudes towards the existing criminal justice system held by judges and prosecutors, and in particular the purposes of punishment and sanctions, and the place of victims within criminal justice procedures. This was followed by an exploration of these officials' views on the demands of their working environment and their roles within criminal justice administration and the wider social structure, and, in addition, towards restorative justice and mediation in particular.

The results of the research are discussed in an analysis of the potential for the successful implementation of the legislation as internalised by the judiciary, and also a recognition that there was a measure of compatibility between the 'traditional' and restorative approaches in a number of practical areas in which the judiciary would exercise their gatekeeping role.

Chapter 4 presents a view from Sir Louis Blom-Cooper QC that the time has come for a 'shift in perspective' in criminal justice in England and Wales, and specifically in the role of the criminal courts. The English trial has two parts: determining guilt and innocence, and sentencing. Judges claim that their function includes crime control, but cases are cited which cast doubt on this. The trial is not always even a search for truth. Only a minority of cases come to trial, but when they do, victims need support and protection.

Crime control can be considered separately from due process; but restorative justice is closer to civil justice or social welfare. Crimes are very varied, and society should respond differently. Many could be dealt with by civil procedure. With offences such as rape, for example, responsibility should be established to a civil standard of proof; only then would a criminal trial be considered. Property lost through fraud can also be recovered through a civil process. Other examples are explored within this chapter, and the role of criminal justice could thus be redefined as being to ensure a fair trial, looking to civil justice to promote crime prevention and community safety.

The ultimate requirement is, as Blom-Cooper concludes, to convince politicians of the need for a more creative and less tramlined outlook on the problems of social control and criminal justice. The first step is to restore consensus among professionals and legislators in criminal justice and penal affairs. Only when the bipartisan, authoritarian approach is abandoned will we be able to re-define the boundaries of criminal justice to promote the prevention of crime, the reduction of reoffending and the public sense of community safety.

In *Chapter 5*, Dr Ann Skelton illustrates, by means of a case study, a number of facets of the difficulties inherent in 'civilising' justice. In many respects her analysis echoes that of Blom-Cooper, though focused more on issues of civil rather than criminal justice. As she notes, the theme of this book arises from the idea that the criminal justice system needs to be civilised. This encompasses two central ideas. Firstly, that current criminal justice practice is uncivilised, and is in need of reform. Secondly, that the advantage of the civil justice system is that it is the resolution of a dispute between the direct protagonists. Restorative justice writers have demonstrated how the victim is no longer a direct protagonist in the criminal justice process, as his or her role has been usurped by the state. A key aspect of civilising the criminal justice process, therefore, is reintroducing the victim as a participant in the justice process.

This chapter raises a slightly different issue. Is the civil justice process itself civilised? Despite the fact that the victim—as plaintiff, applicant or complainant (descriptions differ)—is party to the proceedings, the civil law has also become obfuscated by layers of substantive and procedural rules that frustrate the plaintiff's quest for justice. Lawyers steepen the conflict.

An assumption that a claim expressed in monetary value alone can heal the harm done to the plaintiff is inimical to a restorative justice approach.

The focus in this chapter is on one particular aspect of civil law. The claiming of damages for injury to personality is at the centre of the discussion. South Africa's rich legal heritage has created space to seek inspiration from ancient canon law, Roman-Dutch law, African customary law and modern restorative justice theory and practice in these civil claims. Recent South African case law reveals a cautious willingness to apply restorative justice principles in civil matters, which may result in the civilisation of aspects of the civil law.

The final contribution to *Part I* of this work concerned with 'civilising procedure' is that of Professor Christine Piper and Dr Susan Easton, reviewing sentencing policy in England and Wales as expressed in legislation and guidelines. Punishment is only just if it is proportionate, but how can the criteria be set? Sentencing guidance can allow for aggravation and mitigation including factors such as a more than usually serious degree of harm and the relative 'weights' of harm and culpability, for example in cases of causing death by driving, and domestic violence.

The authors express concern about whether previous convictions should incur a 'premium' or reduced mitigation, especially in the case of minimum sentences ('three-strikes laws'); can this be done without sacrificing proportionality? From a utilitarian standpoint there is little justification on grounds of deterrence, risk reduction through incapacitation, or rehabilitation, but it accords with popular ideas of justice. Balancing consistency, proportionality and populist retributivism will often not be possible. Desert theory and the principle of parsimony may limit the impact of past convictions.

They also point to the difficulties of maintaining a sense of proportionality in cases of persistent and serious offending which attracts the attention of politicians, the media and the general public alike, and of combining this with the principle of parsimony to arrive at just and reasonable sentencing outcomes. In concluding that there are evidently difficulties with the present treatment of past convictions in terms of consistency in practice, the central issue remains that of the extent to which such past conduct should affect sentencing decisions, and how far back into the past such considerations should reach.

*　*　*　*　*

In *Part II*, the focus is on 'civilising theory' in criminal justice. The chapters explore the need for a substantive theoretical underpinning and explanation of restorative justice principles amenable to agreement and adoption at both the moral philosophical and practical levels of justice delivery. This means, in effect, arriving at both a *rapprochement* between the 'maximalist' theoretical and the practitioner approaches *within* restorative thinking, and also the 'accommodations' that must be envisaged to enable 'traditional' and restorative modes of justice to co-exist within mainstream justice administration.

Chapter 7, by Professor John Blad, questions the extent to which it might be contended that in many contemporary democracies criminal justice has become increasingly 'uncivilised' in recent decades, and that this trend has resulted from an ever-increasing manipulation of centralised state power by politicians in response to media and public clamour for increased public protection and severity in sentencing. He traces the genesis of this trend within The Netherlands since the 1970s, and its outcomes and impact upon current criminal justice policies at both the strategic and practical levels.

This form of penal 'instrumentalism' has 'infected' the principles and processes of law and deflected them towards the achievement of political aims that are inconsistent with true justice. Drawing a parallel with David Garland's (2001) analysis of the emergence of a culture of control in the USA and the UK, he questions whether this may ultimately undermine the legitimacy of the nation state in its relationship with its citizens. Indeed, the pursuit of social control may be seen to result almost inevitably in an increase in harshness towards offenders, many of whom already suffer the effects of social marginalisation.

Restorative strategies are perceived in this analysis as one of a number of means by which this trend might be reversed with concomitant social advantages, and it is to this prescription that Blad turns in the later part of his essay. Like Easton and Piper he is critical of the effects of weighting sentencing decisions with considerations relating to previous convictions, of misplaced belief in the efficacy of deterrence, and of reluctance to afford victims of crime a reasonable extent of recognition and participation in justice processes. And like McElrea also, Blad proposes that various 'civilising influences' should be considered in an agenda to bring about a procedural revolution which could bring traditional and restorative justice processes closer together, and ultimately into a partnership of mutual and social benefit.

In *Chapter 8*, Professor Bas van Stokkom questions the claim advanced by some advocates of restorative justice (among others) that expression of remorse by offenders should attract a sentencing discount beyond being considered as a mitigating factor. Just deserts theorists, however, dispute such a notion on the basis that sentencing uniformity is disturbed by such a consideration. He is, notwithstanding, a proponent of mitigation in limiting the harshness of sanctions, though concerned that too great an emphasis tends to be placed on factors that mitigate gravity (harm and culpability), and less on the personal factors and life circumstances of offenders.

The just deserts *versus* individualised sentencing debate has many facets which Van Stokkom acknowledges and discusses: at the least these include considerations of repentance, guilt and harm recognition, acceptance of responsibility, a willingness to make amends, and yet the need for some relativity in treating like cases similarly as a much claimed aspect of 'fairness'. The issue of the place of mercy in the sanctioning process may be viewed as a balancing factor that falls between these considerations, and may provide the 'key' to a dual-track sanctioning process which could deal 'justly', if not necessarily uniformly, with the differing circumstances and attitudes of offenders.

Rationales of personal mitigation and discretion ultimately have to be accommodated alongside those of culpability and harm in sentencing processes: 'humanistic' and 'mechanistic' approaches both have their proponents, but the larger question is that of which serves the cause of justice most effectively. Van Stokkom assesses the value systems that sustain both, acknowledging that both retribution and restoration have a proper place in such considerations. He concludes that the essential difference between the remorseful and the remorseless ultimately justifies a differentiation in the way in which both are treated, and that this is the more likely to promote responsibility and the reduction of crime.

Though far from defending the present-day conduct of criminal justice in Western Europe, Professors Serge Gutwirth and Paul De Hert, in *Chapter 9*, contend that restorative justice is principally an ideological construct that lacks convincing empirical, anthropological or legal foundation, and that rather than attempting to make criminal law more restorative, its advocates would be better employed in examination of the potential of the civil law to provide opportunities for 'horizontal' conflict resolution.

On the one hand, the scope of the criminal law should and could be considerably reduced by strategies of depenalisation and transfer of matters to the sphere of civil law: on the other hand, much can be learned from the creative and constructive way in which restorative writers have been approaching sanctions, which they mistakenly do not call punishments.

The use of criminal punishment, and especially imprisonment, should be reduced to being the ultimate resort, as it should be, and the use of imprisonment should be reduced as much as possible so that criminal procedure does not stand in the way of constructive sanctions that satisfy victims, offenders, and public prosecutors as the representatives of the criminal law. Also, in the civil law domain, much more could be done to make possible adequate repair of the harm caused by offences. But punishment is not repair, and punishment has its legitimate functions that should be recognised. Therefore, to make punishment and restoration alternatives amounts to a distortion of the realities.

In *Chapter 10*, Dr Federico Reggio proposes that while criminal justice is widely in crisis, the restorative approach suggests a decisive change in the way justice is understood. It invites us to rethink the justification, the purpose and the limits of the reaction to crime as a different 'paradigm' of justice. This transcends the purely legal debate, and it cannot be confined to the world of 'social action'. His chapter is a philosophical reflection on restorative justice, deriving from practice and still referring to it: thus the 'holistic' restorative approach to justice assumes a philosophical character.

The restorative approach relies on normative concepts requiring philosophical justification in default of which it risks becoming an 'optional view', chosen or not depending on individual opinions or on general consensus. This requires the restorative approach to reflect on its own conceptual premises and their foundations: a suggestion that may not be popular, and even at odds with a post-modern cultural *milieu* which assumes an anti-foundational perspective as some kind of dogma. It also requires a rethinking of justice beyond the need for solving situational problems, and instead addresses the roots of the question of what justice is and what justice requires.

Connecting classical legal philosophy and the contemporary debate, Reggio explores some ethical and anthropological reflections that move towards a 'dialogical' idea of justice, perceiving 'dialogue' not just as communication but also as a conceptual structure inherent in the human condition. Such a frame of reference may point towards a more humane and ethical approach to justice which, he suggests, already lies behind some of the main proposals of restorative justice, though awaiting a solid philosophical framework.

Emeritus Professor Lode Walgrave, in *Chapter II* contends that in view of the public dimension of crime, an alternative to today's criminal justice system should be a system of public law denouncing crimes, but that this does not imply the necessity for punishment. The ethical choice in responding to crime is to promote further civilisation in criminal justice, and the civilisation process of criminal punishment as described by Elias can and must be continued.

After monopolising violence in the hands of the state, and after making the use of such violence more rational and moderate, the next step is to set aside the use of violence itself in the response to offending, through solutions based on bottom-up deliberation rather than top-down imposed reactions, while preserving norm-enforcement. Restorative justice offers such a paradigm.

The dominion (autonomy) of each legal subject can be protected quite adequately by restorative justice by means of 'inverse constructive retributivism'. The public dimension of restorative justice should be constructed within a frame of 'social life ethics', including notions such as common self-interest, respect, solidarity and active responsibility. Making criminal justice more civilised means making criminal justice more restorative.

*   *   *   *   *

The six chapters that form *Part III* of this work deal with civilising practice in criminal justice, at various stages of development in establishing restorative practices and processes, and of the impact of cultural, social and political influences within the world's contemporary democracies. In other ways also, the contributions demonstrate practical interpretations of the theoretical and philosophical concepts of *Part II,* and of the procedural considerations deriving from the chapters in *Part I.*

In *Chapter 12,* Dr Martin Wright expresses the view that in spite of some humane characteristics, most Western criminal justice systems are flawed because of some of their basic assumptions. In particular, the purpose, justification and effectiveness of punishment and sentencing are discussed with regard to their effects on victims, offenders and societies. He then questions whether systems and practices dominated by restorative justice would be more civilised, stressing the new aim, process, psychology and participants that such a transformation would imply.

Wright points out that the restorative case can be argued two ways: either that in expressing disapproval and sanctions it is painful but differently so; or that the over-arching aim is to persuade people to change their behaviour, not primarily through fear of consequences to themselves, but through empathy for what their act would do to another person. As he further notes, restorative processes and sanctions have to accommodate different degrees of seriousness and harm in offending, even though in appropriate cases of serious offending (some of which he cites) there is no compelling reason why the sentencing response should not be restorative rather than inevitably retributively punitive.

Finally, Wright indicates a number of areas of offending or conflict resolution in which restorative initiatives based on mediation are replacing the traditional punitive (or censorious) responses of former years with proven beneficial effect. This sets the scene for the later contributions to *Part III.*

Chapter 13, by Professor Thomas Trenczek, discusses conflict mediation in a German context. There has been a long-lasting debate about what kind of cases are suitable for such approaches, particularly in relation to violent offending. The process of victim-offender mediation (VOM) in Germany can be appropriate and practicable for domestic violence and other violent crimes.

To explain these developments, Trenczek places the (criminal) conflict in the framework of a continuum of disputes, not focusing exclusively on VOM, but broadening the perspective towards family and other civil conflicts which are appropriate for a restorative justice approach within civil society.

He explains how conflicts escalate in a step-wise manner, and the negative nature of the behaviour of those involved as participants—particularly in court processes. He also indicates the ways in which restorative approaches can reduce this negativity, and the role of mediators in enabling this in both civil and criminal cases.

One of the main obstacles to conflict resolution is the manner in which rigid legal processes co-opt the mediation concept to suit the system's own purposes. The criminal law stands at the end of a long line of measures for social control and is supposed to be a last resort. However, like other contributors, he observes that in modern societies, social problems are increasingly frequently met by a proliferation of laws, definitions of crime, and penalties, all of which militate against the preference for solving such issues through reason, fairness and conciliation.

In *Chapter 14*, Dr Jean-Pierre Bonafé-Schmitt presents an entirely different perspective on the limited development of restorative justice in France, and the reasons for this. He notes that French justice has become more reparative with an increasing awareness of victims, partly due to influences from Quebec and Belgium, and there is a form of informal justice in France, though not as developed as that in the USA. Some restorative work is being undertaken in schools, though this is sporadic and hampered by the lack of a restorative ethic within the mainstream of criminal justice.

In France, mediation in criminal matters is mainly financed by the state, often with probation or victim support. Only prosecutors can propose victim-offender mediation, though with limited scope to do so. Within the various alternatives to formal justice, that of mediation—close to restorative justice—has declined to merely one-third of cases, while those following an entirely instrumental rationale (such as cautions) now represent two-thirds of cases.

Structures are being developed to spread mediation, but the absence of a national organization is unhelpful. Though some statistics are available, there is no culture of evaluation. Bonafé-Schmitt discusses other peace-building initiatives, but concludes that community mediation needs to re-define its relationship with civil society before real progress can be envisaged. There are deeply-embedded historical, cultural and possibly geographical reasons for the slow acceptance of restorative practices in France which, combined with its inquisitorial mode of criminal justice, may explain why that country has preferred to retain its Latin social heritage in contrast with its immediate Northern European neighbours.

In *Chapter 15*, Dr Claire Spivakovsky describes the development of restorative practices in Australia in a manner that has a curious resonance with the preceding chapter, though for entirely different reasons. In that country the young offender and adult elements have reacted entirely differently to the emergence of restorative justice: all Australian states and territories provide some form of restorative approach for their young people, while in relation to the adult system there has been a governmental reluctance to proceed beyond limited discussion of the potential to engage any adult offenders in a system based on restorative justice principles.

In the first part of her chapter she traces the position of the adult offender in contemporary literature and practice, arguing that one of the key problems facing restorative justice proponents is the insular conversations taking place in the justice arena, and a lack of consistency relating to the offender in the rehabilitation, re-integration and restorative literature, and of dialogue between these competing texts.

In the second part, Spivakovsky discusses why certain adult offender populations appear to form exceptions to this divide and, as a result, have been met within the criminal justice system with more restorative approaches. She describes the development of the Koori Courts in Victoria, Australia, to show the conditions that were necessary for Victoria's indigenous offender population to receive a more restorative response, and considers what can be learned from this process about the potential to engage other adult offender populations in a system based on restorative justice principles.

It may be of some encouragement to the reader of this work to note that its two remaining essay contributions present a more optimistic and positive assessment of how significant change can be brought about in civilising criminal justice. In *Chapter 16*, Per Anderson describes the development of restorative justice practices in Norway as an adjunct to both the criminal and civil law, and the relationship between the two in terms of mediation and conflict resolution. In common with other Nordic countries, Norway has extensive social welfare strategies, a relatively equal distribution of wealth, and one of the lowest prison populations in the democratic world. Also, a very small proportion of its population is socially marginalised and prone to higher than average rates of offending.

Involvement of local communities and lay mediators has proved to be a key to the establishment and maintenance of restorative practices, largely at the municipal level, but within a national structure of direction and supervision. The Norwegian Mediation Service, created in 1991, is regarded as part of the criminal justice system, but also has a role in the handling of civil cases. This structure, Andersen argues, had to be changed and reorganized as a state service in 2004 to optimise its cost-effectiveness and strategic direction. Though it is a hybrid system of local and national participation, it has enabled the swift spread of conferencing and mediation services throughout the country.

Andersen sees the future expansion of restorative practices as lying in four key areas: continued diversion of less serious crime; inclusion of both lesser and more serious youth crime; increasing application in dealing with domestic violence; and an enhanced role in civil disputes. He provides a detailed analysis of how this may be achieved, and of the limitations and dilemmas implicit in such a far-reaching and inclusive social endeavour.

The final chapter in *Part III*, by Professor Tapio Lappi-Seppälä, describes the dramatic reduction in the use of imprisonment in Finland in the 1950s and 1960s, which was sustained into the present millennium. In *Chapter 17*, he traces the history of the Finnish criminal justice system and its main legislative strategies during the previous century until the present decade, and in particular the emergence of a new sentencing ideology of 'humane neo-classicism' which aimed to reduce the suffering caused by the crime control system. Proportionality and deliberate reduction of strategies based on deterrence became key features of penal policy, fixing absolute upper limits on the extent of punishment while at the same time stressing the importance of personal responsibility and citizenship.

Lappi-Seppälä emphasises the fact that long-term law reform was the result of a systematic re-appraisal of both social and penal policies underpinned by a consensus between government, academic researchers, the judiciary, practitioners, the media and the public towards reduction of unnecessary cost and preservation of the tolerant Finnish culture within the context of Nordic cooperation. The rapid expansion of mediation services during the

1980s and onwards under the *aegis* of the Ministry of Social Affairs enabled alternative means of conflict resolution to be pursued beyond the confines of the criminal justice system. However, the provisions of the Mediation Act 2006 in relation to domestic and intimate violence were the subject of heated debate, and the Finnish Parliament imposed additional limitations on the use of mediation in such cases which many only resorted to on the initiative of the police or prosecution officials.

The Finnish experience in penal policy development and in particular of decarceration is an outstanding example of a pragmatic and non-moralistic approach built upon a social and political consensus to preserve a responsible and tolerant society. As the author points out, the slogan 'Good Social Policy is the Best Criminal Policy' expresses the essence of the Finnish approach: societies do better by investing in schools, social work and families than in prisons. That this has all been achieved against the tide of rising imprisonment rates, punitive fervour and reactive populist posturing evident elsewhere gives some confidence that it will be maintained in the face of the increasing neo-liberalism that has established a grip in so many Western European and other nations worldwide. The Finnish example has much to say about 'civilising criminal justice'.

At the end of the chapters, we conclude this volume with our own *Conclusions*: a summary analysis of what we perceive to be the main issues emerging from its many and varied contributory texts. Our purpose has been to open and establish a vigorous and reasoned debate about the ways in which criminal justice systems in contemporary democracies might be made more 'civilised'. If it has become evident that this is a many-faceted conversation with realisable possibilities, then our ambition will have been achieved.

References

Brunck, C. (2001), 'Restorative Justice and the Philosophical Theories of Criminal Punishment' in Hadley M. L. (ed.), *The Spiritual Roots of Restorative Justice*, Albany, NY: University of New York Press.

Eglash, A. (1975), 'Beyond Restitution: Creative Restitution?' Original Conference Paper reproduced and available at: http://www.gwu.edu/-ccps/ Bazemore.html; and also in Hudson J and Galway B (eds.) (1977),

Restitution in Criminal Justice: A Critical Assessment of Sanctions, Lexington, MA: Lexington Books, pp.91–101.

Zehr, H. (1990 and 1995), *Changing Lenses: A New Focus for Crime and Justice*, Scottdale, PA: Herald Press.

Zehr, H. (2002) *The Little Book of Restorative Justice*, Intercourse, PA: Good Books.

Part I

CIVILISING PROCEDURE

1

Justice and Punishment: Myths, Mercy and Anglo-Saxon Attitudes

David Cornwell

Setting the Scene

Within the scope of this chapter, an attempt will be made—however diffidently—to address a number of the threads of essential reasoning that emerge from the learned and challenging essay contributions within this volume. In its entirety, the work is rich in the collective wisdoms of the internationally diverse and widely respected group of participants. At its core, the book is concerned with making criminal justice systems more 'civilised' within the context of post-modern democratic societies: such is to suggest that these 'systems', if indeed they can be described as displaying coherent systemic characteristics, stand in evident need of a measure of philosophical renewal to make them 'fit for purpose' in meeting the needs of contemporary societies.

The term 'civilising' requires some explanation at the outset of the discussion. In one sense, it implies the compelling requirement for both criminal justice principles and punitive operational practices to be re-assessed with a view to making them more likely to reduce crime within societies. In another sense, it means enabling the outcomes of justice to deliver social benefits to all of the 'stakeholders' involved in criminal offending, including victims, offenders and communities. In a third sense, and closely allied to that just mentioned, the term 'civilising' entails making justice processes themselves evidently more fair, consistent, understandable and amenable to all citizens whose compliance with laws is a reasonable duty and responsibility.

As will become evident in subsequent chapters also, there is a fourth sense in which the notion of 'civilising' criminal justice could prove to be beneficial socially, economically and jurisprudentially. This lies in re-visiting the traditional classification of certain less serious (and presently criminal) offences with a view to transferring the focus of jurisdiction from criminal to civil courts as 'civil wrongs' requiring a lesser burden of proof in considerations of guilt and culpability. Such a move towards 'decriminalisation' holds a potential for these offences to be dealt with more expeditiously, at a considerably lesser cost, and with a view to mediated settlement between the parties — state, offender(s) and those offended against. The principles and practices of restorative justice provide the potential for such a transition to transform justice systems without diminution of the social or legal disapprobation of less serious wrongdoing.

The title of this chapter deliberately suggests that in Britain, as in many other countries worldwide, there is an urgent need to re-assess some of the traditionally accepted and perpetuated myths, beliefs and attitudes that impede rational progress towards much-needed penal reform. In an era of straitened national and international economic and fiscal circumstances, ways and means have to be considered and implemented towards reducing unnecessary social costs and wasteful practices. Just as important, however, is the need to challenge and re-shape essential services to deliver outcomes based upon prudence and progressive open-mindedness rather than remaining hidebound by change-resistant attitudes and political 'short-termism'. Penal systems tend to stand at the forefront of social provisions resistant to reform, proneness to being used instrumentally[1], and ultimately more

---

1. My friend and colleague John Blad provides an elegant and comprehensive explanation of the phenomenon of 'penal instrumentalism' in his own contribution later in this work. For our purposes here, and by way of a shorthand account of its adverse effect upon the delivery of justice, I confine its definition as the use of penal sanctions and processes for purposes beyond the strict requirements of law and predominantly linked to (largely unwarranted) assumptions about the efficacy of deterrence (both general and specific) within criminal punishment. The main objection lies in the excessive use of sanctions visited upon offenders for the purpose of securing the compliance of others, and to meet political rather than social rather than strictly legal objectives. But see also David Garland's parallel explanation of penal 'populism' as it developed over the closing decades of the 20th century as a means towards crime control

destructive than corrective of those subjected to the exercise of ultimate state power over populations.

An Historical Overview

Penal reform and the means towards its achievement have, over the past three or four decades, become an increasingly sensitive political issue within many democracies throughout the world. The reasons for this are complex and varied, but in criminological terms may be traced back, particularly in Britain and the USA, to the collapse of the 'rehabilitative ethic' during the early 1970s,[2] flirtation with the 'justice model' of proportionate punishment during the late 1970s, the 1980s[3] and into the 1990s, and the emergence thereafter of the 'three-strikes' and 'prison works' era of 'incarcerative' justice and social control into the present millennium.[4] We shall return to this particular sequence of events in subsequent discussion.

With the benefit of historical hindsight it may be claimed that penal reform has been dogged by persistent uncertainties about the morality of the punishment process itself extending through the post-World War II era to the present day. Dominant philosophical justifications for criminal punishment have swerved from pre-War simple retributivism through a *quasi*-medical post-War preoccupation with 'coercive cure' and rehabilitation, and thence towards the deterrence and desert-based concept of proportionality in sentencing encapsulated within the 'justice model' as a reaction to the perceived abuses of the rehabilitative era. However, the justice model with its wide appeal to a number of disparate professional groups[5], was also significantly

---

(Garland, 2002: 145–6), and the seminal account of Anthony Bottoms (1995, 17–49).

2. Known as the 'Nothing Works' era, significantly consequent upon the widely misinterpreted work of Robert Martinson (1974) and of his colleagues Lipton and Wilks (1975) in the USA. See: R. Martinson (1974: 22–54), and D. Lipton. R. Martinson and J. Wilks (1975).

3. Here see American Friends Service Committee (1972); A. von Hirsch (1976); and subsequently, B. Hudson (1987).

4. So described following upon the declaration by Michael Howard, then Home Secretary in the government of Prime Minister John Major, to the Conservative Party conference in October 1993 that: 'prison works' and that he did not flinch from measures which would increase the prison population.

5. The justice model emerged from the coalescence of a number of interest groups all of which were critical of the abuses inherent in the rehabilitative ethic. To lawyers it promised a restoration of due process and the protection of rights; to more radical penal reformers it promised an end to indeterminacy in sentencing and its implicit reliance upon judicial, professional and

flawed due to its foundational emphasis on desert and deterrence, particularly since the latter motivation for punishment was, and remains, an intuitive construct largely impossible of verification or quantification.

Subsequent disenchantment with the justice model and its concept of 'commensurate deserts' as promoted by Von Hirsch and the American Committee for the Study of Incarceration that reported in 1976 became widespread internationally, even though its subsidiary principle of limiting retribution to the minimum extent consistent with the harm caused by offences retained considerable appeal to penal reform groups focused upon policies of decarceration. The demise of the model, slow as it was due to continued (though unfounded) belief in the efficacy of deterrence, created a philosophical vacuum that could only be filled by a return to retributive agendas (in conjunction with deterrence), and a further era of what Norval Morris had described so aptly three decades earlier as 'penal rudderlessness'.[6]

The legacy of these philosophical and operational uncertainties over the justifications for criminal punishment during the post-War decades is reflected in the penal crises of escalating populations that have become persistent in many contemporary democracies across the world at the present time. Of equal concern is the fact that the causes of the crises have become rationalised into forms of political inertia stemming from their apparent inevitability. This leads inexorably to the pre-supposition that 'because things are as they are', continued crisis becomes 'business as normal'. The contributions within this volume challenge such a process of rationalisation and the myths that sustain it. Moreover, until the myths are de-mystified, significant penal reform will remain a pipe-dream. In the section of this chapter that follows, we shall explore these myths and their effects upon the prospects of civilising criminal justice.

Penal Mythology: Fantasy and Folklore

There are a number of anomalies that have traditionally been accommodated and perpetuated within the boundaries of punishment philosophy

---

administrative discretion; and to the increasingly vociferous 'law and order' lobby it promised punishment swiftly administered as 'deserved', and yet in some degree proportionate to the perceived seriousness of offences (Von Hirsch, 1976 *op. cit.*: Hudson, 1987 *op. cit.* 37–39).

6.   N. Morris (1974: 1).

and practices in Britain and in some other countries that have predominantly followed the Anglo-Saxon traditions of criminal justice. Some of these may be seen to have their origins within the punitive discourse as it has developed over centuries past: others are of a relatively more recent nature, emerging from the changing fashions within criminological thinking, particularly during the second half of the twentieth century during which the academic discipline of criminology became a reality and sought to establish its own identity.

The extensive body of literature on criminal punishment is replete with explanations of the 'supposed' justifications for its imposition. There has also existed a broad consensus among philosophers and criminologists that the practice involves the visitation of some form or other of pain or unpleasantness upon an offender for the commission of an offence proscribed by law, and of which he or she has been found guilty following an official investigation or process of adjudication by an authority legally constituted to do so.[7] As to the 'purposes' of punishment, frequently referred to as 'principles', there exists much lesser agreement: in the interest of clarity I shall propose that the former rather than the latter term more accurately reflects the motivations for the infliction of 'sanctions' on offenders proven guilty of committing criminal acts.

Now, it might be further agreed that insofar as the 'purposes' are concerned, there has also existed a widely held acceptance that retribution, deterrence and reform have historically dominated considerations relating to punishment, somewhat later augmented by the term 'rehabilitation' (often in place of reform) when the latter became regarded as an outmoded relic of the penitentiary era in Britain and elsewhere. However this may be, the preference for rehabilitation became widespread in conjunction with the 'treatment and training' model of imprisonment during the post-War period and into the 1970s, founded in the belief that offenders could, either through therapeutic or medical treatment or the processes of acquiring basic literacy and numeracy combined with practical (largely manual) skills, be enabled to live law-abiding lives thereafter.

---

7. Such a definition follows H. L. A. Hart's 'Standard Case' of punishment first set out in his (1960) 'Prolegomenon to the Principles of Punishment' (Hart, 1960: 4–5).

It is at this point that consensus in relation to criminal punishment and its translation into criminal justice policies becomes fragile and even fragmented, and for good reason because serious conceptual difficulties begin to emerge at both the philosophical and operational levels of its justification. For if punishment is to be based upon retribution which is a backward-looking stance focused on past events, then it can only be justified as a response to the free-will and illegal choices of action made by offenders. Moreover, it cannot be justified other than in some sense of strict proportion to the harm caused (or seriousness) of the offence(s) committed. Viewed in such a manner, serious objections must be raised in relation to both indeterminate sentencing[8] and the extension of sentences without release dates for the purposes of public protection.

Where criminal justice sentencing policies are based on the twin purposes of retribution and deterrence[9] the situation becomes even more objectionable. Not only is it 'unknowable' how many actual or potential offenders are in fact deterred from criminal acts by experiencing or witnessing deterrent sentences, but also it is impossible to calculate what proportion of additional punishment (in addition to that imposed in relation to the gravity of crime) is necessary to achieve a deterrent effect. For this reason the extent of sentences imposed for these purposes tends to become inflated and entirely disproportionate to the seriousness of the offence(s) actually committed. Many criminologists regard the concept of deterrence as intuitive and illusory since its effects are incalculable, and also as immoral on the grounds of punishing crimes as yet uncommitted, or of imposing additional punishment in the hope of influencing others. This much stated, however, the notion of deterrence still retains a strong mythical appeal to politicians and policy-makers

8. Indeterminate sentences include life sentences imposed without fixed terms to be served in custody being specified or a release date being calculable. Also falling within the same category would be sentences of imprisonment imposed for public protection (ISPP) or extended sentences for public protection (ESPP) such as have been available in England and Wales, and which carry a tariff period after which release is at the discretion of the Parole Board or a similar administrative body.
9. Here it will be noted that the notion of deterrence takes two forms: that of 'specific' or 'individual' deterrence designed to persuade the offender from further offending, and also of 'general' deterrence designed to dissuade persons who might be tempted to offend similarly from so doing.

who seek to be seen to be 'tough on crime', but the morality of its inclusion among the 'purposes' of punishment remains questionable in the extreme.

The collapse of the 'rehabilitative ethic' during the 1970s, indicated earlier, removed from the punishment 'debate' its only prospective emphasis, and hence also its only 'purpose' that accommodated an element of determinism.[10] Modified sociological and psychological explanations of crime and deviancy accepting an element of determinism have from time to time been advanced, the 'treatment model' within penology also having been predicated on the basis that behavioural change through medical and psycho-therapeutic inter-vention could 'cure' delinquent motivations and 'normlessness', replacing these with pro-social attitudes of a law-abiding nature.[11]

The demise of the rehabilitative 'ideal' went some way towards dispelling the further myth that true rehabilitation of offenders can take place effec-tively within the closed environment of prisons, and without any exposure to the realities of living a law-abiding life within the community. For while it is true that some preparatory work can be done in custody with prisoners in anticipation of their release, they can only resume a full place in society once they are restored to full citizenship with its freedoms and temptations. The justice model brought with it a new 'brand' of rehabilitative discourse which, while sitting somewhat uncomfortably alongside some of its more radical aspirations,[12] at least had the merit of promoting a more caring approach to

---

10. The concept of determinism, in contrast with the doctrine of 'free will' within the study of penology, originated in the Italian positivist school of criminology founded by Cesare Lombroso (1836–1909) and attended also by Enrico Ferri (1856–1929). At its core, determin-ism proposed that human actions were (and are) *caused* rather than *chosen*, and that external stimuli such as deprivation, poverty, and other adverse social conditions, rather than deliberate criminal intent account for much crime being committed. Such claims have been refuted by philosophers and lawyers on the insistence that most human beings are capable of accounting for their actions and motives, other than those suffering from mental impairment or other forms of diminished responsibility.

11. Principal contributions to the literature on deterministic approaches to the explanation of crime and delinquency may be found in the work of David Matza (1964); Howard Becker (1964); and John B. Mays (1970). However, for a comprehensive analysis see E. H. Sutherland and D. R. Cressey (1955: 74–151).

12. Such as the abandonment of indeterminate sentences (other, possibly than mandatory life sentences for murder), sentencing aimed at general deterrence, and discontinuance of coercive therapeutic regimes based on *quasi*-medical models of intervention in prisons. For an account of this development see Barbara Hudson's analysis of the 'new-rehabilitationist' agenda in B. Hudson (1987, *op. cit.*: 170–184), and also F. Cullen and K. Gilbert (1982).

correcting the social and behavioural deficits of offenders both in custody and within the arena of community sanctions.

Whether or not one believes in the practicability of rehabilitation in the prison *milieu*, the aim of rehabilitative programmes in custodial correctional settings is the reduction of crime. The return to retributive and deterrent policies during the 1990s and onwards was motivated by a populist backlash that was to a considerable extent media-inspired, and in the face of which politicians in Britain, the USA and in some European countries also were constrained (for reasons of electoral credibility) to become complicit. The 'tough on crime' mantra resonated with what has been termed 'postmodernist *angst*' (Tonry, 2003: 4; Garland, 2002 *op. cit.*: 145–6) expressed in the form of what Sir Anthony Bottoms (1995 *op. cit.*) had earlier described as 'populist punitiveness'[13], but its shortcoming was that it failed to be correspondingly 'tough on the causes of crime'.

The outcome of these successive gyrations within punishment philosophy was the creation of a 'conceptual gap' between the neo-retributive penal policies designed to achieve crime control through increasingly stringent sentencing combined with wider use of indeterminate measures, and the lingering 'welfarist' preference of academics and correctional professionals[14] for lesser and more constructive use of imprisonment, and an expansion of non-custodial sanctions. Meanwhile, continued (and misplaced) political myopia over the efficacy of deterrence ensured that it retained its status as a 'purpose' of punishment, and enhanced the severity of sentencing as a means towards crime control and public protection.

There were also a number of other 'mythical' constructs and discourses associated with the emerging 'populist' measures designed to secure public confidence in crime control during the late 1990s and into the present millennium. Foremost among these dysfunctional developments are aspects of what Garland has described so aptly as the *naissance* of a reactionary 'criminology of the other' (Garland, 2002 *op. cit.*: 137 and in particular 184–6)

---

13. See: Michael Tonry (ed.) (2003: 4); David Garland (2002 *op. cit.* 145–6); and Anthony E. Bottoms (1995 *op. cit.*: 17–50).

14. Most particularly in the fields of probation and social work, but also within the academic discipline of criminology in which the concept of 'restorative justice' was establishing increasing credibility from the early-1990s and onwards.

that has contributed towards the effective 'demonisation' of certain forms of criminal offending — most notably of a sexual nature and those forms of antisocial and acquisitive behaviour prevalent among marginalised sections of urban populations due to ethnicity and 'alternative' life-style preferences.

Of significance also among the contemporary discourses concerning criminal justice principles and policies are a number of contentious issues relevant to the morality of punishment, particularly in its preoccupation with retribution, crime control and public protection. The first of these issues concerns the morality of measures designed to deliver preventive incapacitation based upon predictions of further serious offending. It is a fact well known to criminologists that predictions of dangerousness are notoriously prone to false-positive outcomes[15] at an unacceptably high rate of incidence (Bottoms, 1977: 82–3; Cornwell, 1989 *passim*). To act on the supposition of such predictions, and also on an indeterminate basis, raises serious moral objections to which we shall return later in this chapter.

The second issue of contention is that the concept of proportionality in making punishments commensurate with the seriousness of offences is impossible of reliable achievement, and therefore that it may reasonably be reduced to the subsidiary intention that such measures should not be manifestly *dis*-proportionate to the harm occasioned and the culpability of the offender. Much of merit has been written about the desirability of proportionate sentencing, particularly during the 1980s and before the advent of 'populist punitivism' (c.f. in particular: Von Hirsch, 1985 *passim*[16]; Hudson, 1987 *op. cit.*: 38–41; Tonry, 2003 *op. cit.*: 114–117), and see also the contributions of Easton and Piper and of McElrea in this volume. Indeed, as Tonry has pointed out, in Britain the Criminal Justice Act 1991 promoted proportionality as the primary rationale for sentencing, though on a retributive and desert-based approach to punishment which argues that justice is best

---

15. False-positive outcomes occur when it is predicted that an offender will re-offend seriously within a foreseeable period of time following release from custody, and it subsequently transpires that he/she does not do so either at all, or within the time-frame predicted. Research completed in this area indicates that the rate of false-positive outcomes can vary between 55% and 70% — see J. Monahan (1975). Also for a concise explanation of the morality of predictive restraint see Anthony E. Bottoms (1977:70–95), and for the outcomes of a research project completed in the UK see David J. Cornwell (1989).

16. Here see: A. von Hirsch (1985: 77–101).

secured by ensuring that punishment is commensurate with the seriousness of the offence (2003: 114). However, as he further indicated, the Criminal Justice Act 1993 and the judicial interpretation of proportionality in the case of *Cunningham* (1993) in the Court of Appeal[17] effectively destroyed the primacy of proportionality in its return to more utilitarian aims of crime reduction and public protection, and perhaps more seriously, by the aggravating effect on sentence(ing) of previous convictions.[18]

The re-introduction of previous convictions into the sentencing process[19] effectively introduced a 'weighting factor' into the process of punishing current offences, ensuring that sentence lengths would increase and that at the same time the prison population in England and Wales would rise swiftly (as it subsequently did).[20] This somewhat cynical and politically inspired initiative adopted by the Conservative government of Prime Minister John Major and his Home Secretary Michael Howard heralded the 'prison works' era, the morality of which has been a divisive issue for two decades past within British criminology, and continues to be so, leaving the criminal justice system of England and Wales considerably isolated within Western Europe with the possible exception of The Netherlands in a contemporary sense.

However arguable the morality of, and the judicial case for, weighing previous convictions into considerations of the seriousness of current offences may or may not be on the grounds of culpability and desert, there remains the fact that 'supplementary punishment' imposed on such a basis amounts to an additional premium imposed for offences already punished previously. It is, in the opinion of many criminologists, a practice equally as objectionable on moral grounds as that of predictive restraint or incapacitation on the presumption of future dangerousness previously discussed.

It is, of course, a matter for judges and magistrates sentencing in the courts to decide, within the extent of discretion available to them and the official sentencing guidelines issued for their consideration of penalties, the

---

17. 14 Crim App R(S) 444.
18. Consideration of which was introduced into the sentencing process as one of the contentious measures within the Criminal Justice Act 1993.
19. In the Criminal Justice Act 1993 which also repealed the unit fines provisions within the Criminal Justice Act 1991.
20. From a average daily level of 46,500 in 1992 to one of 62,298 in 1998 and subsequently to 84,400 in February 2013.

nature and extent of sanctions appropriate in the individual circumstances of offences tried by them. In Britain in particular, the judiciary have proved extremely protective of their independence from the executive, and traditionally resistant to political attempts to curb their discretion: a factor that has tended to create considerable variations in sentencing in both magistrates' and Crown Courts. Historically also, there have been occasions in which judges, reluctant to impose particular penalties available to them, have largely ignored such provisions in their entirety and resorted to other means of sentencing.[21] In her account of the difficulties facing the judiciary of Hungary in meeting the new challenges of 'europeanisation', Dr Borbála Fellegi (in this volume) provides a compelling analysis of the complexities that beset democracies emerging from former totalitarian regimes into the uncertainties that attend a more democratic, even if more socially benevolent criminological future.

In concluding this section of this chapter, I would like to suggest that there are three myths that we need to dispel if we are to 'do justice better'. The first of these is relatively simply stated, and concerns the myth that criminal justice systems are, in fact, 'systematic'[22] — a matter which is subsequently addressed, in the context of England and Wales, by Sir Louis Blom-Cooper in his contribution later in this volume. The second myth is the claim, frequently advanced within the criminological literature, that the practice of

---

21. Such was the case with mandatory suspended sentences of imprisonment in the late-1960s and early-1970s until the measure was repealed in the Criminal Justice Act 1972, and also of the use of preventive detention for public protection in the cases of hardened recidivists guilty of serious offences, and used as an additional sentence to retain them in custody for between five and 14 years (with seven years as the normal minimum). Preventive detention was abolished in the Criminal Justice Act 1967 and replaced by the extended sentence which was similarly disliked by the judiciary, and fell into disuse before being abandoned in the 1980s.

22. Here see Andrew Rutherford's criticism in the following words: 'It is important to place stress on the word *process* as there is a frequent and misleading tendency to view criminal justice as a system. Criminal justice as a system suggests an articulation of purposes and a degree of coordination and coherence which bears no resemblance to reality. One consequence of the system's approach is to invite expectations of criminal justice which cannot be achieved. Alternatively, to view criminal justice as a process allows an appreciation of the loose interconnections between the various stages, of different and sometimes competing goals between and within agencies, of the dynamic nature of the forces which determine shape and direction, of the informal nature of much of what takes place, and of the unanticipated consequences which not infrequently ensue' (Rutherford, 1986: 22).

'bifurcation'[23] within criminal justice is liable to moral objection on the basis of not treating like cases in a similar manner, and is therefore 'unjust'. Professors Serge Gutwirth and Paul De Hert discuss this issue in their chapter in an enlightening manner. The third myth is, perhaps, the most important of all for this work, contending as it does that decarceration is unachievable without a marked increase in public risk. Professor Tapio Lappi-Seppälä dispels this myth with an account of how the Finnish vision of decarceration was achieved through a consensus within government, politics, academic expertise and a moderate media, and became capable of realisation.

Justice 'Systems'

As to the first 'myth' mentioned above, and in spite of the long-overdue creation of a Ministry of Justice (MOJ) from 9th May 2007 in the United Kingdom, the main functional elements of the criminal justice system for England and Wales remain embedded within a sprawling conglomeration of government departments formerly administered by the Department of Constitutional Affairs (DCA), the Home Office, and the Department of the Attorney General. Its main functions include HM Courts Service (HMCS) (since 2011 HM Courts and Tribunals Service), the National Offender Management Service (NOMS) which includes the National Probation Service and HM Prison Service, and, in addition, sponsorship of, or liaison with the judiciary headed by the Office of the Lord Chief Justice with its various component offices, various HM Inspectorates, the Parole Board, Independent Monitoring Boards (formerly Boards of Visitors in prisons), and the Legal Services Commission (LSC). The Ministry had, at formation, also additional responsibilities for sentencing policy, sponsorship of the Sentencing Guidelines Council (SGC), the Sentencing Advisory Panel (SAP), and the Law Commission with its own subsidiary divisions (Gibson, 2008; 2009: 108).[24]

It will be noted, however, that the national police forces of England and Wales remain under the control of the Home Office, as does the UK Border Agency subsuming the UK Immigration Service and the Border Force, each

---

23. A term originally advanced by Bottoms in 1977 (see: Bottoms, 1977 *op. cit.* 88 *et seq. supra*).

24. For a more detailed overview of the Ministry of Justice see: B. Gibson (2008), *The New Ministry of Justice: An Introduction* (2nd Edition), Sherfield-on-Loddon UK: Waterside Press; and (2009), *The Pocket A-Z of Criminal Justice*, also Waterside Press, p.108.

of which have strong, though indirect links with criminal justice agencies in the supervision and operation of Immigration Detention Centres.

The point of issue here is that the structural reforms of 2007 that created the MOJ effectively produced a centralised monolithic structure that in part replaced other monolithic structures (elements of the Home Office and the DCA) and some, though not all of the functions of the judiciary which remain independent of government under the control of the Lord Chief Justice and his/her officers. In addition, the two principal component parts of NOMS (the Probation and Prison Services) have traditionally pursued very different forms of professional ethos within criminal justice: that of the Probation Service grounded predominantly in the non-custodial sector of community justice, contrasting markedly with the mainly exclusive custodial role of the Prison Service. Even though some probation officers undertake secondments to fulfil an important counselling and advisory role within prisons, the two Services require very different skills, training and personal attributes to undertake their professional duties effectively.

Put another way perhaps, the social work ethic inherent in and central to the duties of probation officers, summed up in their traditional 'advise, assist and befriend' approach to dealing with those appearing before courts, those sentenced to non-custodial sanctions, and also those in prisons requiring casework support and preparation for release, sits uneasily alongside the 'security and control' duties that are necessarily central to the work of prison officers. Though the two services 'co-exist' and are to a considerable extent mutually dependent upon one another, theirs is a 'partnership of convenience' rather than of genuine compatibility. Moreover, the original social work ethic of the Probation Service has, over the past two decades in particular, been heavily eroded in favour of risk assessment and public protection,

It is therefore difficult to see how such a vast and disparate organization as the MOJ with its many different and specialised roles and professional requirements can function in a 'systematic' manner other than as the sum of its parts, each having a dedicated role to play in criminal justice administration. That the judicial elements of the criminal justice enterprise function independently of the executive and administrative, not to mention the 'political' influences of government, merely exacerbates the systemic illusion of a cohesive entity.

Bifurcation

As to the second 'myth', the term 'bifurcation' has attracted much debate within criminology and law since it first appeared in the late 1970s at much the same time as the justice model was gaining impetus in the USA and subsequently in Europe. With the benefit of hindsight I should like to suggest that elements of bifurcation have been evident and accommodated within criminal justice for decades past without serious objection: some perceived as beneficial, and others as open to legitimate criticism.[25] For the sake of clarity here, I offer the following explanation of what bifurcation entails. In its core sense, it proposes that there are both moral and practical reasons for departing from the principle of 'treating like cases alike' on the grounds that these *deserve* different consideration in relation to the seriousness of the conduct of persons found guilty of committing criminal (or indeed other) offences.[26]

Here, already, we encounter the first aspect of potential uncertainty about bifurcation since such a definition would suggest a moral case for showing leniency towards the truly repentant and remorseful offender on the one hand, and a supposed justification for being more punitive towards the unrepentant and the incorrigible offender on the other. In considering this dilemma, which admittedly is real, we have to be clear about whether we are proposing to punish the offender or the offence, since the difference is rather more than semantic. The criminal law is constructed on the premise

25. For instance, there is some consensus that the practice of granting parole is an acceptable means of shortening the time spent by prisoners in custody as a response to their positive or remorseful conduct in relation to offences, and that it is reasonable to withhold parole from those displaying a negative attitude towards their offending. On the other hand, there is far less consensus in relation to the morality of extending the sentences of those with previous convictions for similar offences in the past. Both practices involve bifurcation to an extent, insofar as individuals are treated differently subsequent to the commission of offences for which they have been found guilty.

26. The original issue of 'emerging bifurcation' was raised by A. E. Bottoms (1977: 87–9) in a different context from that in which I propose it here, though both have apparent similarities. Bottoms identified a trend to (at that time emerging) to punish serious and persistent offenders increasingly harshly, and lesser offenders more leniently, on largely *economic* grounds relating to the increasing social costs of maintaining penal systems. In this and former works I have proposed a somewhat different explanation of bifurcation as a moral justification for extending a measure of leniency towards offenders who show remorse and accept responsibility for their wrongdoing, combined with a willingness to make an apology and reparation, while showing less tolerance towards remorseless and intransigent offenders within the overall parameters of sentencing.

that certain acts are defined as crimes which, when brought to account in findings of guilt, render those found to have committed them necessarily liable to punishment to an extent prescribed by the law. Viewed somewhat differently, however, each criminal offence is committed by one perpetrator (or possibly more) to an extent of culpability that has to be determined *before* the extent of punishment can be decided upon. In the former instance it is the *act* of breaking the law that 'justifies' the punishment: in the latter it is the *offender* who becomes liable to punishment for the act committed. We cannot, in relation to the first instance, waive the law which is either broken or not, but in the second instance we can decide to deal differentially with those found guilty on the basis of culpability, remorse or their willingness to accept the nature and extent of their wrongdoing.[27]

For a number of reasons to be explained briefly, I shall defend the principle of bifurcation on largely utilitarian grounds within this chapter. I will suggest that the difference between 'positive' and 'negative' bifurcation should be accepted as an inevitable outcome of such an approach.[28] I make this defence because it then becomes possible to envisage a more humane process of justice that could be less inherently retributive, that would relegate deterrence to at the most a marginal consideration in outcome terms as befits its uncertainty, and that would focus on the prospective potential of reparation as a means of repairing the harm caused by offences, and of restoring offenders to full citizenship having made amends for their wrongdoing. This

---

27. In this particular respect H. L. A. Hart's definition of criminal punishment 'of an offender for an offence' becomes awkwardly circular and to an extent ambiguous. As we shall see later in this chapter, considerations of mercy depend critically upon clarity as to who or what is being punished, and to what extent culpability can be mitigated even though a proscribed offence has been brought to account in a finding of guilt.

28. By 'positive bifurcation' I intend the use of penal policies and practices that deal differently with convicted offenders who show genuine remorse, accept responsibility for their wrongdoing, and who are prepared to make an apology and reparation to their victims as a means towards restoration of their status as full citizens within their communities. Such policies and practices are consistent with the implementation of restorative justice within criminal justice and the exercise of mercy to which the next part if this chapter is devoted. I do not, however, wish to suggest that any form of 'negative bifurcation' should be exercised against those offenders not so amenable: they should merely be retained within the 'traditional' penal process, though in prison regimes encouraging reparation and eventual re-integration and restoration within their communities. This differentiation is explained at greater length in D. J. Cornwell (2007: at chapters 4–6), and also more briefly in D. J. Cornwell (2010: 7–20).

may require us to consider the role and virtue of mercy because however outmoded it may seem within the context of our contemporary acquisitive societies, the exercise of mercy in the form of leniency — when it is merited — adds humanity to the process of administering justice to the benefit of the punisher, the punished and to victims of crime who are also legitimate stakeholders within civilised criminal justice processes.

Indeed, to a considerable extent, bifurcation and the concept of mercy become inseparable components of restorative justice if it is to achieve its purposes of limiting retribution, reducing dependence upon custodial sanctions, affording proper recognition to victims of crime, and restoring offenders to law-abiding citizenship within their communities that are also harmed by crime. Within such a view of 'ideal justice', restoration becomes contingent upon reparation having been made, whether directly or indirectly, to victims of criminal acts. Such an approach is also consistent with the moral imperative to limit pain and unpleasantness to the minimum extent commensurate with the seriousness of offences.[29]

Decarceration

The third 'myth' concerns the evident difficulty experienced by many democracies in making strategic plans to reduce custodial penal populations by expanding the use of community sanctions. During the second half of the 20th-century a number of countries designed different strategies to reduce the social costs of incarceration, among which were most notably The Netherlands, Germany, Canada, and Finland. Some of these strategies were relatively short-lived, predominantly for political reasons, yet that adopted in Finland has proved durable and consistently effective.

The history and circumstances in which the Finnish strategy achieved success reveals a remarkable consensus forged between politicians, the judiciary, academics within the social sciences, correctional practitioners, the media and the public, which is elegantly described by Professor Tapio Lappi-Seppälä in his chapter within this volume. His account entirely dispels the myth that

29. Thereby upholding the 'just (or commensurate) deserts' foundation of the abandoned justice model, though tempered with proper consideration of the legitimate needs of offenders to achieve restoration, and of victims to receive appropriate reparation or compensation for the harm caused to them, their dependents and their communities.

reduction of prison populations is impossible to realise and sustain without significant increases in overall crime and public risk. It is an account that every honest politician should read and internalise as a blueprint for penal reform, combined with the social advantages of reduced expenditure and the collateral damage caused by unnecessary and excessive use of custodial punishment.

Mercy: Means and Ends Within Civilised Justice

One of the earliest and most compelling accounts of mercy in its judicial context is to be found in the writings of the Roman Stoic philosopher Lucius Seneca in the first century AD[30], expressed as follows:

> Mercy means restraining the mind from vengeance when it has the power to take it, or the leniency of a superior towards an inferior in fixing punishment…And so mercy may be termed the inclination of the mind towards leniency in exacting punishment. The following definition will encounter objections, however closely it approaches the truth; if we shall say that mercy is the moderation which remits something from the punishment that is deserved or due, it will be objected that no virtue gives to any man less than his due. Everybody, however, understands that the fact of the case is that mercy consists in stopping short of what might have been deservedly proposed. The ill-informed think that the opposite is strictness; but no virtue is the opposite of a virtue. ('On Mercy', II.ii. 2-iv, 1–4).

Following Seneca's reasoning, we may substitute the word 'retribution' for vengeance in the first line of the quotation above, though otherwise it retains a context in which we may detect the potential for its application in a contemporary setting of criminal justice. Restraining the mind from retribution implies allowing other (and possibly more beneficial) considerations to enter the arena of 'purposes' within the justice process without abandoning the

---

30. Lucius Annasus Seneca (*circa* 4BC-65AD) was both a statesman and a philosopher of the Stoic school, and also a tutor and subsequently adviser to the emperor Nero who also condemned him to death for his supposed complicity in a plot to assassinate him. This quotation is taken from Seneca's 'To Nero on Mercy [*De Clementia*]' in *Moral Essays*, Book I, 2-iv, 1–4, [Tr. John W. Basore], The Loeb Classical Library, London: Heinemann.

required balance between desert and proportionality in forming responses to crime on a rational basis.

Inclination of the mind towards leniency suggests being willing to search for mitigating circumstances when sentencing remorseful and amenable[31] offenders, rather than a pre-disposition to escalate penalties on the basis of previous offences for which punishment has already been imposed. It also implies avoiding as far as possible, or at least limiting, the visitation of 'collateral punishment' of the non-guilty who may be relatives or dependents of offenders.[32] In addition, as Alwynne Smart has suggested, where mercy or leniency is extended in certain instances it is to *avoid* an injustice because the law cannot always anticipate all the differences that there might be between offences that appear alike superficially (Smart, 1969: 216).[33]

Here, however, it becomes necessary to include a note of caution since it is frequently (and I shall insist, erroneously) contended that the exercise of leniency or mercy amounts to the condoning of offences, rather than fitting the sanction to the crime where the law is either too inflexible or too unsophisticated to do so. As Smart further indicates, when we condone an offence we do not act merely as if it never happened, but rather as if it didn't matter — in other words, as if it were not an offence (Smart, 1969 *op. cit.*: 217–8). Clearly, such an error has to be avoided, but the impression is frequently evident in reporting of crime and sentencing in the media that where leniency is shown, it is the equivalent of the condoning or overlooking of offences.

Interestingly for our purposes within this discussion, Kristen Bell has helpfully drawn a distinction between what she has termed 'positive' and 'negative' mercy in a judicial context. The former she describes as occurring when judges are not impermissibly departing from rules in pursuit of personal feelings, but are rather serving the Rule of Law in their obligation to uphold just institutions. The latter, on the other hand, occurs when an offender is spared from the full extent of harsh treatment that is strictly

---

31. Amenable in the sense of taking responsibility for their offences, and being willing to make reparation to victims either directly where appropriate, or to victims of crime more generally.

32. In many instances in which custodial sentences are imposed, the immediate families or dependents of offenders suffer the effects of losing their main source of income and even also their homes due to inability to pay rental or mortgage costs.

33. Here, see: A. Smart (1969: 212–228).

deserved (Bell, 2010).[34] Thus, positive mercy is evident where an adjudicator responds 'justly' when unjust social rules call for a harsher response, and negative mercy becomes apparent in the mitigation of penalties where it would be clearly excessive to impose the maximum severity of a sanction prescribed by the law.

Bifurcation within criminal justice becomes necessary to support the principles and purposes of restorative justice, but only insofar as it separates for different forms of judicial response those offenders willing to accept their guilt and make reparation from those unrepentant and unwilling to do so. The moral objection that such practice fails to treat like cases alike may thus be countered by the rather more compelling response that the two classes of offender so separated are distinctly 'unlike', and that it would be manifestly 'unjust' to treat them judicially in an undifferentiated manner.

Whether or not restorative justice is predicated on a form of 'negative mercy' is a moot point, but it can scarcely be criticised for transgressing the concept of 'fairness'. However, in his seminal essay *Justice as Fairness*, the eminent moral and political philosopher John Rawls contested the widely held view that justice and fairness are the same and indistinguishable, maintaining that 'the fundamental idea in the concept of justice is fairness', but that justice can only considered as one of the virtues of social institutions or practices (Rawls, 1961: 80).[35] Though this claim by Rawls may appear at first sight to be somewhat abstruse, it was intended to indicate with some clarity the essential point that justice may, in certain circumstances, involve inequalities, but that these inequalities must work 'for the advantage of every party engaging in it' (1961: 83).

As to desert and proportionality, it may also be argued that offenders who accept responsibility for their actions and commit to making reparation *deserve* some measure of mitigation at the sentencing stage of criminal trials. This is somewhat different from either the practice of plea-bargaining[36] or that of the more recent resort to allowing a 'sentence discount' in the

---

34. This is, it might be suggested, an important distinction. For a full explanation of Bell's stance on this issue, see K. Bell (2010: 9–10).

35. J. B. Rawls (1961: 80–110). (Re-printed from *The Philosophical Review*, vol. LXVII (1958), pp.164–194 and subsequently amended by the author.)

36. In which an accused person agrees to plead guilty to a lesser or different offence from that originally charged in expectation of a lighter sentence.

Civilising Criminal Justice

event that an accused pleads guilty as charged *ab initio*, and thereby saves the court the time and resources necessary to conduct a full trial. Rather, as desert in considerations of culpability and responsibility may be said to establish a reference point in the scale of seriousness of offences, acceptance of genuine remorse and resolve to make amends should logically be weighed in mitigation and expressed in a measure of leniency.

I mentioned earlier that I proposed to defend the concept of bifurcation on the broadly utilitarian grounds that the main purposes of punishment should be forward-looking rather than (as in the case of retributive justifications) predominantly retrospective. By forward-looking here I imply encouragement of a law-abiding or 'crime-free' future lifestyle, and assisted in such achievement by the provision of resources that enable and empower former offenders to become responsible citizens. It further follows from the preceding discussion of mercy that those who repent and resolve to make amends for the harm they have caused have a greater claim on these resources than have the shameless and unrepentant. It also suggests that there is some obligation on the part of 'society' to provide those resources to enable former offenders to do what is expected of them.

However, it has to be shown that by acting in such a discriminatory manner a greater or more universal social benefit may result than would be anticipated from the imposition of retributive and retrospective punishment. In addition, few would, I believe, dispute that to devote such resources to the potential improvement of the unrepentant in a measure equal to, or at the expense of the remorseful would amount to an injustice, and would probably also be wasteful on economic grounds. It is, perhaps in this particular respect that that the *process* and dialogue within restorative justice makes repentance the more likely, though it cannot ensure it.

If, as is the widespread practice at the present time, we wish to continue punishing offenders on a predominantly retributive basis augmented by incapacitation for the purposes of public protection, then the processes of justice become largely merciless towards the repentant while at the same time denying an opportunity to change for the better the lives of the remorseful and of those harmed by their offences. Worse, perhaps, there can be no real prospect of penal reform since when such policies fail to reduce offending, the only recourse becomes that of punishing more harshly. The concluding section of this chapter provides a brief analysis of the contemporary prospects for substantial penal reform, and of the 'Anglo-Saxon' attitudes that presently defy its achievement—most particularly in Britain, but also in many other democracies worldwide.

Penal Reform and Anglo-Saxon Attitudes

Since the purpose of this work is to present a vision of more 'civilised' processes of administering criminal justice, there is an inevitable implication that change is both necessary and considerably overdue. Change within large and complex organizations, particularly on a significant scale, is rarely welcomed and frequently resisted. Penal reform implies that the structures and the principles of justice, and possibly also the way in which it is perceived and delivered, would be better served and more effective in reducing crime if *attitudes* and *behaviours* could be altered. Such change has, at the very least, political, social and philosophical implications, and without some measure of consensus, will remain impossible of achievement.

Stated simply, attitudes embrace mental processes of opinion-and-disposition-forming that subsequently affect behaviours which give them operational impetus. On the one hand, many of our attitudes are learned and developed from traditional and cultural exposure to prevailing influences from childhood onwards, and also from the social environments and value systems in which our developing adult powers of reasoning and inter-personal communication are learned and shaped. Socialisation, on the other hand, is the process by which these powers are adapted and modified to enable us to conform to the norms and demands of social life within the differing tiers of the social structure in which we move and develop relationships. It is this conformity, or the lack of it, that determines whether our behaviours are perceived as law-abiding or deviant, and the sociological and criminological literature of the mid-1970s and onwards is replete with explanations and interpretations of these phenomena.[37]

Attitudes become entrenched within the minds of citizens in relation to the existence and effects of deviant and criminal behaviour within societies, in the minds of offenders whose motivations and rationalisations for

---

37. See, for example, S. Hall and P. Scraton (1981: 460–497), Steven Box (1971: 139–165), and Andrew Rutherford (1986 *op. cit.*: 21–39).

committing illegal acts are many and varied, in the minds of law-enforcement officials whose efforts are devoted towards crime control, and in the minds of politicians whose responsibilities extend to the making of criminal justice policies and legislation. Each of these 'constituencies' is to a greater or lesser extent 'conditioned' by an increasingly influential and sensational media reportage of crime that lays a frustrating emphasis on what is perceived as the persistent failure to curb and reduce socially unacceptable behaviour. Yet levels of crime are endemic within societies in spite of ever more sophisticated methods of surveillance and successful apprehension of offenders. Indeed, within Western Europe in recent years, these levels have generally reduced as this sophistication has increased, as has, by a factor of almost half, the likelihood of the average citizen of becoming a victim of serious crime.

For centuries past, the attitude of most, though by no means all, societies towards crime has been to demand retributive punishment as a 'justified' and reciprocal response. It is essentially a crude response, however understandable, because it insists upon meeting a 'wrong' with what, apart from its legal interpretation, would otherwise be regarded as a further 'wrong' since it involves the imposition of pain or unpleasantness. However, it may be contended that the 'crudeness' lies within the motivation towards revenge, rather than in its reciprocal 'justification'. Put another way, perhaps, there may exist a reasonable justification for responding to a wrongful act, but this need not, of necessity, be retributive: indeed, it may be our Anglo-Saxon prejudice alone that insists upon its reciprocal nature.

If we were able to dispense with the perceived need for and pre-disposition towards reciprocity, and substitute for that the 'satisfaction' of promoting amended behaviour on a morally educative basis, little of social substance would be lost and potentially much prospectively gained. For as Andrew Rutherford has argued: 'the law is only one means of social control and usually less potent than the family, school and workplace. The criminal law tends to be a blunt and cumbersome instrument and may be less effective than arbitration, mediation or other means of resolution based on civil law procedures' (Rutherford, 1986 *op. cit.*: 21). Such was Louk Hulsman's (1982) contention in his description of the 'civilisation' of criminal justice which John Blad takes up later in this work.

The view of Andrew Rutherford quoted above brings us to the second of the four main examples of Anglo-Saxon attitudes that I wish to outline here. It is that offences described legislatively as 'criminal' can (and should) only be dealt with in the criminal courts with a high level of proof as 'beyond a reasonable doubt. For as long as this traditional stance towards the investigation of offences remains largely unchallenged, considerable time, cost, and delay will attend the process of dealing with alleged offenders using the full-blown adversarial or inquisitorial procedures of criminal trials to adjudge not-guilty pleas entered largely on the basis of possible acquittal due to technicalities or of the prosecution having insufficient evidence to prove the offender(s) guilty.

Clearly, where serious offences are alleged, it is necessary that these be fully investigated and the requirements of due process maintained. However, in cases of lesser seriousness[38] there is, as Hulsman has suggested, much merit in treating these as 'civil' matters rather than as crimes, particularly where it may be more expeditious to resolve them through mediation and reparation or compensation (Hulsman, 1982: 38). Moreover, as Rutherford further points out, in many instances of less serious offences against the person or property, it is the victim who decides either to leave the matter unreported, or to decline from invoking criminal law procedures due to the complexity of investigative or legal procedures and the intimidating nature of full criminal trials (Rutherford, 1986 *op. cit.*: 22).

In England and Wales in particular, progress towards reducing the impact of the criminal law has traditionally been resisted both by politicians and by the judiciary, and also considerably impeded by the proliferation of new laws and sanctions—particularly since the late-1990s. Yet, if wider use were to be made of restorative justice processes for resolving disputes of a relatively minor criminal nature, very considerable financial savings could be envisaged and much time saved in reaching satisfactory settlements. Unfortunately, the 'bullish' rhetoric adopted by politicians during the 'Prison Works' era

---

38. Such, perhaps, as theft, shoplifting, non-aggravated burglary, non-injurious assault, criminal damage below specified thresholds of cost, lesser road traffic offences, minor deception or fraud, fine default, and the like, many of which may be settled by mediation, reparation or compensation. It might also be envisaged that breaches of the conditions of non-custodial sanctions such as community service could, in the first instance, be similarly dealt with provided that no further serious offences are alleged in the breach proceedings.

of the mid-1990s and into the present millennium in pursuit of electoral credibility has set back such initiatives very considerably.

Linked inextricably to the situation outlined above in England and Wales, as in some other countries following the 'Anglo-Saxon' traditions and mode of adversarial justice, the predominantly bi-partisan nature of the political arena has exercised a malign influence on penal reform for largely electoral reasons.[39] Worse, perhaps, the pressures exerted on both politicians and political parties by the media, particularly in relation to crime and crime control measures, tend to create a convergence in policy-making and legislation which proliferates law-making and increases the severity of penalties. This 'spiralling' effect makes significant penal reform altogether less likely to attract public support, while fuelling the supposed public demand for increasingly draconian penal measures.[40] It also inevitably results in an escalation in the size of the prison population.

Such legislative behaviour leads to the need to discuss, albeit briefly, the fourth and last of the Anglo-Saxon attitudes that have had a severely limiting effect on penal reform in England and Wales into the present millennium, and which make the prospects for change appear extremely bleak into the immediate future. This situation concerns the morality and the probity of employing measures of predictive restraint, either on a determinate or an indeterminate basis, to imprison supposedly 'dangerous' persons on the prediction of future serious offending, or in other words, for offences as yet uncommitted.

---

39. This situation occurs in countries in which only two main political parties dominate the electoral landscape without the moderating influence of a viable third (or more) other parties that in alliance can dictate the balance of power and exercise a restraining effect on the formulation and implementation of social policies. In bi-partisan states, the dictates of electoral credibility and media influences tend to narrow considerably the 'manifesto gap' between the dominant parties to an extent that policies converge and traditional political alignments become blurred or even almost indistinguishable. This situation occurred in England and Wales in 1977 when, following a general election, the newly formed New Labour government of Tony Blair adopted a number of the penal policies planned but not implemented by the outgoing Conservative government of John Major.

40. Such as, e.g, the introduction of mandatory minimum sentences in the Crime (Sentences Act) 1997, and the indeterminate sentence of imprisonment for public protection (ISPP) and the extended sentence for public protection (ESPP) in the Criminal Justice Act 2003.

In Britain, the 'dangerousness debate' has waxed and waned in intensity since the mid-1970s predicated upon the questionable belief that future dangerousness can be predicted with sufficient accuracy to justify detention to prevent its occurrence. The academic discipline of criminology is almost universally unanimous in the belief that predictions of dangerousness are liable to such a high level of false-positive outcomes as to make the use of such measures both immoral and unjust as we have noted earlier in this chapter. Like the supposed effectiveness of deterrence, future dangerousness is an appeal to intuition rather than a verifiable construct, and is both superstitious and altogether unreliable. It has nothing to do with retributive justice since it punishes no committed offence: it has no foundation in deterrence since it cannot deter because it is preventive: it has no rehabilitative value since its restraining effect denies any such ethic: and it has no reparative potential since there is no victim to whom reparation can be afforded. In short, it is an entirely punitive device serving the sole purpose of incapacitation on the basis of supposition.

Civilised justice should abstain altogether from becoming party to penal measures based on such questionable moral or operational integrity, and yet the practice of predictive restraint remains condoned by judges who impose it, by politicians who for whatever reasons support its use to appease supposed public sentiment, by media unquestioning of its morality, and by the less discriminating elements of the public indifferent towards the fate of those against whom it is used. Until its resurgence in the past decade, preventive detention had been abandoned in England and Wales since the repeal of the Preventive Detention Act 1908 in the Criminal Justice Act 1967. It remains a sad reflection on our punitive and primitive attitudes that its revival in a different form should be tolerated in contemporary justice.

Conclusion: Does the Restorative Ethic Have a Future?

The concept for this volume arose from the conviction that long-overdue penal reform in many countries of the world in this new millennium cannot occur until there has been a seismic shift in attitudes towards punishment of offenders and the structures of justice that could facilitate such change. In many countries also, it is a misnomer to describe what have widely come to be described as 'correctional services' as *systems*, since these conglomerates of functions that contribute towards criminal justice administration in practice display few systemic qualities. To the contrary, the differences of professional ethos and primary operational purpose between the constituent elements of criminal justice delivery make them, at best, a loose-knit alignment of disparate entities each of which in practice pursues its own functional logic.

Moreover, as this chapter has shown, traditional attitudes, myths, pre-dispositions and folk-wisdoms have sustained widely differing criminal justice policies and practices through a succession of changing penal 'fashions' over the past five or six decades, until it has become difficult to discern with any clarity what central purpose the correctional enterprise is, in fact, designed to achieve. And since correctional service delivery is a major consumer of public finances in an era of widespread economic recession, it becomes no more than prudent to question its cost-effectiveness in reducing crime and in contributing to public safety.

National social policies, of which criminal justice policies are an essential and important part, ultimately reflect the dominant moral and social values of their populations. These policies are also expressive of the hierarchy of concerns for the welfare of citizens of all classes in living their daily lives free from socially divisive and dysfunctional influences such as poverty, fear, ill-health, poor education, inadequate housing and other forms of lesser-eligibility.[41] In addition, however, social policies are demonstrative of the extent of tolerance shown towards those particular portions of every population that fail to conform to social norms of behaviour, and become officially excluded or otherwise acted against for the commission of criminal and other forms of offending or antisocial conduct.

Strained economic circumstances within nations naturally lead to the search for means of reducing the cost of public services: it therefore seems extraordinary that in England and Wales in particular, and also in some other democracies, there appears to be no absolute limit sought to restrict the number of persons imprisoned on an average daily basis.[42] Ultimately,

---

41. Such is to include inequalities of access to and outcomes of social provision and welfare amenities that should be freely available to all classes of persons irrespective of age, race, gender, political or religious belief, and the like.

42. By contrast, countries such as Holland (see: Tak, 2001), Denmark (Kvysgaard, 2001), Finland (Lappi-Seppälä, 2001 and in this volume) and Norway (Larsson, 2001) have in the past legally prevented occupation of prisons above the certified level of their accommodation (normally

of course, prison populations, penal policies and punishment patterns are, as Michael Tonry (2003 *op. cit.*: 6) has pointed out, as they are because politicians, however motivated, wished it so. However, when resources are scarce and penal systems compete with other forms of social provision for a share of national welfare and social expenditure, it seems profligate in the extreme to maintain excessive prison populations when other means of reduction are evidently available without unduly enhanced public risk—see Lappi-Seppälä later in this volume.

The principles and practices of restorative justice also provide the means by which many offenders who might otherwise attract custodial sentences could safely be dealt with in their communities, while at the same time making reparation to victims of crime and enhancing public amenity. Though as we have seen this involves a measure of bifurcation within penal policies, it holds the important advantages of enabling a lesser use of custody to be made, while at the same time reducing the overall cost of penal sanctions and avoiding the collateral damage caused by imprisonment to families and close others of offenders who have not broken the law.

Though restorative justice offers no 'soft-options' to those who are willing to accept responsibility for the harm to victims caused by their offences and make apology and reparation, it is more merciful than 'traditional' retributive justice to all the parties involved in criminal offences. For the remorseless and serious criminal offenders there will always remain a need for imprisonment, though it is possible that a reduced need for prison places might result in fewer but less crowded and more effective prisons.

All of these considerations combine to make criminal justice more 'civilised', and also more likely to lead to crime reduction which is its ultimate purpose. If, in addition, there could be a consensus towards 'decriminalising' certain less serious offences and dealing with them as civil wrongs, then

---

less 5% to take account of repairs, refurbishment, etc.). In addition, in Germany in the 1960s and 1970s the use of sentences of six months or less in duration was largely discontinued (Weigend, 2001), reducing the number of such sentences from an annual level of 130,000 to 30,000. In the USA state of North Carolina and also in Canada during the 1990s measures were taken to deliberately reduce the prison populations through the use of non-custodial alternative sanctions (see: Wright, 2002; and Cormier, 2006). France has traditionally favoured the use of amnesties and pardons when its prison population has been considered unsustainably high (see: Kensey and Tournier, 2001) all also quoted in Tonry, 2003 *op. cit.*: 212–3.

the savings in court time and resources could be considerable. In the final analysis, consensus in relation to penal reform holds the key to making it happen. As was the case in Finland, this requires the willing cooperation of politicians, the judiciary, academic advisers and researchers, the media, the correctional services and the public to become a reality. If, however, the myths and attitudes of the past continue to prevail, this uphill path will become even steeper and stonier.

Does the restorative ethic have a future? If the myths and prejudices of former years could be dispelled and dispensed with: if common sense and prudence could overcome the sound-bite politics and rhetoric of retributive predispositions: and if the discourses of reason and social justice be afforded a dispassionate hearing, then the answer to this important question is inevitably affirmative. Many of the texts within this volume attest to this very simple fact.

References

American Friends Service Committee (1972), *Struggle for Justice*, New York: Hill and Wang.

Becker, H. S. (1964), *The Other Side*, Glencoe, ILL: Free Press.

Bell, K. (2010), 'Mercy and Criminal Justice', Ph.D. Thesis, University of North Carolina.

Bottoms, A. E. (1977), 'Reflections on the Renaissance of Dangerousness' in *Howard Journal of Criminal Justice*, vol. xvi, no.2, pp.70–95.

Bottoms, A. E. (1995), 'The Philosophy and Politics of Punishment and Sentencing' in Clarkson C. M. V. and Morgan R. (eds.), *The Politics of Sentencing Reform*, Oxford: Clarendon Press, pp.17–49.

Box, S. (1971), *Deviance, Reality and Society*, London: Holt, Reinhart and Winston.

Cormier, R. B. (2006), 'Were There's a Will There's a Way: A Canadian Perspective on Restorative Justice' in Cornwell, D. J., *Criminal Punishment and Restorative Justice: Past, Present and Future Perspectives*, Sherfield-on-Loddon, UK: Waterside Press, pp.149–162.

Cornwell, D. J. (1989), 'Criminal Dangerousness and Its Punishment: Beyond the Phenomenological Illusion', D. Phil. Thesis, University of York (Part Published).

Cornwell, D. J. (2007), *Doing Justice Better*, Sherfield-on-Loddon, UK: Waterside Press.

Cornwell, D. J. (2010), '*Reparatieve en Herstelgerichte Strafrechtspleging: Een Goed Argument voor Twee-sporigheit in Strafrechtlijk Beleid*' in *Tijdschrift voor Herstelrecht*, vol.10, pp.7–20.

Cullen, F. and Gilbert, K. (1982), *Reaffirming Rehabilitation*, Cincinnati, ILL: Anderson Publications.

Garland, D. (2002), *The Culture of Control*, Oxford: Oxford University Press.

Gibson, B. (2008), *The New Ministry of Justice: An Introduction*; Sherfield-on-Loddon, UK: Waterside Press.

Gibson, B. (2009), *The Pocket A-Z of Criminal Justice*, Sherfield-on-Loddon, UK: Waterside Press.

Hall, S. And Scraton, P. (1981), 'Law and Class Control' in Fitzgerald, M., McLennan G and Pawson J (eds.), *Crime and Society: Readings in History and Theory*, London: Routledge and Kegan Paul, pp.460–497.

Hart, H. L. A. (1960), 'Prolegomenon to the Principles of Punishment' in *Proceedings of the Aristotelian Society, 1959–60*.

Hart, H. L. A. (1968), *Punishment and Responsibility*, Oxford: Oxford University Press.

Hudson, B. (1987), *Justice Through Punishment: A Critique of the Justice Model of Corrections*, Basingstoke: Macmillan Education Limited.

Hulsman, L. (1982), 'Penal Reform in The Netherlands: Part 2 — Criteria for Deciding on Alternatives to Imprisonment', *Howard Journal of Criminal Justice*, 21, 1982.

Kensey, A. and Tournier, P. (2001), 'French Prison Numbers Stable Since 1988, But Populations Changing' in Tonry M. (ed.), *Penal Reform in Overcrowded Times*, New York: Oxford University Press.

Kyvsgaard, B. (2001), 'Penal Sanctions and the Use of Imprisonment in Denmark' in Tonry M. (ed.), *Penal Reform in Overcrowded Times*, New York: Oxford University Press.

Lappi-Seppälä, T. (2001), 'Sentencing and Punishment in Finland: The Decline of the Repressive Ideal' in Tonry M. and Frase R. S. (eds.), *Sentencing and Sanctions in Western Countries*, New York: Oxford University Press.

Larsson, P. (2001), 'Norway Prison Use Up Slightly: Community Penalty Lots' in Tonry M. (ed.), *Penal Reform in Overcrowded Times*, New York: Oxford University Press.

Lipton, D., Martinson, R. and Wilks, J. (1975), *Effectiveness of Treatment Evaluation Studies*, New York: Praeger Publications.

Martinson, R. (1974), 'What Works? — Questions and Answers About Prison Reform', *The Public Interest*, vol.35, pp.22–54.

Matza, D. (1964), *Delinquency and Drift*, New York: John Wiley.

Mays, J. B. (1970), *Crime and its Treatment*, London: Longman.

Monahan, J. (1975), 'The Prediction of Violence' in Chappell D. and Monahan J. (eds.), *Violence and Criminal Justice*, Lexington, DC: D. C. Heath and Co.

Monahan, J. (ed.) (1976), 'The Prevention of Violence' in *Community Mental Health and the Criminal Justice System*, New York: Pergamon Press.

Morris, N. (1974), *The Future of Imprisonment*, London and Chicago, ILL: University of Chicago Free Press.

Rawls, J. B. (1961), 'Justice as Fairness' in F. A. Olafson (ed.), *Justice and Social Policy*, Englewood Cliffs, NJ: Prentice-Hall Inc.

Rutherford, A. (1986), *Prisons and the Process of Justice*, Oxford: Oxford University Press.

Seneca, L. A. (c.30AD), 'To Nero on Mercy' in *Moral Essays*, Book 1, 2-iv, 1–4, (Tr. J.W. Basore), The Loeb Classical Library, London: Heinemann.

Smart, A. (1969), 'Mercy' in Acton H. B. (ed.), *The Philosophy of Punishment: A Collection of Essays*, London: Macmillan, pp.212–228.

Sutherland, E. H. and Cressey, D. R. (1955), *Principles of Criminology* (5 edn.], Chicago, ILL: J. P. Lippincott & Company.

Tak, P. (2001), 'Sentencing and Punishment in The Netherlands' in Tonry M. and Frase R. S. (eds.), *Sentencing and Sanctions in Western Countries*, New York: Oxford University Press.

Tonry, M. (ed.) (2003), *Confronting Crime: Crime Control Policy Under New Labour*, Devon, Cullompton: Willan Publishing.

Von Hirsch, A. (1985), *Past or Future Crimes: Deservedness and Dangerousness in the Sentencing of Criminals*, Manchester: Manchester University Press.

Weigend, T. (2001), 'Sentencing and Punishment in Germany' in Tonry M. and Frase R. S. (eds.), *Sentencing and Sanctions in Western Countries*, New York: Oxford University Press.

Wright, R. (2002), 'Counting the Cost of Sentencing in North Carolina, 1980–2000' in Tonry M. (ed.), *Crime and Justice: A Review of Research*, Vol.29, Chicago, ILL: University of Chicago Press.

2

Restorative Justice as a Procedural Revolution: Some Lessons from the Adversary System

F. W. M. (Fred) McElrea[1]

Why make a film today that is not relevant to today's times? By delving into history, you wind up telling a contemporary story about ourselves:

Shekhar Kapur, Director of 'Elizabeth: The Golden Age',
Telegraph Magazine, 6 October 2007

Introduction

In the course of preparing this chapter I have read a learned and fascinating account of the history of the adversary criminal trial in England: *The Origins of Adversary Criminal Trial* by John H. Langbein (2003). This has been instructive in several respects, not least for the thoughts it throws up about restorative justice.

Although Dr Langbein has a Ph.D. from Cambridge, he is the Sterling Professor of Law and Legal History at Yale University. In 2006 his book was awarded the Coif Biennial Book Award as the outstanding American book on law. It is based on Dr Langbein's study of the Old Bailey Session Papers, which had not previously been used as a principal source of information on the criminal trial.

---

1. This chapter is based on an edited version of a paper originally presented to the first plenary session of the 4th International Winchester Restorative Justice Conference, 10 October 2007.

As Shekhar Kapur suggests in the passage quoted above, by delving into history we can end up telling a story about ourselves. There are three ways in which I have found the historical exercise valuable.

First, we discover that the adversary model is largely unchanged in its essentials since the end of the 18th century—so it is very strongly entrenched, and its ethos tends to overpower alternative models. This, I suggest, is why restorative justice struggles to get off the ground. (Lawyers from the year 1800 could walk into our criminal courts today and recognise most of what they see and hear. The same could never be said of the practice of medicine, or most other professions.) Second, we realise also that the adversary model has its weaknesses as well as its strengths, and when we study these we find that the weaknesses are in the areas where restorative justice is strong. And third, a glimpse back beyond the adversary system reveals trials in which defendants always spoke, without lawyers, and court was not the only solution. Community-based options could be inventive. Restorative justice can help us reclaim some of that history.

For those not familiar with the terminology, a brief word first about the adversary and inquisitorial models of criminal justice. The term 'inquisitorial' is, of course, related to 'inquiry'. In European countries other than the UK, a presiding magistrate is assigned by the court to *inquire* into the truth of the allegations. The court is responsible for deciding which witnesses will be examined, and those witnesses remain under the control of the court, although they may be questioned by counsel for both sides. The accused has a right of silence but nearly always speaks, in order to influence the outcome. All evidence is compiled in a court dossier, and the hearing is based on that dossier.

In the adversary system common in most English-speaking countries, there is a contest rather than an inquiry.[2] The contestants decide which witnesses they will call, and what evidence will be produced to the court. The judge's role is that of an umpire, ensuring that the rules of a fair trial are followed and pronouncing a winner. Most evidence is given orally, not compiled in a dossier. In civil cases, and in summary criminal cases, the judge decides

---

2.   Inquiries are, however, found in some parts of English law, e.g. in the form of a coroner's inquest.

which side has 'won', while in jury trials he or she sums up the case to the jury who bring in a verdict of 'guilty' or 'not guilty'.

The term 'restorative justice' is adequately explained in other chapters of this book and need not be dealt with again here. I have been working in different aspects of restorative justice for 23 of my 25 years as a judge, and speaking and writing about it for the last 22 years.[3] This chapter builds on that experience, but from a new perspective.

Restorative Justice as a Procedural Revolution

In the 1990s it was common to see restorative justice in contrast to retributive justice.[4] That dichotomy has somewhat broken down of late, and I suggest that the more meaningful comparison is a procedural one, contrasting restorative justice with the adversary criminal trial. Restorative justice, understood as a revolution in criminal *procedure*, can enable or lead to a re-ordering of our criminal justice objectives. Indeed, much of the appeal of restorative justice is that its strengths are the weaknesses of the adversary system, and thus the two may be seen to complement each other.

This comparison is possible even though restorative justice and the adversary trial have different roles — the former dealing with admitted wrongdoing and the latter with disputed criminal liability. (Restorative justice therefore cannot be a substitute for a trial system, of either the adversarial or inquisitorial type). Even so, the adversary process colours the sentencing process found in most common law jurisdictions. In particular:

- The sentencing process is under the control of the court with the outcome imposed from above, by a person in authority (the judge).
- Professionals play a major part, especially lawyers, but also probation officers, psychologists and other specialist advisers. The offender usually does not speak.

---

3. I retired from full-time judging in 2008 after 20 years on the Bench, but have continued part-time since then.

4. Probably the most influential text on restorative justice in that period was Howard Zehr's *Changing Lenses: A New Focus for Crime and Justice*, published in 1990. This contrasted retributive and restorative views of accountability — e.g. in the table at p.202. Twelve years later, however, Zehr writes: 'Despite my earlier writing, I no longer see restoration as the polar opposite of retribution' — see Zehr, 2002: 13 and 58–59.

- The process involves two parties, prosecution and defence. Victims are not parties, although their views are sought through victim impact statements or other means.
- In some jurisdictions, including the indictable (jury trial) jurisdiction in New Zealand, submissions are made by counsel for prosecution and defence, emphasising the two-party system. The process is mainly backward-looking, seeking a just punishment for past offending.

This strong imprint of the adversary system on sentencing should not surprise us, for sentencing was originally part and parcel of the trial process. Indeed, an accused could not put forward mitigating factors for sentencing except by giving evidence at trial—something that militated strongly against guilty pleas.[5] And one of the functions of the jury was to 'report any favourable circumstances … [that] appear to them',[6] which the judge took into account in sentencing.

Where sentencing does differ today from determining guilt is that the court has greater power to call for the information it considers relevant. In this area it is not dependent upon counsel and is thus closer to the investigating magistrate of the European courts. (The court is still however dependent on the trial process to provide the facts upon which sentencing proceeds.)

Historical Overview

A study of the history of the adversary criminal trial is instructive in understanding both its strengths and weaknesses, and also in reminding us that the adversary criminal trial is a reasonably modern creature, dating from 18th century England. Although ancient by my country's standards—James Cook first sighted New Zealand in 1769—this is in the 'modern' period of history.

Most law students have heard that before trial by jury, 'the means of proof [were] solemn formal oaths and ordeals designed to elicit the judgment of God'.[7] These included the ordeal of fire (carrying a red-hot iron in the hand), and—after the Norman Conquest of 1066—the ordeal of battle. What is not so well known is that even within the history of jury trials there were

---

5.   Langbein, 2003: 20.
6.   *Ibid.*
7.   Pollock and Maitland, 1952: Vol.1, 74.

two distinct phases prior to the evolution of the adversarial criminal trial in the 18th century.

Initially jurors were local people expected to know what had happened, or at least able find out from local sources. They came to court to speak of what they knew, not to listen to evidence. This type of trial prevailed until the end of the Middle-Ages (about the 15th century). Langbein attributes its demise in part to the vast social dislocations of the Black Death plague of 1348–9, and other social changes.[8] By the 16th century juries were drawn from a much wider area and consequently lost the ability to apply local knowledge. Instead they became passive triers of fact, listening to the evidence of the parties and sometimes other witnesses, in what Langbein calls the 'altercation trial' that lasted throughout the 16th and 17th centuries (the 'early modern' period).

The altercation trial of the 16th and 17th centuries

Langbein takes the term 'altercation' from the commentary of the eminent Elizabethan writer, Sir Thomas Smith, written about 1565. Smith describes a lawyer-free 'altercation' between citizen accuser and citizen accused the purpose of which was to see how the accused responded in person to the prosecution case.[9] In such trials the central questions were: what really happened, and did the accused really do it? The accuser and his witnesses would speak (on oath), the defendant (speaking unsworn) would reply to the accusing testimony, and (said Smith) 'so they stand a while in altercation ...'[10] — or, as Langbein puts it, in 'this unstructured bicker' of accusers and accused.[11] As he notes, such trials 'had a formless or wandering quality that resembles ordinary discourse, a conversation of sorts, lacking the crisp division into prosecution and defense case that we now expect'.[12]

The fuller text of Smith's account in his Chapter 23 is worth repeating:[13]

8.   Langbein, 2003: 64.
9.   Langbein, 2003: 13, 146 and 271.
10. *Ibid.* 13 and 321.
11. Langbein, 2003: 259.
12. *Ibid.*
13. Smith, c1565: 99–100.

The Judge first after they be sworne, asketh first the partie robbed, if he knowe the prisoner, and biddeth him looke upon him: he saith yea, the prisoner sometimes say nay. The partie pursuivant [prosecutor] giveth good ensignes verbi gratia [for example], I knowe thee well ynough, thou robbedst me in such a place, thou beatest me, thou tookest my horse from mee, and my purse, thou hadst then such a coate and such a man in thy companie: the theefe will say no, and so they stand a while in altercation, then he [the prosecutor?] telleth al he can say : after him likewise all those who were at the apprehension of the prisoner, or who can give any indices or tokens which we call in our language evidence against the malefactor. When the Judge hath heard them say inough, he asketh if they can say any more : if they say no, then he turneth his speeche to the enquest [jury]. Good men (saith he) ye of the enquest, ye have heard what these men say against the prisoner, you have also heard what the prisoner can say for himselfe, have an eye to your othe, and to your tuetie, and doe that which God shall put in your mindes to the discharge of your consciences, and marke well what is saide.

While there is no mention here of defence witnesses, Langbein (2003: 51–56) explains that they were allowed, but unlike prosecution witnesses: (i) they were not bound over by the JP to attend at trial (and were unlikely even to be contacted by an accused held in custody); and (ii) until Parliament intervened in 1702, they did not give their evidence on oath. (The accused's evidence remained unsworn until the Criminal Evidence Act of 1898, ostensibly to spare him the choice between defending himself and damning his soul through perjury.)

Langbein notes that the English criminal courts were 'determined to hear the accused speak in person and unaided at oral public trial'.[14] Elsewhere he notes: [15]

The logic of the early modern [altercation] criminal trial was to pressure the accused to speak, either to clear himself or to hang himself. Having to conduct his own defense obliged the accused to become an information resource for the court.

---

14. Langbein, 2003: 61–62.
15. Langbein, 2003: 36.

The altercation trial was defended by the noted 19th-century legal historian Sir James Fitzjames Stephen. Whilst aware of the shortcomings of this system, he explained:[16]

> The trials were short and sharp....They were directed to the very point at issue, and, whatever disadvantages the prisoner lay under, he was allowed to say whatever he pleased; his attention was pointedly called to every part of the case against him, and if he had a real answer to make he had the opportunity of bringing it out effectively and in detail.

Noticeable in these accounts of the altercation trial is the absence of lawyers. Although it must have often worked great injustice, the justification given in the early 17th century by Sir Edward Coke, Lord Chief Justice of England, was that 'a defendant's plea of not guilty goeth to the fact best known to the party'.[17] Or, as it was put a century later by William Hawkins, 'everyone of Common Understanding may as properly speak to a Matter of Fact, as if he were the best Lawyer ... it requires no manner of Skill to make a plain and honest Defence'.[18]

Another feature of the times was the absence of professional prosecutors. Police prosecutions did not commence until the 19th century, after the formation of full-time police forces. Previously all prosecutions were what today would be called 'private' prosecutions. It was up to the complainant (the citizen accuser) to prosecute the case, if it was to be heard at all. Some help was available to the prosecutor from the local (unpaid) justices of the peace, to whom the crime was reported. It was his task to prepare pre-trial 'depositions'[19] by recording the statements of accuser (and any other prosecution witnesses) and accused, before making any committal for trial.[20]

The JPs' role in questioning the accused and other witnesses gave them a role in the investigation of crime similar to that now undertaken by the

---

16. Stephen, 1883: Vol.1, 355.
17. Coke, c.1620s–1630s: 137.
18. Hawkins, 1716, 1721, Vol 2: 400.
19. See further Langbein, 2003: 40–41.
20. Until the 18th century the JPs had no power to dismiss felony charges for lack of evidence—instead the filtering out of weak cases was done by a 'grand' jury of 23, as distinct from the trial jury of 12 citizens (the 'petty' jury).

police. However, while accusers were forced to speak at trial, so was the accused. Since juries were no longer a source of information, the altercation trial induced the accused to disclose what he knew about the matter.[21] This view of the defendant as a source of information is something that has since been lost from the criminal law — (I suggest) to our detriment.

The evolution of the adversary system

Langbein considers that the transition from altercation to adversary trial occurred gradually, with no central design, and without its participants foreseeing the outcome. In essence, the adversary trial evolved in response to a series of problems, particularly for defendants. Some of these have parallels even today.

There were heavy burdens on citizen-prosecutors. The time, effort and cost[22] involved in gathering witnesses and getting their evidence taken by the local magistrate (JP) was a disincentive to many people, so that many crimes were not prosecuted. In response to this, there were formed many mutual associations[23] for the prosecution of felons, and as well solicitors (often the clerks to the JPs) came to play a role in pre-trial work, especially the drafting of indictments and preparing proofs of the evidence for the citizen-prosecutor.

- Solicitors became commonly used by those who could afford them, i.e. the wealthy, but were sometimes disreputable and unscrupulous — the 'Newgate solicitors'.[24] However this assistance to citizen-prosecutors, by JPs and sometimes solicitors, was one-sided and seen as unfair to the accused.

- A further factor against the accused was the practice of offering rewards, equivalent to many years' income for humble folk, which often led to

---

21. Langbein, 2003: 64–65.
22. Court staff were dependent upon fees for their living (Sharpe, 1980: 110–111). Not until the 1750s did Parliament empower the courts to reimburse the costs of poor prosecutors and witnesses who secured the conviction of felons.
23. Langbein, 2003: 131–136.
24. An anonymous tract published in London in 1728 was entitled *Directions for prosecuting thieves without the help of those false guides, the Newgate Sollicitors* [Sic. Eds.] (Langbein, 2003: 124).

perjured evidence (some engineered by disreputable solicitors) and therefore unjust verdicts.

- The unfairness was compounded by some judges who prior to the Act of
  Settlement of 1701 were not independent of the Crown and whose bias
  was seen most clearly in treason trials. Parliament intervened, therefore,
  to allow defence counsel at trial,[25] but only in the case of treason trials
  (the Treason Trials Act of 1696).

- In the early 18th-century, judges started to allow defence counsel in felony
  trials, at first only in special cases, such as with a foreign or sick accused,
  but then more generally. Although by 1753 counsel perceived a 'right' to
  counsel, even at the end of that century only one-quarter to one-third of
  defendants at the Old Bailey had the benefit of counsel.[26]

- However the pressure on the accused to speak was maintained by limiting
  defence counsel to cross-examination of witnesses — they could address
  the judge on legal matters but were not allowed to address the jury on the
  accused's defence.[27] The impact of defence counsel was further limited to
  the few cases in which the accused could afford counsel's fee.

- Defence counsel changed the dynamic of the felony trial by sometimes
  addressing the jury (by surreptitious means[28] — they had no right of
  address until Parliament intervened with the Prisoners' Counsel Act of
  1836), by developing out of the privilege of witnesses a right of silence,

25. Defence counsel had previously been allowed to argue points of law upon the indictment, but
    this was at the pre-trial stage.
26. Langbein, 2003: 170.
27. Langbein, 2003: 254–255.
28. 'In practice … it proved hard to stop defence counsel from making small interjections that
    were argumentative in character' (Langbein, 2003: 297). Sir James Fitzpatrick Stephen
    remarked that 'cross-examination tended to become a speech thrown in the form of questions'
    (Stephen, 1883: Vol.2, 431). Editorial note: There has been some revisionist history in recent
    years and with a high public profile. John Hostettler and William Braby have explained
    how William Garrow and others changed the nature of the trial and the role of counsel: see
    Sir William Garrow: His Life, Times and Fight for Justice (2009), Sherfield-on-Loddon, UK:
    Waterside Press. This was also aided by the BBC's involvement in 'Garrow's Law'.

and by focusing the court's attention on whether the charge had been proved, rather than on the accused's response to it.[29]

- The growing aversion to the death penalty in the second half of the 18th century played a part in these developments.

An Overview of Adversarial and Restorative Processes

Against this background, what are the weaknesses of the adversary system (including those identified by Langbein) and what relevance do they have to restorative justice? I set these out first in summary form and then expand upon my answers.

	Adversarial procedure	Restorative processes
1	Central control with imposed outcomes (requires huge state resources)	Community-based, consensual model (requires some community resources)
2	A two-party system (victims excluded)	Multi-party system, with victims central
3	Process dominated by professionals — hence —	Professionals have support roles only — hence —
4	… system favours the wealthy …	… wealth not a factor
5	… truth often suppressed	… truth is highly valued

29. The standard of proof 'beyond reasonable doubt' appeared in the 1780s, apparently as an initiative of the judges (Langbein, 2003: 263–265).

	Adversarial procedure	**Restorative processes**
6	Focus is on whether offence is proved	Offence admitted — focus on putting right
7	Little incentive on offenders to speak	Offenders do speak, and are valued as a source of information
8	Outcomes restricted by law	Flexible and often creative outcomes
9	Distorted by harsh penalties	Usually avoids harsh penalties
10	Procedure often formalistic and archaic	Informal, adaptable processes
11	A method of prosecution	Can follow or be alternative to prosecution
12	Emphasises the defendant's rights	Emphasises responsibilities

1. Imposed versus consensual outcomes

We are well accustomed to the current, western model of justice in which the outcome is imposed by an authority figure. However the notion of consensual outcomes (now common as mediation in civil disputes) is far from new to English law, even in the context of crimes. Anglo-Saxon (and other) law had a system of monetary compensation known as 'bot' or betterment. The offender could settle the matter by making *bot* to the injured party and paying *wite* to the king, according to an established tariff. As is explained by Pollock and Maitland;[30]

---

30. 1952: Vol.2, 450–451.

> Every kind of blow or wound given to every kind of person had its price ... Gradu-
> ally more and more offences became emendable [able to be paid for]; outlawry
> remained for those who would not or could not pay. Homicide, unless of a specially
> aggravated kind, was emendable; the bot for homicide was the wergild[31] of the slain.

Even in later times, prosecution was far from an automatic response to offending.

> ... for centuries [before the 19th-century] the English system had worked on the
> principle that indictment before a court was the last resort to be tried; there were
> all sorts of alternative informal means which the potential prosecutor might try
> to use short of formal prosecution. What the 18th-century gentry and aristocracy
> valued, was the discretion which the system left them free to exercise ...[32]

(One could add that such discretion to prosecute (or not) remained part of the criminal law and today forms the basis of many alternative measures, some referred to as 'diversion'.)

And from another author:

> ... there was a wide variety of informal sanctions through which indictable behav-
> iour might be controlled or punished: dismissal or chastisement by an employer;
> informal coercion or admonition by a priest or landowner; arbitration; and control
> through the poor law ... It must be remembered, moreover, that the law itself had
> at its disposal a number of means for dealing with the petty offender other than
> by indicting him. Three of these [were] summary conviction before a justice or
> justices, binding over [to keep the peace] and the use of the house of correction ...[33]

A delightful example, from the restorative viewpoint, is that of George Hawkins, caught stealing wood from the landed gentry in 1674. 'Hawkins was made to set his mark[34] to a paper which admitted his fault, expressed

---

31. The statutory sum that would atone for the death.
32. Philips, 1980: 158.
33. Sharpe, 1980: 117–118.
34. He was, we assume, illiterate and had no signature.

his sorrow for it, and contained his promise never to do the like again.'[35] The records of the ecclesiastical courts provide another example:

> When a dispute arose between two women ... a co-parishioner declared 'I would to God yow two were frend[es], for this is not the best meanes for neighbours to sue another.' The two women agreed to settle their differences, and drank a health to each other to symbolize their reconciliation. The deposition relates how 'Katherin tooke the cupp and dranke to the said Emote who thanked her and ... tooke the cupp of her and dranke of yt'.[36]

Perhaps western societies have expected too much of the adversary system, loading it up with more and more responsibilities at the expense of local solutions. History shows that it can co-exist with less formal, more community-based means of dealing with wrongdoing. A change back towards greater use of these alternatives would be consistent with the modern emphases on decentralisation, on strengthening communities, and on concerns about the spiralling cost of court-administered and prison-based criminal justice.

In the process other benefits are likely to ensue. For example, because restorative justice operates only by consent—both in respect of process and of outcomes—it has a higher proportion of reparation agreements fulfilled than the courts achieve with reparation orders. One Canadian study showed that victims seeking restitution for material harm were more than four times as likely to receive it as victims whose cases went to court.[37] In my view this is due to the greater value which people attach to arrangements they have made themselves, compared to those imposed on them.

2. The exclusion of victims

Western legal systems deal with criminal offending as a matter between the State and the defendant. It is the state, or an agent thereof, that prosecutes. In lower courts this is often the police, and in higher courts the Crown.

---

35. Sharpe, 1980: 113.
36. Sharpe, 1980: 112, citing the records of the Archbishop of York's Consistory Court—unfortunately from an undefined time.
37. Reported in Sherman and Strang, 2007: 58. See e.g. the Australian National University research, known as RISE (Reintegrative Shaming Experiments).

Victims are not regarded as parties to criminal proceedings, and their role is usually little more than as witnesses, if they are involved at all.

A large body of literature is now devoted to the problems of victims in our criminal justice systems. Politicians have been alert to the views of lay people on this subject, but lawyers have mostly not understood what all the fuss is about. For me the principal benefit of restorative justice is the fact that victims are involved in, and central to, its procedures.

Langbein does not address the low profile of victims in the adversary system, perhaps because: (i) he favours the inquisitorial system which is still essentially a two-party, state-controlled system; and (ii) victims remained involved as prosecutors (as well as witnesses) in the development of the adversary criminal trial in the 18th century, the period under consideration by Langbein. It was only after the Metropolitan Police Force Act of 1829 that a recognisably modern constabulary was established and took over from citizen-accusers the burden of prosecution.

Indeed, Langbein's account shows victims (accusers) closely involved as prosecutors and witnesses, to the point where it was a burden to them. What restorative justice offers victims is not an engagement in a combative and time-consuming, formal process but a chance for victims to meet offenders in a supportive environment, have their anger and hurt acknowledged by the offender, obtain information that is important to them and (most likely) an apology, and discuss how matters can best be put right.

Restorative justice is, however, more than just victim-offender mediation—indeed, given that wrongdoing must be admitted, it is not mediation at all.[38] It should involve other community members, particularly friends or family of the victim and offender but also people who might help suggest solutions to problems for the wider community. Not only is the larger group usually more resourceful, but it sometimes allows a slightly wider view of responsibility for the offending.[39]

---

38. Mediation makes no assumptions about wrongdoing, and both sides are expected to compromise to reach agreement. See, further, Zehr, 2002: 9.

39. For example, victims may complain of disinterest by the prosecuting body, or contributing actions by other authorities—e.g. poor street lighting not fixed, or delays in providing safe systems.

3. The dominance of professionals

Langbein's account traces in valuable detail the way in which lawyers not only became involved in criminal trials but came to totally dominate them, to the exclusion not only of the accused but in some respects the judge. Lawyers often coached witnesses in what they would say, spoke for and on behalf of the accused, and helped the accused draft his (unsworn) trial statement. They took over from the judges the role of examining the witnesses.[40] Langbein sums up defence counsel's 'commandeering' of the trial as ending the altercation trial, silencing the accused, marginalising the judge, and breaking-up the working relationship of judge and jury.[41]

It is an interesting observation of Langbein that the dominance of lawyers in English criminal trials came about as a 'remedy for one-sidedness', that remedy being 'two-sidedness'. No thought seems to have been given at that time to 'the truth-seeking Continental model', possibly because it still permitted torture (called half proof)[42] and was discredited on that account.

What restorative justice offers is an escape from 'two-sidedness' by including the victim (and others), encouraging the discovery of shared needs and obligations, and limiting professionals' roles to that of supporters. Judges never attend restorative conferences. If lawyers are present, they are not advocates: offenders must be allowed to speak for themselves. Lawyers can give advice if sought, and indeed can be a source of information about the criminal justice system for all present. In New Zealand, police officers are encouraged to attend; they do so not as a prosecutor but as a representative of the public interest whose presence often assists victims. (In youth justice matters, police 'youth aid' officers attend every family group conference, and are highly valued for their professional contributions.)

In fact most adult restorative conferences take place without lawyers or police present. The freeing up of criminal justice from the domination of professional groups is a major advantage of restorative processes. Matters

---

40. The judge's part in questioning the accused seemed not to have the partisan features of cross-examination by counsel. 'The judge commonly questioned the participants to fill out the testimony they volunteered, and called upon the accused to respond' (Langbein, 2003: 253).
41. Langbein, 2003: 17.
42. Langbein, 2003: 84 (re two-sidedness) and 339 (re torture). Torture had been allowed in England between about 1540 and 1640 but only for Privy Council investigations, mostly in cases of treason (Langbein, 2003: 340).

proceed (under the guidance of a facilitator[43]) on their merits, rather than on technicalities; the people most affected by wrongdoing are empowered to deal with the results as best suits them; and the cost to the parties and the state is much reduced.

4. The 'wealth effect' of adversary trial procedure

Adversary criminal procedure privatizes the investigation and presentation of evidence. Such a procedure is intrinsically skewed to the advantage of wealthy defendants, who can afford to hire the most skilled counsel and to pay for the gathering and production of defensive evidence.[44]

It follows from what has just been said under the previous heading that most people do not feel the need of lawyers in restorative processes, and so all parties, rich and poor, are on a much more even footing. (However it is important that the parties are not prevented from getting legal advice, and have access to their lawyer in private when they desire advice.) Accordingly, the wealth effect described by Langbein is absent from restorative justice.

Legal aid has not overcome the problems of the wealth effect, at least to any marked degree. In most legal systems the top lawyers generally do not handle legal aid cases, and the financial restrictions on legal aid mean that there are large numbers of litigants not poor enough to receive legal aid but not rich enough to afford competent counsel for any length of time.

Where wealth can be relevant is in the means available to the offender to make reparation to the victim. This can of course produce different outcomes, which are a fact of life for court and non-court systems, but it does not mean that the wealthy come out of restorative justice better off than the poor, for three reasons.

First, reparation can be made in different forms, including unpaid work for a victim, or for a charity nominated by the victim. The court cannot order such work. Secondly, where offenders attend with family or community supporters, the wider group often accepts some responsibility in the matter, or for other reasons wishes to see the victim compensated. Thus it is common for reparation to be made by one or more members of the wider

---

43. Facilitators must be professional, and in New Zealand are trained according to best practice, but their role is to allow others to express themselves, not to assert their own views.
44. Langbein, 2003: 102–103.

group, usually with reimbursement promised to them by the offender. This sort of result is rare in court processes. Thirdly, victims who have attended a restorative conference are surprisingly understanding of offenders' problems, especially if they see them also as the 'underdog'. In my experience it is almost unknown for a victim not to agree to an outcome because insufficient money has been offered, However, the wealthier offender will be expected to make fuller reparation, precisely because he has more to offer.

5. Suppression of truth — the 'combat effect'

Two-sided partisanship may indeed have been better than one-sided partisanship, but it was still a poor proxy for truth-seeking.[45]

Langbein describes as a 'fundamental structural flaw' the combat effect that became apparent in the later 18th-century:

> By the combat effect, I refer to the incentives to distort or suppress the truth, for example by concealing relevant witnesses, withholding information that would help the other side, preparing witnesses to affect their testimony at trial (coaching), and engaging in abusive cross-examination.[46]

Abusive cross-examination is referred to as 'trying the victim',[47] as is well understood by rape victims. In 1787 Sir John Hawkins, a prominent London magistrate, expressed his concern that such tactics deterred citizen prosecutors from going to court, because they 'may be entangled or made to contradict themselves, or each other, in a cross-examination, by prisoner's counsel …'.[48]

The most aggressive of defence counsel seems to have been one William Garrow. His tactics were the opposite of the counsel of perfection of one Thomas Gisborne in the 1790s:

> [H]e will not defame the witnesses of the adverse party; nor … strive to rob their testimony, which they are of the credit it deserves. He will not overawe [witnesses] … by brow-beating and menaces, nor impose on their simplicity by

---

45. Langbein, 2003: 332.
46. Langbein, 2003: 265.
47. Langbein, 2003: 295.
48. Quoted in Langbein, 2003: 296.

sophistry and cunning. He will not ... insidiously labour to extract from their words a sense foreign to their intentions. He will abhor the idea of drawing those who appear against him into any seeming contradictions and perjury, when he perceives their meaning to be honest and their story in reality consistent.[49]

Few judges today would see this as a realistic account of the role of counsel under the adversary system. Many counsel see it as their job to deprive opposing testimony of the credit it deserves, to brow-beat (though not to menace) witnesses, and to get opposing witnesses to say what they do not mean. While judges can intervene to ensure that witnesses are not treated unfairly, there is a limit to how far they can do so without 'descending into the arena' or 'entering the fray' which they are not meant to do.

A common method of attempting to discredit the evidence of a witness is to point to allegedly inconsistent statements by the witness — e.g. earlier statements not containing the same detail as now given in court. Research summarised at a conference in Cambridge[50] showed that the assumptions made in this form of reasoning are often wrong. A paper presented by Dr Katrin Muller-Johnson, 'Eye Witness and Ear Witness Testimony', explained that:

- In mock crime scenarios, 97 per cent of witnesses provided a later statement with inconsistencies.
- Providing additional information in a later interview is common (found in 98 per cent of one survey), but such information has a high level of accuracy (87 per cent, compared to 95 per cent of the original evidence).
- The difference between the two accounts may be explained by different 'retrieval cues' (e.g. questions) leading to different answers.
- The number of inconsistencies and contradictions was unrelated to the accuracy of the witness's consistent statements.
- Police officers taking statements rarely record all information supplied, yet such information later given by the witness is (wrongly) treated as being especially suspicious.

49. Quoted in Langbein, 2003: 307.
50. Muller-Johnson, 2007.

- Inconsistency between a witness statement and what he or she says in court is probably the single most common cause of wrongful acquittals.

I do not know whether such problems affect evidence given in inquisitorial hearings, but in my judicial experience they are a regular tool of adversarial combat, and one which leaves honest witnesses feeling that their words have been twisted and turned against them.

Langbein correctly diagnoses the combat effect of the adversary process as almost inevitably producing such outcomes. He also correctly notes that there is no obligation on adversaries to put all relevant material before the court, although most countries recognise some obligation of fairness on the part of prosecution counsel. As a result, the court can proceed ignorant of highly relevant material known to one side in the dispute.

The contrast with the restorative approach could not be more marked. There truthfulness is encouraged, as it is part of the process of being accountable and accepting responsibility for wrongdoing. And because there are (ideally) more than victim and offender present, the chances of truth being suppressed are reduced. Someone present is likely to know the fuller story and refer to it. This may even be the victim, who sometimes speaks in support of an offender's explanation.[51] But the most powerful and important form of truth that a victim can receive is an apology.

Further, the requirements of good practice followed by facilitators ensures that there is no 'brow-beating', that each person present is treated with respect and is able to speak without interruption, and coaching of any person present is usually easily detected and unlikely to occur. What is interesting is that lay people find restorative processes to be fairer than court procedures[52] — which is surprising as fairness of process is considered the touchstone of the adversary system. I believe that this is because lay people value truthfulness, dislike a reliance on technicalities, and consider the willingness to hear all affected parties a virtue.

51. For example, the police summary of facts may contain elements that both victim and offender dispute.
52. This also was an outcome of the Australian RISE research, as summarised in Sherman and Strang (2007: 19). Victims experiencing restorative justice had a stronger preference for the process (69% compared to 48%) and greater satisfaction with the outcome (60% compared to 46%) than victims whose offenders were dealt with through the courts.

6. Putting the prosecution to the proof

By assuming the work of defending, and by insisting on the prosecutorial burdens of production and proof, counsel largely (sometimes entirely) silenced the accused. Shutting down the old 'accused speaks' trial changed the very theory of the trial. The purpose of the altercation trial had been to provide the accused an opportunity to reply in person to the charges and the evidence against him. Adversary trial put in place a new conception of the trial, oriented on the lawyers. Criminal trial became an opportunity for defense counsel to test the prosecution case.[53]

Under the next heading we will consider the effect of silencing the accused. For the present the focus is on the notion that criminal liability is a question of whether the prosecution, without reliance on the accused, can prove the charge. Langbein is right in seeing this change brought about by the adversary system as fundamental. Here I wish to repeat what I have said before:[54]

I suggest that one of the key defects in the criminal process today relates to pleading....[A] 'plea' of Not Guilty does not necessarily mean that the defendant denies guilt. It may mean only that the defendant wishes to 'put the prosecution to the proof', i.e. to see if the prosecution can prove its case. This can operate as an incentive not to accept responsibility but instead to deny all responsibility that the defendant or his lawyer thinks cannot be proved. As things stand this is not only permissible but encouraged. Further, with proceedings laid indictably (i.e. intended for trial by jury) the defendant is not even asked to plead until after a preliminary hearing [Taking 'depositions', writing down witnesses' evidence in committal proceedings for transmission to a higher court, is a practice that is now effectively extinct in English committal procedings (Eds.)]. Of course if a key element of an offence does not exist then the defendant should indeed be found Not Guilty. But if instead the prosecution should fail to prove an ingredient of the offence through the absence (or faded memory) of an important witness, or because a witness lies, or through failure to correctly recite the breath-alcohol litany in the witness box, or by simple oversight of the prosecutor, or because relevant evidence is ruled inadmissible, is justice served by a Not Guilty finding?

53. Langbein, 2003: 310.
54. McElrea, 2002.

Where the guilty are found Not Guilty by this process an injustice is done which the positivist approach does not recognise.

I therefore propose that we should do away with the concept of putting the prosecution to the proof, except where the defendant denies the charge or has no means of knowing what happened at the time. Why should not defendants be told the charge against them and asked whether that charge is admitted or denied? If it is admitted then the prosecution should not have to prove it. (Lawyers will have an important role to perform in ensuring that accused persons understand what it is they are admitting to and what defences might be available to them.) If denied it should be proved using the adversary system.

As long ago as 1995 the Attorney-General and Deputy Minister of Justice of Saskatchewan, Brent Cotter, expressed a similar view: he said the criminal justice system encourages offenders to avoid responsibility and deny, and hope you might 'get off'. In a family, such behaviour would be considered dysfunctional. In a community, he suggested, it is still dysfunctional. I agree. By organizing our criminal justice system on this premise we have discouraged personal accountability and promoted evasiveness. A tentative step in the opposite direction was taken by the New Zealand Parliament with section 7 of the Sentencing Act 2002. The list of purposes of sentencing provided by the section reads:

(a) to hold the offender accountable for harm done to the victim and the community by the offending; or
(b) to promote in the offender a sense of responsibility for, and an acknowledgement of, that harm; or
(c) to provide for the interests of the victim of the offence; or
(d) to provide reparation for harm done by the offending; or
(e) to denounce the conduct in which the offender was involved; or
(f) to deter the offender or other persons from committing the same or a similar offence; or
(g) to protect the community from the offender; or
(h) to assist in the offender's rehabilitation and reintegration; or
(i) a combination of two or more of the purposes in paragraphs (a) to (h).

The first two purposes listed were new to our sentencing jurisprudence, although they had been present in our 1989 youth justice legislation. They allow the courts to move in quite a different direction to the largely punitive route of the past. Unfortunately, only judges already familiar with restorative justice seem to have made much use of these provisions. They do however provide a statutory framework for a very different, restorative approach.[55]

Even the humble mark of the thief George Hawkins[56] in 1674 signified 'his promise never to do the like again'. Victims are as much concerned about the future as the past. Once they have been vindicated by the acceptance of responsibility and (in most cases) an apology, most victims want to ensure, if possible, that this trauma will not be inflicted on them or anyone else again. If that can be achieved, some good has come out of their bad fortune. (Is this not why families of people killed in accidents often commit themselves to changing the circumstances that led to their loved one's death?) Instead of encouraging an offender to justify his conduct, and hence the suffering of the victim, restorative justice allows both sides to work towards the elimination of such strife in the future.

7. Silencing the accused

It is true, of course, that restorative justice is not a trial system, and it requires an admission of the wrongdoing before entry into the process. This does not mean, however, that comparisons are not possible under this heading. In fact the contrast between the two approaches, in terms of personal accountability, is stark. Whether appearing in a civil or criminal court, a defendant will probably have been told to admit nothing. In court the defendant says as little as possible, leaving it all to counsel. No concern is expressed for the welfare of the person hurt. There is no opportunity to talk with the victim, let alone make what for many is the natural human response, an apology.

Langbein traces the silencing of the accused as stemming from the decision to allow counsel to address the jury, coupled with the development

---

55. With the leadership of Britain's top judges—eminent legal minds like Lords Woolf, Phillips, Falconer, and Sir Robin Auld—there is some hope that these attitudes could change in the UK, and perhaps beyond. I do however acknowledge the leadership in New Zealand of successive Chief District Court judges.

56. Hawkins, 1716, 1721: 8.

of the onus of proof as a central emphasis of the trial. As noted under the previous heading:

> Shutting down the old 'accused speaks' trial changed the very theory of the trial. The purpose of the altercation trial had been to provide the accused an opportunity to reply in person to the charges and the evidence against him.

In restorative processes, that 'the accused speaks' is taken for granted. This is facilitated by the more natural structure of conversation and the un-adversarial atmosphere. It resembles much more what Langbein said of the altercation trial, which (it will be recalled) 'had a formless or wandering quality that resembles ordinary discourse, a conversation of sorts, lacking the crisp division into prosecution and defense case that we now expect'.[57]

The value of an offender speaking has several aspects. First, the offender is a source of information. It is, on reflection, extraordinary that the common law legal systems allowed that value to be lost.[58] In the home, in the workplace, at school, in recreation, when something goes wrong the very first thing we do is to speak to the people involved, to try and find out what happened, and why. The alleged offenders may have highly relevant information that helps resolve the issue, and/or prevent such problems arising in the future.

In a restorative justice setting, victims have many questions of the offender, and it is a basic need to have those questions answered.[59] These will include questions affecting the security of the victim — why had they been targeted, had the offender planned to strike again, what has been done with stolen property? There may also be questions about the incident itself, especially if the victim has no memory of it, or a loved one has died — where exactly did he die, what were his last words, did he ask for me?

Secondly, victims have a need to speak, to tell their story and to have the offender acknowledge their anger, hurts and anxieties as justified. This is part of the vindication of the victim that is so important to them. It is

---

57. Langbein, 2003: 259.
58. I accept that the UK has allowed some inroads into the right to silence through the provisions of ss.34 and 35 of the Criminal Justice and Public Order Act 1994, allowing appropriate inferences to be drawn from an accused's silence when questioned by the police or at trial.
59. See Zehr, 1990: 26–28.

worth repeating the insight of Dr Nigel Biggar on this topic: 'Justice is primarily not about the punishment of the perpetrator but rather about the vindication of the victim'.[60] So often what victims want to hear most is the offender's acknowledgement of the wrongdoing — that, yes, this did happen to you, and you are right to feel as you do about it. Only the offender who speaks can meet these needs.

Thirdly, the offender can help construct a new order, by participating in discussion as to how these problems might be avoided in the future. Restorative justice looks backward in order to look forward. What can be done differently in future, who should be involved, and how will it be arranged? In part this involves reflecting on the offender's explanations for his conduct, and encouraging him to make the necessary changes in his life. It may also involve changes in the community of which he is part. If he does not speak of these things there is little use other people telling him what to do.

8. Restricted outcomes

It is of the nature of a legal system that it limits the power of those in authority, and in most countries the sentences available to the court are those provided by parliament. Some flexibility arises where courts are empowered to impose special conditions of a sentence, e.g. supervision, but even then the discretion is limited by such criteria as preventing re-offending.

This point of comparison with restorative justice is not one that arises out of Dr Langbein's book. He does not suggest that prior to the advent of the adversary system there were fewer restrictions on the types of sentences. However, Dr Sharpe's essay emphasises the extent of informal punishments available through various types of social control in the 17th-century (i.e. within the span of the altercation trial). Sharpe also notes:

> Students of 18th-century court procedures have shown how the letter of the law was often adjusted to the individual circumstances of offenders once they appeared in court; much of the material assembled in this essay suggests that this flexibility in treatment of the offender was already taking place before he or she came to court.[61]

---

60. Biggar, 1999: 27.
61. Sharpe, 1980: 118.

Flexibility of outcomes is undoubtedly one of the strengths of restorative justice. The story from the Archbishop of York's Consistory Court, about Katherin and Emote drinking each other's health, could have come straight out of a report of a restorative conference. I can think of many similar examples as elements of restorative outcome plans—offenders agreeing to deliver an apology *and* a bunch of flowers to a victim, a newspaper publishing its own apology to an aggrieved community, donations made to community projects, offenders working unpaid for the victim (and then being offered permanent work), new trees being planted and maintained, educative articles being written for ethnic newspapers, acknowledgements of culpability being published in directors' reports to shareholders, and that wonderful Canadian example of the young man who would normally have gone to prison for drunken driving causing the death of his two friends. That was not their families' wish. The outcome of the case after a restorative conference was an educative programme in which the defendant spoke to students at numerous local high schools. The Court of Appeal of Manitoba[62] dismissed the Crown's appeal against the sentence of community work, with one of the appellate judges asking, 'How is the principle of general deterrence better served than by speaking to 8,200 students about the tragedy of drinking and driving?' (The court was right—the resulting reduction in road deaths for young people the next summer was very significant).

None of this should be surprising. When those most affected by wrongdoing are asked what can be done to put things right for them and their communities, the answers will tend to be individualistic and creative, not prescribed or formulaic. This has greater appeal for all parties, including offenders.

It follows that I am not a fan of the modern emphasis on 'proportionality' in sentencing as being the central factor. It *sounds* right that like cases should be treated alike, but in practice it all depends upon how you measure likeness. Usually it is by reference to only a few factors—e.g. in aggravated assault cases, the amount of force used, the injuries inflicted and the nature of the aggravating factors (such as use of weapons). Forced into such a 'sentencing grid' judges produce predictable sentences and appellate judges can

62. *R v. Hollingsby* (1995).

correct 'error' with real ease—indeed in New Zealand it is appellate judges (largely uninterested in restorative justice), not Parliament, that put so much weight on proportionality.

I believe proportionality is also beloved of the news media because it enables them to review the sentences of the courts and encourage public 'outrage' at sentences they adjudge to be too lenient. Outrage encourages higher sales and therefore profits for the media. I make no excuse for being very cynical about that, and the related rise in incidence of 'trial by media'.

However, look more closely at the facts of two 'apparently alike cases' and you will find vast areas of difference. Lay people, in my experience, expect these to matter in sentencing, and do not mind apparently disproportionate sentences when the reasons are explained to them. Indeed, when they participate in devising outcomes in a restorative context, lay people are remarkably inventive and flexible in producing what they see to be a just outcome. It is a far cry from the 'sentencing by numbers' formulas so common in many courts.

9. The undue rigour of the criminal law

The long reign of the death penalty in English law is a memorable aspect of its history. This was not because it took time to reduce the number of capital offences, but because for some time the number of such offences was increased. Radzinowicz quotes from Sir Thomas Buxton's speech in the House of Commons in 1821 on the law of forgery:

> Men there are living, at whose birth our code contained less than seventy capital offences; and we have seen that number more than trebled....It is a fact that six hundred men were condemned to death last year upon statutes passed within that century.[63]

Langbein refers to the 'truth-defeating tendencies' operating at each stage of the criminal prosecution, which judges and others were disposed to tolerate because, in the realm of the criminal trial, 'too much truth brought too much death'.[64] Thus, he reports, prosecutors connived with the clerks

---

63. Parliamentary Debates (1821), N.S. Vol.5, col.926, quoted in Radzinowicz, 1948: 5.
64. Langbein, 2003: 334.

who drafted indictments to charge simple theft rather than burglary or theft from a dwelling house. Judges would construe capital statutes restrictively, and developed exclusionary rules of evidence. (They could also recommend clemency.) Juries would down-value goods, to take the offence outside the scope of the death penalty—a practice referred to by Blackstone as 'pious perjury'—often with the assistance of the judge.[65] By these and other means prisoners might be flogged, (from the 17th century) transported, or (from the 19th century) imprisoned, instead of being hung.

Langbein provides a fine example of the cooperation of judge and jury in this process. He cites the case of Frederick Usop, charged in 1784 with theft from a dwelling-house of clothing valued at 28 shillings. Where the goods exceeded five shillings in value this was a capital offence under an Act of Parliament of 1699. Baron Eyre, the presiding judge, told the jury that the 1699 law was 'made a century ago, [and] that which a century ago was of the value of five shillings, should rather be considered in a case like this, and in favour of life, than what we value at five shillings now; and if you are of that opinion, you may find the prisoner guilty of stealing to the value of 4s. 10d., which will acquit him of the capital part of the indictment'. The jury duly obliged and Usop was transported.[66]

The growing aversion to capital punishment in the second half of the 18th-century 'played an important role in causing the suspect premises of adversary criminal trial to go unchallenged'.

> By that time the understanding was widespread that English criminal law over-prescribed capital punishment, hence that a main function of the criminal trial was to winnow down the number of persons actually executed from the much larger cohort of culprits whom the 'Bloody Code' threatened with death.[67]

It is interesting that Parliament came to see the excessive use of harsh punishment not just as inhumane but as working against the administration of criminal justice. Thus in 1822 Sir James Mackintosh successfully moved in the House of Commons that Parliament should consider 'the means of

---

65. Langbein, 2003: 334–337.
66. Langbein, 2003: 366 footnote 396.
67. Langbein, 2003: 6. And see Chapter 5.

increasing the efficacy of the Criminal Laws, by abating their undue rigour; together with measures for strengthening the Police, and for rendering the punishment of Transportation and Imprisonment more effectual for the purposes of example and reformation'.[68]

What relevance might this have to restorative justice? First, it suggests that without the harshness of criminal sanctions in the 18th century, the adversary system might not have developed as it did. We can therefore speculate that the long reign of the death penalty not only distorted the development of criminal procedure but increased the need for a restorative corrective.

Secondly, part of the appeal of restorative justice to lay people today is that it reduces the use of strongly punitive measures, such as imprisonment. The UK is said to have the highest rate of imprisonment in Western Europe, and New Zealand's rate of imprisonment is even higher, though still much lower than the USA's. A less punitive regime is likely to encourage a greater acceptance of responsibility by defendants, with a reduction in trials.

In both the UK and New Zealand I suggest, prison growth has been driven largely by perceived political advantage for legislators, as it has occurred at a time when offending rates generally have been decreasing, and when criminology has shown that harsher penalties are not a better deterrent. A recent study of restorative justice results in New Zealand, measured after two years, showed a nine per cent reduction in re-offending rates (compared to similar cases not using restorative justice) *coupled with* a 17 per cent reduction in the use of imprisonment, and the use of shorter sentences—and when re-offending occurred it was half the level of seriousness compared to the original offence.[69]

Restorative justice can therefore produce safer societies *at the same time* as reducing the reliance on imprisonment, with its heavy direct and indirect costs. While imprisonment may be seen as inevitable (and be recommended) in a particular case, this is unusual, even for quite serious offending. Community-based sentences are the norm, for obvious reasons—they increase the opportunities for restitution to be made to victims, they enable offenders

---

68. Parliamentary Debates (1822), N.S. Vol.7, H.C. 'Criminal Laws', cols.790–805, quoted in Radzinowicz, 1948: 563.

69. Similar results in other countries are reported by Sherman and Strang, 2007.

to meet their family obligations and continue in employment, and they are forward-looking for victim, offender and their communities.

10. Formalistic and archaic procedures

It is extraordinary the extent to which criminal procedure in New Zealand (and, I suspect, elsewhere) still follows practices laid down in England many centuries ago.[70] At the time of writing, indictable charges still proceed by way of preliminary hearing or 'depositions'. These are usually conducted before justices of the peace. Normally only prosecution evidence is heard. The accused is 'arraigned' upon an 'indictment' and if he pleads not guilty the case proceeds to trial. Similar exclusionary rules of evidence apply at trial as were devised in the 18th century. Even the terms 'guilty' and 'not guilty' are terms of art. 'Not guilty' does not mean 'I did not do it' but 'I am putting you to the proof'. To plead 'Guilty' does not necessarily mean 'Yes, I did it'; it can mean 'I would rather accept a lesser punishment than go through with a trial'.

The danger, of course, is that the law can become divorced from the common touch, and justice can be seen as little more than a game for the lawyers — and an expensive one at that. Further, the whole process can be self-defeating. The more formal and complex the procedures, the greater the chance that they will miscarry — through professional error, or witnesses losing interest in the case, or (with increasing delays) memories fading, files being lost, or other mishap.

No doubt some of these problems may be laid at the feet of lawyers — and in 1844 the *Law Times* claimed the world had long known 'that "an Old Bailey Practitioner" is a byword for disgrace and ignominy'[71] — but the damage to the image of the law is none the less real, and in any event lawyers' conduct in court is under the control of the court.

How refreshing therefore to find a process that is not run by lawyers, that uses the contemporary, informal language of ordinary people, and that can adapt to the culture of participants of different sorts. The comparison with

---

70. The UK Law Commission is expected to review criminal procedure in the near future. There have been attempts to simplify procedure in New Zealand.

71. 3 *Law Times* 501 (28 September 1844), quoted in Langbein, 2003: 307.

court procedures is marked, and helps explain the preference which victims have shown in many countries for restorative procedures.

But is the risk of formalism one that restorative justice also must guard against? I believe there is risk that procedures could become entrenched, and the province of 'the initiated'. There is a delicate balance between insisting on professional competence in facilitators, and creating an elite or inner circle. Any such tendencies can be overcome by constantly refreshing the pool, and the vision, of restorative justice practitioners. Further, maintaining a multi-disciplinary approach to the teaching and practice of restorative justice is a strong incentive against becoming inbred.[72]

11. To prosecute or not

We have already seen in section (1) above that 'for centuries [before the 19th-century] the English system had worked on the principle that indictment before a court was the last resort to be tried'. The adversary system is of course a system of trial. I suggest that it is time once again to see it as a 'last resort'.

A senior South African official once said: 'Court should be the last resort, and not the only formal process'.[73] I wish we could hear that from justice officials in my country! Seen from afar our judiciary, legal profession and justice officials seem in general to be strongly tied to court control and the adversary model. This is a curious anomaly, as overseas people are surprised at the multi-party *political* support for restorative justice in New Zealand, as gauged e.g. in pre-election answers to a Law Society survey in 2005 — support that the justice sector has not taken much advantage of, when others overseas would give their eye teeth for it.

Also, the Treaty of Waitangi might be said to require much more meaningful action to incorporate elements of customary justice into our legal

---

72. AUT University's Restorative Justice Centre of Aotearoa/New Zealand has representatives from many disciplines on its Development Board, partly to maintain the openness of the spirit of restorative justice.

73. Chief Director: Court Services, Pieter du Rand, speaking at the Restorative Justice and Community Prosecution Conference of the National Prosecution Service, Cape Town, 21–23 February 2007.

system (as distinct from our court system). Restorative justice is an obvious way to do this without setting up separate courts for Maori.[74]

Restorative justice can operate as part of the sentencing process,[75] or following sentence, or by way of diversion from prosecution, or from court. It is in its diversionary aspects that I suggest restorative justice may have the most to offer. About one half of youth justice cases in my country since 1989 have been dealt with at family group conferences without referral to court.[76] This resulted in large reductions (of around two-thirds to three-quarters) in the numbers of young persons appearing in court and being held in custodial facilities. I have advocated a type of community resolution centre that would allow diversion for adults to operate on restorative principles.[77] Based on our youth justice experience, this has the potential to take large numbers of adult offenders out of our courts, and out of prison. I am not speaking here of diversion only of first offenders or of minor offences. This is already occurring. It is the additional benefits of diverting reasonably serious offending, even by repeat offenders, that will pay the biggest dividends.

12. Rights and responsibilities

The last point of comparison relates to the question of rights. It seems to be a feature of modern legal process that it is almost entirely rights-focussed, and predominantly it is the defendant's rights that are promoted. The New Zealand Bill of Rights Act, modelled on North American experience, says plenty about defendants' rights but nothing about their responsibilities, and nothing about the rights of victims. Rights are a lawyer's dream, giving ample scope for litigation (sometimes on quite obscure points), plenty of opportunities for delaying trial (and therefore justice); and further scope for the defects of the adversary system to be seen.

We are right to be concerned about false convictions, but at least where they occur there is ample incentive to appeal the result. Appeals by the prosecution are much harder to argue, and most uncommon. This may reflect

---

74. For further comment on the potential role of restorative justice in New Zealand in integrating customary principles and practices into the law, see McElrea, 2007.
75. As to the New Zealand legislation and experience, see McElrea, 2007: 2–5.
76. Conferences of this type are described in McElrea, 2007: 8–9.
77. See e.g. McElrea, 2007: 9–11.

the adage that it is better that ten guilty men go free than that one innocent man be convicted. I suggest that it is dysfunctional to regard a false conviction but not a false acquittal as a miscarriage of justice. The answer lies not in making it easier to gain convictions, but in actively encouraging the acceptance of responsibility by offenders. This is not done by balancing a largely punitive regime with plenty of chances for proof to fail—which is what we seem to do at present.

Some Final Thoughts

I come back to the suggestion that all offenders, young and old, should be asked whether they admit the allegations, and encouraged to find in the benefits of restorative justice an incentive to put things right not just for others but for themselves. This is the way we behave in social groups, whether the family, at work or in clubs and societies. Why should offenders against the law not be treated the same way? I am not suggesting that the answer be given on oath, or that any pressure be allowed to answer in a particular way.

In New Zealand we need to make greater use of the restorative justice facilities available, and the provisions made for restorative processes in the Sentencing Act, the Victims' Rights Act and the Parole Act (all 2002). That effort must continue. However it will not be enough.

The conclusion I have reached is that without strong leadership at the most senior levels of the judiciary, then so long as restorative justice is dependent on the courts, its emergence into a full, mainstream model could take as long as the gestation period of the adversary system, which was about a century. The adversary ethos is so deeply imbedded in our legal structures, the legal profession, and the judges, who (in common law countries) are drawn from the profession, that restorative justice is continually pushed to the margins, despite the encouragement of the legislators.[78]

Without a change in direction I fear that some of Professor Sherman's examples will be apposite, such as the 42 years it took the British Navy to accept the evidence that lime juice could prevent scurvy, or the 56 years it

---

78. Section 9 of the Victims' Rights Act lays a non-enforceable obligation on all lawyers, judges, prosecutors and others to encourage meetings between victims and offenders in suitable cases where there are suitable facilities. In my experience the section is simply ignored by most involved in criminal justice—with of course some notable exceptions.

took to produce a ban on smoking in the workplace and confined public spaces, after publication of the evidence linking smoking with cancer.

I suggest therefore that the answer lies in developing restorative justice both inside and outside of the courts, in parallel structures — e.g. by making the restorative process the normal, or default position, but on a voluntary basis, using community resolution centres that deal with both civil and criminal cases. Only where matters cannot be resolved on a consensual basis in this way — or where the agreed outcome was not implemented — would cases divert to the courts.[79] (Other parallel structures are the education system, where restorative justice is thriving, and the health system — the Copenhagen Centre for Victims of Sexual Assault described by Karin Madsen (2004), is based in the health sector, not the justice sector.)

For only when restorative justice comes out from under the adversary umbrella will it get its share of sunshine and water, and be able to thrive.

References

Biggar, N. (1999), 'Can We Reconcile Peace with Justice?' in Enright R. D. (ed.), *Community Forgiveness and Restorative Justice. Essays from the Criminal Justice System and the Peace Movement,* 27.

Coke, E. (c.1620s–1630s), *The Third Part of the Institutes of the Lawes of England: Concerning High Treason, and other Pleas of the Crown, and Criminal Causes,* London: Posthumous publication, 1644.

Hawkins, W. (1716, 1721), *A Treatise of the Pleas of the Crown,* London.

Institute of Criminology (2007), 'Evidence: Possibilities and Challenges, Validity and Value', Cambridge, 24 September.

Langbein, J. H. (2003), The *Origins of Adversary Criminal Trial,* Oxford: Oxford University Press.

Madsen, K. S. (2004), 'Mediation as a Way of Empowering Women Exposed to Sexual Coercion', *Nordic Journal of Women's Studies,* 12 (1) 58–61.

McElrea, F. W. M. (2002). 'Restorative justice — a New Zealand perspective', Paper for the conference 'Modernising Criminal Justice — New World Challenges', London, 16–20 June 2002.

---

79. I have described such a model in other papers, starting in 1998, and will not repeat it here. See e.g. McElrea, 2007: 9–11.

McElrea, F. W. M. (2007), 'Customary values, restorative justice and the role of prosecutors: a New Zealand perspective', paper given at the conference 'Restorative Justice and Community Prosecution Conference of the National Prosecution Service', Cape Town, South Africa, 21–23 February 2007.

Muller-Johnson, K. 'Eye witness and ear witness testimony', paper presented by.

Philips, D. (1980), '"A new engine of power and authority": the institutionalisation of law enforcement in England 1780–1830' in Gatrell, V. A. C., *et al.* (eds.), *Crime and the Law: The Social History of Crime in Western Europe Since 1500*, London: Europa Publications Ltd., 155.

Pollock, F. and Maitland, F. W. (1952), *The History of English Law Before the time of Edward I*, Cambridge: Cambridge University Press.

Radzinowicz, L. (1948), *A History of English Criminal Law and its Administration from 1750*, London: Stevens & Sons Ltd.

Sharpe, J. A. (1980), 'Enforcing the Law in the Seventeenth-century English Village' in Gatrell, V. A. C. *et al* (eds.), *Crime and the Law: The Social History of Crime in Western Europe Since 1500*, London: Europa Publications Ltd., 97.

Sherman, L. W. and Strang, H. (2007), *Restorative Justice: The Evidence*, London: The Smith Institute.

Smith, T. (c.1565), *De Republica Anglorum*, L. Alston (ed.), Cambridge: Cambridge University Press.

Stephen, J. F. (1883), *A History of the Criminal Law of England*, London.

Zehr, H. J. (1990), *Changing Lenses: A New Focus for Crime and Justice*, Scottdale, Pennsylvania: Herald Press.

Zehr, H. J. (2002), *The Little Book of Restorative Justice*, Intercourse, Pennsylvania: Good Books.

Case

R v Hollingsby (1995) 103 CCC (3d) 472.

3

Retribution and/or Restoration? The Purpose of our Justice System through the Lens of Judges and Prosecutors

Borbála Fellegi

Introduction

This chapter presents the results of qualitative research conducted with Hungarian judges and prosecutors (N=45) about their attitudes towards restorative justice and victim-offender mediation in particular. The semi-structured interviews were undertaken shortly before the implementation of victim-offender mediation under Hungarian criminal law in 2007. As such, it was the last moment to gain a deeper insight into the feelings and views of the future gatekeepers about the restorative approach without them having any empirical experience of its practical mechanisms.

In order to have a more detailed picture of professionals' attitudes towards an approach hardly known to anyone inside the judiciary, it was first necessary to explore their general feelings toward the existing criminal justice system. Hence, this chapter first discusses the interviewees' thoughts about the purpose of punishment in general, about the 'ideal' and the 'realised' goals of sanctioning, and about the position of the victim in criminal procedures.

Next, the everyday working atmosphere of the judiciary is discussed: what can lead to burn-out syndrome and what can be its effect on their support for future reforms? What can be the impact of an isolated and hierarchical organizational setting on attitudes? How heterogeneous are members of the judiciary concerning their personal goals in their work? How do they see their roles in the justice machinery and in society in general?

All the above-mentioned issues are mapped in order to present the 'ground' on which we implement restorative principles and practices. Finally, the attitudes of the interviewees towards restorative justice and mediation are detailed, highlighting the pros and cons they emphasised.

On the one hand, the chapter intends to show what the chances are of a new justice paradigm becoming internalised by the judiciary. On the other hand, it is demonstrated that the restorative principles are, in fact, compatible with the traditional justice system and views on several points. Moreover, it is inevitable that the common ground between the traditional and restorative justice approach should be mapped in order to implement successfully the latter approach, in which the judiciary plays a significant gatekeeping role.

Why did I believe it was necessary to conduct research on legal practitioners in relation to the implementation of restorative justice? First of all, the regulation of victim-offender mediation (VOM) in Hungary grants *discretionary powers* to the prosecutor and the judge on whether the case is referred to mediation. As a result, legal practitioners' individual decisions become particularly critical for the future developments of the case. Secondly, it is a trend that punishments are imposed in an increasingly individualised manner, partly based on the probation officer's report, which allows legal practitioners to learn more about the personal circumstances of the offender and thus impose 'customised' sanctions. However, the weight of the probation officer's report in the judgement also depends on the personal attitude of the decision-maker. Thirdly, it is a question whether judges and prosecutors actually make their decisions on an absolutely objective basis. Or might this objectivity be rather a myth? And, most importantly, how can we combine the demand for objectivity in judicial practice with the subjective nature of the restorative approach?

I would like to emphasise here that the period in which the data were recorded is special, as the interviews were made after the adoption of the mediation law but before the practice started. The framework of its application was known to those with up-to-date information on regulatory reform. However, none of them had any practical experience of the application of mediation. As a result, it was possible to identify the instinctive reactions of legal practitioners to the philosophy and objectives of mediation and whether it was possible to adopt them. A number of studies in Hungary point out that legal practitioners there have limited opportunities to form the legislation. As a result, they are 'officials' in the system rather than 'policy-makers'. As László Sólyom put it in his analysis back in 1985, 'by passing their judgement, courts want to end the legal dispute once and for all, and they want to avoid shaping social developments in a broader sense' (Sólyom, 1985: 21). Another barrier is the prevailing dogma that 'judges are not allowed to make the law, which the author believes is a 'mistake from many points of view' and emphasises that 'the general provisions authorise—indeed, require—the judge to establish new rights' (Sólyom, 1985: 22).

The Methodology and Sample of Research

This qualitative study includes semi-structured interviews with a total of 45 prosecutors and judges. I contacted the professionals by using the so-called 'snowball sampling' technique. Participation was completely voluntary and anonymous. For the purpose of introducing the topic of mediation, I used an edited (14-minute) version of a Belgian film describing the mediation process.[1] The interviews lasted around 90 minutes. It took one and a half hours to get behind the routine answers and find out the actual personal views of the participants. On many occasions it was a considerable challenge for the interviewees to talk about a solution that had not been put into practice yet.

Of the sample of 45 professionals, 28 were prosecutors and 17 judges. The majority of them (41) were working at the first instance of procedure, only four of them at the appellate level. Of them, 70 per cent were dealing with adult offenders, while the remaining 30 per cent specialised in juvenile cases. Ninety per cent of the sample was between the ages of 30 and 50. Twenty respondents were men and 25 women. We wanted to make sure the research would take into account regional differences to a certain extent: 30 per cent of interviewees were judges/prosecutors from Budapest, 25 per cent were from Eastern Hungary and 45 per cent were from the western counties. Of

---

1. The film was made by a Leuven-based mediation centre, BAL, for the purpose of educating the population and peer professions. It was about a specific crime which actually happened and was resolved by mediation. The organization allowed us to use the film for the purposes of the research project.

the respondents, 31 worked at courts or prosecutor's offices located in county towns while 14 of them worked in other towns. Here follow some thoughts about the work of legal practitioners.

Views on the Objectives of Punishment

The majority of the interviewees explained that they had no personal definition of the purpose of punishment and that they did not think about it too much, since 'the Criminal Code gives a very specific definition'. On the basis of the statutory definition, they mostly emphasised the significance of special (individual) and general deterrence. Punishment is necessary to prevent the person in particular and members of society in general from committing crimes.

> P12: People don't think too much about the objectives of punishment. We just do our job. Now that you ask, I cannot really put into words what the purpose of punishment is. We are parts of a system which progresses. The Criminal Code defines the purpose of punishment. That's what we follow when we work.

The interviewees mentioned the following functions most frequently:

a. Retribution

Retribution, they thought, was a reaction expected of them by society. However, it quite often happens that even the legal practitioners themselves do not think that retribution truly achieves justice.

> J01: There is a standard answer, and there is my own answer. Mine is pessimistic. The model answer is what the Criminal Code states: the aim of punishment is to prevent the offenders and others from committing crimes when they experience the punishment imposed. So there are general and special preventive functions. I have been working as a judge for ten years and I have grown a bit pessimistic. I think that in the majority of cases, partly due to the situation of the justice system, partly due to the heavy caseload and partly due to the quantity and type of crimes, we don't do much more than striking a blow. It is the retributive nature of punishment that dominates.

b. Resolving tension

When the case is finally settled by the judgement of the court, and the person found guilty is sentenced to the punishment that he or she deserves, both the victim and the offender can finally leave this procedure, which has caused continuous tension and distress, behind them.

> J03: Punishment releases tension. It is the end of something. It is remorse. I have seen it with juveniles in particular that [the offender] expects the punishment to soothe his or her conscience so that the offender can say that he or she has formally been held responsible.

c. Payback

These are moral considerations in particular. If someone makes gains illegally, the state is required to deprive the offender of such gains so that the balance in society is restored.

> P35: If order is broken on one side, is it OK if we cause similar injury on the other side to balance it out.

> P29: . . . The satisfaction of the victim, I admit, never crosses my mind. It is absorbed by the state's demand for punishment.

d. The communication of norms

By imposing a penalty, the state publicly expresses that the given conduct is unacceptable in society and deserves to be punished, and also supports its citizens in avoiding criminality and in believing in lawful conduct.

> P41: It is a popular opinion, and still a principle of conservative criminology today, that there must be punishment if there is crime. It is certain that the violation of the rules must be declared, because the system of norms regulates the people's behaviour, even if one presumes that two or three times more crimes occur than the number of reported crimes.

The interviewees expressed their scepticism as to whether punishment actually achieves its goals in practice.

P29: I often see that converting [the offender] into a decent person is hopeless. To help them fix their lives. To make sure the judgement helps them in this. The judgement only states what they did and what they get for this. We don't seem to have the tools to fix things.

P41: A talented criminal lawyer presumably knows that criminal law cannot do much more than declaring a person dishonest and stating that [a particular deed] was wrong. But that's all that it can achieve. It cannot reverse the legal order that's been violated. It can only declare that the legal order has been violated. It cannot achieve anything else.

e. The consequence must be seen

Many of the participants in the discussions considered that facing some kind of consequences is the most important factor in sentencing. Moreover, the terms *punishment* and *consequence* are often used by professionals as synonyms, but their meaning is not the same at all. For legal practitioners, *punishment* is necessary to make sure that a reprehensible act does have *consequences*. Meanwhile, the lack of punishment is often seen as a lack of consequences in the eyes of the legal practitioners. Hence, the question is whether it can be guaranteed that, on the one hand, an unacceptable behaviour has consequences, but norms are communicated to society without inflicting pain for the sake of pain (Fatic, 1995: 197).

While asking the interviewees whether it was absolutely necessary for the punishment to actually hurt the offender, many of them slightly altered their opinion. They said that the conduct must have some consequence but it does not have to be painful. (However, they often said that for more serious crimes the response should give the offender pain in one way or another.)

Hence, one can conclude that the interviewees, neither in theory, nor in their practice, justify the necessity of imposing punishment by following any sentencing principle in a consistent way. Instead, they seemed more cynical and dissatisfied with the effectiveness and efficiency of the sanctioning system; they seemed to be missing those sentencing approaches that have visible results. As a result, we see rather frustrated officials, who — while doing their daily routine — avoid asking themselves what the real purpose of their job is. They agree that punishment, as a response, is not effective but must be applied in any case.

> P28: We work hard, we crack one case after the other. But there won't be fewer crimes. Even incarceration doesn't restrain offenders too much from committing crimes.

Views on the Sanctioning System

The interviewees believed that a sanction is effective when the offenders:

- realise the consequences of their crimes for them, actively take responsibility for their actions;
- feel the effect of their crimes themselves;
- feel that society's reaction to their actions is swift;
- are encouraged to think about what they have done;
- feel shame and guilt;
- get feedback;
- get support;
- are given careful supervision;
- realise that the sanction may be imposed for longer periods;
- feel that the sanction is consistent in itself and with other sanctions as well;
- get a response that takes into account their personal circumstances; and
- are prevented from re-offending.

It is interesting that the above mentioned factors apply to the offender only. The interests and needs of the victims and the injured community are entirely missing from legal practitioners' expectations. It is even more noteworthy that the respondents are in general disappointed with the current, quite limited sanctioning system, in which most of the tools available are not sufficient to realise the hopes of the practitioners. The reasons for this are:

a. When probation or a suspended sentence with conditions is applied, offenders often do not realise the seriousness of the sanction and therefore the sanction will have no effect on their future lives.

Jo2: Many people feel, when they get a conditional sentence, that they haven't been punished at all. All right, there's a sentence, but they don't have to serve it, so there's really no punishment. They feel they've got away with it. That's nothing. They don't feel it's serious at all.

b. Community service as a form of sanction would be relevant but very often it does not work and it is not used.

P 28: It would be a useful one, but there is no place to enforce it. There are no employers who would be willing to give work. Probation officers ask us not to use it because they don't have the means to enforce it.

J16: We have recently been informed that in the villages they cannot enforce community service. Not because there's no work. It's because they know [the offender]. They know the kind of person the offender is. That's prejudice, of course. Maybe the poor guy would work hard this time, but they don't give the offender a chance because the person wasted their chances in the past.

Many times monetary fines are converted into imprisonment and therefore have more serious consequences than community service would have, a punishment supposed to be more stringent.

P18: Fines are problematic because offenders don't pay. A fine is in practice imprisonment; sooner or later it is converted into imprisonment and then they have to serve their time.

c. Imprisonment is ineffective and costs the state a lot.

P23: [The deterrent effect of punishment does not work] because punishments are not very serious. Also, due to the fact that each time we have to check how many people we can actually send to prison as they are full up.

This issue is even more pressing in case of the juveniles, as the (irreversible) machinery of the criminal sanctioning system works even faster for them.

J24: The options in the sanctioning system are very limited for juveniles. There are fines, community service, imprisonment and placement in a correctional institution for juveniles. Very often they are already out [on probation], and they'd get a fine, but due to the probation a fine cannot be imposed. Also, if they don't have property of their own, imposing a fine isn't allowed. They're under 18, so community service is not allowed either. So we have conditional sentence to juvenile custody as the next step. A criminal career in the making: when the juvenile is released, he starts off seeing the probation officer occasionally but quickly commits another crime. And this crime might easily result in an unconditional prison sentence that leads to the juvenile institution in Tököl. That's the end of the road: another victim of society.

The judges and prosecutors interviewed were generally satisfied with the correctional institutions for juveniles, and with the probation service. These measures, the programmes promoting community service and other alternative sanctions are backed by the professionals interviewed.

P35: Anything that makes this rigid justice system more flexible is a good thing. Anything, whatsoever.

A key question asked during the interviews was what methods and tools legal practitioners would add to expand the system of sanctions. Many were initially surprised at the question and could not really give an answer. Later, however, some of them said that such sanctions are needed that better represent the above criteria. The majority of participants used the elements of restorative approach to describe the 'ideal sanction', without being aware of it. In practice the idea they have in mind includes the key elements of the restorative approach.

Victims in the Criminal Justice System

The legal practitioners rarely mentioned victim-related expectations when describing the sanctions they considered ideal. It was interesting to observe the level of reactions sympathising with the victims after they had seen the film. Let us discuss which criteria they emphasised the most:

The hard road to receiving financial compensation

Victims have little (if any) chance to be paid damages in the criminal procedure. Enforcing a claim for compensation in the court can only be done through a civil action (*partie civile*) and it is so hopeless that most victims do not even start the process.

> P21: Criminal courts do not like to acknowledge damages because they feel it is the task of civil law courts. The victim can turn to the civil law court when he or she has a copy of the final criminal judgement. There the victim files a claim. The lawsuit starts in the civil law court. Then comes the hearing, when a lot of witnesses must be heard. It's a very lengthy procedure. Even in petty cases, it happens that the accused does not appear in court for one or two years. The judge asks the victim if they *really* want compensation. Then he or she adds that the accused has no assets. Then the victim says 'no thank you', and sighs. This sigh says everything that the victim thinks about the criminal justice system. Quite sad, actually.

The victim as a witness

Since the second half of the 20th-century, numerous criminological studies have been prepared on how victims were downgraded to witnesses in the criminal procedure, how the state's urge to punish and the procedure itself became more important than the acknowledgement of the victim's interests and how victims were denied the right to participate and make decisions in the procedure.

> P10: For me and from a legal aspect, the amount of losses that the victim had is of no relevance. That should be settled with the insurance company. In traffic crime cases, for me a victim is only a victim if they suffered injuries of which the healing takes over eight days. If someone's car is damaged but the person is unharmed, I don't see that person as a victim.

> J25: The other thing is that [communication] should not influence the victim in any way. This is because if charges are pressed and the case goes to court, the victim will be a key *witness*. Mediation should not have any effect on the victim's [subsequent] testimony. Can't you see? In reality [the accused person] is not as scary as one would think. The personal attitude of the victim towards the accused

person definitely shapes the victim's testimony. It is very difficult to bring the victim and the accused person together without making the victim's viewpoint subjective, i.e. biased against or in favour of the accused person when the victim testifies.

Cooperation by order

When the victim is a witness, he or she must appear in court in this capacity; it is mandatory. What is more, he or she is *summoned* to court, which is another sign that the *obligations* applicable to him or her are more relevant to the procedure than the satisfaction of the victim's needs. The studies on secondary victimisation[2] and international documents[3] focus on how the official procedure can victimise the victims again, this time at the hands of the authorities.

> P31: Closing [cases] is often delayed because not only the accused person but also the victim or other key witnesses don't come to the trial as summoned. And even if they do, [the next problem is that] it was a long time ago, and they don't remember. It doesn't matter that the judge says that the witness must testify. The witness still wouldn't care. It sometimes happens that [witnesses] are fined by the court for lack of cooperation.

> BF: Can a fine be imposed if they don't cooperate?

> P31: Or if they don't show up. It is usually quite effective when the [victim as a] witness is told in the summons that a fine of HUF 50,000 is imposed if they don't show up. It is no surprise that they are there for the next hearing.

The victims' interests

The majority of professionals considered that the victims' main interest in and primary expectation of the procedure are to recover the damage they have suffered and to close the case as soon as possible so that the case intrudes into their normal life to a minimal extent.

'Madam, could you please get to the point? We don't have time for the all the details now!'

---

2. See Strang, 2002; Wergens, 1999; Pease, 1998; Görgényi, 2007.
3. See Council of Europe, Recommendation 2006(08), section 3.3.

The rigid regulatory background of criminal procedure does not allow discussion between the victims and legal practitioners of any topics, that have little to do with the 'subject-matter' of the procedure before the prosecutor or the court. Very often the courtroom is the first place where the victims can talk about their sufferings. Nevertheless, even here quite a few judges will ask the victim to talk only about that information which is relevant to the evidence or procedure.

> Jo3: I see all too often that the victims want to speak their mind. In this case, when the judge is impatient and says that this is irrelevant or unimportant, the victim feels even more hurt than if he or she wouldn't get any compensation at all or the offender wouldn't get punished.

Questioning the credibility of the victim

It unfortunately does happen in criminal procedure that the victim, as a witness, falls victim to the defendant's counsel. To refute the charges the defence lawyer can effectively use methods such as questioning the honesty, credibility and reliability of the victim.

The Daily Work of Legal Practitioners: Institutional and Personal Factors

Factors Leading to Burnout

a. Ineffectiveness

Every day legal practitioners experience that their own work, and the criminal justice system as a whole, is ineffective and they do not have the means to actually help people involved in crimes to return to lead the life of law-abiding citizens. This feeling of ineffectiveness and the rigid regulations of procedure are often combined with a reduced level of perceived responsibility. Those questioned often claimed that they cannot reduce the number of crimes, let alone prevent them. Their only goal is to do their job conscientiously.

> P15: Criminal law is meant to make sure the state's urge to punish is enforced and nothing more. Prosecutors are, in a sense, outsiders from the aspect of everyday life. I sometimes think about the defects in the system. But there is little you can do.

J24: I don't have the time or the opportunity to persuade [the offender] to lead an honest life. A criminal procedure cannot repair the damage the parents, the family and society as a whole have failed to repair in 14 or 18 years. I don't have illusions about my work. I don't think I can reform anyone. All I can do is hold some back, those who realise the significance of the whole thing. But it is not my goal to 'redeem' the offender. It is an illusion that they will listen if I [from a superior position] tell them what to do.

b. Lengthy procedures

When the procedure is drawn out, the distance between the reprehensible act and society's reaction grows and the connection between them weakens. This compromises the justice system's function of communicating to those affected and society that the given behaviour is unacceptable and must meet a response.

P18: [When] a trial is held one or two years after a minor crime, nobody's interested other than me, the prosecutor. I find the whole thing pointless. Sometimes [the victim] really has no idea what we are talking about.

c. The assembly-line feeling

Another factor in burn-out is the assembly-line nature of the work, when the caseload is heavy, deadlines are short and therefore there is little time and attention for individual cases and persons. Judges and prosecutors usually get information from paper-based materials only, i.e. they see the other involved parties only in court.

P28: The workload is extremely heavy for us. So when a prosecutor gets a new task, for instance in the mediation procedure, the first thing he or she will check in the text of the Act is that the prosecutor must interview the suspect and the victim before deciding on referring the case to mediation. That's two more interviews.

P34: We deal with a large number of cases here. We work like a manufacturing plant really. It is like working at an assembly line.

P30: What I see is that, after some time, my colleagues tend to get fed up with the whole thing. They deal with cases by thinking that it's just paperwork. This is not good at all. It leads to simplified solutions. They say, let's press charges and we'll see what happens. They stay away from new things.

d. Frequent changes in the law

Legal practitioners expressly state or imply that, when laws change, they experience professional uncertainties and lose self-confidence. It is often claimed that by the time the professionals become reasonably experienced in applying the new law, the rules will change. If laws are rewritten regularly but inconsistently, legal practitioners will grow uncertain, cautious and sceptical. Hence, their resistance towards legal reforms is understandable, since their interest is to minimise the number of possible mistakes (which is high in case of applying new procedures and low if nothing is changed in the procedural routine). So in order to support any new instrument, they need to feel a certain confidence in its application and have to achieve some routine in order to be able to pay attention to the particularities of certain cases. And to achieve such confidence some stability in the legislation is necessary.

J13: Technical changes occur very frequently. I have to say that by the time I learn the new law, I can forget all about it, because the next month they'll change it and replace it with something absolutely new.

P43: The problem is that we are an organization that is slow to react... However, [if we had a bit more time], we would not have to decide the fate of human beings so hastily.

Isolated and Hierarchical Organizational Structures

a. The issue of the independence of judges

Legal practitioners, and judges in particular, refer to judicial independence when explaining the lack of communication within courts and with peer organizations. Is it true that the independence of the judicial profession can only be guaranteed if we do not require judges to communicate with internal or external stakeholders if such a duty were to affect their job? Or is it just a misinterpretation of the concept that can be used as an argument by judges for isolating themselves from the other sub-systems of society?

J09: I'm not sure if communication should be extended. The courts must stay independent. Courts make the decisions; they are not to be influenced by the lawyer or the prosecutor. Consultation would compromise their independence.

BF: Even if this wasn't about specific cases?

J09: Yes. I think both the prosecutor and counsel should have their own opinion.

b. Lack of feedback, supervision and teamwork experience

Legal practitioners have very little knowledge of the activities, skills and viewpoints of other specialised fields. The system does not provide any opportunity to improve self-awareness or for supervision or case discussions, nor does it encourage legal practitioners to do any of these. The lack of a 'feedback culture' also triggers the phenomenon that the court and prosecution system strongly resists learning about studies, research and critiques that analyse their work, and they do not participate in them by discussing their experiences with those preparing the analyses.

BF: Do you think judges should receive self-awareness training?

J24: Yes, it would be essential. It's also a natural result of working as a judge that they become vain and tend to think they are the smartest people in the world. And, due to the nature of the work and the caseload, anyone may get caught up in the work to such a level that they have no time to find a relationship and start a family. I don't know if it occurs here more than in other jobs, but in this job this can really distort personalities

BF: What effect does this have on work?

J24: That they treat people in their courtroom in a really awful way. They show no respect, to say the least, or they look down on them or act aggressively. This happens very frequently.

Jo2: I think there are quite a lot of different judge types. I know a lot of people working here who, I believe, don't show enough empathy for this job. There are colleagues who are unbelievably tense and bad-tempered; they fine people in court for improper conduct and order them to behave.

c. Prosecutors and judges as 'lone fighters' in the justice system

Prosecutors and judges are expected to investigate and react to crimes effectively while they have very little opportunity to cooperate with social and educational services and with the communities of the affected people themselves (families, friends and communities of the offenders and victims). However, they have also learned from their own experiences that the offender's family and small community background is the most important factor in developing the lifestyle of a criminal. Responses by criminal justice, i.e. the official answers to crime are rather 'mandatory exercises' by the officials affecting only the tip of the iceberg and are not able to effectively reduce crime rates.

During the interviews, it was striking to see how limited their knowledge is about the existence, the skills, the responsibilities and competencies of other organizations and professions.

P30: It's not possible for a criminal to be regarded as a victim. You have free will when you are a teenager and that means you could have chosen a different path.

P31: I know families where [the kids] robbed people at the age of six or eight. We all know of such families. We know what to expect from them. In their case, mediation is just pointless.

P34: The truth is that there is nothing we can do about them. In their family, everybody makes a living from crime. They are born into such an environment.

P31: The methods of criminal law won't help here.

BF: What are some methods that could help?

P31: We would have to change the environment and the attitude of the offender completely. But this is beyond the prosecutor's powers.

P33: The problem is that by the time the teenager is on the prosecutor's radar, that is, by the time they have reached the age of 14 and they are punishable, they have been subjected to influences that make it very difficult to convince the teenager to change, even with methods other than the methods of law.

BF: Do you feel in any way a part of the child protection system as a prosecutor?

P31: Minimally. This is not our job. We are the penultimate stop.

BF: Do you think that psychology-related child protection training, further education and information would be useful for you?

P32: The truth is that we don't really have personal contact with juvenile offenders. We are the penultimate stop in the procedure, so we don't really need it.

BF: Do you think that prosecutors and judges would need special training and preparation to be able to handle juveniles?

P31: Yes, we have already been threatened with such training!

d. The legislator's distrust towards the legal practitioners

The strict organizational hierarchy of a system can draw criticism, according to which there is no trust from the top to the bottom (from the legislator to the legal practitioners) and no influence from the bottom up (the experts in the field do not have any influence on regulations). The lack of trust (or, according to a witty remark by an interviewee, the 'meticulous legislator') is apparent in the form of the overly-detailed regulations which provide the legislator's theoretical answers to issues that are only visible in practice.

BF: So, to you, the [mediation] law means distrust?

P35: Not just mediation. Any new legal solution.

BF: Do you think there is a chance that the legislator and the legal profession will start a dialogue as partners?

P35: No. There's too much distrust. It's a general social phenomenon. People want to avoid trouble. They say: there's no trouble if I don't trust people.

e. Limited opportunities to attend training; poor language skills

Hierarchy and isolation have another unfortunate result: in Hungary today, due to the strict hierarchy in appointments, professionals (particularly prosecutors) have limited opportunities to attend conferences and special training. Nevertheless, some judges and prosecutors are willing to train themselves and sometimes they even sacrifice their leisure time and put a lot of energy into getting special training and expanding or updating their knowledge by obtaining a second degree. Some share their professional experiences through publishing papers and opinions. While, at an individual level, many professionals want to learn more, the organization and the motivation system does not support these aspirations. What is more, it is often made difficult for professionals to attend further training. This can easily lead to giving up professional ambitions, not to mention the danger of burn-out in the long run.

Interests and Motives of Legal Practitioners

What personal motives drive judges and prosecutors in their daily work? Experiences can be put into two groups. In the first group—let us call them the *humanists*—human factors, emotions and interpersonal relationships dominate, while in the second group—let us call them the *bureaucrats*—procedural and administrative factors are more significant. Of course, the two appeared in combination in the answers, but the dominance of one or the other could be perceived, nonetheless.

J24: The interest of the prosecutor is to show a high indictment rate, while as a judge, my purpose is to close a file with a final sentence and put it into the archives. Meanwhile, defenders try to reach an optimum: accept any sentence that the accused person accepts.

P21: What interest do I have in having this man sentenced? None. The prosecutor's interest is to secure the lightest sentence possible for the poor guy.

P38: [Our goal is] to close the case in a satisfactory manner, and to make sure the procedure produces some benefit. The important thing is [to make sure the procedure is] more than just a way of imposing punishment: it should bring some hope that the sentenced person will not re-offend.

One factor was surprisingly important for a number of interviewees, namely the feedback and the satisfaction of the parties involved in the procedure. Praise, some positive feedback and the recognition of their work have tremendous impact on professionals. These experiences are very important regarding their perception of professional success.

P39: It never brings satisfaction if we have someone sentenced to years in prison.

P18: It would make me feel good if I didn't meet the offender for the first time [at the hearing or the interrogation] but instead, I had the chance to be like a nice uncle to them. That I could somehow offer them a choice.

P21: Success? Once a plaintiff said to me that what I did was worth more than two sedative pills. It was the greatest success of my life, that I could soothe this person.

J05: I remember it as a great moment in my life that once I got a letter from Baracska [Prison] from an offender. It was written on a piece of paper torn out of an exercise book but this person wrote to me that nobody had ever spoken to this offender as nicely as I did ... It is a great feeling when some down-and-out, miserable person who I sentenced tells me some nice things

J24: Isolation and vanity have a strange result in me: that I crave some kind of praise.

Nevertheless, it is important to note that, according to criminological research (Sherman, 1993: 445), not only do satisfaction-related factors make the participants feel good but they also play a key role in effective crime prevention. Satisfaction and criminal procedure may have a combined effect in reducing crime, while a procedure believed to be unfair may provoke re-offending.

The Typology of Roles of Legal Practitioners

Individual perceptions of legal practitioners concerning their roles

The primary content analysis of the interview transcripts may lead us to the tentative conclusion that the interviewees may be placed into four relatively independent categories on the basis of their emotions, styles and character traits. These are 'self-evaluator', 'teacher', 'philosopher' and 'official'. No character type is 'pure', of course. However, for each interviewee, one of the four styles can be identified as dominant. As a result, their individual attitudes towards mediation were also highly different according to their type (from the very supportive to the very resistant), emphasising different aspects of mediation important for them. *Table 1* summarises the features of the four character types.

Table 1. Some indicators of the four character types

Types of legal practitioners	Description
The 'self-evaluator'	Strong self-reflection and self-criticism; realises own boundaries; emphasises own motivations; emphasises emotional aspects; empathy to clients; primarily uses first person singular; a committed professional; introvert (the only one out of the four); speaks quietly; long pauses in speech, stops to think a lot; micro-level analysis; highly open to mediation.

Types of legal practitioners	Description
The 'teacher'	A provider type; believes in the educational effect of the procedure and the judge/prosecutor; the importance of the legal practitioner's subjective approach in the procedure; categorical thinking; self-confident in role; believes in the possibility of change; pays particular attention to juveniles; very little self-reflection and insecurity; more observations about the external world; community-level (meso-level) analysis; determined style of speech, raised voice, fast speech, no interruptions between arguments; highly open to mediation.
The 'philosopher'	Emphasises general connections of logic; holistic approach; statement of beliefs; self-criticism and criticism of the system; sarcastic approach, but believes in people in general; reserved tone, balanced intonation; reflects 'peacefulness'; macro-level analysis; sceptical but open to mediation.
The 'official'	Organization-oriented, rule-oriented and procedure-oriented; his or her main goal is doing his or her job in a conscientious manner and according to the rules; seeks to reduce the amount of work to a minimum; focuses on possible hindrances and difficulties in connection with the reforms; rigid; considers deviation from standards a problem; lack of criticism of the system; cynical approach to clients; statements rather than questions; lack of emotions; relaxed manner of speech; balanced intonation; brief or lengthy, monotonous narrative; sceptical to mediation.

a. The 'self-evaluator'[4]

J05: This is some form of *psychoanalysis for me,* that *I* thought that it wasn't the criminal that was evil but society. I have this unsystematic *Ars Poetica* that *I developed.* I often grew really *tired* and sometimes even got *sick* because of my job. But, now that you have listened to me speaking for 90 minutes, you probably see that I *enjoy* this profession.

P19: Very often *I feel I that I have to reflect on whether my work has a point at all.* Sometimes I do what I do as a routine and that makes me upset. I could not get used to it in the 20 years of my career. However, I've had to deal with it and accept that I can't save the world. Still, I must try. Otherwise, *there is no point in coming to work* at all.

b. The 'teacher'

P21: I think punishment is [not only about retribution but] also argumentation. At least when the offender hears my argumentation, he or she might realise what he or she has done.

J03: I think I am the 'teacher' type. The accused must feel I'm not angry with him or her. So I behave like a good teacher.

J04: I am very dedicated to helping juvenile offenders…I think it is very important that the offender should never, ever break the law again. I like to use this pedagogical approach in the courtroom.

c. The 'philosopher'

J26: I welcome anything that is new. Whatever that is new in the world could bring positive changes. There is a chance. Some people criticise me for being too humane, a humanist and an optimist. But if we don't believe that something good could happen, we will actually take away the opportunity to let something good happen.

---

4. Emphasis is added in the next quotes.

35: Anything that makes this rigid justice system more flexible is a good thing. Anything, anything at all…I belong to the unfortunate generation who spent one half of their professional career in the Communist regime and the other half in a democratic system and I don't see much of a change. We are just as stupid as we used to be. Was this recorded? Still, it's true.

d. The 'official'

P23: We are the ones who prescribe what should be done. We are usually then ones given some extra task. It doesn't matter how we look at it, this mediation thing will be another extra task.

P42: [Commenting on why it is not feasible to refer the case to mediation if the crime has been committed by multiple persons and not all of them agree to take part in mediation.— BF] The indictment should be delayed for one offender but an indictment must be filed for the other with the court. This case will have to be dealt with twice and we will have to go to court with it twice. A photocopy will have to be made of each and every document to make a separate case. There is a lot of administrative work It's much simpler if I take all three to court and say that the case is not suitable for mediation. So mediation means administrative work. It's much more difficult to carry out the procedure and sometimes it also generates procedural law issues later.

Out of the 45 interviewees, just over half of them (51 per cent) could be labelled as 'officials', 27 per cent as 'teachers', 15 per cent as 'philosophers' and 7 per cent as 'self-evaluators'. If we look at their distribution along independent variables, the age-based differences are the most spectacular. While 60 per cent of those below 40 can be categorised as an 'official', above 40, only 39 per cent of them belong to this category. This may be because a young legal practitioner relies on the procedural rules they learned, and it is more important for young lawyers to gain experience about the procedural rules than to apply the legal solutions that need individualised evaluation. It follows from the above that 'self-evaluators', 'teachers' and 'philosophers' are much more common among older interviewees.

It is interesting that there are no significant differences between the two occupational groups regarding these four character types. The weight of each role is the same within the groups of judges and prosecutors; the proportional differences are relatively small. It is safe to conclude, on the basis of our sample, that the four character types have the same likelihood to develop among judges as with prosecutors. This shows us that the two professional groups are similarly heterogeneous and therefore the role perspectives and attitudes of each legal practitioner (including their willingness to use mediation) depend much more on their general personality traits than the role they have.

Other Factors Influencing Attitudes Towards Mediation

When an interviewee *expressed self-criticism*, it was a sign that he or she is open to mediation.

> P35: You don't always need to know what the truth is. We don't know what the truth is. We just don't. Our approach to things must be very, very humble.

> J26: What's the truth? I'm pretty sure that I'm right when I say that the court sometimes doesn't discover the truth, or only part of it.

Personal dedication and commitment are only key factors for one or two people. After law school, my interviewees chose the profession of judge and prosecutor mostly for practical reasons, that is, depending where they could find job openings. In each case, it has positive results if the interviewee was previously *in other areas of the justice system* (e.g. as a police officer, educator or probation officer).

The *younger* professionals were more *sceptical* and were more likely to have *negative attitudes* and *look for excuses* than their older colleagues. As such, when asked about the changes they had experienced in their work during their professional career, most of them thought that, as a young professional, they used to be much stricter. As they found that their professional knowledge improved and as they could do their work basically as a motor skill, they started to have more energy, attention and ability to look at their activities from the outside.

Their *willingness to punish* is another important aspect. To a certain extent, this research confirms the statement that a large majority of the interviewees believed that the judgements had clearly become more lenient recently and many said that stricter sentences are needed.

> J44: If the state decides not to use its criminal law powers, it promotes the idea of compensating the victim. That's fine and can be argued for, but it's CRI-MI-NAL law, these are CRIMES that must be PU-NISHED! [the interviewee said the words in block capitals in a raised voice and stressed each syllable — BF].
>
> BF: What could the state do to fight crime more effectively?
>
> J44: Sentences should be tougher. They have become softer, frightfully so.

One interviewee even said openly that capital punishment should not have been abolished.

> P11: [With the death penalty being abolished], the state or the community is deprived of the possibility of punishing a person who has brutally murdered someone and thus dishonoured the community and the state.

There are differences between the interviewees' willingness to punish. It is shown well through their perception of imprisonment.

> J24: I have been to a lot of prisons. I've even asked the guards to lock me in the cell or the solitary confinement cell. Oh, that was awful'
>
> P11: If I look at the *prison conditions* alone, what they are like, *going to prison* is no longer a punishment really. If *someone* is imprisoned, they *can* still go home in the weekend, watch TV, listen to the radio, receive newspapers and packages and work out. Is that really punishment? They take away the punishment from the sentence.

Last but not least, it should be mentioned that the *local leader has a key role* in the development of attitudes within the given professional group.

The Opinions of Legal Practitioners on Mediation

Moving on to the next question: with regard to the phenomena discussed above, what is the judges' and the prosecutors' opinion of mediation and restorative justice?

Motives

In the following summary, a specific quote will only be given for one or two factors, as these motive-related factors were not stated specifically by the interviewees but were identified through secondary content analysis. These ideas did not come up specifically related to mediation but as more general observations, when the expectations of sanctions were discussed. As discussed before, expectations of legal practitioners towards sanctioning are highly compatible with the principles and practices of restorative justice.

The interviewees mentioned the following motives the most frequently in relation to the mediation procedure.

a. The victims' interests

The majority of professionals agreed that the main interest of the victims in the procedure and their primary expectation of the justice system are to recover the damage they have suffered and to close the case as soon as possible so that the case intrudes in their normal life to the least extent. The opinions differed on whether victims want harsh sentences. It was many times pointed out that it does not really matter what sentence the offender will get. However, many victims (especially when their losses are heavy) demand a disproportionately harsh punishment, and it is not easy for them to accept that there are statutory upper limits to the sentence.

> P21: I can imagine a case when it is a relative of a victim who insists that the accused must be punished. Especially something serious, such as a parent whose child has been a victim. The kid is mugged, they take away the kid's mobile phone or hat or whatever, it doesn't matter, the important thing is that the child won't be able to sleep at night. And, as I see it, this is a more traumatic experience for the parent than for the child.

b. Effective cooperation with the parties involved in the procedure (offenders, victims and their communities)

A procedure customised to the personal needs of the parties involved in the procedure (victims, offenders, their families and other affected persons) and a personal contact-based approach may help greatly in improving cooperation between the authorities and citizens. As a result, authorities and courts will be able to deal with such cases faster and to the better satisfaction of the parties. They will also face less resistance and therefore their actions will be more acceptable to the parties.

c. The sanction-related expectations concerning the mediation process

As detailed in part 3.2, legal practitioners used several expected factors as their expectations toward an 'ideal' sanction. It became clear that these expectations were highly compatible with the basic principles and practices of restorative justice. It can therefore be concluded that, without being aware of it, legal practitioners in effect summarised some key items of the restorative approach when thinking about the 'ideal' sanction.

d. Advantages of the mediation procedure

The interviewees also emphasised some procedure-related considerations. They gave mediation an important role as its procedure guarantees that:

- there is a dialogue between the parties (as opposed to sentencing without trial, a method of diversion, in which the offender does not have to be present in person at all);
- it provides full information to the parties about the progress of the procedure, the rights and obligations and the possible outcomes;
- the offender confronts his or her actions and the consequences of the actions, and that the related educational benefits are available;
- there is a place and sufficient time to express emotions;
- there is an individualised, individual-focused procedure and outcome; and
- that the 'human' becomes visible in the law case.

P41: Mediation brings back the original meaning of criminal liability and criminal justice, and makes sure the offender does not escape liability through various models and formal solutions. [This is because] the moment the person is sentenced, he or she is exempted from moral and legal liability and is only affected by the correctional system... Today, in legal practice, a criminal procedure is considered 'good' if it involves the least number of persons possible. The best solution is when no trial is held in the procedure as no one has to be heard. The judge, working at home, sits down at a desk and sentences the person on the basis of the papers in the file.

e. Reducing caseload

Short-term, the mediation procedure means additional work for prosecutors and judges, but in the long run the work of prosecutors and judges is reduced as the persons affected by crimes have an opportunity through mediation to come to an agreement voluntarily and close cases themselves if they are willing to and able to do it in the particular case. As a result, the workload of the authorities will be reduced.

f. Transferring the right to make a decision

A surprising result of the research is that the legal practitioners interviewed fully supported the idea of allowing the parties to handle crimes. They appreciate it; what is more, they consider it beneficial if those parties who are affected directly and personally by the case discuss the consequences of crimes on themselves.

The transfer of the right to decide is seemingly acceptable for them if it is guaranteed that procedural law is abided by and fundamental rights are enforced,[5] and the usefulness of the procedure is guaranteed by a formal methodology.

> P21: In my opinion, if the parties cannot settle the conflict themselves — with the assistance of the mediator, for instance — the worst idea is if the authorities intrude in the procedure.

> P28: In the crime-related conflict, it is not the state that is the protagonist but the person who has been beaten up, conned, or whose car, money, computer or

---

5. Hence, private vengeance or other acts not respecting fundamental rights are obviously excluded.

phone has been taken. The victim should be the main character, not the state or the authority asserting the state's demands.

g. The relevance of community sanctions

Despite the previously mentioned difficulties, community-based types of sanction are becoming increasingly acceptable in Hungarian criminal policy, as an increasing number of innovative community service programmes have been implemented and as 'voluntary restitution' has been added to the Criminal Code as a criminal defence or as circumstances allowing the sentence to be reduced without any limitations. It was observed that those interviewees who had doubts about mediation supported and were optimistic about community sanctions. It shows that community sanctions might actually be a bridge between traditional criminal measures and restorative justice approaches.

h. Overcoming prejudices

P26: If a new thing starts to work well and people open up, they start to talk about what has happened to them and say that the person responsible has provided compensation and assistance, even society's simplistic approach to offenders may change.

P41: In the area where I work, everybody is convinced that people steal things because they are filthy Gypsies who commit crimes all the time. Or because they are alcoholic or unemployed. They are not looking for more complex reasons behind the crimes, the small steps that lead to the given action. They label it somehow. Or they give criminological reasons of a biological and psychological nature. Or they explain it through societal deprivation. That, of course, happens with law enforcement workers, too. I see it with my colleagues. By the time they finish law school around the age of 23, 24 or 25 and start work, they have a very specific idea of the causes of crime and they never want to look into the depths of it. Criminal procedure as it is today does not give them the opportunity to reflect on it.

i. Trust in the future probation services providing mediation service

An overwhelming majority of interviewees praised the probation services and their professional cooperation with probation officers.

> P30: [Probation officers,] they're unbelievably nice people. As I see it, every single one of them is really enthusiastic and does it [their job] extremely well. They focus on every detail. They even monitor the offender's behaviour when the prosecutor decides to postpone [charges being pressed]. They write to us regularly about the results [of the postponement]. If they have the energy and the time, this will work and it might work well too.

j. The special role of mediation for juvenile offenders

Those questioned found mediation particularly beneficial for juvenile offenders as 'they still have a chance to realise what they have done and follow the right path'. In other words, the interviewees believed it was a benefit of the procedure that mediation had an educational and re-socialisation effect.

Reservations

a. The fear of the victims

It happens quite often that victims do not come to the trial out of fear or they even request the judge or the prosecutor to allow them to stay away from the trial because they do not want to meet the offender. In a village, where it is well-known who the 'usual' perpetrators are and which community they are from, and the victims and the offenders have known each other for a long time, and where the conflict between them is an ongoing one, it is crucial to avoid the possibility that a mediation meeting might lead to any further victimisation.

b. The lack of 'civil courage'

In the interviews, it was mentioned quite a lot that 'Hungarians', 'Hungarian society' and the 'Hungarian culture of settling disputes' is not ready to use such a method, which requires self-discipline, rationality and a constructive approach to conflict resolution. However, when asked whether they themselves would participate in a mediation procedure, the majority of the interviewees replied that they indeed believe it would seem sensible.

> Jo1: When I was watching this film [at the beginning of the interview], my first thought, among many, was that we would have to reach the level of Western European countries first before mediation can be used. We have to keep in mind the crime rates in Hungary and the characteristics of the criminal population. We have to remember the differences between Central and Eastern European Hungarian society and the societies of the West.

When these doubts are considered, we should remember the period between 2007 and 2010, when 3,000 cases were referred to mediation each year, and the parties could reach an agreement in 80 per cent of mediation cases and 90 per cent of the agreements have been kept.

c. Does diversion mean that crime has no consequences?
In some cases legal practitioners were unaware that, as in other countries, mediation can be used as an additional, supplementary service of the justice system intended to help the victims and can be used in parallel to the traditional criminal procedure.

d. The extension of criminal justice (i.e. the 'net-widening' effect)
Many interviewees mentioned that it was possible that by applying mediation the criminal justice system would punish actions—that were previously only punished through a reprimand—more harshly, as with mediation the offender would have to agree to additional duties. The legal practitioners were therefore concerned that mediation would mean another opportunity of expanding the criminal justice system.

e. Complex procedures

> P29: I wonder how this could be implemented in Hungary. With the caseload I have, for instance, it will be extremely difficult. (…) Although I can see that it will be useful, I'm unsure how it will work in real life.

P10: The postponement of an indictment is a pain in the neck. You have to keep the file on record, open it again and again—we don't have the staff to do it.

f. Lack of guidance and guidelines

Some of the interviewees had reservations about the discretionary character of the method. As they said that until the date of the interview they had not been given guidelines on when it must be used, when it is possible to be used and when it is not advisable to refer the case to mediation. Many of them thought that discretionary methods carry the risk that they would not become an integral part of legal practice. The larger the role discretionary powers and individual beliefs have in a procedure, the more likely it is that legal practitioners will choose not to use it but apply 'tested' and more clear-cut techniques.

P41: Law enforcement officers, like any organization or person in possession of some knowledge, are conservative...If a new legal solution is more complex than an existing one, like mediation is more complicated than the well-known postponement of indictment, law enforcement officers will avoid using it...They don't want the difficult procedure when they can use a familiar and simple one.

g. Infrastructural restrictions

We use the collective term 'infrastructural limits' to describe any doubts the respondents had about the possibility of implementing mediation. These were the following:

- What human, infrastructural and material resources will be available to provide for the effective use of mediation services?
- How will probation officers (who will act as mediators) be prepared for this new role from a professional aspect, as this new role will be quite different from their previous activities?
- How can the mediation service avoid becoming an assembly line type of activity? How can the burn-out of future mediators be avoided?
- How can it be ensured that peer professions and the population obtain full information about the introduction of the mediation procedure, its approach, its procedure and the advantages of its application?

h. Pay and you go?

A few interviewees mentioned that mediation may have the result that offenders with a strong financial background will have the chance to pay instead of going to prison while those from poorer backgrounds who are unable to pay compensation will be denied the opportunity of mediation.

i. Attorneys as mediators

The interviewees' primary concern was whether the future attorney-mediators would be able to represent the basic philosophy of mediation and whether it can be ensured that attorneys would become impartial and neutral mediators.

> P42: I don't think lawyers should be involved in this. I think mediators should definitely be employees of an organization within the justice system that would act independently from the other authorities involved in the procedure ... It's difficult for me to imagine that a lawyer one day defends an offender and the next day acts as a mediator in the criminal case of a relative of the offender the attorney defended the previous day.

> J45: Probation officers can show empathy, but where can you find it with lawyers?

Conclusions

One of the most important lessons of the survey was that the ideal sanctions pictured by the interviewees and the known effects of certain restorative practices overlapped to a large extent. However, it is also true that the 'wish lists of an ideal sanction' visualised by the participants did not include the representation of the victims' and the community's interest and the voluntary side of mediation was also not mentioned.

Both the prosecutors and the judges mentioned that the official procedures do not provide a trained professional, nor time or opportunity for the victims to explain the negative effects the crime had on them, the related needs they may have, their main concerns, etc. The authorities in the procedure are simply inadequate for handling the victim's complaints. On the one hand, their workload is too heavy and they have neither the time/capacity nor the training needed for carrying out such activities, and on the other hand the rigid regulatory background of the criminal procedure does not allow the discussion of any topics between the victims and the legal practitioners that have little to do with the 'subject-matter'. The lack of opportunities to provide psychological and moral support to the victims is frustrating for both the victims and legal practitioners.

The research proved that legal practitioners do not have consistent moral reasoning and penal philosophy when they consider the necessity of punishment or when they apply punishments in everyday practice. And, although they consider deterrence the main objective of punishment, many of them said that punishment itself is not suitable as a deterrent. It can be assumed, on the basis of the interviews, that it is a more important factor in decision-making to make sure there is actually a response to crime and it is a less important criterion that the response should be painful to the offender. This distinction is highly relevant in studying how restorative programmes can be added to our current penal system.

Due to the organizational structure of the prosecutors' office and the court system, legal practitioners rarely have the opportunity to share their recommendations and creative solutions with their colleagues and to have them implemented in practice. Isolation and hierarchy together create a conservative system and make it difficult to implement reforms in practice. This, coupled with other factors, quickly leads to the practitioners' burning out. The lack of external analyses and the resistance to reforms have a double, back-and-forth effect: the less possible (or mandatory) it is for an organization to open up to the public, to become transparent and to reflect on itself, the more important the strategy of avoiding these becomes and the organization isolates itself from the public.

The results of the research support the notion that the restorative and the more traditional sanctioning systems are compatible in many ways, and that the two systems are more similar to each other than they appear to be at first glance. Nevertheless, it is a political (criminal policy) decision where the borderline, above which private agreements must be combined with exercising the state's criminal-justice power representing the interest of the public, is set.

It is a striking result that legal practitioners are willing to hand over the decision-making power to the victim, the offender and other persons affected by the crime. There is a consensus among professionals that to some extent the crime is the parties' private matter, as they are the ones that can express what they need in order to repair the damage and to prevent future crimes. The practitioners believe that handing over the power of decision-making is a rational move if basic personality/moral rights are respected, the procedural rules are kept and it is guaranteed that victims are not re-victimised.

We could see in relation to the introduction of mediation in the criminal procedure that the greatest challenge is to find out how a procedure based on subjective decisions can be organically built into a system which must operate objectively. Nevertheless, this research showed that legal practitioners themselves are different from each other in many respects. Still, they are also driven by personal and positive feedback in their work, just like everybody else. As they emphasised, the appreciative remark of a party in the procedure or any other positive feedback means more to them than their recognition as an authority. It gives them energy from time to time to continue working and make decisions that affect the lives of thousands of individuals and families.

References

Attachment to Parliamentary Resolution 115/2003 (X. 28.) OGY on the National Strategy for Community Crime Prevention.

Barabás, A. T. (2007), 'The Number of Postponed Indictments in Hungarian Criminal Procedures', *Kriminológiai Tanulmányok* (Criminology Studies), Vol.44.

Council of Europe, *Recommendation 2006(08) on Assistance to Crime Victims*, section 3.3 (available at: https://wcd.coe.int/wcd/ViewDoc.jsp?id=1011109&Site=CM).

Fatic, A. (1995), *Punishment and Restorative Crime-handling*, Aldershot: Avebury.

Fleck, Z. (2006), 'The Justice System in the Midst of Reform' in Ágh, A., Somogyvári, I. (eds.), *New Perspectives for the Reform of Public Administration*, Budapest: Új Mandátum Kiadó, 145–164.

Gönczöl, K. (2005), 'Developing Humane Criminal Justice Systems in Democratic Societies: An Update from Hungary', *Journal of Community and Criminal Justice*, Vol.52, No.2, 181–186.

Gönczöl, K. (2007), 'Restorative Justice — Restorable Trust', *Büntetőjogi Kodifikáció* (Criminal Law Codification), No.39.

Harris, N., Walgrave, L. and Braithwaite, J. (2004), 'Emotional Dynamics in Restorative Conferences', *Theoretical Criminology*, Vol.8, No.2, 191–210.

Keijser, J. W. De, Koppen, P. J. and Elffers, H. (2007), 'Bridging the Gap between Judges and the Public? A Multi-method Study', *Journal of Experimental Criminology*, Vol.3, No.2, 131–161.

Keijser, J. W. De (2001), 'Punishment and Purpose: From Moral Theory to Punishment in Action', Amsterdam: Thela Thesis.

Kerezsi, K. (2006), *Control or Support: The Dilemma of Alternative Sanctions*, Budapest: Complex Kiadó.

Kiss, A. (2006), 'The Role of the Victim in the Adhesion Procedure' in Kerezsi, K. (ed.), *The Possibilities of Restorative Justice in Handling Crime*, Budapest: Budapesti Szociális Forrásközpont, 24–33.

McCold, P. (2003), 'A Survey of Assessment Research on Mediation and Conferencing' in Walgrave, L. (ed.), *Repositioning Restorative Justice*, Devon, Cullompton: Willan Publishing, 67–120.

Payne, J. (2007), *Recidivism in Australia: Findings and Future Research,* Research and Public Policy Series, No.80.

Pease, K. (1998), *Repeat Victimisation: Taking Stock,* Home Office, Police Research Group, London, Crime Detection and Prevention Series Paper, No.90.

Sherman, L. (1993), 'Defiance, Deterrence, and Irrelevance: A Theory of the Criminal Sanction', *Journal of Research in Crime and Delinquency,* Vol.30, No.4, 445–473.

Shoham, S. G., Beck, O., Kett, M. (2008) (eds.), *International Handbook of Penology and Criminal Justice.* Florida: Taylor & Francis Group.

Strang, H. (2002), *Repair or Revenge: Victims and Restorative Justice*, Oxford: Clarendon.

Walgrave, L. (2003) (ed.), *Repositioning Restorative Justice,* Devon, Cullompton: Willan Publishing.

Walgrave, L. (2008), Restorative Justice: An Alternative for Responding to Crime? in Shoham, S. G., Beck, O. and Kett, M. (eds.), *International Handbook of Penology and Criminal Justice*, Florida: Taylor & Francis Group, 613–689.

Wergens, A. (1999), *Crime Victims in the European Union,* Umea, Crime Victim Compensation and Support Authority.

4

Crime and Justice: A Shift in Perspective

Louis Blom-Cooper

Preamble

There is no such thing in England and Wales as a criminal justice system — only a series of government departments and public agencies that contribute to a process of justice in response to a variety of criminal events. Each contributor has its own budget and vies competitively for public funding; each has its own agenda for its functioning towards declared aims of criminal justice. Inevitably, there is much overlapping of functions (if not duplication) and even helpful collaboration. Each contributor is answerable and accountable to an arm of government and ultimately to Parliament.

In their impressive work, *Where Next for Criminal Justice?*, David Faulkner and Ros Burnett (2012: 32) argue that when the criminal justice services had to be managed in accordance with the government's Financial Management Initiative, together with policies for efficiency, economy and effectiveness in the 1980s, a system has evolved. Nevertheless they recognise the view of the criminologist Lucia Zedner in her essay 'Reflections on Criminal Justice as a Social Institution' (2010: 69–94) that criminal justice is 'no more than a series of largely independent organizations with different cultures, professional ethos and practices which come together and interact only insofar as is necessary to pursue their respective goals'. System or no system, the independence of the judiciary and the operational independence of the criminal court of trial dictates (as I will demonstrate) a separate identity.

The aim of this chapter is thus to examine the role and function of the criminal courts, *simpliciter*, and their relationship to the other agencies contributing to the overall public response to criminality. The focus is the trial of accused persons for the commission of a criminal offence.

Models of Criminal Trial

The prosecution of an offender is prescribed by Article 6 of the European Convention on Human Rights, whose language and purpose is pure English common law. Our system of trial by judge and jury is fully compliant with the Convention, as the decision of the Grand Chamber of the European Court of Human Rights in *Taxquet v. Belgium* (2010) demonstrated. The defendant is entitled to receive a fair trial in public before an independent and impartial tribunal within a reasonable timeframe. The trial (at least, the English mode of criminal trial) has two distinct parts: determination of guilt or innocence and sentencing. Since the sentence is dependent on a verdict of guilt (which alone legitimises the disposal of the convicted person through a selection of penal sanctions) the prime focus of this chapter is the former aspect. Prosecution of the offender with a view to conviction is all-important. Sentencing of those found guilty is ancillary to the trial process and calls for appropriate disposal by the trial judge alone (strictly speaking, the jury has no role to play in determining the penal disposal of the convicted person).

At the outset it is necessary to consider comparatively the basic models of criminal trial within the criminal processes of the member states of the Council of Europe. It is, however, neither appropriate nor fully accurate to separate the judicial systems of the world into common law and civil law jurisdictions any more than to divide them between those that observe, on the one hand, adversarial/accusatorial traditions (favoured by Anglo-Saxon systems) and, on the other hand, those that are organized according to the inquisitorial model which favours either a professional tribunal or a court of professional judge and lay members. Such a binary vision is gradually adapting to borrowings that increasingly have a tendency to render the two main models more like each other. But while the dissimilarities remain a stumbling block, there is, I venture to think, a consensus of principles encompassed in modern criminal justice that renders the traditional labelling of the modes of trial by practitioners and commentators unhelpful and unrewarding. Under the aegis of the European Court of Human Rights (the international judicial arm of the Council of Europe) with its explicit recognition of the margin of appreciation accorded to the criminal jurisdiction of the member states, there is now a discernible commonality of purpose (in the 21st century) in responding to crime. Accepting that commonality, my starting point is the jurisprudence and practice of the English criminal court.

It is a common, if not universal, claim of judges and criminal law practitioners that they are agents of crime control. To provide an example (Barbara Wootton taught us all that to make any generalisation you need at least two examples), I rely on only one typical, lawyerly statement from the most liberal judge of our time. In *R v. Powell and Another* (1999) Lord Steyn declared that criminal justice 'exists to control crime' (One should observe that New Labour upgraded crime prevention as the main purpose, as distinct from the administration of criminal justice). Their Lordships in *Powell* were dealing, not very satisfactorily, with the case of joint criminal enterprise where a number of individuals (often organized gangs of youths) had been engaged in violent conduct that had resulted in fatal injury inflicted by one (often unidentified) individual with others participating in various degrees of culpability for the victim's death. The reach (indeed, over-reach) of the criminal law to secondary liability in homicide on those participating in violent behaviour often discloses a pronounced judicial desire to affix criminalisation beyond what is either necessary or just. The assumed controlling of criminal conduct through the instant trial dictates an enlargement of criminal responsibility to secondary offenders — an undeclared claim to control of crime in society generally. It is transparently all part of the judicial attitude that reflects its purpose in deterring criminal behaviour by potential offenders.

The latest example of judicial outreach to meet the perceived requirements of public policy is the Supreme Court decision in *R v. Gnango* (2011). The facts were decidedly odd, but simple. A and B voluntarily engaged to fight out their rivalry with pistols. It was a gunfight. A fired the first shot, without effect. B retaliated; one of his bullets killed a young woman who was innocently walking home from work. B has never been found, but A was prosecuted for murder and convicted. Five senior judges in the Court of Appeal quashed the conviction, on the basis that it was impossible to hold A liable for the unlawful killing of the victim. Of the seven justices in the Supreme Court, only Lord Kerr agreed with the Court of Appeal that on orthodox principles there was no room for extended secondary liability because any agreement that A and B may have had did not sensibly include agreement that B should shoot at A. A could be guilty only if he aided, abetted, counselled or procured B in the killing of the victim, who was an innocent bystander. It was obvious that A was not a principal, as he did not actually kill the victim. This was not obvious to the other judges, who in a variety of legalistic principles about joint enterprises were hell-bent on extending the law for policy reasons. In essence they thought that anyone who participates in serious public disorder runs the risk of liability for lethal consequences, whoever is the author of the killing. The net of criminal liability is thus thrown wide open.

Lord Phillips and Lord Judge, with Lord Wilson agreeing, took the extremely pragmatic approach of saying that it matters not whether A was a principal or a secondary party, he and B both acted dangerously in a public place and each should be held accountable for the death of the victim. Either could have killed someone and it was just fortuitous that the person who fired the fatal shot was B. These judges, and Lord Dyson, preferred the secondary liability route to responsibility but they agreed with Lords Brown and Clarke that principal liability could also be used as the basis for liability. Is it right that you can just pluck somebody out of an unruly mob and say that this person could easily be the one who caused the relevant harm, and that he should therefore be held responsible for it, even if it is known that he did not actually do it himself? Can you pretend that he intentionally assisted or encouraged the commission of an offence, when there is no evidence of him meaning to help or encourage its commission? The law must further the interests of the community, but there must be a rational, formalist basis for attributing responsibility for crime. Otherwise we will have a society in which judges can simply say that we should not let a defendant off, so we will hold him liable. Once again, our highest judges are making a mess of a civilised system of criminal justice. They see themselves as instruments of crime control.

The rationale of English criminal justice is quite to the contrary. Crime control by courts is not, and cannot be, an instrument of criminality in the community, other than as satisfaction to the instant victim (if identifiable). The English model of criminal justice is wedded to the adversarial system of due process and does not contemplate crime control, other than as a by-product of individual penal sanctions. Given exaggerated claims of general deterrence from sentencing (the more severe, the greater the deterrent effect, it is rashly claimed) the criminal process has in the past remained stubbornly unresponsive to any external considerations of social control. The contemporary outcrop of terrorism has implanted in the minds of criminal courts their contribution to public safety. But social control and public safety are not, historically, features of a fair trial.

James Fitzjames Stephen wrote in 1883 that 'the object of the lawmaker was rather to reconcile antagonists upon established terms than to put down crimes by the establishment of a system of common law as we understand the term'. And so, broadly speaking, the adversarial trial procedures remain in place, despite some powerful onslaughts from prestigious sources. Jerome Frank, a judge of the famous USA Second Circuit Court of Appeal and a prominent figure among the American realist school of jurisprudence in the 20th-century, wrote in *Courts on Trial* (1949: 80–102.) that the Anglo-Saxon system subscribed to a fight theory of justice rather than a truth theory. The criminal process was and is distinctly not a search for the truth about a criminal event but, far too often, a golden opportunity for defence lawyers to conceal the truth, a method of trial that permits the defence advocate to throw up a smokescreen in front of the jury, what Jerome Frank epitomised as the equivalent of throwing pepper in the eyes of a surgeon performing an operation on his patient. The trial is to ascertain the guilt or innocence of the accused according to a process that is fair in its procedural rules. It might (or might not) produce the right result; the advocates do not have to subscribe to a truthful outcome.

Students of the criminal law are familiar with the writings of another distinguished American commentator, Professor Herbert Packer (1969). He suggested that society may adopt one of two models of criminal justice — the crime control model and the due process model — which are founded on two discrete value systems. The crime control model places a premium on the effective and efficient processing of criminal events so as to optimise society's efforts to exert a dampening influence on the perceived burgeoning rate of crime. The due process model assumes the existence of the control functions outside the jurisdiction of the criminal courts, but it focuses mainly, if not exclusively, on demanding justice for the individual offender facing loss of liberty. Justice to the instant victim and to the public, by catching criminals and punishing them, is at best relegated to an ancillary role. Increasingly, however, there is a public demand to modify the due process model so as to take account of a social policy of remedying harm done to victims and for providing protection to the vulnerable public. The pressures for criminal justice to supply satisfaction other than to the immediate contestants will, if given effect to, distort the existing mode of trial.

Criminal Proceedings

There are three parties to criminal proceedings — the court, the prosecution and the defence. Witnesses (including the victims of criminal events) are not parties to the trial process, providing only evidential material to the court. The essential, residual difference between the adversarial and inquisitorial systems of criminal justice lies in the role and function of the court in relation to the two other parties; prosecutor and accused remain adversaries, whichever system of criminal procedure and trial is adopted. The Royal Commission on Criminal Justice 1991–93 (Runciman, 1993) declined to recommend any fundamental shift away from the principles of an adversarial-based system, but it considered there was scope to widen the judicial involvement in the pre-trial process, as well as the trial process, in order to achieve greater efficiency in the disposal of the caseloads of criminal courts. Legislation implementing a scheme whereby judges are required to hold hearings before trial in order to clarify the issues at trial has been a significant development in court management. As Professor John Jackson noted in his inaugural lecture as Professor of Public Law at Queen's University Belfast on 4 February 1997, there were moves afoot to encourage judges to shed their traditional role of umpire, in favour of a greater managerial role; by the beginning of the 21st-century, court management in criminal proceedings is emerging slowly. As such, it would be merely a shift in court management, not an inroad into the established system of trial by jury (modern-day improprieties by jurors have given rise to a questioning of the integrity of the jury system). Given this restrictive function of criminal justice, can the civil process be used, either in substitution for, or at least in aid of, criminal justice? I defer consideration of that question.

Victims of Crime

To return to the nature of the trial process, witnesses to the criminal event and other evidence are merely the instruments for the actors in the criminal proceedings to use in pursuance of their respective, adversarial functions. Only a fraction of the victims of crime become involved in the criminal process beyond the stage of investigation by the police or some other agency of law enforcement. For the most part criminal justice by-passes the victims of crime.

The evidence about criminal activity strongly — even overwhelmingly — suggests that criminal justice policy and practice can have only, at best, marginal effects on crime levels. As Professor Robert Reiner points out in his (2007) work *Law and Order: An Honest Citizen's Guide to Crime and Control*:

> The police-recorded statistics are problematic, because of the so-called 'dark figure' of unrecorded crime. In the well-worn metaphor, the recorded rate represents only the tip of the iceberg of criminal activity (and, *a fortiori*, culpable harm). At issue is what we can learn about the totality from the part that is visible (Reiner, 2007: 46).

Even the most reliable statistics elicited in the *British Crime Survey*, which are based on the incidence of crime as reported by victims, offers only an alternative source of data capable of mapping trends in interpersonal violence. Victimless crimes, like drug-trafficking offences, are not recorded — and many other crimes go publicly unnoticed. It is, therefore, unsafe if not unwise for those engaged in social policy to do more than take note of apparent trends (both upwards and downwards) in criminal activity. That criminal justice policy should be formulated on such deficient evidence violates the fundamental principle of evidence-based policies. And when it comes specifically to fashioning the role of the criminal courts, with their stated objective of punishing the guilty, even greater caution should be employed. Punishment by the state as a moral response to wrongdoing is a dubious policy. As Professor Reiner (2007: 11) rightly observes, 'there are both pragmatic and ethical grounds for not seeing criminal justice as central to the control of crime'. Just so; indeed, criminal justice is at most peripheral to the control of crime, even though the populace fondly believes that criminal justice is society's revenge for crime.

It is necessary therefore to construct proposals for the support and protection of victims beyond the bounds of criminal justice. Victims of crime are in need of comfort, aid and protection immediately consequent upon the criminal event and not delayed while the criminal process, if any, runs its unpredictable course. The broad areas of need are: receipt of information from the official agencies of crime control of their response to the criminal event; monetary compensation for injury or harm caused by the event; and the ongoing social support of bereaved families of homicide victims and others suffering long-term traumata. There are other issues of secondary victimisation, including financial hardship and health problems which must be addressed through social services and healthcare systems, loss of employment and housing. The due process model of the criminal court is not structured to take care of these needs for victims and for the safety and security of the community disturbed by criminal activity. Victim Support has (December, 2010) introduced a national homicide service, supplied by Victim Support volunteers, to support secondary victims of homicide in coping with their bereavement — an example of public support in pursuance of social (not criminal) justice.

Given the basically unreconstructed adversarial contest, the system can never hope to deliver justice other than, in the restricted sense, to the individuals involved directly in the criminal proceedings and, conceivably, to the immediate community affected by the criminal behaviour. Indeed, it has (as I have explained) never pretended to lead to the truth about the circumstances leading up to, or even surrounding a criminal event, only a highly institutionalised truth, requiring the prosecutor to prove the case according to strict rules as to the admissibility of evidence and the imposition of a high standard of proof beyond reasonable doubt (to use the outworn formula, now to be mouthed to the jury as 'certain so that you are sure'). The possibility of ensuring justice in the widest sense could be reached only as and when the system acknowledged the existence of, and paid respect to, both the interests of victims of crime and of the public generally. But a criminal trial is definitionally not a public inquiry; it has its own institutional function.

The need to acknowledge victimisation is beginning to dawn in quite a few jurisdictions of modern European countries. I pause only momentarily to consider why it is that in the last quarter of the 20th-century the 'victim support' movement has begun to impinge upon the consciences of the administrators of criminal justice, although the scheme of compensation for victims of violent crime, introduced in 1964, is traceable to the writings of Margery Fry in the 1950s (see, e.g. Fry, 1959). Historically, the introduction early in the 19th-century of organized police forces meant that the state entered into a compact with its citizens, whereby the latter agreed to forego self-help and the former undertook to protect the citizen through policing, and to deal appropriately with the offender. According to such social contract theorists as Hobbes, men (and women) surrendered their rights to self-help in return for the sovereign's protection and by such means the state, through its laws, became the guarantor of the individual's freedom from assaults on property or person (I put the two in that order because initially the criminal law was designed to protect the propertied classes). It is not a large step further to assume that the prescriptions of the state, as embodied by law, have a legitimacy, grounded upon its authority alone. Thus the isolation of the victim from the criminal process by a male-dominated justice system was complete by the middle of the 19th-century. Only the existence of the victim's right to bring a private prosecution has survived to give the victim any formal recognition as a party in criminal proceedings. And even today the right to a private prosecution is highly qualified and is even largely theoretical. The power of the Director of Public Prosecutions to take over a prosecution and then drop the proceedings has rendered the private citizen's right to prosecute obsolescent, if not obsolete. Even if the citizen is exceptionally permitted to pursue a criminal prosecution, it is prohibitively expensive and fraught with uncertainty in the result. The case in 1997 of Stephen Lawrence in south London was an example of such a frustrated private prosecution.[1] Strangely, the Law Commission gave support to the continuation of private prosecutions, in recommending a rationalisation

---

1. After Stephen Lawrence's murder, the CPS in 1994 refused to prosecute the accused suspects on grounds of lack of evidence. The dead boy's parents brought a private prosecution, but this failed when a key witness's evidence was ruled inadmissible. [A public prosecution did succeed eventually but only after the law on double jeopardy was changed: Eds.]

of the statutory requirements of prior consent from the Attorney-General or the Director of Public Prosecutions. The fact that the public prosecutor can nowadays judicially review any improper exercise of his discretionary or legal powers suffices to render the private prosecution redundant. It should be pensioned off by Parliament.

It cannot be gainsaid that victims of crime have to be reckoned with by the functions of the criminal process, aided by the civil law. The victim undoubtedly has interests that demand official recognition and protection. Compensation for the injury or loss caused has been with us for over 40 years now, but administered entirely outside the criminal justice system. Compensation for crimes of violence has, since 1996, been put on a statutory footing, administered by a government agency on a tariff system. But there are now efforts to encompass the victim within the criminal process. There are at present, as I see it, two solutions being proffered.

The first is prominently visible by practical reform of existing criminal justice. The point is made that there is an over-emphasis on the rights of the accused. Provisions such as limitations on the consequences of insisting on the right to silence or the greater disclosure of the accused's defence in advance of trial are designedly attempts to redress an inequitable balance. It is claimed that society is over-protective of the offender. The shift towards easing the prosecutor's task of convicting the supposedly guilty is an essay in assuaging the victim's irritation at a system that so often fails to bring offenders to justice. The Criminal Procedure and Investigations Act 1996, moreover, has been widely thought to favour unduly the prosecution in the requirement of disclosure to the defence of relevant material. I do not wish to follow the purpose of this solution in providing an equality of arms. It proceeds, in my view, to sustain, in essence, a criminal justice system that is rightly insistent upon a single, due process model to cope with multifarious criminal events. Availability of all relevant evidential material may require discrimination according to the nature of the criminal activity. Terrorism is one example.

The other solution is to approach the problem of crime control alongside, if not distinctly outside, the due process model of criminal justice. The fundamental principle is that one would start from the position of victims' rights, while in no way forgetting the rights of offenders in jeopardy of their liberty. There is in the dichotomy of the two models a sense that, rights being in competition, the emphasis is to focus upon those areas where the interests of victims and offenders coincide. A prime example of this line of reasoning is where reparation by the offender to the victim leads to the imposition of a more lenient treatment in the labelled offence and penalty by the criminal court. More and more, the interests of victims have been reducing the retributive element in the criminal justice system, although there may be occasional notorious cases where private revenge may surface. Reconciliation and mediation are currently being proposed as devices to circumvent the divisiveness of criminal justice. Restorative justice is the favoured theory of contemporary criminologists (it is even the flavour of the month for many reformists). But does restorative justice have any (and if so, what) role to play in the criminal trial process, or even within the spectrum of the criminal process as a whole? Restorative justice, strictly applied, can operate in any event only at the stage of penal disposal, since it operates only as and when the offender has admitted at least involvement in the criminal event, if not legal guilt, in causing harm to the victim. Much as I favour the process of the victim and offender confronting each other (where appropriate), restorative justice belongs to the field of social action. Justice Sachs (Albie Sachs, the distinguished and recently retired member of South Africa's Constitutional Court) wisely observed in *S v. M* (2007):

> Central to the notion of restorative justice is the recognition of the community rather than the criminal justice agencies as the prime site of crime control.

Like the case for attending to victims' needs, restorative justice fits more easily into the system of civil justice or, less formally, in social welfare and community care.

One thing, however, is tolerably clear. Criminal justice, as we know it, cannot provide (nor can it hope to cope with) the appropriate formulae for all, or indeed many, of the legitimate claims of victims and society. Where then do we go in search of a system of dealing with antisocial conduct which is currently labelled 'criminal'?

An Alternative Strategy

What do the following incidents have in common:

- a number of cars are stolen or vandalised in a leafy suburb of a provincial town;
- a child on a housing estate is discovered to have been sexually abused by a foster parent;
- a bunch of youths cause a serious disturbance in the village community centre;
- a bank clerk disappears with customers' deposits;
- a well-known financier is discovered to have defrauded HM Revenue & Customs over a number of years of substantial sums of money;
- a young woman is raped in an area of town notorious for the commission of sexual assaults;
- an aged couple are found dead in their home from severe injuries inflicted by stab wounds;
- a paedophile ring is uncovered in a residential hostel run by a charitable organization;
- an area of town has been terrorised by persistent burglaries and witness-intimidation by a family of brothers;
- a supermarket finds that its losses are exceeding the acceptable slippage of two per cent of its stock ... and so on and so on?

What, if any, attributes do these disparate, daily occurrences, events, happenstances—call them what you will—share? True, they all indicate the commission of an offence within the country's criminal calendar; more relevantly, they present to an ordered society variegated social problems which call for variable responses from the agencies of social control. How should we as a society in fact respond? Apart from affixing on the convicted offenders the label of criminality to each of the criminal events, each of them automatically becomes susceptible to criminal justice, and then only at the stage of sentencing—itself a process that is not intrinsically judicial, but is rather administrative.

There is no reason why all culprits should be selected for prosecution and hence squeezed into the single straitjacket of the criminal process, as we know it. Indeed, the burden of what I have to say is that there is everything to be said in favour of a selective process whereby variable criminality is assessed and evaluated with a view to differentially appropriate action. It is not simply a diversion from criminal justice, but of constructing alternative ways of effective social control. To speak of crime suggests an analogy with disease, implying that crime, like disease, is a unitary phenomenon, whereas we are dealing with a variety of disparate crimes or, rather, criminal events. We should instantly appreciate that there is no single theory or practical response to all crimes (or criminal events) any more than there is a single theory or cure to be found to explain and treat all diseases. Lord Atkin (1931) once defined crime in the following terms:

> The domain of criminal jurisprudence can be ascertained only by examining what acts at any particular period are declared by the State to be crimes, and the only common nature they will be found to possess is they are prohibited by the State and those who commit them are punished (Atkin, 1931).

Just so, except that I would replace the word 'punished' by action on the part of society to reduce the risk of harm. We would do well if we invariably talked about crimes — criminal events, more accurately — and how society should respond to them. The abstraction of crime is an unhelpful deviance from sensible debate and dialogue.

Is it then axiomatic, as is so often assumed, that a criminal trial of any serious, or less serious offence — I take that to encompass all cases tried at the Crown Court — is a necessary prerequisite to social intervention in the offender's liberty? If the investigation of the event — how, when and why — took place first, without necessarily identifying the perpetrators (just as happens in a Coroner's Court to determine the cause of death), the proceedings would not need to be constrained by the strict rules of evidence in criminal cases which the Law Commission proposed should be relaxed further to allow for the admissibility of hearsay evidence (enacted in the Criminal Justice Act 2003);[2] they would proceed on the basis of the civil standard of proof, the balance of probabilities; and in non-jury trial there

---

2. In July 1995 the Law Commission published *Evidence and Criminal Proceedings: Hearsay and Related Topics*. Its final report appeared in 1997.

would not need to be the inscrutable and inarticulate verdict of a jury. The county court judge would hear the case and deliver a reasoned judgment, indicating what happened, how it happened and (where necessary) who, if anyone, was responsible for the incident, together with an apportionment of any such responsibility among the participants. There are some logistical problems associated with the criminal jurisdiction, namely, bail or custody of the defendant and the protection of witnesses. (The protection of vulnerable witnesses is currently accommodated by procedural safeguards; this may lead to the lessening of orality and a greater use of written statements.)

The complainants of the incident would be an agency, possibly the local authority, but specifically not the Crown Prosecution Service. The police would doubtless have to be the fact-gatherers, working to the orders of the complaining authority. Once the civil court's verdict was delivered, there would be time enough to consider what action, if any, should be taken against any identified culprits. The range of sanctions might conceivably be those currently available, but the decision-makers of what those sanctions should be would not be exclusively the judiciary, high or low, although the county court judge might be the appropriate chair. It would be a composite body, with a large element of the local community most affected by the disturbance. Systems outwith criminal justice should be available, appropriate to the social conduct under scrutiny.

Even if we cannot in some instances dispense with the individualised justice of the due process model, or tailor it to some aspect of crime control, may we not sensibly use the civil process in favour of justice? There is, for example, clearly room for use by local authorities of their protective powers of the local citizenry under the Local Government Act 1972 to proceed by way of injunctive relief against offenders who manage to frustrate the process of criminal justice. In 1995 Coventry City Council was in possession for a whole year of an order from a High Court judge banning two brothers who had terrorised a housing estate from entering a defined restricted zone. The relief thereby afforded to the inhabitants was, if ephemeral, immense. The antisocial behaviour order (ASBO), set up by the Crime and Disorder Act 1998, proved ineffective, if only because it was framed in the context of the criminal courts. Its replacement by the device of civil injunctions seems a much more suitable means of dealing with public disorder. Civil (or social) justice is preferable to the heavy armoury of criminal justice.

Civil justice might also be made available in certain circumstances as a direct auxiliary to the criminal courts as part of a two-way process. A contemporary problem prompts the idea. Only half of the prosecutions for rape end up in a conviction. The victims of these forensic circuses have to undergo the ordeal of reliving the criminal event and frequently do not even have the satisfaction of knowing whether their version of events has been accepted by the jury, let alone the result of a favourable verdict.

The ordeal of the experience in the witness-box is frequently exacerbated by the tenor and temper of cross-examination, particularly aggravated if conducted by the alleged rapist himself, reviving the horrors of the criminal event, rather than by his advocate. The problem appears insoluble so long as the accused's right to defend himself subsists uncontrolled, or, at most, controlled only within narrow judicial constraints. A remedy may lie in a radical proposal. The proposal commended itself to Sir William Utting in his 1997 report to government, 'People Like Us', on the safeguards for children susceptible to abuse. The idea has received a deafening silence.

Whenever the Crown Prosecution Service decides to prosecute an accused with rape or other serious sexual offence, there should be a prerequisite that a certificate to proceed to a criminal trial be applied for in the county court. The civil process would establish, according to the civil standard of proof, the responsibility of the defendant for the commission of the alleged criminal act. Civil liability would be the basis for the certificate, but the court would have to be satisfied that a criminal trial would be appropriate. On past records, many cases would end at the civil stage, the victim at least gaining the important satisfaction of having established her case in the courtroom. The court would always have the additional power to grant an injunction (where appropriate) and even to award damages. The grant of a certificate to proceed to a criminal trial ought to result in a high rate of conviction, thus remedying the present unsatisfactory state of a high acquittal rate. Pleas of guilt would be more forthcoming if the accused's version of the criminal event had been rejected by the certifying court. This proposal is, I think, workable, although it has resource implications for the county court.

There already exist other interesting examples of an alternative system to the process of criminal justice. I refer, first, to the powers of the Inland Revenue and Customs and Excise to administer monetary penalties, up to three times the amount of back duty, on a taxpayer who defrauds the Inland Revenue. Prosecution by HM Revenue & Customs against fraudulent tax evaders is rare, and then only to deal with a new or particularly prevalent form of revenue crime.[3] Second, the investigation and pursuit of white-collar crime is increasingly taking place away from criminal courts. A high proportion of cases being tried today by judges in the Chancery Division of the High Court are effectively criminal cases whose victims — companies and shareholders — have opted for the civil process for the recovery of property lost through fraud. The prediction is that expert consultants, composed of solicitors, accountants and ex-police officers, will in the future offer fraud investigation services. Victims will pay large fees in return for investigation. Whether the results land up in the civil or criminal courts must be a matter of speculation. But the development of private investigation connotes a shift away from the exclusivity of criminal justice. The development of the regulatory system for financial services is a welcome alternative to complex fraud trials.

The trouble about criminal justice today is that it is time-consuming; the outcome is always problematic, and the legitimised penal sanction of imprisonment is costly and cumbersome and, at most, does no more than inflict individualised, temporary incapacitation. As the former Secretary of State for Justice, Mr Kenneth Clarke has said, prison is a waste of public money. There will always be some criminal events which demand the full panoply and majesty of the criminal trial. If only for reasons of symbolism, there is a compelling need, in certain defined circumstances, for all the trappings of the criminal court to be in place — a judge endowed with the Olympian authority of the Crown, festooned with distinctive robes (and, foreseeable for years to come, the wig) sitting in a public building that evokes the might of the state. But for the vast bulk of criminal cases, the run-of-the-mill offences against property and the less serious offences against the person do not call for such elaborate and fancy, hugely institutionalised response, a large proportion

---

3. Compare the far greater number of benefit fraud cases that are currently brought to the criminal courts.

of which are properly handled by the magistrates' courts (The future role and function of the English magistracy is due for a thorough review). The criminal event which exposes unacceptable social conduct and legitimates control of the perpetrator by way of imposition of penal sanctions demands a much less solemn, more expeditious and simpler procedure than is exhibited by the adversarial process of criminal justice. It was Jeremy Bentham who aptly observed that substantive law, by which he meant the basic ingredients of the criminal offence, is never self-enforcing; it is sustainable only by the adjectival law of sound procedures and evidence. The adjectival segment of criminal justice is fraught with difficulties, engendered by the justifiable need to preserve the safeguards against a wrongful conviction.

Apply the alternative approach to the occasion of an affray in the local village. There may well be a case for eliciting, for public view, the circumstances leading up to and surrounding the incident. The civil process of fact-finding, stripped of any sentencing function, would more than adequately provide the forum and pointer for appropriate social action. If the identified miscreants must, for reasons of public protection, be deprived of their liberty, as opposed to any non-custodial sanction, there might have to be further safeguards built into the sentencing process to compensate for responsibility having been imposed by the lesser standard of proof than would ordinarily be a prerequisite to the penalty of imprisonment. The problem is that this process would merely tend to replicate the courts of criminal justice. A differential would need to be devised. We must not forget that many dangerous people are detained under mental health legislation without undergoing the criminal process; their discharge is controllable by resort to the administrative tribunals, the mental health review tribunals. The whole question of detention for the sole purpose of public protection needs to be examined. This may come about as a result of the government proposals as enacted in the Legal Aid, Sentencing and Punishment of Offenders Act 2012, now passed by Parliament.

Concluding Observations

Recent developments surrounding criminal justice are indicative of public unease—a better word would be 'dis-ease'—about its failure to cope with the problem of social disorder. The aim of injecting diversionary tactics into the criminal process is a recognition of a desire to escape the consequences, often unintended, of the pursuit of a criminal conviction. Probation itself was an expression of society's aim to break the iron equation between crime and punishment. The development of non-custodial penalties and forms of intermediate treatment has similarly reflected an attempt to escape the single-minded purpose of criminal justice, to punish the convicted offender. Mediation and conciliation are recent entrants onto the scene to effect avoidance of the treadmill of prosecution, trial, conviction and penal disposal.

Court-based psychiatric assessment should indicate the removal of mentally-disordered persons from criminal justice and the penal system into the mental health system. The apparent clamour of victims of crime for a larger say in the process of decision-making, particularly in influencing the sentencing process, is a clear declaration of some (unquantifiable) public dissatisfaction with criminal justice. But victim support groups have generally remained neutral on questions of sentencing offenders.

Such developments as I have indicated that are afoot at present are peripheral to the main thrust of the criminal court. Rather than providing sensible alternative options of social response to the criminal events, they actually sustain activity within criminal justice. By mitigating the worst features of the process, they positively acknowledge the centrality of the courts and prisons as the instrument to be deployed initially for social control. We start from assuming imprisonment for all serious crimes as the core of the penal system and then work downwards in recognition of the need to avoid the worst effects of the inutility (over and above individual incapacitation) of incarceration.

It is time to review fundamentally the aims of criminal justice, a matter which the Runciman Commission on Criminal Justice (Runciman, 1993) left untouched, mainly for reasons of a restricted remit and a limited timescale for reporting to government. The Chief Constable of Kent in a seminar of the British Academy of Forensic Sciences in 1997 described the Commission's report as 'uneventful ... in recommending nothing of fundamental significance which was not already inevitable [it] endorsed the status quo'; so matters remain largely untouched. What is needed is some theoretical underpinning to the system of social control, some alternative approach to criminality, with the corollary of a justice system tailored to meet particular forms of criminality. This is no wish for an epidemic outbreak of the itch for change—what Chief Justice Hale (1787: Vol. I, 249) described three centuries ago as: 'a certain restlessness and nauseousness of men in what they have, and a giddy humour after something that is new'. It is a plea for a concerted search for something better than today's largely unreconstructed criminal process for which we pay dearly, with too little return for our money. Criminal justice provides naught for our general comfort. At best it provides a patchwork solution to individual cases brought to court, and on its past record too many miscarriages of justice—or should it be 'carriages of injustice'?

How then do we persuade today's politicians of the need for a more creative and less tram-lined outlook on the problems of social control and criminal justice? How do we inculcate in those responsible for policy the need to employ more judicious and, where necessary, judicial means to provide justice for both the victims (the individual and the community) of crime and the offenders? The first step is to restore the erstwhile consensus among professionals and legislators in criminal justice and penal affairs. There is nothing to be gained from the contemporary attitudes that permit politicians to indulge unthinkingly in the rhetoric of law and order. Only when the bipartisan, authoritarian approach is abandoned will we be able to redefine the boundaries of criminal justice and look to civil justice to promote the prevention of crime, the reduction of reoffending and the public sense of community safety. We do not need to swallow the wholesale abolitionist case of Professor Louk Hulsman and his supporters. But we do need a distinct shift away from the deployment of criminal justice, if only because a minimalist approach is more likely to affect the honest politician's attitude to crime control.

Criminal courts should focus exclusively on their task of ensuring a fair trial for the contestants in their courtrooms—adherence to the precepts of due process under the authoritative guidance of Strasbourg—and abandon any notion that they are directly engaged in society's grappling with the problems of criminality. Where criminal justice is appropriately wheeled into place, the sole function of trial by judge and jury is quintessentially to ensure a fair trial. The task of crime control is for the civil authorities.

References

Atkin (Lord Atkin) (1931), *Proprietary Articles Trade Association v. Attorney General of Canada* [1931] AC 310 at 324 (Privy Council).

Faulkner, D. and Burnett, R. (2012), *Where Next for Criminal Justice?,* Bristol: Policy Press.

Frank, J. (1949), *Courts On Trial: Myth and Reality in American Justice,* Princeton, NJ: Princeton University Press.

Fry, M. (1959) 'Justice for Victims', *Journal of Public Law,* no.8, 191–194.

Hale, Sir M. (Chief Justice) (1787) 'Considerations Touching the Amendment or Alteration of Lawes' in Hargrave, F., *Collection of Tracts Relative to the Law of England.*

Law Commission (1995), *Evidence and Criminal Proceedings: Hearsay and Related Topics*, Law. Com. CP 138, Great Britain Law Commission CP 138, London: HMSO.

Packer, H. L. (1969), *The Limits of the Criminal Sanction,* Oxford: Oxford University Press.

Reiner, R. (2007), *Law and Order: An Honest Citizen's Guide to Crime and Control,* Polity Press, Cambridge.

Runciman, W. G. (Lord Runciman) (Chairman) (1993). *Report of the Royal Commission on Criminal Justice*, Cm 2263, 6 July 1993, London: HMSO.

Stephen, Sir J. F. (1883), *A History of the Criminal Law of England,* London: Macmillan.

Utting, Sir W. (1997), 'People Like Us: The Report of the Review of the Safeguards for Children Living Away from Home', London: TSO.

Zedner, L. (2010), 'Reflections on Criminal Justice as a Social Institution' in Downes, D., Hobbs D. and Newburn T. (eds.), *The Eternal Recurrence of Crime and Control*, Oxford: Oxford University Press.

Cases

R v. Powell and Another [1999] 1 AC 1, 14–15. The case was refined in *R v. Rehman* by the House of Lords.

R v. Gnango [2011] UKSC 59, 14 December 2011.

S v. M [2007] ZACC 18.

Taxquet v. Belgium [2010] ECHR 1806, 16 November 2010.

5

Civilising Civil Justice

Ann Skelton

Introduction

The theme of this book arises from the idea that the criminal justice system needs to be civilised. This encompasses two central ideas: Firstly, that current criminal justice practice is uncivilised, and is in need of reform; Secondly, that the advantage of the civil justice system is that it is the resolution of a dispute between the direct protagonists. Restorative justice writers have demonstrated how the victim is no longer a direct protagonist in the criminal justice process, as his or her role has been usurped by the state. A key aspect of civilising the criminal justice process, therefore, is reintroducing the victim as a participant in the justice process.

This chapter raises a slightly different issue. Is the civil justice process itself civilised? Despite the fact that the victim — as plaintiff — is party to the proceedings, the civil law has also become obfuscated by layers of substantive and procedural rules that frustrate the plaintiff's quest for justice. Lawyers steepen the conflict. An assumption that a claim sounding in monetary value alone can heal the harm done to the plaintiff is inimical to a restorative justice approach.

The focus in this chapter is on one particular aspect of civil law. The claiming of damages for injury to personality is at the centre of the discussion. South Africa's rich legal heritage has created space to seek inspiration from ancient canon law, Roman Dutch law, African customary law and modern restorative justice theory and practice in these civil claims. Recent South African case law reveals a cautious willingness to apply restorative justice principles in civil matters, which may result in the civilisation of aspects of the civil law.

Restorative justice and civil justice

Restorative justice is often described as an approach that begins with a consideration of harm. Following an incident, the first question to be asked, according to a restorative justice approach is: Who has been harmed? Harm can be physical (to the body or mind) or to the property of a person. In some cases the harm arises from a criminal act. The mainstream criminal justice system focuses on proof of guilt and, following that, punishment. The focus is rarely on the harm that is done, and where such harm is considered, that usually occurs in relation to sentencing. The more harm done, the more severe the punishment must be. The person harmed is not the focus, and as a general rule the victim does not obtain redress for harm through criminal justice processes. He or she must seek compensation through the civil justice system. In other instances, the harm arises not from a crime, but from an act of negligence, or a failure to act on the part of someone who has a duty. This area of the civil law, which provides for compensation for harm,[1] whether intentional or accidental, is known in some systems as delict, and in others as tort (Cane, 1997: 51).[2] In this chapter the word delict will be used, as the focus of the chapter is on the South African legal system which uses this term.

---

1. A further role of the law of delict/tort is that it aims to discourage wrong or negligent behaviour. This is somewhat at odds with its compensatory role. Cane describes tort law as a complex mixture of principles of personal responsibility for conduct and for outcomes, which are underpinned by different imperatives. The underlying aim of conduct responsibility is to discourage conduct that might attract liability, whilst the purpose of outcome responsibility is to compensate for negative outcomes of conduct (Cane, 1997: 51–52). Most writers are of the view that the civil law is not aimed at punishment or deterrence (see Loubscher and Midgley, 2010: 10–11) but it is apparent that these features do tend to creep into the way that the courts make decisions.

2. The word 'delict' is derived from the Latin 'delictum' which means offence. Originally the word included both civil and criminal wrongs, but now refers only to civil wrongs. Civil law systems that are firmly rooted in Roman law, such as in Scotland, some Continental European countries and South Africa, use this terminology. 'Tort' has French origins and refers to a wrong (other than a breach of contract) for which there is a remedy through compensation or damages. Civil law systems that follow an English common law approach, including the USA, use this terminology.

A person who approaches a court for redress of a civil wrong is in South Africa referred to as a plaintiff. The plaintiff is directly involved with the civil claim because he or she is a party to the proceedings. This is unlike the victim in a criminal matter who is indirectly represented in court proceedings by the prosecutor, and as a result often feels that he or she is neglected or ignored by the system (Green, 2007: 179–181). However, despite the plaintiff's involvement as a party, he or she may still be left with a sense of injustice at the end of the process. The legal process does not generally allow for engagement. Mediation is sometimes offered as an option, but this remains an under-utilised alternative to the mainstream justice system. The plaintiff may be frustrated that there is no acknowledgment of responsibility during the process of a civil claim—sometimes the defendant will try to shift and share blame by pointing out that there was contributory negligence. In such situations there is a limited sense of vindication, even if the outcome is successful. The compensatory order will be framed as a monetary award. This can be important if the harm caused relates to property or personal injury, as the provision of financial compensation may play an important role in the plaintiff's recovery. However, in more abstract cases—such as injury to personality through defamation or other libel, the payment of money in most cases has little meaning, but it is still the only response that the civil justice system has to offer.

In South Africa, academics and judges have been exploring whether this situation could be ameliorated through the application of conciliatory concepts, old and new, Western and African. The rich, pluralistic heritage from which South Africa's legal system derives has offered a unique opportunity of looking at justice in a different way.

Legal Pluralism Reveals Other Ways of Doing Justice

African customary law processes

Before colonisers arrived in South Africa, indigenous South Africans lived under customary law. Although Roman-Dutch law was superimposed over the customary law, the customary law and customary courts never died out entirely, and are still in operation today, particularly in rural areas of South Africa. South Africans who are familiar with customary law practice

immediately recognise the values and practice principles of restorative justice (Skelton, 2002: 507). A reader familiar with modern restorative justice
practice will recognise similarities with essential elements of African customary law processes described here.[3] African customary law processes have the
aim of reconciliation and restoring peace or harmony in the community
(Tshehla, 2004: 16). The process promotes a normative system that stresses
an individual or community duty as well as the rights of the individual
(Gyeke, 1998: 317).[4] Dignity and respect are viewed as central values, and
this links closely to the African concept of *ubuntu*, which will be discussed
later in this chapter.

African customary law processes do not distinguish markedly between
civil and criminal wrongs—a wrong is a harm done to an individual and the
broader community. Simplicity and informality of procedure is an important feature of African traditional conflict resolution processes (Mqeke and
Vorster, 2002: 151). The outcomes in such a process are not based on pro-
nouncements of law by other courts—there is no rule of *stare decisis*,[5] in
other words, the law does not change through precedent. However, customary
law is not static, it is dynamic (Bennett, 1999: 6). Community participation
is very important in African customary law processes. The procedures of an
African customary law court are in themselves powerful. Traditional courts
in Africa are generally carried out with the participants sitting in a circle, a
formation common to many indigenous tribunals in other parts of the world.
African customary law values outcomes such as restitution or compensation.

Roman-Dutch law superimposed

When the British took occupation of the Cape Colony in 1806 under a treaty
of cession with The Netherlands, the new colonial authorities assumed that
the local law was Roman-Dutch. The indigenous people living at the Cape

---

3. The similarities (and differences) of restorative justice processes and African customary law
   processes are described more fully in Skelton (2007).

4. Gyeke asserts that a communitarian ethos underpins African social structures. See also Elechi
   who links this African concept to restorative justice: Elechi (2004).

5. *Stare decisis* is part of English common law, and based on a Latin phrase '*stare decisis et non
   quieta movere*' (stand by decisions and do not disturb settled law). In modern common law
   systems it means that courts are bound by the decisions previously made by other courts
   within the same jurisdiction, particularly superior courts.

at that time, the Khoisan, were unable to assert their own law and customs (Van Niekerk, 2001: 7). A different pattern emerged in the Colony of Natal, which was annexed by Britain in 1845. In 1849 the indigenous law of the Zulus was officially recognised and made applicable to indigenous people (Bennett, 1999: 19). Although customary law was not generally codified, the Code of Zulu Law is an example of such a codification. Section 93(1) of the Code of Zulu Law contains a proviso that no action lies where a defamatory statement was made during a heated quarrel and where 'within a short time thereafter the statement is publicly withdrawn with apology'(Bekker, 1989: 344). There are interesting linkages between this approach and the early approach Roman-Dutch law to defamation.

South Africa's common law of delict is based on a set of principles derived from Roman and Roman-Dutch law actions, namely the *Lex Aquilia*[6] and the *actio injuriarum*.[7] Principles have also been gleaned from the Germanic remedy for pain and suffering,[8] and there have been influences from English law (Loubscher and Midgley, 2010: 25–27).

South African academic Mukheibir (2007a: 583) has described the origins of an old delictual concept, the *amende honorable*. She explains that it can be traced back to medieval canon law, although it is often mistakenly regarded as having originated in Roman-Dutch law.[9] Mukheibir states that the basis of the *amende honorable* is that of Christian forgiveness, as opposed to its punitive counterpart the *amende profitable*.[10]

In medieval times the *amende honorable* arose through praying for pardon in a case of slandering another person. The remedy entailed three aspects: a declaration that the statement was made without intention to defame, a retraction of the defamatory words to repair the injured person's honour, and an acknowledgment of wrongdoing and a request for forgiveness. Both the *amende honorable* and the *amende profitable* became part of Roman-Dutch

---

6. This action is utilised for recovery of patrimonial loss to property or the person.
7. This action is utilised for compensating for invasions of personality, including dignity, privacy, identity and reputation.
8. The action is utilised for compensating pain and suffering and covers injury to the psyche (psychological health).
9. See also Mukheibir (2007b: 38–39).
10. Mukheibir cites Zimmerman (1990: 1072). See *Hare v. White* (1865), *Ward-Jackson v. Cape Times Ltd.* (1910).

law. The *amende profitable* developed into the present day *actio iniuriarum* (Midgley, 1995: 290), and it was thought, until recently, that the *amende honorable* was no longer part of South African law (Mukheibir, 2007a: 585).

Calls for the resuscitation of the amende honorable

The academic debates about the *amende honorable* have considered whether it has fallen into desuetude and if so, whether it should be revived. South African legal academic Mukheibir has argued for the 'revival' of the *amende honorable* (2004: 2).

Whilst most authors seem to be positive about its 'reincarnation', there is disagreement amongst leading academic authors about whether its reintroduction and development should be as a defence or a remedy. Burchell (1985: 315–319) has postulated that retraction and apology should be developed as a complete defence. In other words, where a suitable retraction and apology has been forthcoming, no claim for compensation will lie.

Midgley (1995: 288), on the other hand, was not persuaded by this argument. He pointed out that there may be cases where an apology will be insufficient to assuage the loss suffered, particularly if there is a long delay between the infringement and the apology. Furthermore, an apology will not always be able to reach all who were aware of the original. A published apology might also compound harm (by airing the issues again) and finally, such a defence could be open to manipulation.

The *amende honorable* has recently 'made a comeback' in South African legal debates (Mukheibir, 2007a: 585). A number of recent cases have provided a platform for consideration of the existence or revival of the *amende honorable*, and in each case the discussion appears to approach the concept as a remedy, rather than a complete defence. However, the discussions about *amende honorable* in the case law point to a remedial shift that is more comprehensive than a mere consideration of apology as a mitigating factor. A consideration of the relevant case law illuminates the issues.

The case of *Mineworkers Investment Co (Pty) Ltd. v. Modibane* (2002) dealt with a defamation action in which the applicant proposed, in lieu of damages, that the defendant publish an apology in a full page advertisement of a newspaper. In exploring the rationale and history behind this innovative remedy, Willis J traces the development of the value of apology, starting with

Voet's *Commentary on the Pandects* through to judgments of the South African courts.[11] Willis J held that although the remedy of *amende honorable* seemed to have fallen into desuetude this did not mean that it had been abrogated by disuse. He detected a cautious approach by the courts in applying the remedy, and he identified the core of their reluctance to be the fact that in the days when *amende honorable* was utilised, the enforcement of the remedy was achievable through civil imprisonment. Judges in the modern era were no doubt repelled by this idea.

Another factor Willis J considered as to why the remedy had not been used was an over-reliance by South African judges on English law, whereas *amende honorable* was part of Roman-Dutch (or more, properly, canon) law. He concluded that *amende honorable* had simply been forgotten: '[A] little treasure lost in a nook of our legal attic' (at para. 25).

He further remarked that if he was wrong, and that *amende honorable* was no longer part of South African law, then sound reasons exist for an analogous remedy. He was concerned that if the only other remedy available in a defamation action is damages, then very often an appropriate balance will not be struck between the protection of reputation on the one hand and freedom of expression on the other. He felt that this approach fails in two respects: Firstly, it does not afford an adequate protection to reputation and secondly, it can impose restrictions on freedom of expression.

Amende honorable *meets* ubuntu *and restorative justice*

The Constitutional Court of South Africa has also considered the concept of *amende honorable* in two cases. The first of these was *Dikoko v. Mokhatla* (2006). The case dealt with a civil claim for damages arising from defamation. The applicant sought leave to appeal against a judgment of the High Court that found him guilty of defaming the respondent, and ordered him to pay R110,000.[12] At the time of the incident the applicant was the executive mayor and the respondent was the chief executive officer of the municipality. The defamation arose from the applicant having run up cellular telephone charges grossly in excess of the official limit. When called to account before

---

11. Johannes (Jan) Voet (1647–1713) was a Dutch jurist whose famous work *Commentarius ad Pandectus* is still an important source of South African law.

12. The approximate equivalent of 11,000 euros.

the provincial government Standing Accounts Committee he made allegations to the effect that the respondent was trumping up charges for political reasons. The High Court found that the statement was defamatory, and rejected the applicant's argument that the speech in the legislature was protected by privilege. The appeal judgment of the Constitutional Court split in various different ways, the details of which are not relevant to the current discussion. On the issue of the amount of damages, the majority of the court upheld the award of a substantial claim of financial damages. Whilst Mokgoro J wrote the majority judgment in this matter, she found herself in the minority (together with Sachs J and Nkabinde J) on the issue of quantum of damages.

The minority judgments of Mokgoro J and Sachs J (Nkabinde J concurring) argued for a remedial shift based on the revival of the *amende honorable*, fused with the concept of *ubuntu-botho* and the theory and practice of restorative justice. Both Mokgoro J and Sachs J highlight the importance of a restorative justice approach in their judgments. According to Mokgoro J, the primary purpose of a compensatory measure is to restore the dignity of the plaintiff who has suffered the damage and not to punish the defendant.[13] Focusing on a more apology-centred approach, Mokgoro J states that the focus on monetary compensation diverts attention from two considerations that should be basic to defamation law. Firstly the reparation sought is essentially for injury to one's honour, dignity and reputation, and not to one's pocket. Secondly, courts should attempt, wherever feasible, to re-establish a dignified and respectful relationship between the parties.

> Because an apology serves to recognise the human dignity of the plaintiff, thus acknowledging, in the true sense of *ubuntu*, his or her inner humanity, the resultant harmony would serve the good of both the plaintiff and the defendant. Whether the *amende honorable* is part of our law or not, our law in this area should be developed in the light of the values of *ubuntu* emphasising restorative rather than retributive justice. The goal should be to knit together shattered relationships in

---

13. *Lynch v. Agnew* (1929). See further Mukheibir (2007a: 583 at 585) who states that the *actio iniuriarum* is 'regarded by leading authors on the South African law of damages as having retained an element of punishment and even revenge. In this respect it is anomalous within a system which purports to be compensatory' (Visser and Potgieter, 2003).

the community and encourage across-the-board respect for the basic norms of human and social interdependence. It is an area where courts should be proactive, encouraging apology and the mutual understanding wherever possible (Mokgoro J, para. 69).

In concurring with Mokgoro J, Sachs J proposes a remedial shift in the law of defamation from 'an almost exclusive preoccupation with monetary awards' to 'a more flexible and broadly based approach that involves and encourages apology'(para. 105). The judge was of the view that there should be a greater scope and encouragement for enabling the reparative value of retraction and apology to be introduced into proceedings. The principal goal should be repair rather than punishment.

The judgments of Mokgoro J and Sachs J both make a direct linkage between restorative justice and the African spirit of *ubuntu* or *botho*. According-ing to Mokgoro *ubuntu* does not lend itself to simple definition, nor is it easily translated into English. It is commonly explained by way of drawing together strands of concepts such as *ubuntu ngumuntu ngabantu* which can be translated as 'a person is a person through other people' (Mokgoro, 1998: 15).[14]

In his judgment, Sachs J observes that the spirit of *ubuntu-botho* has been described as a concept highly consonant with the rapidly evolving interna-tional notions of restorative justice. Deeply rooted in South African society, it links up with worldwide striving to develop restorative justice based on reparative rather than purely punitive principles (para. 114). Sachs J recorded that although *ubuntu-botho* and the *amende honorable* are expressed in dif-ferent languages intrinsic to separate legal cultures, they share the same underlying philosophy and goal. 'Both are directed towards promoting face-to-face encounter between the parties, so as to facilitate resolution in public of their differences and the restoration of harmony in the community. In both legal cultures the centre-piece of the process is to create conditions to facilitate the achievement, if at all possible, of an apology honestly offered, and generously accepted.'[15]

---

14. *Ubuntu* is a Nguni word, its *seSotho* equivalent in *botho*. In *seSotho* 'a person is a person through other people' may be translated as *motho ke motho ba batho ba bangwe.*

15. This 'face-to-face' theme is prominent in the jurisprudence of Sachs J. See Skelton (2011).

While finding that there is a need for a significant remedial shift, Sachs J did not suggest that the new, more restorative approach should completely replace the *actio iniuriarum*. He found that 'money, like cattle'[16] could have symbolic value. Sometimes an apology may not be sincere, sometimes it may not be enough. What is required is more flexibility and innovation concerning the relation between apology and money awards. In modern restorative justice practice financial compensation does sometimes play a part in restorative justice outcomes, which is usually where there has been actual financial loss, such as where there has been physical injury or the loss of or damage to property.

A Call for the Recognition of RJ in Defamation Suits is Answered

The second case in which the Constitutional Court dealt with *amende honorable* was the matter of *Le Roux and others v. Dey (Freedom of Expression Institute and Restorative Justice Centre as Amici Curiae)* (2011). This case concerned a civil claim for damages arising from the actions of three schoolboys. They had manipulated a photograph to make a cartoon-like picture of their school principal and deputy principal. The photograph showed two naked men, sitting side by side. The heads of the principal and deputy principal had been superimposed onto the naked bodies. The hands and the genitals of the figures were then covered by the school crest. The manipulation was amateurish and did not look like a real depiction. The photograph was pinned up on the school notice board for approximately 30 minutes and was then removed by a teacher. The electronic image was forwarded via cellular phone short message system (SMS) within the school and was seen by many pupils.

Once the boys were identified as the persons behind the act, they were disciplined by their school in an internal disciplinary hearing, where they were stripped of all their scholastic achievement badges and colours, were demoted from leadership positions and ordered to attend school detention. The boys apologised to the principal who accepted their apology and took no further action. The boys also tried to apologise to the deputy principal, Dr Dey, but he told them his lawyers had advised him not to accept their apology. Dr Dey charged the boys with the criminal offence of *crimen injuria*.

---

16. This is a reference to the value of cattle in African customary law, where the giving or slaughtering of livestock holds both financial and symbolic significance.

The boys were placed on a diversion programme by the magistrates' court and as a result performed 56 hours of community service cleaning cages at the Pretoria Zoo. Extraordinarily, the boys were also sued for damages arising from defamation and *injuria* by Dr Dey. The basis for this civil action rested on the proposition that Dr Dey felt he was portrayed as a homosexual and as a person of low morals who masturbates in public. He asked for damages in the amount of R600,000.[17]

The North Gauteng High Court found in favour of the plaintiff, Dr Dey, awarding a lesser amount of damages than sued for, namely R45,000.[18] The court found that the boys had acted in a wrongful manner, with intent to injure and were liable for defamation. The boys appealed to the Supreme Court of Appeal, but their appeal was dismissed and High Court's order for damages was upheld. The boys appealed again to the South African Constitutional Court. The main argument advanced on their behalf was that the image was not defamatory as it was not representative of reality and a reasonable viewer would not have understood it as conveying any actual facts about the plaintiff. The Restorative Justice Centre[19] (RJC) was admitted as *amicus curiae*[20] and was permitted to make both written and oral submissions. The crux of the RJC's submission was that the common law should be developed to recognise *amende honorable*, infused with the animating philosophy of *ubuntu* and the modern practice of restorative justice. The practical application of this, according the RJC, required the inclusion of a procedural step requiring reasonable engagement before court proceedings relating to a civil claim for damages relating to defamation can be lodged.

---

17. The approximate equivalent of 60,000 euros.
18. The approximate equivalent of 4,500 euros.
19. The Restorative Justice Centre is a leading non-governmental organization in South Africa which promotes restorative justice through advocacy and service delivery. The organization's website address is www.rjc.org.za.
20. *Amicus curiae* means 'friend of the court'. In the South African legal system an *amicus curiae* may be invited by the court or may itself apply to enter. The court can grant permission for the *amicus curiae* to make written and oral submissions. These submissions can play an important role in the outcome of a case. See further Budlender (2006).

In this way attempts to apologise must henceforth be the first resort, that failing, court proceedings may then be implemented.[21]

The RJC compared this new approach of a requirement of engagement with the way in which the old *amende honorable* operated. The procedure was that the plaintiff's initial letter of demand made a demand (without prejudice) for an apology and retraction, failing which an action for a civil claim for damages would be instituted. The RJC proposed that an improved approach—and one more likely to lead to satisfactory results for both the plaintiff and the defendant—would be to demand that a meaningful engagement should take place to deal with the infringement. This would allow for a restorative justice process in which hurt feelings can be expressed and in which a sincere apology can be given space to emerge. If the defendants refuse to engage, or if engagement does not result in a satisfactory outcome, then the path would be cleared for the institution of a civil claim.

In a judgment handed down on the 8 March 2011, the Constitutional Court upheld the appeal by Dr Dey but reduced the quantum of damages to R25,000[22] and ordered the boys make an unconditional apology to Dr Dey. Certain significant adjustments were made to the costs awards, in favour of the boys. The majority of the Constitutional Court found that the image did amount to defamation. There were two dissenting judgments: the first was a joint judgment by Froneman J and Cameron J. They found that Dr Dey was not defamed, but that his dignity was actionably injured. The second dissenting judgment is that of Yacoob J who concluded that Dr Dey's claim should have failed entirely. Skweyiya J concurred with Yacoob J, and set out his reasons in a separate judgment. Both of these latter judgments are based strongly on child law principles.

It is significant that the only portion of the judgment that was subscribed to by the whole court is contained in the paragraphs of the judgment about

---

21. The idea of 'meaningful engagement' has been stressed by the South African Constitutional Court in a line of cases relating to the right to housing and protection from eviction. The cases include *Republic of South Africa v. Grootboom* (2001); *Port Elizabeth Municipality v. Various Occupiers* (2005); *Occupiers of 51 Olivia Road and 197 Main Street v. City of Johannesburg* (2008); *Residents of Joe Slovo Community, Western Cape v. Thubelisha Homes and Others (Centre on Housing Rights and Evictions and Another, amici curiae)* (2010); *Abahlali Basemjondolo Movement SA and Sibusiso Zikode v. The Premier of the Province of Kwazulu-Natal* (2010).
22. The approximate equivalent of 2,500 euros.

apology. The court decided that it was time to develop the Roman-Dutch common law. The judgment pointed out that the only claim for one who has suffered an infringement of a personality right is one of damages. There is no provision enabling one to claim an apology even if apology would be the most effective way of restoring the dignity of that specific person. A person who is genuinely sorry about an infringement of another's rights cannot raise an immediate apology and retraction as a defence to a claim for damages. The court found that had South Africa's Roman-Dutch law given due recognition to the value of an apology and retraction things might have turned out differently. Instead the matter went to court which deepened and steepened the conflict. The court stated that 'it is time for our Roman-Dutch common law to recognise the value of this kind of restorative justice'. The court was of the view that this could be done in a way that draws from the shared values of fairness in both our common law and customary law systems.

The court discussed the two Roman-Dutch law remedies for injury, the *amende honorable* and the *amende profitable*. The court observed that the *amende honorable* which consisted of retraction and apology, seems to have fallen into disuse over the years. The court did not reinstate it, but rather developed the law in accordance with equitable principles also rooted in Roman-Dutch law. The court explained the reasons for developing the law as follows: Respect for the dignity of others lies at the heart of the constitution and the society we aspire to. That respect breeds tolerance for one another in the diverse society we live in. Without that respect for each other's dignity our aim to create a better society may come to naught. It is the foundation of our young democracy. And reconciliation between people who opposed each other in the past is something which was, and remains, central and crucial to our constitutional endeavour. Part of reconciliation, at all different levels, consists of recantation of past wrongs and apology for them. That experience has become part of the fabric of our society. The law cannot enforce reconciliation but it should create the best conditions for making it possible. We can see no reason why the creation of those conditions should not extend to personal relationships where the actionable dignity of one has been impaired by another (at para. 202).

Conclusion

The civil law of delict appears to have lagged behind the developments of the criminal justice system regarding the use of restorative justice principles. Although any civil law process may seem to involve the victim because the plaintiff is a party to the action, in reality the plaintiff may be also be alienated from a sense of justice. Christie's observation that the conflict had been 'stolen' from the protagonists in a criminal law conflict (1981: 93–94) may be equally applicable to parties in a civil suit. In the case of *Le Roux v. Dey* (2011), the plaintiffs tried to apologise but were sent away by the defendant who had been told by his lawyer not to talk to the plaintiffs.

It is incredible that the defamation case about three schoolboys making a cheeky cartoon of their teachers in *Le Roux v. Dey* managed to battle its way through three expensive tiers of the South African court system. The silver lining is that the development of the Roman-Dutch law in this case holds promise for the future resolution of delictual claims through a process of apology. This will allow for the promotion of respect for one another, the preservation of dignity, and for reconciliation between parties. Civil law, like criminal law, can benefit from this development. The South African Constitutional Court drew on the rich heritage of South African law to make this finding. This is a reminder that restorative justice principles are both old and new, Western and African, indigenous and universal.

References

Bekker, J. C. (1989), *Seymour's Customary Law in Southern Africa*, Cape Town: Juta.

Bennett, T. W. (1999), *Human Rights and African Customary Law under the South African Constitution*, Plumstead: Juta and Co. Ltd.

Budlender, G. (2006), 'Amicus Curiae' in Woolman, S., Roux, T., Stein, A., Chaskalson M. and Bishop M. (eds.) *Constitutional Law of South Africa* (2nd edn., Original Service), Cape Town: Juta.

Burchell, J. (1985), *The Law of Defamation in South Africa*, Cape Town: Juta.

Cane, P. (1997), *The Anatomy of Tort Law*, Oxford: Hart Publishing.

Christie, N. (1981), *Limits to Pain*, New York: Columbia University Press.

Elechi, O. (2004), 'Human Rights and the African Indigenous Justice System', unpublished paper presented at the 18th Conference of the International Society for the Reform of Criminal Law, Montreal, 8–12 August 2004.

Green, S. (2007), 'The Victim's Movement and Restorative Justice' in Johnstone G. and Van Ness, D. W. (eds.), *Handbook of Restorative Justice*, Devon, Cullompton: Willan Publishing.

Gyeke, K. (1998), 'Person and Community in African Thought' in Coetzee P. and Roux A. (eds.), *The African Philosophy Reader*, London: Routledge.

Loubscher, M. and Midgley R. (eds.) (2010), *The Law of Delict in South Africa*, Cape Town: Oxford University Press Southern Africa.

Midgley, J. R. (1995), 'Retraction, Apology and Right to Reply', *Tydskrif vir Hedendaagse Reomeins Hollandse Reg*, 288–296.

Mokgoro J. Y. (1998) 'Ubuntu and the Law in South Africa', paper to the first Colloquium *Constitution and the Law*, 31 October 1997, Seminar Report, Johannesburg, RSA: Konrad-Adenauer-Stftung.

Mqeke, R. B. and Vorster, L. P. (2002), 'Procedure and Evidence' in Bekker, J. C., Labuschagne J. M. T. and Vorster, L. P. (eds.), *Introduction to Legal Pluralism in South Africa: Part 1, Customary Law*, Durban: LexisNexis Butterworths.

Mukheibir, A. (2004), 'Reincarnation or Hallucination? The Revival (or Not?) of the *Amende Honorable*', *Obiter*, 288–296.

Mukheibir, A. (2007a), 'Ubuntu and the Amende Honorable — A Marriage Between African Values and Medieval Canon Law', *Obiter*, 583–589.

Mukheibir, A. (2007b), 'The wages of delict — compensation, satisfaction, punishment?' Unpublished thesis, University of Amsterdam.

Skelton, A. (2002), 'Restorative Justice as a Framework for Juvenile Justice Reform', *British Journal of Criminology*, Vol.42, 496–513.

Skelton, A. (2007), 'Tapping Indigenous Knowledge: Traditional Conflict Resolution, Restorative Justice and the Denunciation of Crime in South Africa' in Van der Spuy, E., Parmentier S. and Dissel A. (eds.), *Restorative Justice: Politics, Policies and Prospects*, Cape Town: Juta.

Skelton, A. (2011), 'Face to Face: Sachs on Restorative Justice', *South African Public Law Journal*, Vol.25, 94–107.

Tshehla, B. (2004), 'The Restorative Justice Bug Bites the South African Criminal Justice System', *South African Journal of Criminal Justice*, Vol.17, 1–6.

Van Niekerk, G. (2001), 'The Plurality of Legal Domains in South Africa: The State's Historical Legislative Intrusion into the Field of Urban Popular Justice and Customary Law' in Scharf W. and Nina D. (eds.), *The Other Law: Non-state Ordering in South Africa*, Lansdowne: Juta.

Visser, P. J. and Potgieter, J. M. (2003), *Law of Damages*, Cape Town: Juta.

Zimmerman, R. (1990), *The Law of Obligations—Roman Foundations of the Civilian Tradition*, Oxford: Clarendon Press.

Cases

Abahlali Basemjondolo Movement SA & Sibusiso Zikode v. The Premier of the Province of Kwazulu-Natal 2010 (2) BCLR 99 (CC).

Dikoko v. Mokhatla 2006 (6) SA 235 (CC).

Hare v. White (1865) 1 Roscoe 246.

Le Roux and Others v. Dey (Freedom of Expression Institute and Restorative Justice Centre as amici curiae) 2011 (3) SA 274 (CC).

Lynch v. Agnew 1929 TPD 974.

Mineworkers Investment Co. (Pty) Ltd. v. Modibane 2002 (6) SA 512 (W).

Occupiers of 51 Olivia Road & 197 Main Street v. City of Johannesburg 2008 (3) SA 308 (CC).

Port Elizabeth Municipality v. Various Occupiers 2005 (1) SA 217 (CC).

Republic of South Africa v. Grootboom 2001 (1) SA 46 (CC).

Residents of Joe Slovo Community, Western Cape v. Thubelisha Homes and others (Centre on Housing Rights and Evictions and Another, Amici Curiae) 2010 (3) SA 454 (CC).

Ward-Jackson v .Cape Times Ltd 1910 WLD 257.

6

Seriousness: A Disproportionate Construction and Application?

Christine Piper and Susan Easton

Introduction

The weakness, as well as the strength of retributivist theory, is that a punishment is just only if it is what the offender deserves, if it is proportionate to his or her culpability and the harm he or she has caused. This is problematic for two reasons. First, the amount of punishment the offender is deemed to deserve depends on the way the seriousness of his offending is calculated and, secondly, proportionality depends on the level at which the anchoring point for sentencing is set. Yet constructing what counts as more or less 'serious' is by no means an arithmetical and objective calculation unless the harm done can be translated easily into financial loss. Whilst research suggests there is some societal consensus as to what offending is most serious in broad terms, there is little agreement beyond that as to exactly how seriously one should classify different elements of harm and culpability. Therefore, if 'just deserts' based sentencing is to be 'just' sentencers need to be provided with guidance which imposes some form of consistency at the crucial stage of calculating seriousness as well as in setting proportional sentences.

In practice what has emerged in England and Wales—and in many other jurisdictions—is a model of sentencing which delineates factors that would make the form of offending in question more or less serious—in other words what would aggravate or mitigate seriousness. Aggravation and mitigation are, therefore, not only consistent with desert theory but integral to it in the determination of the level of seriousness. This chapter will review some of the guidance, notably from the Sentencing Council and its predecessors in the UK, to illustrate how seriousness is calculated and discuss whether this acts as a restraint on discretion and on the 'over-calculation' of seriousness.

In particular, we focus on the role of persistent recidivism in this stage of the sentencing process. Increasingly, in the UK and elsewhere, past convictions have been used to communicate particular messages but they do so by aggravating seriousness. By so doing, they inflate sentencing levels in a way which could be deemed disproportionate. Indeed, it could be argued that pure desert theory is incompatible with any premiums for past offending but desert theorists have tried to accommodate past offending within retributivist approaches to sentencing. So, whilst the role of past convictions in desert theory is problematic, we will assess the most appropriate and fairest way of dealing with them in constructing seriousness for sentencing purposes.

Calculating Culpability and Harm

Although we argue for a properly structured 'just deserts' system of sentencing we acknowledge that sentencing on retributivist principles is very difficult. The construction of 'seriousness' (gravity) which is at the core of retributivist sentencing requires the assessment of two elements — 'blameworthiness' (or culpability) and harm — and this dual process is now enacted in section 143(1) of the Criminal Justice Act (CJA) 2003: 'In considering the seriousness of any offence, the court must consider the offender's culpability in committing the offence and any harm which the offence caused, was intended to cause or might foreseeably have caused'. This apparently simple statutory requirement entails a very complex process: harm and culpability in sentencing, as in everyday life, are very problematic concepts.

In the last decade the policy pressure to tighten sentencing guidance further was given impetus by the Halliday Report which argued specifically that sentencers had insufficient guidance on the measurement of seriousness (2001: 1.9). The 2003 Act responded to that criticism in enacting section 143(1) but also in setting up (by section 167) the Sentencing Guidelines Council (SGC). The Labour government had introduced a Sentencing Advisory Panel (SAP), which started work in July 1999, to assist and advise the Court of Appeal by making proposals for new guidelines which the court could issue when a suitable case came up. However, this compromise solution was viewed as too slow a method of producing a clear sentencing framework of guidance. The SAP continued as an advisory body to the new SGC, chaired by the Lord Chief Justice until the Coroners and Justice Act 2009 mandated the establishment of a Sentencing Council for England and Wales to replace those two bodies. Its remit is much broader, including reporting annually and assessing the resource implications of its guidelines. Lord Justice Leveson, a Court of Appeal judge, was appointed chairman of the Sentencing Council which began work in 2010. That Council now has the task of issuing new guidance, revising existing guidelines and ensuring that the guidance establishes a principled and inter-locking sentencing framework.

The SGC published early guidance on the process of calculating seriousness (SGC, 2004). In focusing on culpability it concentrated on the 'amount' of intention to cause harm and identified four 'levels' for sentencing purposes:

Where the offender:

(i) has the **intention** to cause harm, with the highest culpability when an offence is planned. The worse the harm intended, the greater the seriousness.

(ii) is **reckless** as to whether harm is caused, that is, where the offender appreciates at least some harm would be caused but proceeds giving no thought to the consequences even though the extent of the risk would be obvious to most people.

(iii) has **knowledge** of the specific risks entailed by his actions even though he does not intend to cause the harm that results.

(iv) is guilty of **negligence**.

(SGC, 2004: 1.7; emboldening as in original)

The SGC also provided a list of 'Factors indicating a more than usually serious degree of harm' which includes 'multiple victims', 'an especially serious physical or psychological effect on the victim, even if unintended', 'a sustained assault or repeated assaults on the same victim' and offending committed in the presence of friends or relatives (SGC, 2004: 1.23). Yet this points up the problematic connections between the two elements of culpability and harm. What counts as more or less harm also depends on personal, social, religious and political factors and an intention to cause the greatest harm entails the greatest culpability. The apparently factual judgment about the amount of harm is, then, also not an easy judgment.

Further, there is a particular difficulty when the 'amounts' of harm and culpability are very different. The 2004 Guideline acknowledges this:

- sometimes the harm that actually results is greater than the harm intended by the offender;
- in other circumstances, the offender's culpability may be at a higher level than the harm resulting from the offence (SGC, 2004: 1.16).

Guidance must try to establish relative 'weights' for these different elements — weights that may well have to be adjusted over time as social ideas about culpability change, as has happened in relation to sentencing those who have caused death by their driving. The definitive guideline had to make its approach clear:

Because the principal harm done by these offences (the death of a person) is an element of the offence, the factor that primarily determines the starting point for sentence is the culpability of the offender. Accordingly, the central feature should be an evaluation of the quality of the driving involved and the degree of danger that it foreseeably created. These guidelines draw a distinction between those factors of an offence that are intrinsic to the quality of driving (referred to as 'determinants of seriousness') and those which, while they aggravate the offence, are not (SGC, 2008a: 2).

So 'determinants of seriousness' include the degree of carelessness and/or intoxication and these in turn place an instance of offending within a certain level of seriousness (*ibid*: 3–4). The aggravating factor noted, on the other hand, is whether more than one person was killed whilst the mitigating factor concerns the effect on the offender of injury to himself or death/injury to a relative or friend (*ibid*: 5). Factors to be allowed as personal mitigation are also listed (*ibid*: 6). The determinants of seriousness place the offence into one or other of three levels, the aggravating and mitigating factors move the offence above or below the starting point. This is the approach taken by many guidelines. What then reflects the arguably now greater seriousness accorded to death by driving is the level at which the proportionate sentence is set for each of the levels of seriousness: Level 1 reflects the increase in the maximum penalty for death by dangerous driving and for causing death by driving under the influence of alcohol or drugs (implemented 2007) and the new offences of causing death by careless or inconsiderate driving and causing death by driving: unlicensed, disqualified or uninsured drivers introduced in 2006 (implemented in 2008). However, the new statutory maxima and the guidance are not without their critics. Research commissioned by the then SAP found the public to be generally in favour of the new guidelines but the researchers made the following comment:

> [T]he research also clearly shows that the public thinks the maximum sentence of two years' imprisonment for the new offence of causing death by driving while unlicensed, disqualified or uninsured is too low. Interestingly, for many, this offence is perceived as being more serious than the new offence of causing death by careless driving which has a maximum sentence of five years (Hough *et al*, 2008: Foreword p.ii).

The guidance on assaults classified as 'domestic violence' (SGC, 2006) is another example of a guideline reflecting the wider denunciation in social and political life of a particular form of offending—in this case assaults against spouses and partners: 'This guideline makes clear that offences committed in a domestic context should be regarded as being no less serious than offences committed in a non-domestic context. Indeed, because an offence has been committed in a domestic context, there are likely to be aggravating factors present that make it more serious' (2006: 1). Assessing domestic assault as being at least as serious as non-domestic assault—as opposed to its earlier downgrading as 'just' a domestic—is a development to be found in other jurisdictions. Research in New South Wales, Australia, provides data that clearly shows that the more serious instances of offending are now punished with imprisonment although it is not able to compare this with non-domestic assault (see Ringland and Fitzgerald, 2010).

In relation to these offences, therefore, seriousness has been inflated in relation to the more serious instances of the offending whilst in other instances seriousness has been reduced. That, to a large extent, reflects opinion, it increases consistency and — overall — it constrains the use of excessive punishment. However, the guidelines cannot always reflect a majority societal consensus, either because there is no consensus or because popular punitiveness conflicts so strongly with the policy pressure, within the context of monitoring resource impact, to reduce the use of custody. The guidance for domestic burglary is a case in point.

In response to advice from the SAP (2002), the Court of Appeal, in *R v. McInerney, R v. Keating* (2002), issued new guidance on sentencing for burglary in a dwelling under which a domestic burglar who previously would have been sent to prison for 18 months or less should in future receive a community sentence. That guidance was criticised in Parliament and by the press and Police Federation, and it led Lord Woolf CJ to issue his *Statement in response to inaccurate comments on the guidelines issued by the Court of Appeal as to the sentencing of domestic burglars* (14 January 2003). Nevertheless, the guidance led to a reduced rate of custody for burglary. After the *Saw* (2009) case, the court re-examined *McInerney* and offered fresh guidance in which, apart from cases where a low-level burglary involved minimal loss and damage, custodial sentences were said to be normally appropriate (SAP, 2010b: 9). Burglary in a dwelling is considered serious because, apart from the loss or destruction of possessions, as the court in *Saw* pointed out, '[s]omething precious is violated by burglary of a home'. A new Definitive Guideline issued in 2011 gives a 'high level community order' as the 'starting point' only for the lowest category of seriousness (Sentencing Council, 2011a: 9).

Establishing Aggravation

Assessing seriousness, as the above examples illustrate, entails a normative judgment about wrongfulness but there is very little consensus even as to which crime counts as most or least 'wrong' once murder at one end of the continuum — and possibly parking offences at the other — are eliminated from the analysis. As Tonry noted: 'Like the Recording Angel's, most people's judgements of others' blameworthiness depend on knowledge of their circumstances' (Tonry, 1996: 18) and yet sentencing guidance must also generalise. In relation to sentencing judges Cross identified — over 30 years ago — wickedness, social disapproval, social danger, and social alarm as factors affecting their assessment of culpability (Cross, 1981: 178–182) and current guidance embodies these ideas when it endorses as aggravating factors aspects of the offending such as targeting the vulnerable or dependent victim, using replica guns to cause fear, and domestic burglary during the night.

The SAP were also asked in 2008 to review the 2004 SGC guideline on sentencing principles and issued a consultation paper before publishing their advice (SAP, 2010a). These normative judgments about culpability are also reflected in the SAP's advice on '*Factors indicating higher culpability*'. Included are 'An intention to commit more serious harm *than actually resulted from the offence*' and 'Abuse of power or a position of trust'. Further, the list of '*Factors indicating a more than usually serious degree of harm*' includes 'A sustained assault or repeated assaults on the same victim' and 'In property offences, high value (including sentimental value) of property to the victim' (*ibid:* 84).

However, some particularly problematic sentencing issues have become more pressing in recent years. One of these, the discount for a guilty plea, is outside the scope of this discussion, because it is not part of the process of calculating seriousness and determining a proportionate sentence. It is a discount at the end of the process done for reasons other than just deserts. It simply rewards those who give administrative and financial benefits to the state by avoiding a trial. It is criticised, therefore, because of its effect on the length or content of a sentence which has been carefully constructed according to retributivist principles. It is no longer a discount which includes an element for remorse and so goes neither to culpability nor to harm except in so far as it benefits a victim who might not have wished to give evidence at the trial.

The other most problematic issue — that of aggravating culpability because of previous offending — is one which is integral to the retributivist exercise. Indeed the guidelines reviewed above have been required to deal with that issue since the CJA 2003 because section 143(2) of that Act mandates the consideration of previous convictions at the sentencing stage. That provision states that:

> ...the court must treat each previous conviction as an aggravating factor if (in the case of that conviction) the court considers that it can reasonably be so treated having regard, in particular, to–
> (a)   the nature of the offence to which the conviction relates and its relevance to the current offence, and
> (b)   the time that has elapsed since the conviction.

So, e.g., advice for the Sentencing Council on burglary in a dwelling included the following proposal relating to previous convictions:

> [T]he Court endorsed the statement in *Brewster* (as it had done in *McInerney*), that 'the record of the offender is of more significance in the case of domestic burglary than in the case of some other crime'. The Panel considers that recent and similar dishonesty offences, such as domestic or non-domestic burglaries and distraction thefts from the homes of elderly occupiers, should aggravate an offence of domestic burglary (SAP, 2010b: 58).

The move towards cumulative sentencing clearly did not begin with the CJA 2003 and evidence would suggest that some judges at least have always weighted seriousness by adding an amount for past offending (Halliday Report 2001: 1.3 and Appendix 3, Table 1). However, legislation from 1991 to 2003 shows a clear trend towards punishing persistence. The CJA 1991 had made clear in section 29 that sentencers could not normally use previous convictions to aggravate seriousness.[1] However, after criticism the government repealed section 29 and substituted a new section 29 by the CJA 1993 which stated that, 'In considering the seriousness of any offence, the court may take into account any previous convictions of the offender or any failure of his to respond to previous sentences'. The Powers of Criminal Courts (Sentencing) Act 2000 re-enacted this provision in section 151 and also re-enacted, in sections 110–111, minimum sentences for a third burglary

---

1.   Although this provision could, arguably, have allowed a progressive loss of mitigation approach (see below).

or drug offence which had been introduced in the Crime (Sentences) Act 1997. Such sentences allowed, therefore, for a potentially disproportionate sentence for a recidivist burglar or drug-dealer. The move to mandated cumulative sentencing was more apparent in the Halliday Report which argued that 'Clarification needs to be based on a clear presumption that sentencing severity should increase as a consequence of sufficiently recent and relevant convictions' (2002: 2.7). *Justice for All* also noted that prison must be 'reserved for the serious, dangerous and seriously persistent offenders' (Home Office, 2002: Executive Summary, 8).

The result was the provision in the CJA 2003. This has created problems for the retributivism and potentially allows sentencing to be harsher than it would otherwise have been.

Previous Convictions

We acknowledge that in most sentencing systems there will be harsher sentences for repeat offenders. Even if there is no statutory premium for past convictions, recidivists cannot rely on good character in mitigation and, in practice, a recidivist premium has proved popular with sentencers, governments and the public. Indeed, this may be an area where academic debates on the appropriate level of enhancement or its justification have made little impression on governments. However, where the basis and justification for enhancing sentencing on account of previous convictions is not clear then consistency and justice are in doubt. Moreover, there are problems in justifying enhanced sentences for persistence on either of the main justifications of punishment, desert or utilitarianism.

The political and social context will be crucial too as the emphasis in recent years has meant increased focus on the victim rather than the offender and under the Labour government, 'rebalancing' the criminal justice system in favour of the offender. Although the coalition government has questioned the value of imprisonment and is committed to some reductions in prison numbers, the rationale of the recidivist premium was not considered in its 2010 Green Paper, *Breaking the Cycle* (Ministry of Justice, 2010). Given that the increase in sentence length and the increased use of custody has contributed to prison expansion in the last twenty years, the role of previous convictions may be a significant factor in adding to the prison population. The Green

Paper noted that there is a core of prolific offenders and it calculates that there are over 16,000 active offenders who each have over 75 previous convictions, and have been to prison on average 14 times (*ibid*: 6). Yet figures for 2008 had shown that '44 per cent of offenders serving sentences of six months or less at the end of June 2008 had 15 or more previous convictions or cautions; for those serving four years or more (excluding indeterminate sentences) the figure was 25 per cent (Ministry of Justice, 2009: 82).

However the Crown Court Sentencing Survey states that '59 per cent of offenders with one to three previous convictions taken into account were sent to immediate custody. This increased to 78 per cent for offenders with 10 or more previous convictions taken into account' (Sentencing Council, 2011b).

Although Kenneth Clarke, former Secretary of State for Justice, pledged in 2010 to reduce the daily prison population by 3,000 within four years, the projected numbers in prison for the immediate future are still likely to exceed 80,000. Proposed measures include increasing the work opportunities for prisoners, increasing support for offenders leaving prison and amending the Rehabilitation of Offenders Act 1974 to improve work prospects and making prisons more cost-effective. While the focus is also on developing viable alternatives to custody the government is, at the same time, committed to continuing custody for persistent offenders, although using shorter sentences where appropriate, so the rationale for punishing for persistence is still very pertinent.

Prima facie sentencing enhancements for recidivists would seem incompatible with pure desert theory as the emphasis should be on the current offence. If the offender has already served his or her sentence for the past offence, then the debt to society has been cancelled and on the principle of double jeopardy he or she should not be punished again for that crime. Moreover, if the effect is a disproportionate sentence, then the principle of proportionality has also been violated. Strict desert theorists such as George Fletcher[2] would argue that no premium should be imposed, but all offenders should be sentenced on the basis of the current offences and we should not discriminate between offenders on the basis of past and already punished crimes. The focus should be squarely on the current crime.

---

2.   See Fletcher (1978).

Nor should the system of punishment administer punishment on the basis of the individual's past good or bad character or attitudes, but simply focus on the culpability for the current offence. However, this approach is difficult to 'sell' to the public. So modern retributivists have considered ways of justifying an increase by focusing on the ways in which the persistent offender might be seen as more culpable than a first offender who lapses from generally good behaviour.

One way of dealing with the problem of recidivism is to focus on the progressive loss of mitigation, an approach advocated by Von Hirsch and Ashworth.[3] So here a first offender will be given a discount but this will be progressively reduced in the case of subsequent offences until the offender reaches a point where the discount is removed so the full penalty is given. So the principle of proportionality here will place a limit on the severity of the sentence. On this approach a concession is made to human frailty and the individual's claim that he has lapsed from a previously law-abiding life may be persuasive for a first offence, but is less so with subsequent offences as our tolerance will decline. In the case of young offenders we may be more willing to grant concessions because of their immaturity.

For Von Hirsch and Ashworth the point at which the discount is lost would usually be the third offence, but there may be disagreements over the exact point at which it should be limited or indeed whether a discount for a first offence is appropriate where we are dealing with very serious offences. Moreover, we cannot be sure that first offenders are first offenders as studies of self-reported crime such as the *British Crime Survey* suggest a considerable amount of unrecorded and unpunished crime. Moreover, if some crimes are so severe or so pre-meditated, then the concession to a lapse on the part of the individual is hard to justify even for a first offence. Concessions on the basis of human frailty still mean that recidivists are denied tolerance which means that ultimately they are being punished again for their bad character. Roberts[4] argues the progressive loss of mitigation approach is only legitimate if applied to minor crimes but is not appropriate to more serious crimes, and that at most the concession should be given sparingly, as previous

3.   See, for example, Von Hirsch and Ashworth (2005).
4.   Roberts (2008a; 2008b; 2010).

convictions can justify harsher punishment by increasing culpability and to reflect community values.

Justifications for a recidivist premium may also focus on whether the harm to the victim may be increased by the knowledge that the offender is a recidivist especially in crimes of violence, sexual crimes or invasive crimes such as burglary, if there is concern that the assailant may return and may require more protective measures to guard against a pattern of behaviour than a one-off opportunistic offender.[5] But at the time of the current offence, the victim may not have this knowledge.

One further way of defending the premium is to focus on the fact that the repeat offender has been through the process of the criminal trial and is aware of the court's and society's censure of him and of the impact on the victim and harm caused and is therefore more blameworthy than a first offender. But if we are punishing persistent offenders because they have ignored the court and society's judgement or failed to accept any help offered by the criminal justice system, we are still focusing the offender and ultimately his bad character rather than what he has done in the instant case. It is difficult to say that the harm of the current offence is greater or the offence is more serious, because a similar or even dissimilar offence has been committed on past occasions, or because of the perpetrator's bad character.

One pragmatic solution may be to adapt a modified form of retributivism to negotiate increased sentences for recidivists without sacrificing proportionality. So for example, Morris (1974) and Tonry (2010) advocate a limiting retributivism. On this approach past convictions will be a factor which may justify an increased sentence along with other factors, but the final sentence should not go beyond the upper limit of the range for that offence. The first offender, on the other hand, would enter the sentencing grid at the lower level. However, striking the optimum point for according sufficient but not excessive weight to past convictions may still be subject to disagreement between sentencers and penologists.

There is also the problem of how precisely past offences are dealt with. If they are committed very recently they may be taken into consideration and dealt with concurrently, so the seriousness of the offending is aggravated by

---

5.   See Frase (2010).

the most serious of the offences. But if the prior offence was committed some time ago, then this might lead to greater seriousness and to a proportionately harsher penalty, but it is difficult to distinguish between the two situations in terms of culpability or harm. In any event, at the point of sentencing for the current offence the court will not re-examine all previous crimes in any detail and may not have the same information as the earlier court. However, if we do accept the general principle of punishing persistence, then the increases need to be kept within boundaries to avoid an escalation or we could reach the disproportionate levels of three-strike laws in the USA which constitute an extreme response to this problem.

Other Justifications?

If desert theory finds it difficult to justify enhancing seriousness because of persistence, we also find problems in doing so on utilitarian theory. Cumulative sentencing clearly also raises problems for utilitarians. To justify the additional expense of further imprisonment especially in the current economic climate, there would need to be a benefit in terms of deterrence, risk reduction by incapacitation, or rehabilitation. But it is difficult to find conclusive evidence of the deterrent efforts of imprisonment, or of longer imprisonment and the issue of deterrence is subject to considerable debate. Defenders of a recidivist premium might argue that if repeat offenders pose a greater threat to society, they may need a stronger sentence to incapacitate them or need more time in rehabilitative programmes to ensure their rehabilitation or to protect society for a longer period. Previous criminal career is a key factor in the prediction of future offending so from a utilitarian perspective, incapacitation could be relevant. There are many difficult issues here, given the problems of predicting risk, the negative effects of incarceration and the limited effects of imprisonment on crime reduction. We also know that removing offenders from a community may not solve problems of crime in the locality as others may take over their territory. Furthermore, we also know that the longer offenders are in prison they may adapt to imprisonment in ways which make it less likely they will desist from future offending. But even if the deterrent effect could be established, a utilitarian rationale would need to apply the principle of parsimony, to establish if the same effect could be reached by less costly means. So if other measures might achieve the same goal it would be difficult to justify the additional costs of a recidivist premium.

Bagaric argues strongly against a recidivist premium from a utilitarian standpoint, that it cannot be justified on the basis of incapacitation, deterrence or rehabilitation: 'the available empirical evidence does not support the view that either incapacitation or deterrence are effective sentencing objectives, at least from the perspective of justifying harsher sentences' (Bagaric, 2001: 246). Given this, 'deterrence cannot be used to justify heavier penalties *per se*, let alone for repeat offenders' (*ibid*). Moreover, weighting for prior convictions discriminates against offenders with deprived backgrounds. On the other hand, ignoring previous convictions, he argues, would ensure greater consistency in sentencing and address the problem of discrimination against those offenders from poorer social backgrounds. As it is difficult to establish a link between a recidivist premium and deterrence or incapacitation, we cannot assume that a longer prison sentence results in greater deterrence.

The link between deprivation and previous convictions is universal but is especially marked in the USA where offenders from African-American communities may have most previous convictions. While the impact of drug crimes in these communities is devastating, the effect of removing young males from the community for longer periods will exacerbate the social and economic impact on those communities as well as on the families of offenders. The reasons for the high number of African-Americans within the USA prison system have been widely discussed elsewhere, in relation to social policies and sentencing law and policy, especially in relation to drugs offences.[6] The fact that a recidivist premium is likely to affect some groups more than others raises problems for both utilitarians, in terms of social impact, and desert theorists as it has implications for equality in treatment of offenders and equality of impact of punishment.

In the USA the most extreme recidivist premium is found in 'three-strikes' laws, where the punishment for a third offence may result in a highly disproportionate sentence for the third offence. The effect of such policies in California has had enormous financial implications swelling the prison population and increasing the costs and contributing to the fiscal crisis.

---

6. See, for example, Wacquant (2007) and Clear (2007).

Three-strikes laws, which are intended to both incapacitate and deter, impose a 25-year minimum sentence for a third felony, resulting in both excessive and disproportionate sentences where the focus is heavily weighted on the past rather than the current offence and cannot be justified on either desert or utilitarian theory. Constitutional challenges to three-strikes laws failed in *Lockyer v. Andrade* (2009). The Supreme Court also upheld the constitutionality of a 25-year sentence in the case of a minor theft of three golf clubs in *Ewing v. California* (2003). In the view of the court it was not grossly disproportionate and did not breach the Eighth Amendment, although for desert theorists this would clearly be excessive. Moreover, for utilitarians it would be difficult to justify the extremely high costs of incarceration here for a minor theft, and on Bentham's principle of frugality it would seem a massive expenditure for an uncertain and best limited result.

But even in states in the USA without such laws, past criminal history has assumed greater importance in sentence calculation in the past 20 years. This partly reflects the general rise in punitiveness and the fact that past criminal history is a significant predictor of future risk of crime. Sentencers there seem to have less discretion than those in the UK on this issue.

There is also the problem of how to measure desistance, to ascertain whether recidivists have 'slowed down' in their rate of offending or are committing less serious offences, or attending relevant programmes, and if so, should they then be treated differently from other persistent offenders who lack these qualities? The issue of desistance is complex and little research was undertaken on this until the 1970s and 1980s. It may be linked to age, gender, peer group involvement and other factors.[7] We also know that imprisonment, insofar as it disrupts family and work relationships, may make it harder for offenders to readjust to life in the community. Research on 'what works' has shown the importance of shaping responses to particular groups of offenders. But we do know that nearly 50 per cent of adult offenders and 75 per cent of those sentenced to youth custody in England and Wales re-offend within one year.

It would seem that using previous convictions to aggravate the seriousness of an offence—and thereby justifying a sentence which would otherwise

---

7.   See Farrall and Calverley (2006).

be disproportionate to the offending—is an aspect of sentencing against which it is currently impossible to argue. Punishing persistence accords with popular ideas of justice. Its use therefore needs to be more controlled and restrained through specific guidance.

Conclusion

Providing guidance to ensure consistency and restraint in the calculation of seriousness in a retributivist sentencing framework is, as we have seen, a complex and difficult issue. Political and populist concerns cannot be ignored and finding a consensus on issues of harm and culpability will often not be possible. Nevertheless, the SAP, SGC and the Sentencing Council have produced ever more detailed guidance in relation to seriousness, sentencing principles and the allowable aggravating and mitigating factors for various specific offences (Ashworth and Roberts, 2013). However, it is the mandatory aggravation of seriousness on account of previous offending which now threatens to alter significantly these calculations and lead to disproportionate sentences.

As we have seen there are particular problems in justifying punishments for persistence on the major theories, nonetheless the reluctance of sentencers or the public to relinquish the recidivist premium makes change difficult. Negotiating public opinion is one of the major problems facing governments in introducing change but we need more information on the public's knowledge and perceptions of sentencing practice[8]. Neither the public nor sentencers would accept that no weighting should be given to prior convictions. However, what concerns the public most is inconsistency in sentencing and sentences which are disproportionate to the offence, particularly in relation to more serious offences.[9] But the situation in *Ewing* would be seen as disproportionate for most people and proportionality does not necessarily mean severity.

This may be illustrated by the fact that where desert is the key influence on sentencing, the regimes may be less punitive than regimes where it is less important. As Von Hirsch and Ashworth observe, 'The Finnish and Swedish examples demonstrate that ... adoption of desert and proportionality as

8.   See Henham (2012); Mitchell and Roberts (2012).
9.   See Mitchell and Roberts (2010).

guiding principles does not lead to greater severity'.[10] Here some proportionality has remained central to the sentencing process which has served to limit sentence severity. In Sweden there is a strong presumption against imposing custody unless the offence is serious and the past convictions are limited to those committed in the previous three or four years. So the principle of proportionality is also shaped by the principle of parsimony. However, in recent years there has been more pressure in Sweden to increase the premium for previous convictions.

Those states in the USA whose sentencing guidelines give greatest weight to desert, such as Minnesota, have amongst the lowest imprisonment rates compared to states such as Texas and Nevada whose guidelines are not primarily based on desert. In the current Minnesota Guidelines the primary focus is on the current offence and the offender's criminal history plays only a secondary role.[11] Moreover, the guidelines distinguish sharply between the levels of seriousness of the past convictions and offences committed more than 15 years ago will not be included.

Clearly, there are difficulties with the current treatment of past convictions and problems of inconsistencies and disparities in practice. However, arguably, desert theory offers a greater hope of limiting the impact of past convictions if tempered by the principle of parsimony. A key objective for the Sentencing Council must, therefore, be that of giving clear guidance, in revising past guidelines and publishing new ones, as to the extent to which past convictions should aggravate seriousness. Clear guidance is needed on both limbs of section 143(2) — relevance and the time lag — such that the discretion inherent in this provision is used wisely and well to ensure that the primary focus is on seriousness and proportionality. Both of these may then limit excessive sentencing.

References

Ashworth, A. and Roberts J. (eds.) (2013) *Sentencing Guidelines*, Oxford/New York, Oxford: Oxford University Press.

Bagaric, M. (2001) *Punishment and Sentencing: A Rational Approach*, London: Cavendish.

---

10. Von Hirsch and Ashworth (2005: 78).
11. See hwww.msgc.state.mn.us/guidelines/guide10.pdf.

Clear, T. (2007), *Imprisoning Communities*, New York: Oxford University Press.

Cross, R. and Ashworth, A. (1981) *The English Sentencing System*, London: Butterworths.

Farrall, S. and Calverley, A. (2006), *Understanding Desistance from Crime*, Maidenhead: Open University Press.

Fletcher, G. (1978), *Rethinking Criminal Law*, Boston: Little Brown.

Frase, R. S. (2010), 'Prior-conviction Sentencing Enhancements: Rationales and Limits Based on Retributive and Utilitarian Proportionality Principles and Social Equality Goals' in Roberts, J. V. and Von Hirsch, A. (eds.), *Previous Convictions at Sentencing: Theoretical and Applied Perspectives*, Oxford: Hart, 117–136.

Halliday Report (2001) 'Making Punishments Work: Review of the Sentencing Framework for England and Wales', London: Home Office.

Henham, R. (2012) *Sentencing and the Legitimacy of Trial Justice*, London, Routledge

Home Office (2002) *Justice for All*, Cm 5563, London: The Stationery Office.

Hough, M., Roberts, J., Jacobson, J., Bredee, A. and Moon, N. (2008), *Attitudes to the Sentencing of Offences Involving Death by Driving*, Sentencing Advisory Panel Research Report, 5.

Ministry of Justice (2009), *Offender Management Caseload Statistics 2008*, London: Ministry of Justice.

Ministry of Justice (2010), *Breaking the Cycle: Effective Punishment, Rehabilitation and Sentencing of Offenders*, Cm 7972, London: Ministry of Justice.

Mitchell, B. and Roberts, J. (2010), 'Public Opinion and Sentencing for Murder: An Empirical Investigation of Public Knowledge and Attitudes in England and Wales', www.nuffieldfoundation.org/

Mitchell, B. and Roberts, J. 'Sentencing for Murder, Exploring Public Knowledge and Public Opinion in England and Wales', *British Journal of Criminology* (2012) 52 (1): 141–158.

Morris, M. (1974), *The Future of Imprisonment*, Chicago: Chicago University Press, 44.

Ringland, C. and Fitzgerald, J. (2010), *Factors Which Influence the Sentencing of Domestic Violence Offenders*, Crime and Justice Statistics Issue Paper No.48, NSW Bureau of Crime, Statistics and Research, Australia, www.

bocsar.nsw.gov.au/lawlink/bocsar/ll_bocsar.nsf/vwFiles/bb48.pdf/$file/bb48.pdf.

Roberts, J. V. (2008a), 'Punishing Persistence: Explaining the Enduring Appeal of the Recidivist Sentencing Premium', *British Journal of Criminology* (2008) 48(4), 468–481.

Roberts, J. V. (2008b), *Punishing Persistent Offenders, Community and Offender Perspectives*, Oxford: Oxford University Press.

Roberts, J. V. (2010), 'First-offender Sentencing Discounts: Exploring the Justifications' in Roberts J. V. and Von Hirsch, A. (eds.), *Previous Convictions at Sentencing: Theoretical and Applied Perspectives*, Oxford: Hart, 17–35.

Sentencing Advisory Panel (2002), 'Advice to the Court of Appeal: Domestic Burglary'.

Sentencing Advisory Panel (2010a), 'Advice to the Sentencing Guidelines Council: Overarching Principles of Sentencing'.

Sentencing Advisory Panel (2010b), 'Advice to the Sentencing Guidelines Council: Sentencing for Domestic Burglary'.

Sentencing Guidelines Council (2004), *Overarching Principles: Seriousness,* Guideline.

Sentencing Guidelines Council (2006), *Overarching Principles: Domestic Violence,* Definitive Guideline.

Sentencing Guidelines Council (2008a), *Causing Death by Driving*, Definitive Guideline.

Sentencing Guidelines Council (2008b), *Theft and Burglary in a Building Other than a Dwelling*, Definitive Guideline.

Sentencing Council (2011a) *Burglary Offences,* Definitive Guideline. London: Sentencing Council.

Sentencing Council (2011b) *Crown Court Sentencing Survey, October 2010 to March 2011 Results,* London: Sentencing Council.

Tonry, M. (1996), *Sentencing Matters*, Oxford/New York: Oxford University Press.

Tonry, M. (2010), 'The Questionable Relevance of Previous Convictions to Punishments for Later Crimes' in Roberts J. V. and Von Hirsch, A. (eds.), *Previous Convictions at Sentencing: Theoretical and Applied Perspectives*, Oxford: Hart, 91–116.

Von Hirsch, A. and Ashworth, A. J. (2005), *Proportionate Sentencing*, Oxford: Oxford University Press.

Wacquant, L. (2007), *Urban Outcasts: A Comparative Study of Advanced Marginality*, Cambridge Polity Press.

Woolf, H. (Lord Chief Justice) (2003), 'Statement in Response to Inaccurate Comments on the Guidelines Issued by the Court of Appeal as to the Sentencing of Domestic Burglars, 14 January'.

Cases

Ewing v. California 538 US 11 (2003).

Lockyer v. Andrade 538 US 63 (2009).

R v. McInerney, R v. Keating [2003] 2 Cr App R.

R v. Saw [2009] EWCA Crim 1.

Part II

CIVILISING THEORY

7

Civilisation of Criminal Justice: Restorative Justice Amongst other Strategies

John Blad

Introduction

Is criminal justice becoming more and more uncivilised and, if so, how could this be explained? Could it be related to the approach of the criminal justice system as an 'assembly line' that should produce punishments and effective crime control in the most cost-effective way, dominated by an instrumentalist rationality, instead of viewing criminal justice as a normative system of checks and balances promoting the values of a purportedly democratic society within the Rule of Law? If certain tendencies towards de-civilisation can be demonstrated, to what extent and how could the implementation of restorative justice then contribute to a return to more civilised criminal justice? Could re-civilisation of criminal justice by implementing restorative justice also contribute to reducing relapse into crime?

These are the questions that will be explored in this chapter, in an attempt to elaborate the intuition that restorative justice could function as a new civilisation movement for criminal justice.[1] But not only restorative justice: other strategies can also contribute, as several other chapters in this book argue, and these strategies seem interlinked and could well be combined.

---

1. A first concept of this contribution appeared in Dutch as J. R. Blad (2012) '*Herstelrecht en civilisering van de strafrechtspleging*' in Marie-Claire Foblets, Mireille Hildebrandt and Jacques Steenbergen (eds.), *Liber Amicorum René Foqué*, Gent/Den Haag: Larcier/Boom Juridische Uitgevers, pp. 169–188.

Criminal Justice and Civilisation

It is highly plausible that the institution of criminal justice has contributed importantly to the civilisation of the populations of the European nation-states during the long process of state formation and, in this framework, the construction and consolidation of the monopoly of violence of the central state. Around 1800, all states became a '*Rechtsstaat*', ruled by law, with an important function for the 'legality principle' that rules the functioning of the criminal justice system, thereby normatively controlling the exercise of state (or, sociologically more correct: collective) power.

By effectively implementing this monopoly of violence an increasingly large and stable social domain came into existence during this long process, in which citizens—increasingly protected by and subjected to the law—learned (because they were able to) to take account of each other's needs and interests, not only in their relations as 'legal subjects' but also in socio-economic and other, private and public, relations. People learned to reckon with fellow-citizens in ever longer 'chains of mutual dependence', to be thoughtful of the consequences of their own behaviour for themselves and for others and to exercise self-discipline (Elias, 2000: 370–373). Increasingly, the individual came to live in circumstances in which he learned to think about and foresee the consequences of his own momentary actions in the future, several steps ahead in the chain of interrelated actions and events: enabled by the relatively calm and safe circumstances of life he was in. Both the 'psychogenesis' and the 'sociogenesis' of the civilised citizen are related to his development into a legal subject, secured by the monopoly of violence that was itself subordinate to, and controlled by, the Rule of Law.

Importantly, Elias observed that the citizen's self-control becomes 'dispassionate' and models itself after the external processes of social control, which show an increasing differentiation of interrelated functions, producing a 'dense web of interdependencies' that counteract and prevent uncontrolled outbursts of (disturbing) affects. In the situation without monopoly of violence the uncertainties and the unpredictability of events in life meant that one could indulge in 'extreme cruelty' (towards others) and in 'extreme enjoyment of pleasures': if one declined those attitudes there was the option of 'extreme asceticism' (Elias, 2000: 373) .When these conditions of what Hobbes has termed the natural state slowly disappeared by the establishment of the monopoly of violence, the pacified war of all against all was transformed in a permanent internal struggle to control the types of passions, which would naturally resist such control (drive-satisfaction versus drive-control) (Elias, 2000: 375).

In his Freudian analysis Elias defines a successful individual civilisation as a pattern of conduct that on the one hand responds to the functional expectations that adults are confronted with (in the societal chains of mutual dependence), offering on the other hand sufficient personal satisfaction of needs. The civilising processes of socialisation in which the human comes into being are however never complete, nor permanently effective, and egocentric affects can and will often be indulged in at the cost of others. When the legislator has foreseen this possibility and considered the consequences unacceptable, penal consequences can be imposed on the basis of penal law provisions.

On the grounds of the legality principle thoughtful legal subjects can foresee this and in this way the legality principle not only limits and controls the exercise of state power (its normative function) but also potentially informs and shapes behavioural choices to be made by legal subjects. This criminal-political function provides the criminal law with a certain, although limited, instrumental value. This dual functionality (of the legality principle) characterises all other key principles of the classical criminal law which began to reign in Europe soon after 1800: equality before the law, personal responsibility, (internal and external) publicity, proportionality and finally that of subsidiarity (*ultima ratio*). These all made criminal justice more predictable, more equal, more controlled and moderate and at the same time more functionally effective (Dupont, 1979). Torture (to obtain confessions) and secret penal procedures disappeared in the context of doing justice publicly, with both more impact and more accountability to the public, but also corporal punishments and other excessive and highly dysfunctional punishments, such as the declaration of 'civil death' and the general confiscation of all possessions of the culprit—and also of his dependants—were abolished. The punishment of imprisonment began slowly to drive out the death penalty, but the general and cultural developments also brought a certain moderation in the use and execution of this custodial punishment.

In penological terms there was the moderating influence of classical retributivism that focussed on administering the punishment in proportion to the degree of individual guilt and the degree of severity of the crime. Particularly in The Netherlands this moderating effect seems to have been quite strong, probably above all influenced by the Catholic, and later more humanistic and existentialist views of the famous 'Utrecht School', which could explain why The Netherlands was close to having the lowest (relative) prison-population in the 1970s (Van Ruller, 1986). Utilitarianism brought along a predominant focus on rehabilitation and reintegration of convicts as useful and productive members of society, which contributed in its own way to moderation and avoidance of excessive severity of punishment. Influenced by developments in anthropology, conditional sentencing was introduced, the requirements of which implied alternative types of sanctioning, and were also recognised as valuable ways of avoiding the social and economic costs of imprisonment, when this punishment is not absolutely inevitable. Differentiation of penal regimes for juveniles and offenders with serious mental problems made criminal justice potentially both more humane and subtle and more effective.

One can conclude from this introduction that in the civilising social networks of interdependence, there is a high degree of differentiation of mutually dependent functions and a similar complexity of interwoven chains of reciprocal dependence. This makes it necessary to be thoughtful, prudent and careful, decisional attitudes which are facilitated by the ability to take a distant (ex-centric) view of these networks and chains and through awareness of one's own place and functions in them.

The incremental loss of civilisation in criminal justice today
Norbert Elias' analysis concerns a process spanning many centuries in which the developments were not permanently nor unequivocally progressive, but sometimes they were predominantly or partly regressive. Still the unplanned result in the long run was that of an enhanced level of civilisation.

If we want to suggest in this chapter that there may be a regressive tendency in the level of civilisation in actual criminal justice practices we can only search for indicators of such a development, because interpreting developments in which one is deeply immersed in one's own lifetime is much more hazardous than interpreting historical processes. One can only try to ground one's intuitive analysis on the relevant documentary evidence that one can find, perhaps overlooking other processes that take place at the same time. What is presented here is however not a subjective, but at least an inter-subjective analysis, based on contemporary writings of various professionals witnessing the same tendencies.

Mindful of Elias' analysis, a loss of civilisation (in criminal justice) should be seen as a process of a broader, societal, socio-economic and cultural nature that is expressed and manifests itself in the contemporary uses of criminal justice. What is contended is not that there are inherent, immutable charac-teristics that might get lost or are endangered by internal changes in criminal justice itself (the institutions of law are no agents), but that there are wider and continuing processes which produce a certain degree of rough and toughness and induce an inclination to stress certain functions of criminal justice, such as its capacity to punish, at the cost of other functions such as offering individual suspects protection against the power of the social col-lective, exercised through the state.

Substantively one could think of the degree to which doing criminal jus-tice is still based on thoughtful, prudent and careful consideration, in the context of an institutionally guaranteed, distanced, (and dispassionate) delib-eration of all interests which are at stake when using the state's monopoly of violence. To what extent have there been developments that have changed or even undermined the *checks and balances* between the agencies of crimi-nal justice (the legislator included) and to what extent has this given rise to a situation in which criminal justice can no longer be an institutional brake on spontaneous outbursts of cruelty and excessive harshness, but to the con-trary a way of forcefully expressing these — more or less collective — affects?

In The Netherlands, a country that was formerly famous for its humane and lenient penal system, some developments which are alarming in this regard can be discerned. Especially giving rise to concern is the fact that in the recent decades the traditional distance between the politically responsible minister of justice and the Public Prosecution Service (PPS) — which always served well to prevent a politicisation of everyday justice — expressed in the 'doctrine of the velvet glove' was replaced in 1999 by an explicit power of the same minister to give instructions with regard to every task and (legally mandated) power of the PPS (Blad and De Doelder, 2008).[2] Since the Minister himself is accountable to Parliament this has enabled the traditionally feared, but now desired politicisation of doing justice, which expresses itself in unlimited meddling by politicians in any criminal event that is covered by mass media, creating and amplifying an impression that criminal justice is massively failing to perform its purported main function, namely crime control.

Another landslide that has happened in our criminal justice system is that the PPS has been given an autonomous power to impose punishments ('penal dispositions' which may not imply custodial sanctions) (Hartmann, 2008). This competence of the PPS to punish will, in the near future, replace most of the formerly consensual settlements between the PPS and the suspect, the so-called 'transactions', to avoid prosecution on certain agreed conditions such as compensating the victim. The initiative to address an independent court now has to be taken by the citizen who faces a punishment already imposed by the PPS: therefore he should oppose the decision by default (i.e it will have effect unless he does so). This new procedural arrangement has in this context two relevant consequences: the first is that the everyday sanctioning levels in a massive amount of cases can be directly steered by the Minister of Justice (in view of the latter's unlimited power to instruct the PPS). And the second is that the independent courts tend to be marginalised in determining what justice implies in very frequent incidences of crime, dealt with routinely by the prosecution service. The power of the PPS will be increased and that of the courts decreased further when the mandatory minimum sentences that have been proposed become law:[3] the courts will then, under normal circumstances, not be able to escape the duty to impose the mandatory sentences (50 per cent of the maximum penalty), but the PPS has the power to decide whether to bring a criminal charge that *does*, or *does*

---

2. In the review of the Act on Judicial Organization (*Wet Rechterlijke Organisatie*) of 1999, in which section 127 RO gives an unlimited competence to the Minister of Justice to issue both negative and positive instructions to the Public Prosecution Service.

3. The cabinet of Liberals and Christian-Democrats, supported by the PVV that introduced the Bill, had fallen before it was accepted by Parliament but the pressures in this direction continue. The new cabinet announced that the guidelines for sanctions to be demanded by the PPS will be adapted to obtain more or less the same result.

not imply a legal construction of the putative offence that would oblige the courts to impose a mandatory sentence upon conviction (De Doelder, 2011).

The system's internal capacity to discuss and consider prudent action in doing criminal justice is undermined by these developments. In this regard it should also be mentioned that, while the limits of substantive criminal law are drawn ever wider, become more vague and sometimes even imply the liability to be punished for mere (ascribed) intentions, the criminal procedural law is to a certain degree de-formalised, leaving it to the courts e.g. to decide what should be the legal consequences of serious flaws — and even transgressions — in the preparatory investigations by police and PPS. The legal scholar Mevis has interpreted this as signs of a 'withdrawing legislator' — letting the courts down by weakening the legal sources of legitimacy of the courts' verdicts (Mevis, 2008) — but it is much more appropriate to see these developments in legislation as conscious and purposive action of the legislator, facilitating political steering of criminal justice much more effectively than strict legality would.[4] As noticed by the legal scholar Klip (2010: 588), by the ever-increasing power to punish the necessity to make choices and set priorities in law enforcement becomes also greater and more urgent, because it is impossible to react to each and every (putative) offence, but these choices are no longer made in transparent legislation, grounded in a democratically open and public debate, but in the everyday decisions about investigation and prosecution, hidden from the public view.

Penal Instrumentalism

These developments in The Netherlands can be interpreted as evidence of the increasing instrumentalisation of criminal justice since the middle of the 1980s, which has been analysed and criticised by the legal scholars A. C. 't Hart and R. Foqué (1990a) as a fundamental problem in the context of a modern relational theory of law. In this relational approach law should provide and guard the foundations of a democratic state under the Rule of

---

4. For the attentive reader of Dutch professional literature on the functioning of criminal justice the signs of political steering of legal action are many. Recently, Stevens (2012) demonstrated the strong influence of 'risk-management' on decisions about the use of pre-trial detention: all legal aspects that should be weighed by judges are in daily practice overruled by one political necessity: to avoid any risk.

Law as a model for a balanced society, orientated towards the realisation of equality, equal liberty and equal opportunities for participation of all legal subjects. Quoting A. C. 't Hart (2004: 210), the founding fathers of the modern Rule of Law were searching for:

> ...a construction [meaning 'structure'] in which power would be divided between participants who acknowledge each other reciprocally and wherein law would function in the first place as the structure constituting the relations between the participants in power. Law is then not a pure instrument of the exercise of power, but is understood as a pattern of relations...expressing a comprehensive structural equilibrium that allows limitation and diffusion of the exercise of power. (My translation).

On this view, in as far as law can be an instrument, it is an instrument only for the preservation of the comprehensive equilibrium in the long run. It does so by maintaining the 'counter-factual' legal, aspirational model of the democratic Rule of Law as expression of an ethical-political ideal, wherein the rights and liberties of each legal subject are equally protected, both in his horizontal legal relations to fellow-citizens and in his hierarchical legal relations to government and authorities. From this legally guaranteed position all legal subjects can participate freely in public debate about the fabric of society and the polity of the state.

Instrumentality of and protection by law are in this view inseparable: protection by law is instrumental. But it is a kind of instrumentality that transcends the short-term political aims, interests and practices, which should normatively be limited by legal policies geared to the long term balances.

Very different from this kind of instrumentality is the 'penal instrumentalism' that has become predominant in the last 25 years in criminal justice policies. Penal instrumentalism places effectiveness of law in combating crime as sole priority and inherently views provisions of legal protection of citizens against state powers as obstacles that should be removed as much as is (constitutionally) acceptable (Foqué and 't Hart, 1990b: 194). The realisation of short-term political aims should be smoothly facilitated with the means of criminal justice, conceived as and reorganized to be an assembly-line of the politically desired output, instead of an autonomous system of check-and-balances that imposes limits on political programmes and agendas.

Penal instrumentalism could be defined as:

> the tendency to overlook and overstep the inherent limits of penal instrumentality (that is the limited capacity to reach certain aims with the means of the penal law), which leads to an incremental weakening of the legal protection of individual citizens against oppressive tendencies in society and the powers of state authorities (Blad, 2008: 38).[5]

Analytically two types of limits are being overstepped. Firstly there are the functional limits inherent in the capacity to achieve certain goals by means of the penal law: as a means of influencing conduct in the direction of 'norm-conformity, the threat and imposition of punishment only have a very limited efficacy'. This depends upon various personal and societal (educational, socio-economic, cultural) conditions, which are not within the reach of the penal law. Moreover, there are almost always negative and even counter-productive effects of penal repression.[6] These limits are increasingly disregarded.

The concept of inherent limits to the capacity of the penal law to achieve certain aims implies that to overstep these limits produces no positive results (no surplus value in terms of reducing crime-levels) but merely implies more costs in terms of loss of rights and liberties. The latter is caused by the transgression of the second type of inherent limitations, the ethical-normative limits which — in the relational theory of law used here — follow from the social contract as the foundation of state and civil society and of the legality-principle ruling the exercise of power: predominantly the safeguarding of privacy, personal life and human equality. The one-sided stress on combating, not only crime but now also issues of nuisance and even mere feelings of un-safety (often without much objective reason) leads to an increasing

---

5. One could think of the distinction that H. L. Packer (1968) made between the crime control versus the due process model, which is certainly implied, but here the intuition is that — while marginalising the due process aspects — penal instrumental does in fact not deliver more or more effective crime control. See also Wright, 1996: 138–139.

6. A well-known example is the worldwide war on drugs that is correctly identified as a failure with devastating consequences by a Panel of the United Nations in 2011.

number of invasive powers of the criminal justice agencies, foremost the police, many of which are called 'preventative' but are in fact of a repressive character. Examples are the so-called 'preventative search'[7] and the obligation to be able to show an ID when required, which can be at any occasion in public. Other examples are invasive means of investigation and detection such as systemic electronic surveillance of private homes and communications.

While these invasive powers of the criminal justice agencies are increased and more frequently used, their use is becoming more and more selective, informed and directed by social and political discourses negatively stereotyping certain sections of the population as *the* source of our crime problems. Although the (most often marginalised) sections of the population that are under popular attack vary fashionably in time, the politically exploited repressive talk, distributed and amplified by the mass media, prepares the population at large continuously for new invasive powers and repressive interventions in a dramatic projection of a moral battle of 'us against them'. Groups that have been socially constructed as our enemies are various ethnic minorities labelled, often inaccurately, as 'Antillians', 'Moroccan youth', or 'Gypsies'; they also include 'street-terrorists', which are groups of youngsters causing (sometimes serious) nuisance, and nowadays for instance Polish workers and motor-cycle clubs such as, or resembling, the Hell's Angels.[8]

Typical for this era is that politicians do not any more dissociate themselves from these social constructions of 'folk devils' or try to neutralise them — as they would have done until the 1980s — but accept them as images, feelings and desires that the population has a right to maintain (Hallsworth, 2000). Penal instrumentalism is framed in, and frames, the development of a predominant 'culture of safety', that projects and seeks to protect a majority of presumably law-abiding, well-integrated citizens against less integrated and relatively more deprived groups, perceived as the source of criminal risks and danger (Van Swaaningen, 1997). As a result, instead of promoting a

7. A search on the body, all goods carried and one's car, which is allowed in so-called risk zones without the demand of having good reasons to suspect a person of having committed or committing an offence.
8. A. C. 't Hart (1983) demonstrated how this kind of language can stigmatise and degrade social groups, making them vulnerable for political manipulations which decrease their actual and equal protection by the law. Manipulations which would not have been publicly accepted without the prior dissemination of stigmatising labels.

democratic society of equals, this use of criminal justice merely reproduces and reinforces the structure of inequality and relative deprivation at the bottom of the socio-economic ladder (Frehsee *et al*, 1997 among others).

David Garland's analysis (1996; 2001) of the waning of 'penal welfarism' and the gradual development of a culture of penal control, indicated *inter alia* by the decline of the rehabilitative ideal and the political exploitation of fear of crime and a re-dramatisation of crime against which the public must at all costs be protected, was based on the USA and the UK but is very applicable to the developments in The Netherlands, even more so since 2001, the year of publication of his book. In particular, the discovery of the symbolic figure of the victim as a source of legitimacy for penal control developed in The Netherlands only after 2001. Penal instrumentalism is based on populism and coupled with managerialism, leaving less and less room for professional discretion in doing justice. Not only scientific expert knowledge, but also legal professionals are politically 'denigrated', as Garland correctly observed (2001: 13), and public opinion serves as the privileged, almost exclusive source of political discourse and crime policies.

A prominent explanation in penal sociology for the drastic changes in the penal climate in so many western countries is the thesis that complex and interrelated technological, socio-economical and cultural changes in connection with globalisation have undermined traditional certainties and forms of (informal) social control. While situational and informal social control mechanisms have been weakened the increasing wealth and mobility has increased the opportunities for criminal activity. Also in The Netherlands a strong increase in recorded (property) crime in the 1970s has produced a legitimation-crisis for the nation state, which derives a great deal of its legitimacy from the capacity to protect its subjects against crime.

Politicians and policymakers have responded by adapting the criminal justice system in order to make it a seemingly more efficient system of crime control, with an increasing emphasis on deterrence and incapacitation by longer terms of imprisonment. But what is most striking is that the criminal justice system is still made more severely punitive now, while overall registered crime levels are decreasing. Management of fear seems to be an overriding political aim here (Van de Bunt and Van Swaaningen, 2004; Van Swaaningen, 2009), and it seems to induce an acceptance of unduly harsh punishment and control levels on offenders, which will now be discussed as an indication of de-civilisation.

Conditions and Expressions of Harshness

Referring to the increasing punitiveness of criminal justice in the USA, Jonathan Simon has suggested that there seems to be a growing acceptance of an *'entitlement to cruelty'*. Cruelty is defined by him as:

> …the trend towards penalties that are painful, vengeful, and destructive for life chances. By cruelty I also mean to foreground a feature of the public presentation of these penalties as something more than a belief in the necessity of harsh punishments to provide some crime control benefit, or even to satisfy some philosophically abstracted notion of retribution. By cruelty I mean satisfaction at the suffering implied by, or imposed by, punishment upon criminals, as well as emotions of anger and desire for vengeance taking violence (Simon, 2001: 87).

The cruel forms of punishment that Simon discusses are the death penalty (defended nowadays also as offering the victim or bereaved relatives the possibility of 'closure'), the ever increasing lengths of terms of imprisonment (even for relatively small third offences under 'three-strikes' legislation) which he interprets as 'life-thrashing sentences' , and the wide scale of different sanctions aimed at 'shaming', such as uniformed work in 'chain gangs'.

Tendencies towards public shaming are not very strong as yet in The Netherlands, but it has been suggested that offenders sentenced to a community sanction should carry out their community work wearing brightly-coloured jackets with words printed on them indicating that this work is done for punishment.[9] More disturbing is the tendency to impose ever longer terms of imprisonment, with the unprecedented rise in life-imprisonment and the announced introduction of mandatory sentencing in cases of recidivism involving crimes causing an infringement on the personal integrity of the victim, within a ten-year time span after a previous conviction. All institutional advisory boards in The Netherlands have rejected this proposal on professional legal and scientific grounds, but the bill has been introduced anyway,

---

9.   Folkert Jensma, 'Het daderhesje deugt niet', *NRC-Handelsblad*, 5 August 2011.

with even more severe provisions. The serious and deep conflicts between the professional legal elite—most particularly judges, now announcing forms of civil and legal disobedience—and populism that have been developing in the last two decades in The Netherlands seem to culminate in drastic fettering of the courts in their traditional power to determine sentences on the grounds of individualised considerations of the offence, the offender and the circumstances of the case.

The sociologist Boutellier (2002: 111 ff; 2004) perceives a development towards 'urgent criminal justice' (as opposed to criminal justice as *ultima ratio*), predominantly geared to deterrence and selective incapacitation, but the legal scholar Professor Klip (2010: 592) speaks more sharply of a tendency towards 'total criminal justice': 'a justice system with severe punishments that have to be applied always and everywhere', implemented by a political elite that is only interested in the punitive aspect of the justice system, but not in the legal aspects of it and that would preferably make the courts redundant. From the advanced and subtle system based on personal culpability the Dutch legislator is slowly turning back to the medieval system of offence-oriented justice in which only the abstract severity of the crime is relevant. Another legal scholar, Professor Groenhuijsen, discussing a legislative initiative taken by the very right-wing populist Freedom Party (*Partij Voor de Vrijheid*: PVV), concludes that this initiative involves a party-political programme encompassing the 'complete field of criminal justice', most strikingly without any relevant substantial justification and explanation:

> Drastic increases in maximum penalties across the board, the introduction of severe and sometimes massive minimum penalties, the corruption of the foundations of juvenile justice and the application of preventative detention in many, many categories of offences (Groenhuijsen, 2010: my translation).

A younger academic, Claessen (2010: 100), and a group of his colleagues observe an 'unprecedented punitive climate and austerity of penitentiary law'. The penitentiary specialist Emeritus Professor Kelk, in an overview of developments, unreservedly notices a clear regression 'from humane to hard-hearted'.

Jonathan Simon tries to explain the apparent change of mentality, already noticed by Garland, that expresses, promotes and accepts the need for satisfaction by cruel, vengeful punishments, in two different ways. Firstly he wonders whether the evolution from mechanical towards organic solidarity, as proposed by the famous sociologist Durkheim, could be in reverse now:

> The bloody rituals of the scaffold reflected the characteristics of the conscience collective under mechanical solidarity. Under conditions of organic solidarity justice is increasingly reconceived as restitutive. There is less intense collective emotion and what there is valorizes things like individuality, rationality and choice, which mitigate against cruelty. (Simon, 2001: 97)

In this regard he mentions the street-culture of various youth-groups coming from the lowest socio-economic classes, but also the fact that many of the Californian supporters of the 'three-strikes' legislation were those 'who feared the breakdown of a common moral order as reflected in the family or in the demographic make-up of the state (Simon, 2001: *ibid.*)'.

Secondly Simon attempts to find an explanation in terms of Elias' theory of civilisation. Are there signs of a certain de-civilisation, a decrease in shame and embarrassment when expressing or regarding the expression of cruelty? Elias posited a homology (an identity in form and style) between psychical order and self-control on the one hand and social order and social control on the other, and this presupposes a close relation between individual and society. When citizens exercise self-discipline and give up satisfying 'improper' needs, this must indicate the existence of a certain solidarity with fellow-citizens and a willingness to accept the obligations associated with it: the welfare state was promoted by this and in turn the welfare state rewarded solidarity with adequate and reliable care in case of mishaps and disasters in personal life. But, says Simon:

> The larger political and economic strategies of neo-liberalism tend to place many of the burdens back on individuals. What remains of organized forms of social solidarity is further problematized by increased immigration and growing fragmentation of the society into geographically segregated class and race enclaves.

These changes may be breaking down the psychical equilibrium that the civilising process presupposed (Simon, 2001: 95).

Pratt, also in a reflection based on Elias, reminds us that the theoreticians of the 'risk-society' have demonstrated that the 'networks of interdependence' in that type of society have dramatically changed and have above all become more unpredictable and more fluid:

> It is as if all the road maps of everyday life which the state had previously drawn up on our behalf have been removed: in the new ones that replace them, the state only sketches in vague landmarks around which we must then undertake our own cartography (Pratt, 2005: 265).

Our situation of growing uncertainties about our identity that goes together with the weakened or even dissolved networks of reciprocal dependency promotes the construction of:

> …common, easily identifiable enemies who seem to put us further at risk, whether these be particular types of criminal or new categories of unwanted citizens, such as refugees. Under these circumstances, the habitus of self-restraint begins to give way to more unrestrained outlets of emotion, as all the assurances which had allowed us to take uncertainties and vicissitude in our stride, or to tolerate those whose conduct or character seemed undesirable, begin to unravel. Indeed, we now live in an era of road rage, hospital rage, and so on — as if, without the social solidity of the pre-1970 period, *ad hoc* outbursts of anger can now become our response to delays, frustrations, and inconveniences; and a new intolerance — zero tolerance — of those not making a contribution to social wellbeing (*ibid.*).

Pratt is more assertive in his conclusions than Simon:

> There is less self-restraint on the part of individuals but a simultaneous yearning for stronger and clearer responses from the state, (Pratt, 2005: 265)

Political elites — and not so much the bureaucratic and professional groups working in the criminal justice system (Hallsworth, 2000: 154) — have responded to this 'yearning for stronger and clearer answers' to a seemingly dissolving social structure and the concomitant occurrence of crime and nuisance, not with rational self-restraint but by embracing what Garland has termed a 'criminology of the other', which allows for an aggressive, populist criminal policy (sold under the guise of efficacy in terms of protection against crime). Garland circumscribes this 'criminology of the other' as a:

> criminology of the alien other which represents criminals as dangerous members of distinct racial and social groups which bear little relation to us. It is, moreover, a criminology which trades in images, archetypes and anxieties, rather than in careful analysis and research findings — more a politicised discourse of the unconscious than a detailed form of knowledge-for-power (Garland, 1996: 461).

This type of criminology is one of the aspects of a political strategy of 'denial' of the increasing failure of traditional criminal justice to deal adequately with modern phenomena of crime from the centre of the national state (2001: 137–138).

The observable call for punishments that are so hard that they can be called cruel, could according to Simon, also be explained by the success of the civilising process itself. The features contributing to civilisation also contribute to a greater fear of violence and a stronger empathy with victims, which may induce a willingness to accept very harsh measures:

> Because we see punishment as an instrumentally useful security device, we may not respond to it as an act of violence (Simon, 2001: 96).

In this respect it is important that the bureaucratic and professional elites administrating criminal justice have made the execution of punishment quite invisible for the public and are expected to perform their duties in a calm and dispassionate way, despite passionately punitive political rhetoric. We must and may hope that this is still to a certain degree the case with our public prosecutors and our judges, although the former are brought more directly under the political direction of the minister of justice and the latter are nowadays publicly criticised for being too lenient. The right-wing populist party PVV has even proposed abolishing the appointment of judges for life and dismissing those judges who have been punishing too leniently. This proposal will not be supported broadly, but the possibly incremental introduction of mandatory minimum sentences may also do the job of harnessing judicial discretion, with the result that they will be obliged to mete out punishments which they might consider not *justified* in the case at hand.

What has been outlined above is a sketch of the most important developments in public discourse and criminal policy in The Netherlands to show the probability of an actual decrease of the level of civilisation in Dutch criminal justice. At the very least conditions are building up for a kind of justice that no longer counteracts and checks tendencies towards cruelty but celebrates them. The degree to which legal professionals in various functions manage to mitigate these developments is an empirical question that cannot be discussed and answered here. In so far as there are ways to sidestep punitive expectations, many will try to do so when they perceive more positive forms of tailored sanctioning. It is known, for example, that Dutch criminal courts are much less inclined to impose the measure of detention for repetitive offenders—with a minimum duration of two years—when it becomes apparent that the administration will not promote rehabilitation for the convicted offender but only aims at temporary incapacitation (Struijk, 2008: 367).

In reaction to the proposed introduction of mandatory minimum penalties in cases of recidivism many judges have announced that they will do all that is within their power to avoid having to impose them, just as courts have done historically at times when legal punishments were (seen by them as) excessively harsh.[10] Quite correctly they insist that allowing mandatory punishments for recidivism will in the foreseeable future imply the introduction of mandatory punishments for first offenders. They fear that the predictable instrumental failures of the mandatory sentence for recidivists will be interpreted as proof that the first punishment was already inadequately low, since all functional expectations of the punishment depend on its harshness.

10. The editorial of the important Dutch newspaper *NRC-Handelsblad* of 14 September 2011, p. 2, reports under the heading 'No need for judges': 'Judges and prosecutors will avoid unreasonable consequences. They will be the last who are still taking account of the offender's interests. When the punishment can no longer be tailored, then messing about with the charge might be the only way to do justice.' (My translation, J. R. B.). The editorial comment rightly states that this will have an undermining effect and will lead to a crisis of trust.

Problematic publicity

A last relevant factor to mention in connection with the punitive populism that dominates Dutch criminal policies is the functional role of the mass media in amplifying fear of crime and promoting the simplistic 'solution' of punishment. Not only crime, but also the way the justice system functions has increasingly become 'media-dominated'. In a reconstruction of the relations between the justice system and the media in several consecutive decades, Brants and Brants demonstrate that attention has shifted from 'serving the common public interest together' to a battle between justice system and media based on conflicting interests.

Where initially there was mutual trust and consensus about the common interest and its implications, there grew an increasing distrust in the way the criminal justice agencies supposedly served it. The loss of trust became almost total in the era 1980–1990, precisely when the criminal-political discourse sounded the alarm because of a highly increased level of recorded (property-) crime and made a drastic turn away from the traditional Dutch reticent politics — of parsimony with punishment and predominant use of social policies — to an attempt to 'regain' trust in criminal justice by a 'consequent, consistent and credible' use of repression. In the context of this new punitivism the PPS itself began actively to use the media to show the public that they were 'now' really fighting crime with tough measures.

Paradoxically, however, this led to the opposite image of justice as failing to achieve its ends. In the post-2000 era, Brants and Brants witness a spiral of highly tuned up expectations and deep disappointments. There is an interaction between the justice system and the media in which the latter continually stress that the Rule of Law is threatened [by crime], that criminal justice has no adequate response, is incompetent, makes mistakes, covers up cases — making it unlikely that the justice system can be entrusted with the important duty of serving the common, public interest:

> This message however is not given in a vacuum. In political discourse there are constant promises that the more severely punitive approach, that the public anxiously asks for, indeed offers the solution. The justice system brags with new legislation, reorganizations of the Public Prosecution Service and the police, all geared to more efficient and cost-effective performance. The picture that arises

from the media is however that the situation is only getting worse. (Brants and Brants, 2002:24. My translation)·

Professor A.C. 't Hart (2001) has drawn attention to the inherent fundamental tensions between the mediating functions of law in a democratic state and the way in which news — about crime and society, criminal justice and adjudication — is constructed and presented. Whereas the (principles of) 'internal' and 'external ' publicity of adjudication have both an instrumental and a legal-protective function, the protective dimension is often totally lacking in mass-media publicity, especially in television coverage, about crime and the allegedly involved suspects and victims. Where the penal law and procedure have the obligation and capacity to make multiple interests, needs and perceptions compatible in a legal conceptualisation of problems and conflicts, and to solve the latter in terms of the law, the media tend to suggest a direct access to the 'one and only truth' of the matter, described in everyday language.·

Criminal justice can only perform its function of mediating various and often conflicting perceptions of truth by keeping its artificial, legal concepts as open as possible, thus avoiding the monopolising of the meaning of legal concepts by one or more of the conflicting parties. This leaves space for a possible recognition of other ways of viewing reality and of being human (alterity: that is, the inherent right and capacity to be different). But the media powerfully ontologise (hypostasise) one image of reality: in this way they disturb and undermine the procedural, distanced and dispassionate mediation of different views on truth and reality by creating the illusion that there is such a thing as an easily knowable, obvious truth ('t Hart, 2001: 158). ·Perhaps needless to say, but important to note in the context of this contribution, is that the 'criminology of the other' — the criminalising imagery about certain social groups (most recently 'biker gangs') — is disseminated by mass media, as well as traditional imagery about innocent victims and predatory offenders, carved as it were in a culturally available dualistic frame of thinking. Not only the pluralistic nature of democracy itself, but also the capacity to live together as citizens in our (temporary) capacities as offenders and victims tend to be denied in much mass-media coverage of crime and justice.

Restorative Justice and Other Strategies of Civilisation

It is one thing to try to demonstrate that certain developments seem to bring about a tendency of de-civilisation, but quite another to indicate the ways in which we could try to counter such a tendency. It is evidently not just a matter of making different political decisions regarding criminal justice, but also of building public support for those other decisions and of more objective social and social-economic conditions. But we will not focus here on the ways in which change could be brought about, but only on the ideas that might convince our fellow-citizens of the desirability and even necessity of certain changes in justice policies. Hopefully, opinion-leaders will one day succeed in publicly defending an alternative view on criminal justice, reviving old valuable principles and introducing new principles appealing to emancipated and consciously democratic citizens (Lissenberg, 2005). The greatest challenge here seems to be breaking through the 'instrumentalist syndrome', nowadays apparently broadly accepted, that deconstructs criminal justice in its classical, legal protective dimensions to facilitate an oiled machinery — an assembly-line of punitive interventions.

Reconfirming the classical protective functions — protective of the suspected individual in his conflict with the state that criminally charges him through the penal procedure and based in narrowly circumscribed offences in the substantive law — could and should be combined with a new set of ideas with regard to how criminal justice could achieve its other aims, besides legal protection of suspects. Amidst those other aims, general and special prevention, conflict resolution and channelling vengeful feelings, a special new aim — introducing new problems — is giving voice and recognition to the victims, who have returned to the arena of criminal justice after having been almost completely excluded since the development of the central nation-state with its monopoly of violence.

Restorative justice not only offers foundations for a strong involvement of victims, and procedures in which they can be involved if they wish, it also is grounded in a much more modern set of ideas about responding to offences and offenders: a modern anthropology that is far removed from the utilitarian anthropology of Bentham and Beccaria, which provided the classic criminal law with its predominant functional model of influencing the general conduct of legal subjects: threatening with punishments. It is because these threats have to be credible, that punishment must always follow upon a crime, as Feuerbach argued. Only then a certain 'psychological force' can be assumed to go from the threat itself. The actual imposition of the promised amount of pain can then also be justified as retribution for the fact that you, suspect, have not been deterred. It is this deeply ingrained belief in deterrence that causes criminal justice to be easily perverted into an inhuman system of pain-infliction. Inhuman, but also highly ineffective in view of large scale recidivism and the social reproduction of crimes and criminals through the cultural and structural organization of the criminal justice system, with the prison as its symbolic core institution (Quinney, 1970; Christie, 1981).

The inadequacy of continuing to reason within the classical models of deterrence and retribution is demonstrated by the discourse of Easton and Piper in their chapter in this book. Discussing the influence of past convictions on sentencing they argue that on principle, retributive (deserts-) theory offers a greater hope of limiting the impact if tempered by the principle of parsimony, concurring with Von Hirsch and Ashworth who state that the examples of Finland and Sweden *'demonstrate that ... adoption of desert and proportionality as guiding principles does not lead to greater severity'*. This is what has also been brought forward in The Netherlands with regard to retributive philosophy in general.

Judge and scholar, Otte (2002) argued for a revival of the retributive approach to punishment, complaining about the apparent boundlessness of actual, consequential sentencing: but without any noticeable effect. In one of the very few other (more or less recent) defences of retribution, it is argued that punishment is viewed much too rationally in consequentialist approaches and that there is a certain element of 'irrationality' in sentencing that can be accommodated with or expressed in retributive sentencing (Knigge, 1988). But should we really escape from our theoretical and practical difficulties into an acceptance of irrationality and irrational state responses to crime? Where are the limits then?

Easton and Piper also show how in the UK past convictions have become elements to take into account when determining the punishment for the case at hand. This is something which would not be in conformity with pure desert theory, which would focus attention on the case at hand, when previous offences have already been punished. But political and popular opinion seem to stress the importance of the criminal record for the determination of punishment, and retributive theorists have been trying to accommodate their theories to allow for that. Perhaps with the same feeling that Easton and Piper express:

> …it would seem to us that using previous convictions to aggravate the seriousness of the offence is … an aspect of sentencing against which it is currently impossible to argue. (This volume, *Chapter 6*, 'Other Justifications?').

They go on to say:

> Punishing persistence accords with popular ideas of justice. Its use therefore needs to be more controlled and restrained through specific guidance. (This volume, *Chapter 6*, 'Establishing Aggravation')

They are not saying which guidance they would prefer substantively, but note that providing such guidance to 'ensure consistency and restraint in the calculation of seriousness in a retributivist sentencing framework is a complex and difficult issue.' Agencies in the UK such as most recently the Sentencing Council have produced ever more detailed guidance but:

> …it is the mandatory aggravation of seriousness on the account of previous offending which now threatens to alter significantly these calculations and lead to disproportionate sentences. (This volume, *Chapter 6*, 'Conclusion')

Above I have mentioned that the same pressures—towards mandatory, more severe punishment in cases of recidivism[11]—are evident in The Netherlands and theoreticians of penal law and penological scientists seem not to be able to do much more than adapt their reasoning to allow for these pressures, deliver futile protest statements, or stay out of the public debate.

---

11. For the same reason as was given in the English CJA 1993 which stated that: 'In considering the seriousness of any offence, the court may take into account (any previous convictions of the offender or) *any failure of his to respond to previous sentences'* [emphasis added]. Failure to be deterred becomes itself a proof of moral degeneration.

As for judges, practically involved in sentencing on a daily basis, they are aware of the various theoretical legitimations of punishment and they have their preferences for, for example, retribution, deterrence, rehabilitation or even restoration.

But when one examines their actual imposed sentences, these appear to have no relation to their personal beliefs: the imposed punishments cannot be explained on the grounds of the theoretical preferences of the judges with regard to legitimate punishment (De Keijser, 2000). Institutional arrangements, such as the functional relation between the PPS and the courts, sentencing guidelines (PPS) and 'punishment orientation lists' (of the courts) and the fact that the most serious cases are decided by courts of three judges, determining the sentence together, are factors that bring about a sentencing praxis that seems to be uncontrolled rather than controlled by any actor in the system. In view of the wide discretion that is built into the system, predominant political discourse must be assumed to have a strong, if not decisive, influence.

Beliefs in deterrence seem to be decisively influencing abstract scales of just desert, through the legislative process of enhancing the threatened punishments on existing crimes and offences. Once the substantive law has been adapted to express a higher level of perceived severity of the crime, the level of retribution follows from that in each individual case. Fundamentally, what is wrong here is that a *normative dimension*, the severity of a crime, is supposed to be given expression in *factual, quantitative terms*: the number of years of incarceration and such. Since the normative dimension really cannot be factually weighed and measured, there is no intrinsic limit to expressing the abstract severity of a crime. It could be placed on a scale (or ladder) of a number of crimes, differing with regard to their relative severity, but then the whole scale could be moved up or down in severity without any objective foundation or touchstone.[12] These problems seem to

12. Louk Hulsman wrestled with this problem of 'severity' and 'severity-scales' without really finding a solution. See: L. H. C. Hulsman (1981), 'Waarover beslist men eigenlijk in het strafrechtelijk systeem?' in *Beginselen. Opstellen aangeboden aan G. E. Mulder, Arnhem*: Gouda Quint, pp. 107–116. Abstracted severity (as in penal law provisions) seems often misleading, for concrete severity remains contextual and contingent. Perhaps participatory justice, involving victim and offenders and significant others, does indeed offer a more reliable way of assessing severity, as Hulsman must have surmised.

have become more serious in their consequences now that there is so much 'surrogate participation' of citizens (non-victims and non-offenders) in the social drama of crime, through the means of the mass-media. Criminal justice has become more 'responsive' but it is a responsiveness to often deeply misleading images of offenders and victims, the nature of crime, crime-causation and—prevention.

As Louk Hulsman has remarked, civil (private) law seems to function quite well in preventing and redressing serious wrongs without the use of notions such as deterrence[13] and retribution: so should they not be ignored in designing a better system of public (criminal) law? More participation of the victim and a different participation of the offender in procedures of criminal justice, by putting compensation (or restitution) for the victim central: these were Hulsman's suggestions for a way out, projecting a reform program implying making a default use of civil law (Hulsman, 1968). Could it indeed not be the case that the most strategic decision we could make, with regard to our criminal justice system, is to make criminal justice fundamentally participatory for and dialogic with those directly or indirectly involved in and touched by (the consequences of) a criminal offence? Indeed, this is what McElrea contends when he stresses that restorative justice is above all a 'procedural revolution' (This volume, *Chapter 2*). Hulsman claimed that we should give relatively more influence to those directly involved in deciding what should be done, than to those who are only involved as a consumer of stories of crime and punishment without any real experience or knowledge of the reality of criminal events (Hulsman, 1979).

This does not imply privatisation of the problem of crime and the response to it, but the much more difficult task of reforming public (criminal) law on well-defined grounds, with different foundational concepts and different practices, which could be defined as hybrid practices in the sense that in the domain of criminal justice procedures will be allowed that are predominantly of a civil law nature like forms of mediation. Gutwirth and De Hert express amazement that restorative justice protagonists devote so little attention to the civil law domain and they rightly maintain that there is a much closer link between restorative justice and civil law than with today's

---

13. This is correct when one looks at civil law doctrine itself, but the idea of deterrence plays a role in legal economics, mainly in terms of monetary consequences.

criminal law arrangements and theory. They would like to maintain a more reduced criminal justice system — with much less use of imprisonment, which they call a monstrosity (this volume, *Chapter 9*) and want to achieve that reduction by transferring certain categories of criminal offences to the civil law system and, perhaps, also by depenalisation in the sense of down-scaling penal sanctions.[14] This is an interesting strategy, but the same result (in terms of reducing the scope of penal law and punishment) could also be achieved by adapting the criminal justice system in ways that allow restorative procedures to be used in a maximum number of categories of criminal offences. This is what Walgrave proposes to do: maximise the use of restorative procedures and sanctions in criminal justice:

> Pushing back as much as possible the punitive premise in the response to crime
> is the logical next phase in the civilisation process. That means less coercion and
> less pain-infliction in a top-down imposition of a formal legal order, but more
> space for voluntary, non-violent bottom-up responses. (This volume, *Chapter 11*)

Van Stokkom's proposal implies reducing the applicability of imprisonment by a bifurcated criminal policy that allows no custodial sanctions for offenders who show themselves to be trustworthy and responsible by a recognisable degree of remorse:

> Remorse indicates that the offender is connected with the values the law is appealing to. He is morally approachable. Genuine remorse points at a positive moral disposition, a commitment to comply, an indication that trust can be renewed. (This volume, *Chapter 8*, 'Facilitating Responsibility')[15]

These three strategies of reform carry differing implications of course, which need to be looked at further. But it is obvious that each implies legislative operations which need to be thoroughly discussed and consciously

---

14. The Report on Decriminalisation of the Council of Europe speaks about depenalisation in two ways: the first is the abolition of a penalising provision as such, the second is penalisation at a lower level of punishment.
15. This path has also been trodden by David Cornwell in *The Penal Crisis and the Clapham Omnibus* (2009), Ch. 11, pp. 149–163.

prepared in a democratic legislature: this need for a democratic, broad debate is not a disadvantage of some kind, but refers to the crucial social-political condition of political legitimacy—and therefore plausibility and feasibility of legal reform.

Integrating both the foundational and the practical procedural aspects of restorative justice into the criminal justice system can be done and would bring not only more 'civil law'-like procedures into its domain but also promote more civilised responses to criminal offending. Provided, of course, that the integration is carefully designed to leave room for classical due process of law, enabling the accused to dispute a charge that could lead to imposition of punishment, whenever that appears to be necessary. All legal subjects should keep their classic, procedural human rights, such as the right of access to an independent court, to adequate defence and to full participation in a fair trial. When restorative procedures are allowed and followed, these should be legally framed in such way that they do not implicitly undermine procedural rights the participants would have in a criminal trial.

Leaving aside the question whether De Hert and Gutwirth are not a bit too critical in their reading of Walgrave's approach, as summarized in his contribution to this book, and of Braithwaite's work, they are right in drawing attention to possible regressive implications of a specific way of integrating restorative justice into criminal justice. The challenge is to *preserve* the concepts of substantive criminal law while at the same time accepting a system in which the presumption of punishment[16] as the only acceptable response to a criminal offence is abolished. It should be noted that indeed, as De Hert and Gutwirth remark (this volume, *Chapter 9*), the criminal justice system is not as radically punitive as restorativists often claim.

A lot of responses that the criminal justice system produces (and allows) are already today not really punishments in a strict sense. And on a theoretical level punishment is still seen as acceptable only as the last resort. But one of the problems is that the centrality of the notion of punishment in the criminal justice system has induced a legal culture in which the normative connection between 'crime and punishment' dominates the dogmatic,

---

16. Punishment is here taken in its classical definition as a deliberately intended imposition of pain. An alternative way of reasoning would be to say that we should change the meaning of the word punishment. As Walgrave notes, this might be like trying to find dry water.

systematic ordering of all possible legal answers to criminal offending, placing all responses which are 'not punishment' as (allowable or not allowable) deviations from the normative answer 'punishment'. And this legal culture seems to be changing nowadays into one that allows more easily the imposition of what is intended as punishment, but without fair trial (e.g. the penal dispositions of the PPS introduced in The Netherlands). Penal instrumentalism, as Klip (2010) remarked, loves punishment but it is not very fond of law.

McElrea is undoubtedly right when he claims that restorative justice implies above all a procedural revolution: indeed conferencing as introduced in New-Zealand is a remarkable innovation, but in view of the multiple and endlessly varied situations to which the criminal justice system has to respond it is important to recognize that it should have — and already has — various kinds of procedures available[17] to deliver the kind of response deemed most appropriate. And the introduction of new procedural forms — even new types of participants such as victims, offenders or their relatives — must be taken to express new ways of thinking about appropriate aims and procedures and changing insights about how law can best be maintained. Besides the recognition of victims as participating stakeholders, there is also a growing belief that offenders should be approached and engaged in a different way, implying inherently different roles also for legal (and other) professionals.[18] It could be that these 'new' insights are in fact anthropological insights that have been around longer and that are and should be rediscovered: with Reggio I think that this is the case. Penal instrumentalism should be viewed as an extreme expression of the 'modern' image of man as an objectified and manageable individual, a self-sufficient free-floating particle. It is this image of man as a 'closed personality' that Norbert Elias rejected as a consequence of the inextricable connection he discovered between 'inner' and 'outer' civilisation. His image of man is that of an 'open personality who possesses a greater or

---

17. For The Netherlands one can discern procedures which (begin and) end at the level of the police, such that end at the level of the PPS and such that end at a court level, before or after trial. From the most appropriate aims we could mention cautioning, diversion, influencing conduct through specific conditions, avoiding prosecution, and the imposition of punishment.
18. The 'problem solving courts' in the USA and their link to the approach of 'therapeutic jurisprudence' and other forms of 'non-adversarial justice' could be mentioned as one of the most telling developments besides RJ: see M. King, A. Freiberg, B. Batagol and R. Hyams (eds.) (2009).

lesser degree of relative (but never absolute and total) autonomy vis-à-vis other people and who is fundamentally orientated towards and dependent on other people throughout his or her life. The network of interdependencies among people is what binds them together' (Elias, 2000: 481).

This open, relational image of man has become one of the core elements of the relational theory of justice that is defended and developed in the Dutch speaking countries by A. C. 't Hart and R. Foqué, offering the foundations for a radical critique of penal instrumentalism. It is only this open, relational image of man that enables us to understand the importance of how symbolic interactions in (and around) law enforcement contribute to the 'production' of the criminal we fear or the law-abiding citizen we hope for: the importance of 'normal smithing' taking place and not 'deviant smithing' (Maruna, 2001) as is often the case.

As Reggio correctly observes (*Chapter 10* of this volume), criminal justice and restorative justice may not be totally opposed or even mutually exclusive, but restorative justice's presuppositions, normative assertions and goals are distant from those of criminal justice and are even alternatives to them, reacting to the modern understanding of law and justice. Firstly, RJ pays much attention to 'relational textures' while modern criminal justice is characterized by a mainly individual (and often utilitarian) anthropological model. Secondly, RJ attempts to envision an idea of legal order that is experience-based, context-sensitive and open to complexity, while the modern world-view contains an abstract, rationalistic, mathematic-geometrical, standardised conception of—all kinds of—order. In consequence the restorative approach to justice tends to conceive a 'horizontal', 'relational' and 'context-sensitive' idea of legal order, as opposed to the hierarchical conception of legal order within the context of the state as a monopolistic actor.

Assuming that indeed criminal justice and restorative justice are neither totally opposed nor mutually exclusive, the most important decision that legislators should take is when restorative justice or punitive justice should have precedence. This is on the legislative level above all a decision about the *categories* of crimes and offences in which a decision-making process between the two most involved citizens—victims and offenders—may or should have a chance to develop. And of course, what types of legal consequences could be attached to the results of such deliberations.[19] On the basis of these generic decisions, abstracted from specific cases, in each concrete case it will depend on the attitudes and wishes of those directly involved whether the offer to engage in a deliberative procedure leads to mediation or conferencing with certain results, to be determined together within the limits of the law. Criteria could be developed for referring cases which were selected for prosecution and punishment to a restorative procedure: for instance when victims in the particular case, despite the legislator's expressed preference for punitive justice, express a pre-dominant desire for consensual agreement and this seems to be achievable in view of the attitude and wishes of the offender(s) in the case. Transfers from an initially restorative procedure to a penal process should also be possible and regulated, with special attention to safeguards for offenders and victims. At least *this* flexibility should be made possible, when it is not already there.

It is striking that in developing 'soft', supra-national European law, this kind of reform of the criminal (and criminal procedural) law is actually asked for. The EU Framework-decision of 2001 with regard to (strengthening) the position of victims in the criminal procedure (2001, nr. 6335/01, Article 10 s. 1)[20], obliges the member states to promote 'mediation in criminal cases for offences which it considers appropriate for this sort of measure'. The second section of Article 10 stipulates that each member state shall ensure that 'any agreement between the victim and the offender can be taken into account.' Mediation in criminal cases is defined as 'the search, prior to or during criminal proceedings, for a negotiated solution between the victim and the author of an offence.[21]

---

19. This decision should be categorical in order to safeguard equality in terms of the law and to avoid arbitrary allocations of restorative and punitive procedures on the basis of discriminatory prejudices with regard to individual offenders. It is also necessary to create foreseeability for victims and offenders of the consequences of engaging in a restorative procedure. In sum, for reasons of legality.
20. In The Netherlands this framework-decision has led to changes in the code of criminal procedure, in force from 1 January 2011 (Title IIIA concerning the rights of the victim). The Framework-decision has been transformed into a Directive with the same purport but with more explicit guarantees for victims who are offered a mediation procedure.
21. Article 1 sub e. This framework decision is now being transformed into a Directive, with changes relating to safeguards for victims in mediation, but these core elements are maintained.

The Strategic Value of Agreements

In a strategy of reforming criminal justice to make it more restorative the importance of legal permissibility of agreements, reached by mediation and conferencing ('extended mediation') cannot be overestimated. For the primary parties (victim and offender) themselves, for society in general and for the criminal justice system the allowance of agreements will have many functions and effects.

The *UN Handbook on Restorative Justice Programmes* (2006) — speaks of 'restorative outcomes' , described as 'an agreement reached as a result of a restorative process'.[22] It states:

> The agreement may include referrals to programmes such as reparation, restitution and community services, "aimed at meeting the individual and collective needs and responsibilities of the parties and achieving the reintegration of the victim and the offender". It may also be combined with other measures in cases involving serious offences. (p. 7)

The combination of the agreement with 'other measures' allows for imposition of sanctions besides and above the obligations for the offender included in the agreement; these often imply restitution or compensation for damages, community service, obligations to address criminogenic factors etc., which could often also be imposed by a public prosecutor or court. The close connection between the *'restorative process' and 'restorative outcomes'* — the participatory, direct and oral character of restorative procedure — is assumed to make the crucial difference with traditional imposition of punishments. Through this close connection, this dynamic, the 'process goals' of restorative procedures are served. These goals are described in the above handbook as follows:

- Victims who agree to be involved in the process can do so safely and come out of it satisfied;

---

22. A restorative process is defined as: 'any process in which the victim and the offender and, where appropriate, any other individuals or community members affected by a crime participate together actively in the resolution of matters arising from the crime, generally with the help of a facilitator' (p. 7).

- Offenders understand how their action has affected the victim and other
  people, assume responsibility for the consequences of their action and
  commit to making reparation;
- Flexible measures are agreed upon by the parties which emphasise repairing the harm done and, wherever possible, also address the reasons for the
  offence;
- Offenders live up to their commitment to repair the harm done and
  attempt to address factors that led to their behaviour; and,
- The victim and the offender both understand the dynamic that led to
  the specific incident, gain a sense of closure and are reintegrated into the
  community. (p. 9)

The second, third and fourth procedural aims have a direct relation with
the content and the intention of the agreement and demonstrate that the
obligations that can be agreed upon are to be subsumed in at least two
categories: firstly restorative obligations vis-à-vis the victim and secondly
obligations of the offender to address what has been going wrong in their
own life and what contributed to their offending conduct. In view of the
fact that restorative justice aims to be a part of the public law system, there
are also interests of the society at large to be satisfied: the public will want
to know that the response to the offence was adequate and that the obligations are creating conditions for better conduct in the future and a return
to the norms and values of legitimate behavioural expectations.

This is why promising to enter, for instance, a drug-rehabilitation programme is called a restorative outcome. If needed, in view of the nature and
circumstances[23] of the offence, some restorative obligations may be agreed to
'make good' with society, for instance by doing community service. When the
latter type of obligations (Aim No. 3) is not discussed and proposed by the
parties themselves a judicial authority — public prosecutor or court — might
wish to add it, broadening the scope of the agreement. It should be noted
that the legal entitlement for the parties to reach an agreement, and the
possibility that judicial authorities might change the agreement, preferably
with the consent of the parties, implies that we are really looking at a 'three

---

23. E.g. a high level of media coverage following the event.

party agreement' with a mixed private-public character. And of course the civil parties cannot reach results which would imply incarceration: only equivalents of non-custodial sanctions could be proposed, since custodial sanctions can only be imposed by courts in view of the required stronger protection of human rights.

Integrating restorative justice into the criminal justice system, by allowing the use of restorative procedures in many categories of offences, would imply that—when cases are cleared up and there are no doubts about the facts—communication and deliberation between all stakeholders becomes the core dynamic of maintaining the law when the parties make use of restorative procedures. Emotional and material impact of the offence on victims, perceptions of the offending conduct from victim, offender and others, normative and moral reasons for condemning the offending conduct and for taking account of interests and needs of fellow-citizens, thinking through how the wrong and harms can best be repaired and how a better life can be promoted: all these become objects of oral, face-to-face communication in order to discuss what should happen with the aftermath of the offence. In the stage of developing an agreement, and also later, when the resulting agreement is scrutinized by judicial authorities, the necessity to be thoughtful, prudent and considerate, to take the roles of others and to take account of all sorts of reciprocal dependence will be evident in view of the aim, to reach an agreement (and to avoid as much as possible an imposition of unhelpful sanctions). In this way integrating restorative justice may push towards a re-civilisation of criminal justice. Three specific aims could be discerned of this strategy of grounding (a part of) criminal justice in private-public agreements: 1) de-victimisation of victims, 2) decriminalisation of offender-identities and 3) depenalisation (in the sense of downscaling) of criminal justice sanctions. These aims will be briefly discussed now.

De-victimisation of victims (injured parties)

Injured parties should be enabled to liberate themselves as soon as possible from the status of being a 'victim', because experiencing this status and the social and cultural connotations of victimhood are detrimental to their own self-image (personal identity, feelings of self-worth) and worldview. This has been demonstrated among others by the Dutch victimologist Van Dijk

(2006): the label 'victim' carries conflicting social expectations. On the one hand it is expected that the '*victima*' will liberate offenders and others from their guilt by forgiveness.[24] On the other hand it is supposed that the victim will have an almost boundless desire for revenge, that needs to be constrained and controlled by the criminal trial, keeping the victim sidelined and sublimating damaging emotions as much as possible. Legal scholar Verrijn Stuart (1994) has drawn attention to the circumstance that when victims remain victims too long and become predominantly perceived as victims by others, they risk becoming socially isolated and excluded from their social networks (as being a problematic person, hard to cope with).

Victims should be taken seriously and be approached in their strength, not in their weakness ; on the grounds of an assumption of competence to stand up for themselves, not of helplessness and need of care. After the Austrian case of Natasha Kampusch — the girl who was incarcerated for years in the cellar of her kidnapper's house — Groenhuijsen and Van Dijk (leaders of the Tilburg International Institute for Victimology) claimed that Kampusch made very clear in her conduct after liberating herself: victimhood is no disease.[25] A Dutch report on the needs of victims (Ten Boom and Kuijpers, 2008) placed these needs in a hierarchical order, making use of Maslow's scale. At the bottom there are physiological needs which are generally not endangered after surviving victimisation. The second level is that of primary needs for immediate safety and the need to prevent repetition, and the emotional needs for shelter and support, coping with and closure of the shocking event. On the third level there are the needs for love, belonging and positive relations to others, sometimes including the offender. The highest-placed needs are those of self-realisation and autonomy.

The experience of victimisation is a source of existential uncertainty, of doubting personal competence, doubting others and a shaken belief in the inherent justice and predictability of the social world. One often cannot understand how and why one has become a victim and has a need to understand the situation and to be understood by others. Against this background

---

24. Van Dijk contends that the archetype of the Christian *victima* (sacrifice) is Jesus Christ, who would turn the other cheek.

25. *NRC-Handelsblad* 13 September 2006: '*Kampusch doet normaal, wij niet.*' ('Kampusch acts normally, we do not')

the psychologist Mooren described the potential functions of a successful mediation between offenders and victims of violence, for the victims, as follows:

> Voluntarily confronting the offender means that the victim again takes his own life in hand. Facing his own fear, without letting this fear dominate, strengthens the experience of competence. The situation of violence may have caused an acute loss of control. Meeting the offender in a situation where he (the offender) is no longer in control and in which he needs something from the victim contributes to the recovery of the victim from the experience: the balance of power is now fundamentally different from that during the violent offence. The fact that the victim can confront the offender with what he has brought about, against the background of a hardly defined but definitely existing moral right, shifts the balance of power to the advantage of the victim (Mooren, 2001: 32. My translation)

The process of mediation in criminal matters is fundamentally about re-vindication — with the support of the judicial authorities — of the right to be free from criminal intrusions in personal life and the recognition — in various forms — of injustice done to the victim and the need to restore justice. Walgrave (2008: 140–155), following Braithwaite and Pettit (1990), speaks of the restoration of the 'dominion' (autonomy) that law should guarantee for all.

Decriminalising offenders' identity

Just as it is an existential shock to become a victim of a crime it is also a shock to have become the perpetrator of one, causing many moral, psychological and social questions and problems. Even though a person might have contemplated committing an offence before the act, the various consequences of actually doing so are highly unclear and largely unpredictable. Often offenders realise only after the fact what they have actually done and how it may impact personal life perspectives and chances. Also for offenders the most urgent questions will relate to how to cope with the offence and its consequences and how the social relations to 'the other' in general will be in the future. The Dutch legal scholar and judge Pompe (1954), discovering symbolic interactionism in the early 1950s, observed that the first condition for becoming a 'criminal' was to commit a crime. But the second and more important condition is the development of an intimate bond between offence and offender, defining his identity and keeping his personal life organized around the fact of his crime. The fully developed 'criminal' will not think of himself as having committed a theft, but will say he is a thief. The (partial) status of criminal offender becomes a dominant status.

A striking result of a recent evaluation of so-called 'victim-offender-conversations' is that many requests for such conversations came from offenders, although the talks were explicitly stated to have no impact upon the penal process whatsoever (and sometimes are requested after the offender has been sentenced). So even without any hope for diminished punishment many offenders feel the desire to explain their actions to their victims and to apologise (one of the stated aims of the talks) (Van Garsse, 2012).

Restorative procedures in general have as a pre-condition that the offenders who are addressed in the intake-stage acknowledge the basic facts of the criminal offence and are willing to take responsibility for the harmful consequences of their wrongful act. In this way a situation is created in which the offender can do two things at the same time (Duff, 2001; 2002): he can accept ownership and responsibility and at the same time he can dis-own his conduct and declare that this type of conduct is not typical for him: 'I am sorry I stole from you and I am not a thief.' In this way and by proposing and accepting several obligations to 'morally repair' the wrong and 'factually restore' the harm as well as possible, he can limit the damaging impact of his wrong act on his personal identity, which is in fact in the interest of the common good (Blad, 2011).

Fundamental in the restorative philosophy and practice is to avoid defining the person of the offender by his offence. It is the harmful act that is morally rejected, not the person of the offender. This arrangement makes it possible to avoid the attribution of a criminal identity to the person of the offender or to weaken this identity if it was already formed or in the process of formation: the offender can demonstrate how he relates now to his offence, which becomes an objectified historical life-event, the implications of which can be discussed with others. The offender is not made responsible in a passive way — by making him suffer the pain of punishment but actively responsible for restoring the harmful consequences to the best of his abilities.

The moral censure that is implicitly and explicitly communicated in restorative procedures, in combination with restorative obligations laid down in a consensual agreement, mean that restorative procedures are inherently sanctioning wrongful behaviour, while avoiding the ascription of a criminal identity. This avoidance is in the common interest, since fully formed criminal identities are expected and will allow themselves to keep on committing crimes, as is clearly demonstrated in 'desistance'-studies.

It should be noted that opening up and offering restorative procedures (in many categories of criminal offences) is necessary to achieve the type of bifurcated criminal justice that Van Stokkom proposes in this volume. For the choice of the type of penalty and to assess the offender's amenability to rehabilitation we require information about his degree of self-control, his empathy to the victim, his willingness to undergo rehabilitation, and many other subjective factors. (This volume, *Chapter 8,* 'Examining the offender's soul')

Van Stokkom agrees with Steven Tudor who claims that we need to respect the offender's moral autonomy and dignity, and that it is precisely this respect that requires us to pay attention to the moral attitudes of wrongdoers:

> To ignore a person's remorse can be to shun a fundamentally important aspect of his moral self, and can manifest a fundamental disrespect (this volume, *Chapter 8,* 'Facilitating the Offender's Soul').

Responsible and remorseful offenders deserve to receive only non-custodial sanctions, but for a reliable intersubjective evaluation of the offender's attitude towards his offence we need to follow voluntary restorative procedures (Blad, 2011).

This line of reasoning shows another important implication of integrating restorative justice into the criminal justice system: the categories of offences which the legislator pre-selects for restorative procedures will be those that can in general be sanctioned sufficiently with only non-custodial sanctions.[26] This is not to say that we should decide this question based on our actual

---

26. By preferably those proposed by the parties as a result of a restorative meeting, if necessary imposed, as proposed by Walgrave, with restorative aims.

patterns of imposing prison sentences: reconsidering when incarceration is in general absolutely inevitable is implied in designing an integrated system.

Depenalisation of criminal justice

As Walgrave argues, the satisfaction offered by the offender to the victim can be interpreted as a moral form of 'inverse retribution': the offender 'pays back' his ' just dues' to the victim.[27] When this goal of the restorative procedure is achieved judicial authorities should be obliged to take account of this in their formal decisions about the case. Should this not be so, the moral and functional merits of the restorative procedure would be annulled. The 'contractual' obligations included in the agreement can easily be recognised and accepted as equivalents of the non-custodial sanctions that are widely available nowadays for both public prosecutors and courts. The important change that is brought about by following restorative procedure is that, when agreed obligations are proposed to the judicial authorities, the legitimacy of approving these proposals will be almost complete, especially when and because the victim in the case is one of the parties proposing to take the agreement as sufficient sanction. Importantly, voices in the media of 'surrogate victims' demanding firm punishments can then be contradicted by the expressed opinions of the real victim in the case and the authority can show itself to be really responsive on the grounds of the detailed agreement by the parties involved. Additionally imposing the condition that the offender fully complies with the agreement will in most cases be sufficient. All this amounts to an opportunity to 'depenalise' — in the meaning of deescalation of punishment (Council of Europe, 1980) — an important part of criminal justice.

That the greater good can be served by a successful and officially sanctioned restorative procedure seems evident: the restorative procedure is inherently communicating censure and the offender works consciously towards a future without relapse and new victimisations. Succeeding in this the offender will

---

27. But it could maybe better be argued, on historical grounds, that making apology and compensating for damages is retribution, and the state's monopoly of violence is a surrogate form of retribution: often defended because in history sometimes 'compositions' and restitutive agreements did not follow or were not complied with, leading to revenge and sometimes feuds. How often this happened, and under which specific conditions, might be worthy of research.

receive rewards facilitating the development of a (more) positive self-image and social re-integration. The legally facilitated and supported restorative procedures can in this way become the workshops for 'smithing' (Maruna, 2001) the 'normal' law-abiding citizen we would like to see as our neighbour, avoiding the most destructive sanction of imprisonment.

Civilised justice and functionality

Van Stokkom, Walgrave and Reggio all claim that it is an ethical choice and even a duty to install a restorative kind of criminal justice. The latter does so explicitly referring to the 'open and relational' image of man, which Elias deduced from his civilisation study, and the need for a permanent communication between humans in search for truth which means that 'each person is responsible for searching for those contents that, given a certain context, provide the best reasons.' This attitude to knowledge supports a 'relational concept of humanity', because the search for truth is then not solipsistic but structurally open to dialogue. This has important ethical implications:

> In the search for truth, no human being is superfluous; no human being can be silenced or set free from asking and providing reasons; and no one, in fact, is provided with definitive reasons or arguments for claiming that another human life is meaningless and therefore able to be treated as though it was an 'object'. Indigence requires from each person a constant attitude to dialogue and it means that all human beings are reciprocal to each other and mutually involved as subjects entitled to ask questions and offer answers. Denying this dialogical principle embodies both a contradiction (denying the condition of indigence) and an act of violence. (See Reggio, this volume, *Chapter 10*, under 'The "Indigence of Truth", etc.')

Applied to questions of crime and punishment the 'dialogical principle' means that crime can be viewed as a serious form of denial of the same principle:

> It represents a violent act through which someone states his/her own will as absolute, and imposes (violently or with fraud) upon someone else undesired consequences (without considering each other's reasons in a dialogical way). (See Reggio, this volume, *Chapter 10* under 'Implications of the Dialogical Principle')

Crime embodies both a personal and an inter-personal violation. It is therefore inappropriate to view crime entirely in terms of a specific legal violation that is sanctioned with a form of punishment regulated by penal law. The criminal conduct is non-legitimate not only because it infringes a certain legal order: it is intrinsically wrong because (and only if) it becomes anti-dialogical as a result.[28] It requires a response not just because it is illegal, but because acquiescence to crime assumes the unacceptable ethical meaning of validating violence. This principle means that the reaction to crime cannot assume forms which themselves violate the dialogical principle. It should avoid the self-absolutism[29] of the crime and also avoid imitating the violent act itself.

The first element that the reaction to crime should incorporate is the attempt to re-balance the violation of mutual respect and dialogical reciprocity that the crime created: this includes the necessity to re-empower the victim and to ask the offender to give reasons for his behaviour. This means that indeed the reaction to crime ought to be participatory and designed to allow a dialogue between the various stakeholders.

The second element is to respect and treat the offender as a responsible and relational being including the dialogical dimension. A reparative approach to the reaction to crime then appears to be the most suitable reaction, because it neither seeks to imitate violence through retaliation, nor aims in some way at 'transforming' the offender in ways that supposedly respond to the need for recreating a certain social order. In the process of responding to a crime the situation of dialogue and mutuality should be restored to repair the damage caused, but also in order to ameliorate the social situation(s) that generated the offence(s).

The ethical merits of Reggio's approach, I hope, will easily be recognized. But it should be noticed that there are strong indications in research that restorative practices, performed well, can have remarkable effects in preventing recidivism. The ethical choice is, in other words, also a functional one.

---

28. i.e. the relation is no longer based on dialogue but on force. See Reggio under heading 'Implications of the Dialogical Principle, etc.' in *Chapter 10* of this volume.

29. i.e. the character of any action that is performed without consideration of any interests, feelings or the needs of others.

The general picture rising from the empirical evaluations of effects is that there is less recidivism, that the time between the restorative intervention and the relapse is comparatively longer and that offenders relapse, when they do, into less serious forms of criminal offending (Morris and Maxwell, 2001; Sherman and Strang, 2007; Shapland, *et al.* 2008). Of course this type of research is full of methodological problems and pitfalls but one can hardly escape from the impression that treating and approaching people humanely and decently[30] increases the likelihood of future norm-respecting conduct. Morris and Maxwell concluded with regard to juvenile offenders (in New Zealand) that family group conferences contribute to the lessening of future re-offending (even when other important intervening variables are taken into account) when young people 'are having a conference that is memorable, not being made to feel a bad person, feeling involved in the conference decision-making, agreeing with the conference outcome, completing the tasks agreed to, feeling sorry for what they had done, meeting the victim and apologising to him/her, and feeling that they had repaired the damage' (Morris and Maxwell, 2001: 261). Strikingly, more or less the same conclusion was drawn with regard to adult offenders in the UK, by Shapland *et al.*:

> The way in which the offender had experienced the conference did relate to decreased subsequent offending. In particular, the extent to which the offenders felt the conference had made them realise the harm done; whether the offender wanted to meet the victim; the extent to which the offender was observed to be actively involved in the conference; and how useful offenders felt the conference had been, were all significantly and positively related to decreased subsequent reconviction.

A possible theoretical interpretation is also given for this phenomenon:

---

30. Decency implies here above all the avoidance of a merely instrumental approach that does not see nor value the equal human being in the offender, an equal with legitimate desires and wishes. The Dutch legal scholar Pompe (1928) warned in this respect that the personality (of the offender like every other) is full of secrets, 'one can only guess about, with very little chance of guessing right and much danger of arbitrariness'. See W. P. I. Pompe (1928), p. 3. (My translation).

…the value of restorative justice conferences in promoting desistance in adult offenders: where offenders have decided to try and stop offending, a conference can increase motivation to desist (because of what victims and supporters said) and provide the support offenders may need to help tackle problems to their offending (Shapland *et al.*, 2008: iv.)

In their research synthesis of police-led conferencing Sherman and Strang (2007) mentioned three examples of conferencing projects that appeared to deliver counterproductive results. The three examples all are characterized by a (context of) communication of disrespect, not only for offences, but more importantly, for offenders (Sherman and Strang, 2007: 74 ff.).

References

Blad J. R. and De Doelder, H (2008), 'Rechtshandhaving door het Openbaar Ministerie' in J. R. Blad (ed.) *Strafrechtelijke Rechtshandhaving, Aspecten en actoren voor het academisch onderwijs belicht* (2nd. edition). Den Haag: Boom Juridische Uitgevers, 105–131.

Blad J. R. (2008), 'Strafrechtelijke Rechtshandhaving' in J. R. Blad (ed.) *Strafrechtelijke Rechtshandhaving*. Den Haag: Boom Juridische Uitgevers, 21–42.

Blad, J. R. (2011), 'Het sanctieconcept van het herstelrecht', *Sancties, Tijdschrift over straffen en maatregelen*, 4, 232–250.

Blad, J. R. (2012), 'Herstelrecht en civilisering van de strafrechtspleging' in Marie-Claire Foblets, Mireille Hildebrandt & Jacques Steenbergen (eds.), *Liber Amicorum René Foqué*. Gent/Den Haag: Larcier/Boom Juridische Uitgevers, 169–188.

Boom, A. ten, Kuijpers, K. F. and Moene M. H. (2008), *Behoeften van slachtoffers van delicten*. WODC reeks Onderzoek en Beleid, 262. Den Haag: Boom Juridische Uitgevers.

Boutellier, Hans (2002), *De Veiligheidsutopie*. Den Haag, Boom Juridische Uitgevers.

Boutellier, Hans (2004), *The Safety Utopia. Contemporary Discontent and Desire as to Crime and Punishment*. Dordrecht: Kluwer Academic Publishers.

Braithwaite, J. and Pettit P. (1990), *Not Just Deserts. A Republican Theory of Criminal Justice*. Oxford: Oxford University Press.

Brants, C. and Brants K. (2002), 'Vertrouwen en achterdocht. De driehoeksver-houding justitie-media-burger', *Justitiële Verkenningen*, jrg. 28, 6, 8–28.

Bunt, H. G. van de and Van Swaaningen R. (2004), 'Van criminaliteitsbestri-jding naar angstmanagement' in Muller, E. R. (ed.) *Veiligheid. Studies over inhoud, organisatie en maatregelen.* Alphen aan de Rijn: E.M. Meijer Instituut/Kluwer.

Claessen, Jacques (2010), *Misdaad en straf, een herbezinning op het strafrecht vanuit mystiek perspectief.* Nijmegen: Wolf Legal Publishers.

Christie, Nils (1981), *Limits to Pain.* Oxford: Martin Robertson.

Cornwell, David (2009), *The Penal Crisis and the Clapham Omnibus*, Sherfield-on-Loddon, UK: Waterside Press.

Council of Europe (1980), *Report on Decriminalisation.* Strasbourg: Expert Com-mittee on Decriminalisation.

Dijk, Jan J. M. van (2006), 'The Mark of Abel: Reflections on the Social Label-ling of Victims of Crime'. Inaugural lecture, Tilburg: Intervict.

De Keijser, J. W. (2000), *Punishment and Purpose: From Moral Theory to Punish-ment in Action.* Leiden: Thela Thesis.

Doelder, H. de (2011), 'Minimumstraffen en de scheiding der machten', *Sancties. Tijdschrift over straffen en maatregelen*, 337–346.

Duff, R. A. (2001), *Punishment, Communication and Community.* Oxford: Oxford University Press.

Duff, R. A. (2002), 'Restorative Punishment and Punitive Restoration' in Lode Walgrave (ed.) *Restorative Justice and the Law.* Devon, Cullompton: Wil-lan Publishing, 82–100.

Dupont, Lieven (1979), *Beginselen voor een behoorlijke strafrechtsbedeling.* Antwer-pen/Arnhem: Kluwer/Gouda Quint.

Elias, Norbert (2000), *The Civilising Process. Sociogenetic and Psychogenetic Inves-tigations.* Revised edn. edited by Eric Dunning, Johan Goudsbloem and Stephen Mennel. Oxford: Blackwell Publishers.

Foqué, R. and Hart, A. C. 't (1990a), *Instrumentaliteit en rechtsbescherming.* Arn-hem/Antwerpen: Gouda Quint/Kluwer,

Foqué, R. and Hart A. C. 't (1990b), 'Strafrecht en beleid: de instrumentaliteit van rechtsbescherming' in Fijnaut C. and Spierenburg P. (eds.) *Scherp Toe-zicht.* Arnhem: Gouda Quint, 181–218.

Frehsee, Detlev, Gabi Löschper and Gerlinda Smaus (eds.), (1997) *Konstruktion der Wirklichkeit durch Kriminalität und Strafe*. Baden-Baden: Nomos Verlagsgesellschaft.

Garland, D. (1996), 'The Limits of the Sovereign State', *British Journal of Criminology*, 445–465.

Garland, D. (2001), *The Culture of Control*. Oxford: Oxford University Press.

Groenhuijsen, M. S. (2010), 'Wijziging van het sanctiestelsel, wijziging van de leeftijdsgrenzen in het strafrecht en aanscherping van de bepalingen inzake voorlopige hechtenis', *DD* , 9, 105–118.

Hallsworth, Simon (2000), 'Rethinking the Punitive Turn: Economies of Excess and the Criminology of the Other', *Punishment & Society*, vol. 2 (2), 145–160.

Hartmann, A. R. (2008), 'De procespositie van de verdachte en de Wet OM-afdoening: een passende verandering?' in Blad J. R. (ed.), *Strafrechtelijke rechtshandhaving: aspecten en actoren voor het academisch onderwijs belicht*, (2nd. edn). Den Haag: Boom Juridische Uitgevers, 133–155.

Hulsman, L. H. C. (1981), 'Waarover beslist men eigenlijk in het strafrechtelijk system?' in *Beginselen: opstellen aangeboden aan G. E. Mulder*. Arnhem: Gouda Quint, 107–116.

Hulsman, L. H. C. (1968), 'De strafrechtelijke sanctie en zijn maat', *Wijsgerig Perspectief*, 207–232.

Hulsman, L. H. C. (1979), 'Een abolitionistisch (afschaffend) perspectief op het strafrechtelijk systeem' in *Problematiek van de strafrechtspraak*. Baarn: Bosch en Keuning, 50–73.

Kelk, C. (2011), 'Strafrecht in de maalstroom van de tijd: van humaan naar hardvochtig' in Spapens, T., Groenhuijsen, M. and Kooijmans T. (eds.), *Universalis, Liber Amicorum Cyrille Fijnaut*. Antwerpen/Cambridge: Intersentia, 153–166.

King, Michael, Arie Freiberg, Becky Batagol, Ross Hyams (eds.) (2009), *Non-Adversarial Justice*. Sydney: The Federation Press.

Klip, A. H. (2010) 'Totaalstrafrecht', *DD*, 34,

Knigge, G. (1988), *'Het irrationele van de straf'*. Inaugural lecture. Arnhem: Gouda Quint.

Lissenberg, Elisabeth (2005), 'Een elite voor herstelrecht', *Tijdschrift voor Herstelrecht*, (5), 3, 3–4.

Maruna, Shadd (2001), *Making Good: How Ex-convicts Reform and Rebuild their Lives*. E-book, Wolters-Kluwer.

Mevis, P. A. M. (2008), 'De positie van de strafrechter' in Blad, J. R. (ed.), *Strafrechtelijke rechtshandhaving*. Den Haag: Boom Juridische Uitgevers, 177–218.

Mooren, J. H. (2001), 'Recht maken wat krom is: herstelbemiddeling in het perspectief van zingeving', *Tijdschrift voor Herstelrecht*, 2, 26–36.

Morris, A. and G. Maxwell (2001), *Restorative Justice for Juveniles Conferencing, Mediation & Circles*. Oxford and Portland (OR): Hart Publishing.

Otte, M. (2002), 'Reële kansen en kansloze verwachtingen van de straf in een veranderende samenleving. Schuld en boete in de sleutel van een ruim vergeldingsbegrip', *DD*, 943–957.

Packer, H. L. (1968), *The Limits of the Criminal Sanction*. Stanford: Stanford University Press.

Pompe, W. P. I. (1928), *De persoon des daders in het strafrecht*. Utrecht/Nijmegen: Dekker & Van de Vegt.

Pompe, W. P. I. (1954), 'De misdadige mens', *Tijdschrift voor Strafrecht*, 153–171.

Pratt, John (2005), 'Elias, Punishment and Decivilization' in Pratt, J., Brown, D., Brown, M., Hallsworth S and Morrison W. (eds.), *The New Punitiveness: Trends, Theories, Perspectives*. Devon, Cullompton: Willan Publishing, 256–271.

Quinney, Richard (1970), *The Social Reality of Crime*. Boston: Little, Brown and Company.

Ruller, S. Van (1986), 'Honderd jaar vrijheidsbeneming in cijfers' in De Jong, D. H., Van der Neut, J. L. and Tulkens, J. J. J. (eds.), *De vrijheidsstraf*. Arnhem: Gouda Quint, 57–76.

Shapland, J. *et al* (2008), *Restorative Justice: Does Restorative Justice Affect Reconvictions?* The Fourth report from the evaluation of three schemes. Ministry of Justice Research Series, 10/08, Ministry of Justice, UK.

Sherman, L. and H. Strang (2007), *Restorative Justice: The Evidence*. Report to the Smith Institute London (www).

Simon, Jonathan (2001), 'Entitlement to Cruelty: The End of Welfare and the Punitive Mentality in the United States' in Stenson K and Sullivan, R. R. (eds.), *Crime, Risk and Justice: The Politics of Crime Control in Liberal Democracies*. Devon, Cullompton: Willan Publishing, 125–143.

Stevens, L. (2012), 'Voorlopige hechtenis in tijden van risicomanagement. Lijdende of leidende beginselen?', *DD* 2012/36, 382–405.

Struijk, S. (2008), 'Rechtshandhaving en veelplegers: ontwikkeling van drang naar dwang' in Blad J. R. (ed.) *Strafrechtelijke rechtshandhaving*. Den Haag: Boom Juridische Uitgevers, 345–370.

Swaaningen, R. van (1997), 'Beginselen van strafrecht in een risicomaatschappij' in Blad J. R. and Mevis, P. A. M. (eds.), *Het gelijkheidsbeginsel*. Deventer: Gouda Quint, 53–68.

Swaaningen, R. van (2009), 'Fear and the Trade-off Between Security and Liberty' in M. Hildebrandt, A. Makinwa, A. Oehmichen (eds.), *Controlling Security in a Culture of Fear*. Den Haag: Boom Legal Publishers, 47–56.

't Hart, A. C. (1983), 'Strafrecht: de macht van een verhaalstructuur' , in André de la Porte, E. (ed.), *Bij deze stand van zaken*. Arnhem: Gouda Quint, 181–218.

't Hart, A. C. (2001), 'Strafrecht en tv' in A. C. 't Hart, *Hier gelden wetten, over strafrecht, openbaar ministerie en multiculturalisme*. Deventer: Gouda Quint, 131–166.

't Hart, A. C. (2004), *Openbaar ministerie en rechtshandhaving*. Arnhem: Gouda Quint.

United Nations, Office on Drugs and Crime (2006), *Handbook on Restorative Justice Programmes*, Vienna, New York, UN Criminal Justice Handbook series.

Van Garsse, Leo (2012), 'Daders en herstel: tussen plicht, behoefte en capaciteit' in Weijers, I. (ed.), *Slachtoffer-dadergesprekken in de schaduw van het strafproces*. Den Haag: Boom-Lemma, 59–72.

Van Ruller, S.(1986) 'Honderd jaar vrijheidsbeneming in cijfers' in De Jong, D. H., Van der Neut, J. L. and Tulkens, J. J. J. (eds.) *De Vrijheidsstraf*. Arnhem: Gouda Quint, 57–76.

Verrijn Stuart, H. (1994), 'Via onschuld naar macht; slachtoffers in het strafproces', *Justitiële Verkenningen*, jrg. 20, 2, 94–115.

Walgrave, Lode (2008), *Restorative Justice, Self-interest and Responsible Citizenship*. Devon, Cullompton: Willan Publishing.

Wright, Martin (1996), *Justice for Victims and Offenders: A Restorative Approach to Crime* (2nd edn.), Sherfield-on-Loddon, UK: Waterside Press.

8

Tempering Justice with Compassion: Rationales of Personal Mitigation in Sentencing

Bas van Stokkom

Introduction

In his book *Crime, Punishment and Restorative Justice* Ross London argues that the expression of remorse constitutes an important instrument for restoring trust in an offender and therefore would operate to reduce the demand of punishment (2011: 176). It is a widely accepted and well-settled legal principle that remorse should be treated as a mitigating factor in sentencing (if it is proved to the sentencing court's satisfaction). But there is comparatively little sustained explanation for its rationale, in either case law or jurisprudential commentary (Proeve and Tudor, 2010: 115).

When offenders show remorse and take responsibility, what are exactly the consequences of imposing punishment? I will argue that a 'remorse discount' is not always logical; offering a non-custodial sanction-track may sometimes be more convincing.

In justifying a sentencing discount several issues obstruct a clear discussion. The grounds on which to grant a possible discount differ. In this chapter I will try to offer more coherent reasons to legitimate less severe sentences (mitigation), be it a discount or a non-custodial sanction. Now mitigating considerations of justice can be oriented at culpability, operating within the logic of just deserts. For example when an offender has mental disabilities and therefore is deemed less accountable. But I will focus on personal mitigation factors, especially offenders who *ex-post-facto* apologise and want to make good. In considering these factors there is not always a connection with the wrongdoing, e.g. when an offender is allocated a non-custodial punishment in order to maintain his family obligations. So I will not discuss factors that mitigate gravity (harm; culpability), but only personal factors (features of the offender's personality and life circumstances).

I will try to bring more order in these factors and explicate several rationales, but I will focus on remorse. Indeed, this remorseful attitude, the 'change of heart' and the willingness to make good, is in the centre of many restorative justice theories. Although recently the debates on restorative justice have focused much attention on responsible offenders, personal mitigation is still an under-theorised aspect in punishment theory.

Many judges—and the public—do recognise the importance of personal mitigation factors, but just deserts theorists regularly object because sentencing uniformity should prevail. They tend to disqualify offender-related factors and focus on harm and culpability. For those and other reasons theories of just deserts have often been criticised (Braithwaite and Pettit, 1990). According to Michael Tonry (2011: 217) the (strong) proportionality principle has three fundamental problems. First, by giving priority to equality in suffering for 'like-situated' offenders, it often requires imposition of more severe and intrusive punishments than are required. Second, it misleadingly objectifies punishment, by allocating generic penalties and using terms as 'like-situated offenders'. Third: it ignores the problem of 'just deserts in an unjust society' (ignoring social deprivation and problems of social injustice).[1]

I will interpret the tendency to reject personal factors—as philosopher John Tasioulas does—as 'just deserts reductionism'. My contention is that 'special' concerns about the offender—mercy, tolerance, taking responsibility—are as important as 'regular' just deserts. The theory of Tasioulas opens up 'one-dimensional' accounts of retributive desert and allows varying values (just deserts, prevention, mercy) to compete under the aegis of the justified censure. Within this perspective mercy has a firm place in deliberation about criminal punishment. Now mercy has a 'baroque reputation' in

---

1. Also retributivists recognise that just deserts theory seems to be 'unremittingly in its zeal to expose individuals to the sufferings and indignities of legal punishment' (Lippke, 2009: 378). Lippke agrees that the use of strict retributivism tends to be pernicious. He pleads for various forms of reduction in punishment.

punishment theory, a 'relic of a defunct political absolutism or a religious mentality' (Tasioulas, 2003: 120). Philosopher Jeffrie Murphy refers to the modern belief that mercy must be a 'product of morally dangerous senti-mentality' (Murphy, 1988: 167). Despite these views, I will point out that mercy is a structural feature in sentencing practices.

I will re-interpret Tasioulas' theory and argue that mercy can be viewed as one aspect of a broader category of special concern and care for the offender and the persons affected (his dependants/those to whom he owes something). The several grounds for personal mitigation do have a com-mon ethical basis: by giving attention to specific interests and needs justice can be tempered with compassion. Within this perspective we can facilitate responsibility and devise individualised sentences, giving counterweight to abstract justice orthodoxies.

The question of the sentencing discount is not peripheral, as just deserts theorists would argue. It is one of the core questions in penal justice. I believe the issue of mitigation deserves more attention in the current debate on punishment and high custody levels. Christine Piper (2007) argues that populist punitiveness has led to an inflation of calculations of seriousness at policy and sentencing levels; offenders with a criminal history are often sent to prison in case of relatively minor offences. According to Piper there seems to be a reduced acceptance of mitigation factors, which prevents the 'cusp cases'—lying on the community/custodial sentence boundary—from being moved down the penalty ladder. However, Jacobson and Hough (2007) found that personal mitigation plays the largest part in tipping the balance away from the imposition of a term of custody.

Like Shapland (2011) I will argue that personal mitigation should move from the margins to the centre stage of sentencing guidance. By doing so, there can be more concern for encouraging the offender to desist from crime, as well as to make reparation. If mitigation is to play a more profound role, judicial discretion needs more structure (Jacobson and Hough, 2007). On which principles is personal mitigation based? Principled distinctions need to be made between factors that relate to unusual difficult circumstances, factors that affect the offender's suffering and factors that facilitate non-custodial sentences. Because I will focus on these mitigation rationales, the particularities of offenders are in the forefront. I will not really deal with mediation in penal matters and its negotiated outcomes (like compensation). I will only discuss sanctions as authoritative responses by the state.

In the next section I will discuss the gap between just desert orthodoxy (and its objections against individualising punishment) and sentencing practices in which personal mitigation factors do play a large role. Consequently I will briefly explore John Tasioulas' argumentation, in which censure functions as an overarching principle of justice. His theory breaks open the hierarchy of sentencing principles, counteracts just deserts and puts repentance and mercy in the centre of attention. I will then discuss some critical issues with reference to mercy and offender-characteristics. Is mercy an intrusion into judicial sentencing as philosopher Antony Duff contends? Is it reasonable to examine the offender's soul to assess remorse and other attitudinal aspects? How does mercy relate to another leniency-rationale, the principle of greater tolerance to first offenders? I will argue that the offender's willingness to apologise and take responsibility restores trust and justifies a non-custodial sanction-track. Finally the rationales of personal mitigation are presented together and the question whether social deprivation is a mitigation-factor is dealt with.

Just Deserts and Personal Mitigation: Theory Versus Practice

Some retributive thinkers are prepared to include remorse in their reasoning. Contrition and repentance can provide the grounds for genuine inner restoration: punishment aims at expiation of the wrongdoer's guilt (Garvey, 1999). Jeffrie Murphy (1997) argues that repentance can repay the victim for the blow to his dignity and erases the message of inferiority that the offender *prima facie* conveys to the victim through the criminal act. But he admits that this message will not always be absorbed by the public. The public might respond cynically: 'express remorse and escape punishment'.

But many retributivists stick to the doctrine of just deserts: offenders should be punished because they deserve it. Classical retributivism is looking backwards and is only concerned with the wrongful act. Post-offence remorse, apology, or repentance cannot lessen the culpability of the act itself. Just deserts emphasises, in the name of fairness, the standardised treatment of all offenders, so that individualised concerns with repentance (or rehabilitation or reparation) are overlooked.

Andrew von Hirsch criticises the instrumental role of punishment in securing repentance, because it threatens to undermine proportionality. Restrictions on severity in order to facilitate the achievement of penitence would sacrifice proportionality (Von Hirsch, 1993: 75–76; Von Hirsch and Ashworth, 2005: 104–105).

Likewise Antony Duff endorses a strict retributivist theory: repentance does not have a punishment-reducing significance. Deserved hard treatment is considered as an integral part of repentance: punishment enables the offender to repent through undergoing the deserved punishment as a penance. Thus, the crime, not the offender is the focus of punishment. The offender is censured for the crime committed and not for his character. Nothing the offender does or feels after the crime alters the nature and seriousness of the crime committed. Besides, Duff points out that the assessment of remorse would require an intrusive interest in the offender's inner life, as will be evident later in this chapter.

The standard arguments against mercy focus on equality. Mercy violates the rational norm of treating like cases alike and thus flouts the demands of penal justice. Mercy amounts to treating identical cases differently, showing leniency to one wrongdoer yet withholding it from another. It is unfair to those who do not receive a lenient sentence and allows unequal treatment. Moreover, excusing the offender from punishment belittles the crime and the harm done. Victim and the public interpret the failure to punish to mean that the crime is not really wrong and that the offender is free to keep doing it. Therefore we should eliminate mercy from the possible range of mitigation justifications (Markel, 2004). [2]

Retributive proportionality, as a system of uniform sentencing, necessarily shoehorns cases into crude abstract categories. But two ostensibly identical crimes can have widely different harms and consequences for their victims and other stakeholders, as offenders' families. There is no consideration of the real-life human being who committed the offence. Ensuring proportionality between the punishment and the criminal offence (if such a thing

---

[2]. From a different viewpoint, see Garvey (1999). Imposing too light a punishment can undermine the public's appreciation of the value of the victim, and the latter's self-esteem. It conveys the message that the criminal act was not, after all, so evil, thereby adding to the harm done to the victim.

is altogether possible; see Wright, 1999), means that neither the offender's characteristics nor his past conduct may legitimately be considered in determining an appropriate sanction. It follows that a remorseful offender should not be treated differently from a contemptuous, indifferent offender. And it follows that an experienced criminal should not be punished more severely than an infrequent or first-time offender. To circumvent this kind of reasoning Von Hirsch devised a theory of greater tolerance to defend mitigation for first offenders (see below). Obviously personal factors matter after all!

Just deserts theorists want us to believe that only the wrongfulness of the act and the harm to the victim matter, thereby deliberately restricting the scope of justice. They reject differential treatment between offenders based on their history of prior offending, their demonstration of remorse and rehabilitation needs. Fortunately, sentencing practices give another picture. Judges automatically take into account the content, nature and importance of personal mitigation. Remorse often has a moderating effect on the severity of sentences.

In the US remorse, although marginal in the guidelines and in proceedings, does play a far more prominent role than often is thought. When it comes to the sentencing decision, judges seem to weight expressions of remorse and apology heavily. The perceived remorse can significantly reduce the likelihood that a jury will impose severe punishments. When discussing release decisions parole boards take remorse into account (Bibas and Bierschbach, 2004).

In their overview of some common law jurisdictions Proeve and Tudor point out that the prosecutor's decisions are influenced by remorse and apology, including decisions not to charge, to accept proposed pleas and cooperation agreements, and to recommend favourable sentences (2010: 85–87). Some studies have found that offenders who deny committing serious offences receive significantly higher sentences than those who admitted guilt. Sometimes offenders who exhibited no contrition for their offence received sentences four times the length of those who were highly contrite. When offenders have an extensive prior history of alcohol use, remorse may have the opposite effect of more severe sentences: these offenders may be seen as insincere.

Jacobson and Hough (2007) examined the role of personal mitigation in sentencing in the English Crown Court. Personal mitigation takes many forms, for example relating to the offender's past (e.g. productive life; financial pressures; psychiatric problems; etc), the response to the offence (e.g. remorse, acts of reparation, willingness to address problems that led to the crime; etc) and the offender's prospects (e.g. family responsibilities; capacity to address problems; etc.).[3] The authors conclude that personal mitigation plays an important part in the sentencing decision. 'It can be the decisive factor in choosing a community penalty in preference to imprisonment … In just under a third of the 127 cases where the judge made the role of mitigation explicit, personal mitigation was a major — usually the major — factor which pulled the sentence back from immediate custody ' (2007: vii) .

Does the public share the judiciary's tendency to take into account personal mitigation, when the offending is serious? Research on public opinion and personal mitigation shows that the effects of personal mitigation on sentence are sometimes quite significant (Hough *et al*, 2009).

Although offence related factors dominate in assessing aggravation,[4] and there is less consensus among respondents in justifying mitigation, there is widespread support for taking into account these factors. The background, circumstances and individual 'story' of the offender are deemed to be critical factors that should feed into the sentencing decision. When examining mitigating factors, most respondents seem to display an attachment to individualised sentencing and are willing to take personal factors into account. 'The public tends to attach weight to personal mitigation, even if they are disinclined to regard specific factors as universally applicable' (2009: 54). There is strong public support for considering an appeal to leniency on behalf of the victim and there is a significant level of acceptance of alternative sanctions. Two thirds of the public believes a community sentence is justified (definitely or probably) in the absence of previous convictions,

---

3. Jacobson and Hough (2007: see table 2.3. at 13).
4. The authors stress that aggravating factors are offence- rather than offender-related, and are seen as more generally applicable (as a matter of principle) to sentencing decisions. Offender-related mitigating factors are by definition highly contextual and less clear. They depend heavily on personal and case characteristics which cannot be specified in advance.

even in cases of a serious assault. Other important offender-related factors are: 'offender caring for children', 'offender remorse' and 'offender is young'.

In an American study Gromet and Darley (2006) found that respondents sent a majority of low-seriousness cases to restorative procedures. As crimes increase in seriousness, respondents sent a majority of cases to a mixed procedure (retributive and restorative), even though they had the option to use the traditional court system. This suggests that in case of an offence of a serious nature people are willing to allow also restorative measures. The more potential they see for the offender to be rehabilitated, the more likely they are to apply restorative measures. This is consistent with the finding that people who are most supportive of restorative measures are the ones who believe in the possibility of rehabilitating offenders. By contrast, there may be offenders who are thought of as 'un-rehabilitative', who regardless of the seriousness of crime, will not be qualified for restorative measures (Gromet and Darley, 2006).

We may conclude that criminal law professionals accord much weight to personal mitigation factors, also expressions of remorse. Bibas and Bierschbach offer a convincing answer: 'In the eyes of judges, they indicate that an offender is not 'lost', that he has some self-transformative capacity that justifies (or requires) a lesser punishment.'(2004: 94). Concerning public opinion, we may conclude that people's intuitive judgments depend not only on the wrongfulness of the act, but also on their assessment of the actor's attitudes and other contextual factors, including the possible damage of the punishment to the web of people and relationships.

Beyond Just Deserts Reductionism: Tasioulas' Theory

According to John Tasioulas just deserts theory tries to sideline mercy and other considerations in order to save the consistency rationale. But this primacy of consistency and predictability is misplaced. 'The long history of philosophical disputation about punishment teaches us that a cut-and-paste assembly of disparate principles is the best we can realistically hope for' (2006: 282).

Tasioulas is in favour of value pluralism within an overarching structure of communicating censure for wrongdoing. He regards the communication of justified censure (through hard treatment) as the general justifying aim of punishment.[5] So punishment is not merely the communication of deserved blame. This retributive norm of just deserts is a fundamental norm, but it is not the only one. We should not allow just deserts to take up all the space of penal justification at the expense of other values as crime prevention and mercy.

Tasioulas offers a revised communicative theory, in which the formal end of condemnation encompasses many values. Desert is a fundamental, but not necessarily exhaustive, determinant of what punishment is justified. Desert may determine the just quantum of punishment only within a broad range. Even when the circumstances of the crime are fully specified it is not possible to determine the exact punishment that is proportionate to crime. Of course this indeterminacy does not render the idea of just desert vacuous. Considering fairness (treating like cases alike) and ordinal scaling remain instructive.

But Tasioulas' formal theory of communicative censure does not equate justified punishment with deserved punishment. There are other considerations. So mercy can have a bearing on justified punishment independently of any impact on judgments of desert. Also preventative considerations can play a role in determining the amount and type of punishment to be inflicted in particular cases.

When discussing which amount of punishment is justified, there is a conflict between reasons of desert to punish and reasons of mercy to show leniency. There may be 'an unavoidable sense of excess in insisting on the full infliction of the deserved hard treatment' (Tasioulas, 2006: 318). A decent concern for the offender's welfare can justify us in tempering the punishment deserved. So Tasioulas argues that it is perfectly legitimate to widen one's field of vision beyond the wrongful act—to take account of the nature of the agent and his broader circumstances.

Repentance is a central consideration within the communicative enterprise aimed at conveying justified censure for wrong-doing (and resists being

---

5. Within retributive theories hard treatment is supposed to communicate justified censure for the offender's wrongdoing. I think 'hard treatment' is a fallacious term because it suggests that sanctions should be threatening and that moral learning (facing-up to what you have done) is not important (Van Stokkom, 2005). I prefer 'burdening'. As I will argue later on, we may conceive two sanction-tracks that both involve burdens, one disciplining, the other restoring.

subsumed under the norm of retributive desert). Repentance is the experience of the burdens of guilt, 'burdens that can dominate a person's mental horizon, sapping their capacity to engage with what ordinarily gives life its value' (Tasioulas, 2007: 493). By repenting the offender re-integrates himself with the moral values and works towards healing the rift with the community by the work of apology, reparation and moral regeneration. It is the intrinsically correct response by the wrongdoer, a righting of one's wrongdoing, not just a change for the better in its aftermath.

Tasioulas contends that 'antecedent repentance', manifested prior to the infliction of punishment, figures as a *pro tanto* ground for mercy to the offender, a reason, for inflicting a more lenient punishment (Tasioulas, 2006: 316–321). On the other hand, punishment could help spark in the offender the remorseful recognition of his wrongdoing that leads him to undergo his punishment as a penance (Tasioulas, 2007: 496). But a consistent proponent of punishment as repentance should reject all forms of punishment that inhibit the willingness to reconsider one's wrongdoing. Custody but also 'shaming' punishments, in terms of Tasioulas, are 'deficient both as a penance and as a means for encouraging repentance' (2007: 496). 'Subjection to the scornful gaze of others … is more likely to inhibit, rather than facilitate, the offender's development of a penitent understanding of his deed' (2007: 497). For that reason sentencing authorities should select forms of punishment which are judged more likely to foster the offender's repentance. The sentencing authority should select 'among equally deserved punishments, that which would be more effective in inducing a penitent state' (2007 *idem*). In this way Tasioulas is more realistic than other expiation theorists.[6]

Tasioulas criticises the notion of repentance as self-inflicted punishment. In this view (Murphy, 1997; Nozick, 1981) it may be obligatory to show leniency to the repentant offender, because we can take the exhibited repentance as a form of suffering. This can in turn be seen as punishment he has already undergone. This argument suffers from two difficulties: first it lacks

---

6. Retributivists like Duff who set a premium on expiation tend to take no account of the adverse effects of regular imprisonment (and seem unaware of labelling theory). Most convicts develop a hardened attitude, as Nietzsche emphasised. Punishment intensifies the feeling of alienation and strengthens resistance. In effect, it is the practice of punishment itself which hinders the development of a sense of guilt (Van Stokkom, 2005).

an imposed burden, and secondly it lacks a public meaning accessible to the victim and the wider community (2007: 504, 505).

Tasioulas' theory of communication enables us to view repentance as a ground for mercy. Mercy is responsive to the plight of the wrongdoer and 'embraces reasons for leniency that arise out of a charitable concern with the well-being of the offender' (2006: 312).[7]

Merciful acts are not discretionary or 'gift-like' as is often assumed, nor is mercy distinguished from justice by its 'particularity'. Tasioulas (2007) masterfully shows why these 'dogmas' are implausible and explains why judges have an obligation to grant mercy to offenders in appropriate cases.[8] Of course this obligation possibly conflicts with the obligation to impose the deserved punishment. Tasioulas adds that the interest of the offender alone is not sufficient to create a duty to grant mercy. 'Mercy is a great common good, one that makes our communal life more humane' (2003: 128).

Mercy offers reasons for the suspension or reduction of a penalty. What sorts of facts provide grounds for mercy and wherein lies their normative significance? Tasioulas (2003) addresses four.

1. The offender's history and upbringing; the formidable obstacles he may have encountered to forming a decent and law-abiding character.
2. Cases that pose unusually severe obstacles to law-abiding behaviour (for example, the plight of a battered woman).
3. Offenders who suffered a grave misfortune which will be cruelly exacerbated by the infliction in full measure of his just deserts (e.g. losing your child as a result of drink-driving).
4. Offender repented his wrong-doing.

The general idea behind these grounds is that the imposition of the sentence warranted by the retributive norm is an excessive hardship. Their salience consists in their bearing on a humanitarian concern, one that looks

---

7. Compare Bibas, 2007: mercy does not obliterate the need to punish. But although the offender deserves punishment, mercy may lessen the deserved punishment (see also Bibas and Bierschbach, 2004).
8. The offender cannot earn mercy and has no subsequent right to mercy. At most offenders might have a right to present a case for mercy (Bibas, 2007).

to the impact of a proposed punishment on the offender's well-being in the light of their prior moral conduct, life history and the broader context of their wrongdoing (2003: 119). It is harsh and, at the limit, cruel in such cases to communicate the full extent of censure that would have been warranted.

Personal Factors and Leniency: Criticism and Contra-criticism

Tasioulas' hybrid theory allows taking into account remorse and other personal factors in sentencing decisions. That is an attractive starting point because in practice sentencers have to select and combine varying and sometimes conflicting punishment considerations. However, and not surprisingly, his theory, and many other accounts of sentencing leniency, have induced a lot of criticism. I will deal with two issues: the intrusion of mercy in judicial sentencing, and the examination of the offender's soul. Consequently I will argue that mercy is but one of the leniency rationales. Condoning a 'lapse' of an offender without prior convictions is another. Andrew von Hirsch recognises the importance of this justification of personal mitigation and tries to integrate this rationale in his model of retributive desert.

The intrusion of mercy

Could mercy play a proper role in the criminal justice system? Duff's answer is clear: mercy 'intrudes' into the criminal process. Punishment must aspire to be a process of communication from the offender to those he wronged. The communicative aim of punishment is to bring the offender to face up, to focus on the wrong he has done, as something he should repent. By contrast, mercy focuses on what the offender himself has suffered. It cannot communicate an appropriate message to the victims.

Moreover, the sentencer has no reason to mitigate the punishment, since whilst repentance motivates to undertake reparative action, it cannot affect the wrongdoing. The repentant offender deserves no less severe a punishment than the unrepentant offender. There is no reason to mitigate. Duff concludes: 'The claims of mercy conflict irremediably with the demands of justice' (2007: 387).[9]

---

9.   Duff (1993) stresses that (later occurring) repentance does not make the crime less serious. The same is true for the defiant criminal: defiance does not make the crime worse.

However, Duff argues, sometimes the sentencer should have her eyes open for the offender's suffering. When the depth and intensity of an offender's repentance is obvious, a sentencer, as human person, might reasonably be moved to leniency. But still mercy cannot operate within the perspective of criminal punishment; it is not a virtue of sentencers but rather a virtue of human beings. In other words: as persons, sentencers can and should feel sympathy and compassion, but these feelings are irrelevant to the performance of their role as sentencers.

So Duff tries to sustain the claim that mercy is only discretionary. By contrast, Tasioulas tries to convince us that mercy can and should be obligatory. Only a duty to grant mercy could possess normative force needed to justify deviation from the judge's duty to implement justice. He defends a legal duty for judges to show mercy in sentencing when undefeated grounds for it obtain (2003: 129). This duty to grant mercy concerns a subclass of (unusual) cases in which offenders find themselves in miserable circumstances. This means that judges are not required to show mercy in cases where no grounds for it obtain. There is no potential overburdening of punishers.[10]

Tasioulas recognises that procedural fairness will be violated. But 'it may be judged worth the cost of introducing an element of inconstancy into the penal system if it is thereby rendered more humane' (2003: 130). Seen from this perspective, mercy should properly play a role in the criminal process. Protecting human worth should be part of the criminal justice institution. For example, it cannot tolerate verdicts that amass public suffering upon grave private suffering.

Another relevant point in Duff's reply to Tasioulas is that liberal law involves abstraction. Therefore sentencers should not allow the assessment of changes within the conduct of the offender and the examination of other concrete particularities of the individual offender and the social context from which his offence emerged. Duff recognises that abstraction involves

---

10. Proeve and Tudor (2010) distinguish a strong version (remorse must always be a mitigating factor; eliminate discretion) from a weak version (remorse may be treated as a mitigating factor: large degree of discretion). They opt for a middle ground position: remorse should be a mitigating factor in a limited range of cases. A failure to consider personal mitigating factors requires explanation (in a fully articulated set of reasons for sentence). This preserves judicial discretion, but within certain constraints. This middle ground version both reflects settled law and practice and seems to be the more plausible approach.

a source of individual injustice. And he also recognises that individualised particularities constantly irrupt into the law, thus destroying its pretensions to rational coherence. But still, he prefers the law's abstract reasoning. He seems to accept that this view brings along an impoverished discourse of censuring that eliminates the articulation of human circumstances, including the ways how the offender has processed guilt and accounts for the harm done. The abstract censure he pleads for contains messages without many opportunities to internalise moral norms. Remarkably, this contrasts Duff's plea for two-way communication. Viewed from that angle one might expect that the censure is not only about crime categories and punishment measures, but also made to a particular human being who has to face up to what he has done (see Van Stokkom, 2007).[11]

Examining the offender's soul

Duff stresses that the criminal law has to respect its citizens' privacy. A liberal system of criminal law should not allow an inquiry into the defendant's life and character. Judges should only attend to those factors that the law defines as directly relevant to guilt (2007: 376).

Von Hirsch expresses similar arguments: the liberal state may impose a penalty on the offender as a means of moral censure, but it may not require any attitudinal response to that censure because, if it did, the personal autonomy of the subject would be violated. Requiring or even encouraging defendants to apologise for their conduct would extend the reach of authority of the state beyond its legitimate function of controlling harmful behaviour and would become intrusive into a person's autonomy (Von Hirsch, 1993: 82, 84).

Encouraging offenders to acknowledge and repudiate their crimes is seen by many liberals as an invasion of conscience. Generally liberals have trouble with what they call 'penetrating the criminal's soul' (Markel, 2004). The

---

11. It seems that many desert theorists inconsistently switch between abstract and concrete ways of reasoning. On the one hand they devise objective measures of penal deservedness. But on the other hand they focus at individual blameworthiness and its particularised judgments about moral responsibility (self-defence, knowing, mental illness, duress, etc.). If punishment is principally related to blaming, Tonry says, it is relevant 'whether the offender was mentally impaired, socially disadvantaged, a reluctant participant, or moved by human motives' (Tonry, 2011: 229).

examination of the offender's character is deemed tricky and could undermine individual autonomy. Indeed, 'character' is a tricky question. Punishing character, Nigel Walker says, is 'to engage in moral book-keeping, using previous records as an index of total moral worth' (cited in Bagaric, 2000).

There are good reasons to limit the scope of the criminal law to the conduct of the offender rather than to his thoughts and beliefs. As Tasioulas says (2007: 487) we should not embrace a 'character' version of retribution (see Murphy, 1997) which would require that the state delves into the privacy of its citizens to make an exhaustive accounting of features of our lives that form part of our moral characters. This means that sentencers should focus on the outer features of attitudes, as apologising, rather than the inner moral state of the offender.[12]

How to justify attitudinal considerations? London (2011: 200) offers two important reasons. First, demonstrations of attitudinal change, including apology and the expression of remorse, are never required. Evaluation of attitudes may be made, including the offender's personality, but only if the offender agrees. For example, he may refuse to answer any questions that may be incriminating, but also waive the rights against self-incrimination when it appears in his best interest to do so. So offenders may apologise voluntarily if they believe it is in their interest to do so. In sum, what is morally objectionable is not the assessment of specific attitudes, but the possibility that the state will coerce an individual into adopting an attitude that contradicts his values and beliefs.

Second, liberal criminal sentencing does not bar considerations of an offender's attitudes. Personal factors are relevant in devising adequate sanctions (London, 2011: 200). To assess which type of punishment is suitable, and to assess the offender's amenability to rehabilitation we require information

---

12. Often liberals resort to cheap rhetoric. For example, Lippke (2008) portrays state officials as inquisition fanatics, intruding the rights of offenders. In the words of Tudor: 'he paints the picture of untrustworthy legal officials probing the moral souls of hapless offenders who languish in their grip for indeterminate periods.' (Tudor, 2008: 271). In reality much of the so-called 'intrusive' monitoring is already in place in the form of parole boards and with good reasons: checking improvements in self-reform, work-attitudes, responsible conduct, etc. There is little disturbing in this: it is routine for parole boards and sentencing courts to assess offenders' self-perceptions, attitudes, behavioural patterns, etc.

about his degree of self-control, his empathy to the victim, his willingness to undergo rehabilitation, and many other subjective factors.[13]

In other words, the judge has to take into account offender attitudes, just as she takes the social circumstances of offenders and their families into account. If you adhere to the principle that the offender 'has to learn a lesson' it is good to know if he has learning disadvantages or lacks self-control. Moreover: suppose the judge does not take into account the offender's motives, attitudes and social situation. This would stimulate the offender to cope with the imposed sanction in cynical and indifferent ways and to make no effort to respond positively.

Another argument that is often raised is that taking account of remorse would reward those offenders who succeed in displaying the appropriate sentiments. Concerning the problem that many offenders portray themselves as less blameworthy than they are, there is an adequate reply: we can trust judges to discern sincerity and honesty. Besides, other moral states such as the credibility of witnesses are also not easy to verify. The assessment of these states always brings along practical fact-finding problems (Bibas and Bierschbach, 2004: 142).[14]

Of course we need to protect offenders against close supervision of their moral selves. We should respect the moral autonomy and dignity of persons. But, as philosopher Steven Tudor says, it is precisely this respect that requires us to pay attention to the moral attitudes of wrongdoers. 'To ignore a person's remorse can be to shun a fundamentally important aspect of his moral self, and can manifest a fundamental disrespect' (Tudor, 2008: 271–272). Basic respect may sometimes not allow the probing of conduct, but respect may also require recognition of human needs.

---

13. Of course the determination of appropriate punishment is also presumed to serve the purpose of preventing future crime. Inquiring the offender's history of offending and his beliefs as to the wrongfulness of his actions is justified because it has a significant bearing on the assessment of the risk he poses to society.

14. When it comes to assessing remorse and its genuine expressions, research shows that judges are led by four sorts of indicators: co-operative (providing information etc), reparative (restitution to the victim), reformative (change his behaviour) and self-punitive (imposing a burden on himself) (Proeve and Tudor, 2010: 96, 97).

Tolerance

Tasioulas suggests that when we take notice of the plight of offenders, automatically mercy is involved. I think he tends to overstretch the domain of mercy. We need a more refined approach of rationales involved when concern for offenders is at stake, including tolerance for incidental 'lapses', taking responsibility and prevention of harm.

Like Duff, Von Hirsch would also reject mercy as a ground for leniency, calling it a subjective feeling that misses references to offender-interests. But remarkably, he defends a first offender discount, exactly on the basis of sympathy feelings. We should sympathise with 'human frailty'.

Von Hirsch (2001) develops a 'principle of greater tolerance' in the application of penal censure to juveniles and first offenders. Adolescence is a time of testing limits and making mistakes, including those that harm others. A milder punishment convention for juveniles would preserve the young person's opportunities and prospects. In certain situations, Von Hirsch argues, 'we should entertain a certain degree of sympathy for the predicament of those punished—and hence utilize more forgiving standards of blame' (2001: 231). Even an ordinarily well-behaved person can have his moral inhibitions fail in a moment of wilfulness or weakness. 'Such a lapse reflects a kind of human frailty for which some sympathy would be shown' (*idem*). Recognising fallibility—the human susceptibility to lapse—calls for a limited tolerance of failure, expressed through some diminution of the initial penal response.[15]

In other words, the reduced response for the first offender serves to accord some respect for the fact that the person's inhibitions functioned before, and to show some sympathy for the all-too-human weakness that can lead to a lapse. Such a loss of self-discipline is the kind of human frailty for which some understanding should be shown (Von Hirsch, 1998: 194).[16]

Thus, the offender should get less when first convicted, but the discount should progressively be reduced thereafter. The repeated offence can less and less plausibly be characterised as a lapse, an aberrant failure of moral

15. I think the lapse-discount can be viewed as a 'condoning rationale' based on moral credibility (recognition and approval of the attributed moral quality to be trusted, to be worthy of confidence).
16. This comes very close to Tasioulas' arguments. He points out that mercy makes a concession to human frailty in many cases, to the failure of basically decent people to exercise the rational self-discipline in difficult conditions.

inhibition. We should give up the discount after a number of repetitions because the offender has chosen to disregard the disapproval visited on him, thus not responding to the requisite effort at self-restraint (Von Hirsch, 1998: 193).[17]

The lapse discount, Von Hirsch goes on, reflects not only sympathy, but it is also granted on the assumption that humans are capable of something worthy of respect — namely, paying attention to others' censure. In viewing the offender as a moral agent, we assume him capable to attend to the disapproval visited on him, and thus give him a second chance. The assumption is that the offender takes the condemnation of his acts seriously. What is hoped for is that the offender not merely desists in the future, but desists because he shares the recognition of the wrongfulness of the act.

I think this argumentation is important: believing in the moral capabilities and trustworthiness of the offender. We trust him to take the lesson to heart. It is based on the assumption of taking notice: bear in mind, consider and process the censure. Mercy seems to lack this agency aspect: suffering or vulnerable offenders are not really morally approachable. They are more likely to be concerned with their own pain than with the harm they have caused to others.

Facilitating Responsibility

In this section I will concentrate on other grounds for personal mitigation which are more related to future interests. A case in which leniency might be warranted is the defendant's effort for the advancement of an important social good (e.g. giving employment) or a socially valuable invention (e.g. the discovery of a cure for cancer). Custody would threaten to thwart these valuable contributions. This consequentialist rationale is especially relevant when considering the adverse effects of prison. For example, many judges show leniency to offenders because the just penalty would entail harm to innocent dependants. It is the sentencer's duty to prevent this. Preventative approaches are much more open to post-offence factors that may play a role in determining the effectiveness of the sentence.

---

17. Von Hirsch points to other relevant questions. Does the lapse-discount apply to any criminal conduct, however grave? Does the most heinous conduct fall outside the scope of human fallibility?

But in this section I will discuss another future-focused rationale: the offender's intended efforts to 'make good' and to change his conduct. These efforts may very well have preventative effects, but the rationale is not instrumental and is based upon remorse and its inducement to take responsibility (to repair or to rehabilitate). The offender recognises the wrongfulness of his conduct.

A complicating factor is that remorse can have two different mitigation justifications.

Remorse considered as grave suffering, accompanied with inner turmoil and consuming torments, may induce mercy and take the form of 'a less severe sentence'. But remorse considered as a concern to relieve the victim's suffering and a promise to change yourself, does not have the logic of counterbalancing an excess of public punishment. Thus, remorse can invoke mercy (avoiding an excess of suffering) but it may also be matched with self-committed efforts to repair/self-reform. Importantly, in the context of restorative justice remorse is valuable not because it is painful, but because it reinforces the victim's worth and promotes the offender's moral reform.

What justifies mitigation in the case of the offender's remorse and apology? Proeve and Tudor (2010) argue that remorse implies the recognition that the offender is worthy of social respect. He is listening to his conscience. By taking account of a morally appropriate response to a reproach, you are acknowledging the wrongdoer's efforts. Therefore the reproach can be modulated.

I think we should extend this reasoning: we can trust the responsible offender (Van Stokkom, 2005; London, 2011). As stated, remorse indicates that the offender is connected with the values which the law is appealing to. He is morally approachable. Genuine remorse points at a positive moral disposition, a commitment to comply, an indication that trust can be renewed. The willingness to repair the harm done not only indicates that the offender acknowledges that he committed a wrong, but also that he will respect other person's rights in the future. By contrast, if an offender says 'when I am free I will steal again', he cannot be trusted. Threatening to continue criminal behaviour is a promise to harm other persons in the future and implies a breach of trust.

Remorseful offenders do change the claims between the involved parties: offender, victim and state. If the offender admits guilt and is willing to repair the harm, there is no conflict between offender and the state, at least in the sense of a 'clash of opinions'.[18] What the preventive punisher wants is there: a commitment to avoid future victimisation. And what the retributive punisher aims at is also fulfilled: the offender has called himself to order and subscribes the legal norms. If there is no such conflict between the offender and the state, one can argue that the offender may become the co-author of his sanction-plan and that the interests of the victims involved can be dealt with. The victim comes in and is allowed to have a say in determining the plan.

Does remorse—as willingness to repair/self-reform—imply a reduction of the sentencing amount? I think allocating a less severe kind of sentence is more appropriate. Let's first discuss some arguments in favour of reduction. A radical version of remitting / reduction of sentencing is the redundancy rationale. In this account the offender has done (at least part of) what the sentence would have done. The offender has 'pre-empted' the sentence. Redundancy fits the consequentialist rationale of Bentham: the remorseful person is less likely to reoffend in the longer term.[19] But as stated before, it is a misdescription to say that the remorseful person is already punishing himself. Punishment is imposed from without. Self-punishment cannot simply be a substitute for the censure by the judge (Proeve and Tudor, 2010).

Jeffrie Murphy (2011) claims that repentance is a relevant ground for a reduction in criminal sentence. In his view repentance is a direct repudiation of the message of contempt carried by the criminal wrong. Withdrawing the contemptuous message, he argues, lessens the harm and wrong in significant ways. I think this is correct in respect with spontaneous remorse right after the offence (before the offender is arrested by the police). The offender is less culpable. But in cases of later occurring remorse Murphy's argumentation does not convince. It is not obvious that in such situations apologising words would in itself lessen harm and wrong. Admittedly the offender shows a zeal to 'elevate' the status of the victim, but he should combine his remorse with real efforts.

---

18. In terms of violation of legal norms there is of course a conflict.
19. There is much empirical support for this proposition. For an overview see Proeve and Tudor (2010: 120–121).

Ross London argues in a similar way as Murphy and claims that trust should lead to reduction of sentencing terms. 'Intuitively we demand less punishment for those who strive to restore trust by every means within their power. We feel they simply do not need to be punished further' (2011: 121).[20] But I think the severity of punishment cannot be reduced by the demonstration of indices of trust. Trust cannot and should not be rewarded with a punishment discount. It is an everyday obligation of citizens to behave trustworthily.

Offenders who demonstrate a trustworthy attitude do not deserve a sentencing discount, but a non-custodial sanction. In that way courts can promote the development of responsible behaviours in offenders. Ideally these sanctions confer a positive meaning to the burden that is imposed upon the offender, oriented at self-reform and reparation. By contrast, custody tends to interrupt ordinary 'good behaviour' routines and social obligations. Custody is disempowering; it is an ineffective method of communicating normative standards to offenders or eliciting compliance with those standards. Offenders would have relatively little incentive to accept a reparation package, if they necessarily had to suffer 'hard treatment' in terms of a dull prison regime.

To be clear, there is a difference between the willingness to make good and the actual accomplishment of reparative tasks. Fulfilling the obligations that were agreed to in a restorative proceeding (e.g. carrying out tasks in order to compensate the victim), may go hand in hand with remittal / reduced punishment.[21]

Rationales of Personal Mitigation

I have discussed several grounds for personal mitigation: mercy, tolerance, prevention and responsibility. They are part of the judge's duty to show

---

20. London's theory contains a related implausible argument. He states that those offenders who manifest no signs of trustworthiness must correspondingly be punished more severely (2011: 295). But remaining untrustworthy (or unrepentant or unresponsive) is not a good reason to impose aggravated sentences (see Proeve and Tudor, 2010: Chapter 7). It is a good reason, I think, to impose a disciplining sanction track.

21. In reality full restitution of considerable harm appears seldom and is difficult to achieve. English restorative schemes do not show so much direct gifts (except those embodied in apologies), nor restitution, but very considerable expression of potential self-reform. Offenders take responsibility to change themselves to make the victim and society feel better (Shapland, 2006: 518).

sensitivity and concern for offenders and those affected by his wrongdoing, focusing on their specific needs. In the scheme below the four rationales are presented in terms of the judge's object and core legitimation, characteristics of offenders and their life circumstances.

A. Sentencing reduction

1. Mercy. Counterbalance an excess of suffering or misfortune.
Extreme vulnerability of the offender / miserable plight (illness / old age / loss or severe illness of beloved / long term separation from beloved); battered woman; consuming pains of remorse) (possibly: formidable obstacles to compliance in case of socially deprived offenders).

2. Tolerance. Condone a lapse.
Offence 'out of character': assumption of predominant compliance or good reputation in case of first offenders; long time elapsed since offender's last previous offence.

B. Non-custody sanction-track

3. Active responsibility. Facilitate (planned) efforts to make good / self-reform.
Trustworthy offenders taking responsibility.

4. Prevention. Avoid harm to the offender and the offender's dependants.
Young offenders. Petty repeat offenders. Offenders maintaining a family/ bringing-up children.

These four types of personal mitigation are outside the logic of reduced culpability. All four are grounded in concern for the well-being of the offender and those affected, tempering the claims of just deserts. As stated, the first two could lead to reduced sentencing measures. Both are based on a 'unduly harsh' logic. Three and four are more future focussed and justify sanction-tracks that facilitate responsible behaviour and/or lessen the destructive impact of penal sanctions. The rationales can be combined, for instance a sentence discount for a lapse and facilitating efforts to make good.

The judge has a legal duty to take into account personal mitigation factors when undefeated grounds for it obtain. If the judge would set aside the mentioned rationales he could compromise interests, not only the offender's interests but also those of the victims and the offender's dependants. If mercy is bypassed the inflicted 'punitive-extra' could lead to relentless and even cruel forms of harm. Not incorporating the plight of a battered woman in sentencing considerations would be more than unreasonable. In case of the responsible offender: not honouring his attitudinal change would mean that he is fundamentally discredited (a cause to be distrusted and disbelieved). Maybe Tonry's term 'malign neglect' is a better qualification: a wilful lack of care and attention. Excluding offender-responsibility as a factor to determine which sanction track is appropriate may have many adverse effects. Suppose a responsible offender is informed that he is not allowed to escape a disempowering sanction-track. Then it would be far more difficult to discuss with him in constructive ways which reparation might be offered or in which ways he might rehabilitate/change his life.

The fourth rationale in particular aims to protect the interests of the offender and the offender's dependants: prevent damage to their life prospects. Possibly the attitudes of the offender himself remain unchanged. So our concern to the offender is mainly consequentialist: it relates to the less injurious consequences of a non-custodial sentence.

Of course there are more classes of mitigating factors and there are certainly many more reasons for sentencing mitigation. For example the case of an offender who has already been punished independently of formal legal procedures (e.g. through vigilantes or social ostracism). A complicating factor is the class of cases honouring the wishes of victims, which are often idiosyncratic and difficult to order/rationalise.[22]

Particular circumstances are often subject to variable interpretations which create the possibility of discrimination and inconsistency. Therefore discretion should be exercised for reasons, without partiality, that is, in rule-following

---

22. It is good to realise that leniency in sentencing need not possess moral value. Some mitigation factors are merely prompted by expediency as rewarding offenders for cooperation (pleading guilty; giving evidence against another defendant). Mitigation may also be justified by reducing the escalating costs of the penal system. Acts of leniency may even be grossly unjust, as in cases in which mild sentences are motivated by class prejudice (Tasioulas, 2007: 501).

ways (Walker, 1995; Roberts, 2011). Some reasons are capable of being made the subject of rules, although not all acts of leniency can be satisfactorily determined by rules. Rules 'constrain' and we may argue that rule-following is not necessarily 'being just'. Not all rules fall within the definition of just deserts. So under the rationale of mercy we have to treat like cases alike, as much as retributive desert does, although the criteria of relevant similarity are different. From the perspective of compassion for the offender's suffering, it treats like cases alike (Duff, 2007).[23]

Accounting personal mitigation factors involves many practical problems of implementation. For instance, judgments of proportionality across punishment-modes and tracks are harder to make. But at the same time it seems to be possible to make publicly clear that a lighter sentence does not imply a less serious crime (Duff, 2007: 385).[24]

In the case of serious and abhorrent crimes apologising words will often fail, no matter how honestly and eagerly expressed. Repentance and the urge to repair are outweighed by a shocked sense of justice. For that reason imprisonment will often have (temporary) priority. The offender is not yet conferred the status of 'co-director of his own sanction'. First, the retributive emotions must erode before we can grant him a dialogue on the subsequent modelling of his punishment. In other words, some crimes are so serious that the willingness to repair is not sufficient and an incapacitating punishment-track seems to be indicated.

Remorseful offenders do not have a right to a restorative sanction-track. They have to convince us that trust is justified. An initially cooperative

23. Often the categories of just deserts are stretched to achieve the desired result of a less severe punishment (accountability; excuse; etc). Consider the battered woman who kills her partner in a burst of anger. The woman may be assessed as having a mental illness that renders her not fully accountable for her actions. Or she was provoked and acted out of self-defence thus she retained her rational competence. However, I agree with Tasioulas (2003) that she is primarily a case for mercy on the grounds that her hopeless situation properly elicits our compassion.

24. Tonry (2011) argues that judges should impose the least severe sentence (applying the principle of parsimony). Proportionality only has the role of setting upper limits to punishment. This way of thinking introduces robust departures from parity requirements. According to Von Hirsch and Ashworth this means a sacrifice of equality. In their view parity is an important requirement of fairness, not just a marginal constraint (2005: 161). I agree, but not with their conclusion that this justifies only modest deviations. Serious deviations should be allowed (and are widely applied in sentencing practices: conditional sentences, acquittal, accord, etc).

convict who agreed with a reparation-plan but fulfils no obligation at all, forfeits our trust. Conversely, the sentencing authorities cannot impose a restorative sanction-track to an unrepentant or recalcitrant offender. Many offenders seem to be 'tigers': not responsive to moral considerations or capable of governing their conduct (Von Hirsch, 1993). Their punishment takes place in a hostile context that will probably 'harden' them. But as soon as they want to take responsibility they should be allowed to change to more constructive sanction-tracks. For that reason it should be possible to invert a disempowering sanction to a constructive one. This means that, during the term of a sentence, offenders—conditional upon their behaviour—could be referred to other tracks.

Viewed from the perspective of trust and responsibility, a dual track system seems a convincing model. In principle (under the system described), judges have the duty to convey a referral order to responsible offenders—also in serious cases. This should still be the case when victims are not willing to participate in a restorative procedure, or in case of absent or abstract victims.

Is social deprivation a mitigating factor?[25]

An extensive group of offenders has experienced a tragically disadvantageous upbringing. Some of them will have significant cognitive and emotional disabilities (lack of understanding of other persons' basic interests; deficient command of impulses). This may justify reduced culpability and the imposition of treatment or assistance.

In his study *Malign Neglect* (1996) Michael Tonry re-introduces an individualised approach to sentencing in order to humanise the decision-making process. A system of punishment based on 'social culpability' would take account of all the particulars of an offender's life. He aims to reverse the American trend to impose long punishments on disadvantaged groups (especially young black males), based on a system of rigid guidelines. This system 'generally forbids judges to mitigate sentences to take account of the offender's background and personal circumstances' (Tonry, 1996: 127).

Tonry argues that judges should consider an offender's exposure to social adversity in mitigating sentencing. Those whose chances of life have been

---

25. Social deprivation is an issue far too complex to discuss in this text. I only will present some preliminary considerations.

diminished by forces beyond their control are less blameworthy for their resulting misconduct than those who suffered no such disadvantages. Many face an overwhelming temptation or undergo great pressure to commit crime. Tonry assumes that it is not morally wrong to sympathise with those who gave in to those pressures and help them resist temptation next time.[26]

Although having a 'deprived background' does not seem to be a sufficient reason, there are many areas in which the judge could exercise mercy. Candidates for merciful treatment are (Misner, 2000):

- non-violent crimes that have not invoked strong emotional responses by society;
- criminal conduct that is questionable in terms of moral culpability (e.g. begging; using drugs);
- criminal conduct that did not cause injury;
- criminal conduct that did not create particularised victims;
- criminal conduct that actually disadvantaged the offender over the long haul.

So there are good reasons for sentencing reduction. But is mitigation feasible? There are many obstacles. The population might think that a large number of indigent but criminally active offenders are 'getting away' with reduced punishment (Von Hirsch and Ashworth, 2005). Mitigation could give the message that disadvantaged offenders are to a lesser extent responsible. Obviously they do not have the duty to be responsive to moral norms. In this way they are persistently excused (London, 2011: 252). So it is not

---

26. For similar arguments see retributivist thinkers such as Lippke (2009) and Von Hirsch and Ashworth (2005). Lippke points out that severe social deprivation tends to undermine the capacity to behave in responsible ways. Although socially deprived offenders are more or less blameworthy, some sentencing reduction seems in order. The criminal justice system, Lippke says, is 'rightly perceived as weighting more heavily upon them than upon equally ill-deserving others, thus earning their distrust if not contempt' (2009: 386). Von Hirsch and Ashworth argue that in a severely deprived social environment the social incentives to compliance are reduced. If social supports for law-abidingness are lacking, the deprived offender is in a more troubled situation, 'one in which the temptations to offend become harder to resist' (2005: 68). This predicament, the authors argue, warrants a degree of compassion and could in theory justify a sentencing reduction.

always wise to sympathise with 'overwhelming temptation' and 'great pressure' to commit crime.

Ross London believes that restorative sanction-tracks will offer more prospects. I agree, but an important question is: to what extent is the willingness to self-reform and 'making good' dependent on social class? London contends that an attitude of defiance is as prevalent among privileged offenders as it is in underprivileged offenders. Both groups are receptive to social controls. But still we may assume that the verbal capabilities to empathise and take responsibility seem to be distributed unevenly among social classes. For example, middle class offenders seem to have fewer difficulties with the language of peace-making and apologising in mediation settings (Presser and Hamilton, 2006).

Many socially deprived repeat offenders are not prepared to face up to what they have done. I think the rationale of prevention of harm by keeping non-dangerous repeat offenders with naïve and chaotic lifestyles out of custody is still relevant. Behavioural orders and removal to sanction regimes with much supervision and social support might be indicated.

Conclusions

Does focusing on specific needs and human characteristics introduce inequality? Some judges are quick to grant mercy. Some offenders and some victims are more eloquent and attractive than others, which also may stimulate or discourage mercy. As Bibas (2007) says, all these concerns are legitimate but far from fatal. Discrimination, arbitrariness, and variations in temperament, eloquence, and attractiveness are endemic problems in criminal justice. Bringing them into the open can help reasoned deliberation and public scrutiny. The option to have more rules and less discretion is understandable, and to an extent discretion can be channelled effectively. Therefore we could try to bring more structure to personal mitigation decisions.

Treating like cases alike is a value, but not the only one (Bibas, 2007: 347). Equality should not trump other relevant values, thereby sacrificing individualisation. Doing justice demands a balance of competing values, and taking into account mercy, tolerance, and responsibility keeps justice from being inexorable and rigid. Doing justice involves more rationales than only just deserts. Penal law should also protect the human worth of offenders and all those they affected. Crime has a human face and there is no need to suppress it by employing tight sentencing guidelines.

Jacobson and Hough (2007) contend that greater attention to personal mitigation could help contain the burgeoning prison population. If sentencers are allowed to deviate from proportionality in high risk cases (imposing long-term preventative sentences to dangerous offenders) they should also have the possibility to do so in cases where the risks are low. The authors add that the significance of mitigation in sentencing is not recognised by policymakers. They are much readier to promote long-term preventative sentencing and tend to assume that the public is fed up with 'soft' treatment of criminals.

Punitive preferences are booming in a populist drama-democracy and probably will be booming, in spite of dropping crime figures. The philosophy of just deserts cannot defend itself against this long-term trend of rising demands for severe punishments. In America, the introduction of sentencing guidelines did nothing to undo the trend of meting out disproportionate sentences to young black males. An appropriate answer to penal populism and distorted offender images is individualisation: putting the offender back into sentencing.

Just deserts theory fails to take account of differences in personal circumstances and individual effects of punishment. I believe this rejection of offender specific factors has contributed to the growth of unreasonable and unjust sentencing systems that in many ways discourage initiatives to desistance and reparation. An important fact is that the public supports personal mitigation factors (Hough *et al*, 2009; Lovegrove, 2011). Robinson's research (2012) shows that laypersons support mitigation of punishment when offenders show true remorse or when punishment would render a hardship on the offender's family. The author points out that strict proportionality deviates from the community's shared intuitions of justice; the moral credibility of the criminal law could be undermined if mercy is not exercised.

As Tasioulas has exemplified we should go beyond just deserts reductionism. There are competing moral imperatives that justify sanctions. Doing justice presupposes that proportionality constraints (standard cases and punishments) are loosened and that judges take account of the variety of offender circumstances, offence contexts, and punishment dimensions (Tonry, 2011: 235).

We could strive for a multi-track sanction-system. When defendants—also of serious crimes—are willing to take up responsibility, they may be eligible to a restorative sanction-track. Disciplining sanctions (which are inevitably disempowering) might be reserved for defendants who keep responsibility at bay. As argued, the trustworthiness of the offender is decisive in assessing which sanction-track could be followed. The availability of restorative and disciplining tracks—or a mix of measures—could result in a decreased reliance on the prison system for handling offenders. These arguments fit in with the ideas of David Cornwell, Jim Dignan, Daniel Van Ness, Catherine Hoyle and many others who advocate a sanction-system in which restorative justice has its proper place. They share the view that in this system retribution is a necessity, but at the same time its application should be restricted.

Many protagonists view restorative justice as incompatible with retribution. This is still a grave impediment to accommodate restorative schemes in the mainstream of criminal justice practices. I agree with London that—at least for serious crimes—punishment is needed to underscore the public denunciation of the crime (London, 2011: 185). Of course, imposing punitive sanctions can be undesirable for many reasons. Serving one's time in prison obstructs moral education: understand and account for wrongdoing. Offender and society interests are damaged, like the preservation of social networks, caring for children, finishing school, etc. Therefore we should take—under the umbrella of the justified censure—personal attitudes and circumstances into account, consider the needs of those concerned, and protect human worth.

References

Bagaric, M. (2000), 'Double Punishment and Punishing Character: The Unfairness of Prior Convictions', *Criminal Justice Ethics*, 19, 1, 10–28.

Bibas, S. (2007), 'Forgiveness in Criminal Procedure', *Ohio State Journal of Criminal Law*, Vol. 4., 329–348.

Bibas, S. and Bierschbach, R. A. (2004), 'Integrating Remorse and Apology into Criminal Procedure', *Yale Law Journal*, 114, 85–148.

Braithwaite, J. and Pettit, P. (1990). *Not Just Deserts*, Oxford: Oxford University Press.

Duff, R. A. (1993), 'Choice, Character, and Criminal Liability', *Law and Philosophy*, 12, 345–383.

Duff, R. A. (2001), *Punishment, Communication, and Community*, Oxford: Oxford University Press.

Duff, R. A. (2007), 'The Intrusion of Mercy', *Ohio State Journal of Criminal Law*, Vol.4, 361–387.

Garvey, S. P. (1999), 'Punishment as Atonement', *UCLA Law Review*, 1804–29.

Gromet, D. M. and Darley, J.M. (2006), 'Restoration and Retribution: How Including Retributive Components Affects the Acceptability of Restorative Justice Procedures', *Social Justice Research*, 19, 395–432.

Hough, M., Roberts, J. V. and Jacobson, J. (2009), *Public Attitudes to the Principles of Sentencing*, Sentencing Advisory Panel, Research Report-6, London.

Jacobson J. and Hough, M. (2007), *Mitigation: The Role of Personal Factors in Sentencing*, Prison Reform Trust.

Lippke, R. L. (2008), 'Response to Tudor: Remorse-based Sentence Reductions in Theory and Practice', *Criminal Law and Philosophy*, 2: 259–268.

Lippke, R. L. (2009), 'Retributive Parsimony', *Res Publica*, 15: 377–395.

London, R. (2011), *Crime, Punishment, and Restorative Justice. From the Margins to the Mainstream*, Boulder/London: First Forum Press.

Lovegrove, A. (2011), 'Putting the Offender Back into Sentencing: An Empirical Study of the Public's Understanding of Personal Mitigation', *Criminology & Criminal Justice*, 11(1): 37–57.

Markel, D. (2004), 'Against Mercy', *Minnesota Law Review* 88, 1421–80, http://papers.ssrn.com/sol3/papers.cfm?abstract_id=392880.

Misner, R. L. (2000), 'A Strategy for Mercy', *William and Mary Law Review*, 41 (4): 1303–1400.

Murphy, J. G. (1988), 'Mercy and Legal Justice' in Murphy, J. and Hampton, J., *Forgiveness and Mercy*, Cambridge: Cambridge University Press, 162–186.

Murphy, J. G. (1997), 'Repentance, Punishment and Mercy' in Etzioni A. and Carney, D. (eds.), *Repentance: A Comparative Perspective*, Lanham Maryland: Rowman and Littlefield, 143–170.

Murphy, J. G. (2011), 'Repentance, Mercy, and Communicative Punishment' in Cruft, R., Kramer M. H. and Reiff, M. R. (eds.), *Crime, Punishment, and Responsibility*, Oxford: Oxford University Press, 27–36.

Nozick, R. (1981), *Philosophical Explanations*, Oxford: Oxford University Press.

Piper, C. (2007), 'Should Impact Constitute Mitigation? Structured Discretion Versus Mercy', *Criminal Law Review*, 141–155.

Presser, L. and Hamilton, C.A. (2006), 'The Micropolitics of Victim-offender Mediation', *Sociological Inquiry*, 76 (3): 316–342.

Proeve, M. and Tudor, S. (2010), *Remorse. Psychological and Jurisprudential Perspectives*, Farnham: Ashgate.

Roberts, J., Hough, M. and Ashworth, A. (2011), 'Personal Mitigation, Public Opinion and Sentencing Guidelines in England and Wales', *Criminal Law Review*, 7, 524–530.

Robinson, P. H. (2012), 'Mercy, Crime Control, and Moral Credibility' in Sarat, A. (ed.), *Merciful Judgments and Contemporary Society. Legal Problems, Legal Possibilities*, Cambridge and New York: Cambridge University Press, 99–123.

Shapland, J. (2011), 'Personal Mitigation and Assumptions about Offending and Desistance' in Roberts J. V. (ed.), *Mitigation and Aggravation at Sentencing*, Cambridge: Cambridge University Press, 60–80.

Shapland, J. *et al.* (2006), 'Situating Restorative Justice Within Criminal Justice', *Theoretical Criminology*, Vol.10(4): 505–532.

Tasioulas, J. (2003), 'Mercy', *Proceedings of the Aristotelian Society* CIII, 101–132.

Tasioulas, J. (2006), 'Punishment and Repentance', *Philosophy*, 8, 279–322.

Tasioulas, J. (2007), 'Repentance and the Liberal State', *Ohio State Journal of Criminal Law*, Vol.4, 487–521.

Tonry, M. (1996), *Malign Neglect. Race, Crime and Punishment in America*, New York: Oxford University Press.

Tonry, M. (1994), 'Proportionality, Parsimony, and Interchangeability of Punishments', reprinted in Tonry, M. (ed.), *Why Punish? How Much? A Reader on Punishment*, Oxford: Oxford University Press, 2011.

Tudor, S. (2008), 'Remorse, Reform and the Real World: Reply to Lippke', *Criminal Law and Philosophy* 2: 269–272.

Van Stokkom, B. (2005), 'Does Punishment Need Hard Treatment? A Reply to Duff' in Claes, E, Foqué, R and Peters T. (eds.), *Punishment, Restorative Justice and the Morality of Law*, Antwerp — Oxford: Intersentia, 165–178.

Van Stokkom, B. (2007), 'The Expressive Function of Restorative Punishment. A Public Interest Perspective' in Bošnjak, M, Deklerck, J, Pelikan, C, Van Stokkom B and Wright M. (eds.), *Images of Restorative Justice*, Frankfurt-am-Main: Verlag für Polizeiwissenschaft, 151–167.

Von Hirsch, A. (1993), *Censure and Sanctions*, Oxford: Clarendon Press.

Von Hirsch, A. (1998), 'Desert and Previous Convictions' in Von Hirsch, A. and Ashworth, A. (eds.), *Principled Sentencing. Readings on Theory and Policy*, Oxford: Hart, 191–197.

Von Hirsch, A. (2001), 'Proportionate Sentences for Juveniles. How different than for Adults?', *Punishment and Society*, 3(2): 221–236.

Von Hirsch, A. and Ashworth, A. (2005), *Proportional Sentencing: Exploring the Principles*, Oxford: Oxford University Press.

Walker, N. (1995), 'The Quiddity of Mercy', *Philosophy*, 70, 27–37.

Wright, M. (1999), *Restoring Respect for Justice*, Sherfield-on-Loddon, UK: Waterside Press.

9

To Punish or to Restore? A False Alternative [1]

Serge Gutwirth and Paul De Hert

En droit, croire que le jugement console, fait le deuil, c'est typiquement une erreur de catégorie. Car le droit ne fait pas le deuil, il ne transporte pas quelque chose qui s'appelle de la thérapeutique, ou du salut.... C'est comme téléphoner à quelqu'un qui doit vous livrer une pizza, et dire: 'Faxez-la moi.' Erreur de catégorie typique. Il n'a pas compris que le mode de transport qui fait la commande n'est pas le mode de transport de la livraison. Eh bien, demander au droit de transporter vos peines, la fin du deuil, c'est la même chose.

Bruno Latour[2]

Introduction

The restorative justice movement is in full bloom. The practical applications of its various propositions go far beyond the tremendous production of theoretical texts and discourses. Indeed, in certain countries one can even see the development of fervent restorative initiatives in the margins of criminal

---

1. This chapter is a translation of Gutwirth S. and P. De Hert, 'Punir ou réparer? Une fausse Alternative' in Fr. Tulkens, Y. Cartuyvels and C. Guillain, *La Peine dans Tous Ses États. Hommage à Michel van de Kerchove*, Larcier, Bruxelles, 2010, 93–114 by Margaret Malmquist-West.

2. Fossier and Gardella (2006), translation (MMW): 'In law, to believe that sentencing consoles, mourns, is typically a categorical error. Law does not mourn, it does not provide something that one might call therapeutic or salvific ...It's like telephoning someone who is supposed to deliver a pizza and saying: "Fax it to me". A typical categorical error: he didn't understand that the mode by which he ordered the pizza is not the mode by which it is delivered. So, to ask law to bear your sorrows, to bring an end to your mourning, it's the same thing'.

law. Here, we have chosen to call this dynamic 'restorativism', as we see it above all as an ideological movement[3] and not, moreover, evidence of the new 'paradigm' that has purportedly been developed in criminology or in criminal law studies.[4]

Early on, proponents of restorativism requested that they be allowed to work *pragmatically*. They did not want their material efforts to be impeded by a debate on the movement's theoretical foundations. Accordingly, some even asked for a moratorium on all theoretical discussion: an understandable request supposing the purpose of the movement was, first, to facilitate the development of new ideas and, second, to prevent these new ideas from being killed off prematurely (Von Holderstein Holtermann, 2009: 191). Today — now that the birth of the movement has been traced back to the 1970s and 1980s and the conduct of restorativists has proven to be more brazen than benevolently assertive — this respectful moratorium is over. Faced with the genuine antiquity and the political and ideological impact of restorativism, we would like to resume the debate about its theoretical foundations, from both juridical and scientific perspectives.

Restorativism comprises at least two trends that need to be differentiated. One trend, called 'maximalist', is radical and aims to replace criminal law with restorative practices. Proponents of the maximalist programme maintain

---

3. This contribution is part of a series of individually and co-authored texts in which we began the discussion with proponents of restorativism. The series includes, notably, De Hert (2004 and 2009); Gutwirth (2009) (a reaction to Lode Walgrave's 'locomotive text' in the same volume); Gutwirth and De Hert (2001, 2002 and 2004).

4. In the context of the debate with restorativists, we use the concept of 'paradigm' strictly in the sense that Thomas Kuhn defined it. In this contribution, as we simply need to distinguish the restorative ideology from scientific and juridical approaches, we prefer to avoid calling them all 'paradigms' and thus implying, wrongly, that they all refer *a priori* to the same scientific 'genre'. For our prior explanations of this use, see Gutwirth (2009: 569–570) and van de Kerchove (2009: 12). Also, a paradigm *imposes itself* on the practitioners of a discipline: it is not a choice, but a scientific/methodological work and practice. Thus, contrary to what L. Walgrave wrote, the 'paradigm' is neither a critical position that one would like to adopt nor an epistemological status that one could claim under the pretence of developing another vision of things; cf. Walgrave (2009a, particularly 20–21) and Walgrave (2008: 24): 'By claiming a paradigm status, restorative justice advocates make clear their ambition to present more than a complementary scheme and to challenge the evidence and presuppositions of the current criminal justice system'. In our opinion, these sentences very clearly show that restorative justice comprises a 'platform', not an ensemble of preconditions that form the rules by which a discipline validates its findings.

that punishments imposed by criminal law, which they find ethically unacceptable, must be abolished and replaced by 'bottom-up', 'participatory' mechanisms that are negotiated amongst the perpetrator, the victim(s), and the 'community'. The other trend is more moderate. This trend recognises both the necessity and the influential presence of traditional criminal law and as such envisions both the installation and operation of 'switching points' or 'intersections' between traditional criminal law and the restorative processes of reparation or of reconstruction. In the first part of our contribution, we will examine the viewpoint of radical or 'maximalist' restorativists, exemplified by our Belgian compatriot Lode Walgrave; in the second, we will look at the work of the moderates, best represented by the Australian John Braithwaite.

Before we proceed, let us be clear on one point: our rejection of the restorative ideology does not imply that we defend the criminal system as it exists and functions in contemporary Western nation-states, whether in the Anglo-Saxon world or on the European continent. On the contrary, we find the 'criminalisation' of our societies to be cause for alarm and so for some time we have systematically defended policies of decriminalisation (fewer crimes) and reduction of criminal responses (fewer criminal prosecutions, fewer implemented punishments).[5] In parallel, we favour the re-valorisation[6] of civil law and, more specifically, of civil liability (judiciously called 'quasi-delictual' liability in continental law). Within such a framework, one could successfully develop a legal system based on compensation, reparation, restoration and, perhaps, on reconstruction. We are convinced that punishment must first be symbolic, and, above all, must denote both the rejection of the act (not its author) and the re-establishment of the order that has been flouted.[7] In our opinion, the penalty of imprisonment is a monstrosity to be avoided. Yet, if one must incarcerate — that is, if physical imposition of a penalty is required in addition to the penal sentence — we favour the implementation of more positive measures that encourage re-socialisation

---

5. As, e.g., one can read in: De Hert, Gutwirth, Snacken and Dumortier (2007); De Hert and Gutwirth (2005); Gutwirth and De Hert (2001 and 2002).

6. Re-valorisation means 'giving attention again to the implicit or inherent values' in something/some arrangement etc. or attributing new values to it.

7. On this, see also Hildebrandt (2002a); Van de Kerchove (2009: 269 ff); and of course Van de Kerchove (2005).

and rehabilitation or measures that are reparative, reconstructive, and (re)
integrative. To this end, we are not abolitionists: we do not seek to abolish
criminal law; we defend its minimal use in exceptional cases. We are radical
reductionists with regard to imprisonment, and we recognise *incapacitation*
as its only, purely negative, function.[8]

Nevertheless, we know that the history of the stabilisation of relationships
and conflicts in Western societies has been, for at least the past 2,000 years,
a *juridical* history. Law, and its particular application, characterises Western
civilisation[9] and as such it will not vanish overnight—at least not without
serious repercussions—in the face of a couple of good ideas. The knowledge
of this does not however prevent us from defending the principle that civil
law should occupy the most important legal role, the *default* role, and that
criminal law remains, as stated in its manuals, the last resort, the *ultima ratio*.

Restorativism Instead of Law

Maximalist restorativism positions itself as a challenge (Walgrave, 2001: 24
and 2009b: 531) and as an alternative[10] to criminal law. Following this logic,
criminal law and restorativism can neither agree with nor accommodate one
another. Indeed, according to Walgrave the two engage in a 'duel', and, as
we all know, duels often end in death (2001: 97–109).

For Walgrave, the goal of the maximalist programme is to remove as
much as possible of the criminal law's presumption of punishment in order
to replace it with a 'reparative presumption'. Thus the alternative: *to punish*
or *to restore* (Walgrave, 2008: 65).

Restoration: the only legitimate objective

Walgrave defines maximalist restorativism as 'an option for doing justice after
the occurrence of an offence that is primarily oriented towards repairing the
individual, relational, and social harm caused by that offence' (Walgrave,
2008: 24). In analysing the structure of this particular definition, one can

8. On this reductionism, inspired as much by criminological and penological analysis as by
    human rights and constitutionalism, see Van Zyl Smit and Snacken (2009); Snacken (2006).
9. See Latour (2002); Gutwirth (2010).
10. Walgrave (2009a: 19) 'So basically I still consider that restorative justice must be regarded as a
    valid alternative which will eventually replace the criminal law currently in force.'

easily see the form taken by the maximalist tendency. Such a conception puts all the weight on the reparative objective of the restorative response while at the same time disregarding at least three processes particular to criminal law: first, the defining of an 'offence'; second, the criminal procedure by which this offence is attributed to a person; and, third, the denunciatory and symbolic character of the subsequent criminal sentencing.[11] Walgrave's maximalist restorativism concentrates all effort and attention on the reparative objective, and it is precisely this concentration that allows him to explicitly ignore the process of defining the 'offence' as either a 'juridical fact' or an 'ontological entity'(Walgrave, 2009b: 524).

All this leads to the belief that under restorativism there is an offence as soon as there is personal, relational or social harm. Therefore, it is necessarily an offence that starts the process of horizontal mediation that in turn leads to the material and emotional reparation of individual, relational, and social harm. Evidently, maximalists envisage a radical replacement of criminal law: it is no longer the perpetration of an offence as provided for by criminal law that spurs the intervention we now call 'doing justice', but the occurrence of harm. What is more, this intervention is no longer a legal procedure, but an ethical evaluation left as much as possible in the hands of those directly affected by the incident, the 'community' included. Thus, the maximalist ideology proposes 'bottom-up' instead of 'top-down', ethics instead of law, and community member instead of legal person (Walgrave, 2008: 30).

Even more remarkable than this plan to replace criminal law is the fact that restorativism instinctively presents itself as a 'philosophy', 'a complex and lively realm of different… beliefs and options, renovating inspirations and practices in different contexts', a social movement, a domain of scientific research, but also part of a 'larger socio-ethical and political agenda' (Walgrave, 2008: 11). Unsurprisingly, such a mix of genres—in which philosophy, ethics, belief, political engagement, law and science find themselves interchangeable[12]—permits both the adoption of extreme analytical standpoints as well as the construction of ideological Utopias. But it fails when its critical discourses are applied to real and lasting practices like law, science, and

11. On the difference between the 'characteristic' and the 'objective' of penalty, see Van de Kerchove (2005: 35–36).
12. We critiqued this aspect in Gutwirth (2009).

politics that are not only distinct, each functioning in its own way, but that also, collectively and individually, constitute our cultural heritage.[13]

The premises of maximalist restorativism can be presented in three steps: firstly, punishment and *a fortiori* incarceration are not efficacious methods and are moreover socially and ethically undesirable; secondly, criminal law ignores what is really at stake in a conflict, notably the victim, his or her bereavement, material, social, and emotional harm, and compensation; and, finally, people and their communities must be given back their rightful conflicts, conflicts that were expropriated from them by the cold and indifferent machine of criminal law. By adhering to these positions, maximalist restorativism roots itself in an approach based on the victim, in a criminological abolitionism, and in a normative communitarianism. Although in his recent writings Walgrave attempts to refine these ideas with warnings against the excesses that could result from them, this fundamental ideological extremism remains unmistakably present. The alternative that maximalist restorativism proposes is the horizontal resolution of conflicts and the collective management of victims and perpetrators by the community — analogous to the 'extended family' — that is in turn helped by benevolent mediators or 'facilitators' , presumably trained in the social sciences or in criminology.

For these reasons as well as several others, we consider maximalist restorativism to be both highly problematic and questionable.

Utopianism

Firstly, there is to our knowledge no empirical evidence even of the possibility of this proposed alternative to criminal law. On the contrary, far from replacing criminal law, implemented restorative initiatives have simply related themselves to it. Though undoubtedly legislators have created sectors of horizontalism,[14] these sectors have always been overseen by criminal law. Here, not only does criminal law supervise the process, but it takes over if the affair cannot be regulated horizontally. This type of architecture — where spaces of soft and voluntary resolution are overshadowed by the intervention of the state and by prison walls — creates a continuum in which the threats

---

13. *Ibid.*

14. Decision-making or conflict resolution between those directly concerned, not imposed by a higher authority.

of intervention and of incarceration resound even in the softest corners of the justice system.[15] In these sectors, penal pressure remains efficaciously present and the suspect has noticeably fewer legal protections. These sectors are not simply 'versions' of restorativism or of criminal law; in our eyes, they would be more accurately described as 'perversions'. Here, we agree with Walgrave when he argues that one must separate radically from the traditional criminal system in order to preserve the identity and the singularity of restorativism. Now, the logicality of this last point notwithstanding, our argument remains that in contemporary Western societies, whether we like it or not, restorative practices occur not instead of but under the surveillance of traditional criminal law. And Walgrave, in defending the Utopian dimension of maximalist restorativism, implicitly reinforces this argument (Walgrave, 2009b: 539).

Anti-legalism

It is clear that horizontal, non-legal, and reparative conflict regulation occurs in situations preceding legal intervention. For example, A crashes into B's car. A and B get out of their cars, converse, and decide to settle things privately. A gives B 300 dollars and avoids an increase on his insurance premium. Or, A and B get in an argument in a public place, fists fly and blood spatters. Bystanders separate A and B, speak to them, and together all decide that it would be better to not call the police. A and B go to their respective doctors to be treated. These are, we feel, two examples of maximalist restorativism. And yes, they are effectively laudable since they divert from heavier legal interventions, and all parties leave on an equal footing. But then again, one cannot deny that legal action, even the mere possibility of it, is fundamental. For if A and B cannot agree, it will be law, either civil or criminal, that assigns responsibility, stabilises relationships, and sets up the 'truce'.[16] From this angle, maximalist restorativism finds itself in a very contradictory position because it tries to impose spontaneity, informality, and community where they would not spontaneously arise, i.e., precisely where, in practice, horizontal reconstruction does not work out.

---

15. See the description of this power continuum in the systems of protection of youths and mentally-ill in Belgium in Gutwirth (1993). See also Cohen (1985) and Deleuze (1990).
16. *'La trève'*. See Rigaux (1998).

The above examples also demonstrate the necessity of a third-party arbiter. In a conflict, there is more at stake than the interests of the victim and his or her 'immediate community'. This third-party arbiter serves to uphold general or public interest (that of society at the state level), concerned with both the resolution of the conflict as well as 'distributive justice'. If one of the protagonists is simply not able to pay the amount wanted by the other (or the other and the community), the third party finds a different solution in light of criteria other than the means and demands of those involved and the ethical convictions of the community.

The first example reveals yet another remarkable aspect of the restorativist ideology, one to which we will return in the second part of this chapter. This type of conflict falls under civil, not criminal, jurisdiction. This is hardly surprising given that restorativism resembles civil law—and more specifically civil liability—much more than it does criminal law. It is surprising, however, that the vast majority of restorativists remain radically blind to civil law: surprising, of course, because how could one seriously defend a restorativist treatment of criminal matters without doing so in civil matters in addition, or even as a starting point?[17] .

Maximalist restorativism is thus much more than a penal or criminological abolitionism. Though the writings of Walgrave suggest positions that seemingly call for legal intervention,[18] maximalist restorativism is plainly and simply anti-legal. If in his writings Walgrave does open the door to legal intervention, his aim is not to employ law as *law*, but to mobilise a judicial power that can legitimately and forcefully impose reparative sanctions upon recalcitrant and/or irrationally negative offenders, upon nonconformists, and upon those who resist communal pressure, voluntary mechanisms, and the

---

17. Walgrave responds to this question, but only in order to introduce the larger maximalist agenda: 'Maximalist restorative justice cannot be limited to settling a tort according to civil law, but deals with crimes which are considered also to be public events, traditionally dealt with by criminal law' (2008: 26). It is not infra-juridical and civil affairs that interest Walgrave, but exactly those that are taken up by criminal law, or, more accurately, offences that mobilize traditional criminal law and public prosecution. If civil law is not present in Walgrave's work, it is precisely because he wants to move immediately to serious affairs, because he leapfrogs civil law, its systems of liability and its compensatory damages.
18. See Walgrave (2008: e.g. 8) and Walgrave (2009a: 20).

good intentions of restorative facilitators.[19] Though maximalist restorativism prefers voluntarism and horizontalism, this preference does not eradicate the need to be able to force reparation or reconstruction on a non-cooperative offender: thus restorativists appeal to the legal system to impose the 'reparative sanction'. But this invocation of legal power—where law is mobilised by restorativists simply as a means of coercion—is in no way a friendly reunion with law. Even after having got rid of civil and criminal law, even after having replaced law (in theory, fortunately) with an alternative and maximally restorative system (the 'pyramid of restorative law enforcement' (Walgrave, 2008: 144–155)), Walgrave realises the need for coercion in order to induce those who would resist and/or refuse to participate in the deliberative ceremonies of shame, forgiveness, and reparation to value the restorative alternative. Thus, when restorativism fails, Walgrave calls on the legal system to wield the big stick and to impose 'restorative sanctions'. The nature of this judicial appeal—where 'law' is put into the service of a non-legal programme purely as an instrument of force—exposes the strong anti-legal inclination of maximalist restorativism.

In the light of this anti-legalism, it is not surprising to see restorativism inspired by indigenous, historical, religious, and other systems of conflict resolution that arise in communities where law as we know it does not exist or that are/were governed by mechanisms of pacification and of conflict resolution based on moral values, the authority of old sages, the interests of the group, etc. But what is more, this anti-legalism makes painfully obvious the radical nature of the maximalist tendency. From its utopian standpoint, maximalist restorativism permits itself to disregard the history of Western societies in which law, since even before the Romans, has functioned as a particular 'mode of existence' or 'regime of enunciation' (according to Bruno Latour), as a 'practice' (following Isabelle Stengers), or as a 'great cultural formation' (to use the term of Clifford Geertz).[20] Now the history of law in the West teaches us that law has always—regardless of the political system

---

19. And worse, for certain 'serious offenders who are unwilling to participate in deliberation, and who are likely to re-offend seriously', despite everything, Walgrave sees no other solution than, in the name of danger and risk management, incapacitation (see Walgrave, 2008: 153–155).
20. See Latour (2002); Geertz (2002); Stengers (2004); Gutwirth, De Hert and Desutter (2008).

under which it was active—stabilised links, set up truces, and assigned the responsibility for acts, things, and words. Therefore, the anti-legalism of maximalist proponents is, to say the least, unhistorical and slightly naïve. The presence of a juridical regime in our civilisation and in our various forms of secular 'Rule of Law' (*Rechtsstaat*)—both characterised by a complex system of checks and balances—is much more deep-seated in and constitutive of our Western identity than it is believed to be by those who want to replace it with a 'pyramid of restorative law enforcement' or with that which one could rather meanly call a system of institutionalised palavers overseen by those whom the Dutch call 'reparation workers' (*herstelwerkers*).

Foregoing due process

The extremism of the maximalist ideology never ceases to amaze. If it were up to Walgrave, the justice system would sideline the legal rights provided for by the criminal system and endorsed in Article 6 of the European Convention on Human Rights. Indeed, he unhesitatingly calls for the disregarding of due process in the name of the so-called new restorativist paradigm (Walgrave, 2009b: 532–533 and 2008: 155 ff). Thereby, the magnitude of the restorativist programme would be great enough to justify de-emphasising, even foregoing, the political principles and traditions emphasised in the Convention's preamble and, more particularly, the pre-eminence of law or the 'Rule of Law'. These political principles and traditions are characteristic of our society, signifying that power can only be exercised constitutionally, that we are governed more by law than by humans, and that, in the case of conflict, an independent judge will intervene heeding the rights and liberties of citizens, laws, and the fundamental principles of law. Since we live under a 'Rule of Law' we can always find recourse in law and the rights protected by it. These principles, one will do well to remember, came into being during the age of political Enlightenment and the ensuing revolts against the arbitrary and absolute sovereignty of the former rulers in England (1689), America (1776) and France (1789). Fortunately, law will not disappear simply because one introduces another ideological programme, even if this programme is presented as a paradigm shift and even if one amasses a political and moral majority around it. Whether it is a paradigm, a radical alternative to criminal law, a 'socio-ethical' programme or an ideological movement, restorativism—like all other political and ideological programmes—cannot downplay the respect existing for constitutional or legal principles.

Restorativism Alongside Law

Three premises

At first glance, moderate restorativism is more acceptable than its counterpart: this less extreme tendency aims not to replace criminal law but to ameliorate it. Dissimilar agenda notwithstanding, the premises of the moderates remain nonetheless akin to those developed by maximalist restorativists.

First premise: moderates claim that the reparation of the harm suffered by the victim lies at the heart of the debate, yet traditional criminal law attaches very little importance to it.

Second premise: compensation, reparation, and restoration are objectives linked to the restorativist preference for deliberative processes in which the persons concerned ('stakeholders') participate voluntarily ('victim-offender mediation', 'conferencing', 'circle') and that are closed to the public in order to ensure privacy and confidentiality.

Third premise: ultimately, moderate restorativism also rejects criminal (penal) laws because the latter, by definition and often for the wrong reasons, punish: where restorativists favour reparation, criminal law reprimands and/or cautions. Moderates maintain that, cynical objections aside, criminal punishments—*a fortiori* incarceration—do not work and that as such criminal law should only be called upon when there is no other option, as a last resort. For moderate restorativists, criminal law intervenes only if the voluntary and deliberative processes occurring amongst stakeholders fail: for example, if malefactors refuse to cooperate or are found obstinate, recalcitrant, malevolent, or dangerous.[21]

---

21. 'I part company with those who see punishment as a respectful way of raising our children, of dealing with criminals or with nations we disagree with. Compared with restorative dialogue…punishment is less respectful. That is not to say we should never resort to it. But when we do it should be on consequentialist grounds—because there is no alternative way of resisting injustice. We should then do so as respectfully as we can, but without deluding ourselves that hitting or confining can be inherently respectful' (Braithwaite, 2003: 2).

Criminal law does not work, but it can be a last resort

We will begin with the last premise, according to which restorative justice would be the default course of action and criminal law the exception. Hence, in moderate restorativism, the switching point between the two systems functions in terms of subsidiarity: if the processes of restorative justice do not work, the case can be sent to the back-up, to traditional criminal law.[22] However and importantly, this interchange or transfer mechanism between the two systems remains undefined and thus brings up several significant questions concerning the fundamental differences between restorative justice and criminal law. When exactly will a case be transferred to criminal law? After having been transferred to criminal law, is it possible to return to the restorative system? And, with all this in mind, what happens to the rights of the accused that according to certain restorative thinkers will (or should) be less comprehensive?

Without precise answers to these questions, one cannot seriously consider this proposed system of cooperation between the restorative approach and criminal law. Indeed, as Jakob von Holderstein Holtermann has expertly shown, these answers are too often absent. Restorative thinkers have neither clearly defined nor overtly treated these interchanges between restorative justice and traditional criminal law. Where is the gateway between the two situated? How does this interchange function and who operates it? Even John Braithwaite, the most eminent thinker in the school of moderate restorativism and undoubtedly one of the most eloquent restorativists, remains unclear. One is indebted to Von Holderstein Holtermann for his long analysis of Braithwaite's vast work (Von Holderstein Holtermann, 2009: 187–207), an analysis to which we remain faithful in the following paragraphs.

Braithwaite envisions the intervention of criminal law when, for example, a recidivist persists even after having been given a warning (Braithwaite, 2002a: 29–43). At some point in his or her career and after having passed numerous times through the restorative system, a known offender will be confronted by the latter and presented with a choice: either adapt to the

---

22. 'Principals to any restorative justice process about a legally significant matter, not just criminal matters, should have a right to appeal the restorative solution to a court of law and a right to resolve the dispute in a court of law in preference to a conference/circle' (Braithwaite, 2003: 10).

norms of society or be subject to intensified police surveillance. If still the offender persists, he or she would no longer be given a choice and all new infractions would be processed criminally. As Von Holderstein Holtermann justly remarks, the person identified as a known offender — who is moreover not suspected of a specific crime at the moment of confrontation with the restorative mechanism — will not truly be at liberty to refuse a restorativist offer. That is, if the person refuses, he or she would necessarily be 'sanctioned' by intensified police surveillance. If this is the case, where are we with the principles of respect and of non-domination advanced by restorativists?[23]

In further contradiction, though respect for the victim is supposedly restorativists' primary concern, in no way does their proposed system take into account those who suffer at the hands of a recidivist. In Braithwaite's example there is not yet a victim: when confronted, the known offender must face an ensemble of persons (family, workplace ...) who are not truly victims but who are instead concerned persons willing to help him or her.[24] In short, this proposal is neither restorativism nor traditional criminal law, but a third system, and one that would undoubtedly please classical utilitarians. This system aims not to repair but to prevent further infraction (Von Holderstein Holtermann, 2009: 194–195). As such, the future victims of this known offender will not be given the chance to go through a restorative process (and thus will not benefit from the advantages attributed to it by its proponents) simply because the author of these infractions previously refused to adapt himself or herself and to voluntarily obey the restorative propositions that were made to him or her (Von Holderstein Holtermann, 2009: 195).

Yet the situations that warrant transfer to the criminal system are not for known offenders only. Ultimately, traditional criminal law is much more present in Braithwaite's work than one might expect, for Braithwaite envisions

---

23. On these principles, see Braithwaite (2003: 10–11), and below.
24. Cf. the notion of 'affected communities': 'Restorative justice programmes must be concerned with the needs and with the empowerment not only of offenders, but also of victims and affected communities. Programmes where victims are exploited as no more than props for rehabilitation of offenders are morally unacceptable. Deals that are win-win for victims and offenders, but where certain other members of the community are serious losers, worse losers whose perspective is not even heard, are morally unacceptable' (Braithwaite, 2003: 10).

blocking access to restorative justice and transferring the suspect to a criminal court in at least four other situations:

(i)   when a suspect overtly refuses to participate in a process of reparative justice;

(ii) when the criminal suspect claims his or her innocence;

(iii) when the agreements reached through a process of reparative justice are more severe than those prescribed by criminal law for the same infraction; and

(iv) when the participants in a process of reparative justice cannot come to an agreement.[25]

To say the least, these four situations make up a significant portion — and certainly more than that of the known offender — of all existing and possible procedures and as such numerous cases would be transferred to a traditional criminal court. Protocol is straightforward in the first situation, when the suspect refuses to participate in a process of restorative justice and opts for a criminal trial. Situations (ii), (iii) and (iv), on the other hand, are much more complicated. In light of the above-mentioned premises and principles, these three situations pose several insurmountable problems to the restorativist approach. Here, the restorative process took place, but the results of this process were then transferred to a traditional criminal judge for verification or revision.

In these three cases, the recourse to traditional criminal law is far from being neutral or innocent. Often, it is beneficial for the suspect to avoid traditional criminal law (creation of a criminal record, subjection to traditional penalties, etc.). Even the alleged victim could benefit from avoiding a

---

25. Braithwaite is very imprecise when he addresses these four situations and nowhere in his work does he address them fully and all at once. They must instead be localised through interpretation and in doing so one runs the risk of being reproached for reading in his work things which he did not write. On this interpretive reading and its risks, see Von Holderstein Holtermann (2009: 195) with specific references to Braithwaite's work.

traditional criminal procedure (and its public debates). In order to prevent pressure or even the blackmailing of one concerned party by the other (either the victim who threatens the suspect with a criminal process if the latter remains inflexible or the suspect who refuses to accept the given schema of compensation unless he is compelled), the judge would need to come up with methods and standards by which one could evaluate a 'correct' process of restorative justice. Not only is this a difficult task, but it prefigures a return to paternalism and thus the end of the horizontal and self-managed conflict resolution that restorativists so eagerly propose (Von Holderstein Holtermann, 2009: 204).

There are additional problems specifically when a suspect is sent to a criminal tribunal because the schema of compensation and restoration agreed upon through a restorative procedure is more severe than the upper-limit penalties prescribed by criminal law for the same act (situation (iii)). According to Braithwaite, victims are reasonable and well-behaved; neither vengeful nor subject to unpredictable or unbalanced emotions. If the behaviour of victims were truly so serene, bringing forth what Braithwaite lyrically calls the 'collective wisdom of stakeholders' (Braithwaite, 2002b: 158; and Von Holderstein Holtermann, 2009: 199), situation (iii) would rarely occur, and rare occurrence would implicitly both minimise and justify the exceptional transfer to criminal law. Rarely does not mean never. Clearly proponents of restorativism accept in principle a situation in which a criminal court reverses the collective decision made through and conforming to all the rules of a reparative process. For Von Holderstein Holtermann this creates a problem of incommensurability: if restorativists employ better and different methods of punishment (and this is at least what Braithwaite and other proponents of restorative justice claim), how can one accept that a traditional judge could intervene afterwards to make the necessary corrections (Von Holderstein Holtermann, 2009: 199–200)?

Also particularly problematic is situation (ii), when a criminal suspect claims he or she is innocent, his or her case is transferred to a criminal court. Under these circumstances, the restorative process would become a space for plea-bargaining where the suspect, under threat of a criminal trial and/or harsher treatment within the restorative system, would be pressured into pleading guilty. Again, given restorativism's characteristic respect for protagonists' freewill and its preference for horizontality,[26] this would be a situation to avoid. As evoked above, the threat of a criminal trial and its influence on the decisions made in a restorative process ultimately pervert the restorative approach. This tension could be resolved by giving the suspect claiming his or her innocence the opportunity to return to a restorative process after having been convicted by a traditional judge, but regardless of its nature, this exception seems to us above all to lead to another failure on the part of this proposed restorative system. It is extremely difficult on one hand to maintain that restorativism is based on the principles of non-domination with horizontal and self-managed conflict resolution while on the other to plan on calling in a judge when, in practice, these principles do not hold (Von Holderstein Holtermann, 2009: 198).

Deliberative processes closed to the public

Our criticism of the third premise of moderate restorativism also casts doubt on its second premise, the preference for horizontal and deliberative processes closed to the public so as to guarantee the spontaneity, privacy, and confidentiality of participants.[27] As we have seen, criminal law is well and truly present in *all* restorative practices, but this presence is much more blatant in the moderate approach where the referral to a traditional criminal judge is a veritable *right*. If we follow a restorative logic, this unspoken 'right to criminal process' seems contradictory and thus raises several questions. The continuing presence of criminal law serves as a form of intimidation: it puts pressure on those who refuse to participate in the 'spontaneous and private' ceremonies of restorativism. Malefactors, dissidents, and even those who dare to plead their innocence—in short, all those who do not admit their wrong doings with the full desire to repair them and/or those who do not satisfy the congregation of stakeholders—are sent back to the chopping block of criminal law. While Braithwaite promotes the empowerment of participants,

---

26. 'But a programme is not restorative if it fails to be active in preventing domination. Any attempt by a participant at a conference to silence or dominate another participant must be countered' (Braithwaite, 2003: 9).

27. 'Not all of the accountability mechanisms of criminal trials, however, seem appropriate to the philosophy of restorative justice. For example, if we are concerned about averting stigmatisation and assuring undominated dialogue, we may not want conferences or circles to be normally open to the public' (Braithwaite 2003: 10).

mutual and respectful listening, non-domination, and horizontality as the essential values of the restorative process, he ignores the fact that the possibility, even the *guarantee*, of access to a criminal judge is a way for the victim to dominate the suspect for whom, the victim quickly realises, a criminal trial would most likely be disadvantageous. Paradoxically, this entanglement with criminal law impedes the spontaneity, intimacy, and confidentiality that moderate restorativism places at the heart of its preoccupations.

To add to this, the simple fact that the conditions under which a case can be transferred to a criminal court are unclear collides with the principle of due process. Whether or not Braithwaite values due process, to us it is fundamental. Restorative justice, Holtermann rightly observes, is faced with serious intrinsic problems, due process being one of them: if it wants to be implanted in the centre of the justice system, its proponents must fundamentally consider the effect of the axe of criminal law, ever-ready to fall on the processes of reparative justice (Von Holderstein Holtermann, 2009: 206). Restorativists will need to find a way to counter the dissemination, even 'metastasis', of the threat of criminal action through the continuum created by the links between the two systems.

The reparation of harm lies at the heart of the problem, yet traditional criminal law attaches very little importance to it

Now, let us return to the first premise. Moderate restorativists maintain that the reparation of harm occasioned to the victim should be given priority in the process, yet this priority is flagrantly denied by criminal law. This claim, we feel, derives from an incomplete and inaccurate understanding of the history of criminal law and its function.

The history of criminal law is heavily marked by vengeance, feud, and private justice. The story is well known: in communities where there is neither centralised power nor law, perceived harm triggers an act of vengeance that in turn triggers retribution and so on until the series degenerates into a great *vendetta* or clan war. Here, vengeance is horizontal and remains so even when taking it becomes a right. This right is negotiable (the *Lex Talionis* of the Code of Hammurabi, the Old Testament, and the *Lex Duodecim Tabularum*) and can eventually lead to the *compositio* or the payment of *weergeld*. In vengeance, protagonists are equals and there is no authority that can intervene on their behalves. Law does not pre-exist, it is produced through negotiation. Without negotiation, there is war.[28] If vengeance is retributive, it is thus not 'punishment' in the contemporary sense that presupposes the existence of an institutionalised power.[29]

M. Hildebrandt defines 'punishment' as a voluntary infringement of the rights and liberties of a person who has violated a legislative norm, executed by an institutionalised power with a view to (re)establishing the authority of this norm (Hildebrandt, 2002a: 103–146). If this definition is accurate, the differences between (rightful) vengeance and punishment are significant. Where vengeance and its derivatives play out horizontally and between free and independent equals, punishment requires the involvement of an authority who vertically and hierarchically opposes the transgressor. There-fore, modern punishment can only be retraced to situations where life was regulated by a central power. Thus, and again according to Hildebrandt, it was the 12th-century that saw the birth of the modern concept that 'punish-ment' can only be based on a law decreed by a sovereign.[30]

In this sense, the restorativist concept focusing on the victim and the preference for horizontal justice could be considered as a step backwards, since they are simply rediscovering what the criminal law replaced almost one thousand years ago. It is thus not surprising that proponents of restora-tivism emphasise the positive aspects of vengeance or that which Garapon, Gros, and Pech call 'vindictive justice': the horizontality of relations, the non-domination of one party over another, and the self-management of conflicts by those concerned. Consequently, the development of criminal

---

28. On this, see our previous works cited in Footnote 3.
29. See Hildebrandt (2002a); Hildebrandt (2002b: 184): 'The lack of any hierarchical relation excludes the imposition of punishments. Upholding the law in the *"sibbe"* (the community of blood-relatives) is a consensual matter and can in principle be initiated by any free man. Pri-vate vengeance reacting upon a breach upon the honour of a free man was therefore the most usual form of punitive maintenance of the law. In order to prevent feuds that could severely disrupt common social life, the *"ping"* (gathering with judicial power) will urge towards a reconciliation: the *"zoen"* (reconciliation agreement) is an agreement between the parties that does not restore the honor by punitive revenge but by the payment of a *"weergeld"* (com-position) to the kinship of the victim. Private vengeance and composition are according to Immink and Radbruch no predecessors of state punishment, but they are gradually marginal-ised and pushed out precisely when central governments develop.' (Translated J. R. B.)
30. Cf. Hildebrandt (2002a: 147–315).

law appears as a process by which humans are unjustly and cruelly relieved of their conflicts (cf. N. Christie) and all the more so when the concept of vengeance is spun with the Nietzschean grandeur of a question of honour where the adversary is seen as a respected equal[31] instead of being associated with resentment, humiliation, irrationality, exaggeration, and hate.

History thus shows that the sovereign — the state — has reserved for itself the right to punish; this much is evident when one looks at the inquisitorial criminal systems in the countries of continental Europe. Even though criminal law has always been the state's prerogative, political changes and our societies' history have not neglected its evolution. The contemporary state is no longer that of medieval kings or of the Old Regime and the same goes for criminal law. Indeed, if criminal law and the right to punish started out as the prerogative of the more-or-less absolute and authoritarian power of a sovereign and if they were exclusively or most importantly used in order to preserve the interests of the state, things have certainly become more complex under the contemporary 'Rule of Law'.[32] Today, criminal law is supposed to uphold and protect the juridical order of a democratic 'Rule of Law', a juridical order in which the protection of constitutional principles (balance of power, legality of exercising power) and the fundamental rights and liberties of individuals are just as important as the interests of the state and of the government. Criminal law is thus taken in a 'double bind': it must legally protect citizens *and* uphold the legal order. In this way, criminal law

---

31. See Fr. Gros's argument in Garapon, Gros and Pech (2001: 112–138 and 132): '[T]he avenger does not obey a blind and evil rage; he neither humiliates nor abases the other, but his vengeance is a proud reaction that makes of the other a rival, not a prey offered up to his desire to destroy. Vengeance is not structured by a logic of hate that eats away at and corrodes the relation of the avenger and his adversary, but by a logic of exchange that unites them in opposition' (trans. M.M.W.).

32. This does not mean that criminal law no longer serves and safeguards the interests of the state; on the contrary, this dual role is unmistakably present throughout the history of criminal law. Indeed, there is a long list of crimes against the interest of the state placed under the second heading of the Belgian Criminal Code. This prioritised placement confirms that criminal law is still designated for the sovereign's privileged use and therefore the danger of abuse and over-criminalisation is very real, as we see when criminal law intervenes and regulates in, e.g., economic, social, financial, and environmental law. For more on this subject, see De Hert, Gutwirth, Snacken and Dumortier (2007); and Gutwirth and De Hert (2002).

functions autonomously.[33] Even though criminal law remains exclusively 'vertical' in the sense that in principle it places the state and the accused in opposition to one another, it nevertheless takes into account interests other than those of the state; these other interests, as we shall see below, include those of the victim.[34]

To add to this, criminal law should in principle be the *ultimo ratio*, to be used only as a last resort. Lamentably, this is not the case in practice. For some time now, we have defended both legislative decriminalisation and the creation of the possibility of decriminalising a case while a trial is in process, a sort of 'revocation without possibility of return' and the transfer to a civil judge.[35] This, however, is beside the point of this contribution. The point is that civil law exists alongside criminal law, and, more importantly, since 1804, civil liability takes charge of the resolution of conflicts arising from harmful acts. Since the Napoleonic Era, law recognises both civil and criminal liability. While the principle that operates the distribution between a criminal and a civil wrong remains unclear,[36] the difference between their outcomes—the former resulting in punishment and the latter in compensation—remains devastatingly apparent. While civil wrong leads to a 'horizontal' process that legally balances opposed parties in order to compensate (or even 'to repair'), criminal wrong leads to a 'vertical' process where, under the eye of a judge, the accused faces the state and risks censure, public stigmatisation, and punishment, i.e. a direct infringement of his or her rights and liberties. Through civil law, the victim is compensated; in criminal law, even as the state (re)establishes juridical order, the victim is not barred from access to civil action and compensation. Though both civil and criminal law undoubtedly remain within a legal system, they are fundamentally different and serve dissimilar purposes: civil liability stabilises the relations between parties, assigns responsibility, and puts an end

---

33. On this conception of criminal law, see above all Foqué and 't Hart (1990a). See also Foqué and 't Hart (1990b: 193–209); 't Hart (1994); 't Hart (1995). For a short summary of Foqué and 't Hart's work in French: Gutwirth (2001: 305–342 (part III.B)).

34. Braithwaite evidently knew the history of criminal law, but for him it was no more than an 'obscure idea to have been taken seriously by the intellectuals of the North Atlantic for all these centuries' (Braithwaite, 2003: 16).

35. See Gutwirth, S. and De Hert, P. (2002), *op. cit.*

36. *Ibid.*: 127–140.

to the conflict through compensation; criminal law (re)establishes and (re) asserts the violated juridical order. To criticise criminal law because it does not satisfy the victim's expectations is to make a categorical error; it is like trying to 'fax a pizza'.

In light of all the above, we are still surprised by the fact that restorativists remain radically blind to civil law and to civil liability when these practices possess a multitude of aspects that correspond to their requirements. Civil law and civil liability place the highest of importance on the concerns of natural persons and, in comparison with criminal law, practitioners employ much more refined methods for measuring harm and compensation, less emphasis is placed on the rights of the accused, and the burden of proof is distributed differently. Indeed, there are even numerous systems of 'expanded' responsibility in the sense that parents, family, or employer can be implicated in the procedure and even required to pay part of the compensation.

Moreover, even in criminal law things are much less radical than restorativists want us to believe. Despite its singular history and the particular function that has been assigned to it, criminal law remains open to the victim. Legislators have not been deaf to the demands of the victim and classical criminal law has significantly evolved. Of course, criminal law is still *law* and is, of course, still riddled with problems, but the interests of the victim have always been present and influential; after all, victims are also part of the electorate. Today, all over Europe and the world, the instruments that a victim can use in order to obtain just satisfaction are more and more promising in a procedure that is more and more considerate of his or her perspective.

As Garland remarked in 2001, 'the victim is no longer an unfortunate citizen who has been on the receiving end of a criminal harm, and whose concerns are subsumed within the "public interest" that guides the prosecution and penal decisions of the state. The victim is now, in a certain sense, a much more representative character, whose experience is taken to be common and collective, rather than individual and atypical' (2001: 11). In Belgium, for example, one can already join a claim for civil damages (*partie civile*) to criminal proceedings and/or demand civil action as well as take action through private prosecution and summon the accused directly before a trial jury (*'la citation directe'*). Indeed, the Franchimont Law of 12 March 1998[37] grants the injured person—the new player on the criminal stage—several specific rights: the right to aid and representation by counsel, the right to submit documents, the right to be informed, the right to request specific investigative measures, and the right to send delayed trials to an appeal court. The 1994 introduction of criminal mediation as a mode of conflict resolution demonstrates that criminal law is opening up to horizontalism,[38] even if, as we wrote above, the opening of the former undoubtedly risks the perversion of the latter.

Conclusion

At the end of our itinerary, it seems that the fundamental ideas of 'maximalist' and 'moderate' restorativism are very similar. Clearly, both tendencies reject criminal law in favour of horizontal and communitarian conflict resolution that is based on the moral, material, and relational reparation of victims and the reconstruction of the community. Rather, it is in their proposed applications of restorative justice that the two ideologies differ: for 'moderates' like Braithwaite, the restorative approach must accept, incorporate, and be dependent upon criminal law; for the 'maximalists', restorative practices

---

37. Cf. Franchimont *et al.* (1998); Franchimont, Jacobs and Masset (2006).

38. With an eye to compensating the victim and to repairing damages, article 216*ter*, paragraph 1 permits mediation under the aegis of a public prosecutor. 'Reparation' is not limited to financial amends, but it could also include oral and written apologies, restitution, the defining of rules of tolerance and reciprocity, symbolic reparation, etc. If, for example, a victim's exorbitant demands or an offender's derisory offers prevent agreement, the case is taken up by a prosecutor. If, on the other hand, an agreement can be reached, the criminal case is dropped. In 2005, the Belgian criminal system was enriched by a similar act: article 3*ter*, written as follows, was inserted in the Preliminary Title of the Code of Criminal Procedure: 'the possibility of employing mediation is offered to persons having a direct interest in the given legal proceedings, in accordance with the relevant legal stipulations. Mediation is a process that permits persons in conflict to actively participate, with their consent and in complete confidentiality, in the resolution of difficulties arising from an infraction, with the aid of a third party using a predetermined methodology. The objective of mediation is to facilitate communication and to help the parties concerned to reach an agreement concerning the modalities and conditions of conflict resolution and reparation' (trans. M. M. W and M. W.). In article 195 of the same Code, a fourth paragraph was inserted, which reads: 'If elements of mediation are brought to the attention of the judge in accordance with Article 555, § 1, these elements are referred to in the sentencing. The judge can take into account these elements, and in that case mentions this when sentencing' (trans. M.M.W. and M. W.).

.should replace criminal law, preferably in its entirety. Moderates must in consequence not only spell out the relations and exchanges between both systems, but also and more importantly confront the fact that threat of criminal action and of the involvement of a criminal judge permeates through the restorativist continuum and thus links their processes of 'doing justice' to criminal procedure. In comparison, maximalists are more consistent, but this does not diminish the number and significance of the problems with which they are faced: the Utopian and ideological dimension of their project, the utter lack of practical applications that would demonstrate that their 'out-of-court' proposals are really viable, the minimisation of the right to a fair trial and the rights of the accused, and, of course, the unhistorical and naïve disregard of the role of law in the West, especially now in this era of democratic constitutional states.

As we have said from the beginning, our criticism of restorativism can in no way be interpreted as a defence of criminal law in its present form and we certainly do not count ourselves amongst the supporters of the criminalisation of society. On the contrary, we support the minimal and exceptional use of criminal law and the default use of civil law (of an *enriched* civil law). We take very seriously the principle that criminal law is the last resort and that as such de-criminalisation is a priority. We also think that after the disapproval and symbolic rejection resulting from sentencing, one must avoid the imposition of destructive and lethal penalties such as prison.[39] But on the other hand, we know that law will continue to produce, following 2000 years of history, stability in our Western society. Law is neither therapeutic nor salutary: it provides legal security, it resolves, it passes judgment, and it measures and defines the responsibility of the condemned or the acquitted. Law ends cases which without it could remain the subject of eternal discussion and boundless interpretation. Law produces neither truth nor justice, but stability, and establishes a truce. Whether or not an outcome is satisfying, we can be confident that law will resolve that which we cannot resolve ourselves.

Restorativism clearly lacks empirical, anthropological, philosophical, and juridical underpinning. The latter is all the more detrimental since

---

39. On these positions, see Gutwirth and De Hert (2002).

restorativists are blind to civil law (even if here too there is much to criticise) despite the fact that it is more in tune with their objectives. 'To punish' is not 'to restore'; the two are not interchangeable, but are distinct and different and moreover are the concerns of different legal registers. If the moderate and realist tendency of restorativism truly aims to construct a robust and effective relationship to law, it must take an interest in civil law and in the complex division of labour that links civil law to criminal law. Horizontalism and compensation lie at the heart of civil law, whereas the primary concern in criminal courts remains the state's reaction to the act that violated the legal order, regardless of whether or not this violation was caused by an infringement of the rights and liberties of a victim. In criminal law, the state confronts the offender: the objective is to correctly punish the offender and not to satisfy the victim's needs. Criminal law transcends private interests; it is characterised instead by its public dimension.

Now, since our particular juridical order — that of a democratic 'Rule of Law' — represents its citizens and their aspirations as victims, there is no reason why the legal system, be it criminal or civil, should not benefit from restorativism's propositions. Therefore, why not create mechanisms that, on one hand, provide for the irreversible decriminalisation of a criminal case and its transfer to a civil judge if the victim and the prosecution service agree to do so and that, on the other, give the civil judge enough flexibility so that he or she may allow the parties to prepare and propose a fair and reparative solution. As regards the execution of punishments, i.e. what happens after the criminal sentencing, criminal law could learn a lot from restorativism and its creativity in constructive and reparative sanctions (that some, like Walgrave, refuse to call 'sanctions' but which are nevertheless punitive reactions). Since the law of 17 April 2002, Belgian criminal law has added labour as an autonomous penalty. Indeed, if one broadens the number and type of available penalties, one could diminish incarceration and even replace it with sanctions that contribute to the material and moral reparation of victims and the community as well as to the reintegration of perpetrators into the community.

Punishment and restoration are two very different things. The former is carried out by criminal law and exclusively by criminal law. This exclusivity is important not only because the state prohibits us from taking justice into our own hands, but also because in criminal law more than in any other branch of law the state must in principle respect the strictest of rules that protect us against its power should we find ourselves accused in a criminal trial. The latter, restoration, occurs either outside of law, when we (or our representatives) are able to settle things amongst ourselves, or within civil law, where the interests of opposed parties are compared and balanced under the watchful eye of the judge, guarantor of the law.

To say that one must restore instead of punish is thus to propose a false alternative. Now, this does not prevent one from asserting, rightfully moreover, that it is time to start thinking about how *better* to punish and how *better* to restore.

References

Braithwaite, J. (2002a), *Restorative Justice and Responsive Regulation*, Oxford: Oxford University Press.

Braithwaite, J. (2002b), 'In Search of Restorative Jurisprudence' in Walgrave, L. (ed.), *Restorative Justice and the Law*, Devon, Cullompton: Willan.

Braithwaite, J. (2003), 'Principles of Restorative Justice' in Von Hirsch, A. *et al*, *Restorative Justice and Criminal Justice*, Oxford: Hart Publishers.

Cohen, S. (1985), *Visions of Social Control: Crime, Punishment and Classification*, Cambridge and Oxford: Polity/Basil Blackwell.

De Hert, P. (2004), 'Schaamte en rechtvaardigheid. Twee pijnpunten voor restorative justice' in Van Stokkom, B. (ed.), *Straf en herstel: ethische reflecties over sanctiedoeleinden*, Den Haag: Boom Juridisch, 169–194.

De Hert, P. (2009), 'Waarom herstel niet tot de kerntaken behoort', *Tijdschrift voor Herstelrecht*, no.3, 39–46.

De Hert, P. and Gutwirth, S. (2005), 'Gij zult straffen om de mensenrechten te beschermen! De strafbaarstelling als positieve staatsverplichting' in Verbruggen, F., Verstraeten, R., Van Daele D. and Spriet B. (eds.), *Strafrecht als roeping. Liber Amicorum Lieven Dupont*, Leuven: Universitaire Pers, 729–755.

De Hert, P., Gutwirth, S., Snacken, S. and Dumortier, E. (2007), 'La montée de l'état pénal: que peuvent les droits de l'homme?' in Cartuyvels, Y., Dumont, H., Ost, Fr., Van de Kerchove, M and Van Droogenbroeck, S.

(eds.), *Les droits de l'homme: bouclier ou épée du droit pénal?*, Brussels: Publications des Facultés Universitaires Saint-Louis/Bruylant, 235–290.

Deleuze, G. (1990), 'Contrôle et devenir' and 'Post-scriptum sur les sociétés de contrôle' in *Pourparlers, 1972–1990*, Paris: Les Éditions de Minuit, 227–247.

Foqué, R. and 't Hart, A. C. (1990a), *Instrumentaliteit en rechtsbescherming: grondslagen van een strafrechtelijke waardendiscussie*, Arnhem and Anvers: Gouda Quint/Kluwer.

Foqué, R. and 't Hart, A. C. (1990b), 'Strafrecht en beleid: de instrumentaliteit van rechtsbescherming' in Fijnaut C. and Spierenburg P. (eds.), *Scherp toezicht: van 'Boeventucht' tot 'Criminaliteit'*, Arnhem: Gouda Quint, 193–209.

Fossier, A. and Gardella, E. (2006), 'Entretien avec Bruno Latour' in *Tracés. Revue de sciences humaines, genres et catégories*, no.10 February: 19 March 2010 from http://traces.revues.org/index158.html.

Franchimont, M. *et al* (1998), *La loi belge du 12 mars 1998 relative à l'amélioration de la procédure pénale au stade de l'information et de l'instruction*, Brussels: La Charte, 1998.

Franchimont, M., Jacobs, A. and Masset, A. (2006), *Manuel de procédure pénale* (2nd edn.), Brussels: Larcier, Collection of the Law Faculty of the Universisty of Liège.

Garapon, A., Gros, Fr. and Pech, Th. (2001), *Et ce sera justice: punir en démocratie*, Paris: Odile Jacob.

Garland, D. (2001), *The Culture of Control: Crime and Social Order in Contemporary Society*, Oxford: Oxford University Press.

Geertz, Cl. (2002), 'Local Knowledge: Fact and Law in Comparative Perspective' in *Local Knowledge. Further Essays in Interpretive Anthropology*, New York: Basic Books, 167–234.

Gutwirth, S. (1993), *Waarheidsaanspraken in recht en wetenschap: een onderzoek naar de verhouding tussen recht en wetenschap met bijzondere illustratis uit het informaticarecht*, Brussels and Anvers: VUB Press/Maklu, 237–361.

Gutwirth, S. (2001), 'Une petite réflexion sur l'importance de la filibusterie épistémologique des littéraires: Dostoïevski, la criminologie, les sciences, le droit et la littérature' in Ost, F., Van Eynde, L, Gérard, Ph., and Van de

Kerchove M. (eds.), *Lettres et lois: le droit au miroir de la littérature*, Brussels: Publications des FUSL, 305–342 (part III.B).

Gutwirth, S. (2009), 'Blurring als methode, ideologie als resultaat: Walgrave's restorativisme' in Bruggeman, W., De Wree, E *et al* (eds.), *Van pionnier tot onmisbaar: over 30 jaar Panopticon*, Anvers: Maklu, 564–576.

Gutwirth, S. (2010), 'Composer avec du droit, des sciences et le mode technique: une exploration', http://works.bepress.com/serge_gutwirth/14/.

Gutwirth, S. and De Hert, P. (2001), 'Een theoretische onderbouw voor een legitiem strafproces: reflecties over procesculturen, de doelstellingen van de straf, de plaats van het strafrecht en de rol van slachtoffers', *Delikt en Delinkwent* 31, December, 1048–1087.

Gutwirth, S. and De Hert, P. (2002), 'Grondslagentheoretische variaties op de grens tussen het strafrecht en het burgerlijk recht: perspectieven op schuld—risico—en strafrechtelijke aansprakelijkheid, slachtofferclaims, buitengerechtelijke afdoening en *restorative justice*' in Boonen, K, Cleiren, C. P. M., Foque, R and De Roos , Th. A. (eds.), *De weging van 't Hart: idealen, waarden en taken van het strafrecht*, Deventer: Kluwer, 121–170.

Gutwirth, S. and De Hert, P. (2004), 'Vergelding: een kernbegrip van het strafrecht ?', *KriTies. Liber amicorum et amicarum voor prof. mr. E. Prakken* in Klip, A. H., Smeulers A. W. and Wolleswinkel, M. W. (eds.), Deventer: Kluwer, 295–312.

Gutwirth, S., De Hert, P. and Desutter, L. (2008), 'The Trouble with Technology Regulation from a Legal Perspective' in Brownsword R. and Yeung K. (eds.), *Regulating Technologies*, Oxford: Hart Publishers, 193–218.

Hildebrandt, M. (2002a), *Straf(begrip) en procesbeginsel: een onderzoek naar de betekenis van straf en strafproces en de waarde van het procesbeginsel naar aanleiding van de consensuele afdoening van strafzaken* (dissertatie Rotterdam), Deventer: Kluwer.

Hildebrandt, M. (2002b), 'Eenheid en verscheidenheid in de punitieve rechtshandhaving: over doel en betekenis van straf en strafproces' in Gaakeer J. and Loth M. (eds.), *Eenheid en verscheidenheid in recht en rechtswetenschap*, Arnhem: Gouda Quint, 184.

Latour, B. (2002), *La fabrique du droit: une ethnographie du Conseil d'État*, Paris: La Découverte.

Rigaux, Fr. (1998), *La loi des juges*, Paris: Odile Jacob.

Snacken, S. (2006), 'A Reductionist Penal Policy and European Human Rights Standards', *European Journal of Criminal Policy and Research*, Vol.12, 143–164.

Stengers, I. (2004), 'Une pratique cosmopolitique du droit est-elle possible?', *Pratiques Cosmopolitiques du Droit. Cahiers théoriques pour l'écologie politique*, no.8, Paris: l'Aube, 14–33.

't Hart, A. C. (1994), *Openbaar ministerie en rechtshandhaving*, Arnhem: Gouda/ Quint.

't Hart, A. C. (1995), *Mensenwerk?, Over rechtsbegrip en mensbeeld in het strafrecht van de democratische rechtsstaat*, Mededelingen van de Koninklijke Nederlandse Akademie van Wetenschappen, Afdeling Letterkunde, Noord-Hollandsche, Amsterdam, Nieuwe reeks, Deel 58, no.4.

Van de Kerchove, M. (2005), *Quand dire, c'est punir: essai sur le jugement pénal*, Brussels: Publications des Facultés Universitaires Saint-Louis.

Van de Kerchove, M. (2009), *Sens et non-sens de la peine: entre mythe et mystification*, Brussels: Publications des Facultés Universitaires Saint-Louis.

Van Zyl Smit, D. and Snacken, S. (2009), *Principles of European Prison Law and Policy: Penology and Human Rights*, Oxford: Oxford University Press.

Von Holderstein Holtermann, J. (2009), 'Outlining the Shadow of the Axe — On Restorative Justice and the Use of Trial and Punishment', *Criminal Law and Philosophy*, Vol.3.

Walgrave, L. (2001), 'Herstelrecht en strafrecht: duet of duel?', *Justitiële Verkenningen*, no.3, 97–109.

Walgrave, L. (2008), *Restorative Justice, Self-interest and Responsible Citizenship*, Devon, Cullompton and Portland: Willan Publishing.

Walgrave, L. (2009a), 'Een maximalistische visie op herstelrecht', *Tijdschrift voor Herstelrecht*, no.3, 19–38.

Walgrave, L. (2009b), 'Criminologie en strafrechtelijk beleid' in Bruggeman, W. De Wree, E. *et al* (eds.), *Van pionnier tot onmisbaar. Over 30 jaar Panopticon*, Anvers: Maklu, 531.

10

Dialogical Justice: Philosophical Considerations for Re-thinking the Reaction to Crime in a Restorative Way

Federico Reggio

Viewing Restorative Justice from a Philosophical Perspective

In an era in which there is a wide and consensual agreement about the long-lasting state of crisis in criminal justice both in its conceptual premises and its practical applications, restorative justice emerges as a very peculiar proposal. Such an approach, in fact, does not simply identify and criticise 'what is wrong' or malfunctioning in contemporary criminal justice: rather it suggests a decisive change in the way justice is understood and envisioned, both as a practice and as an idea.

This can explain why such a perspective has increasingly been gaining attention from outside the sector of criminological studies, since it seems to transcend the purely legal debate.[1] On the other hand, although much of restorative justice actually originated from practice and still constantly refers to it, it would also be inappropriate to confine the restorative approach to the world of 'social action', since its invitation to understand crime and

---

1. Remarkable examples of the interdisciplinary nature of studies on restorative justice can be found both in the literature and the current debate, which tends to reconnect different sectors of human sciences as well as scholars and practitioners differently involved in the field of conflict resolution.

punishment differently aims at globally and conceptually revising the role, the justification and the limits of criminal justice.[2]

Despite the superficial perception that sometimes occurs within the context of legal doctrine, the restorative approach does not merely propose some programmes or techniques as an alternative to the traditional idea and practice of both the legal process and punishment.[3] Restorative justice aspires to represent a different and autonomous 'paradigm' of justice.[4] Thus if restorative justice challenges both the *practice* and (most of all) the *idea* of criminal justice, it also invites a discussion of the underlying *philosophy* that informs criminal justice as a system and as an idea. For these reasons, it is appropriate to reflect on restorative justice from the perspective of legal philosophy — as this chapter attempts.

The 'Foundations' of the Paradigm: Restorative Justice and the Challenge of Ethics

The ambition of representing a different paradigm of justice requires that restorative justice provides solid conceptual premises to sustain its different understanding. Here, nevertheless, several scholars have noticed that restorative justice encounters some difficulties concerning the 'ring of vagueness' which seems to affect the concept of restorative justice itself.[5]

Some authors have suggested, therefore, that a further clarification could be provided by exploring some fundamental concepts that lie — under different names (values, principles, assumptions, axioms) — at the base of the restorative approach[6]. Without a further exploration of these core concepts,

---

2. Remarkably, approaching the issue of crime and punishment within a wholesome, all-encompassing vision recalls a typical feature of a philosophical attitude, regardless that its proponents explicitly wanted to assume it: according to a classical notion, in fact, philosophy is a 'discipline of the whole', which approaches reality within a systemic, global perspective, rather than through a 'technical' and analytical lens, which is typical of other disciplines.

3. As Kay Pranis observes, 'Restorative justice as a field flows back and forth between practice that informs philosophy and philosophy that informs practice' (Pranis, 2007: 49).

4. This expression is usually attributed to Howard Zehr. See, for instance, Zehr (1985 and 1995).

5. Johnstone and Van Ness suggest therefore that restorative justice is an 'internally complex concept' (2007: 7), while Wright and Zernova (2007) offer an overview of the different (and not always fully compatible) visions of restorative justice. The problem of the 'vagueness' that affects the idea or the underlying premises of restorative justice has been variously remarked on. See, e.g., Braithwaite (2003); Mackay (2007).

6. See, e.g., Pavlich (2006); Von Hirsch, Ashworth and Shearing (2003). Referral to 'values' can

underlying assumptions and arguments, there is the risk of basing restorative justice's appeal just on its '*pars destruens*' (effectively its critique of the way in which criminal justice is traditionally conceived and practised in the western world), or on its proposal of a (necessary but as yet unclear) alternative to weakly justified and malfunctioning criminal justice systems. This way, though, the previously mentioned vagueness risks becoming a 'double edged' sword: on the one hand it certainly helps to build and maintain some consensus around some wide and very general core-ideas, but on the other, such general agreement might turn out to be more apparent than real.[7]

The question about the ethical basis of restorative justice emerges at this point as a vital issue for two main reasons: first, some of its core ideas have an intrinsically normative character; and secondly, restorative justice is based on — and seeks to promote — a set of values like (for instance) mutuality, participation, recognition, respect, responsibility, care for relationships and attention to the context.[8]

Normative concepts (like, e.g. 'crime creates obligations' or 'the central obligation is to put right the wrongs') require adequate formulation in order to be theoretically justified. The question about the source of such 'normativeness' and its real cogency (that is, the arguments that explain and justify such normative claims) naturally requires investigation of the soundness of the ethical basis of the restorative approach: there is, otherwise, the risk of confining restorative justice to being an 'optional view' that can be chosen (or not) depending on individual opinions or general consensus.[9]

Moreover, if it is true that restorative justice is based on — and seeks to promote — a set of values, the question about their 'ethical justification' assumes a central importance, since it invests the solidity of the whole restorative paradigm: why those values and not others? What makes them

---

be found, e.g., in Howard Zehr and Lode Walgrave; John Braithwaite mentions restorative justice 'principles', while the expression 'axioms' has been recently used by Martin Wright.

7. See Roche (2001). For an analysis of three main frequently used conceptual references (alternativeness; community; restoration) and the ambiguity that makes of these 'commonplaces' some rather problematic standpoints, see also, Reggio (2010).

8. See, for an overview, Pranis (2007).

9. The importance of a reflection that helps underline that restorative justice outlines an ethically preferable model has been remarked on by several scholars. See, e.g., Sawatsky (2008); Wright (2007); Bošnjak (2007).

preferable? What are the principles that ground and sustain them? Such questions show that restorative justice proponents should face the challenge of moving beyond the (still rather important) arguments of effectiveness as an alternative to traditional criminal justice if they truly aspire to advocate for more than a 'vision of the world' which tends to be chosen by people who already agree on some general values and, most of all, on the necessity of moving beyond the contemporary theory and practice of criminal justice.[10]

In other words, the ambition to represent an *idea* (and maybe also an *ideal*) of justice obliges the restorative approach to face the challenge of providing a philosophical basis for its proposal: nevertheless, such an ambition may nowadays sound unpopular, or even be rejected by a cultural *milieu*—such as the *postmodern* one—which is deeply embedded in an anti-foundational perspective.[11] The questions at stake are, of course, too complex and deep to be fully explored here: this chapter does not aspire, therefore, to offer answers, nor a map capable of clearly orienting the debate on such issues. It only offers some philosophical considerations, hoping to serve as a theoretical 'compass' or 'signposts' to help the debate on restorative justice in the process of structuring its innovative and courageous proposals within a clearer and more solid philosophical frame.

Orienting RJ: Beyond Modernity and Postmodernity

As some scholars have argued, it is not correct to see restorative justice and the traditional conception of criminal justice as totally opposed or even mutually exclusive:[12] nevertheless, a systematic analysis of the restorative paradigm's conceptual frame shows that many of restorative justice's presuppositions, normative assertions, and goals are distant from those that

---

10. Restorative justice proponents can of course offer several important arguments about the effectiveness and the usefulness of their proposals. These arguments clearly are open to deeper ethical questions about the purposes and goals on which usefulness and effectiveness are measured (see, on this point, Wright (2008), *passim*).

11. Throughout this writing I will not, as some authors do, distinguish between 'postmodernism', 'postmodernity', 'the postmodern' or 'postmodernism'. I use them all to refer to the same philosophical sub-category. Although it is rather hard to outline a commonly accepted definition of 'postmodernity', I will for the moment define it as 'an attitude of mistrust and disillusion towards the possibility of reaching stable—or at least durable—notions and values'. For an overview see Connor (1989); Lyotard (1984).

12. See e.g., Zehr (2002) and, most especially, Walgrave (2007 and 2008).

traditionally inform the majority of contemporary criminal justice systems, and are sometimes even alternative to them,[13] reacting to the modern understanding of law and justice. I would like to underline three main frictions between the restorative and the modern understanding:

(1) RJ pays much attention to 'relational textures' (e.g. considering the impact of crime on interpersonal relations and the need of putting relations at the centre of the justice process; putting a strong accent on interconnectedness and mutuality) while modernity is characterised by a mainly individualistic and utilitarian approach;

(2) RJ attempts to envision an experience-based, context-sensitive and open-to-complexity idea of legal order while one of the modern worldview's main features is an abstract, rationalistic, mathematic-geometrical, standardised conception of (natural, societal, political, legal) order;

(3) RJ, therefore, tends to conceive a 'horizontal', 'relational' and context-sensitive idea of legal regulation while one of the products of the modern conception of law is the idea of legal order as a hierarchically organized system of norms, placed within the pyramid of the state's articulations and enforced by the sanctions that the state can dispose of as a monopolistic actor.[14]

On the other hand, it is important to clarify that, while distancing itself from modernity, restorative justice does not fully fit within the postmodern perspective. Postmodernity has a critical attitude towards many aspects of the modern worldview about knowledge, anthropology, society and law.[15] Some

---

13. See, most notably, some of the 'milestones' of restorative justice literature, such as: Zehr (1990); Wright (1991); Cragg (1992).
14. I had the chance to express such considerations more widely at the international conference 'Doing Restorative Justice in Europe — Established Practices and Innovative Programmes', organized by the European Forum for Restorative Justice in Bilbao (17–19 June 2010). About the modern understanding and its legal-philosophical implications my main sources are: Gentile (1983); Zanuso (1994); Cavalla (ed.) (1997). With specific reference to the different 'paradigms' of criminal justice, see also Zehr (1990), *passim*.
15. By promoting a higher consciousness of the structural limits of human knowledge, the postmodern sociological/political studies abandoned the abstract, geometrical idea of order typical of modernity (and its legal representation, the state) in favour of concepts like 'complexity'

of these criticisms are indeed consistent with important arguments outlined by advocates of restorative justice: there is a tendency to refuse abstract, hierarchical and geometrical conceptions of legal/social order, typical of the modern understanding, in favour of conceptions that emphasise complexity and inter-relatedness. Such concepts are in any case more suitable to the horizontal, context-sensitive, participatory and non-standardised model of conflict resolution that typically characterises the restorative approach.[16]

Postmodernity is not only critical of many of modernity's claims, since it encompasses a general 'disillusionment' with the idea of enduring, non-renounceable concepts: short-term, low-range solutions are preferred to wide and extended projects. In the legal world, visible effects of such perspective can be found — e.g. — in the weak attitude of contemporary legislation towards 'thinking globally', and in the subsequent preference for specialised, technical types of knowledge.[17] Finally, the postmodern *milieu* is characterised by a highly relativistic attitude, most especially in the sector of ethics.[18]

These elements contrast with some of restorative justice's main characteristics: for instance, the aspiration of considering restorative justice as a *paradigm* of justice reveals an intrinsically 'global' attitude, and such 'holistic' propensity can also be found in the tendency to reconnect and bring together scholars and practitioners belonging to different fields of knowledge (legal, psychological, sociological, educational, communications). Further, supporters of the restorative approach also seem to contrast the predominantly 'technical' approach of the contemporary culture by adopting a generally humanistic attitude, often not explicit but still visible as a 'texture' that filters from their arguments. Finally, restorative justice — as previously noted — advances clearly normative proposals, such as claiming that victims' needs *should* be addressed; promoting the shift towards a system in which offenders are expected to take active responsibility for the outcomes of their conduct; promoting the involvement of stakeholders within a *constructive* and *respectful* dialogue; and the idea that harms ought to be 'repaired'. As

---

(see, e.g., Bauman, 2000), 'risk assessment' (see, e.g., Beck, 1992), or 'interconnectedness' (i.e., in the lesson of sociological communitarianism, Karp, 2000).

16. See, for further reflections on this point, Pelikan (2007).
17. Zanuso (1998).
18. See Slob (2007).

already mentioned, such proposals all rely on more or less explicit values (dialogue, mutuality, participation, recognising personal needs and individual dignity), which play a very important role in informing and sustaining the whole 'grammar' and 'rationale' of restorative justice.

Postmodernism's aversion towards global thinking, and its resistance to discourses that may appear 'foundational' (that is, those that ground their proposals on a set of values claimed to be preferable to others) shows that restorative justice might not find adequate philosophical support within the postmodern approach. As George Pavlich asks, 'is an approach to ethics that seeks universal principles of restorative (as opposed to criminal) justice viable, given the broader intellectual *milieu* facing us today?'[19]

Should we not instead think of postmodernity as a good 'companion along the road' just as long as we distance ourselves from the many mistakes and the limits of the 'modern' understanding? Should we not also then be ready to leave such company when moving from criticism to the attempt to investigate and consolidate the conceptual ground in which restorative justice's roots are planted? Analysing and discussing George Pavlich's interesting reflections on 'ethics, universal principles and restorative justice' — which are explicitly inspired by a postmodern perspective — might help us find some conceptual references that can orient our possible answers to these questions.

The Risk of Undermining Restorative Justice: An Example

In considering several different approaches to restorative justice's underlying values, George Pavlich concludes that 'there is no clear consensus of values or principles deemed to define specifically restorative justice' (Pavlich, 2007: 619). Consequently, the debate 'leads to a dissonant chorus of ethical voices', which result in a 'disaffection with the very grammar of an ethics that revolves so centrally around universal principles' (Pavlich, 2007: 620).[20] According to Pavlich, the restorativists' approach to justice endorses 'an ethical frame of reference that is difficult to sustain in the late modern contexts' (Pavlich, 2007: 620). He suggests, therefore, abandoning the common assumption 'that essential principles are discoverable and so one finds a corresponding

---

19. Pavlich (2007: 616).
20. For a more detailed description of the different dimensions of such dissonance, see Pavlich (2005: Chapter V).

commitment to locate these' (Pavlich, 2007: 620). Such a perspective would belong to a typically 'modern' understanding, the conceptual columns of which crumble, leaving only the ruins of failed philosophical attempts: consequently, today we would be 'unable to point to a universally common *telos* (goal), or even a widespread belief in the intrinsic value of universal maxims' (Pavlich, 2007: 620).

Joining the typically postmodern 'incredulity' 'towards any "meta-narratives" that claim an ability universally to declare one version of emancipated, restored, just, peaceful, etc., social relations', this scholar invites us to completely renounce ground principles or foundational discourses. Ethics—as he puts it—are 'intrinsically unfounded and open-ended' (Pavlich, 2007: 620).[21]

If such a critical perspective towards universalism serves—according to the author—as 'a stinging reminder of our mortal finitude' and makes us conscious of the 'immense responsibility' that any ethical decision entails, some rather heavy doubts emerge while we start analysing Pavlich's conclusions and the implications that such a view might have for restorative justice. For instance, it would no longer be appropriate to talk of 'victim' and 'offender'—as if a 'naturally defined ethical subject' already existed: to do so 'would return ethics to ontology (the absolute being of natural subjects, or even of universal rights)', so eclipsing 'the distinctively indeterminate realm of ethics' (Pavlich, 2007: 624).

In dissolving the difference between victim and offender, though, also the notion of 'harm' becomes rather evanescent. Consequently also the restorative goal—at least where intended as a reparation of the harm done—tends to be cut down to size or even denied. The fundamental goal of a restorative approach—according to Pavlich who here explicitly recalls Derrida—is to allow two conflicting subjects to meet and reciprocally welcome each other as 'hosts': 'if the hosting relation is to continue'—he explains—both host and guest 'can begin to negotiate the contours of the unjust events, perhaps name them in precise ways, and contemplate the promise of future (just) relations'.[22] Accordingly, harm, injustice, and violation of relationships do

---

21. Pavlich explicitly recalls authors like Lyotard, Thebaud, Bauman (most especially his reflection on postmodern ethics) and Derrida, who typically are placed (or self-co-located) in the postmodern view.

22. Pavlich (2007: 625). For the notion of *hospitality*, that the author draws from Derrida, see

not pre-exist the latter encounter, yet are the outcome of a negotiation between responsive persons who seek a better future in their relationships: within such negotiation — Pavlich explains — 'ethical subjects might be implored to dissociate from the mode of being that they define as unjust', and to 'lay the groundwork for contemplating new, future modes of being' (Pavlich, 2007: 626).

We can have doubts about the compatibility of this perspective and the core ideas of a restorative approach, which can be summarised — according to Zehr — in three main propositions: 'crime is a violation of people and relationships; violation creates obligations; the central obligation is to put right the wrongs' (Zehr, 2002: 19). But, most of all, the underlying philosophical perspective that Pavlich adopts appears itself unsustainable, due to the contradictions that characterise its presuppositions, and to the unacceptable practical outcomes that it implies.

Firstly, thinking that individuality emerges as a product of responses and negotiations — as Pavlich suggests — is a conceptual mistake: being responsive, relational and able to negotiate presupposes the existence of an individual capable of relation, and does not 'create' such a subject. Secondly, when Pavlich claims that the resolution of the conflict requires 'hospitality' — meaning an attitude of welcoming the other as a host and negotiating, through a dialogue, a new, hopefully positive relationship — does he not thereby assume 'hospitality' and 'dialogue' to be cogent values themselves? Otherwise there would be no reason why a different relationship should be sought between victim and offender: violence appearing in the conflict would be just 'another way to manage interpersonal relationships' (we don't want to return to ontology and ethically 'label' violence!) and there would be no reason why the offender should or could not go back to repeating non-hospitable and non-dialogical behaviours towards the victim.[23]

If instead, as it seems, dialogue (as a way to negotiate past, present and future relations) and hospitality are assumed as values — be it only for the

---

Derrida and Defourmantelle (2000).

23. As Inge Vanfraechem notices, 'it is not clear to what extent "hospitality" could avoid exclusion ... Does it entail a responsibility of taking into account the other, hosting him as a guest? Or does it leave room to decide what people you will or will not consider as a guest, thereby excluding certain people from your hospitality?' (2007: 79).

chance they offer to help in (re)creating peaceful and mutual relations — then their denial is a disvalue. Furthermore, if the violence that crime expresses emerges also as an 'interruption of a dialogical bond and of welcoming the other as a guest' then there is no reason to refuse to conceptually distinguish victims and offenders. Talking about 'victim' and 'offender' does not mean 'applying predetermined ethical roles', yet it helps in recognising that — in certain situations — two different roles emerged: respectively the perpetrator of a violent act and the person subjected to it.

Thinking otherwise would lead to the unacceptable outcome of putting the behaviour of victim and offender on the same moral level: consequently, violence could be regarded as just one of the many equally valid ways in which an interpersonal relationship can take place. Moreover, there would be no argument for thinking that the perpetrator of a violent act might want to dissociate from that conduct; to agree to meet the person who was subjected to such violence; to 'negotiate' with that person and, finally, to try to find new ways of creating a future, non-violent relationship.[24] As Zehr reminds us, crime results in harm to people and to relationships: through his conduct, the offender imposes his own will on the victim and thereby exempts himself from 'negotiating' those reasons within a communicative and reciprocally hospitable attitude.[25]

In conclusion to this part, although he refuses to join an *anything goes* vision of ethics, Pavlich's arguments strongly risk falling into the unsustainable contradictions of a relativistic approach to ethics. Consequently, also the possibility of ethically sustaining restorative justice's proposal is undermined.[26]

---

24. This should not surprise us since, as Van Huyssteen notices, 'non-foundationalism is unable to explain why we choose some viewpoints, some language games, or some networks of belief over others, and thereby undercuts its own position' (1997: 26).

25. Viewing crime as a 'violation of people and relationships' is one of restorative justice's most important and ground-breaking statements. See Zehr (1990); Wright (1991). About the 'relational' impact of crime and the forgiveness of such factors in the modern approach to crime and punishment, see also, outside the debate on restorative justice, the contributions of Ancel (1966); Cavalla (1979); Eser (2007).

26. As Wouter Slob puts it, relativism 'digs its own grave. In order to make this point, it must claim that *its* conclusion is not culturally relative. Applying the theory of self-referentiality, its validity only extends to the select subculture of Western academic anthropologists and supporting friends' (2002: 51). See also Vendemiati (2007).

Beyond Dogmatism and Scepticism

These reflections assist in showing that total rejection of foundational dis-courses leads to contradictory conclusions as well as to unacceptable practical implications. Still, the anti-foundational perspective which has been criti-cised previously contains a very important warning about the risks of naïvely approaching discourses about foundations. Although we should not with-draw from the challenge of philosophically grounding the ethical premises of a discourse on justice, this does not mean that we can derive from such grounds a full-fledged (and fully developed) 'code' of values. As Bauman has pointed out, 'the foolproof— universal and unshakeably founded— ethi-cal code will never be found'.[27] Therefore, if it is possible to agree on the importance of 'grounding' the normative proposals of restorative justice, then discourses about 'foundations' can be rather problematic.[28] How can, for instance, underlying concepts and values be put at the base of a theory of justice? How have they been arrived at? Have they been simply hypotheti-cally assumed as valid and preferable premises by persons who have already agreed upon their basic content? Such questions are obviously too wide and complex to be fully addressed here, although some brief considerations can be suggested.

We can firstly propose, for instance, that assuming a set of values and normative proposals as axioms can become rather problematic. What is the source of their validity? If it is, for instance, general consensus, we can observe that a general and total consensus on a proposition is practically impossible and, most of all, it would be just a fact that does not explain the normative nature of the contention itself. If, on the other hand, we are thinking of a situational and contextual consensus, its range remains limited, while the validity of its generalisation results to be rather problematic.

---

27. Bauman (1993: 10).

28. Such a question is of course too complex (and still open in the contemporary debate) to be fully stressed within this chapter, but it is still possible to outline a few considerations that might help orienting our path. On the contemporary debate on the issue of foundations see the interesting overview offered in Slob (2002: 50–65). The author here underlines the impli-cations of radically 'anti-foundationalist' discourses, which are full of doubts and objections and sometimes contradictory, yet he meanwhile draws interesting indications from the more careful and prudent reflections of 'post-foundationalist' approaches. See also Schrag (1992) and Vendemiati (2007).

If, instead, these normative concepts and values were said to be 'self-evident', what would happen in a situation of conflict between such concepts and others, or in case of doubt whether they were really self-evident? One would probably need to demonstrate under which premises a concept can be regarded as self-evident, and, again, whether such premises might need further grounding, thereby entering an endless spiral.[29] Apart from these rather simple arguments, the idea of 'assuming' some contents as axiomatic hides an invalid claim of 'possessing the truth' which is usually identified, in classical philosophy, as 'dogmatism'.[30]

Recognising the equivocal or even fallacious characteristics of the dogmatic perspective might lead us, on the other hand, to think that any attempt to find philosophical grounds for a theory is necessarily invalid and bound to fail.[31] It would then be possible to argue about the usefulness of theories and paradigms — or even about their degree of consensus — but no philosophical arguments would be able to show that some underlying premises (capable of grounding a discourse on justice) are in any sense preferable to others.[32] In other words, values and ethical principles would be only optional,

---

29. Such a model — as Harold I. Brown states — requires 'that rationally acceptable claims be justified, and that the justification proceed from rationally acceptable principles in accordance with rationally acceptable rules. Each of these demands leads to an infinite regress until we can find some self-evident rules from which to begin, but these have not yet been found, and there is no reason to expect that they will be forthcoming' (Brown, 1988: 77). See, for a further analysis of this confutation, Williams (1996: 60ff).

30. As the Italian philosopher Francesco Cavalla points out, truth can never be denied nor possessed as an 'object' of thinking, because both these claims result to be contradictory. Considering the 'truth' as an object requires an impossible operation of 'seeing the world from nowhere', whose fallacy had already been outlined within the context of the early philosophical debate. See, on this point, Cavalla (1996). Similar considerations can be found in the Anglo-Saxon context with reference to the common limits of two apparently opposite approaches, such as realism and relativism. As Hilary Putnam pointed out, 'Like Relativism, but in a different way, Realism is an impossible attempt to view the world from Nowhere. In this situation it is a temptation to say, "So we make the world" or "our language makes up the world" or "our culture makes up the world"; but this is just another form of the same mistake. If we succumb, once again we view the world — the only world we know — as a *product*' (1990: 28–29). See, for an overview of such debate's influence in the contemporary Anglo-Saxon legal philosophy, Patterson (1999).

31. Such an attitude has been critically discussed, in recent times, also within a dialogue between theology and epistemology, by the theologian Joseph Ratzinger (Pope Benedict XVI) and the philosopher Marcello Pera: see Ratzinger and Pera (2006).

32. We already found such a position, for instance, in Pavlich, according to whom 'it may be

---

because of the impossibility of defining criteria to justify them. Arguing that values are optional, though, leads to a problematic *impasse* typical of relativism: if values are optional, does this mean that their contents are irrelevant or even unimportant? Are they merely based on subjective—ultimately non-arguable—choices?

According to this relativistic view, it would be impossible to prove that some values can be preferred to others except by referring to a certain context that the interlocutor is not obliged to assume.[33] Such a conclusion depends on a sceptical approach which assumes that 'no truth can exist or ever be found', and therefore every instance of human knowledge—at least in ethical matters—is just a matter of 'opinions' or 'practices', or 'meta-narratives' or even 'games' of inter-personal interaction.[34] The question about the existence of 'universally recognisable' values—should be left aside, because it embodies an impossible claim, the 'universalistic' perspective of which might even hide a violent, 'totalitarian' risk.[35]

Although much of the contemporary context helps to develop a more critical and conscious attitude towards the limits of human reason, and to abandon naïve approaches to universalistic ethical claims, sceptical relativism is itself unsustainable since it is based on self-contradictions. For instance, it implicitly or explicitly denies the truth by claiming to say something true; it states that all is relative or contextual by expressing a non-relative and

---

important to refuse a modern intellectual blackmail that commands us to come up with founded, universal ethical principles to guide our actions or be condemned as unethical, immoral and even just plainly irrational' (2007: 617).

33. Sometimes, such a view is incorporated in contextualistic claims, according to which 'no act or practice can be assessed as right or wrong, good or bad, etc., without the full explanation of circumstances and context' (Wiggins, 2006: 347). A contextualistic claim can develop into a full-fledged relativism, though, as it transfers its context-dependence from the problem of 'translating values into practices' to the claim of 'assuming that each content is valid only within a certain context'.

34. Such a position is a common point of various forms of scepticism: both a first 'general, all-encompassing wholesale version, which attacks the very idea of objective truth about anything, and a limited, selective version that concedes objective truth to "descriptive" claims, including mathematical ones, but denies it to "evaluative"—moral or ethical or interpretative or aesthetic—ones' (Dworkin, 1996: 88). The terms 'meta-narratives' and 'games' immediately recall some typical postmodern arguments. See Connor (1989: 10–12).

35. Pavlich (2007: 627). All we can actually do—according to a widespread understanding within postmodernist approaches—is to invoke instead a general 'tolerance' and disposition to compromise, in order to prevent a violent conflict from arising between particular opinions.

non-contextual sentence (otherwise such claim would be only contextually true, and therefore unable to express any general validity). In other words, the sceptical relativist—in order to express his own theory—needs to ground his own claims on statements that ought to be valid for 'all' the situations, and, therefore, no longer relative, this way contradicting himself.[36]

So far, such reasoning may look like a—perhaps abstract—exercise in logic. This subject is nevertheless deeply involved with justice issues, since it leads to the heart of the problem of conflict-resolution in human experience. The reduction of ideas, beliefs, conceptions, to the rank of mere opinions (all potentially equal to the others in terms of value) is apparently inviting tolerance and the avoidance of totalitarian risks embodied in some forms of universalism; instead, however, it is very dangerous, since it never provides true arguments against violence.[37] As long as values, beliefs and conceptions are seen as mere opinions or practices, the absence of rational criteria to state a preference between them in case of conflict leads to leaving the solution of such controversy to a merely factual outcome. When a compromise cannot be adopted, the only criterion left to solve the conflict is 'force': be it the force of 'numbers' that form consensus, the force granted by weapons, the force of the state, the force of a subtle and not rationally controlled persuasion, still the method that solves the dispute is merely quantitative and not qualitative.

---

36. As Dworkin correctly noticed, 'these influential theories are "archimedean", since they purport to stand outside a whole body of belief, and to judge it as a whole from premises or attitudes that owe nothing to it. Of course they cannot stand outside thought altogether, to deny real truth to every thought. For even archimedeans need some place to stand, as their progenitor conceded. They must assume that some of what they think (at an absolute minimum their beliefs about the good reasoning) are not just their own or their culture's invention, but are true and valid- indeed "objectively" so' (Dworkin, 1996: 88). As I am willing to show, the base on which those ideas try to stand is contradictory with the content of those ideas themselves. With similar argumentations, Slob critically observes about Derrida's deconstructivist approach, that 'the deconstruction of truth must itself claim to be true if it is to have any force. If this is accepted, deconstructivism either would annihilate itself, or would have to re-struct the notion it only seemed to de-struct' (2002: 64).

37. If we even agreed that any 'truth' can be formed only by the consensus between a defined number of 'actors' within a certain context, there is no reason why such a consensus *should* be sought. Why not violence? Why not coercion? Why not subtle persuasion? If there's no definitive reason why they should not be applied.

Is There a 'Third Way'? Suggestions from the Past

In the light of these considerations, neither modernity nor postmodernity seems to offer conceptual frameworks able fully to sustain the restorative paradigm. Much of the contemporary reaction to the limits of the modern approach seems in fact to be unable to sustain proposals which — like restorative justice — suggest a global rethinking and also rely on rather strong normative propositions.

We have also noted that detecting the contradictions of a relativistic approach to ethics does not immediately authorise us to think that a universally valid 'code' of ethical principles can be found. Should we then conclude that we have come to a dead end? Should we just acknowledge the intrinsically problematic nature of the ethical discourse and renounce our exploration, in favour of more viable, practical issues?[38]

No: *de vita nostra, de moribus res agitur!* — the issue at stake deals with our lives, with our behaviours! — as Augustine of Hippo reminds us in his book *Contra Academicos* (386 A.D.).[39] Therefore, the issue should not be set aside. In relation to the unsustainable positions of both scepticism and dogmatism there is the temptation to think that there is no way out: nevertheless, such an act of surrender — according to Augustine — is both ethically and logically wrong. A brief exploration of Augustine's argument might help us in pondering whether there is a 'third way' between two apparently opposite positions that did not turn out to be sustainable.

In his *Contra academicos*, the philosopher — who had formerly adopted a substantially sceptical approach — challenges two of his scholars with the question about '*sapientia*' (wisdom): 'What is the real wisdom — Augustine asks Licentius and Trigetius — namely that type of knowledge that, being granted by the truth, proves to be universal, eternal, non-defy-able and non-confutable?'[40] In answering their mentor's question, the scholars respectively

---

38. Similar questions explicitly came out also in the debate on the underlying values of the restorative paradigm: shouldn't we just withdraw from questioning about them and instead focus on more practical questions? As Zehr and Toews asked 'is it a problem that there is no agreed definition or set of principles? Should there be? Could there be?' (2004: 405).

39. Augustine (1951: 52–54).

40. I am here quoting the reflections on of Augustine's dialogue with his scholars *Licentius* and *Trigetius* written by Francesco Cavalla. See Cavalla (2000) (the quotation is taken from page 225, my translation).

adopted a dogmatic and a sceptical position: one contended that it is possible to rationally outline a series of self-evident principles from which one can deduce a set of certain and accepted notions or values. In showing the fallaciousness of such a perspective (see, e.g., the problem of 'self-evidence' that we have already explored in this chapter), the other scholar concluded, instead, that 'no truth exists' and that the real wisdom would be acknowledging the entirely unfounded nature of notions and values. Such a conclusion, though, was promptly challenged by the first scholar: denying the existence of the truth by claiming to say something true is simply contradictory.[41]

The two disputing scholars both appeared to be wrong. Such a dilemma, though, does not lead to a dead end. According to Augustine it requires us instead to 'elevate' the reflection to a higher consciousness: both of his scholars had said something right and something wrong; their discourses, though apparently opposite, did not exclude each other, they rather integrated with each other. Augustine argued that the reciprocal confutations of his scholars helped in discovering two opposite mistakes which can and should be avoided. Moreover, the philosopher showed that there is indeed something we can learn from those contradictions: *we cannot logically deny the existence of the truth, nor can we claim to possess it, as if it was an 'object' that can be fully grasped, possessed and analysed by human reason.*[42]

Applying a dialectical reasoning that excludes contradictions and 'mediates' between the opposites by letting common contents emerge, Augustine suggested—locating his considerations in the 'Socratic' tradition of classical philosophy—that human beings are 'bound to an endless search, intended to continuously transcend historically contextualised orders, knowledge and values' (Cavalla, 2000: 226). Still, this does not mean that any content is ethically equal: the 'non-definitiveness' of human knowledge does not mean that criteria of preference between values and contents do not exist. Being 'in the truth' and 'for the truth' obliges endless searching for such criteria and finding appropriate arguments to support choices. One of the most important logical tools that can be used for such a purpose is the dialectical ability

---

41. We can easily notice the similarities between such types of dilemma and the reflections outlined above in trying to explore the problem of 'grounding' restorative justice.

42. This means, in other terms, that when we're thinking of the 'truth'—as Francesco Cavalla puts it—we must not confuse *un-objectivability* with *non-existence*. See Cavalla (1990).

to find and expel contradictions, and identify common contents, as in the example given by Augustine himself in his dialogue with his two scholars.

The 'Indigence of Truth' and the 'Dialogical Principle'

Acknowledgement of the limited extent of human knowledge does not fully deprive of legitimacy the contents that human reason can outline, neither does it mean that such contents are radically unfounded and undeterminable, as some of postmodernity's main discourses seem to suggest. Some incontrovertible principles can be found, for instance, by showing that any attempt to contradict them is logically bound to fail (to recall a previously explained example, *the truth exists and it cannot be possessed*). Meanwhile, human limitedness implies that the possibility of precisely outlining definitive contents—such, for instance, as a fully developed and clear set of ethical standards, universally valid in all situations—is out of human reach.

Such considerations, which apparently might seem paradoxical, help in revealing something about the human condition.[43] If we can reach some incontrovertible conclusions but at that moment are unable to give definitive shape to their implications, then this means—as Francesco Cavalla suggests—that human beings are '*indigent of truth*'.[44] Despite its evidently problematic character such a conclusion should not paralyse our reflection, since from such a standpoint some important anthropological and ethical considerations can still be drawn.

First of all, if 'indigence of truth' implies that none of our concrete expressions—be these rules, behaviours, or procedures—can be proved to be definitively and ultimately 'true', this does not mean that the contents of such expressions are ethically or epistemically unimportant: it means, instead,

---

43. Recognising that the human condition is 'limited' does not only have a defective characterisation, since such limit determines our condition, so it also has the 'positive' function of setting a 'conceptual borderline' that helps us understand something about ourselves. See, on this point, Illetterati (1996).
44. See Cavalla (1990: 150–180). The lesson of classical philosophy about the relationship between the limits of human knowledge and the research for the truth has continued—although often sustained by a minority—throughout the whole modern age. In the late-modern Italian debate such lesson has been inherited and refreshed also by the approach of 'classical metaphysics'. See, for an overview, Berti (2006). As for the contemporary Italian legal philosophy, see Cotta (1991); Cavalla (ed.) (1996).

that each person is responsible for searching for those contents that, given a certain context, prove to be the 'best reasons'.[45]

It is no surprise that this attitude to knowledge supports a relational concept of humanity: if being conscious of human limitedness means entering an unending search for what the truth 'is', 'implies' and 'requires from each one of us', then one must also recognise that this research is not solipsistic but structurally open to dialogue.[46] The latter point has also some remarkable ethical implications. In the search for truth no human being is superfluous; no human being can be silenced or set free from asking and providing reasons; and no one, in fact, is provided with definitive reasons or arguments for claiming that another human life is meaningless and therefore able to be treated as though it was an 'object'.[47]

Indigence requires from each person a constant attitude to dialogue. In a situation in which no contingent expression or idea can claim to be definitive, everyone is bound to a dimension of continuous 'asking' that expresses both her/his own inherent limitedness and her/his own capacity to try and search for answers and provide reasons in support of personal convictions. In such a situation—which we may call a *dialogical dimension*—all human beings are *reciprocal* to each other and mutually involved as subjects entitled to ask questions and offer answers.[48] Indigence—limitedness—opens and binds human beings to enter a dialogue with each other: denying such *dialogical principle* embodies both a contradiction (denying the condition of indigence) and an act of violence.

Ethics, therefore are not totally unfounded and undeterminable: they are rather problematic and complex, but still grounded in the dialogical principle.

45. 'This involves'—according to Wouter Slob—'that transversal rationality must be substantial: to every problem there is one best rational solution' (2002: 57). As the author remarks in another part of his book, 'this makes scepticism in any form an impossible positions, but also it supports the idea that we must accept responsibility for our convictions'(2002: 178).
46. 'Identity is understood in a "chronotypical" (to mean, contextual) way and there is nothing mysterious or alarming about the idea that people simply differ in their biographies and hence their ideas about the world. We should be careful, however, not to confuse chronotypicity with solipsism' (Slob, 2002: 178).
47. See Cavalla (1990) *passim*.
48. Considering the main political and legal values as realised and saved 'in the course of an uninhibited dialogue grounded in mutual recognition'(Pelikan, 2007: 41) has been underlined—within a different philosophical tradition', by Habermas (2003).

The human *dialogical condition* offers a foundation to ethics, since it is both undeniable and propels us towards a continuous research through dialogue.[49] Moreover, dialogue (intended as a structural human dimension of potential and actual relatedness and not just as a situation of communication) is both a value and a source of other — complementary — values, since it requires the recognition and the protection of a condition of *mutuality* and *reciprocal respect* among human beings.[50] The impossibility of drawing from such fundamental principles a fully developed set of universal standards does not deprive the values of their cogency, rather it binds each person in the problematic and dialogical search for the best way of actualising (and protecting) such values and principles in each situation that emerges from human experience (including the experiences of crime and conflict).[51]

At this point we can also better understand how the dialogical perspective that has been briefly outlined distances itself from the sceptical postmodern approach. Postmodernity turns the perception of limits into a full 'incredulity' concerning the possibility of grounding and arguing ethical discourses: this can probably best be explained by noticing that in the background of postmodernity there still remained the modern idea of grasping and possessing

---

49. The confutation of modern individualism and the adoption of a relational anthropological model has emerged through the late-modern context within the reflection of various philosophers from different traditions, which is impossible to fully quote here. I would like to refer, here, to the important contributions of Buber (1947), Mounier (1949) and, in the Italian legal-philosophical debate, of Capograssi (1953).

50. We are 'reciprocal' with each other, because we are all sharing our asking and answering and nobody is provided of arguments that may show that someone else is indifferent or worthless: common indigence is also, in this case, a common *value*, since everyone — in this dialogical condition — is worthy and entitled to contributing to the endless common research that human limitedness requires. See, for the implications of such a principle in a philosophy of punishment, my own *Giustizia Dialogica* (190–203). An interesting and deep analysis of the concept of 'mutuality' as the source and the legitimating factor of the legal dimension can be found in Fuselli's work on Hegel's *Philosophy of Law*: Fuselli (2001).

51. See Cavalla (ed.) (2007). As Manzin comments, 'Rhetorical conclusions consist of a truth that, being *concrete*, stands constantly 'at the door' between past and future, while the rigid and abstract truth of formalised discourses (such as geometric demonstrations) can be repeated in the same way indefinitely. This kind of repeatability is typical of all things that, being abstract (like triangles or circles), never properly 'occurs'. The rhetorical method, on the contrary, is deeply rooted in the concrete occurring of human experience: it is 'practical rationality' capable of giving discourse persuasion based upon logic'.

the truth.[52] Discovering that such possession is illusory led to entire denial of the possibility of achieving true contents, instead of re-thinking in more humble terms the relationship between human knowledge and truth. This reminds us of what happened in the conclusions of Augustine's sceptical scholar, who, after confuting his dogmatic colleague, kept the idea of relating to the truth as if it was an object: non-existing—as he said—but still (and therefore) thought of as an object.

Yet, as the Italian philosopher Giambattista Vico (1668–1774) pointed out in his *De antiquissima italorum sapientia* (1711) 'neither dogmatists know everything nor sceptics know nothing'.[53] In his most famous work, *The new science* (1744), Vico—who criticised the modern approach within the modern age by re-interpreting a classical approach—offers an interesting argument about the relationship that epistemology, anthropology and ethics can have around the notion of 'human limitedness'.[54] Assuming consciousness of one's own structural limitedness, according to the Italian philosopher, emerges firstly as a feeling of *pudor* (shame) and later on as a rational knowledge which can also become a source of *virtus* (virtue). Such virtue can have a double dimension: *ethica* when it promotes a moral change, and *dianoetica*, when it promotes the search for more solid and wider knowledge. Limits act both as a warning against *self-absolutism* (which happens both when someone claims to deny the truth and when someone claims to possess it), and as a *propulsive factor*. Being conscious of a structural limitedness opens the way both to investigation (*virtus dianoetica*) and to relationality (*virtus ethica*) and each of these dimensions is ethically cogent for human beings, whose

---

52. On the elements of continuity between modernity and postmodernity, despite the many differences, see Zanuso (2000).

53. Vico (1711/2003: 191).

54. Giambattista Vico's philosophy offers interesting and stimulating arguments now that—in the 'post-modern' age—we can critically outline and experience the outcomes (and the failures) of modernity. Underrated, and probably also misunderstood, by many of his contemporaries—for his critical approach towards several aspects of the evolving modern thought at the beginning of Enlightenment—Vico (1668–1744) developed, through a 'solitary' although not isolated path, a diverse and original philosophy, deeply related with the humanistic tradition of classical thought. Such a view nowadays appears to be for many aspects alternative to the modern vision, and, for that reason, rich with interesting suggestions for the contemporary reflection, also in the field of legal philosophy. On the relationship between Vico and modernity see Lilla (1993).

freedom is continuously challenged by the possibility of choosing between acting in respect of, or in violation of them.[55] Vico's lesson has probably something to say in our times, too.

Implications of the Dialogical Principle for the Theory and Practice of Criminal Justice

As we have seen, the *dialogical principle*, rooted as a corollary of the human condition of *indigence of truth*, helps in connecting an 'epistemology of limit' with a relational anthropology and, subsequently, with a dialogical idea of ethics.

From here on, some considerations can be applied also to the theory and practice of criminal justice. As previously mentioned, though, the following considerations do not aspire to offer either answers or a detailed map to guide reflection on the problem of punishment: they should instead be considered as some conceptual references that might help in orienting further reflection and dialogue among the scholars who are differently involved in this debate.

If we then agree on the soundness and on the cogency of the previously mentioned dialogical principle, we can also try to show some implications that such an ethical standpoint can have with regard to the problem of crime and punishment. More specifically, we can draw some considerations regarding three main core-themes: first, the idea of crime as a harm to persons and relations; second, the impossibility of considering punishment as a mere 'application of legal norms'; and third, the consequent refusal of a self-referring and self-grounded idea of legal order, in favour of a conception of law that is itself consistent with the dialogical principle and respectful of its implications.

If relatedness — as we have previously suggested — is more than an experience of communication, but rather represents a non-deniable dimension intrinsic to the human condition and grounded in the human indigence of truth, then violating such a dimension immediately assumes an ethical

---

55. See, for a reconstruction of such theory with reference to Vico's doctrine of nature's law, Bellofiore (1954). Also, with reference to Vico's moral philosophy, Verene (2008). About the relationship between human limitedness, self-absolutisation and Vico's reflections on crime and punishment, see Reggio (2004). See also, for an overview on Vico's peculiar perspective, Reggio (2012).

meaning.[56] Denying reciprocity represents both a contradiction and an act of violence when such denial emerges as 'silencing' someone else by imposing upon that person undesired consequences without allowing any opportunity to enter into a dialogical discussion on the issue at stake. Violence includes, therefore, a form of self-absolutism as well as an act of treating someone else as an 'object' rather than as someone who is reciprocally involved in dialogue, and so worthy of respect. Violence, consequently, represents a harm that can affect both some identified persons (those who have been actually subjected to the violent act) and the intangible (but still existing) relational bond which, inherent in the human condition, is always at stake when violence occurs.[57]

Also, within this understanding crime can be viewed — in its conceptual structure — as a particularly serious violation of the dialogical principle. It represents, more specifically, a violent act through which someone states his or her own will as absolute, and imposes (violently or with fraud) upon someone else undesired consequences (without considering each other's reasons in a dialogical way).[58] As also proponents of restorative justice observe — through arguments often drawn from an experience-based approach — crime embodies both a personal and an inter-personal violation: if mutuality and reciprocity (and of course the overall respect that grants such dimensions) are corollaries of the dialogical principle, any act of violently breaking this condition and the values that stem from it invokes consequences both at a personal and at an inter-personal or societal level.[59] It is therefore inappropriate to view

---

56. Not all violations, though, have the same ethical meaning. If one denied the principle of dialogue just by affirming that it is not a principle, such violation would just assume the form of a contradiction (trying to deny the principle of dialogue by using a communicational way). If instead someone radically tried to prevent or defeat any dialogical confrontation by imposing on someone else undesired consequences without providing any space for confronting each other's reasons, such 'putting into silence' any 'opposition' would represent an act of violence, and not just a logically weak discourse.

57. On the dimension and the value of 'interconnectedness' see Lederach (2005), and, with specific reference to restorative justice, Zehr (2002) *passim*; Sawatsky (2008) *passim*.

58. I am here following some important considerations expressed in Cavalla (1998: 84–85).

59. Many different cultures put an accent on the relational (or at least communitarian) dimension of crime. Concepts like e.g. '*ubuntu*' (for some parts of the African culture) or '*koru*' (for the Maori culture) express a 'common belonging' and the existence of a 'societal network' that is always at stake when inter-personal conflicts occur. As for the Western culture (in which such conceptual referrals tended to lose importance due the rise of an individualistic

crime entirely in terms of a specific legal violation that is sanctioned with a form of punishment regulated by penal law.

Certainly the occurrence of crime (understood in the manner discussed above) immediately challenges the social and the legal order and needs to be addressed: yet explaining the need for responding to crime merely by invoking the application of legal procedures and mechanisms is a rather unsatisfying and weakly argued justification.[60] The criminal behaviour is non-legitimate not only because it infringes a certain legal order: it is intrinsically wrong because (and only if) it becomes anti-dialogical as a result. Therefore it requires a response not just because this is legally prescribed, but because acquiescence to crime assumes the unacceptable ethical meaning of validating violence. On the other hand, though, the (ethical) need to respond to crime cannot assume forms which themselves violate the dialogical principle.[61] Stated in another way, the reaction to crime must be subjugated to the dialogical principle, in order to avoid that self-absolutism which—as we noted previously—belongs to the structure of violent acts.

For each of these reasons, the first element that the reaction to crime should incorporate is the attempt to rebalance the violation of mutual respect and dialogical reciprocity that the crime created: this includes the necessity of re-empowering the victim and meeting his or her needs, as well as an attempt

anthropological and ethical model during the modern age), important references can be found in the Jewish idea of 'shalom' (see Zehr, 2002: 125–133; Yoder, 1987) and in the concepts of 'harmonia' and 'kosmos', which emerged within Greek philosophy (see, e.g., Moro 1996). Such ideas found a very important development in the Christian tradition, in which the lessons of Jewish prophetism and classical philosophy found a peculiar synthesis (see on this Ratzinger 1992). For a brief overview of the ancient and early medieval conceptions of punishment and their relational character, see Velo Dalbrenta (2000).

60. See, among the several, diverse voices that support such a critical attitude towards theories of 'crime as law-breaking', Barnett and Hagel (eds.) (1977); Cavalla (1979); Mathieu (1978); Bianchi (2004); Christie (1977); Zehr (1985); Wright (1991); Cragg (1992).

61. As Cavalla puts it, the legal order is valid only when it does not assume itself as definitive. The validity of any human order, including the legal system, requires that such order is always open to be discussed and overwhelmed. See Cavalla (1998: 77). According to such a view, the protection of the dialogical condition can never be perpetrated in violation of subjectivity and relationality, in order not to contradict the reason why such a protection is invoked: therefore, all the issues of 'prevention' and 'social control' must be directed to promoting and protecting sociality and subjectivity as undividable, interconnected and complementary dimensions. This includes also the problem of facing social dangerousness. See, for some reflections, Reggio (2010b).

to restore a situation of mutuality between victim and offender, which happens at first when the latter is asked to provide reasons for his behaviour. It is at that moment, in fact, that the offender ceases to be an 'absolute' and is required to provide reasons for his behaviour and accept the objections that are intended to show that his acts were ultimately unjustified.[62] For such reasons, the reaction to crime ought to be *participatory* and designed to allow a dialogue between the various (direct and indirect) stakeholders.[63]

Furthermore, the need to honour each person as a relational and responsible being implies that the legal order, in reacting to crime, should try its best to avoid any forms of 'imitation' of violence.[64] In addition, the offender must be honoured as a responsible and relational being, included — however horrible his conduct might have been — in the dialogical dimension. A reparative approach to the reaction to crime appears to be the most suitable to these needs, since it neither seeks to 'imitate' violence through retaliation, nor aims at in some way 'transforming' the criminal in ways that supposedly respond to the need for (re)creating a 'social order'. Reparation tries to 'put right the wrongs', so it recognises the harm and the need for assessing its seriousness, though in a constructive way.[65] As Brunk observes — following Cragg — 'criminal sentencing should aim to go as far as possible in this by seeking to repair the damage caused by the offense, but also by ameliorating the conflict situation that produced the offences'.[66] The first way of seeking

---

62. The latter elements are undoubtedly common to a restorative approach to justice. Such reflection moves towards understanding law as an instrument finalised to fostering and protecting the dialogical dimension, and that tries to restore it when it is violated. The dialogical dimension would become both the justification and the limit of law of its binding (and sometimes also coercive) power. See, for a more detailed argumentation, Reggio (2010: 190–212). I saw an embryo of such perspective also in Vico's theory of nature law and in his approach to the problem of punishment. See, for an overview, Reggio (2004: 253–295).

63. See also, in an interesting comparison with an example taken from ancient Greece, Zanuso (2009).

64. About the 'imitation of violence' that occurs within the retaliatory structure of retribution and the risks of unjustly instrumentalising the offender within preventive theories (deterrence, neutralisation or rehabilitation approaches) my main references are: Brunk (2001); Zanuso and Fuselli (eds.) (2004).

65. I am here referring to Zehr's typical expression (2002), *passim*.

66. See Brunk (2001: 46); Cragg (1992), *passim*.

such amelioration is in trying to restore a situation of dialogue and mutuality in the *process* of responding to crime.[67]

Restorative Justice and the Challenge of Complexity

At this point we can see that many of restorative justice's premises and proposals assume a consistent and global characterisation when confronted with the philosophical-ethical reflections previously outlined.

First, by proposing not to consider crime exclusively as 'law-breaking' and in proposing a notion of crime as a harm to people and relationships, restorative justice challenges the predominantly 'technical' and 'abstract' vision of law that still informs the theory and practice of criminal justice. In doing so the restorative approach appears to suggest a sort of 'Copernican revolution', according to which the person — as an individual and as a relational being — is to be considered 'central' and not peripheral. Consequently the reaction to crime can never be reduced to the mere 'application of norms' but is informed by a relational idea of law and society.

Secondly, we can also understand the terms in which restorative justice proposes to set free the issue of responding to crime from 'the idea that criminal punishment has to "pay back" the offender with a harm of some kind', and also 'from a definition of justice in terms of an appropriate amount of harm (either "just desert" or "sufficient deterrence" or "neutralisation"). It is free to explore all kinds of ways in which a sentence can realise a proper restoration' (Brunk, 2001: 647). This does not mean, of course, that the reaction to crime has to be seen as the mere result of some sort of negotiation or bargaining, or even as a chance dependent outcome.

As we have noted with reference to the issue of the 'indigence of truth', determining the correct reaction to crime is always, in any case, a complex question that never responds to a pre-determined measure. This does not mean, of course, that such a determination should not respond to criteria of reasonableness, equity and adequacy: it means that the referral to these principles will have to be discussed from time to time among those who have a stake in a specific controversy. The participatory character of restorative practices, for such reasons, can be seen as a way to enable a dialogical

---

67. The word 'process' does not refer to a specific form or instrument of conflict resolution, therefore it should be intended in general and abstract terms.

consideration of how to respond to the harm that crime created. In other words, participation can offer an actualisation of a dialogical approach to justice in which the confrontation between stakeholders searching for 'what justice requires' is meant to put into practice the common search for rationally agreeable and acceptable solutions.

Third, allowing the participation of victim(s), offender(s) and other stakeholders is important in order to restore a situation of dialogue and mutuality that, as we have seen, is essential to restoring the reciprocity that is inherent in the dialogical condition.

And finally, the reparative connotation of the concept of restoration acquires a further philosophical consolidation, when considering the reaction to crime in reparative terms appears most suitable to a concept of legal order that is itself respectful of the indigence of truth and of the dialogical condition that characterises human beings and human institutions.

This should confirm that both the participatory and the reparative dimensions that restorative justice proposes are not just 'optional' elements of an 'optional' paradigm of conflict resolution: rather, they are an attempt to apply practically a *dialogical idea* of justice that considers complexity as a challenge and not an excuse for refusing to constantly (and dialogically) search for what justice requires. Here, both the philosophical need to provide best reasons, and the practical concerns of those who aspire to re-envision criminal justice through a restorative lens, can perhaps look in the same direction.

References

Ancel, M. (1966), *La défense sociale nouvelle*, Paris: Cujas.

Augustine (1951), *Against the Academics*, New York-Ramsey: Newman Press.

Barnett, R. and Hagel, J. (eds.) (1977), *Assessing the Criminal: Restitution, Retribution and the Legal Process*, Cambridge: Harvard University Press.

Bauman, Z. (1993), *Postmodern Ethics*, Malden-Oxford-Carlton: Blackwell.

Bauman, Z. (2000), *Liquid Modernity*, Cambridge: Polity Press.

Beck, U. (1992), *Risk Society: Towards a New Modernity*, London: Sage.

Bellofiore, L. (1954), 'La dottrina del diritto naturale' in Vico, G. B., Milano: Giuffré.

Berti, E. (2006), 'Il richiamo alla "metafisica classica"' in Berti, E. (ed.), *Filosofie 'minoritarie' in Italia tra le due guerre*, Roma: Aracne, 22–34.

Bianchi, H. (2004), *Justice as a Sanctuary. Towards a Non-punitive System of Crime Control*, Bloomington-Indianapolis: Indiana University Press.

Bošnjak, M. (2007), 'Some Thoughts About the Relationship Between Restorative Justice and the Law' in Mackay, R., Bošnjak, M, Deklerck, J., Pelikan, C., Van Stokkom B. and Wright M. (eds.), *Images of Restorative Justice Theory*, Frankfurt-am-Main: Verlag für Polizeiwissenschaft, 93–111.

Braithwaite, J. (2003), 'Principles of Restorative Justice' in Von Hirsch, A., Roberts, J, Bottoms, A., Roach J., and Schiff, M. (eds.), *Restorative Justice and Criminal Justice: Competing or Reconcilable Paradigms?*, Oxford: Portland (Or), 1–20.

Brown, H. I. (1988), *Rationality*, London and New York: Routledge.

Brunk, C. G. (2001), 'Restorative Justice and the Philosophical Theories of Criminal Punishment' in Hadley M. L. (ed.), *The Spiritual Roots of Restorative Justice*, Albany: State University of New York Press, 31–56.

Buber, M. (1947), *Dialogisches Leben*, Zurich: Gregor Müller.

Capograssi, G. (1953), *Introduzione alla vita etica*, Milano: Giuffré.

Cavalla, F. (1979), *La pena come problema. Per un superamento della concezione razionalistica della difesa sociale*, Padova: Cedam.

Cavalla, F. (1990), 'Sul fondamento delle norme etiche' in Angelini, G., Cavalla, F. and Lecaldano, E., *Problemi di etica: fondazione, norme, orientamenti*, Padova: Gregoriana (Lanza Foundation), 142–202.

Cavalla, F. (1996), *La verità dimenticata. Attualità dei presocratici dopo la secolarizzazione*, Padova: Cedam.

Cavalla, F. (ed.) (1997), *Cultura moderna ed interpretazione classica*, Padova: Cedam.

Cavalla, F. (1998), 'La pena come riparazione. Oltre la concezione liberale dello stato: per una teoria radicale della pena' in Cavalla F. and Todescan F. (eds.), *Pena e riparazione*, Padova: Cedam, 1–109.

Cavalla, F. (2000), 'Libertà da, libertà per: ordine e mistero' in Bassani L. *et al.*, *L'insopportabile peso dello stato*, Treviglio-Bergamo: Leonardo Facco.

Cavalla, F. (ed.) (2007), *Retorica, processo, verità*, Milano: FrancoAngeli, 1–101.

Christie, N. (1977), 'Conflicts as Property', *British Journal of Criminology*, No.17, 1–8.

Connor, S. (1989), *Postmodernist Culture. An Introduction to the Theories of the Contemporary*, Oxford: Oxford University Press.

Cotta, S. (1991), *Il diritto nell'esistenza. Linee di ontofenomenologia del diritto*, Milano: Giuffré.

Cragg, W. (1992), *The Practice of Punishment. Towards a Theory of Restorative Justice*, London — New York: Routledge.

Derrida, J. and Defourmantelle, A. (2000), *On Hospitality*, Stanford: Stanford University Press.

Dworkin, R. (1996), 'Objectivity and Truth: You'd Better Believe It', *Philosophy and Public Affairs*, no.25, 87–139.

Eser, A. (2007), 'The Nature and Rationale of Punishment', *Cardozo Law Review*, no.28/6, 2,427–2,437.

Fuselli, S. (2001), *Processo, pena e mediazione nella filosofia del diritto di Hegel*, Padova: Cedam.

Habermas, J. (2003), *Truth and Justification*, Cambridge: Harvard University Press.

Illetterati, L. (1996), *Figure del limite. Esperienze e forme della finitezza*, Trento: Verifiche.

Johnstone, G. and Van Ness, D. (2007) 'The Meaning of Restorative Justice' in Johnstone G. and Van Ness D. (eds.), *Handbook of Restorative Justice*, Devon, Cullompton: Willan Publishing, 5–23.

Karp, D. (2000), 'Sociological Communitarianism and the "Just" Community', *Contemporary Justice Review*, no.3, 153–173

Lederach J. P. (2005), *The Moral Imagination. The Art and Soul of Building Peace*, Oxford: Oxford University Press.

Lilla, M. (1993), *G. B. Vico, The Making of an Anti-modern*, Cambridge: Harvard University Press.

Lyotard, J. F. (1984), *The Post-modern Condition. A Report on Knowledge*, Minneapolis: University of Minnestota Press.

Mackay, R. E. (2007), 'Law as Peacemaking: Beyond the Concept of Restorative Justice' in Mackay, R., Bošnjak, M., Deklerck, J., Pelikan, C., Van Stokkom B, and Wright, M. (eds.), *Images of Restorative Justice Theory*, Frankfurt-am-Main: Verlag für Polizeiwissenschaft, 112–128.

Manzin, M., *An Outline on Legal Rhetoric*. Available online at the website of the Center for Research on Legal Methodology (Cermeg): www.cermeg.it/eng.

Mathieu, V. (1978), *Perché punire? Il collasso della giustizia penale*, Milano: Giuffré.

Moro, P. (1996), 'L'essenza della legg: saggio sul minosse platonico' in: Cavalla, F. (ed.), *Cultura moderna e interpretazione classica*, Padova: Cedam, 113–168.

Mounier, E. (1949), *Le personnalisme*, Paris: Presses Universitaires de France.

Patterson, D. (1999), *Law and Truth*, Oxford: Oxford University Press.

Pavlich, G. (2006), *Governing Paradoxes of Restorative Justice*, London: Glass House Press.

Pavlich, G. (2007), 'Ethics, Universal Principles and Restorative Justice' in Johnstone G. and Van Ness. D. W. (eds.), *Handbook of Restorative Justice*, Devon, Cullompton: Willan Publishing, 615–627.

Pelikan, C. (2007), 'The Place of Restorative Justice in Society: Making Sense of Developments in Time and Space' in Mackay, R., Bošnjak, M., Deklerck, J., Pelikan, C., Van Stokkom B, and Wright, M. (eds.), *Images of Restorative Justice Theory*, Frankfurt-am-Main: Verlag für Polizeiwissenschaft, 35–55.

Pranis, K. (2007), 'Restorative Values' in Johnstone G. and Van Ness, D. W., *Handbook of Restorative Justice*, Devon, Cullompton: Willan Publishing, 59–74.

Putnam, H. (1990), *Realism with a Human Face*, Cambridge: Harvard University Press.

Ratzinger, J. (1992), *Introducing Christian Doctrine*, Grant Rapids-Cambridge: Eerdmans.

Ratzinger, J. and Pera, M. (2006), *Without Roots*, New York: Basic Books.

Reggio, F. (2004), 'Una riflessione sui concetti vichiani di "pena" e "penitenza"' in Zanuso F., Fuselli S. (eds.), *Ripensare la pena*, Padova: Cedam, 253–295.

Reggio, F. (2010a), *Giustizia dialogica. Luci e ombre della restorative justice*, Milano: FrancoAngeli.

Reggio, F. (2010b), 'Facing Dangerousness or Creating New Dangers? Community and Informal Cocial Control in the Debate on Restorative Justice' in S. Tzitzis (ed.), *Peine, dangerosité—quelles certitudes?*, Paris: Dalloz, 323–340.

Reggio, F. (2012), 'A Discarded Image. Rediscovering Vico's Lesson as a Topical Heritage for Contemporary Reflection on Law and Justice', *L'Ircocervo* 1, 1–29.

Roche, D. (2001), 'The Evolving Definition of Restorative Justice', *Contemporary Justice Review*, No.4, 341–353.

Sawatsky, J. (2008), *Justpeace Ethics. A Guide to Restorative Justice and Peacebuilding*, Eugene: Cascade Books.

Schrag, C. O. (1992), *The Resources of Rationality. A Response to the Postmodern Turn*, Bloomington: Indiana University Press.

Slob, W. (2002), *Dialogical Rhetoric. An Essay on Truth and Normativity after Postmodernism*, Dordrecht: Kluwer.

Van Huyssteen, W. (1997), *Essays in Post-foundationalist Theology*, Grand Rapids: Eerdmans.

Vanfraechem, I. (2007), 'Community, Society and State in Restorative Justice: An Exploration' in Mackay, R., Bošnjak, M., Deklerck, J., Pelikan, C., Van Stokkom, B. and Wright, M (eds.), *Images of Restorative Justice Theory*, Frankfurt-am-Main: Verlag für Polizeiwissenschaft, 73–85.

Velo Dalbrenta, D. (2000), 'Il diritto penale al cospetto di Dio' in Cavalla F. and Todescan, F. (eds.), *Pena e riparazione*, Padova: Cedam, 340–412.

Vendemiati, A. (2007), *Universalismo e relativismo nell'etica contemporanea*, Genova: Marietti.

Verene, D.P. (2008), 'Vichian Moral Philosophy: Prudence as Jurisprudence', *Chicago-Kent Law Review*, No.83, 1107–1130.

Vico, G. B. (2003), *De antiquissima italorum sapientia* (1711), Roma: Storia e Letteratura.

Vico, G. B. (1744), *La Scienza Nuova*, 3rd edn. (See, for the English edition, Vico G. B. (1968), *The New Science of Giambattista Vico*, transl. by T. G. Bergin and M. H. Fisch, Ithaca: Cornell University Press).

Von Hirsch, A., Ashworth, A. and Shearing, C. (2003), 'Specifying Aims and Limits for Restorative Justice: A "Making Amends" Model?' in Von Hirsch, A., Roberts, J and Bottoms, A. E. (eds.), *Restorative Justice and Criminal Justice: Competing or Reconcilable Paradigms?*, Oxford-Portland, 21–41.

Walgrave, L. (2007), 'Integrating Criminal Justice and Restorative Justice' in Johnstone G. and Van Ness, D. (eds.), *Handbook of Restorative Justice*, Devon, Cullompton: Willan Publishing, 559–579.

Walgrave, L. (2008), *Restorative Justice, Self Interest and Responsible Citizenship*, Devon, Cullompton: Willan Publishing.

Wiggins, D.(2006), *Twelve Lectures on the Philosophy of Morality*, Cambridge: Harvard University Press.

Williams, M. (1996), *Unnatural Doubts: Epistemological Realism and the Basis of Scepticism*, Princeton: Princeton University Press.

Wright, M. (1991), *Justice for Victims and Offenders*, Philadelphia: Open University Press. (2nd edn. 1996, Sherfield-on-Loddon, UK: Waterside Press). (2007),

Wright, M. (2007), 'Punishment and Restorative Justice: An Ethical Comparison' in Mackay, R., Bošnjak, M., Deklerck, J., Pelikan, C., Van Stokkom, B. and Wright, M. (eds.), *Images of Restorative Justice Theory*, Frankfurt-am-Main: Verlag für Polizeiwissenschaft, 168–184.

Wright, M. and Zernova, M. (2007), 'Alternative Visions of Restorative Justice' in: Johnstone G. and Van Ness, D. (eds.), *Handbook of Restorative Justice*, Devon, Cullompton: Willan Publishing, 91–108.

Yoder, P. B. (1987), *Shalom: The Bible's Word for Salvation*, Newton: Faith and Life Press.

Zanuso, F. (1994), *Conflitto e controllo sociale nel pensiero politico-giuridico moderno*, Padova: Cleup.

Zanuso, F. (1998), 'Post-modernità e pena: alcune riflessioni sulla "Just Desert Theory"', *Diritto e Società*, 4, 615–657.

Zanuso, F. (2009), 'Les avantages de la justice réparatrice et la sagesse du tribunal de l'Héliée' in S. Tztzis (ed.), *Déviance et délinquances. Approches psycho-sociales et pénales*. Paris: Dalloz, 331–357.

Zanuso, F. (2000), *A ciascuno il suo: La retribuzione da Kant a Norval Morris*, Padova: Cedam.

Zanuso, F. and Fuselli, S. (eds.) (2004), *Ripensare la pena. Teorie e problemi nella riflessione moderna*, Padova: Cedam.

Zehr, H. (1985), 'Retributive Justice, Restorative Justice', *New Perspectives on Crime and Justice*, No.4.

Zehr, H. (1990) *Changing Lenses. A New Focus on Crime and Justice*, Scottsdale: Herald Press.

Zehr, H. (1995), 'Justice Paradigm Shift? Values and Visions in the Reform Process', *Mediation Quarterly* XXII, no.3, 207–216.

Zehr, H. (2002), *The Little Book of Restorative Justice*, Intercourse: Good Books.

Zehr, H. and Toews, B. (eds.) (2004), *Critical Issues in Restorative Justice*, Monsey-New York: Criminal Justice Press.

11

From Civilising Punishment to Civilising Criminal Justice: From Punishment to Restoration

Lode Walgrave

The title of this volume contains an ambiguity, which may be deliberate. 'Civilising Criminal Justice' indeed can have two main or principal meanings. For some, 'civilising criminal justice' means making criminal law into civil law. For others, the same expression stands for making criminal law more civilised. The latter is what I understand by it.

Preserving a Criminal Justice System

Abolitionists argue for abolishing criminal justice (Hulsman, 1979; Bianchi, 1994). Instead, they propose a model of deliberation between conflicting citizens that should be made available and accessible to all. The remaining matters of conflict are to be subjected to civil courts. The main arguments for this radical option are the cruelty of 'man-inflicted pain', even if it is inflicted under the label of punishment (Christie, 1981), and the destructive impact it has on human relations. In the abolitionists' view, the concept of crime would disappear or be reduced to extreme behaviour. In principle, all norm transgressions are seen as conflicts between citizens. In Christie's figurative language, the state's criminal justice system 'stole' the conflict from its owners, and this conflict should be given back to them (Christie, 1977). Abolitionists believe in the potential of citizens to find solutions through deliberation. Only if necessary and as a last resort, a very reserved state power would cut the knot in conflicts where deliberation among citizens does not result in an agreement. The state's intervention would be based on civil law procedures.

Not surprisingly, this view emerged in the critical 1960s and 1970s, and was part of a larger social critical movement that believed in the spontaneous human potential to organize peaceful emancipating communities with marginalised state power only. The enthusiasm of the movement however overlooked a crucial dimension. It may become clear through two examples. What shall happen if a lonely homeless person is murdered? The settlement of this event cannot be reduced to deliberation among individual citizens, because one of the crucial stakeholders in 'the conflict' would remain absent for ever. Yet, a disapproving and norm enforcing response to the murder of this person is indispensable. Probably, the community in one or another form will have to be involved as an interested third party, and not only as arbiter.

The second example may seem simplistic and down to earth. Imagine that I steal a car. If I am not caught, I have the car. If I am caught, I have to settle 'the conflict' with the owner. Probably, I will have to give the car back to the owner, and pay some compensation. When that is done, I can try again tomorrow, hoping that I will be luckier this time. All in all, that does not seem the best response. The intuitive feeling is that something more is needed to respond adequately to the theft of a car.

Obviously, stealing or committing private violence is more than a just a conflict between two (or more) citizens. The procedural differences between civil law and criminal law clearly reflect this. Civil law is reactive. It acts only in response to a complaint. Criminal law, on the contrary, is proactive. Criminal procedures can be activated on the initiative of criminal law agents themselves. While most criminal justice procedures start in practice after a complaint by citizens, the possibility to start up itself shows that other principles are involved here. Not just the victim and the offender, but also 'society' is concerned by what is called an offence. In crime something more is at stake than in a tort. What is that 'something more'?

Criminal justice as a moral messenger?

Many scholars believe in the moral function of criminal justice. In that view, the function of criminal law is not just to resolve conflicts between citizens. Criminal law also sends a public moral message (Duff, 2001). Basically, this position suggests an overlap of criminal justice with social ethics. Crime must be punished to mark the wrong, they state, in line with Kant. Boutellier

(2004: 27) quotes Durkheim saying that the criminal trial is a 'celebration of public morals'. This statement provokes three types of question: (1) what is a wrong?; (2) Does the criminal justice system reflect the rejection of the wrongs?; and (3) Is punishment the only possible way to express the rejection of a wrong? We now deal with the first two questions.

Defining the wrong is quite a challenge. Surprisingly, retributivists seldom question the ethical value of the norm system itself, which the punishment is supposed to enforce. Most retributivists seem to uncritically equate legal order with moral order. But that is far from being evident.

Would there be an intrinsic wrong, linked to human nature? Do *mala in se* exist, and how are they defined? Freud argued that our morality is basically a psychodynamic construct to keep our libido within socially acceptable channels. For Durkheim, the function of morality is to preserve cohesion in society. Both godfathers of social sciences have grounded a scientific tradition that stripped ethical systems from their unworldly dogmatic nature, and reduced it to what they are: a pragmatic system to keep living together liveable. As Elias describes, the gradual development of these rules has penetrated social life and individual persons so deeply that they seem to have become intrinsic to human psychology, a basic characteristic of human existence and an indispensable part of our civilisation (Elias, 2000).

Nevertheless, rejecting a 'wrong' appears to be not really inspired by a general human attachment to 'the right', which would be given by nature. It is a pragmatic aversion from what we experience as a threat for our personal and social lives and our comfort.[1] Deep down, ethical categories, distinguishing the right from the wrong, seem to rest upon self-interest. What we can only hope is that self-interest is understood in terms of being a participant in harmonious communities leading to mutual respect, solidarity and taking active responsibility. And, fortunately, it mostly is (Putnam, 2001).

It is difficult to maintain that criminal justice reflects the aversion from an abstract 'wrong'. While a number of criminal stipulations indeed reflect a kind of moral consensus about what is intolerable, not all of them are rooted in moral beliefs. Many are meant to preserve social interactions within a

---

1. *'Le crime ne blesse les sentiments que d'une façon secondaire et dérivée. Primitivement, ce sont les intérêts qu'il lèse'* (Crime does not injure feelings except in a secondary and derivative way. Primarily, it is people's interests that it harms.) (Maxwell, 1914, cit. in Debuyst, 1990: 357).

given community or even simply to serve the interests of particular population groups, mostly linked to the powerful in society. The least we can say about some criminal regulations in some regimes is that they are themselves morally doubtful. Inversely, many immoral acts are not criminally punishable. The death penalty, killing in war, using power for self-interest, causing harsh living conditions for populations, all are actions which could be called 'intrinsically immoral', but which are committed in and by self-declared 'model democracies'. In political and in business life, lying and cheating is common. In sports, committing so called 'professional fouls' is the rule.

Criminal punishment is used to enforce any legal system. It is used in our democratic regimes, and in the most dictatorial regimes as well. It is an act of power to express disapproval, possibly to enforce compliance, but it is neutral about the value system it enforces. Basically, criminal justice is nothing more than a system of discipline within a given political regime (Foucault, 1975). Ethical questions about legal order must be asked, including about the legal order in our Western democracies. Why, for example, is penal law predominantly geared to public order, individual physical integrity and property, and not, for example, to social peace, solidarity, and social and economic equity?

Maybe, the very pragmatic actuarial approach to criminal justice (as described by Feeley and Simon (1992)) is stripping criminal justice too much from its moral dimension. However, the link between moral wrongs and criminal justice is far thinner than some rhetoric suggests, and the penetration of morals in criminal justice is partial and selective.

And that is a good thing. Prosecuting all acts which are judged to be immoral by those in power would yield an ethical absolutism, a suffocating cultural and social climate grounding totalitarian regimes. We have witnessed such development for example in Afghanistan ruled by the Taliban. And the 'Talibanisation' of society, losing the achievements of the Enlightenment, is not what we want.

Harm to social life

What then grounds the selection of conducts to be criminally punishable, to mark the crucial difference between a tort and an offence? Where lies the fundamental justification of proactive public intervention in individual behaviour? It is the harm certain conduct is supposed to cause to the quality of social life.

It is not moral beliefs that ground the criteria for designating criminal behaviour, but the concept of public order. Public order and norm enforcement must be limited to what is needed for the quality of public life. Why, for example, is it debated whether criminal justice should intervene in some types of sexual behaviour among consenting adults or in the use of illegal drugs? While there may be a large majority who consider such behaviours undesirable or even unethical, there is no agreement on whether they are so harmful to other people or to social life that they justify the authorities' intrusion into individual rights and freedoms. Authorities cannot interfere coercively in our lives unless it serves to prevent harm to fellow citizens or to public life. Here is the criterion to define a 'public wrong', as the reason for public intervention: the harm it causes to fellow citizens and to social life in general.

In an article with Jareborg, Von Hirsch distinguishes four types of 'damages to standards of living' (physical integrity, material support, freedom from humiliation and privacy/autonomy: Von Hirsch and Jareborg, 1991). Boutellier (2000) advances 'victimalisation' as the 'moral minimum' to underpin a commonly acceptable criminal justice system. John Braithwaite and Philip Pettit speak in terms of 'intrusion into dominion' (1990). They all consider the harm or damage to others and/or to collective life as the reason to criminalise certain behaviour.

And rightly so. In a crime, not only the interests and needs of an individual victim (and his or her community of care) are infringed, but also those of the social context as a whole. Crimes are considered also as public events, traditionally dealt with by criminal law.

What makes an offence a collective or public event? After a burglary, for example, restitution or compensation for the individual victim's losses could be private, to be arranged by civil law. But we are all concerned that the authorities respond to the burglary. Let us imagine that the authorities did nothing, or limited the intervention to registering the crime and identifying the burglar, and then inviting offender and victim to try to find a solution, without exerting pressure on the burglar. Probably, most burglaries would remain unresolved, provoking private actions to 'make things even', leading to an escalation in mutual revenge, and dragging down security in the community as a whole.

The disinterested attitude by the authorities would also hurt all citizens' trust in public rules, in their right to privacy and property, and in the authorities' power and willingness to preserve order and justice. Not only would peaceful life in the community be lost, but also order and justice in society. 'While the government is responsible for preserving a just public order, the community's role in establishing and maintaining a just peace must be given special significance' (Van Ness and Heetderks Strong, 2002: 42). Both order and peace are threatened by the crime, and need a public response.

The public dimension of crime lies in the threat and the harm it causes to public trust in norms and norm enforcement.

Dominion

The notion of dominion, as presented in Braithwaite and Pettit's Republican theory of criminal justice (Braithwaite and Pettit, 1990), helps us to understand this.

Dominion (or 'freedom as non-domination')[2] can be defined as the set of assured rights and freedoms. It is the mental and social territory of which we freely dispose, guaranteed by the state and by the social context in which we live. The assurance aspect of rights and freedoms is critical. The assurance element marks the decisive distinction between the social concept of 'freedom as non-domination' and the liberal concept of 'freedom as non-interference'. In the latter, the rights and freedoms of the individual citizen end where the rights and freedoms of the other citizens begin. The set of rights and freedoms is conceived as a stable given, which must be distributed as justly as possible. All other citizens are possible interferers in my freedom and rivals in my struggle to expand my freedom. State intervention is pushed back as far as possible and strictly limited to what is vital to preserve individual liberties. Justice and jurisdiction are settlements of conflicts of interests between citizens, and between citizens and the state.

---

2.   In more recent publications, dominion has been renamed as 'freedom as non-domination'. This may make it easier to oppose it to the liberal concept typified as 'freedom as non-interference', but I see no other advantage in complicating the wording. I will therefore stick to the old naming, dominion.

In the Republican view, on the contrary, rights and freedoms are a collective good. Dominion is not a stable given but a value to be promoted and expanded by individual and collective action. Fellow citizens are allies in trying to extend and mutually assure dominion as a collective good.

The citizens and the state seek to extend and deepen dominion by promoting equality through more participation in democracy, more education, equitable socio-economic policy, welfare policy and the like. Criminal justice is the defensive institution. Its aim is not to extend or deepen dominion, but to repair it when it has been intruded upon by crime (Walgrave, 2000). The intrusion most hurts the assurance of dominion. In the case of the burglary, for example, it is not the legal right of privacy and possession that is lost, because these rights remain legally defined. What is lost, or at least shaken, is the *assurance* that fellow citizens respect these rights. The victim is confronted with the fact that, despite the legally guaranteed home safety, he did not enjoy this safety.

But, contrary to the position taken in the 'civilisation thesis', the impact of the burglary goes beyond the individual victim. As we have just seen, the civilisation thesis replaces criminal law by a system of—legally monitored—compensatory mechanisms (Hulsman, 1982). In that view, the restitution or compensation of the victim's losses could be private, to be arranged as a tort in civil law. If the victim and the burglar then agree about restitution and compensation, all is settled. However, that would mistakenly neglect the public side (Johnstone, 2002; Bottoms, 2003). The burglary not only damages the individual victim's trust that his or her privacy and possessions will be respected by his or her fellow citizens. The particular victim stands as an example of the risk run by all citizens. If the authorities did nothing against the particular burglary, it would undermine all citizens' trust in their right to privacy and possession.

Hence, public intervention after a crime is not primarily needed to redress the balance of benefits and burdens, or to reconfirm the law, as traditional penal theories suggest. It is needed first of all to enhance assurance by communicating the message that the authorities take dominion seriously. The intervention must reassure the victim and the public at large of their rights and freedoms. It must restore these rights and freedoms into a fully-fledged dominion through clear public censure of the intrusion and through public actions involving, if possible, the offender in reparative actions. Voluntary cooperation by the offender is more effective in restoring assurance, but it is imperative that it is backed by public institutions. The reassurance comes not only from the offender's repentance and apologies, but also from the authorities' determination to take the assured rights and freedoms seriously.

Referring the matters which are now subject to criminal justice to civil procedures would drop this 'public dimension' in the response to crime. Yet authorities' assurance that they take dominion seriously is necessary for peace in communities and public order, which are both indispensable conditions for developing social life. A criminal justice system that includes the public interest in the quality of social life is crucial to express this assurance. We must preserve such a system, addressing conduct that is not only unjust, not always ethically wrong, but is considered to threaten the quality of social life as a whole.

This principled position is not a defence of the current public order as defined by the current criminal laws. The selection of conducts currently subjected to criminal justice is debatable. As suggested a few paragraphs ago, a number of scholars find that the current penal law is too one-sidedly oriented towards safeguarding physical integrity and individual property, and neglects crucial social goods such as social peace, solidarity, and social and economic equity. But that is another debate which goes beyond this chapter.

The question now is which kind of criminal justice can best assure dominion.

Making Criminal Justice More Civilised

Let us be serious: if the reason for criminalising certain behaviour is defined in terms of harms to social life, then the functioning of criminal justice must logically be evaluated in terms of its contribution to the avoidance or the reparation of these harms.

Current criminal justice systems are characterised by the premise that crimes must be responded to by inflicting punishment to the offender. The essence of punishment is the deliberate infliction of pain on the one who is considered to have committed an unacceptable conduct. As Von Hirsch writes: 'Punishing someone consists of visiting a deprivation (hard treatment) on him, because he supposedly has committed a wrong...' (1993: 9).

Three elements are distinguished: hard treatment, the intention of inflicting it, and the link with the wrong committed.[3] If one of these elements is lacking, there is no punishment. Painful obligations that are imposed without the intention to cause suffering are not punishments. That is the key difference between a fine and taxes. 'Pain in punishment is inflicted for the sake of pain …' (Fatic, 1995: 197).

A few penal theorists try to release the link between criminal punishment and pain infliction (De Hert, 2009). They understand that too easy and too intensive infliction of pain is problematic, and they seem to strive for a kind of penal justice without pain infliction. It is like searching for dry water. If you take away the intentional infliction of pain, you cannot call it a punishment and the punitive premise of criminal justice disappears. The paradigm of penal justice fades away.

The essence of punishment is not that the response to the undesired behaviour is painful, but that *we want* it to be painful (Wright, 2003). It is the intention of the punisher to impose hard treatment that counts, not the perception of the punished. The question that now arises is, whether the link between criminal justice and the civilisation process inevitably implies that criminal justice should remain based on the premise of punishment.

Civilisation of punishment

In Elias' conception, the process of civilisation involves a transformation of human behaviour, which is based on changing patterns of social interactions and a consequent modification in psychical structures (2000). Increasing differentiation and specialisation in labour and in services yield an intensification of mutual dependency. Mutual dependency creates the necessity of finding ways of dealing constructively with each other, self-control and discipline. Aggression in daily relations must be reduced, peace and security enhanced. Control over individuals becomes more strict and differentiated.

This development over generations has an impact on the psychological functioning of individuals, and especially on their drives and emotions. Gradually, the restraints are internalised; instinctual pleasures are repressed

---

3. Contrary to Von Hirsch, I do not add the dis-approbatory message as another characteristic. Punishment in practice is often administered routinely, and it is experienced as a price to be paid, without any moral reflection at all.

by way of moral emotions like shame, embarrassment, anxieties. The levels of delicacy and sensitivity heighten. Others are increasingly seen as fellow humans, worthy of respect.

One of the societal consequences of this process is that violence in individual relations is rejected, and actually is decreasing, while it is monopolised in the hands of the central power. The criminal justice system is the preeminent system of state violence. But also here, refining sensibilities have their impact. The cruelty of criminal punishment decreases. Punishment is reconsidered as a moderate response with constructive objectives.

Garland has expanded on Elias's approach to the developments in criminal punishment (1990). The most crucial expression of civilisation in criminal justice is the disappearance of the scaffold and the growing capacity of the central states to impose a decent level of law and order in an orderly way (see also Spierenburg, 1984). More and more 'punishment is nowadays undertaken in special enclaves removed from public view' (1990: 234). Sensitivities have made the imposition of painful punishments to the offender a painful event to the spectator himself or herself, so that it is now executed 'behind the scenes', in order not to shock the more delicate feelings of the public. 'The civilisation process in punishment is also apparent in the sanitisation of penal practice and penal language' (1990: 235). Physical violence has almost disappeared, penal regimes are rationalised and professionalised, stripped from emotional bias. '"Guards" become "officers", and "prisoners" become "inmates" or even "residents"' (1990: 235). Finally, Garland considers the 'extension of sympathy to the offender' as the most obvious expression of the civilisation process (1990: 236). The capacity to feel companionship with social inferiors and enemies is a high point in the process. It is obvious in the welfare and rehabilitation approach which has penetrated the criminal justice system and its sanctions, modifying the penal system into what has been called by Garland 'the penal welfare complex' (2001).

De-civilisation?

Civilisation does not develop in a straight line. Elias recognised that the structure of social organization and the structure of human personality yield other factors and dynamics which may influence deeply the development of human interactions. Garland refers to several social structures and other sensibilities that may curb, retard or stop the civilisation process of criminal punishment. Social inequalities and particular interests, 'the need to maintain proper levels of deterrence, security, and reprobation' (Garland, 1990: 237), political groupings that frame crime and justice issues in ideological terms. Garland insists most on the Freudian concept that repressed instincts do not disappear completely and continue to express themselves in 'hidden' forms, including fantasy and irrational behaviour. Fascination with and fear of crime are one of these irrational expressions. 'In a society where instinctual aggressions are strictly controlled and individuals are often self-punishing, the legal punishment of offenders offers a channel for the open expression of aggressions and sanctions a measure of pleasure in the suffering of others' (Garland, 1990: 240).

Pratt goes a step further. He speaks straightforwardly of de-civilisation (1998). Civilisation is characterised among other things by the concentration of violence and penal practice in the hands of the state, including rationalisation and professionalisation. Pratt observes that the axis of penal power has shifted. 'Whereas previously the public was kept away from the process of punishment by a powerful penal bureaucracy ... it now became more and more involved in penal affairs' (Daems, 2008: 90). Penal bureaucracies lost their grip on penal policy to the benefits of public emotions penetrating penal practice.

It is worth noting here that the loss of legitimacy has touched the authorities' apparatus as a whole. We are currently living in an era dominated by the obsession with risk, uncertainty, un-safety, and anxiety, which is often projected on fear of crime. Governments are powerless in governing the foundation of these obsessions, which is capitalist globalisation, and try to maintain their legitimacy by focusing on crime problems and giving in to penal populism (as, for example, described by Bauman (2000) and Walgrave (2008)).

Pratt concludes that we are witnessing a new punitiveness, as can be observed in more and more exclusivist punishment in recent decades. 'Populist punitiveness' is reflected in Pratt's interpretation of penal change: public involvement (populist) and harsher punishments (punitiveness) (Daems, 2008). It marks, for Pratt, the de-civilisation of punishment.

It may be somewhat too quick a conclusion. Pratt's analysis reaches over recent decades only, while the historical reach of Elias, Spierenburg or Garland goes over centuries. Cultural developments over several centuries never go straightforwardly, but with fluctuations. A more optimistic account is that the current comeback of punitiveness is not a definitive turn in the civilisation, but rather a temporary deep in the fluctuating process that would remain fundamentally enhancing.

Boutellier sees it even more optimistically (2004). In his conception, the re-emergence of punishment of recent decades is not a relapse in civilisation, but part of the civilisation process itself. The recent punitive turn may witness a revival of moral awareness. The humane tendency for compassion with the offender has 'bolted' into too permissive tolerance for offending, and thus a loss of social norms. It is a good thing that social norms are currently being reconfirmed with vigour. The mission of civilisation is to combine this persistent norm enforcement with an increasingly humane way of punishing norm transgression. Boutellier points to restorative justice developments as a possible track to find such combination.

In my view, Boutellier is right that the pursuit of more humane responses to crime has been confused sometimes with norm erosion. But I am less optimistic than he is, in my interpretation of the punitive trend of today. After the riots in 2011, for example, the British prime minister repeatedly declared that human rights are the least of his concerns in his 'combat' against the troublemakers. That does not seem to me an expression of increasing civilisation.

Civilisation as an ethical challenge

The debate suggests anyhow that civilisation is not an evident, automatic process. While social structures and dynamics may influence, canalise, orient, slow down or accelerate the process, it is also a matter of options and choices. It is what we want, a social ethical objective. Civilising is a verb, a mission for humanity.

As Elias rightly points out the ground of this process is the mutual dependence of humans. We cannot live without others. We benefit from living together and cooperating peacefully. This human condition is even rooted in our biology. Neuroscientist Cacioppo writes: 'The distinctive human adaptation is to be socially cooperative in a way that allows us to optimise the advantages of the group while retaining our own individuality' (2008: 197). Throughout history, human cooperation has made life longer, less dependent on natural elements, more self-determined, more comfortable and more pleasant. Other human achievements however have caused new insecurities and threats, such as global warming, corruption, poverty and war.

An intrinsic tension subsists between pursuing individual self-interests (as represented in extreme Liberalism) and living as a conscious member of the community (as advanced by Communitarians). Communitarianism can go too far, when it creates the illusion of community consensus. Pushing individual self-determination too far turns into selfishness, creating an everlasting struggle and exploitation of the weakest by the strongest. Both are not favourable to civilisation. Civilisation is also a matter of social-ethical choices.

We have no choice about living with others and being dependent on them, but we have a choice about *how* we live together and how we organize mutual dependency. To grasp the tension between self-interest and mutual dependency, I have advanced the notion of common self-interest (Walgrave, 2008). I shall come back to this notion later in this chapter.

Civilisation thus is more than a sociological and cultural process. It is also a Sisyphean Utopia, orienting social ethical options.

From civilisation of punishment towards civilisation of criminal justice

Roughly, the civilisation process of punishment has taken three steps so far. The first step concentrated violence in the hands of the central power. Private violence was reduced as much as possible so that private social life would be less guided by threat and fear. The second step hid the infliction of punishment away from public sight in order not to shock the sensibilities which were an internalisation of the ongoing civilisation process. The third step made the infliction of pain in punishment itself more civilised, by making it less brutal, more rational and moderate, in the hands of penal professionals.

It looks as if this process is threatened or already blocked in recent decades. The—appropriate—concern for reconfirming the social norm includes a risk of excesses into heavy punitiveness and cruelty (Simon, 2001). It poses the ethical question whether responsible citizens simply undergo these developments or continue pursuing the advancement of civilisation.

The answer to this question is the social ethical option for a new, fourth step in the civilisation of the authorities' use of violence through punishment. This fourth step is the reduction of violence itself to an absolute minimum. Pushing back as much as possible the punitive premise in the response to crime is the logical next phase in the civilisation process. That means less coercion and less pain infliction in a top-down imposition of a formal legal order, but more space for voluntary, non-violent bottom-up responses. Whereas current 'civilised' criminal justice implemented violence with kid gloves, we now advance criminal justice using less violence, but with bare hands. It is not punishment we civilise, but the criminal justice system as a whole.

This option brings us logically to restorative justice (Blad, 2011; Boutellier, 2004).

Restorative Justice[4]

This is not the place to extend the debate between different and even competing visions of restorative justice. Let me just recall how I understand it. Restorative justice is for me 'an option for doing justice after the occurrence of an offence that is primarily oriented towards repairing the individual, relational and social harm caused by that offence' (Walgrave, 2008: 21). For reasons of clarity, the definition focuses on doing justice after the occurrence of an offence. The — very worthwhile — restorative processes after injustices and conflicts in other social contexts are kept out of the definition. The definition presents a 'maximalist' vision. Priority is given to voluntary deliberation among all direct stakeholders as the best possible way to achieve restoration. However, under some conditions, judicial sanctions also are considered as being (partially) reparative. The ambition is to change the punitive premise in current criminal justice into a restorative premise.

Restorative justice is not alternative punishment

The obvious unpleasantness of being involved as an offender in a restorative process has led several scholars to consider restorative justice as an 'alternative punishment', not an 'alternative to punishment'. Duff, for example,

---

4. The ideas in this section have been expanded much more in Walgrave, 2008: 46–62.

considers all hard burdens imposed or accepted under pressure as punishments (1992). However, this position overlooks some critical differences between punishment and restoration.

There is, first of all, an intrinsic difference. Punishment is a means used to enforce any legal and political system, in democratic societies as well as in the most dictatorial regimes. It is neutral about the value system it enforces. Restoration, on the contrary, is not a means, but a potential outcome. Restorative justice is characterised by the aim of doing justice through restoration. The broad scope of harm amenable to possible reparation inherently demonstrates its orientation to the quality of social life, as a normative beacon.

Punishment, meaning intentional infliction of suffering, is not at all an appropriate tool in the pursuit of restoration. On the contrary, the *a priori* option of punishment is a serious obstruction.

The second difference points at the heart of the social ethical debate. Even if participating in a restorative justice process and complying with the agreements may be a heavy burden, its unpleasantness is not the aim.

The crux of punishment lies in the intention of the punisher (Wright, 2003). It is the painfulness in the intention of the punisher that counts, not in the perception of the punished. The punisher considers an action to be wrong and wants the wrongdoer to suffer for it. Many may find the obligation to repair very hard and call it 'a punishment'. But actually it is not a punishment if the intention was not to cause suffering, but to obtain a reasonable reparative contribution.

However, even if there is no *intention* to inflict pain, there must be an *awareness* of the painfulness. Knowing that something will hurt, and taking the hardship into account, is not the same as intentionally inflicting pain. In punishment, the painfulness is the principal yardstick, and its amount can be increased or decreased in order to achieve proportionality. In restoration, on the contrary, a relation may be sought between the nature and seriousness of the harm and the restorative effort; awareness of painfulness can lead to a reduction of the effort required, never to an increase. And that is an ethically crucial distinction.

Arguments in favour of criminal punishment do not stand up

Most ethical systems consider the deliberate and coercive imposition of suffering on another person as unethical and socially destructive. Nevertheless, punishment of offences by criminal justice is considered as self-evident. The question arises why the general ethical rule not to inflict pain on others does not apply to responding to offences. Penal theories advance instrumentalist and retributivist arguments.

According to instrumentalist approaches, penal law is only acceptable if it serves higher social aims. Roughly, the instrumentalist aim is purchased in two different ways, by generally deterring those who are considering committing a crime, and by individually deterring or re-socialising those who already committed one.[5] The tenability of instrumentalist theories can be tested empirically. A long tradition of research leads to the conclusion that punishment is not effective for any of these goals (Tonry, 1995; Sherman, 2003; Andrews and Bonta, 2003).

Despite a systematic failure to demonstrate the instrumental value of punishing offenders, punishment is still maintained as the mainstream position. Apparently, the instrumentalist illusions are grafted onto retributive emotions.

According to retributivism punishing the wrong is simply inherent in moral conduct. It is a categorical imperative (Kant). The reasons for inflicting pain are sought in a concept of equality (by rectifying the illegitimate advantage obtained by the crime), or in the expression of blame. Retributivists advance several arguments to except the punitive infliction of pain from the general disapproval of pain infliction. They can be reduced to: (1) criminal punishment is needed to reconfirm the criminal law and the morals that inspire the law; and (2) criminal punishment must channel moral indignation and feelings of revenge provoked by the offence into the principles of a constitutional democracy.

---

5. Incapacitation is sometimes also considered as a possible purpose of punishment. I hesitate to do so. There is a fundamental difference between the preventative aims of punishment and the security concerns in incapacitation. In the first, offenders are locked in because *they* have committed an offence and as an attempt to 'improve' them. In incapacitation, offenders are locked in because *we* are afraid of them.

Both arguments must be taken seriously. But restorative justice appears to fulfil these retributive aims in a more constructive way.

Restorative justice as inverse constructive retributivism

Retribution basically consists of three elements: (1) the blameworthiness of the unlawful behaviour is expressed, (2) the responsibility of the offender is indicated and (3) the moral imbalance is repaired. Restorative justice shares these components, but in a constructive version, which may contribute directly to the quality of social life, while avoiding the ethically negative premise of pain infliction.

(1) Blaming norm transgression

Restorative justice clearly articulates the limits of social tolerance. It intervenes because a crime has been committed, and the crime is disapproved of. Restorative justice thus provides the essential elements of censuring. But restorative censuring is distinguished from punitive censuring. In current criminal justice, the offender is condemned according to formal criminal procedures because he has transgressed an article of penal law. Restorative censuring, on the contrary, is rooted in social relations. The offender's behaviour is disapproved because it caused harm to another person and to social life, and he is invited (under pressure) to consider the kind and amount of harm caused. Restorative censuring refers to the obligation to respect the quality of social life.

A problematic aspect may be that the restorative process is, by preference, confidential (Hildebrandt, 2005). Censuring in court indeed conveys the message of disapproval to the public at large. Restorative processes, on the contrary, are internally confidential. But they are organized under a public mandate. The public thus gets the message that the authorities do not let things happen, that they disapprove the criminal act, and are committed to giving a response. An additional message to the public is that the main stakeholders are given a chance to contribute decisively to a response, which should be as constructive as possible to social life. This public address is what Blad (2004) calls positive general prevention, contrary to the negative deterrence in punitive justice.

(2) Responsibility

In responsibility, the offender is considered as a moral agent. The person is linked to his acts and its consequences. As in punitive retributivism, restorative justice raises the responsibility of the offender. But there is a remarkable difference. Punitive retributivism is based on a passive concept of responsibility. It is the criminal justice system which makes the relation between the suspect and the act. The offender is confronted with his responsibility by the system, and must submit to the punitive consequences imposed on him by that system. He has no active role to play, other than organizing his defence, and to try to get away with the least possible punishment. Passive responsibility is retrospective, in that it is imposed because of an act committed in the past.

Restorative justice relies on a concept of active responsibility. The offender is invited (under pressure) to take active responsibility, by participating actively in the deliberations in order to assess the crime-caused harm, and to make active gestures that contribute to the reparation of this harm (Braithwaite and Roche, 2001). If this active commitment does not succeed, a sanction will be imposed on the offender, requiring from him or her an active effort as part of a (symbolic) reparation. Active responsibility is raised because of the act committed in the past, but also oriented towards an action or a situation in the future. Active responsibility, therefore, is both retrospective and prospective.

(3) Balance

In punitive retributivism, the balance (whatever this balance may be) is restored by paying back to the offender the same amount of suffering and harm he or she has caused. It is supposed that things are then evened out: both parties suffer equally. The problem is, however, that 'balancing the harm done by the offender with further harm inflicted on the offender … only adds to the total amount of harm in the world' (Wright, 1992: 525). The amount of suffering is doubled, but equally spread.

In restorative justice, the offender's paying-back role is no longer passive but active: he or she must himself or herself pay back by repairing as much as possible the harm and suffering caused. The balance is now restored, not by doubling the total amount of suffering, but by taking suffering away.

Retribution in its genuine meaning is achieved, in a constructive way. *Retribuere* in Latin is a contraction of *re-attribuere*, to give back, and that is what restorative justice seeks to do. One could see in this reversed restorative retributivism also a kind of proportionality. It is based, however, not on 'just deserts', but on 'just dues'. Restorative justice asks the question which 'debt' the offender has, and what he or she owes to pay back reasonably for the losses he or she has caused.

All in all, restoration and retribution 'may be seen as two sides of a coin, rather than a pair of opposites' (Baehler, 2007: 290). Zehr lists the commonalities as: 'a basic moral intuition that a balance has been thrown off by a wrongdoing. Consequently, the victim deserves something and the offender owes something ... There must be a proportional relationship between the act and the response' (Zehr, 2002: 59).

'Because crime hurts, justice should heal' (Braithwaite, 2005: 296). Restorative justice does not add more hurt, but tries to take hurt away by inversing punitive retributivism into constructive restorative retributivism. Facing the common concern of both punitive and restorative justice to rebalance the consequences of a wrong helps to indicate more precisely where the fundamental difference lies (Blad, 2003): it is the way the balance is going to be restored. Punitive retributivism assumes that intentional pain infliction is indispensable to balance the wrongful behaviour and to censure it. That is a principle that restorative justice cannot encompass.

Sticking to the premise that the response to crime must inflict 'pain for the sake of pain' (Fatic, 2005), while more constructive responses to crime are instrumentally at least as effective and social ethically less charged, is in itself an unethical position. It is an obstacle to the further civilisation of social institutions and of social life in general.

Ethics of social life instead of public order
Aiming at restoration instead of accepting the punitive premise, and giving full space for deliberation processes among stakeholders instead of imposing a top down decision procedure, are grounded in different views on human relations and on social institutions.

Why is it forbidden to steal or to commit private acts of violence? Because if it were not forbidden, severe victimisations would occur. The absence of a formal response would provoke counteractions to make things even, leading to an escalation in mutual victimisation. Constructive social life would be impossible and be dominated by abuse of power and fear. To avoid such escalation and to make social life liveable, civilisation has concentrated the use of violence in the central power's hands. Criminal justice has its roots in the concern for preserving living together. Hence, what is logically the first concern of the social response to crime? It is to repair — as much as possible and in an orderly way — the harm done to the victim and the damage to social life.

Restorative justice recalls the fundamental *raison d'être* of the criminal justice system. Instead of the abstract legal order, the quality of social relations and social life is (re)positioned as the fundamental reason for criminalising certain behaviour. The aim is to restore this quality, and not primarily to enforce public order. Both are not contradictory *in se*, but different accents are possible.

The question now is what this quality of social life is.

Individual liberties create ethical obligations

Freud and Durkheim teach that we are all driven by self-interest. Each individual has the desire to shape his or her own life, but we must include this desire in our social embedding. We cannot but live together. The behaviour of others affects my opportunities, and my behaviour has an effect on the others' lives. That creates mutual entitlements and responsibilities. I am entitled to demand an ethical account from the others. The drunk driving of one driver is a risk for us all, so that we are entitled to stop such driving. The brutality of one neighbour disturbs social life in the neighbourhood, which makes other neighbours entitled to demand more decent conduct instead.

My individual rights and liberties to make my own choices confront me with my social responsibilities. I can opt for ruthless, selfish choices, or I can include the interests of others and of social life in the choices I make. Liberties are a crucial good to cherish, but the full use of all rights and freedoms is not always ethically advisable. It has to be balanced with the interest of others and of social life in general.

This balance is the crucial issue of the debate between Liberals and Communitarians. It cannot be resolved empirically or by new laws and rules. It is a matter of socio-ethical understanding.

Opting for common self-interest

Instead of considering the others as competitors, I can bundle self-interest with that of others. The others then are seen as allies in a common project for more autonomy, and my self-interest is integrated in what I have called 'common self-interest' (Walgrave, 2008). It merges in one notion the seeming contradiction we are all living in: we are individuals with particular needs, wishes and ambitions, but we also are living with others, with whom we cannot but share opportunities and goods. Indeed, to gain more autonomy, we need each other. The more smoothly mutual dependencies operate, based on mutual respect, the more space there will be for each individual to enjoy liberty and live his life as he wishes. Living in a community that gives all its members maximum space, based on respect for plurality and solidarity, is the common self-interest.

It is self-interest, because I invest in such a community for my own profit. I promote such a community life, not because I am an unworldly idealist, but because I hope to get the maximum possible benefits from being part of it. But it is more than self-interest, because I am not alone in going for these benefits. If we all invest in social life, we all profit from its high quality. We do not divide the benefits, together we increase them.

I am in good company to see a version of self-interest as the basic drive in high quality social life. Robert Putnam, for example, writes that our good citizenship is not because we obey 'some impossibly idealistic rule of selflessness, but rather because we pursued self-interest rightly understood' (Putnam, 2000: 135). John Braithwaite and Philip Pettit (1990) advance 'dominion' as a social conception of freedom. The mutual assurance that fellow citizens and the state will respect individual rights and freedoms increases the individual enjoyment of those rights and freedoms. In Bloomfield, we read 'one's well-lived life, one's happiness, is not independent of one's self-respect and one's self-respect is not independent of how one treats others' (Bloomfield, 2008: 8).

Common self-interest as a norm

It is not given by nature that we invest our self-interest in the project of common self-interest. It is an ethical advice. Obvious disrespect is easily observed. Some will say 'Well, that's life', but it is my ethical choice not to accept such a way of life. I am entitled to do so because of our fate to develop our lives together. Giving in to cynicism would be a kind of self-fulfilling prophecy. It would drag social life down into being an arena of ruthless struggle for the survival of the fittest. But rejecting cynicism is accepting active responsibility in the everlasting struggle for a better social life. While knowing that we shall never reach the ideal, we must keep trying. Continuously trying to do better is the only way of avoiding degradation into much worse.

Inversely, some people seem to act against their own self-interest, to serve others or social life in general. Mothers seem to sacrifice their life for their child, or firemen in a blaze. Self-sacrificing people are often called heroes. It expresses the admiration for them as exceptional people, who far exceed our own modest capacities.

But erasing self-interest completely in favour of common interest is not the ideal. Not only is it unrealistic, it also would relegate us to a community with suffocating social pressure, or bring about a totalitarian regime without personal initiative, progress, or pleasure. Examples of such communities and regimes exist, and they are not attractive.

Sympathy as a ground for developing common self-interest

Sceptics may protest that believing in common self-interest is naïve. Referring to the current hardening of social life and punitive populism, they may suggest that there is little hope for such idea.

However, it is an old wisdom that humans are bound by a basic empathy. We spontaneously feel compassion when mass media show the miserable situations of refugees and victims of war, crimes, or natural disasters. We are also positively moved by the happiness of others, and we enjoy the conclusion of peaceful agreements in which we are not directly involved. It is the basis of our potential for mutual understanding and solidarity, despite differences in opinions and immediate interests.

For several reasons, the potential for mutual empathy is not always activated to the same degree. We are more likely to sympathise with family members than with more distant people. We support the football team of our own country, even if they play badly and brutally. Empathy may be diminished or blocked. Sometimes, the luck or success of others is experienced as a threat to our own prestige or interests, so that envy may prevent us from enjoying other people's good fate. War situations lead to de-humanising the enemy. But these are variations and exceptions, which do not alter the ground position that average people do feel in general empathy with other people.

Such unavoidable human relationships are the key, for example, in the work of the French philosopher Emmanuel Levinas (1966). It is a deep philosophical account of the fact that people are sensitive to others and unavoidably appeal to ethical responsibility.

The capacity for empathy and for sympathy (which is not always activated) is the intuitive ground on which common self-interest can be developed.

Crucial attitudes for developing common self-interest

The quality of social life depends on the commitment of the individuals concerned. Developing citizens' commitment to the project of common self-interest is based on three basic attitudes, respect, solidarity and active responsibility. Respect for humans recognises and esteems the intrinsic value of human beings. It is made concrete through the Universal Declaration of Human Rights, for example. The international community recognises that a number of rights are due to all humans, for the simple reason that they are human.

Respect for human dignity is a bottom-line obligation for all social institutions. It is the minimum condition for making living together possible. Respect for persons and groups in the community leads to acceptance of pluralism and multiculturalism. Disrespect is actively rejected. Crime is an expression of disrespect. Racist political parties disrespect immigrants. Fundamentalist Muslims disrespect non-Muslims. 'Freedom of speech' may conflict with the fundamental necessity of mutual respect. Such phenomena threaten the quality of social life in our heterogeneous societies. They intrude upon our common self-interest. If persuasion is not effective, they must be confronted actively, and their behaviour may be criminalised and possibly referred to coercive justice interventions.

Solidarity presupposes more commitment than does respect, because it includes a form of companionship and reciprocity of support. It draws on the basic inter-human sympathy described earlier, and it is crucial in bundling our individual self-interests into the project of common self-interest. If combined with pluralism (a consequence of respect), solidarity yields more freedom.

Unlike disrespect, lack of solidarity cannot be actively suppressed. We are entitled to *demand* from each other not to degrade social life (through disrespect); we only can (and should) *promote* acting so as to improve social life (through solidarity).

Responsibility links a person to his acts and their consequences. It confronts the self with its own actions. Active responsibility is an awareness of the link between the self and the actions, and behaviour that reflects this (Braithwaite and Roche, 2001).

Active responsibility is typical in leadership, but does not automatically lead to ethically positive actions. Many tyrants and criminal gang leaders probably take active responsibility for their choices and actions. That is why active responsibility must be exerted in view of ethically desirable objectives.

Active responsibility of citizens is indispensable to the quality of social life. Indeed, a good society depends on committed participation by its citizens. Participants in social life must take their responsibility, and respond actively and autonomously to the obligations of social life. In the ideal situation, members take active responsibility for combating disrespect and promoting solidarity.

If these three attitudes were held by most citizens, freedom would result automatically from it and justice as a separate value would be redundant.

Ethical attitudes in traditional criminal justice versus restorative justice

At first glance, advancing respect, solidarity and active responsibility as the basis of socio-ethical behaviour may seem to be mere rhetoric. Who would object to these virtues? Let us examine whether they also guide the current criminal procedures.

Is respect an ethical guideline in the current criminal justice? Respect for the victim is absent, because he or she is not included in the punitive reflections. Possible claims through civil procedures are subordinated to the public procedure. Punitive retributivism is focused on the offender. Criminal justice respects the offender as a responsible person, understanding right and wrong and able to make free choices and decisions, and as a citizen with guaranteed rights. But the respect is not complete. In the end, the offender has to submit to a proportionate punishment. The offender is judged as a moral agent to be considered guilty, but not as a morally and socially competent citizen who might be motivated to contribute to a constructive response to the problems caused by his or her crime.

I do not see solidarity in the prioritisation of punishment. The response does not support the victim. The victim's witness is used to assess the guilt of the offender. Support to victims is located at the margins of the criminal justice system, and allowed only in so far as it does not impede the criminal justice investigation and procedure aimed at punishing the offender. The punishment usually hampers possible reparation. In restorative justice, principled solidarity with the victim is evident, though practice sometimes fails in this regard. Solidarity with the offender appears through the attempt to avoid social exclusion. The offender is encouraged to make up for his conduct, in order to preserve his or her position as an integrated member in social life.

Responsibility is central to retributivism. Current penal justice holds the offender responsible by imposing on him the obligation to respond for his misconduct; but again, the responsibility is incomplete. It is a passive, retrospective form of responsibility, to which the offender is submitted by the criminal justice system. He is not supposed to take active responsibility to find a constructive solution to the problems he created. The victim's only responsibility is to contribute to the criminal procedure by reporting the crime and acting as witness. Current criminal justice burdens its agents with active responsibility: they must censure criminal behaviour and impose proportionate punishments, according to legal procedures and other standards. On the contrary, restorative justice largely relies on active responsibility in the stakeholders. The offender's active responsibility includes the obligation to contribute actively to the reparation of the harm. The victim is encouraged to assume the general citizen's responsibility for trying to find peace-promoting solutions. Restorative justice also stands for responsible collectivities, bound by obligations to search for socially constructive responses within the rules of law.

Clearly, socio-ethical attitudes such as respect, solidarity for all and active responsibility, are more inherent to restorative justice than to the prioritisation of punishment. Hence, restorative justice is more likely to contribute constructively to social life and relations. The priority for the quality of social life underlies the bottom-up approach in restorative justice. It appears through a priority for informal regulations, as opposed to imposed procedures and outcomes. The point of departure for restorative justice, as in social life ethics, is that solutions must primarily be sought through the human and social resources in social life itself. This is opposed to the top-down approach in traditional criminal justice, where decisions are imposed according to strict rules, leaving restricted room for the views and interests of those directly concerned.

Conclusion

According to Elias, the civilisation process is a pathway towards societies and communities with constructive relations among its citizens, avoiding as much as possible the use of violence and coercion. The increasing complexity of social and economic life creates tighter interdependence, which would ground more mutual respect and understanding, increasing refinement and civilisation in our relations.

Such a statement seems to be unworldly in the current hardening of the social and economic world. But the civilisation process, as described by Elias, is to be seen as a very slow development over centuries, including decades of relapses, differentiations among geographical regions, social groups and cultural fields, due to degrees of altruism or selfishness, economic or other interests, power relations, long-term or short-term visions, anxieties and fears. Many forces can deviate, delay or block the civilisation process and thus also threaten the quality of social life and human relations. The Egyptian and Greek civilisations were overcome by the Roman civilisation. For the leading Egyptians and Greeks, this must have been experienced as a loss. But the Romans created a stronger legal ground for the development of society. The French Revolution was brutal and cruel. Part of the artistic achievements and etiquette of the aristocracy were lost, but democracy emerged. More refinement and sensitivity in human relation is a desirable progress, also if it extends towards the humble and the offending. But, if misunderstood, it may lead to norm erosion.

Social life is a differentiated complex of relations and forces. It is oriented by material facts and events, but also by social, ideological and socio-ethical movements. The civilisation process is not an automatic deterministic process that we simply have to undergo. It is also a matter of choices. That brings civilisation under the umbrella of social ethics. Civilising forces must navigate through the wildly surging waters of social life, with a view to a social ethical objective: communities and societies that are based on mutual respect and solidarity, driven by participating citizens who take active responsibility in the pursuit of common self-interest.

But even the best possible mode of living together will be in need of clear norms and norm enforcement. The ethical choice in responding to crime is to promote further civilisation in criminal justice. There is no reason to believe that the civilisation process of criminal punishment, as described originally by Elias, would have reached its finish. It can and it must be continued. After monopolising violence in the hands of the state, after making the use of violence more rational and more moderate, the next step is to push aside the use of violence itself in the response to offending. That means giving priority to solutions based on bottom-up deliberation, rather than top down imposed reactions, while keeping clear norm enforcement. Restorative justice is a paradigm that offers such a way of dealing with the aftermath of crime. Making criminal justice more civilised equals making criminal justice more restorative.

References

Andrews, D. and Bonta, J. (2003), *The Psychology of Criminal Conduct* (3rd. edn.), Cincinnati, OH: Anderson.

Baehler, K. (2007), 'Justifying Restorative Justice' in Maxwell G. and Liu, J. (eds.), *Restorative Justice and Practices in New Zealand: Towards a Restorative Society*, Wellington (New Zealand): Institute of Policy Studies, Victoria University, 289–299.

Bauman, Z. (2000), 'Social Uses of Law and Order' in Garland, D. and Sparks, R. (eds.), *Criminology and Social Theory*, Oxford: Oxford University Press, 23–46.

Bianchi, H. (1994), *Justice as a Sanctuary: Towards a New System of Crime Control*, Bloomington: Indiana University Press.

Blad, J. (2003), 'Community Mediation, Criminal Justice and Restorative Justice: Rearranging the Institutions of Law' in Walgrave, L. (ed.), *Repositioning Restorative Justice*, Devon, Cullompton: Willan Publishing, 191–207.

Blad, J. (2004), '*Herstelrecht en general preventie. De normbevestigende werking van herstelrecht en herstelsanctie*' ('Restorative justice and general prevention. The norm confirming function of restorative justice and reparative sanctions) in Van Stokkom, B. (ed.), *Straf en Herstel. Ethische Reflecties over Strafdoeleinden*, Den Haag: Boom, 91–112.

Blad, J. (2011), '*Herstelrecht en de civilisering van de strafrechtspleging*' ('*Restorative justice and the civilisation of criminal justice administration*') in Foblets, M.-C., Hildebrandt, M. and Steenbergen, J. (eds.), *Liber Amicorum René Foqué*. Brussels: Larcier.

Bloomfield, P (ed.) (2008), *Morality and Self-interest*, Oxford: Oxford University Press.

Bottoms, A. (2003), 'Some Sociological Reflections on Restorative Justice' in Von Hirsch, A., Roberts, J., Bottoms, A., Roach, K. and Schiff, M. (eds.), *Restorative Justice and Criminal Justice: Competing or Reconcilable Paradigms*, Oxford: Hart, 79–113.

Boutellier, H. (2000), *Crime and Morality. The Significance of Criminal Justice in Post-modern Culture*, Dordrecht: Kluwer Academic Publishers.

Boutellier, H. (2004), '*Beschavingspretenties van straf en herstel*' ('The civilisation pretentions of punishment and reparation') in Van Stokkom, B. (ed.), *Straf en herstel. Ethische reflecties over sanctiedoeleinden*, Den Haag: Boom Juridische Uitgevers, 25–42.

Braithwaite, J. (2005), 'Between Proportionality and Impunity: Confrontation => Truth => Prevention', *Criminology*, 43(2), 283–306.

Braithwaite, J. and Pettit, P. (1990), *Not Just Deserts. A Republican Theory of Criminal Justice*, Oxford: Oxford University Press.

Braithwaite, J. and Roche, D. (2001), 'Responsibility and Restorative Justice' in Bazemore G. and Schiff, M. (eds.), *Restorative Community Justice. Repairing Harm and Transforming Communities*, Cincinnati: Anderson, 63–84.

Cacioppo, J. and Patrick, W. (2008), *Loneliness. Human Nature and the Need for Social Connection*, New York: Norton and Company.

Christie, N. (1977), 'Conflicts as Property', *British Journal of Criminology*, 17(1), 1–15.

Christie, N. (1981), *Limits to Pain*, Oxford: Martin, Robertson.

Daems, T. (2008), *Making Sense of Penal Change*, Oxford: Oxford University Press.

De Hert, P. (2009), '*Waarom herstel niet tot de kerntaken behoort. Bedenkingen bij Walgrave's onbehagen*' ('Why restoration is not a core business. Reflections on Walgrave's discomfort'), *Tijdschrift voor herstelrecht* 9(3), 39–46.

Debuyst (1990), '*Pour introduire une histoire de la criminologie: les problématiques du départ'. Déviance et Société*, 14(4), 347–76.

Duff, A. (1992), 'Alternatives to Punishment or Alternative Punishment?' in Cragg, W. (ed.), *Retributivism and Its Critics*. Stuttgart: Steinder, 44–68.

Duff, A. (2001), *Punishment, Communication and Community*, Oxford: Oxford University Press.

Elias, N. (2000), *The Civilising Process. Sociogenetic and Psychogenetic Investigations*, revised edn. by Dunning, E., Goudsbloem, J. and Mennel, S. Oxford: Blackwell Publishers.

Fatic, A, (1995), *Punishment and Restorative Crime-handling*, Aldershot: Avebury.

Feeley, M. and Simon, J. (1992), 'The New Penology: Notes on the Emerging Strategy of Corrections and its Implications', *Criminology* No.30, 451–471.

Foucault, M. (1975), *Surveiller et punir*, Paris: Gallimard.

Garland, D. (1990), *Punishment and Modern Society*, Oxford: Clarendon.

Garland, D. (2001), *The Culture of Control. Crime and Social Order in Contemporary Society*, Oxford: Oxford University Press.

Hildebrandt, M. (2005), 'Restorative Justice and the Morality of a Fair Trial: A Reply to Brochu' in Claes, E., Foqué, R. and Peters, T. (eds.), *Punishment, Restorative Justice and the Morality of Law*, Antwerp/Oxford: Intersentia, 89–99.

Hulsman, L. (1979), 'An Abolitionist Perspective on Criminal Justice and a Scheme to Organize Approaches to "Problematic Situations"', Paper presented at the University of Louvain-La-Neuve (Belgium).

Hulsman, L. (1982), 'Penal Reform in The Netherlands. Reflections on a White Paper Proposal', *Howard Journal of Penology and Crime Prevention*, No.21, 35–47.

Johnstone, G. (2002), *Restorative Justice. Ideas, Values, Debates*, Devon, Cullompton: Willan Publishing.

Levinas, E. (1966), *De totaliteit en het oneindige: essay over de exterioriteit* (*Totality and infinity: an essay on exteriority*), Rotterdam: Lemniscaat. Translated from the French: *Totalité et infini: essai sur l'extériorité* (1961).

Pratt, J. (1998), 'Towards the "Decivilisation" of Punishment?', *Social and Legal Studies*, 7(4), 487–515.

Putnam, R. (2000), *Bowling Alone*, New York: Simon and Schuster.

Sherman, L. (2003), 'Reason for Emotion: Reinventing Justice with Theories, Innovations and Research', *Criminology*, 41(1), 1–37.

Simon, J. (2001), 'Entitlement to Cruelty: The End of Welfare and the Punitive Mentality in the United States' in Stenson, K. and Sullivan, R. (eds.), *Crime, Risk and Justice: The Politics of Crime Control in Liberal Democracies*, Devon, Cullompton: Willan Publishing, 125–143.

Spierenburg, P. (1984), *The Spectacle of Suffering: Executions and the Evolution of Repression*, Cambridge: Cambridge University Press.

Tonry, M. (1995), *Malign Neglect: Race, Crime and Punishment in America*. New York: Oxford University Press.

Van Ness, D. and Heetderks Strong, K. (2002), *Restoring Justice*, (2nd ed.), Cincinnati: Anderson .

Von Hirsch, A. (1993), *Censure and Sanctions*, Oxford: Clarendon Press.

Von Hirsch, A, and Jareborg, N. (1991), 'Gauging Criminal Harm: A Living-Standard Analysis', *Oxford Journal of Legal Studies*, No.11, 1–38.

Walgrave, L. (2000), 'Restorative Justice and the Republican Theory of Criminal Justice: An Exercise in Normative Theorising on Restorative Justice' in Strang H. and Braithwaite, J. (eds.), *Restorative Justice: Philosophy to Practice*. Aldershot: Ashgate.

Walgrave, L. (ed.) (2002), *Restorative Justice and the Law*, Devon, Cullompton: Willan Publishing.

Walgrave, L. (2008), *Restorative Justice, Self-interest and Responsible Citizenship*, Devon, Cullompton: Willan Publishing.

Wright, M. (1992), 'Victim-offender Mediation as a Step Towards a Restorative System of Justice' in Messmer, H. and Otto, H. U. (eds.), *Restorative Justice on Trial. Pitfalls and Potentials of Victim-offender Mediation*, Dordrecht/Boston: Kluwer Academic Publishers, 525–539.

Wright, M. (2003), 'Is it Time to Question the Concept of Punishment?' in
    Walgrave, L. (ed.), *Repositioning Restorative Justice*, Devon, Cullompton:
    Willan Publishing, 3–23.

Zehr, H. (2002), *The Little Book of Restorative Justice*, Intercourse, PA: Good
    Books.

Part III

CIVILISING PRACTICE

12

Could a Restorative System of Justice be more Civilised than a Punitive One?

Martin Wright

Introduction

A case can be made—by being selective—for saying that modern Western criminal justice systems are civilised. Many countries base their social control on the Rule of Law (Bingham, 2011). More is being done for victims. For the accused there are many safeguards, such as trial by jury (in some countries), rules about police interviews, provisions for accused people to have a defending lawyer, rules of evidence, not being re-tried after being acquitted (*ne bis in idem*), and so on. But the ultimate sanction in most civilised Western countries and those which have been influenced by them is imprisonment. Even in the best prisons, despite some constructive regimes and facilities for relatives and friends to visit in acceptable surroundings, there is seldom enough work, education, and training, especially when prisons are overcrowded. There is bullying and self-harm.[1] Many prisons are in remote

---

1. Taking England and Wales as an example—neither the best nor worst of prison systems—in December 2011 the prison population was over 87,000 (156 per 100,000 of the population), but the number of work places was only about 24,000. Ten prisons were from 159% to 196% overcrowded. Although about 48% of prisoners are at or below the level expected of an 11-year-old in reading, 65% in numeracy and 82% in writing, only about a fifth of prisoners with serious literacy or numeracy needs enrol on a course that would help them. In 2010 there were 26,983 incidents of self-harm in prisons, nearly half by women although they comprise only 5% of the population in custody (Prison Reform Trust, 2011, pp. 4, 17, 67, 64, 53).

places, difficult and expensive for families to visit. The list of problems is too well known to need repeating here (Wright, 1982: ch.2, 3).

Assumptions on Which the System is Based

Problems arise because of the assumptions on which the system is based: that there is a clear dividing line between civil and criminal law; that if an action can be treated as criminal, it should be (the 'legality principle'); and that criminals should be punished. This chapter will examine some of these problems, and recent moves to overcome them, the most prominent of which at present is restorative justice.

Civil and criminal law

We need to begin by clarifying: what is crime? It may appear obvious that, e.g., certain actions such as theft and causing bodily injury are always crimes, but they are not; for example, if a person made an honest mistake, or acted in self-defence or under duress, or was mentally-ill. Crimes are forms of harm which have been defined by law as public wrongs, so serious that the state intervenes against the wrongdoer. A definition thus far could be: a crime is committed when one person or group harms, or imposes their will on, another without their consent and in a way defined by law as crime. It is the last phrase that causes the fluidity of the dividing line: actions are being criminalised (or less often de-criminalised) all the time. As Thomas Trenczek and Per Andersen (this volume, *Chapters 13* and *16*, respectively) remind us, Nils Christie proposed that crime can be seen as a conflict and handled accordingly; Andersen suggests that this should at least be done for young people.

Criminal law as first resort

Two assumptions are commonly made here. The first is that when an action falls within this definition, it should be treated as a crime. But many such acts (or omissions) are also civil wrongs or torts in English law (originally Norman French): the injured party can decide to claim redress in the civil court rather than report the harmful action to the police, and if necessary the state assists him or her in enforcement. In England and Wales the prosecutor may discontinue the case if he or she decides that it is not in the public interest to proceed, or there is not enough evidence for a reasonable prospect of conviction. Then the injured party can only go to the civil court, or do nothing. To take one example among many, early in 2012 it came to light that major British banks had knowingly mis-sold a form of insurance known as payment protection to between four million and 12 million customers. The policies were supposed to pay out in the event that redundancy or sickness prevented the policyholder from working, but contained exclusions which meant that people were not able to claim the benefits which they thought they had purchased. Some might argue that this should have been regarded as a crime, such as obtaining a pecuniary advantage by deception, but instead the five major banks have set aside over seven billion pounds to reimburse customers. Although this was no doubt painful for those responsible, it was not imposed *because* it was painful, but by requiring the banks to make amends, it was of more benefit to the victims than merely prosecuting and fining the banks. Combined with the damage to their reputations, and more rigorous regulation, this should help to persuade banks to behave better in future, although that result appears to be slow in coming[2].

Dealing with wrongdoing by criminalising it does not necessarily help to maintain a well-behaved society. People may decide not to report a crime, especially if it was committed by someone they know, because they fear that 'justice' will be too heavy-handed, or that they will suffer retaliation, or simply that the process will be time-consuming and distressing. The use of a civil procedure would not necessarily remove these problems, but it could mitigate them. In the coal industry, for example, the shift from punitive to restorative justice (that is, from criminal prosecution to persuasion involving dialogue on safety between workers and management) led to a reduction in the number of miners killed in British pits from about a thousand a year in the late-19th-century to 44 in 1982–83 (Braithwaite, 2002: 63–64). In nursing homes, similarly, the Australian government changed from a policy of inspection based on prosecution for breaches of the hundreds of regulations, to

---

2. At the time of writing yet more examples have come to light, involving mis-selling of insurance and falsification of interest rates. Barclays Bank has been fined £290 million by regulatory authorities. The large pharmaceutical company GlaxoSmithKline has been fined $3 billion for illegally marketing to young people the anti-depressant drug Paxil (Seroxat in Britain), widely reported as having potential links to suicide. The settlement included criminal fines and civil penalties, but newspaper reports do not mention compensation (Foley, 2012).

discussions between residents, care groups, management, owners and unions. This led to the adoption of just 31 standards, with regular meetings of all concerned to monitor performance (Braithwaite, 2002: 17–18). Braithwaite does however consider that the criminal model should not be abandoned completely and that persuasion should be backed up by the possibility of punishment. There is a wide range of actions which could be called 'crimes of the powerful'. In some cases they have been defined as crimes, in others not, for example because a large company can persuade the legislator not to do so,[3] or not to enforce the law.[4]

Some would argue that cases like these should be criminalised; but it is also suggested that it would be in the interests of victims or potential victims if some actions, currently treated as crimes, were to be 'civilised' and the victims could personally have a facilitated meeting with the directors of the company (not their lawyers: this is not a case of lawyers 'stealing the conflict' but offenders paying them handsomely to take it away). In 2006 a British government report on regulation recommended that restorative justice should be used, at least as a first stage in dealing with such cases:

> Victims will often be very raw and sensitive about the physical, emotional or financial harm that has been inflicted on them. Offenders, on the other hand, will often be very nervous about facing those whom they have harmed. ... [The agreed remedy] could amount to a significant burden on the offender, for example, financial compensation or a commitment to undertake unpaid work (Macrory, 2006: 72).

Or, it might be added, to use their considerable wealth to endow charitable foundations. A similar approach might be more effective than civil litigation or prosecution in cases such as environmental poisoning by the

---

3. Early examples of this process were the Enclosure Acts in England, by which common land and smallholdings were 'enclosed' (i.e. appropriated) by large landowners, leaving the tenant farmers as landless labourers. This process was legalised by nearly 4,000 private Acts of Parliament, from 1709 until 1845 (Arnold-Baker, 1996: 686).

4. For instance, nine sectors of the USA economy, including pharmaceuticals, oil and gas, and insurance, each spent more than one billion dollars on lobbying in the years 1996 to 2012 (Center for Responsive Politics, http://www.opensecrets.org/lobby/top.php?showYear=a&indexType=i, accessed 27 June 2012). Non-enforcement has been termed 'de-facto decriminalisation' by the Expert Committee on Decriminalisation (Council of Europe, 1981).

Union Carbide Corporation (now owned by the Dow Chemical Company) in Bhopal, India (see e.g. Sinha, 2009) and by the Chevron Oil Company in the river Amazon in Ecuador (Adams, 2011).

Punishment and Sentencing

The second assumption is that if the state prosecutes and the perpetrator is found guilty, the result should be punishment. It has been pointed out that in some countries this assumption is built into the language: *droit pénal* in French, *Strafrecht* in German and Dutch, and in Russian even *ugolovnoe pravo* (capital law). In the 20th-century other measures were added, such as rehabilitation (probation) and reparation (monetary compensation or work for the victim or the community). These may be painful or inconvenient, but they are ostensibly not imposed for that reason, so here they will be described with other words such as 'consequences' or 'measures'.

The response

It is worth looking in more detail at two questions: What is punishment? and What is punishment for? We will consider whether it 'works': its effects on victims, offenders and society. We will then discuss the two paradigms on which the response is based, and how to decide the amount of the response. As we have seen, punishment can be defined as the imposition of a measure intended to cause pain (such as imprisonment) or inconvenience or hardship (such as fines) on a person who has done wrong, by a person or agency with power and/or authority. Without this authority, the punitive action would itself be a crime. To lock a person in a cell, with authority, is law enforcement; to lock him or her in a cellar, without authority, is the crime of false imprisonment.

Treating an action as criminal can have advantages, e.g. the state takes on the burden of prosecution, and if the accused person is found guilty and the offence is serious enough, the offender is imprisoned and their opportunity to re-offend temporarily curtailed. But punishment also has disadvantages. Because its effects are so serious, the criminal justice system requires a higher standard of proof of guilt ('beyond reasonable doubt' rather than 'on the balance of probabilities' as in civil cases) and other safeguards which make it more difficult to secure a conviction; moreover, the accused is likely to go to greater lengths to avoid conviction, such as finding procedural loopholes, bribing police officers or intimidating (or even killing) witnesses. It could be said that the more severe the threatened punishment, the less likely the offender is to confess.

What is punishment for? Unfortunately it is trying to do incompatible things. In England and Wales, e.g., the Criminal Justice Act 2003, as amended by the Criminal Justice and Immigration Act 2008 (sections 142 and 142A) lists five purposes. Four of them are the punishment of offenders, the reform and rehabilitation of offenders, the protection of the public, and the making of reparation by offenders to persons affected by their offences. The fifth one is different for offenders aged 18 or over: the reduction of crime, including its reduction by deterrence, and for those under 18, to prevent offending or re-offending, having regard to the welfare of the offender (the welfare of adult offenders is somehow omitted).

But is it justifiable for the state deliberately to hurt a citizen who has committed a crime? Firstly, one school of thought argues that it is self-evidently right: there is a moral equivalence between the wrong caused by the offender and the pain inflicted on him or her. This ignores the effect on the offender's future conduct, implying that retribution is justified even if it results in worse behaviour (this argument is clouded by the fact that punishment often takes the form of imprisonment, which prevents offending for a time, but it ignores the notoriously high reconviction rate after release). It may be regarded as instrumental, not in the usual sense of achieving a measurable aim such as preventing re-offending, but in a symbolic, intangible way, by expressing society's condemnation of the crime.

Secondly, a more pragmatic question is whether it makes society a better place. It could be argued that, although the infliction of pain is normally unacceptable, it may be justified if it 'works' better than more constructive methods. The answer to this appears to be that there is no such evidence,[5] and considerable evidence of harmful side-effects, especially in the case of

---

5. 'Court-ordered community sentences are more effective (by eight percentage points) at reducing one-year proved re-offending rates than custodial sentences of less than 12 months for similar offenders' (Prison Reform Trust, 2011: 74).

imprisonment.[6] The closer punishment comes to being inhuman and degrading, the more damaging it is to its recipient. It could be argued that you don't make people behave well by treating them badly. Punishment gives the wrong message: that the way to impose your will on other people is to threaten them. As we have seen, there is a litany of all-too-well known disadvantages of prisons, deriving ultimately from the underlying philosophy based on punishment. Whether punishment 'works' can be considered in three parts: the effects on the victim, the offender and the society.

Effects on victims

It is often said that victims want 'justice', but that word means different things in different contexts. For some, it means retribution: the offender should experience the pain which he or she has caused to someone else. Others simply want acknowledgement of the hurt they have suffered. They do not like it, e.g., when an offender pleads guilty to a less serious crime in order to reduce the punishment which the actual crime would incur. A common reaction is to want action that will make future offending less likely. For example:

> In a survey of 1,087 victims of non-violent crime, 81 per cent would prefer an offender to receive an effective sentence rather than a harsh one, and nearly two thirds (63 per cent) disagreed that prison is always the best way to punish someone. Eight in ten (81 per cent) of victims in the UK would be in favour of community sentences if they prevent an offender from re-offending. Fifty-eight per cent of victims agreed that it would be harder for an offender to face up to their problems in the community than receiving a short prison sentence. Only 49 per cent said that punishment was the most important part of an offender's sentence, with reparation ('payback') second (43 per cent) and rehabilitation third (36 per cent) (Ministry of Justice, 2007).

---

6. For example, '[m]aintaining contact with children is made more difficult by the distance that many prisoners are held from their home area...in 2009 there were 753 women held over 100 miles from home.' 'Imprisoning mothers for non-violent offences has a damaging effect on children and carries a cost to the state of more than £17 million over a 10 year period' (Prison Reform Trust, 2011: 29).

This report was, however, issued by the Ministry of Justice under the headline 'Victims of crime want punishment', presumably because of a political belief that this would resonate with the public.

Effects on offenders

As for offenders, psychological research amply demonstrates that the effects of punishment are at best short-lived and at worst counterproductive, generating resentment and damaging the individual's belief in his or her ability to do better (Wright, 2007; 2008: Ch. 2). Educationalists advise against it because it encourages self-centred thinking and is based on the principle 'Don't do as I do, do as I tell you' (Faber and Mazlish, 1980: Ch. 3; Rosenberg, 1999: Ch 10, esp. pp. 121–2; Hopkins, 2004: Ch. 8). It is a truism among criminologists that deterrence depends on the probability of conviction and whether the offender even pauses to consider this. An example is the fact that even the risk of ruining their careers has not deterred some British politicians from falsely claiming a few thousand pounds of expenses. As for behaviour after the punishment, the stigma makes it harder to be re-integrated e.g., by obtaining legitimate employment, whereas reparation allows a person to earn some credit to offset against the stigma.

Effects on society

There is a danger in relying on an ineffective remedy, because it undermines the search for a better one. Marshall Rosenberg identifies two questions that reveal the limitations of punishment. One is 'What do I want his person to do that's different from what he or she is currently doing?' For this, punishment may seem effective, at least in the short run. But the second question is, 'What do I want this person's reasons to be for doing what I'm asking?' There are other relevant questions, such as 'What are this person's needs, to enable him or her to behave in a way that respects others and gains their respect?' A civilised society is surely one in which people do not merely conform through fear but respect each other's needs and feelings, 'acknowledge responsibility for our own actions, and are aware that our own well-being and that of others are one and the same' (Rosenberg, 1999: 122–3).

This list does however need two qualifications. Firstly, as Braithwaite has suggested, even if restorative regimes exist, there may need to be an ultimate sanction for those who are unwilling or unable to cooperate with them. Secondly, there are individuals who need time away from their everyday lives before they realise that they have taken a wrong turning and decide to change the direction of their lives: this is similar to the idea of sanctuary (Bianchi, 1994). But the prison regime should be designed to encourage such a change; it should not be a solely punitive one in which change happens in spite of it, not because of it. In England there is one prison, Grendon, whose regime has always been based on the concept of the therapeutic community and not on punishment; its purpose is to make prisoners think and feel about what they have done. A former governor of Grendon therapeutic prison, Tim Newell, has co-authored a book about how this can be done (Edgar and Newell, 2006); there is now a second Grendon-type therapeutic regime at Dovegate Prison and also quite a few therapeutic communities within larger prisons (Cullen and Mackenzie, 2011). For those who subscribe to the first of these arguments, that those who cause pain should also suffer it, this provides an answer: those who experience remorse do suffer pain, but it arises from empathy for the victim and what he or she has suffered, not from fear of what the authorities will inflict on them.

Two Paradigms

Thus we have two approaches based on different philosophical and psychological principles. One takes it as axiomatic that wrongdoing should be followed by punishment, either because that is right in itself ('poetic justice'), or because it symbolises society's disapproval, or because it is intended to persuade the individual not to repeat that behaviour and other individuals not to do it in the first place. For the sake of fairness the punishment should be proportionate to the seriousness of the offence. The principal punishment is imprisonment, and the amount is measured by the number of time-units, usually months or years (just as in bygone times, and still to-day in some countries, it was measured by the number of lashes with a whip). This number bears no relation to the amount required to induce the offender to change his or her behaviour.

The punishment consists in the deprivation of liberty; within that parameter, the more humane penal systems offer courses relating to behaviour-change or to earning a living after release (but usually only to limited numbers of prisoners) and facilities for recreation and exercise to make the experience more tolerable and the prison easier to manage. The basic principles are fear and shame on the part of the offender, and control by other members of society. Although attempts are made to safeguard people from being wrongly convicted, or inhumanely treated after conviction, this approach has inescapable drawbacks: punishment is inherently damaging, including pain caused to families, it only 'works' when people believe that they will be caught, and it is likely to produce unwanted consequences (denial of the offence, resentment) rather than compliance. There are also questions about how much punishment is appropriate, and whether it should be influenced by public opinion, even if it is assessed by a more reliable instrument than newspaper headlines. There is a recent tendency to rely on risk assessment, which gives little weight to personal relationships, and electronic control, which is liable to technical or human error and to fraud by surveillance companies.

The second approach is based on a different paradigm: that it is at least equally axiomatic that the society should respond by requiring the perpetrator to do what he can to repair the harm or make amends for it, and by doing everything possible to persuade and enable him not to do it again. There should be an opportunity for dialogue with those affected. The dialogue is partly an end in itself, providing a setting in which the offender can understand, and express regret for, the harm he or she has caused to someone else, rather than the pain that will be inflicted on him or her; both sides are more likely to feel empathy. And partly it is a process for deciding on appropriate reparative action by the offender. The basic principles are empathy and self-worth on the part of the offender, and trust from the victim and other members of society. These have the advantage that they can influence a person's behaviour even when it is not likely to be found out. They work in harmony with rehabilitative measures, whereas punishment counteracts them. Physical containment would be necessary, but only as a last resort for public protection or persistent non-compliance. The empathy of course may not always develop, the trust may on occasion be betrayed, but the claim of advocates of a restorative philosophy is that these 'soft' methods may turn out to be more effective in persuading people to behave well to each other, and conducive to those states of wellbeing called by such names as *shalom* and *ubuntu* (see below).

Deciding on the response

After considering what punishment is, and what it is for, a third question now arises: if we impose a sanction, how much should it be? This takes us from the idea of punishment to its application: sentencing. The effect of sentencing on criminality is very limited, compared to the strongest influences on people which generally occur in early childhood (Gerhardt, 2010: 314) and, in the case of sentenced offenders, after the end of the sentence. Maxwell and Morris (2001), for example, found that aspects of family group conferences, such as feeling involved in the conference outcome and not being made to feel a bad person, were indeed associated with not being reconvicted; but a much larger number of other factors were associated with reconviction. In early life there were 'significant deficits' such as not being cared about as a child, harsh punishment as a child, and witnessing family violence; after the conference there were 'subsequent life effects' such as not gaining employment or not having close friends. As we have seen, it is a psychological truism that general deterrence depends more on the probability of being caught than on the severity of the sentence. Individual deterrence and rehabilitation pull the offender in opposite directions. The stigma of punishment is intended to communicate social disapproval of wrongdoing (an extremely crude method of communication, as Mathiesen (2000) remarks) but it makes it harder for the wrongdoer to do better. There are unintended consequences, such as the pain and financial hardship suffered by the offender's family,[7] and separation from those who might have a good and supportive influence on the offender after release.[8] As for rehabilitation, the content of the sentence depends more on probation and prison officers than on the judge.

Community sentences are often perfectly adequate. In England and Wales, a number of provisions were made in the Criminal Justice Act 2003 for

---

7. 'The average personal cost to the family and relatives of a prisoner is £175 per month' at a conservative estimate (Prison Reform Trust, 2011: 28).

8. 'During their sentence 45% of people lose contact with their families and many separate from their partners'; 'the odds of reoffending were 39% higher for prisoners who had not received visits whilst in prison compared to those who have;' 'an average of 40% of prisoners reported difficulties with sending or receiving mail' (Prison Reform Trust, 2011: 30).

rehabilitative programmes (section 177).[9] These aimed to persuade and enable the offender to become a good citizen, something contradicted by punishment which tends (or even aims) to influence them through fear, and to stigmatise people, the majority of whom will have already been experiencing disadvantages. This is not a question of what they deserve, but of what is more likely to influence their behaviour in the desired direction. For the protection of the public there are restrictive requirements in community orders, such as curfews and prohibited activities, for a maximum of three years; for imprisonment there are various maxima which are loosely related to the perceived seriousness of the crime, and tend to be increased when a particular crime catches public attention, but they are not based on the estimated length of time required to influence behaviour. The making of reparation is a relatively recent, and welcome, addition to the aims; it leaves open the question of whether the reparation should be in the form of money or work, for the victim or the community, and it does not always mention the possibility that the victim and offender could have the opportunity to agree on what form it should take, which can be empowering for the victim, and can make the offender more likely to fulfil the requirements.

Can sentencing be proportionate? Sentencing judges conscientiously make elaborate calculations to try to match the sentence to the seriousness of the offence (as Easton and Piper show in this volume, *Chapter 6*); Andersen, however (also in this volume, *Chapter 16*), points to the discrepancy between the needs of individuals and time-oriented sentences. There have been numerous attempts to assess public opinion about sentencing. They have found that generally the public does not know the current level: 'People underestimate the severity of sentencing practice. Many believe that courts are retreating from the use of imprisonment, when the reverse is the reality' (Hough and Park, 2002: 164).

Would Restorative Justice be More Civilised?

Restorative justice has an ancient and a more recent history. Community-based justice has been practised for centuries by indigenous peoples of

---

9.   Including activities which 'may consist of or include activities whose purpose is that of reparation, such as activities involving contact between offenders and persons affected by their offences' (section 201(2)). Later replaced by a more general provision.

Canada, New Zealand and, as Claire Spivakovsky (this volume, *Chapter 15*) reminds us, by the Koori people of Victoria and other parts of Australia. More recently, various initiatives in Canada and the USA led to the development of victim-offender mediation, while independently in New Zealand and Australia a related method called family group conferencing was developed (Wright, 1996: 174ff). The practice is spreading beyond the justice system, for example to mediation in communities and workplaces and schools, as Trenczek, Bonafé-Schmitt and Spivakovsky have each separately noted in this volume (*Chapters 13, 14* and *15*, respectively). In schools the idea has extended from conflict resolution to a 'whole-school approach'. The generic term 'restorative practices' is being used to cover this approach; this volume focuses particularly on its relationship with the justice system, increasingly known as 'restorative justice'.

The concept of restorative justice brings with it four new features: a new aim, in which the desired outcome is healing and the repair of harm; a new process, which prefers to address conflict by informal conflict resolution, civil law and criminal law, in that order; a different psychological approach based on empathy, relationships and consent as the primary aim; and new participants: the process should where possible include dialogue between those affected, involving those who have caused and suffered the harm and members of the community, to decide the measures needed in the interests of all concerned.

A new aim

The new aim is to heal or repair the harm that has been caused, and if possible to restore (or create) the state which South Africans call *ubuntu*, in which people recognise that everyone's well-being depends on recognising other people's needs as much as on meeting their own (Skelton, this volume, *Chapter 5*). The early Israelites called it *shalom,* meaning not only peace but health and material prosperity, living in peace without enmity, with the right social, economic and political relationships, and honesty (Zehr, 1995: 130–2). This has the effect of giving a new aim to sentencing. It is by no means lenient, as shown by the example given in the Discussion below; there are 'burdensome' consequences (to use the word favoured by Duff, 2003), but they are purposeful ones. Restorative justice advocates claim that its aims are more civilised than those of punishment, and that it is better able to achieve them. It should also be able to observe another, negative one: *primum non nocere,* the first requirement is to do no further harm, and especially not to those who were not responsible for the original offence.

A new process

We need to remember that restorative justice only applies after admission of involvement in the crime or harm; but it may be argued that a restorative response and a relatively informal procedure would make such an admission more likely. Once the accused has accepted responsibility, the procedure is restorative, or 'dialogic' as Federico Reggio calls it (this volume, *Chapter 10*); instead of focusing merely on 'who did what?' it can explore who was affected, what were their thoughts and feelings, what are their needs now, and how can things be made better, and unlike the adversarial court procedure, this process itself contributes to those ends. Many cases could be diverted from the system to an informal procedure, or treated as torts in a civil court; only when this was not possible would it be necessary to refer them to the criminal court (as McElrea and Gutwirth and De Hert suggest in this volume: see *Chapters 2* and *9*, respectively).

A new psychology

This raises the question, Can the positive force of empathy be as strong a motivator as the negative force of fear? Is the restorative process powerful enough to restore the victim's trust that the offender will not re-offend, the offender's trust that his participation will be respected, and the community's trust that the state has made a strong enough response to show the offender, and everyone, how seriously the offence was taken? This relates both to its effectiveness as a preventive measure, and its symbolism of condemnation. Trust is essential to the return of the wrongdoer to society (London, 2011); but innovations such as electronic tags are signs of a lack of trust, and do not even work well: the Inspectorate of Probation has found that more than half of tagged criminals break their curfews (Judd, 2012: 19).

The basis of this is a different psychology. Conventional justice assumes that punishment is imposed; restorative justice provides an opportunity for voluntary[10] reparation first. A willing apology means more to the recipient and the giver than a forced one. At its best the process, with its emphasis on thoughts and feelings, encourages feelings of empathy (though of course it does not guarantee them). It facilitates catharsis, which is not a painless process but the pain has a purpose: not to instil fear and humiliation (and often resentment), but to cleanse, purging anger, guilt, fear and other destructive emotions. To adapt a saying of the 19th-century British statesman Gladstone, it is based on trust in the people, qualified by prudence, whereas the conventional system is based on mistrust of the people, qualified by fear.

New participants

In accordance with Christie's ideas, the restorative process gives the conflict back to its owners. In victim-offender mediation, this usually means the victim and the offender, with each often bringing a supporter; in family group conferencing extended families can also be brought in, and may contribute to implementing the agreed plan. Another method, also based on the traditions of Indigenous peoples, is the sentencing circle, practised in some parts of Canada; sitting in a circle creates a different dynamic from a conventional courtroom, and, as Claire Spivakovsky (this volume, *Chapter 15*) points out, it encourages the participation of members of the community and (re)integration of the individual; whereas rehabilitation implies addressing shortcomings and problems of the offender only, without considering his environment.

Another way in which restorative processes involve the community is by the use of lay mediators, as in the original programme in Kitchener, Ontario (Peachey, 1989). This policy has been adopted by law in Norway (Andersen, this volume, *Chapter 16*); others, such as Poland, use lay mediators but the law requires certain conditions: they must (*inter alia*) be Polish citizens, over 26-years-old, with qualifications in fields such as psychology, education, sociology or law (Czarnecka-Dzialuk, 2010). The management of mediation services also provides an opportunity for community involvement, if they are run by non-governmental organizations, supported and

---

10. Not entirely voluntary, since the alternative is that a sanction will be imposed; but the offender (we can now use this word, since he or she has admitted involvement) does have a choice.

regulated by a national organization such as the (German) Service Bureau for Victim-Offender Mediation and Conflict Resolution (*Servicebüro für Täter-Opfer-Ausgleich und Konfliktschlichtung*), the Polish Centre for Mediation (*Polskie Centrum Mediacji*) or, in England, the Restorative Justice Council. This is a practical matter which advocates of RJ need to address.

Discussion

The restorative case can be argued two ways: either that it is painful, but in a different way: the pain comes from the realisation of the harm caused to another person and the fact that the offender is not making the most of his or her life (painful acceptance), rather than being imposed by an external agency (pain likely to cause rejection, resentment, determination to get revenge and not be caught next time). Or that the question of pain is a side-issue: the aim is to persuade people to change their behaviour, not primarily through fear of consequences to themselves, but through empathy for what their act would do to another person. The restorative process, unlike the criminal justice process, is likely to engender empathy. It gives the offender the opportunity to earn the trust of other people that he or she will behave acceptably in future.

As we have seen, it is argued that instead of pain for its own sake the restorative process causes the offender the pain of realising what he has done: an internal pain, which does not require additional punishment to be imposed. It can also be said that what is required is not the passive endurance of pain but positive effort: physical effort of constructive work for the victim or the community, or the effort of courage to face the person who has been harmed—or both. It is true that some offenders cannot or will not face their victims, and prefer to undergo the punishment; but for most, because it is less painful, or a more acceptable kind of pain, the offender is more likely to admit involvement in order to 'wipe the slate clean'. This would be more satisfactory for the victim, for whom a recognition of the offence and the harm it has caused is an important need. This is the psychology of the Truth and Reconciliation Commissions in South Africa and elsewhere, which were not perfect but dealt with traumatic experiences to the satisfaction of many, lending support to the argument that the threat of punishment can be the enemy of truth.

The case for restorative justice as an alternative method in less serious cases, and as an addition to punitive sentences in more serious cases, is now supported by ample evidence of good results for all concerned, the high satisfaction rate of victims and offenders and the reduced rate of re-offending. The question is, can an entirely restorative process be advocated including the most serious cases, and those where reparation and dialogue are for any reason not possible (for example where the offender shows no remorse or the victim is unwilling)?

After criticising punishment, and advocating restorative justice, it seems illogical to revert to punishment imposed by a court in cases where a restorative process is not suitable for any reason. There is an intuitive feeling that when someone has caused great harm, the response should be substantial; but given the disadvantages of punishment, does it have to be a punitive response? Is restorative justice adequate? It is argued that the restorative process is not based on the offender's fear of pain caused to himself or herself, but on fostering his or her empathy for the pain caused to the victim. As we have seen, this cannot of course be guaranteed to 'work'; but neither can a system based on fear, or electronic control, and for many people, a society based on encouraging concern for others would be preferable to one based on fear for oneself.

What about the man (it is usually a man) who has shown extreme cruelty, perhaps to numerous people, shows no sign of remorse, and is unwilling to co-operate or cannot be trusted to respond to the restorative process in a way that will help the victim or anyone else? The civilised response is surely not to descend to his level. As is well-known, many serious offenders come from damaging backgrounds, and need programmes such as Enhanced Thinking Skills or Cognitive Behavioural Therapy to overcome their effects. That need not exempt them from a restorative process, which should, on the contrary, reinforce other treatment. It could be combined with other methods such as democratic therapeutic communities (Cullen and Mackenzie, 2011: 59–60, 67). The offender may be required to make amends by community service. The length of the prison sentence would express condemnation, but could be suspended if he was co-operative, in which case it would in effect be a period of close supervision. This would revert to imprisonment if this became necessary to compel him, or for the protection of the public. The keywords would be firmness, requiring amends, ensuring public protection, but not 'toughness' or punishment for its own sake. A more likely form of non-co-operation is that the offender would 'go through the motions' with no change of heart, but if the work is useful, at least there is some benefit, and there is a better chance of the wished-for change of attitude. The individual is shown that there is a more effective way to gain self-respect and the respect of others than by exploiting other people. The Probation Service would have to provide support as well as supervision, following perhaps its English 20th-century motto, 'Advise, assist and befriend', at least as much as the recently introduced, impersonal 'enforcement, rehabilitation and public protection'.

Restorative sentencing

Examples of how restorative sentences can be used for the most serious offences come from South African courts. In one case a woman who killed a young burglar but was unlikely to commit further violence, and who had four dependent children, was given a sentence of eight years' imprisonment suspended for three years, on condition that *inter alia* she apologise to the victim's mother (High Court of South Africa, Transvaal Provincial Division, *State* v. *Maluleke and others*, CC 83/04). Another case was cited as a precedent, in which community service coupled with suitable conditions was imposed for homicide (*State* v. *Potgieter* 1994(1) SACR 61(a)) (both cited in Wright, 2010).

More recently in the case of *DPP* v. *Thabethe*, a man had coerced his step-daughter (aged just below 16 years) into having sex with him, and was convicted of rape. Dr Ann Skelton, Director of the Centre for Child Law in the Law Faculty at the University of Pretoria, appeared as *amicus curiae,* a legal procedure which might well be used more in England and Wales. The trial judge, Eberhard Bertelsmann, took the unusual step of respecting the needs and wishes of the victim and her mother: that the victim had forgiven him and did not want him to go to prison,[11] that he was the family's sole breadwinner, that he had apologised, been reconciled to the girl's mother and continued to support the family. He therefore imposed a restorative sen-

---

11. The judge interviewed the girl separately, accompanied only by his clerk, to ascertain that she was not speaking under pressure.

tence: a ten-year prison sentence, mandatory for such an offence, to reflect its seriousness and public condemnation; but this sentence was suspended for five years, and combined with a reparative package with numerous conditions. If these were met for that period, the prison sentence would not be implemented. It is worth setting out the conditions at length:

- The accused is not convicted, during the period of suspension, of a crime involving violence or a sexual element or both;

- That he remain in the employment of Mr Roussow unless he is laid off [through no fault of his own];

- In such event, he must immediately do everything necessary to find alternative employment;

- From his income, at least 80 per cent must be devoted to the support of the victim and her family. In particular the accused must accept responsibility for the victim's schooling and, if applicable, for her tertiary education;

- Such support for the family is to continue even if his relationship with the victim's mother is terminated for whatever reason;

- The accused must report on one day each weekend (subject to his work programme, which normally entails working one day each weekend) to the probation officer at Delmas and participate in any programme that such officer might prescribe;

- Such programmes must include a Sexual Offender's Programme to be attended at the accused's cost;

- The accused is to perform 800 hours of community service of a nature to be determined by the probation officer during the period of suspension

[This represents the maximum number of hours the accused can serve as he is only available on one day of every weekend].

DPP v. Thabethe (619/10) [2011] ZASCA 186 (30 September 2011)

Thus the sentence took account not only of the seriousness of the crime (expressed by the length of the sentence, which was not affected by the victim's statement) but also of the needs, wishes and best interests of the offender's family, including the victim (met by the conditions imposed). It suggests the additional principle proposed above: *primum non nocere*, the first priority is to do no harm; to the offender, by making it more difficult for him or her to live within the law, nor to the victim and others affected, by depriving them of their breadwinner. However, the DPP appealed to the Supreme Court on the grounds that the sentence was not appropriate, the appeal was upheld, and the defendant sentenced to ten years' imprisonment, not suspended. An appeal to the Constitutional Court was considered (Wright, 2012) but does not appear to have been pursued. This approach could have far-reaching implications for the principles of sentencing.

The conditions were designed not to cause 'collateral damage' by depriving the offender's family of his support. He would remain a productive (and presumably tax-paying) worker, and do additional work for the community, instead of being a burden on the state. The length of the sentence serves the denunciatory function of sentencing. This method of what could be called 'holistic' sentencing deserves further consideration, in cases where there is no substantial risk of absconding or committing further offences. There are however three further reservations. Firstly, there is a risk of piling on extra onerous conditions to make the sentence look 'tough' despite not including immediate imprisonment, but making excessive demands on the offender, and thus setting him up to fail. Secondly, unnecessary conditions could be added to community sentences where prison was not in prospect, which in other words would 'widen the net' of control over the person's life. Thirdly, even if supervision is intensive, the measure depends on the person's co-operation: it is impossible to compel someone to work if he is totally un-cooperative, whether through resistance to authority or, in the case of politically-motivated offences, because of refusal to recognise the regime.

So can restorative justice replace punishment? Ross London (2011) argues that restorative justice is not enough on its own, and needs to be reinforced by punishment. He admits that punishment on its own is also not effective, and that it should be kept to a minimum; the greater the restorative element, the less punishment will be necessary. He is not very clear about what the punishment should consist of, but implies that it need not be prison with all its disadvantages. In the 19th century, the punishment of turning the crank or the treadmill was aggravated by the knowledge that it was not only hard work but unskilled and completely useless: it was raising sand that would then fall, or 'grinding the wind'. If effort is to be required of offenders, it seems only sensible that it should be of benefit to someone and/or facilitate their reintegration into the community. At present much of the punishment consists of the boredom of having nothing to do.[12]

If different victims of similar crimes agree to different amounts of reparation, is that unjust? It could be argued that the outcomes are equal and therefore fair, because the victims are equally satisfied. London (2011) maintains however that there is an additional criterion: enough must be done to maintain the public's trust that the state is taking crime seriously. His solution is to complement the restorative activity with an amount of punishment; the argument in this chapter is that this should be done instead by imposing further reparative activity. Similarly if no agreement takes place, or the offender is un-cooperative and un-remorseful, there should not be punishment for its own sake, but compulsion to do useful work. But in either case, how much? A judge cannot know for how long an individual will have to undertake restorative work in order to change his attitude; nor are indeterminate sentences the answer, because a parole board cannot be sure either.

So despite the arguments above, that sentence lengths are arbitrary and bear no relation to the length of time required for the offender to make reparation or to change the offender's attitude, it is difficult to argue for any other criterion than proportionality to the harm caused by his action. This will be complex to work out. For how long was the victim unable to work? For how long did she suffer post-traumatic stress? If the victim was

---

12. In England and Wales, only about one third of prisoners have work, much of it menial, and the average working week in 2009–10 was 11.8 hours (Prison Reform Trust, 2011: 67).

paralysed for life, would that mean a whole life sentence, which would thus be the same as for homicide?

There are other considerations which cannot be explored in detail here, for example the use of feedback. The non-accusatory nature of the restorative process encourages the exploration of factors behind the criminal event itself; an opportunity is being wasted if information about the social and economic background is not collected and used in the formation of public policy and the promotion of social justice. This process would be assisted if the management board of the programme included senior representatives of relevant statutory and non-governmental agencies from education, social services, children's services and so on. It is taken a step further in the Zwelethemba model in South Africa, where for each case handled, a small amount is paid into a community fund; when a sum has accumulated, it is used for local improvements (Froestad and Shearing, 2007).

Another question is whether the principles of restorative justice can be maintained if it is absorbed into the criminal justice system, or would be better safeguarded by being contracted out to NGOs single-mindedly committed to the restorative ideal; this could perhaps be evaluated by action research. Its proponents also need to show that 'community involvement' is not just an aspiration but a vital part of the concept: employers, owners of accommodation, and other NGOs have an important role in enabling offenders to fulfil the undertakings they make during their restorative meeting.

Conclusion and Outlook

It is possible that, as Claire Spivakovsky suggests in this volume (*Chapter 15*), a dramatic event will provide the spark to ignite a major transformation of the system of doing justice. More likely, perhaps, is a gradual process. Is this a feasible vision? It is already beginning with preventive work through the introduction of restorative practices in schools, where the next generation can grow up understanding how to use dialogue and 'conferences' to make decisions and prevent or resolve conflicts. The city of Hull, in northeast England, has set about training everyone who works with young people in restorative principles, with the aim of becoming a 'restorative city', and others are following its example.

Another approach is to create local community-based mediation centres, such as *Die Waage* in Germany (Trenczek, this volume) and comparable NGOs in the United Kingdom. People with conflicts could ask mediators to help resolve them; the centres could also spread knowledge and understanding of restorative decision-making, conflict prevention and resolution, just as local environmental groups promote energy conservation and recycling. There could be a network of such centres, accredited and supported by a national NGO, which would require them to maintain restorative principles and good practice, as well as good governance. In order to have roots in the local community they would use trained lay mediators; their management could also be drawn from the local community, probably with representatives of statutory services, or the service could be provided by local municipal authorities, as in Norway, regulated and supported by a national council. In either case there should be state funding so that they could concentrate on the development and quality of their work rather than on fund-raising.

Cases referred (or self-referred) could be, firstly, civil disputes in families, neighbourhoods, workplaces and so on. Secondly, they could include cases capable of being treated as criminal, where the parties (usually those who already knew each other) did not choose to involve the courts. Thirdly, they could be referred from the criminal justice system, where the accused had admitted involvement. The prosecutor could refer a case in which, if it were satisfactorily resolved in a restorative process, it would no longer be in the public interest to prosecute. More serious cases would go to court after an admission (or finding) of guilt; the case would be referred to a restorative conference of those affected by the offence, which would recommend a suitable action plan to be included in the court's sentence. Experience in the New Zealand juvenile system suggests that, in about 80 per cent of cases, the judge would endorse the recommendations of the conference. Community involvement would also mean that relevant local agencies, employers, and NGOs would provide the facilities to enable the offender to fulfil the undertakings he made.

Cases where the accused denied guilt would have to go before a judge. So would more serious offences, although the level of seriousness at which this became necessary could gradually be raised in the light of experience and public acceptance. What of the cases where mediation is inappropriate or even impossible, for example because the victim or offender is unwilling to take part, or the offence so serious and the offender so lacking in remorse that any meeting is likely to be traumatic? If the victim was aware of the situation and wanted to proceed, and there was no physical danger, a meeting could be considered: it has been argued[13] that the offender did not give his victim a choice, so it is fair for him not to have one. If the reparative actions agreed by the victim and offender are considered inadequate for such a serious crime, or if no such agreement takes place, how can London's criterion (2011, see above) be met, with a response that marks the seriousness and restores the trust of the public that the state has taken adequate action? London proposes that it should be done by punishment, but does not say what form this should take or how to overcome its disadvantages.

The proposal here is, firstly, to replace punishment with restorative measures, which are fit for purpose in that they aim directly at what they want to achieve, and not merely at causing pain to the offender. They can be very demanding and deprive the offender of considerable liberty, but with as little unintended pain as possible for others. They do not aim to make the offender feel worthless, but to show him, and others, that he is capable of doing better. These measures, however, do not fulfil one of the aims of sentencing, which is to symbolise the seriousness of the offence and the public condemnation of it. The proposal is that this should be done by means of a prison sentence which should have a declaratory function: it would, by its length, denounce the seriousness of the offence, but would normally be suspended, unless the offender was at serious risk of absconding and re-offending, or was refusing to co-operate. Thus the purposes of imprisonment would be limited, firstly, to persuading and enabling the offender to make reparation and become re-integrated with the law-abiding community, where less restrictive measures were ineffective, and secondly, physically to contain those few who are considered to present a serious risk of committing further serious offences.

There is an opportunity for progressing step-by-step along a continuum, making increasing use of measures agreed through dialogue, and decreasing use of an adversarial procedure leading to imposed sanctions. As more people have experience of it, including victims, offenders and mediators,

---

13. By Guy Masters, when manager of a youth offender team.

their families and friends, and those who work within the system, so public acceptance can be encouraged to grow, accompanied by research to identify and promote good practice, building a society based on respect rather than fear, and a system which repairs harm rather than adding to it. [14]

References

Adams, G. (2011). 'A dirty fight: a giant oil corporation has been fined $8.6bn for an environmental disaster that has been called "the Amazon's Chernobyl but .. it may end up paying nothing.' *Independent*, 16 February, 14.

Bianchi, H. (1994). *Justice as Sanctuary: Toward a New System of Crime Control*. Bloomington: Indiana University Press.

Bingham, T. (2011). *The Rule of Law*. London: Penguin Books.

Braithwaite, J. (2002) *Restorative Justice and Responsive Regulation*. New York and Oxford: Oxford University Press.

Cullen, E., and J. Mackenzie (2011) *Dovegate: A Therapeutic Community in a Private Prison and Developments in Therapeutic Work with Personality Disordered Offenders*. Sherfield-on-Loddon, UK, Waterside Press.

Czarnecka-Dzialuk, B. (2010) 'The Quest for Sustaining Research: Empirical Research on Restorative Justice in Poland' in Vanfraechem, I., Aertsen I and Willemsens, J. (eds.) *Restorative Justice Realities: Empirical Research in a European Context*,The Hague: Eleven International Publishing.

Duff, A.. (2003) 'Restoration and Retribution' in Von Hirsch, A., Roberts, J. V., Bottoms, A., Roach, K. and Schiff, M. (eds.), *Restorative Justice and Criminal Justice: Competing or Reconcilable Paradigms?*, Oxford and Portland. OR: Hart Publshing.

Edgar, K., and T. Newell (2006) *Restorative Justice in Prisons: A Guide to Making it Happen*, Sherfield-on-Loddon, UK: Waterside Press.

Faber, A., and E. Mazlish (1980). *How to Talk so Kids Will Listen and Listen so Kids Will Talk*, New York: Rawson, Wade Publishers/Avon Books.

Foley, S. (2012). 'Glaxo pays £3bn for illegally marketing depression drug' i*ndependent*, 3 July, p. 48.

Froestad, J., and C. Shearing (2007) 'Beyond Restorative Justice: Zwelethemba, a Future-focused Model Using Local Capacity Conflict Resolution' in

---

14. I am grateful to Helen Curtis for helpful comments, but responsibility for the views, and any errors, is mine.

Mackay, R., Bošnjak, M., Deklerck, J., Pelikan, C., Van Stokkom, B and Wright, M. (eds.), *Images of Restorative Justice Theory*, Frankfurt-am-Main: Verlag für Polizeiwissenschaft.

Gerhardt, S. (2010) *The Selfish Society: How We All Forgot to Love One Another and Made Money Instead*, London: Simon & Schuuster.

Hopkins, B (2004) *Just Schools: A Whole School Approach to Restorative Justice*, London and NewYork: Jessica Kingsley Publishers.

Hough, M., and A. Park (2002) 'How Malleable are Attitudes to Crime and Punishment? Findings from a British Deliberative Poll' in Roberts, J. V. and Hough, M. (eds.) *Changing Attitudes to Punishment: Public Opinion, Crime and Justice*. Devon, Cullompton: Willan Publishing.

Judd, T (2012) 'Tagging offenders is expensive and archaic, says report', *Independent*, 24 September.

London, R. (2011) *Crime, Punishment and Restorative Justice: From the Margins to the Mainstream,* Boulder, CO, and London: First Forum Press.

Macrory, R. (2006) 'Regulatory Justice: Making Sanctions Effective', Final report. London: Better Regulation Executive.

Mathiesen, T. (2000) 'Towards the 21st Century: Abolition—An Impossible Dream?' in West W. G. and Morris, R. (eds.), *The Case for Penal Abolition*. Toronto: Canadian Scholars' Press.

Maxwell, G. and A. Morris (2001) 'Family Group Conferencing and Reoffending' in Morris, A. and Maxwell G. (eds.), *Restorative Justice for Juveniles: Conferencing, Mediation and Circles*. Oxford and Portland, OR: Hart Publishing.

Ministry of Justice (2007) Survey by ICM for MoJ, press release on 16 November 2007. Originally accessed on http://www.justice.gov.uk/news/newsrelea-se161107a.htm

Peachey, D. (1989) 'The Kitchener Experiment' in Wright M and Galaway, B. (eds.), *Mediation and Criminal Justice: Victims, Offenders and Community*. London: Sage.

Prison Reform Trust (2011) Bromley Briefings: Prison Factfile. London: PRT.

Rosenberg, M. B. (1999) *Nonviolent Communication: A Language of Compassion*. Del Mar, CA: PuddleDancer Press.

Sinha, I. (2009) 'Bhopal: 25 years of poison.' *Guardian*, 3 December.

Wright, M. (1982) *Making Good: Prisons, Punishment and Beyond*, Sherfield-on-Loddon, UK: Waterside Press.

Wright, M. (1996) *Justice for Victims and Offenders: A Restorative Response to Cime* (2nd ed.), Sherfield-on-Loddon, UK: Waterside Press.

Wright, M. (2007) 'Punishment and Restorative Justice: An Ethical Comparison' in Mackay, R., Bošnjak, M., Deklerck, J., Pelikan, C., Van Stokkom, B. and Wright, M. (eds.), *Images of Restorative Justice Theory*. Frankfurt-am-Main: Verlag für Polizeiwissenschaft.

Wright, M. (2008) *Restoring Respect for Justice* (2nd ed.), Sherfield-on-Loddon, UK: Waterside Press.

Wright, M. (2010) *Towards a Restorative Society. A Problem-solving Response to Harm*, London: Restorative Justice Council.

Wright, M. (2012) 'Making Restorative Justice Available: A South African Perspective'. Paper prepared for Khulisa, Johannesberg, with the assistance of the European Union.

Zehr, H. (1995) *Changing Lenses: A New Focus for Crime and Justice* (2nd edn.), Scottdale, PA: Herald Press.

Beyond Restorative Justice to Restorative Practice

Thomas Trenczek

Crime as Conflict

Victim-offender-mediation (VOM) is usually defined as a process which is offered to the parties of a dispute arising from the commission of a crime. VOM refers to a communicative process in which the harm done is addressed, facts and feelings are ventilated, and — in ideal, successful cases — an apology and compensation/restitution are part of a holistic redemption which may lead to some understanding and psychological closure. With the assistance of a neutral mediator the parties identify the disputed issues of the harm done, develop options, consider alternatives and endeavour to reach an agreement about reparation.[1] The goal is to get the act out of the system of both victim and defendant; sometimes VOM may even lead to reconciliation.

Victim-offender mediation is just one model of restorative justice but in the present European context the most important one (Pelikan and Trenczek, 2006). Restorative justice (RJ) is seen as a broad approach oriented on repairing as far as possible the harm caused by crime (Zehr, 1985; Wright and Galaway, 1989; Zehr, 1990; Wright, 1996; Cornwell, 2006; Wright, 2008: 199–200; Trenczek, 2012). In 'modern', 'Western' societies the criminal justice system defines crime in terms of a violation of the laws of the state. Therefore, the state alone becomes responsible for determining punishment and, therefore, the accused is protected from the personal revenge or retribution

---

1. Reparation (German: *Wiedergutmachung*) is different from restitution which is a narrower concept, replacing or repairing what was damaged; reparation addresses also non-material damages and can also include symbolic actions.

which might be exacted upon him or her by a victim or victim supporters. The function of the criminal justice system is to protect rights, to determine guilt and to decide punishment. Therefore, the focus is on due process and a fair trial. However, victims often feel that they are left out or even used by the system rather than having their needs attended to. When victims are included in the procedure it is usually to act as witnesses in the contest between the accused and the state. In this role their story of victimisation is often questioned, and consequently victims often report feeling re-victimised by the court procedures.

RJ places the victim with the offender at the centre of the process. Instead of defining crime in terms of breaking the law, the restorative justice approach defines it in terms of the harm done by one person to another. The focus of interest is not on the abstract violation of the peace under the law, but rather the problems of the persons directly involved: victim and offender. In general, a bad deed is not committed against the state (except in so-called victimless crimes such as consumption of illegal drugs, violation of immigration rules, tax fraud, etc.) but first and foremost crime is a physical and emotional violation of the integrity of a human being. This is true not only for personal, violent crime but for property offences as well (Maguire, 1980). In Europe we owe to Nils Christie the revival of the understanding of *crime as* a cause, expression and consequence of a *conflict*, of difficulties and problems of and between victim and offender (Christie, 1977:5; *cf.* Hanak *et al.*, 1989; *Figure* 1).

With regard to relevant criminal offences and the relationship of the victim and the defendant we distinguish at least *two levels of conflict*. The first relates to the act committed itself. Anger, rage and frustration may come over a victim after being attacked and violated. The victim has an interest in the whereabouts of stolen goods or may want compensation for the material loss, obviously contrary to the interest of the perpetrator. Within our mediation practice we call these cases 'situational conflicts,' in which there was no prior contact between the victim and the defendant. But now there is emotional stress as well as financial damage:

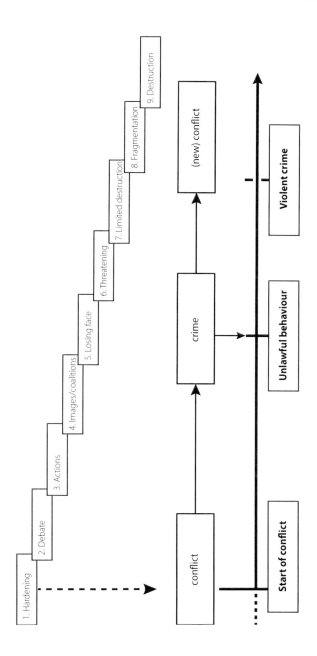

Figure 1: Crime as Conflict

One evening, the apartment of a lady was burgled by a young, unemployed man. At this time she was living under quite stressful circumstances. Just divorced, with financial problems, she took the crime as just another piece in the chain of her unfortunate fate for which she could not blame anybody other than herself. On the other hand, the perpetrator also had a huge number of problems, no work, addiction, facing criminal charges, and no future...

Both the victim's and the offender's lives have been disrupted. Both have been distressed and are looking for ways to restore equity but these may contradict the attempts of the other. The victim may try to achieve material or psychological compensation; the defendant may use techniques of neutralisation to justify the wrongdoing.

The second level of conflict relates to the problems the parties have had prior to the offence. In more than two thirds of the 600 cases referred annually to *Die Waage* ('The Scales') Dispute Resolution Centre in Hanover, both victim and offender have known each other prior to the offence and the offence was the result and expression of unresolved conflicts. In the case of long-lasting conflicts between two people the boundary line between the role of the offender and the role of the victim is sometimes nebulous and dependent on the fact of who files a charge first or whose act is defined as unlawful because of the involvement of law enforcement officials.

> Two men quarrelled for a long time about some neighbourhood issues and the ownership of some borrowed material until the one who was labelled the offender broke into the dwelling of the other and took the things he claimed to be his own.

According to Friedrich Glasl conflicts tend to develop in (nine) *escalation steps* (*Figure* 1), from an initial hardening of arguments to a dispute followed by early actions (instead of words) to threatening strategies and total destruction (Glasl, 2011: 33). On each level of conflict escalation the dispute gets more and more polarised, the parties manoeuvre themselves into negative roles and fight each other until an established concept of enemies fosters strategies of limited damage and, finally, the destruction and downfall of the hostile party are pursued intensively. Highly escalated conflicts tend to turn into violence; Kathleen Turner and Michael Douglas have shown a copybook example in the black comedy 'The War of the Roses', directed by Danny DeVito in 1989, a movie which is used intensively in family mediation training in Germany. As you may know, Oliver and Barbara's quarrel culminated in a horrific bloodbath as the two crashed from the ceiling together with the chandelier.

In reality *domestic violence* is not a comedy and violence in relationships is not a rare experience. According to a survey of the German Government about every fourth woman is (at least) once beaten or abused physically or emotionally by her (ex-)spouse (Müller and Schöttle, 2005).[2] Domestic violence is widespread but in public perception a mostly taboo problem which does not occur only in 'antisocial' problem families or in 'macho-cultures' but is a phenomenon of society in general. Violence very often occurs in highly escalated partner conflicts, when couples break up, especially when there is a fight about the custody of the children or access rights. In these cases violent people act dreadfully and unjustifiably because they are swamped and unable to cope with the conflict situation in a decent way (Trenczek and Petzold, 2011; Dietrich and Paul, 2006: 13; Krabbe, 2008: 49). Violence in relationships often expresses intricate and complex fabrics of power and love, of dependency and sexuality (Pelikan, 2002). Violence is mostly a sign of weakness; violent persons want to establish power but are actually weak in person. This is not said to remove the taboo from violence but rather to understand the mechanics and the circle of the violence to prevent further aggression. Violence happens often at the end of highly escalated conflicts. Hence, any process which supports the parties in de-escalating the conflict, and is empowering to the parties in conflict, will prevent violence.

From the beginnings of restorative justice the theme of domestic violence and the use of criminal law interventions have sparked controversy (Pelikan, 2002: 1; Krieger, 2002). The core of this critique and even rejection was whether mediation is an instrument that should and could be applied to cases of domestic violence at all; particular criticisms are the supposedly defective consideration of structural power imbalances in the mediation procedure and inadequate training of mediators

---

2.   In our daily practice most victims are female, about 5% to 10% are male.

to look behind the culprit's justifications, and to recognise the true power relations and relations of violence behind the women's non-genuine readiness to agree to an arrangement (Pelikan, 2002: 3).

Meanwhile the refusal has changed to a differentiated perception and a willingness to co-operate (Pelikan, 2010: 17ff.). This is especially true with the Hanover Intervention Programme Against Violence in Families (HaIP), described below, a network of women's support groups, the equal opportunities office, the woman and child crisis intervention shelter, the police and prosecutor's office, immigrant organizations, *Die Waage* Dispute Resolution Centre and others (http://www.waage-hannover.de/html/haip.html). The specific approach of intensive counselling with elements of mediation

is likely to work in complicated conflict situations taking into account the individual living conditions and needs of the parties involved, regardless of the juridical facts of the matter. In this respect the suitability of mediation particularly for special relations and life situations is especially great (Glässer, 2008: 157).

However, it is necessary that

the perception of the woman is taken seriously in the procedure, further the perpetrator needs to be led in separate one-to-one counselling to an understanding of the grief which he has caused to the woman and, finally that these perspectives can be communicated in a professional setting … (Pelikan, 2010, 26).

Restorative justice, including victim-offender-mediation, is different from the legal way of dealing with crime, it is victim-oriented but not predominantly against the offender. This is especially the case in family disputes. *Family mediation* deals quite often with violence and crime, despite the terminological resemblance, even more than the so-called victim-offender-mediation approach. By definition restorative justice is not a process that aims for punishment. It is not 'penal mediation' (as the French say), but *mediation in penal matters*, which means conflicts that have become relevant within the criminal justice system (cf Europe Committee of Ministers, 1999; Trenczek, 2003). Regardless of whether or not the act is defined as criminal, or prosecuted, mediation is a systematic approach which aims at autonomous and consensual conflict resolution. VOM is not a completely new or unique process but finds its roots in the way many indigenous cultures have traditionally dealt with deviant, disruptive or victimising behaviour within their communities. In New Zealand, Maori and Pacific Island communities, when dealing with offending within their own communities in family group conferences, are able to follow their own protocols for the conduct of meetings, use their own language, and produce outcomes that are culturally appropriate (Maxwell and Morris, 1993; McElrea, 2011). On the other side of the world victim offender mediation as part of the restorative justice movement in Europe stands on a theoretical foundation very close to the work of the Norwegian criminologist Nils Christie who stated as early as 1977 that conflicts are important elements in society:

> It is the *conflict itself* that represents the most interesting property taken away, not the goods originally taken away from the victim (Christie, 1977: 5, emphasis in original).

Justice as Fairness — Justice as Participation

'Justice as Fairness' is the title of an article by John Rawls (1921–2002) published in 1958 on which his main work *A Theory of Justice* (1971) is based, one of the most important works of legal theory (Rawls, 1958). According to Rawls fairness is the basis of justice. In this view fairness is very much linked to a fair procedure, an approach on which the Anglo-Saxon common law is based. Different from the German (continental) statutory law, the common law system is founded mainly not on material legal positions, but is traditionally process-oriented and develops its legal orientations to a great extent from the case-law of precedents. Hence, it is not surprising that mediation was rediscovered in the USA, after the end of the 1960s. If the conflict is dealt with in courts the litigants fight to win, but they do not solve the conflict. Once the verdict is decided by the court the parties very seldom know why they have won or lost. Lawyers and other experts who have taken over tell them that they have fought intensively; if the case was lost, this is unfortunate, but the court is to blame. Lawyers are trained to deal with conflicts of their clients, which means: 'conflicts are ... taken away from the directly involved parties'. This is especially true for victims:

> Criminal conflicts have either become *other people's property*—primarily the property of lawyers—or it has been in other people's interest to *define conflicts away* ... (Christie, 1977: 5, emphasis in original).

> Lawyers are particularly good at stealing conflicts (Christie, 1977: 4).

For law enforcement agencies conflict means a violation of law, rules and standards, which is not acceptable and therefore needs to be avoided. However, to deny a conflict is to avoid its value (Shonholtz, 1981). Quite in line with the notion of Nils Christie, within restorative justice the conflict of the people involved is central. Instead of understanding justice simply in terms of guilt and punishment, the RJ framework attempts to understand justice in terms of responsibility. From the perspective of RJ, equity and justice are achieved through the offender accepting responsibility for his or her actions and taking steps to make amends. This reflects an *interactive, conflict-oriented perspective on crime*, a move towards an integrative approach which is sensitive to the needs and problems of both victims and offenders.

RJ and mediation focus on equity and balance. The German word *Ausgleich* (literally translated as 'balancing') means both the process of dispute resolution and problem solving as well as the settlement. RJ goes beyond restitution or reparation and connotes a dynamic dimension and an *interactive process* of establishing justice and fairness. With its focus on conflict resolution the central objective of RJ is to facilitate self-determination and participation to re-establish fairness and justice (Netzig and Trenczek, 1996). In Europe the initiation and facilitation of a controlled forum for settling and resolving conflicts is at the centre of the VOM philosophy. Active participation of the parties concerned forms *a core element of RJ*. Thanks to its participatory nature, mediation is likely to produce a more comprehensive solution to the problems arising from the offence or which have led to the offence than the criminal justice system can do alone. Hence, VOM processes are best characterised by a direct meeting of the victim and the accused.[3] It is in the communicative process that the harm done is addressed, facts and feelings are ventilated, and — in ideal, successful cases — the dialogue itself, apology and compensation are part of a holistic redemption which may lead to some understanding and psychological closure.

In the process of victim-offender mediation it is the parties that decide. The *mediator's role* is not to advise them or to determine the content of the dispute or the outcome of its resolution. They are given the chance to handle their own conflict, to represent their own interests. Mediation gives those involved the necessary freedom and space to cope with or make good both the emotional and material consequences of criminal acts, and thus actively participate in reducing and resolving conflicts. Consensus is inconceivable without the active participation of the parties themselves. Therefore, *empowerment* is related to mediation's essential element of active participation. It is based on the premise that full participation in the process of mediation requires the capacity of both victim and offender to stand up for themselves and their interests, to speak out and to be able to 'agree and to disagree' (Pelikan and Trenczek, 2006: 66).

Mediation in Criminal Conflicts and in Civil Disputes — A Community Justice Orientation

In Germany mediation in violent conflicts is not limited to victim-offender mediation. *Die Waage* Dispute Resolution Centre (DRC) which offers mediation in both criminal and civil conflicts handles violent acts in several ways with a special focus on cases of domestic violence. The DRC acts as a crisis contact point for victims of violence (called: BISS = *Beratungs und Interventionsstelle: Counselling and Intervention Centre*) and also counsels and mediates both kinds of cases, criminal cases of domestic violence which are referred by the prosecutor's office as well as highly escalated disputes concerning custody and access rights referred by the family court. Alongside these programmes, *Die Waage* DRC pursues VOM in 'normal,' situational (criminal) conflicts

---

3.   In Germany to participate in a victim-offender mediation programme the 'offender' (defendant) does not have to confess legally, but just has to admit involvement in and responsibility for the incident. Due to Article 6 European Convention on Human Rights (presumption of innocence), a person not yet sentenced by a court is still a 'defendant' or an 'accused person'.

with adult offenders and was the first VOM programme in Germany which was permitted to act as a conciliation board in civil disputes.

The know-how of *Die Waage* Hanover programme dealing with violent conflicts is based on a 20-year constantly developing practice focusing especially on cases of domestic violence. Since 1997 *Die Waage* has been part of the Hanover Intervention Programme Against Violence in Families (HaIP) which has led to a constant increase of referrals of partnership offences. The public prosecutor's office of Hanover assigns to *Die Waage* programme more than 500 criminal cases per year, all committed by adults.[4] In the meantime domestic violence cases make up more than 60 per cent of VOM cases of *Die Waage*. Such offences within social proximity are mostly linked to a long-time (previous) history and numerous conflicts such as

- violent disorders in connection with the separation of a partnership/ marriage;
- continuing harassment (e.g. telephone terror, ambush, threat) of desired partners ('stalking')
- violent disorders as one-time escalation
- ongoing violence in partner relationships.

Cases of intra-familial violence usually involve a considerably higher amount of work in comparison with VOM procedures in situational conflicts. The (mostly female) victims are invited to a first interview in order to weigh up the pros and cons of VOM. Often it leads to extensive consultations about relevant aid organizations (e.g. empowerment centre, women's centre, marriage guidance, alcohol therapy, etc.) and possible action alternatives. The perpetrator is contacted only at the request of the victim.

The underlying conflicts are often complex and may require indirect mediation, joint meetings or both. It is about all issues within a marriage and family: children and partnership issues, money, maintenance and (separation) alimony, household division, quite often alcohol/drinking problems and violence. The results of these mediations in domestic violence cases are diverse, for example:

---

4. The victim-offender programme with juveniles in Hanover is run by the youth court service programmes of the municipalities with approximately 500 further cases a year.

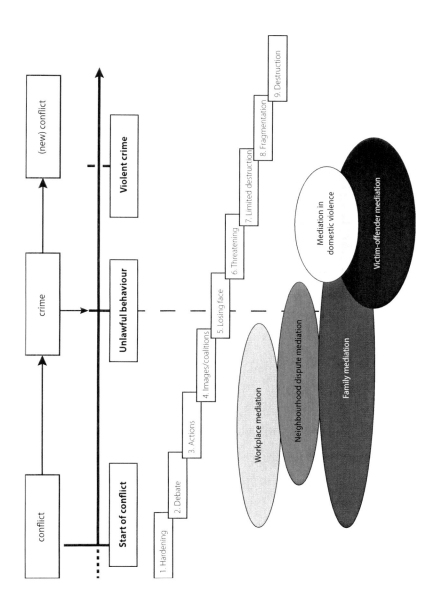

Figure 2: Mediation in different kinds of conflicts

- an open talk about the sincerity of the desire for separation arrangements on different aspects concerning the move out clarification of material issues (finances, ownership of certain items, division of property, etc.)
- arrangements for future contact
- regulation of visits regarding children of both spouses
- compensation for pain and suffering.

If the parties agree to participate, they reach a consensus and positive result in more than 90 per cent of cases. The empowering of the injured parties is essential. In a substantial number of cases the counselling and mediation process supports the victims to enable them to separate from their spouses and leave the violent relationship behind. In cases in which the separation took place before the offence, but had not been accepted by the accused, requirements that ensure the avoidance of any future contact are paramount also. Contrary to common opinion and despite violent escalations not all (female) victims want to separate; some prefer to stay together with their spouse. What victims want is an end to violence. Within counselling, *Die Waage* makes very clear that violence is a taboo, therefore in these cases the parties often agree on outcomes such as:

- beginning a programme of alcohol and behaviour treatment of the accused;
- marriage counselling;
- rules of conduct concerning the handling of future conflicts.

In these cases material reparation payments are only rarely stipulated as those involved usually run a household together.

In collaboration with the family court of Hanover and the child welfare agency of the child protection services of Hanover *Die Waage* has also run a project for 'counselling and mediation in highly escalated family disputes' since 2009. The aim is to support parents in finding a mutual solution in such disputes about custody and access rights and to shape the processes of development with regard to the welfare of the child. Mediation in custody and access issues has been especially emphasised within the accelerated pro-cedure regarding the new family procedure code (*Familienverfahrensgesetz,*

FamFG) becoming effective on 1 September 2009 (cf. §§ 36, 156, 165 FamFG); however, conflicts that have become violent have been officially ruled out from the speedy procedure. What has not been considered is that in practice the violent background is usually not ventilated by the parties before the proceedings begin and once a case is pursued in the accelerated procedure it does not make any sense to rule them out again, especially not in the interest of the children, who need parents who do not use violence. By German law not only both parents have a legal right to contact with the child, but the child has a legal right to contact with both parents regardless of the conflicts they have with each other, and they have a legal right to violence-free education (§ 1631 Abs. 2 BGB).

Parents who are prone to (physical, verbal, psychological) violence need special support to make them realise that their violent behaviour harms their children. It has to be made clear that they have to give up violence in order to exert their parental responsibilities properly. In a specific counselling setting with elements of mediation *Die Waage* wants to support the parents for the benefit of their children. With regard to domestic violence cases Ulla Glässer has pointed out that

> the mediation procedure, unlike the court process, is likely to work on complicated conflict situations by taking into account the individual living conditions and needs of the partners as much as possible, regardless of the juridical facts of the matter. Therefore mediation seems to be very well suited for these special relationships and life situations (2008: 349).

In 2009, within a pilot study, ten cases of highly disputed custody and access rights proceedings were processed: in eight cases *Die Waage* could foster amicable arrangements, in two cases one party did not keep its promises and therefore the court was able to impose a court ruling. In 2010, 24 cases were recorded, of which six were concluded in 2010. In the first half-year of 2011, another 19 cases were recorded, of which seven have already been concluded. Altogether, 28 cases had been concluded by July 2011. There is no typical course of events and conclusion in the treatment of these cases. The cases are very different and the partners are in different stages of the separation. Although all cases are different, the consultation is always intense.

As a rule several separate counselling sessions take place with both parties; in addition the mediator holds intensive and frequent telephone contacts with both of them. Due to the highly escalated conflicts the counselling and mediation process is time-consuming and requires specific competencies of the counsellors/mediators. Cases concluded so far have required five to 15 hours, but in some current cases this is being extended to about 20 hours.

The counselling and mediation proceed in small steps forwards—and sometimes backwards. In some cases the partners are so deeply in the phase of coping with their own vulnerabilities and trauma that no readiness exists to cooperate with the other parent. Here the intensive consultation work serves first to work on their own situation to create the base for mutual cooperation.

It has become apparent what could be achieved by the generation of a protected dialogue in the framework of *Die Waage* approach:

- mothers who had been exposed to long-time violence could receive offers of specific counselling and therapy and protective measures could be demonstrated to them;
- for children, a way has been paved to specific support schemes for children's and adolescents' institutions (e.g. Hanover Children's Shelter);
- regulations to ensure non-violent contact with children have been agreed upon; both parents accepted a renunciation of violence;
- parents agreed to supervised contacts.

In the cases processed to date, sustainable solutions have been worked out and in some cases, because of the counselling process, the family court was able to impose appropriate rulings. As a result, the number of court applications typically filed in these (highly escalated) cases has been significantly decreased and therefore legal costs were saved for both the courts and the families. According to the estimation of the Hanover family court the potential savings amount to up to 50 per cent with regard to the highly contentious proceedings regarding custody and access rights.

Finally, in November 2008, *Die Waage* DRC was the first non-profit mediation organization in Germany to be officially recognised by the state justice department as a state-approved conciliation agency[5] which is able to broker enforceable mutual agreements in civil disputes. With this project *Die Waage* wants to open a 'low-threshold' access to out-of-court and fair conflict resolution to citizens. As a conciliation centre *Die Waage* jurisdiction covers the area of the judicial district of Hanover (which is bigger than the city and region of Hanover) and pecuniary and non-pecuniary claims. As a non-profit/charitable mediation centre, *Die Waage* is not limited to a geographic area and can be engaged in all (civil law) disputes by the parties involved. However, conciliation agreements are only enforceable within the jurisdiction of Hanover. Further with respect to freelance mediators *Die Waage* does not deal with 'normal' separation and divorce cases nor with mediation in and between companies (business mediation).

In 2010, *Die Waage* DRC received 30 requests; however nine cases were unsuitable because parties were not willing to pay the conciliation fee or expected (partisan) legal assistance. In other cases parties have not been interested specifically in a conciliation procedure but in (civil) mediation. In eight of the 21 remaining cases only one party wanted to get information and counselling with regard to the conciliation procedure but did not file a claim. In two cases the parties concerned came to a mutual agreement after an initial contact with *Die Waage* DRC but without a mutual mediation session. In two cases a conciliation file was lodged but the respondents did not agree to mediation. In seven cases mediation was undertaken, of which three cases were still in process at the start of 2011. Issues were family disputes (especially inheritance disputes) or team, partner and neighbourhood disputes. Shortly before the end of the year, two lawyers' offices lodged a conciliation application (*Güteantrag*). In these cases it can be presumed that it was primarily to suspend the statute of limitation. Meanwhile (in 2011) one of these cases was settled by mutual agreement.

A case in the mediation and conciliation programme is more time-consuming than a VOM case. This concerns especially the sometimes long-term family disputes that cannot be settled in one session. The conflict processing takes its course over a longer period of time which enables the people involved

---

5. Voluntary conciliation centres (German: *Gütestelle* or *Schlichtungsstelle*) differ from mediation in that the agreement is enforceable and the offer of conciliation is time-limited; further the conciliation process can be initiated by one party to suspend the limitation period.

to deal or cope with the changes. For instance in one case an 87-year-old lady asked herself if she wanted to move into sheltered accommodation or if she preferred to be looked after at home by her daughter in law. To resolve these issues several mediation sessions were held. Equally this also applies to another case of inheritance matters with various parties and issues, a dispute in which several mediation sessions were scheduled. In this case mediation was successful but it took over six months before an accompanying notary was able to formulate the mutual agreement.

Die Waage DRC has only just started to offer its mediation and conciliation services and therefore the case figures are still quite low. The potential is much higher; however, in conflicts in Germany people are used to seeking legal advice and filing a law suit. The German legal system is significantly more attractive for consumers than those of common law systems. It is less expensive due to the fees and cost structure, as well as the availability of legal aid and legal costs insurance. Therefore, clients of the German legal system have not suffered the same level of inability to access justice as their Anglo-Saxon counterparts. Accordingly, in Germany it may, in fact, be more expensive to mediate a case than to take it to court. Because of its low fees this is not true with regard to *Die Waage* DRC. However it takes time to overcome the traditional attitudes and way of dealing with conflicts. In any case, the offer of mediation in civil cases is an additional and necessary component towards a community justice orientation.

Restorative Justice Goes Further

In legal theory, criminal law stands at the end of a long line of measures for social control; it is supposed to be a last resort (*ultima ratio*). However, in modern society, social problems are very often addressed by new legal provisions and often by more law enforcement but not by participation of citizens. The direct involvement of the parties in conflict, rather than focusing on punishment, does not mean that injurious and violent behaviour is accepted or played down; on the contrary it indicates recognition of the ownership of conflicts and the limitations of the justice system in dealing with them. In an earlier paper I have pointed out that the current criminal justice system is not only too rigid and mediation-unfriendly but co-opts the mediation approach for its own purposes (Trenczek, 2002). As Howard Zehr has put it with reference to Malcolm M. Feeley (1983), the justice system seems to be

> so impregnated with self-interest, so adaptive that it takes in any new idea, molds it, changes it until it suits the system's own purposes (Zehr, 1985: 3).

From a sociological perspective such a self-referencing co-optation seems to be necessary because the alternatives are threatening to the system. That is, according to Feeley and Zehr, the reason why simple reforming solutions have to fail. Victim-offender reconciliation in Germany has not failed, but has stayed quite marginal even though it used to be one of the biggest fields of mediation in Germany between 1985 and 2000 (Trenczek, 2003).

Therefore *Die Waage* DRC does not focus on victim-offender-mediation any more, but offers mediation regardless of whether the dispute is seen as criminal or labelled as a civil dispute. The restorative justice approach opens up the vision of a community-related conflict culture that is close to people's needs. Family court judges in need of an appropriate way of dealing with domestic violence have given an important impulse in establishing mediation in family conflicts. And further, in our practice quite a few citizens do not wait until a case is referred to *Die Waage* DRC by the state prosecutor's office, courts or other official bodies; they take up the offer of mediation right away by themselves once they have been informed by police or flyers, etc. But still mediation is not used as much as it could be. The industry of lawyers is still powerful and it is not in their interest to give the disputes back to the owners of conflict but rather bring a case to court.

On a continuum of possible stages for facilitating conflict resolution, victim-offender-mediation is not the only or ideal way, but on a continuum of possible steps for the treatment of conflicts it only represents one possible application. A community justice centre where criminal conflicts as well as civil disputes (e.g. family, neighbourhood, and consumer conflicts) can be dealt with would be in keeping with the fact that there is no such thing as crime per se but rather that behaviour from a certain point on a continuum is defined as criminal (see the section of this chapter, 'Crime as Conflict', above). VOM represents an alternative way of thinking; it serves less to augment criminal justice decision-making programmes, and is more in keeping with principles of autonomous conflict resolution, fairness and justice (see the section 'Justice as Fairness—Justice as Participation', above). Community justice forums need to provide the means for the early expression and potential resolution of conflict. They need to provide support and participation in order to mediate in conflicts as they emerge and before they become court statistics. Mediation and community dispute resolution centres however will not replace the judicial system, but offer an additional way to justice, parallel to the judicial system which often is quantitatively and qualitatively overstrained with the resolution of conflicts.

References

Christie, N. (1977), 'Conflicts as Property', *British Journal of Criminology,* 17 (1), 1–15.

Cornwell, D. J. (2006), *Criminal Punishment and Restorative Justice: Past, Present and Future Perspectives*, Sherfield-on-Loddon, UK: Waterside Press.

Council of Europe Committee of Ministers (1999, 15 September). Recommendation No. R (99) 19 of the Committee of Ministers to member States concerning mediation in penal matters. https://wcd.coe.int/ViewDoc.jsp?id=420059&Site=DC.

Dietrich, P. S. and Paul, S. (2006), 'Hochstrittige Elternsysteme im Kontext von Trennung und Scheidung' in Weber, M. and Schilling, H. (eds.), *Eskalierte Elternkonflikte: Beratungsarbeit im Interesse des Kindes bei hochstrittigen Trennungen*, pp. 13–28. Weinheim: Juventa-Verlag. Bundeskonferenz für Erziehungsberatung.

Feeley, M. M. (1983), *Court Reform on Trial: Why Simple Solutions Fail*, New York: Basic Books.

Glasl, F. (2011). *Konfliktmanagement: ein Handbuch für Führungskräfte, Beraterinnen und Berater* (10th edn.), Bern: Haupt.

Glässer, U. (2008), *Mediation und Beziehungsgewalt: Möglichkeiten, Bedingungen und Grenzen des Einsatzes von Familienmediation bei Gewalt in Paarbeziehungen*, Baden-Baden: Nomos.

Hanak, G., Stehr, J. and Steinert, H. (1989), *Ärgernisse und Lebenskatastrophen: über den alltäglichen Umgang mit Kriminalität*, Bielefeld: AJZ.

Krabbe, H. (2008), 'Rosenkriege—Ist Mediation Scheidungspaaren möglich?', *Zeitschrift für Konfliktmanagement,* 2, 49–52.

Krieger, S. (2002). 'The Dangers of Mediation in Domestic Violence Cases', *Cardozo Women's Law Journal,* 8, 235ff.

Maguire, M. (1980). 'The Impact of Burglary upon Victims', *British Journal of Criminology*, 20(3), 261–275.

Maxwell, G. M. and Morris, A. (1993), 'Families, Victims and Culture: Youth Justice in New Zealand', Wellington: Social Policy Agency/Ropu Here Kaupapa and Institute of Criminology, Victoria University of Wellington.

McElrea, F. W. M. (2011), 'Twenty Years of Restorative Justice in New Zealand: Reflections of a Judicial Participant', *Journal of Commonwealth Criminal Law* 1, 44–54.

Müller, U. and Schöttle, M. (2005), *Lebenssituation, Sicherheit und Gesundheit von Frauen in Deutschland: eine repräsentative Untersuchung zu Gewalt gegen Frauen in Deutschland,* Berlin: Bundesministeriums für Familie, Senioren, Frauen und Jugend. Hauptstudie des Bundesministeriums für Familie, Senioren, Frauen und Jugend.

Netzig, L. and Trenczek, T. (1996), 'Restorative Justice as Participation: Theory, Law, Experience and Research' in Galaway, B and Hudson, J. (eds.), *Restorative Justice: International Perspectives*, pp. 241–260. Monsey NY: Criminal Justice Press.

Pelikan, C. (2002, January), 'Die Wirkungsweise strafrechtlicher Interventionen bei Gewaltstraftaten in Paarbeziehungen. Der Strafprozess und der Aussergerichtliche Tatausgleich im Vergleich — Qualitative Methoden der Datenerhebung und der Datenanalyse', *Forum: Qualitative Social Research* 3(1), Art. 16.

Pelikan, C. (2010), 'Der (österreichische) Aussergerichtliche Tatausgleich (ATA) bei Gewaltstraftaten in Paarbeziehungen', *STREIT Feministische Rechtszeit-schrift,* 1, 17–26.

Pelikan, C. and Trenczek, T. (2006), 'Victim Offender Mediation and Restorative Justice: The European Landscape' in Sullivan, D. and Tifft, L. (eds.), *Handbook of Restorative Justice: A Global Perspective*, pp. 63–90. London: Routledge.

Petzold, F. and Trenczek, T. (2011), 'Eskalierte Trennungskonflikte — Ist Vermittlung in Rosenkriegen möglich?', *Zeitschrift für Konflikt-Management* 6, 178ff.

Rawls, J. (1958, April), 'Justice as Fairness', *Philosophical Review* LXVII (2), 164–194.

Rawls, J. (1971), *A Theory of Justice,* Cambridge MA: Harvard University Press.

Shonholtz, R. (1981), *Ethics and Values of Community Boards: Developing Concept Tools for the Work of Community Members*, San Francisco CA: Community Board Program.

Trenczek, T. (2002), 'Victim-offender Reconciliation: The Danger of Cooptation and a Useful Reconsideration of Law Theory', *Contemporary Justice Review* 5 (1), 23–34.

Trenczek, T. (2003). 'Mediation im Strafrecht', *Zeitschrift für Konfliktmanagement* 3, 104–109.

Trenczek, T. (2012): 'Vermittlung in strafrechtlich relevanten Konflikten' in Trenczek, T., Berning, D. and Lenz, C. L. (eds.), *Mediation and Conflict Managment Handbook*, pp. 589–585. Baden-Baden: Nomos.

Wright, M. (1996). *Justice for Victims and Offenders: A Restorative Response to Crime* (2nd. edn.), Sherfield-on-Loddon, UK: Waterside Press.

Wright, M. (2008). *Making Good: Prisons, Punishment and Beyond*, Sherfield-on-Loddon, UK: Waterside Press.

Wright, M. and Galaway, B. (eds.) (1989), *Mediation and Criminal Justice: Victims, Offenders and Community*, London: Sage.

Zehr, H. (1985, September), 'Retributive Justice, Restorative Justice', Mennonite Central Committee Office of Criminal Justice, Akron PA, *New Perspectives on Crime and Justice* (Issue #4). Reprinted in Johnstone, G. (ed.) (2003), *A Restorative Justice Reader: Texts, Sources, Context*. Devon, Cullompton: Willan.

Zehr, H. (1990), *Changing Lenses: A New Focus for Crime and Justice*, Scottdale PA: Herald Press.

14

Restorative Justice and Penal Mediation: The French Exception

J-P Bonafé-Schmitt

Introduction

The concept of restorative justice (RJ) has not known the same success in France as in other countries such as the USA, Canada and New Zealand, despite the development of alternatives to formal justice, such as penal mediation,[1] over many years (Umbreit and Coates, 1992; Messmer and Otto, 1992; Aertsen and Peters, 2003; Aertsen *et al*, 2004; Faget, 1997; Jaccoud, 2003; Mbanzoulour, 2004; Cario,2005; Bonafé-Schmitt, 2010). This observation stems from the first evaluations at international level of the development of this paradigm for conflict-management in the different countries examined (Mirsky, 2004; Lauwert, 2003; Carpentier, n.d.; Faget, 1997). In order to try and understand these differences in development, comparative research will need to be developed, while remaining conscious of the fact that it can be difficult to 'compare the incomparable' (Maurice, Sellier and Sylvestre, 1992), due to both the socio-cultural differences which exist between the different countries, and the blurred outlines of this field of study. Depending on the authors and countries, there are differences in the definition and boundaries of RJ, since this term was originally limited to the criminal domain and has for some years been extended to the civil. Referring only to the criminal domain, where it started generally, the first comparative studies reveal

---

1.   The French term *médiation pénale* is commonly used for 'mediation in criminal matters'.

both similarities and differences in the models of RJ developed in different countries (Mirsky, 2004; Carpentieri, n.d.).

Even if all authors agree with the idea that these experiments with restorative justice express the emergence of a new model of justice, they differ in their description of its nature and content (Jaccoud, 2003). Without going into the debate about the notion of diversification or fragmentation of the model of justice, we would like to focus our analysis, firstly, on the reasons for the poor development of the principles of RJ in France and, secondly, on its progress, and particularly its institutionalisation. To explain these differences, we have to stay away from purely cultural or universalist approaches and adopt the view that there is a societal effect that requires us to take account of the specific systems of social order proper to each country (Maurice, Sellier and Sylvestre, 1992). As we have been able to show in earlier research (Jaccoud, 2003; Bonafé-Schmitt, 2010) France constitutes a good example of the necessity to take account of a societal effect when explaining the differences in the acceptance and implementation of the principles of RJ.

Context of the Development of Restorative Justice in France

The concept of RJ, as underlined by J. Faget (n.d.), has appeared recently in France and has been developed only over the last couple of years, stimulated by people from Quebec and Belgium. Nevertheless, since the beginning of the 1980s France has witnessed the development of forms of consensual conflict management, such as mediation, reparation and conciliation which are forms of RJ.

Similarities in restorative justice

Although, as has been highlighted by several French authors (Faget, n.d.; Jaccoud, 2003), the concept of RJ is hardly known in France by academics or practitioners, it remains true that countries on either side of the Atlantic have known comparable developments in conflict management in the criminal domain. However, in order to understand the emergence and development of this model of conflict management, we should relocate it to the broader context of the crisis in social order models. This crisis does not simply impact the sphere of criminal justice alone, but all domains of social life: the family, neighbourhood, schools, workplace, etc., and this explains, as we shall see later on, the success of the concept of RJ in many fields of social life.

To return to the criminal domain, analysis of French and English-language literature shows that authors on both sides of the Atlantic bring forward similar factors to explain the emergence of this movement towards a more 'reparative' model (Jaccoud, 2003). Firstly, they mention the increasingly severe criticism with regard to the 'punitive' model of justice, in relation to both its procedures and its results in terms of prevention of recidivism. Secondly, they underline that the emergence of the victims' rights movement has increased this critique of a model of justice that deprives the parties of their conflict and this only to the benefit of the state. Finally, they remind us more broadly that the crisis of intermediate structures of social order (e.g., family, school, workplace) has brought about the disintegration of social relations, bringing more and more police and criminal justice interventions to resolve conflicts. Indeed, the judicial system is no longer even capable of dealing with the massive increase in cases to be adjudicated upon; to be convinced of that we need only look at the French reports for 2008: of the 4,726,539 cases dealt with by the public prosecution offices, 3,226,128 have been discontinued[2] (*Annuaire Statistique de la Justice, 2010*).

A review of the literature shows that there are also strong similarities in the definition itself of the content and meaning of RJ as a model of conflict management. If one refers to the meaning given to restorative justice by the most prominent authors, who are mostly Anglo-Saxon, one notices that France has seen a similar development in the models of consensual conflict management such as mediation in criminal matters, in the neighbourhood and in schools. In fact, over the years, the perimeter of restorative justice has constantly been refined and enlarged, so as to also include various forms of mediation (victim-offender-mediation and community mediation), as well as the different forms of 'conferencing' (family group conferencing and community group conferencing), not forgetting the three forms of 'peacemaking circles': peacemaking circles, talking circles or healing circles (Mirsky, 2004).

At first, the RJ movement was developed mainly within the criminal domain, to be extended later to the family and schools, as is testified by

---

2.   In French: *classées sans suite:* no further legal action was taken.

a number of studies (Bowen, Belanger, Rondeau, Corriveau, Beaumont, Desbiens and Janoz, 2011; Burssens and Vettenburg, 2011). With the exception of 'conferencing' and 'peacemaking' circles one can see that France has experienced a similar development of consensual models of conflict resolution and it has, in some ways, done RJ without knowing it. For this reason we have always pleaded for the development of comparative research on an empirical basis. Using this approach we have been able to show in earlier work (Bonafé-Schmitt, 2010) that there are great similarities in the development of these consensual models of conflict management and that it makes sense to overcome the problems of terminology to analyse their main characteristics.

Thus, we have some 40 years' experience of the paradigm of conflict management to look at, but the history of its emergence and development still has to be written. It is important to analyse the historical context, for this will allow us to examine several received ideas in France about having allegedly imported an American model of mediation. It is true that in this era of global exchanges, one cannot deny the role played by the USA in the diffusion of their models of mediation throughout the world, as witnessed in the former Communist countries after the fall of the Iron Curtain. But historical analysis taking account of the differentiated tempo tends to demonstrate that, although both sides of the Atlantic are witnessing a renewal of consensual models of conflict management such as conciliation and mediation, it cannot really be ascertained that one of the countries has influenced the other(s) decisively. In fact, comparative analysis shows similarities in the development of non-judicial models of conflict regulation, because in the 1970s there was talk of 'informal justice' in the USA and of '*justice informelle*' in France; later in the 1980s we had 'alternative dispute resolution' (USA) and '*modes alternatifs de résolution des conflits*' (MARC) or '*modes alternatifs de résolution des litiges*' (MARL) in France. However, the terminology of MARC or MARL has not had the same success as ADR had in the USA and the French have, unjustifiably, preferred to use the general term of mediation to categorise all models of alternative dispute regulation (Bonafé-Schmitt, Dahan, Salzer, Souquet and Vouche, 1999).

If one looks at the two principal components of RJ, mediation in criminal matters and community mediation, strong similarities can be seen in the development of these two types of mediation in France and the USA. In the criminal domain, the victim-offender-mediation movement has structured itself and developed rapidly, prompted originally by the Victim-Offender Reconciliation Programne (VORP), which was transformed in 1988 into the Association for Victim Offender Mediation, and then became known as the Victim Offender Mediation Association (VOMA) in 1997. The movement has developed on the American continent as well as internationally, particularly with the creation of the European Forum for Restorative Justice in Europe in 2000, on the initiative of mainly Belgian academics and practitioners.[3] The forum has played a major role in the diffusion of the RJ-paradigm in Europe, including France. The particular role of academics and practitioners from Quebec should be mentioned concerning the diffusion of the idea of RJ in Europe and especially in France; they have contributed to making the concept known by translating the principles of RJ into French (Jaccoud 2003). This is not the first instance in which people from Quebec have played a leading role in the diffusion of North-American ideas of mediation in France. Such was the case for family mediation, where some mediation-pioneers went to Quebec for training and then called on their trainers to contribute to the first courses in mediation to be organized in France. On the other hand, concerning mediation in criminal matters there has been no such link which could partly explain the poor development of RJ in France, where it has mainly developed on the initiative of two national associations, the *Institut National d'Aide aux Victimes et de la Médiation*[4] (INAVEM) and the *Comité de Liaison des Associations Socio-éducatives de Contrôle Judiciaire*[5] (CLCJ). These two national organizations have benefited from the support of the state, particularly that of the Ministry of Justice and the *Délégation Interministerielle à la Ville*[6] (DIV), which has allowed for a rapid structural build-up of this movement nationwide from the end of the 1980s.

It should be emphasised that not all RJ-theoreticians agree that 'the second component of RJ', 'community mediation', is in fact a part of RJ and this is also firmly disputed among those who are involved in the movement for

---

3. The European Forum for Restorative Justice (2000) was originally called the European Forum for Victim-offender Mediation and Restorative Justice: www.euforumrj.org.
4. National Institute for Victim Support and Mediation.
5. CLCJ took the name *Citoyens et Justice* (Citizens and Justice) in 2001.
6. Interdepartmental Delegation for Cities.

community mediation (Mirsky, 2004), Nevertheless, one can see a certain convergence between the USA and France in the development of this type of mediation involving inhabitants of neighbourhoods in managing their own conflicts. Such involvement of the community in conflict management is one of the founding characteristics of the paradigm of restorative justice, the re-appropriation by the community of the power to resolve conflicts generated within its own boundaries (Zehr, 2003). This type of mediation, most often established on the initiative of civil associations, developed on both sides of the Atlantic in the mid-1980s, with only a slight lead for the USA, as was also the case with mediation in criminal matters. The 'community mediation' movement has known a greater development in the USA than in France and has structured itself mostly around a national organization, the National Association for Community Mediation (NAFCM), which is not the case in France.[7] However, one cannot say that the community mediation projects either in France or in the USA refer directly to the principles of RJ, as is the case with VOMA. With some exceptions, these two movements have developed in autonomous ways, separated from their early start, but this does not imply that there have been no exchanges at all between the two movements (Bellard, 2000).

Mediation in schools does not escape from manifestations of RJ, but just like community mediation, one cannot say that the movement for mediation in schools in France and the USA drives the principles of RJ. It is mainly RJ organizations such as the Victim-Offender Mediation Association (VOMA) or the European Forum for Restorative Justice (EFRJ) which are advocating the development of RJ principles within school organizations.[8] Although such projects are in the minority, some experiments in the USA, Canada and Europe claim to follow the principles of RJ. In France, the notion of RJ is beginning to make its way in the domain of education, for example in the work of the *Assises Nationales sur le Harcèlement à l'École*,[9] organized by the Ministry of National Education. The contribution of the *Conseil*

---

7. The National Association for Community Mediation (NAFCM) includes approximately 300 community mediation services, some of which acknowledge RJ principles.
8. The fourth conference of the European Forum for Restorative Justice: 'Restorative Justice and Beyond—An Agenda for Europe', which took place on 15–17 June 2005 in Barcelona: www.euforumrj.org/Activities/conferences.Barcelona.htm.
9. National Consultations on Bullying at School.

Scientifique des États Généraux de la Sécurité à l'École[10] stresses that in cases of proven violence 'the interventions may vary between a punitive sanction and restorative justice practices using a non-punitive perspective'.[11] In their arguments for the practices of RJ, the Scientific Council cites the works of Howard Zehr and John Braithwaite and makes reference to evaluative studies conducted in schools in Australia, Belgium and the UK. A national assessment conducted in schools in the UK has shown that 'Ninety-two per cent of the sessions have been positive and that six months later 96 per cent of the agreements were still respected'.[12] Despite these very positive results, one may wonder how these RJ practices are accepted and implemented in French schools, especially considering the very limited response to them in the penal domain, as we shall see below.

Finally, the last components of RJ, 'conferencing' and 'peacemaking' circles are directly linked to a renewal of the old ancestral models of conflict management of the indigenous peoples of New Zealand, Canada and the USA. This historical particularity explains to a great extent the absence of development of these forms of conflict management in France. Nevertheless, it should be noted that in recent years, we have been witnessing the emergence of a number of experiments inspired by RJ principles such as the '*rencontres détenus-victimes*' (victim-prisoner encounters) but projects of this kind remain marginal (Cario, 2011). They are completely in line with the proposals of the report published by a working-group on restorative justice, which was established at the request of the National Council for Victim Support (*Conseil National de l'Aide aux Victimes*) (Cario, 2007). The report proposed a number of restorative justice measures such as family group conferences and restorative conferences, '*groupes de parole*',[13] restorative conferences between convicted persons and victims, and other restorative meetings (Cario, 2007).

---

10. Contribution of the *Conseil Scientifique des Etats Généraux de la Sécurité à l'École* (Scientific Council of the States General on School Safety) to the *Assises Nationales sur le Harcèlement à l'École* (see above, note 9) organized by the *Ministère de l' Education Nationale*, 2/5/2011, Paris, www.esen.education.fr/fr/actualites/actualites-de-l-education/.

11. *Ibid.*

12. *Ibid.*

13. Group where each party has the right to speak and be heard and supported, in the French sense of *parole* meaning 'word'.

To complete this issue it should be mentioned that there are other initiatives in the domain of the family, such as '*points rencontres*' ('meeting points'), especially in cases where the right to visit is problematic, or '*groupes de parole des parents*' ('talking and listening groups for parents'), which might seem to belong to the 'conferencing' movement, but analysis of these projects shows that they are at some distance from the Anglo-Saxon models.[14]

Differences in Matters of Restorative Justice

To explain these differences in the French development of RJ, it is necessary to overcome linguistic, cultural and chronological problems concerning acceptance of this paradigm in France. Above all, questions should be raised on the semantic level about the different terms used by Anglo-Saxons and Francophones to define the different forms of mediation. In fact, to define penal mediation, Anglo-Saxons use the term 'victim-offender-mediation' even though the word 'penal' exists in English, and comparable questions can be raised with regard to 'neighbourhood' or 'community mediation' (see below). On the other hand, for mediation in schools, there is no difference concerning the use of the term 'school mediation'. Besides these semantic remarks, it is necessary to reflect upon these different terminologies because they translate, as we have found in our earlier research, societal differences which are expressed in different models of social order (Bonafé-Schmitt, 2010). One cannot, in fact, understand the position and the role played by different forms of mediation without reference to the model of social order developed by each country (Crawford, 1996)

The socio-cultural dimension is the first variable to be taken into account because the analysis of the phenomenon of mediation and more generally of RJ cannot be reduced to a simple technique of conflict management. Above all, it represents a new form of action, a new model of social order implying a restructuring of the relations between the state and civil society. In order to analyse this revival of mediation on both sides of the Atlantic, we should like to insist on the notion of the historicity of action-systems and on the

---

14. *Points rencontres* are spaces for contact with the parent who does not have residence rights in a contentious divorce. Parental *groupes de parole* are spaces where parents can find someone to listen to them as well as support them (terminology defined in the French directives of 9 March 1999 and 20 March 2001).

necessity to place the actions of players in the structural framework of each country. In fact, important differences exist between countries according to their different traditional socio-juridical systems: on the one hand the 'Roman law' countries, such as France, characterised by a tradition of written law, and on the other hand those with a 'common law' tradition, such as the USA (Crozier, 1980; D'Iribarne, 1989). Thus, the French system is based on instruments of centralised regulation, functioning in a hierarchical model, appealing to a very prescriptive conception of law, whereas the American system would be more decentralised and contractual. This different legal culture is also linked with a certain conception of the state and the juridical culture: in the Roman Law countries such as France, there exists a 'culture of the law' equal for all and applicable to all, especially in penal matters, which explains to a great extent the difficulties in implementing plea-bargaining,[15] and every other form of negotiation in the context of the penal process. In the common law countries, such as the USA, there exists a 'culture of negotiation' in which processes such as plea-bargaining allow for negotiation between the parties at every stage of the penal procedure (Golberg, Green and Sander, 1985).

We could add to this the differences in the conception of the state and its relation to civil society, with a strong tendency to make the state fulfil a welfare role in the Latin countries, such as France, while this is much less the case in Anglo-Saxon countries, particularly in the USA. France has remained loyal to the Colbertist[16] tradition of interventions by the state and mediation has not escaped from this phenomenon, both with regard to the forms of its institutionalisation and the financing of its activities. The state, through the Minister of Justice, has swiftly provided a framework for the first experiments with mediation, first with the guideline of 15 November 1989 and then with a law in 1993 (Bonafé-Schmitt, 2010). Unlike the USA where numerous foundations exist, in France the structures which practise mediation depend almost exclusively on state finances, which often makes them para-judicial associations depending directly on state or para-state policies.

---

15. *La transaction pénale* corresponds to plea-bargaining.
16. Jean-Baptiste Colbert, 1619–1683, French Minister of Finances, with a control-oriented approach to the economy.

On the cultural level, we can also not ignore the impact of the Catholic religion in the construction of social relations and representations in Latin countries, and of the Protestant religion in Anglo-Saxon countries. It should not be forgotten that the original foundations of RJ principles must be sought, to a large degree, in the programmes developed by the religious movement of the Mennonites. It is amongst their members that we find both the pioneers of the first VORP projects and the first theoreticians of RJ (Bonafé-Schmitt, 2010). The same goes for the Quakers who have been heavily involved in the development of community mediation and mediation in schools. In France, the Catholic movements have a very limited involvement in mediation with only a few individuals or a very small syndicate, the *Confédération Française des Travailleurs Chrétiens*.[17] This depends essentially on the office of public prosecutors which has exclusive legislative power to send cases to a mediation project, without judges in court having even a possibility of proposing mediation based on the nature of the case or at the request of the parties. In addition, the way mediations are done comes under the close supervision of the public prosecutor and the same goes for the content of mediation, since the mediator is obliged to inform the prosecutor of the results, which makes him a true auxiliary of justice.

The two countries also differ in their models of social integration, which have influenced the forms of mediation (Crawford, 1996). It is customary to contrast the French and American models of social integration, referring to what is called the 'universalist' or 'Republican' model on the one hand and the 'differentialist' or 'communitarian' model on the other (Schnapper, 1991; Todd, 1994). In France, integration would take place on an individual basis, through the notion of citizenship, whereas in the USA, integration is produced on a more collective basis, that of the community. These differences of model explain why North Americans talk more of 'community mediation', whereas in France one refers more often to 'social mediation' or 'neighbourhood mediation'. This kind of integration through and on the basis of community in the USA explains why the mediators, in community mediation projects, organized in relation to certain dwelling zones, essentially come from ethnic communities: black, Hispanic, Asian or American-Indian.

---

17. French Confederation of Christian Workers.

On the other hand, in France, in so far as one can perceive the existence of community mediation, with the introduction of 'intercultural mediators', the neighbourhood mediation projects most often bring together residents from different communities.

Thus, to explain these differences in the acceptance of RJ principles in the different countries, certain authors (Lauwaert, 2003; Jaccoud, 2003) refer to 'radically different cultural and political traditions' such as 'the presence of indigenous populations or of a traditional society'. This is most notably the case in New Zealand where the authors of the family group conferencing projects are fundamentally inspired by aboriginal practices and also in Canada with sentencing circles, largely influenced by the ancient practices of autochthonous Amerindian communities.

Difficulties in the Development of Restorative Justice in France

To explain the difficulties in the development of RJ in France and particularly the existence or not of a societal effect, it would be appropriate to develop comparative research on the European and international level. Several authors have insisted on the hypothesis that 'a typically European conception of restorative justice and victim-offender mediation is gradually developing'. According to one of them, Katrien Lauwaert, 'the European approach to restorative justice that shapes the programmes of victim-offender mediation on the continent is a more pragmatic and modest conception' (Lauwaert, 2003). She adds, 'in practice these programs are often diversionary and they remain therefore limited to minor delinquency. That is their main disadvantage'. This assessment, as we shall see, is particularly correct in the case of France but one may wonder whether there really is a 'typically European conception of restorative justice' or if it would not be more appropriate to distinguish different approaches in the countries of southern Europe, those of the North and even those of central Europe. Since there has been a greater development of RJ practices in the northern European countries, we could ask whether there is a 'northern model' that is differentiated from a 'Latin model' of RJ shared by France, while keeping in mind that it is difficult to model the modes of regulating social order (Bonafé-Schmitt, 2010).

The difficult development of the components of restorative justice

Unlike the situation in the USA, in France it is the state that plays a dominant role in the development of mediation, above all in criminal matters, by
integrating it in a redefinition of its criminal policies, constituting a 'third
way' between disposing of cases with no further action and formal prosecutions. This influence of the state is less noticeable in the other components
of RJ such as community or school mediation.

In the case of penal mediation, even if it is true that a number of victim
support associations or probation/parole agencies ('*contrôle judiciaire*') stood
at its cradle, the fact remains that these structures are also essentially financed
by the state.[18] This type of financing is associated with the presence of various law professionals, most notably magistrates, and has led to para-judicial
associations, which have left their mark on the particular character of the
development of penal mediation in France (Bonafé-Schmitt, 2010; Faget,
1997). It has often been prosecuting attorneys who have taken the initiative
or recognised the merits of developing that type of mediation and who have
referred cases to such associations: for this reason the term 'delegated mediation' has been used (Lazerges, 1992). These experiments in penal mediation
conform to a logic of case management, because the judicial institution
is inundated by cases 'en masse' with the proliferation of offences against
property (e.g. thefts from caravans, criminal damage, assaults and wound-
ing, fights on the public road, family conflicts, neighbourhood disputes).

It is hardly surprising that the first experiments with mediation were done
by these types of organizations because they respond to an instrumental vision
of mediation, perceived as a form of reparation for the victims, promoted
and facilitated by victim support agencies, or as a means of reintegrating
offenders under the auspices of the probation services. This instrumental
vision of penal mediation can also be found in the structure of national
organizations which aim at structuring penal mediation. In this way, the
Institut National d'Aide aux Victimes et de la Médiation,[19] established in 1986,

---

18. Among the most representative early experiments, we can cite the AIV (*Aide Information aux Victimes*) in Grenoble, ACCORD (*Association Conviviale de Coordination pour la Réinsertion des Détenus, la Prévention et l'Aide aux Victimes*) in Strasbourg, the AAVI (*Association d'Aide aux Victimes d'Infractions*) in Besançon, *Victimes Assistance* in Limoges, the Prado and the ARESCJ (*Association de Réadaptation Sociale et de Contrôle Judiciaire*) in Bordeaux.

19. National Institute for Victim Support and Mediation.

regroups and brings together under its umbrella both the victim support agencies and the organizations for mediation. The same goes for the other organization, *Citoyens et Justice*[20] (Bonafé-Schmitt, 2010). Most recently the *Association Nationale de la Justice Restaurative*[21] was founded in September 2010. Although this structure seems to have few supporters to date, its creation testifies to the penetration of RJ ideas in France.

The reinforcement of this instrumental vision of mediation has continued with the creation, at the end of the 1980s, of the '*Maisons de Justice et du Droit*' (MJD). Although in the beginning the great majority of mediations were carried out by voluntary associations, over time with the development of the Centre for Justice and Law (MJD) or '*Antennes de Justice*' (AJ), a high proportion of mediations are done in the latter. It should be noted that through the experimentation with the MJD, the state has not only sought to improve the efficacy of the judicial system, but also developed new policies of conflict management, calling on a social and not only a judicial response to conflict matters. The creation of these structures illustrates quite well the will of the state to pacify social relations in the neighbourhoods on the basis of cautions and with new disposal-methods for minor delinquency such as discontinuance under condition of reparation, cautions, reparative measures and mediation. Over the course of the years, this ambition of social pacification, coupled closely with managerial preoccupations to cope with the increasing flow of penal cases, has been strengthened and has led the state to institutionalise the MJD.[22]

The dominance of this instrumental rationale does not in the least mean that the movement for penal mediation is not influenced by other rationales close to the principles of RJ. This is well-demonstrated by the national survey conducted by J. Faget (Faget, n.d.) distinguishing two models of practice. The first model, which he classifies as 'judicial', represents two-thirds of the practices observed, grounded in a purely instrumental rationale. This type of mediation takes place mostly in court buildings or in the MJDs and

20. Citizens and Justice.
21. National Association for RJ, www.anjr.fr.
22. By the law of 18 December 1998 in the case of the MJD, and by the decrees of the 29 January 2001 and 27 September 2004 for the delegates of the state prosecutor (assistants appointed by the state prosecutor to administer cautions), the mediators of the state prosecutor and the prosecutorial penalties (*la composition pénale*).

they are conducted by 'active or retired lawyers who have not received any training in mediation' (Faget, *ibid*). The second model, which he calls 'restorative' because it is close to the philosophy of restorative justice, represents one third of all the observed practices (Faget, *ibid*). This restorative model is most often implemented by associations and by trained mediators. It is above all in these non-governmental organizations that the acceptance of RJ principles has been most significant, even if it comes a bit late, as is testified by the publications of the organizations for penal mediation (Faget, *ibid*).

While penal mediation has shown some development in France, the same cannot be said with regard to community mediation, which remains in an embryonic state. In spite of promising starts, thanks to the support of a number of state organizations such as the DIV (*Délégation Interministérielle à la Ville*), the mediation projects which involve the residents of neighbourhoods have not progressed. Whilst in the USA, some community mediation projects have been inspired by the principles of RJ, this has not been the case in France where the movement has remained distant from RJ. It is true that the absence of any national organization comparable to the NAFCM does not help to develop this type of mediation, nor its receptiveness to new ideas like the philosophy of RJ. Today, we can count fewer than 50 projects in France plus an effort to group their structures in a network, the *Réseau National d'Accès au Droit et à la Médiation* (RENADEM).[23] The aim of this network is to reorganize the structures in order to develop services of access to justice and/or mediation in neighbourhoods, calling on inhabitants to perform mediation functions. But this network does not make any reference to principles of RJ in its founding documents, nor in the documents published since its creation.

Mediation in schools, like community mediation, struggles to develop in France since the implementation of the first programme of peer mediation at the beginning of the 1990s. Some organizations like *Générations Médiateurs*, the *Institut de Formation et de Recherche du Mouvement pour une Alternative Non-Violente* (IFMAN)[24] and also the *Association de Médiation de Lyon*[25] (AMELY) try to develop programmes of mediation or conflict management

---

23. National Network for Access to Justice and to Mediation.
24. Institute of Training and Research of the Movement for a Non-violent Alternative.
25. Lyon Association for Mediation.

programmes in educational institutions, but without real support on the part of the responsible academic administrations. None of these organizations refers explicitly to the principles of RJ.

Instrumental rationales trump restorative rationales

We could have expected a broader development of RJ principles in France over the course of the last decade because of the proliferation of European directives and the activities of European organizations, but progress has been minimal. In fact, the recommendations of the Council of Europe (1999), just like the European programmes or even the activities of the European Forum have had only a limited effect in France. The absence of a genuine organization for penal mediation in France as in other countries, has not helped the development of an autonomous mediation policy and it is the state which over the years has imposed its own policies in matters of penal mediation. Engrossed in a desire for social pacification after the urban riots that have shocked France from time-to-time, and preoccupied by management problems, in view of the massive increase in penal cases, the state has been led to develop the MJDs, and 'cautioning' procedures as well as setting up the plea bargain (*'transaction pénale'*), which are all a long way from RJ principles. On an institutional level this is expressed by the acknowledgement of new actors in the field such as the Delegates of the State Prosecutor (*Procureur de la République*)[26] and the Mediators of the State Prosecutor and it has led to a decline in the application of RJ principles. This new statute has actually caused the mediator, as is indicated by his name, to become an auxiliary of the state prosecution service, and we are witnessing increasing pressure on a number of guarantees preserving his or her independence and impartiality.[27]

Paradoxically, at a time when mediation is becoming the dominant discourse we observe that penal mediation is increasingly called into question in favour of 'differentiated treatment' of prosecutions with measures such as 'plea bargains', 'cautions', and 'measures of penal reparation'. The judicial statistics seem to correlate these developments with the strong increase in alternative procedures to prosecution which have increased from 101,341

---

26. See above, note 22.
27. Cf. French decrees of 29 January 2001 and 27 September 2004 (above, Footnote 22).

cases in 1997 to 250,051 in 2000 and to 544,715 in 2008,[28] which represents 19.3 per cent of all cases which were dealt with by the public prosecution service in 2000 and 36.3 per cent in 2008. However, these quantitative data should not surprise us because the recent developments in penal policies, with the institutionalisation of the 'plea bargain' and of 'prosecutorial assistants[29] and mediators', will indicate, as we have already pointed out, that penal mediation has been marginalised in favour of measures which are nearer to the more managerial and retributive end of the spectrum of alternatives to prosecution and sentencing. Thus, the number of mediations has been reduced from 33,391 in 2000 to 24,471 in 2008 while the number of cautions has increased from 116,694 to 2,692,002 over the same period. If we add mediations and reparation orders, we find that over the years, the percentage of these two components of RJ have steadily decreased from 15.2 per cent in 2000 to 6.1 per cent in 2008, while cautions went up from 46.7 per cent to 49.4 per cent in the same period,[30] The same can be seen with regard to 'plea bargains' which have increased from 1,511 in 2001 to 67,230 in 2008, thus confirming the managerial rationale of case-flows on the part of the Ministry of Justice.[31]

If we analyse penal mediation cases between 2002 and 2008 more precisely, there are significant trends. The number of mediations in cases of theft fell from 3,097 in 2002 to 1,178 in 2008.[32] On the other hand, we can see a big increase of in cases relating to intra-family violence which went from 5,150 to 6,043 over the same period, whereas cases of 'other voluntary assaults and woundings' dropped from 11,238 to 7,487. When reading these figures, we note that family conflicts represent 38.1 per cent of the total number of mediated cases for 2008. The increase in the number of family cases referred to mediation fits quite well within the rationale of RJ, but this positive result should not disguise the quantitative reduction of the other categories such as theft and voluntary assaults and woundings. This mixed result well conveys

---

28. In 1997, the 101,341 cases dealt with by alternatives to prosecution comprised: 33,270 conditionally discontinued, 48,154 mediations, 11,874 mediation-reparation for juveniles and 8,054 therapeutic orders. Source: *Ministère de la Justice, Direction des Affaires Criminelles et des Grâces.*
29. See above, note 22.
30. *Annuaire Statistique de la Justice*, editions 2006, 2008, 2009–10.
31. *Ibid.*
32. *Ibid.*

the instrumental rationale that drives the services of the public prosecution office, which refers private conflicts to mediation, those within the family that cannot be resolved in a purely repressive way, whereas other infractions such as thefts, assaults and woundings are increasingly dealt with by caution procedures.

Looking at the results of mediations, we observe that the percentages of success show a great stability between 2001 and 2008, varying between 54.5 per cent and 54.7 per cent. A purely quantitative analysis of these results would lead to a conclusion that penal mediation is not very efficient because the success rate is hardly above 50 per cent but we need to reflect critically upon the notion of success in mediations beyond purely quantitative criteria in favour of more qualitative criteria. Thus, studies (mostly American, e.g. Umbreit and Coates, 1992) assessing the degree of satisfaction of those mediated (with regard to this model of conflict management) and also regarding the question of recidivism, have shown the advantages of mediation compared to traditional justice. In France, we don't have this culture of evaluation, and the systems arrive or disappear without any evaluation of their efficacy, in either quantitative or qualitative terms[33] (Ben Mrad *et al,* 2008).[34]

To this list one should add 'night pastors', mediators who work in teams during evening-hours on the city streets to promote peaceful order, the AMIS,[35] etc., and the proliferation of these new 'third parties' intervening in neighbourhoods, public transport, and institutions, has contributed to the dilution of the notion of mediation. As we have already emphasised, although these new third parties indisputably perform mediation activities, they are not mediation agencies. In fact, the functions of these social mediators in most cases are much more similar to missions of public protection or 'public tranquillity'—to use their own terminology—than to genuine mediations. Thus we are far from the principles of RJ which inspired the mediation projects in neighbourhoods involving the participation of inhabit-

---

33. In France there are few studies on the evaluation of mediation outcomes, but see: Bonafé-Schmitt, Charrier and Robert (2007); Bonafé-Schmitt and Charrier (2009). On penal mediation, see Fabbrini and Palmer (2008).

34. These professionals can be requested to intervene in troubles in many contexts, such as the street, public transport, companies etc. and also they can function more as 'street-workers', intercultural mediators etc. There are also '*correspondants de jour*'.

35. *Agent de Médiation, Information, Services.*

ants acting as mediators. In fact, the different governments since 2000 have put the accent on the development of this type of social mediation — to the detriment of neighbourhood-mediation projects — which have taken the term 'citizens' mediation' to distinguish themselves from these 'public tranquillity'-type social mediation projects.

The integration of these mediation facilities, such as the ex-ALMS (*Agents Locaux de Médiation Sociale*), into local security contracts (CLS) testifies to the dominance of the public protection rationale to the detriment of the more restorative rationales to be found in neighbourhood-mediation projects. On the quantitative level, in 2001, there were 3,697 ex-ALMS in the 500 existing CLS which is not a negligible number compared to the number of neighbourhood mediators in neighbourhoods which has not been above 500 (at most) in the same period. Even when the change of government in 2002 put an end to the policy of recruiting ex-ALMS in the framework scope of youth employment policies, this did not prevent the continuation of a policy of developing agencies of social mediation, most notably with the creation of professional diplomas such as the one for the *Agent de Médiation, Information, Services* (AMIS).[36] To respond to an increasing demand from local authorities, this social mediation movement has become more structured since 2008 with the creation of a national association in 2008: *France Médiation*.[37]

School mediation does not escape from this dilution of the concept of mediation because we are witnessing an inflation of intervening actors in the educational establishments such as the *adultes-relais* (adult intermediaries),[38] educational mediators and also the most recent addition 'mediators for educational success'. The plan of the former Minister of Education was to

---

36. Training for diploma of *Agent de Médiation, Information, Services*: www.afpa/fomation.
37. Cf. See the history and objectives, in French, on the website of *France Médiation*: www.france-mediation.fr.
38. These *adultes-relais* offer support, information and mediation in many contexts; mediation in the sense of helping to resolve small conflicts arising in daily life. The other functions are: to contribute to social relations in the neighbourhood and to linking people and associations; to inform and accompany citizens in their affairs with administrations and public services; to improve and preserve social order by facilitating dialogue between generations and to support parenthood; to support and strengthen social life by developing capacities for initiative etc. (social capital). Source: website '*Vos droits et démarches*': http://vosdroits.service-public.fr/F1019.xhtml

recruit more than 5,000 of these mediators to combat truancy and school dropouts in 2009.[39] So we are far from the practices of mediation inspired by the principles of RJ and the role of these interveners is located more in the rationale of social order or pacification of social relations.

Conclusions

The debate around the notions of restorative, negotiated or participative justice illustrates the emergence of another paradigm of conflict management that will be the bearer of a new model of social order in many countries.

The development of the RJ movement should not make us forget, as Ivo Aertsen expressed so well (Aertsen and Peters, 2003), that it has progressed through a 'mixture of ... preventive and reparative logics' and that its institutionalisation by states risks 'giving it a function of legitimation or reinforcement of the dominant policies or the existing institutions'. In France, we can see that, over the years, instrumental rationales seem to be trumping the restorative rationalities, as is shown by the decline in the number of penal mediations in favour of cautionary procedures (cautions). In reference to the typology used by Martin Wright (2000), these would be 'unilateral and authoritarian forms' of restorative justice that gain the upper hand over 'democratic forms'. It should be noted that the movement for penal mediation in France has never sought to make itself independent from the judicial system, which partly explains why instrumental considerations of managing the penal caseload, and of 'penal treatment of social issues' have prevailed over restorative concepts that characterised the original projects of penal mediation (Bonafé-Schmitt, 2010; Faget, n.d.; Mary, 2003). There has been a tendency of states to criminalise social relations. The development of these RJ practices could only happen if there were a redefinition of the relations between the civil society and the state, and more particularly, of the legitimacy of the power of government to regulate (legal) disputes. It would imply, particularly in France, calling into question the attitude of 'it should

---

39. On the tasks of the mediators for educational success see: www.education.gouv.fr/cid23676/mediateurs-de-reussite-scolaire-dans-le-second-degre.html.

be done by the state' acquired in the decades of the social welfare state, and such a cultural revolution cannot come about in months nor even years.[40]

References

Annuaire statistique de la justice (2010), edn. 2009–10.

Aertsen, I. and Peters, T. (2003), 'Des politiques européennes en matière de justice restauratrice', *Journal International de Victimologie*, Tome 2, n.1.

Aertsen, I. *et al.* (2004), '*Renouer les liens sociaux: médiation et justice réparatrice en Europe*', Strasbourg: Conseil de l'Europe.

Bellard, J. (2000), 'Victim offender mediation', *The Community Mediator,* Autumn 2000. www.voma.org/docs/bellard.pdf

Ben Mrad, F., Marchal, H. and Stébé, J-M. (2008), *Penser la médiation*, Harmattan—Collection: Le Travail du Social.

Bonafé-Schmitt, J-P., Dahan, J., Salzer, J., Souquet, M. and Vouche, J-P. (1999), *Les médiations, la médiation*, Erès-trajets.

Bonafé-Schmitt, J-P. (2010), *La médiation pénale en France et aux Etats-Unis*, (réédition et mise à jour), collections Classics, LGDJ Lextenso-Edition .

Bonafé-Schmitt, J-P. and Charrier, P. (2009), '*Evaluation des effets des processus de médiation familiale sur les médiés*', *Empan* no.72, 81–97.

Bonafé-Schmitt, J-P., Charrier, P. and Robert, J-C. (2007), *Evaluation des effets des processus de médiation familiale sur les médiés.* Unpublished report, *MODYS-groupe d'étude médiation,* FENAMEF et CNAF.

Bowen, F., Belanger, J., Rondeau, N., Corriveau, D., Beaumont, C., Desbiens, N. and Janoz, M. (2011), '*La médiation par les pairs à l'école primaire: conditions de réussite et perspectives de recherche*', 30 August 2011, www.jidv.com.

Burssens, D. and Vettenburg, N. (2011), '*Assises nationales sur le harcèlement à l'école*', 2–3 May 2011, www.education.gouv.fr.

Cario, R. (2005), *Justice restaurative. Principes et promesses*, L'Harmattan Coll. *Traité de sciences criminelles*, Vol. 8.

Cario, R. (2007), *La justice restaurative: rapport du groupe de travail, Conseil National de l'Aide aux Victimes*, www.inavem.org/index.

---

40. Translated from the French by John Blad. The author and editors would like to express their thanks to Sheila Guyot-Sutherland, Faculté de Droit et de Science Politique, Université Lumière Lyon 2, for her considerable help with the translation.

php?option=com_content&view=article&id=83&Itemid=163 l'aide aux victimes.

Cario, R. (2011), '*Les rencontres restauratives en matière pénale: de la théorie à l'expérimentation des RDV' [rencontres détenus-victimes]*', AJ Pénal, June 2011.

Carpentieri, L.(n.d.), 'Restorative justice in France: obstacle for the application of a truly restorative approach to French dispute resolution' in *Restorative Justice Online*, www.restorativejustice.org, accessed August 2012.

Council of Europe. Committee of Ministers (1999) *Recommendation No. R (99) 19 … to member states concerning mediation in penal matters*. Reprinted in Aertsen I. *et al* (2004), *Rebuilding Community Connections: Mediation and Restorative Justice in Europe,* Strasbourg: Council of Europe.

Crawford, A. (1996), 'Victim-offender mediation and appeals to community in comparative cultural context: France and England and Wales', Mediation Seminar, 6–7 June 1996, International Institute for the Sociology of Law, Oñati.

Crozier, M. (1980), *Le mal américain*, Fayard.

D'Iribarne, P. (1989), *La logique de l'honneur. Gestion des entreprises et traditions nationales*, Seuil.

European Forum for Victim-Offender and Restorative Justice (ed.) (2000), *Victim Offender Mediation in Europe: Making Restorative Justice Work*, Leuven University Press.

Fabbrini, M. and Palmer, N. (2008), *La médiation pénale pour mineurs dans le canton de Fribourg. Suivi de recherche dans le cadre de l'Observatoire européen de la médiation,* Mémoire Diplôme Universitaire de médiation, IUKB.

Faget, J. (1997), *La médiation: essai de politique pénale*, Erès-trajets.

Faget, J. (2010), 'Les fantômes français de la restorative justice: l'institutionnalisation conflictuelle de la mediation' in *Restorative Justice Online*, www.restorativejustice.org. Accessed August 2012

Golberg, S., Green, E. and Sander, F. (1985), *Dispute Resolution*, Boston: Little Brown and Company.

Hansen, T. (2005), *Restorative Justice Practices and Principles in Schools*, Center for Restorative Justice and Peacemaking, University of Minnesota, www.cehd. umn.edu/ssw/rjp/resources.

Hopkins, B. (2005), '*La justice "restauratrice" dans les écoles*' in *Médiation en milieu scolaire, Les politiques sociales,* n.1–2, 2005, *Pratiques réparatrices de groupe en milieu scolaire.*

Jaccoud, M. (ed.) (2003), *Justice réparatrice et médiation pénale: convergences ou divergences,* L'Harmattan-Sciences Criminelles.

Lauwaert, K. (2003), 'Le cadre légal de la médiation victime-auteur en Europe continentale', *International Journal of Victimology,* Vol. 1, no.4.

Lazerges, C. (1992), '*Essai de classification des procédures de médiation*', *Archives de Politique Criminelle,* no.14/1992.

Mary, P. (2003), *Insecurité et pénalisation du social,* Ivry-sur-Seine: Labor Sciences Humaines.

Maurice, M., Sellier, F. and Sylvestre, J-J. (1992), '*Analyse sociétale et cultures nationales. Réponse à Philppe d'Iribarne*', *Revue Française de Sociologie,* Vol.32, 75–86.

Mbanzoulour, P. (2004), *La médiation pénale,* L'Harmattan.

Messmer, H. and Otto, H-U. (eds.) (1992) 'Restorative Justice on Trial: Pitfalls and Potentials of Victim-offender Mediation'. *International research perspectives,* Dordrecht, Netherlands: Kluwer Academic Publishers.

Mirsky, L. (2004), 'A summary of "Survey of assessment research on mediation and Restorative Justice" by Paul McCold', Restorative Practices e-forum, 29 June 2004, www.restorativepractice.org.

Schnapper, D. (1991), *La France de l'intégration. Sociologie de la nation en 1990,* Paris: NRF-Gallimard.

Todd, E. (1994), *Le destin des immigrés; Assimilation et ségrégation dans les démocraties occidentales,* Seuil, Paris.

Umbreit, M. and Coates, R. (1992), *Victim-offender Mediation: An Analysis of Programs in Four States of the US,* Citizens Council Mediation Services, School of Social Work: University of Minnesota.

Wright, M. (2000), 'Restorative Justice: for Whose Benefit?' in European Forum for Victim/Offender Mediation and Restorative Justice, *Victim-offender Mediation in Europe,* Leuven: Leuven University Press. Also available in French: '*À qui profite la justice restauratrice?*' in Gailly, P. (ed. and trans.) (2011), *La justice restauratrice,* Bruxelles: Larcier.

Zehr, H. (2003), *The Little Book of Restorative Justice,* Intercourse, PA: Good Books.

15

Positioning the Offender in a Restorative Framework: Potential Dialogues and Forced Conversations

Claire Spivakovsky

Introduction

Australia, like many other colonised countries, has two histories of restorative justice. The first is interwoven in the long history of the traditional owners of Australia, the Aboriginal and Torres Strait Islander peoples. Although this history is much broader than simply a history of restorative justice, restorative principles are so prominent within these traditional approaches to law and justice that proponents of restorative justice often present indigenous peoples' approaches as the origin of contemporary restorative justice (see, for example, Consedine, 1995; Shearing, 2001; Weitekamp, 1999).[1] Indeed, recognition (albeit not always explicit) of this apparent link between traditional, indigenous justice and restorative justice practices has seen many Western criminal justice systems develop restorative court processes specifically for indigenous offenders, under the guise of culturally appropriate practice.[2]

The second 'history' of restorative justice in Australia is the much shorter history of restorative practices in the youth justice arena. This history begins

---

1. For a critique of the relationship between contemporary 'indigenous' restorative justice approaches and the traditional, indigenous justice, see: Cunneen, 1997 and Tauri, 1998.
2. For example, the Koori Courts, Murri Courts, and the New South Wales Circle Courts have all emerged within the past two decades within the Australian criminal justice system to address the specific needs of indigenous offenders.

in the early-1990s, when Australian practitioners tried to replicate the success of their New Zealand counterparts in reducing youth offending by providing family group conferencing and other alternative forms of mediation for young people. Notably, 20 years after its inception, very little has changed in the genealogy of restorative justice in Australia; restorative justice as an explicitly recognised objective, has remained largely restricted to the youth justice arena.[3]

This is not to say that there have been no developments in restorative justice practices in Australia. Strang's (2001) detailed report on restorative justice programmes maps the numerous police-initiated mediations and family group conferencing processes that have been implemented across Australia's six states and two mainland territories over a period of a decade. However, as this report exemplifies, each of these developments aimed to create better outcomes for young offenders, with little to no consideration of the potential of restorative justice practice for adult offender populations. Moreover, in the limited instances when the subject of expanding restorative justice practices has been discussed in the Australian literature, the conversation has tended towards expanding the practice *beyond* the justice arena, for example, in relation to addressing school bullying (Morrison, 2002 and 2006), rather than *towards* adapting it to adult offenders.

This chapter is concerned with both of these Australian histories of restorative justice, and in particular, their recent intersection in relation to addressing indigenous offenders in Australia's criminal justice system. Accordingly, this chapter will explore the following two issues: (1) why conversations about restorative justice have gained limited audience in relation to adult offender populations; and (2) why certain adult offender populations, such as indigenous offenders, appear as exceptions to this rule.

---

3. Indeed, one only needs to perform a brief search of the publication records of Australia's national research and knowledge centre on crime and justice, the Australian Institute of Criminology, to find that the majority of restorative justice research undertaken in the past two decades has centred on the role that this practice can play in addressing juvenile offending (see, for example: Cunningham, 2007; Richards, 2009 and 2010; and Snowball, 2008).

Part 1: The position of the Adult Offender in Contemporary Literature and Practice

There are numerous potential impediments which can explain why conversations about restorative justice have gained a limited audience in relation to adult offender populations. Broadly, these can be grouped into three categories; political, practical, and legal. The 'law and order' discussions that tend to gain prominence around the time of elections are an excellent example of political barriers. These discussions commonly centre around politicians' need to be seen as 'tough on crime' (e.g. harsher sentences, mandatory sentencing, and greater powers for the police), and as a consequence usually result in the Government rejecting any proposed criminal justice reform that could be interpreted as being 'soft on crime'. Practical barriers can take myriad forms, however they usually present as a lack of funds or other resources needed to create the restorative spaces and environments often described in restorative justice literature. And, there are the legal barriers, such as the often impossible task of reforming legislation in order to create new restorative sentencing options for the courts.

Each of these three barriers has clear implications for anyone seeking to create a criminal justice system based on restorative justice principles, and each has already received attention in restorative justice literature (see, for example, Beale, 2003; Braithwaite, 1999a; Marshall, 1996). What has not been discussed, however, is the impediment created by the inconsistency in the ways that scholars and practitioners in the field of criminology position offenders, the community and the criminal justice system in relation to the notion of enacting justice. The lack of consistent construction, and its impact on the furtherance of restorative justice principles and practice, is the focus of this first part of the chapter. Through tracing the positioning of the offender, community and justice system within the offender rehabilitation, reintegration and restorative justice literatures, this chapter will illuminate how both the lack of consistency surrounding this positioning process, and the lack of dialogue between these competing texts, limits the potential for future discussions about restorative justice approaches.

Offender rehabilitation

If you were asked to write a brief account of the emergence of contemporary approaches towards offender rehabilitation, you would need only to focus on three main points. First, prior to the 1990s, correctional agencies across the world had little faith in the effectiveness of offender rehabilitation, and were quite willing to believe that 'nothing works' (see, for example, Martinson, 1974; Andrews, Zinger, Hoge, Bonta, Gendreau and Cullen, 1990). Second, many Western correctional agencies renewed their faith and interest in offender rehabilitation with the advent of the Risk Need Responsivity Model (RNRM) in the early-1990s (see, for example, Andrews, 1999; Gendreau, 1996; Hollin, 2002). Finally, the faith of correctional agencies in the RNRM has not wavered since the 1990s, and the RNRM still guides correctional practice in Canada, the UK, Australia and several states of the USA (see, e.g., Birgden and McLachlan, 2004).

What is missing from this brief account of offender rehabilitation, however, is something quite critical for the purposes of this chapter. The RNRM did not simply capture the attention of many correctional agencies across the Western world, rather, it fundamentally changed the way that many Western correctional audiences understood and discussed the roles of offenders, the justice system, and the broader community in relation to the notion of justice. To illustrate this point, let us briefly consider the positioning of roles taking place in the first two guiding principles of the RNRM: risk and need.

The purpose of the risk principle is to instruct correctional agencies in the tasks they must complete in order to correctly classify their offender population. To this end, it provides correctional agencies with two key guidelines. First, the principle indicates that correctional agencies must use a risk assessment tool (e.g. the Level of Service Inventory — Revised) to correctly classify their offenders into three different levels of risk: low, medium or high. This tool works by assessing risk based on the number and nature of each offender's static and dynamic 'risk' factors. For example, an offender who was first arrested under the age of 16, has two or more prior adult convictions, has some criminal friends, and has attitudes or orientations which are supportive of crime, will be assessed through this risk assessment tool, as posing a medium level of risk to the community. In contrast, an offender who has been using drugs or alcohol for the past year and who also has poor or a non-rewarding relationship with their parent(s) may only be assessed as posing a low level of risk.

Once the classification process has been completed, the risk principle further instructs correctional agencies about the importance of classification for treatment: correct intervention levels. The principle states that correctional agencies must ensure that they provide offenders with a level of treatment and intervention that matches the gravity of the offender's risk (Andrews, Bonta and Hoge, 1990; Andrews and Bonta, 1994). Indeed, correctional agencies are warned that providing too much or too little intervention can elevate the risk of re-offending for some offenders. Accordingly, an offender who is assessed as medium risk should be provided with a greater level of targeted intervention than an offender who is only assessed as low risk. What is envisioned by the term 'targeted intervention' is clarified by the *need* principle.

The *need* principle states that if correctional agencies aim to lessen and then manage the risk that their offender population poses to the community, they must deliver treatment that targets their offender's 'criminogenic needs'. This means that correctional agencies must focus their attention on addressing antisocial attitudes, values and associates, poor problem-solving skills, a lack of employment skills, and several other dynamic factors that have been directly associated with criminal behaviour in psychological research (Andrews and Bonta, 1994). Thus, using the previous example once more, the individual that was assessed as posing a medium risk of reoffending would not only receive a greater level of intervention than their low-risk counterpart, but the medium-risk offender's treatment would also primarily focus on addressing their antisocial attitudes and relationships with criminal associates, as these factors have been identified as associated with both this specific individual's pattern of offending behaviour, as well as offending behaviour in general.

While it is not the purpose of this chapter to deny how important it has been for correctional agencies to gain empirically proven, easy-to-follow guidelines for classifying and treating offender populations, it is its purpose to show how these simple guidelines also provide correctional agencies with a particular way of identifying, discussing and understanding the roles and responsibilities of offenders, correctional authorities and the broader community in relation to the notion of justice. Indeed, as this brief review of the principles illustrates, the RNRM provides clear roles for these three key figures in the justice arena.

The offender is presented as plagued by a set of criminal attributes. What is interesting about these attributes, is that they appear in the literature as characteristics which are not simply common, and thus defining, of offender populations, but more specifically, as characteristics of civilised society which the offender lacks. Thus, it is not merely that the offender is shown to possess criminal associates, values and attitudes, but more specifically, that they possess *antisocial* associates, values and attributes. Perhaps this emphasis on antisocial characteristics helps explain why, even if an offender only presents with one antisocial characteristic they are presented as a risk to the community, and as requiring some form of intervention or monitoring to ensure that the risk that they pose does not escalate. In response to these fundamentally antisocial figures, the correctional authority (or more broadly, the justice system) is presented with two interlinking roles. The justice system is positioned as the only entity capable both of managing the individuals who represent the antithesis of social values, and consequently, of protecting the vulnerable community from the ongoing risk that these antisocial individuals pose to them. Thus, finally, by implication, the community is provided with no real role in this construction of justice; the community are neither responsible for the onset of the offending behaviour, nor its subsequent management.

This is the construction of justice which permeates the offender rehabilitation literature, and, as indicated earlier, many correctional agencies practising offender rehabilitation in the Western world. Yet, as it will now be shown, while this construction dominates the correctional sphere, the roles of justice have been reshuffled in other criminal justice arenas. Indeed, if we turn our attention to a process seemingly more closely aligned with restorative justice, the process of offender reintegration, we are provided with quite a different notion of justice.

Offender reintegration
The offender reintegration literature positions the dynamic of responsibility between the offender, community and justice system in a markedly different way to the offender rehabilitation literature. Rather than presenting the

offender as possessing a series of criminal characteristics, which by their very antisocial nature mean that the offender poses some level of risk to the community, the reintegration literature presents the offender as a struggling member of the community, who only poses a risk of reoffending *if* the community and social justice system fail them. In fact, the majority of offender reintegration literature begins with the proposition that the goal of service agencies is not to *re*integrate an offender back into society, but rather to *integrate* the individual for the very first time (see, for example, Baldry, McDonnell, Maplestone and Peeters, 2003; Ward, 2001).

Of course, this process of (re)integration is not an easy task for the justice system or the broader community. While in the rehabilitation literature the offender-community-justice triangle revolved around the almost tangible notion of antisocial risk (i.e. the individual who presents with it, the community who suffer from its effects, and the justice system capable of its management), the centroid of the offender reintegration triangle is far less finite. In the reintegration literature, the problem is not the offender, but the absence or lack of support and services provided to this vulnerable individual. The problem, in this literature, is the *injustice* of society. To illustrate this point more clearly, let us briefly consider one of the key issues covered in the offender reintegration literature: accommodation.

The issue of accommodation is often raised in Australian offender reintegration literature to highlight how little attention has been paid by governments and social justice agencies to the needs of individuals returning to the community. For example, Baldry and colleagues' research into housing and prisoner re-entry, highlighted the multiple challenges that offenders returning to the community face, and often fail to address (Baldry, McDonnell, Maplestone and Peeters, 2003 and 2006). This research indicates that although returning offenders struggle to find accommodation, Australian government agencies consistently fail to provide sufficient funding to service providers to resolve the ongoing problem of housing and homelessness. As a result, many offenders returning to the community lack the stability afforded by short-term or long-term housing options, which contributes to their reoffending and, ultimately, their return to prison (for further research into homelessness and reintegration in Australia see Borzycki and Baldry, 2003; Willis, 2004). Thus, the 'problem' in the offender reintegration literature is not simply the lack of accommodation provided by government funded service providers to offenders returning to the community, but more specifically, the lack of attention paid by governments to resolving this endemic, escalating social justice problem.

Notably, research reported in the reintegration literature has begun to map the relationship between the struggles of returning offenders and the lack of acceptance and care of the broader community. For example, Graffam, Shinkfield and Hardcastle's (2008) research into the perceived employability of ex-prisoners and offenders in Australia. This research showed that potential employers perceived people with other forms of disadvantage, such as chronic illness, physical and sensory conditions or a communication problem, to be more likely to obtain and maintain employment than an individual with a criminal background. Thus, once again, the issue brought to the forefront in this literature, is not just that offenders returning to the community face a lack of employment options, but more specifically, they face a lack of willingness and support from the community to provide them with meaningful employment based on their skills (and not their past).

Thus, it would seem that while the construction of the antisocial, 'risky' offender may successfully dominate the correctional sphere, the constructions of the vulnerable offender and the unjust society have captured the attention of post-release service providers across the world (see, e.g., Cortes and Rogers, 2010; Kraszlan, 2009; Visher, LaVigne and Travis, 2004). Moreover, as any reader versed in the dialogue of restorative justice would know, while this notion of integrating a vulnerable offender into a resistant and almost neglectful society governs the offender reintegration literature, this notion is inconsistent with the term 'reintegration' as a restorative process often described and promoted by restorative justice proponents (Braithwaite, 1999b). Thus, it is now time to turn to the restorative justice literature, not simply to illustrate yet another contrasting process of positioning and constructing justice, but also to consider the implications of these separate, contrasting processes, for criminal justice reform (in particular, towards restorative practices).

Restorative justice

While there is no agreed definition of restorative justice, many authors use Tony Marshall's (1999: 37) definition as a guideline for restorative justice discussions. Marshall states that restorative justice is: 'a process whereby all the parties with a stake in a particular offence come together to resolve collectively how to deal with the aftermath of the offence and its implications for the future'. It is also commonly agreed that those 'with a stake' are: offenders, victims and the community.

Clearly, this definition of restorative justice sits in contrast to the offender-justice-community dynamics presented in the offender rehabilitation and reintegration literatures. Indeed, this definition does not just reshuffle the dynamic of this triangle, but rather, fundamentally changes its formation. In restorative justice literature and practice, the figure of the justice authority has been replaced by the figure of the victim. Moreover, the victim does not simply replace the *role* of the justice authority, but rather, the appearance of the victim changes the whole interplay of justice taking place between those 'with a stake'. Thus, when discussing the topic of justice, restorative justice proponents emphasise the *process* of discussing and resolving the problematic actions by an offender and their impacts on their victim and community, rather than the importance of the role that a single party with a clearly defined role (e.g. the justice system) can play in *delivering* justice to a specific construct of the offender.

It is this altered notion of justice, and the different ways of being it implies for key stakeholders, which, while freeing restorative justice proponents from having to engage with the restrictive positions previously attributed to the offender, community, and justice system, also limits the potential for restorative justice principles and practice to gain a footing with adult offender populations. Let there be no mistake, this chapter is not arguing that this altered notion of justice has no potential, or that a focus on a just process rather than an unjust or antisocial individual or community would not provide adult offenders with a different opportunity to become established in society. Rather, what is of concern here, is how, by altering the notion of justice in this way, restorative justice proponents limit their ability to converse in most current conversations about conventional criminal justice.

To illustrate this point, let us consider the two main ways that restorative justice proponents approach this conversation. First, there is a small collection of literature that attempts to present this altered notion of justice as something within which conventional criminal justice practices could be incorporated. For example, Bevan, Hall, Froyland, Steels and Goulding (2005: 195) propose that 'the ability to refer offenders to appropriate treatment programmes is as important for restorative justice models as it is in the application of rehabilitation approaches'. Yet, as this chapter has illuminated, current treatment programmes in many countries not only approach offenders as if they pose a constant risk to the safety of society due to their fundamentally antisocial nature, but also present justice authorities as the only party capable of protecting vulnerable, uninvolved communities. As such, there are likely to be significant differences between the content and aims of a programme perceived as 'appropriate' to restorative justice compared with one considered 'appropriate' within a rehabilitation approach, as well as significant differences in relation to the correct participants in such programmes. Moreover, in light of the likely differences, the overall place of restorative justice programmes within a contemporary rehabilitation framework becomes unclear, which in turn diminishes the value of the analogy presented by Bevan and colleagues. Thus, while some parts of the restorative justice literature may seek to position restorative justice as something which does not require a complete overhaul of conventional justice approaches, these discussions rarely acknowledge the severity of the gap between restorative and conventional approaches, or provide the steps that would be required to bridge this gap.

There is also a collection of literature which, acknowledging the significant gap between conventional and restorative approaches, proposes that restorative approaches should not be compared to existing conventional approaches. For example, Morris (2002: 597), in her critique of the key criticisms of restorative justice, states that: 'restorative justice has to be evaluated against the values it represents and not against those it attacks and seeks to replace'. While it can be agreed that the latter types of evaluations may unfairly expect restorative justice practices to address or fix a problem that has not been resolved by conventional justice approaches, some comparative evaluation is still required. The detailed examination required to engage in a meaningful comparison serves to draw out the primary similarities and differences between the approaches, without which the steps needed to base a criminal justice system on restorative justice principles and practice (or move an existing system towards such principles and practices) cannot be deduced.

In light of these discussions, it seems that one of the key problems facing restorative justice proponents is not the lack of effort by them to develop alternative principles and practices of justice, but the lack of dialogue and common language between competing processes of justice. What this first part of the chapter shows, is that while the offender rehabilitation literature presents techniques for the delivery of justice to an antisocial population, the offender reintegration literature provides the space for the narratives of injustice which has been experienced by offenders returning to society, and the restorative justice literature presents the principles and practices for 'justice' to appear as a process. Accordingly, while restorative justice proponents either refuse to enter conversations which compare conventional and restorative justice (and by implication, the roles of the justice system, offender and the community presented therein), or only enter these conversations superficially, the principles and practices of restorative justice will appear too divorced from conventional justice.

Of course, it is reasonable to ask at this stage, is it not the point of an alternative process of justice to appear in contrast to conventional justice? Yes, it is. However, while these parallel, insular discussions continue, we will continue to see the growth of practices such as offender rehabilitation, reintegration, and restorative justice kept in silos within different sections of the criminal justice arena, with fewer and fewer opportunities presented for practitioners to traverse the entire landscape of justice with a single, comprehensive approach. Accordingly, until restorative justice proponents can establish a dialogue for engaging with contrasting constructions of justice, and articulate how criminal justice systems can bridge the gap between them, restorative justice will remain a separate practice, seemingly too different from conventional justice to warrant further consideration as a mainstream approach.

Part 2: Adult Offender Populations that are Exceptions and Therefore Have Been Met with Restorative Justice Approaches

The above conclusion suggests that the capacity of restorative justice principles and practice to form the basis of a criminal justice system is tempered by the capacity of restorative justice proponents both to engage in alternative conversations about justice, and to create the necessary dialogue and common language to bridge the gap between alternative constructions of the offender-community-justice dynamic. This does not mean, however, that there have been no exceptions to the proposition that restorative justice approaches have not taken shape in the criminal justice system in relation to adult offender groups. Indeed, as this second part of the chapter will now demonstrate, Victoria's indigenous offender population, the Koori offender population, have been met with the Koori Court, a criminal justice approach that is closely aligned with restorative justice principles. However, as this second part will also show, what allowed this process of justice to take shape were some very clear dialogues about the roles and responsibilities of the offender, community and criminal justice system in both broader society and the justice process (something which is currently missing from the restorative justice literature).

Accordingly, the purpose of this second part of the chapter is both to trace the development of the Koori Court in Victoria, and to consider what can be learnt from the development of this more restorative response to Koori offenders for the potential to engage other adult offender populations in a system based on restorative justice principles. In order to perform these tasks, this chapter will draw on both the official documents of the Victorian Department of Justice and data from interviews undertaken with key Indigenous staff members of the Victorian Department of Justice.

The Victorian criminal justice system and the Koori Court

There are three tiers in the court system in the Australian State of Victoria; with the Supreme Court as the highest court with jurisdiction to hear criminal matters at first instance, and an appeal from the two lower courts, the county court and the magistrates' court. It is at the lowest court within Victoria's system that a further three specialised magistrates' courts have taken shape. These are: the drug court, the family violence court division and the Koori Court.

Each of these specialised courts provides offenders and victims with pathways to justice alternative to the traditional magistrates' court, and each provides the Victorian criminal justice system with new approaches to delivering justice. For example, the drug court and family violence court division practise a form of justice that is based on the principles of therapeutic jurisprudence. Accordingly, both of these specialised courts use the law and the criminal justice system as a 'therapeutic agent' (Wexler and Winick, 1991). In practice, this means that these courts not only consider an offender's circumstances prior to an offence, but also act to address some of those circumstances through court intervention. Thus, a serious offender with a drug and alcohol dependence, who has committed offences under the influence of drugs, or to support their habit, will often receive a drug treatment order (DTO) from the drug court instead of a traditional custodial sentence from a magistrates' court. The DTO not only requires the offender to avoid engaging in further criminal behaviour, but also requires him or her to commit to a treatment and rehabilitation programme to address their underlying addiction. Similarly, at the family violence court division, victims of family violence who seek an intervention order against their offending family member, are not only afforded the opportunity to obtain this order, but are also provided with specialist help from family violence support workers, who provide emotional support on the day of the hearing, and provide referrals to further support in the community.

While the drug court and the family violence court division provide both victims and offenders with an alternative experience of the justice system, neither deviate greatly from the traditional offender-community-justice dynamic presented in the offender rehabilitation literature. Indeed, even though the law is administered as a 'therapeutic agent' in these specialised courts, the law is still seen as the sole body capable of achieving justice; the offender is still presented as a figure of risk, plagued by their antisocial attitudes, values and behaviours, and requiring some form of specialised treatment or intervention to be put in place to address them; and the community are still deemed too vulnerable to be involved in any part of the decision-making process.

The other specialised court in Victoria, the Koori Court, however, represents a break from these conventional configurations of enacting and delivering justice, and one of the first moves towards a criminal justice system that embodies restorative justice principles and practice.

The Koori Court Division of Victoria's magistrates' court (the Koori Court) was first piloted in 2002 in two locations; Shepparton, a regional city of Victoria, and Broadmeadows, a western metropolitan suburb of Melbourne, Victoria. The Koori Court was established with both criminal justice and community building objectives. Accordingly, the Koori Court aimed to both decrease the negative effects of the criminal justice system and Koori people's contact with it, and increase the Koori community's awareness, ownership and participation in sentencing members of their community.

After a two-year pilot, the Koori Court was evaluated, with several positive findings presented. Most notably, recidivism rates were shown to be significantly lower, with only 12.5 per cent of those persons sentenced at the Shepparton Koori Court, and 15.5 per cent at the Broadmeadows Koori Court re-offending within two years of release, compared to a 29.4 per cent recidivism rate for the remainder of defendants in Victoria (Harris, 2006a: 85). As a result of this, and several other positive findings, a further five Koori Courts with magistrates' jurisdictions, two children's Koori Courts and one Koori Court with county court jurisdiction have been established around Victoria.

One of the key factors contributing to the success of the Koori Court is the opening of traditional legal spaces to the Aboriginal community. For example, in the Koori Court, Koori elders or respected persons, the offender's family and other community members are invited to contribute to the court hearing. Moreover, each of these participants are invited to sit together with a magistrate at a round table to discuss the offence, and the impact it has had on everyone involved.

This alternative approach has facilitated the environment needed for new discussions to take place. Rather than simply presenting the facts of a case, determining guilt, and arriving at a proportionate sentence for the offender, it is not uncommon for Koori Court sessions to include times when elders and other community members both confront individual offenders about their actions and the impact on the Koori community, and also emphasise the value of the individual within the community and their long ancestry in Australia (Harris, 2006b). The importance of this new environment and approach to delivering justice with Koori offenders is aptly expressed by the following two Indigenous staff members of the Victorian Department of Justice:

> I think it [the Koori Court] helps refocus people a bit, whereas in the old days, magistrates are all over the place now, whereas you have that local community connection sitting at the table, it makes a big difference I feel. Especially if it is their first time, it does a lot of really good diversion.

and

> The elders and magistrates, they identify when someone comes back if they are improving, they also know when someone is bullshitting to them, and they have a crack at them.

What is interesting about these reflections is that they not only indicate why this new approach to working with Koori offenders is important (providing both a good diversion for first time offenders, and those in authority with the ability to see change in repeat offenders), but also indicate the different dynamic of justice this court empowers. Both these statements and the previous observation about the types of conversations taking place in the Koori Court indicate that: (1) the Koori offender is not a subject of risk which is fundamentally antisocial, but rather, an individual who has not lived up to their role in the Koori community, and will need to understand the important part they play in that society before they can address their behaviour; (2) the Koori community is not some vulnerable population that requires protection from their own people, but rather, they are capable of identifying and addressing problematic behaviour in their community;; and (3) the formal criminal justice system is not the sole authority in matters of justice, but is only one voice amongst many others. In other words, the Koori Court appears to empower an offender — community — justice dynamic that closely aligns with the principles and practices of restorative justice, where the emphasis is on the process and conversation of justice that can take place between all stakeholders.

In light of the above findings, it is necessary to ask, how has this come to be in Victoria? Why have Koori offenders been met with an approach to justice that neither matches the approaches of the traditional magistrates' court, nor the other specialised courts? Why has the process of justice changed in this particular specialised court?

The Royal Commission into Aboriginal Deaths in Custody

There is a clear answer to the above line of questions: the Royal Commission into Aboriginal Deaths in Custody (RCIADIC). In 1989, following the deaths of 99 Aboriginal people in police custody and prison over the period of a decade, the RCIADIC was established. Amongst other things, the RCIADIC provided governments and their agencies with 339 recommendations in a Final Report (*Royal Commission into Aboriginal Deaths in Custody,* 1991). The purpose of these 339 recommendations was twofold. First, the recommendations demonstrated for governments across Australia the necessity both to redress the past and present disadvantage experienced by Indigenous people, and to reduce the over-representation of Indigenous people in the criminal justice system. Notably, in a similar vein to the reintegration literature reviewed in Part 1 of this chapter, the focus of many of these recommendations was on bringing to light the *injustice* Indigenous peoples had experienced at the hands of the government, and the strong connection between this injustice and Indigenous offending. Second, the recommendations provided governments with guidelines for achieving these tasks. What these recommendations sparked in Victoria was a series of investigations, reviews and documentations which changed the landscape of delivering justice to and with Koori peoples. What follows below is a brief recounting of this process.

For six years after the release of the Final Report, Australian state and territory governments were allowed to develop their approaches to the recommendations, and in 1997, all states and territories of Australia were called to meet at the Australian National Summit on Indigenous Deaths in Custody. This summit was held to assess the implementation of the recommendations from the Final Report of the RCIADIC by these states and territories. In response to this summit, the state government of Victoria set about develop-ing an agreement between itself and the Victorian Koori community. This agreement was entitled the 'Victorian Aboriginal Justice Agreement: Phase One' (VAJA 1) (Department of Justice and Department of Human Services, 2004), and was launched by the Department of Justice in 2000.

Interestingly, while the accusations and findings of the RCIADIC may have mirrored the claims of injustice which we still hear echoed in the reintegration literature today, the response of the Victorian Government was not restricted to the dialogue of reintegration. The VAJA 1 focused on addressing the underlying issues facing Indigenous communities in order to reduce Indigenous over-representation in the criminal justice system.[4] Accordingly, this document outlined a set of principles and objectives to guide 'the working relationship' between the Koori community and the Vic-torian Department of Justice (Department of Justice and Department of Human Services, 2004: 5). These principles and objectives included: increas-ing community participation; developing culturally appropriate programmes and services; developing a co-ordinated and strategic approach; delivering fair and equitable justice services for Aboriginal people; and, recognising the impact of dispossession of traditional lands, the separation of children and families, and past policies on Aboriginal people. In other words, the response of the Victorian government was to open up the spaces of justice in Victoria to include the voices of Aboriginal people and their experiences, because these people were understood as key stakeholders in Indigenous jus-tice issues. Notably, it was pursuant to this first opening of the justice arena that the Koori Court was developed.

In addition to these principles and objectives the VAJA 1 outlined several smaller initiatives to be taken up by the Victorian Department of Justice. One of these required the Department of Justice to conduct a review to identify if, how and when it had implemented or met the recommendations of the RCIADIC. This review began in 2003 and was completed in 2005 with the publication of the *Victorian Implementation Review of the Recommendations*

---

4. This was a common focus for all Justice Agreements developed in Australia at this time: see, for example, the 'Western Australian Aboriginal Justice Agreement' (Department of Justice *et al.*, 2004) and the 'New South Wales Aboriginal Justice Agreement' (New South Wales Aboriginal Justice Advisory Council, 2003).

of the Royal Commission into Aboriginal Deaths in Custody ('the Implementation Review') (Implementation Review Team, 2004).

The Implementation Review was conducted both by, and in consultation with, Indigenous peoples of Victoria. It spanned more than 700 pages and contained eight sections. The purpose of these sections was to:

- outline the main findings and recommendations of the Final Report of the RCIADIC;
- consider how these findings and recommendations were implemented in the Victorian justice system through the VAJA 1;
- determine what issues remained unresolved; and
- present a new set of recommendations that outlined problematic areas still needing to be addressed by the Victorian Department of Justice.

Around the same time as the publication of the Implementation Review (2004), the Victorian government also published the *Victorian Government Response to the Implementation Review of the Recommendations of the Royal Commission into Aboriginal Deaths in Custody* ('the Victorian Government Response') (Jackomos, 2005). The purpose of this document was to provide a way forward, building on the Implementation Review. Accordingly, while the Implementation Review provided an outline of the existing success and failure of the Victorian Government in implementing the recommendations of the RCIADIC, the Victorian Government Response provided an outline of new approaches the Victorian Government would take in order to further their success and remedy their failure. The response provided an outline of the process by which the findings of the Implementation Review would lead to the development of a new phase of the Victorian Aboriginal Justice Agreement. This phase was realised by the Victorian Department of Justice with the launch of the Victorian Aboriginal Justice Agreement: Phase Two (Department of Justice, 2006).

The 'Victorian Aboriginal Justice Agreement: Phase Two' (VAJA 2) was developed by the Victorian Department of Justice as both a response to the progress and limitations of Phase One (as indicated by the Implementation Review and the Victorian Government Response), as well as a response to the necessity to renew the commitment between government and the Koori community towards addressing over-representation.[5] Like VAJA 1, VAJA 2 comprised several principles and objectives aimed at reducing the over-representation of Koori people in the criminal justice system. In VAJA 2, these principles and objectives included: making mainstream services more responsive and inclusive of the needs of the Koori community; providing crime prevention and early intervention techniques; reducing the level of victimisation that Koori communities experience; and increasing the rate at which the court system delivers Koories from more serious contact with the criminal justice system. It was pursuant to the last of these objectives that the Koori Court system was expanded. VAJA 2 is the final document (to date) in this series of publications about Victoria's past and present relationship, commitment and partnership with the Victorian Koori community.

The above account of the trajectory and impact of the RCIADIC in Victoria holds two implications for the current discussion about restorative justice. First, what this account shows is that the Koori Court and other more restorative approaches towards Indigenous peoples which have taken shape within Victoria's criminal justice system, did not arise from the effort of restorative justice proponents to move the system in this direction, but rather was one part of a broader political shift occurring at the time. Second, this account also shows that what allowed this shift to take place was not simply the concerted effort of the authors of the Final Report, who, like restorative justice proponents, questioned the type of justice that was and could be delivered without the involvement of all of those with a stake in the process, but also the inescapable demand of the Final Report for a response to this question (something which is currently lacking from restorative justice literature).

Positioning Koories in Victoria's criminal justice system

Clearly the RCIADIC changed the landscape of delivering justice to and with Indigenous peoples in Victoria. As the above account indicates, the RCIADIC led to changes in both the structure of Victoria's criminal justice system (e.g. the development of culturally appropriate programmes and services), and its objectives (e.g. the need to recognise the impact of

5. The Victorian Government is the only Government to date in Australia both to undertake a review of the original Aboriginal Justice Agreement and to renew a commitment with more objectives to be met through a second agreement phase.

dispossession on Indigenous populations). However, what the RCIADIC also prompted, was a change in the way that the offender-community-justice dynamic could be constructed in relation to Indigenous offenders. We can see this change more clearly when we look at the way in which the four major documents to emerge in Victoria in relation to Indigenous offenders (VAJA 1, VAJA 2, Implementation Review and Victorian Government Response) present Indigenous offenders, Indigenous communities and the criminal justice system.

Both the Koori offender and the Koori community are presented within the official documents of the Victorian Department of Justice as marred by their 'difference'. More specifically, these documents indicate that in Victoria, Indigenous offenders are 'different' from non-Indigenous offenders, not because they are a different type of offender, or because their offending behaviour is connected to their different experiences from non-Indigenous offenders (see Spivakovsky, 2009 for a discussion about this distinction), but rather because all Indigenous peoples in Victoria (and Australia) are 'disadvantaged', 'over-represented' and plagued by a collection of 'underlying issues or factors'. For example, the VAJA 1 states that:

> We know that over-representation will not be reduced until the disproportionately high levels of disadvantage experienced by the Aboriginal community are tackled by all parts of government (Department of Justice and Department of Human Services, 2004: 5).

Similarly, the VAJA 2 acknowledges that:

> The Royal Commission identified that the overwhelming reason for Indigenous over-representation in the criminal justice system was their social, economic and cultural disadvantage. With respect to Victoria, this disadvantage is the direct result of Koories having been dispossessed from their land and culture and being forcibly removed from their families (Department of Justice, 2006: 13).

Thus, it would seem that in Victoria's official documents, both the Koori offender and the Koori community are characterised by their 'difference'. Indeed, these positioning quotes indicate that the Koori offender, like the

Koori community, needs to be spoken of as 'disadvantaged', 'over-represented' and plagued by 'underlying issues' because difference (as understood in these terms) is the defining object in their lives.

This is not, however, the only position provided for the Koori community in these official documents. What the Victorian documents also make clear is that because the experiences of Koori offenders are so tightly linked to the experiences of Koori peoples in general, the Koori community must be provided with a greater role in addressing Koori offending: it is the Koori community that knows what is best for their people. Thus, as the VAJA 1 states:

> The Government recognises that the Aboriginal community has the right to develop its own structures to service its needs, while maintaining the right to use mainstream services (Department of Justice and Department of Human Services, 2004: 11).

Similarly, as the Implementation Review states:

> The Victorian Government acknowledges Aboriginal people as the rightful owners of their heritage and as having primary responsibility for its control and management (Implementation Review Team, 2004: 19).

Thus, in the Victorian documents, the experiences that mark the Koori offender as being 'different', are the same experiences that mark the Koori community as capable of managing Koori offenders.

Notably, the Koori offender and community are not the only figures to undergo transformation in Victoria's official documents; Victoria's justice system has also taken on a new role. One of the most striking features of these Victorian documents is the way that they present past and present Government agencies (such as the Victorian Department of Justice) as responsible for the disadvantage, over-representation and underlying issues or factors that Koories experience. For example, the VAJA 1 states that:

> The Government understands that previous policies of separating indigenous children from their families continue to have a profound and lasting effect on

economic, social and cultural outcomes of indigenous people in Victoria (Department of Justice and Department of Human Services, 2004: 21).

Similarly, the Victorian Government Response states that:

> The Victorian Government accepts that past policies resulting in the removal of children have contributed significantly to the worse health and well-being of Koori families and communities. It is undertaking a number of initiatives to redress these disadvantages (Jackomos, 2005: 24).

Thus, as both these and the previous extracts illuminate, the traditional justice system is constructed as an underlying catalyst for much of the difference that Koori peoples experience, offenders and communities alike. Moreover, as the following reflections of an Indigenous member of staff show, it is because the traditional justice system has played this role in Koori people's lives, that it must now step back and let the Koori community manage the outcomes and experiences of their peoples:

> …government has tried for 200 years to have a corrections and justice system for all people including Aboriginal people, and it didn't work. So you have Aboriginal people breaching their community based orders at twice the rate, over-representation in prisons at 14–15 times, not accessing any of the services and programs that are available in the system …and the RCIADIC said if you are going to solve these problems, the solution has to come from within the Aboriginal community, and you have to work with the Aboriginal community as equal partners to solve these solutions. And the VAJA has just picked up on that, it is Victoria's response to the RCIADIC. Everything about the VAJA is working towards letting us, the Aboriginal people, have our say in these issues that affect us.

When we look at the broader history of Victoria's criminal justice system, and the way that it has positioned and responded to Koori offenders, it should come as little surprise that the Koori Court approaches the offender-community-justice dynamic in a different way to both the traditional Magistrates' Court, and either of the other two specialised courts in Victoria. Indeed, what the above account of the RCIADIC, and its impact in Victoria, reveals is that all practices with Koori offenders, including the practices of the Koori Court, present the construct of 'justice' in a particular way. All Victorian practices present the Koori offender as being an inseparable part of the Koori community, and as needing to be reminded that they have a particular role to play in the history of their community. All Victorian practices present the Koori community as capable of contributing to the direction of outcomes for Koori offenders. Finally, all Victorian practices present the formal elements of the justice system as needing to be reduced from the role of sole authority on justice, to just one voice amongst many others in a conversation about achieving and delivering justice for Koori peoples.

Observations and Conclusions

In light of the connection between the development of the Koori Court and the changing landscape of Victoria's criminal justice system, this chapter can now draw some final observations and conclusions. What the above account of the Koori Court reveals, is that in order for a shift to occur in the way that a jurisdiction constructs the offender-community-justice dynamic, two key things must often occur. First, something must occur outside the control of justice authorities (e.g. an external review of deaths in custody), but which also holds implications for both the operation of the criminal justice system and Government-population relationships more broadly. Second, whatever occurs outside the control of justice authorities must have enough clout so that it forces a change in criminal justice conversations from that point onwards; that it creates the right positions for a new or alternative construction of justice to operate. This is what is currently missing for restorative justice proponents, and what the RCIADIC did for Victoria's criminal justice system. As the then Attorney-General notes in the forward to the VAJA 1, 'the Royal Commission into Aboriginal Deaths in Custody was such a moment—a profound wake-up call that put the country's leaders on notice to stand up and take responsibility' (Department of Justice and Department of Human Services, 2004: 3). Thus the power of the RCIADIC came not from its ability to present yet another alternative way of practising justice, but rather, from its ability to present undeniable, damning truths about government-population relationships that resulted in all other conversations taking place in the criminal justice system (e.g. about antisocial individuals, vulnerable communities and solely capable justice systems) losing their meaning.

This observation implies something interesting for restorative justice proponents. Criminal justice reform is not just about proposing alternatives, or even presenting the steps to make those alternatives take shape (as was argued at the conclusion of Part 1 of this chapter); it is *also* about finding the right time to have these conversations. Indeed, there is no doubt that the Koori community had advocated for criminal justice reform prior to the VAJA 1, or had known what steps would be needed to make this reform come into effect, but the opportunity for their voices to be heard did not exist until the RCIADIC silenced all other conversations. As one Indigenous staff member of the Victorian Department of Justice explains:

> The Koori community has always seen things as holistic and related and linked, and the Government is organized into these functional agencies which don't really align with how people live their lives, or how the Koori community understands things and wants to respond to issues. So the RCIADIC was classic in that it really highlighted the underlying issues for the Government to see. The Koori community had always wanted those underlying issues addressed. So that is where the RCIADIC has had an impact, because it made Governments more aligned with how Koori people live their lives.

Thus, in conclusion, what this chapter has shown is that criminal justice reform is not just about having the right words or dialogue to present the offender-community-justice dynamic in a different formation, it is also about knowing how and when to engage in conversations about population management, both within and beyond the justice arena.

References

Andrews, D. (1999), 'Principles of Effective Correctional Programs' in Serin, M. (ed.), *Compendium 2000 On Effective Correctional Programming*, Ottawa: Correction Service Canada.

Andrews, D. and Bonta, J. (1994), *The Psychology of Criminal Conduct*, Cincinnati: Anderson Publications.

Andrews, D., Bonta, J. and Hoge, R. (1990), 'Classification for Effective Rehabilitation: Rediscovering Psychology', *Criminal Justice and Behavior*, Vol.17, No.1, 19–52.

Andrews, D., Zinger, I., Hoge, R., Bonta, J., Gendreau, P., and Cullen, F. (1990), 'A Human Science Approach or More Punishment and Pessimism: A Rejoinder to Lab and Whitehead', *Criminology*, Vol.28, no.3, 419–429.

Baldry, E., McDonnell, D., Maplestone, P. and Peeters, M. (2003), *Ex-prisoners and Accommodation: What Bearing Do Different Forms of Housing Have on Social Reintegration?*, AHURI Final Report, No.46, Melbourne: Australian Housing and Urban Research Institute.

Baldry, E., McDonnell, D., Maplestone, P. and Peeters, M. (2006), 'Ex-prisoners, Accommodation and the State: Post-release in Australia', *Australian and New Zealand Journal of Criminology*, Vol.39, no.1, 20–33.

Beale, S. (2003), 'Still Tough on Crime? Prospects for Restorative Justice in the United States', *Utah Law Review*, Vol.10, 413–437.

Beven, J., Hall, G., Froyland, I., Steels, B. and Goulding, D. (2005), 'Restoration or Renovation? Evaluating Restorative Justice Outcomes', *Psychiatry, Psychology and Law*, Vol.12, No.1, 194–206.

Birgden, A. and McLachlan, C. (2004), *Reducing Reoffending Framework: Setting the Scene, Part No. 1.*, Melbourne: Victorian Department of Justice.

Borzycki, M. and Baldry, E. (2003), 'Promoting Integration: The Provision of Prisoner Post-release Services', *Trends & Issues in Crime and Criminal Justice*, No.262, Canberra: Australian Institute of Criminology.

Braithwaite, J. (1999a), 'Restorative Justice: Assessing Optimistic and Pessimistic Accounts', *Crime and Justice: A Review of Research*, Vol.25 (ed. Tonry, M.), Chicago: University of Chicago Press, 1–127.

Braithwaite, J. (1999b), *Crime, Shame and Reintegration*, New York: Cambridge University Press.

Consedine, J. (1995), *Restorative Justice: Healing the Effects of Crime*, Lyttelton, NZ: Ploughshares Publications.

Cortes, K. and Rogers, S. (2010), *Reentry Housing Options: The Policymakers' Guide*, New York: Council of State Governments Justice Centre.

Cunneen, C. (1997), 'Community Conferencing and the Fiction of Indigenous Control', *Australian and New Zealand Journal of Criminology*, Vol.30, No.3, 292–311.

Cunningham, T. (2007), 'Pre-court Diversion in the Northern Territory: Impact on Juvenile Reoffending', *Trends & Issues in Crime and Criminal Justice*, No.390, Canberra: Australian Institute of Criminology.

Department of Justice (2006), 'Victorian Aboriginal Justice Agreement: Phase Two', Melbourne: Indigenous Issues Unit, Department of Justice.

Department of Justice and Department of Human Services (2004), 'Victorian Aboriginal Justice Agreement: Phase One', Melbourne: Department of Justice.

Department of Justice, Department for Community Development, Department of Indigenous Affairs, Western Australia Police Service, the Aboriginal and Torres Strait Islander Commission, the Aboriginal and Torres Strait Islander Services and Aboriginal Legal Service of Western Australia (2004), 'Western Australian Aboriginal Justice Agreement', Perth: Department of Justice.

Gendreau, P. (1996), 'Offender Rehabilitation: What We Know and What Needs to be Done', *Criminal Justice and Behavior*, Vol.23, No.1, 144–161.

Graffam, J., Shinkfield, A. and Hardcastle, L. (2008), 'The Perceived Employability of Ex-prisoners and Offenders', *International Journal of Offender Therapy and Comparative Criminology*, Vol.52, No.6, 673–685.

Harris, M. (2006a), *A Sentencing Conversation: Evaluation of the Koori Courts Pilot Programme, October 2002 –October 2004,* Melbourne: Department of Justice.

Harris, M. (2006b), 'The Koori Court and the Promise of Therapeutic Jurisprudence', *eLawJournal (Murdoch University electronic journal of law)*(special series), no.129, https://elaw.murdoch.edu.au/archives/issues/soecial/The_Koori_Court.doc.

Hollin, C. (2002), 'An Overview of Offender Rehabilitation: Something Old, Something Borrowed, Something New', *Australian Psychologist*, Vol.37, No.3, 159–164.

Implementation Review Team (2004), *Victorian Implementation Review of the Recommendations from the Royal Commission into Aboriginal Deaths in Custody: Discussion Paper*, Melbourne: Department of Justice.

Jackomos, A. (2005), *Victorian Government Response to the Implementation Review of the Recommendations from the Royal Commission into Aboriginal Deaths in Custody*, Melbourne: Indigenous Issues Unit, Department of Justice.

Kraszlan, K. (2009), 'To Study the Development, Provision and Evaluation of Re-entry Services for Prisoners — USA, Israel', Report to the Winston Churchill Memorial Trust of Australia, Canberra: Winston Churchill Memorial Trust.

Marshall, T. (1996), 'The Evolution of Restorative Justice in Britain', *European Journal of Criminal Policy and Research,* Vol.4, No.4, 21–43.

Marshall, T. (1999), *Restorative Justice: An Overview.* London: Home Office Research Development and Statistics Directorate.

Martinson, R. (1974), 'What Works? Questions and Answers about Prison Reform', *The Public Interest,* Vol.35, 22–54.

Morris, A. (2002), 'Critiquing the Critics: A Brief Response to Critics of Restorative Justice', *British Journal of Criminology,* Vol.42, 596–615.

Morrison, B. (2002), 'Bullying and Victimisation in Schools: A Restorative Justice Approach', *Trends & Issues in Crime and Criminal Justice,* No.219, Canberra: Australian Institute of Criminology.

Morrison, B. (2006), 'School Bullying and Restorative Justice: Towards a Theoretical Understanding of the Role of Respect, Pride and Shame', *Journal of Social Issues,* Vol.62, No.2, 371–392.

New South Wales Aboriginal Justice Advisory Council (2003), *NSW Aboriginal Justice Plan: Beyond Justice 2004–2014*, Sydney: NSW Aboriginal Justice Advisory Council.

Richards, K. (2009), *Juveniles' Contact with the Criminal Justice System in Australia,* Monitoring Report No.7, Canberra: Australian Institute of Criminology.

Richards, K. (2010), 'Police-referred Restorative Justice for Juveniles in Australia', *Trends & Issues in Crime and Criminal Justice,* No.398, Canberra: Australian Institute of Criminology.

Royal Commission into Aboriginal Deaths in Custody (1991), *Royal Commission into Aboriginal Deaths in Custody Final Report*, Canberra: Australian Government Publishing Service.

Shearing, C. (2001), 'Punishment and the Changing Face of the Governance', *Punishment & Society,* Vol.3, No.2, 203–20.

Snowball, L. (2008), 'Diversion of Indigenous Juvenile Offenders', *Trends & Issues in Crime and Criminal Justice,* no.355, Canberra: Australian Institute of Criminology.

Spivakovsky, C. (2009), 'The Construction of the Racially Different Indigenous Offender', Australian and New Zealand Critical Criminology Conference 2009: Conference Proceedings (online), www.arts.monash.edu.au/criminology/c3-conference-proceedings/index.php.

Strang, H. (2001), *Restorative Justice Programmes in Australia: A Report to the Criminological Research Council,* Canberra: Criminology Research Council.

Tauri, J. (1998), 'Family Group Conferencing: A Case-study of the Indigenisation of New Zealand's Justice System', *Current Issues in Criminal Justice*, Vol.10, No.2, 168–182.

Visher, C., LaVigne, N. and Travis, J. (2004), 'Returning Home: Understanding the Challenges of Prisoner Re-entry: Maryland Pilot Study: Findings From Baltimore', *Research Report for the Urban Institute*, Washington, D.C.: Justice Policy Centre.

Ward, J. (2001), *Transition From Custody to Community*, Melbourne: Office of the Correctional Services Commissioner, Victoria Department of Justice.

Weitekamp, E. (1999), 'The History of Restorative Justice' in Bazemore, G. and Walgrave, L. (eds.), *Restorative Juvenile Justice: Repairing the Harm of Youth Crime*, Monsey: Criminal Justice Press.

Wexler, D. and Winick, B. (eds.) (1991), *Essays in Therapeutic Jurisprudence*, Durham: Carolina Academic Press.

Willis, M. (2004), *Ex-prisoners, SAAP, Housing and Homelessness in Australia: Final Report to the National SAAP Coordination and Development Committee*, Canberra: Australian Institute of Criminology.

16

Development of Restorative Justice Practices in Norway

Per Andersen

Introduction

Norway and the rest of Scandinavia have some interesting common trends in criminal justice policy or practice, at least compared to England, several other European countries, New Zealand and not least the USA. We have relatively fewer prisoners per 100,000 inhabitants as is the case also for other Nordic countries: Norway has 73, Sweden 79, Denmark 74, Iceland 64 and Finland 60 per 100,000 (2010: figures from the International Centre for Prison Studies, *World Prison Brief*).

What Nordic countries have in common are extensive welfare strategies and societies with a relatively equal distribution of wealth. If this is the reason why we don't have overcrowded prisons, the best way to 'civilise criminal justice' is to create the fairest possible society (Wilkinson and Pickett, 2009). It seems also that Scandinavian societies are in reasonably good balance: the institutionalised public system is generally conceived as legitimate and there are no really serious conflicts going on. It is more a question how we distribute wealth, rather than intense class or ethnic struggles. Alternatively or as a supplement to this we can find an explanation in the way Nordic countries have responded to crime. This chapter will for the most part focus on different possible responses to crime.

Nils Christie and others have stated that prison should be the last resort and should be used as little as possible (Christie, 2004). I will not argue for or against this statement, but rather take it as a normative precondition in what follows. If so, it is necessary to develop alternatives to punishment as pain delivery. I will call them interventions, because for several reasons we have to put new meaning into the concept of punishment.

Christie himself is still an active supporter, and at the same time a 'friendly critic' of restorative practices in Norway. He is concerned about how Western societies are developing; the school system creates dropouts who later become losers in the labour market and adult life. Differences in economic and cultural capital are rising. Local communities are disintegrating; citizens become alienated and are strangers towards each other. Society becomes individualised. Our reliance on the criminal justice system gets more and more important with these structural changes accelerating. The curve of the prison population has been rising. Christie's argument is quite simple: If we do not take this into account we can work night and day with RJ practices without moving from where we started. Christie points out that the criminal justice system is some sort of mirror of society. In the worst case, restorative justice practitioners risk being the soft front of a predominantly punitive system. Good restorative interventions can absolutely be carried out in a punitively oriented society, as can be seen in the USA. Those interventions do not change systems, but can help easing some of its worst negative effects.

The good thing about restorative practices in Norway according to Christie has to do with the involvement of local communities and the use of non-professional, lay mediators. The civilising of criminal justice has to take the local community into account and encourage local democratic discussion and participation. To involve communities in this work is essential. By such a strategy we can achieve less dependency on the formal criminal justice system and the use of punishment. This is a difficult and seemingly impossible task, in a society on its way to centralisation and an individualised way of living.

Norwegian criminal justice policies are at the moment a project with a dual personality. We have on the one hand a new criminal law extending punishment with longer sentences and new areas of regulating social behaviour. On the other hand we have strong emphasis on different restorative practices and probation. The present Government (in 2012, left-centre) has also a strong emphasis on rehabilitation within the prison system.

Parallel developments can be observed within the criminal justice system and in public opinion. For those who argue for a shift in criminal policy away from the pain-delivering system, this can seem like a paradox and a problem. As a practitioner, or organizer, I prefer to see opportunities. Restorative justice strategies should work as a counterforce and aim at reducing the need and legitimacy for retributive responses to acts of wrongdoing. Restorative justice in Norway at the moment has great opportunities.

Restorative Justice Practices as a Realistic Option

The overall question is to bring restorative justice practices (RJP) to a position where such practices can be perceived as a more effective, realistic and legitimate alternative (by the public, the press and the political system). It is not enough to pinpoint the negative effects, or the lack of positive results within the retributive system. It is not enough to argue about the normative and ethical problems within the prevailing criminal justice system. The traditional retributive system is a strong one, and it is powerful. It is not easily changeable. The system legitimates itself with what is necessary at any moment. What is ethically good is often secondary to necessity and it is always easy to find ideological reasons to make different punitive practices seem appropriate.

RJP has to prove itself as a realistic and legitimate alternative. The best way this can be done is by institutionalising RJP. We also need secure regular funding for the practice. The alternative can be a lot of good local initiatives and projects, helpful for some communities, helpful for some victims and offenders but it will never be a realistic alternative to the criminal justice system. In some European countries there is competition and even hostility between different restorative practice initiatives on the grounds of professional or theoretical disagreements. Such a situation will be the certain death of restorative justice as a realistic alternative. Different practitioners or services will keep their professional and theoretical purity, but will be hopelessly impotent. What are needed are compromises and common strategies. We do not have to make things difficult.

The criminal justice system has some important characteristics, especially the Rule of Law and a state-wide institutionalised system to manage it. RJP needs to learn how to come to a position where we can challenge existing punitive systems or at least parts of it.

RJPs need a constant and ongoing reflection and discussion to remain as an alternative to punitive systems. At the same time RJPs need to think about organizational structure, create national cooperation between services, build common strategies; learn how to influence administrative and political decision-makers, how to influence public opinion through the media, get researchers' attention and so on. To be an alternative we need to be consistent with the ethics of RJ and at the same time we have to be organizers and actors in systems where decisions are taken.

RJPs are Connected to the Criminal Justice System (in Norway)

The background for establishing a system of mediation between offender and victim in Norway dates back to two central events in the late 1970s. The debate in Norway started with the article 'Conflicts as Property', written in 1976 by Nils Christie (1977). The other event was the government's *Report on Criminal Justice* of 1978, by the then Minister of Justice, Inger Louise Valle. Conflicts represent a potential for activity, learning and participation. In his article, Christie argues for establishing an alternative to the penal system and to professionals who deal with conflicts, such as lawyers, psychologists etc. Crimes represent conflicts between victim and offender and they should be enabled to handle them personally.

Another argument for creating an alternative to the established systems dealing with crime is to find a system that is more orientated towards the victim, and the victim's needs and wishes. The article 'Conflicts as Property' implies a wish to revitalise and strengthen the local communities in modern society through an alternative way of dealing with conflict resolution.

The Norwegian Mediation Service was created in 1991 by the Municipal Mediation Service Act. Its underlying philosophy rests on two main viewpoints:

(1) One was based on the aim to extend and revitalise the civil sphere by solving criminal matters through mediation on a local level with active participation from the parties and the local community, as suggested by Christie.

(2) The other viewpoint is originally based on the wish to avoid serious penalties for juveniles such as imprisonment, and aims at crime prevention (governmental policy).

So, already from the beginning we have had two principles for developing mediation in Norway. The two principles are not necessarily in harmony with each other — or are they?

It may be helpful to outline some principles of how Norwegian society works (and possibly the rest of Scandinavia). Social work and welfare systems are executed through public institutions (municipalities, county and state). NGOs play a very modest role in the provision of services. Especially the CJS is considered as a state-owned, public task. There is for example no local municipal police force in Norway.

Mediation in Norway would then naturally be placed in some kind of public setting (not an NGO), especially because it is perceived as a part of the criminal justice system. This was implied in the mediation law of 1991.

The first principle for RJP in Norway was outlined from Nils Christie's article: what we can call a community model, where the local community (municipality) was considered as the most important brick in building society. The second principle was outlined from the authorities — not as part of a wish for restorative practices but as part of a new, more humane and presumably more effective way of responding to crime and then consequently also part of a crime reduction strategy. Even if the authorities back in the 1990s had no research confirming the effects of RJP on crime reduction and recidivism, this was taken more or less for granted. Or, they believed the introduction of RJP (known as mediation at that time) could not be worse than the existing system. Changes in the direction of less formal procedures were anyway considered positive.

The mix between Christie's thinking and the governmental policy did result in another structure connected only indirectly to the CJS. The mediation services were given the responsibility for handling civil cases. Typical civil cases could be: conflicts in family matters, different types of youth social interaction, neighbour conflicts — or any other conflicts relevant to citizens and the local community. In practice many of the civil cases handled by mediators are found in the area between criminal and civil law. Restorative practices can also be used in cases of what citizens conceive as socially unacceptable behaviour which is still not regulated by criminal law (or which should be according to general norms or public opinion), or it could be an escalating civil conflict with some potential later to become a challenge for the police and criminal law. The wish to include civil cases is in direct line with Nils Christie's thinking about crime as conflicts. The better we handle conflicts—informally and at the lowest possible level—the better for society and communities. It makes communities less dependent on the formalised CJS (if we suppose communities are harmonious).

Organizing RJP in Norway

Following the second principle would typically place the Mediation Service within or as a part of the criminal justice system and not at community level. In 1991 mediation services were, however, placed at community level according to Christie's principle of local orientation. The services were placed within the administration of the municipalities. The Ministry of Justice[1] kept the professional and economic responsibility. From 1991 up to 2004 there were between 38 and 42 Municipal Mediation Services interconnected professionally through the Ministry of Justice and through an NGO umbrella organization called Forum for Mediation Services. This NGO worked with typical professional questions concerning policy, common training of mediators, mediation techniques and methods, coordination of meetings and so on. The municipal model did not work for several reasons. The municipalities did not take responsibility for the services; overall they considered RJP (even if they also had civil cases) and crime prevention as part of the state's responsibilities, while the municipalities—as a part of a national plan for specialising within the public sector—had responsibilities for the production of welfare-oriented services to its citizens. RJP was not considered as a part of this. The municipalities welcomed the state ownership in 2004. Maybe this also can be explained by the way the law of 1991 was drafted and its strong emphasis on the connection between mediation and the CJS (which is a state task in Norway). The fact that the ministry kept the professional

---

1.   Changed to the Ministry of Justice and Public Security after the terror attack of 22 July 2011.

responsibility for the services meant that it was not realistic for the municipalities to be responsible.

During their first ten years, municipal mediation services were perceived
as part of the CJS rather than of local communities. The fact that almost
90 per cent of all cases were referred from the police and the prosecutor's
office underlined the connection to the CJS. In many ways the attempt to
create a mediation service as an integrated part of local communities failed.
There was never a call from local communities for mediation. It was rather
conceived as a state initiative. This was obvious also for those who worked
in the services up till 2004.

Nils Christie's thoughts about local communities as an important brick in
building society are in general not realised in Norway. On the contrary, we
are going in the opposite direction with strong emphasis on centralisation,
larger companies, larger police districts, larger municipalities, specialisation
and so on. More welfare for less money, and the most efficient and cost-
effective ways of delivering welfare are considered the best. Welfare systems
have to a large extent replaced tasks or functions previously performed by
local communities. Communities can take action and can be revitalised in
some degree (for examples in RJ conferences, during crises and so on), but
in everyday life Norwegian communities are in general sleeping entities.
Citizens can no longer be relied on for functions which in theory local communities can or could offer.

A State Service

For these reasons RJP (including its civil side) was reorganized as a state service within the Ministry of Justice in 2004. The structure of the service is
organized in the same way as the police (and other state institutions) with
a central administration (directorate) and 22 regional mediation services,
funded by the state. Since then the connection to the CJS has been even
more obvious.

Every type of organization has its upsides and downsides. The positive
side is the ability to adapt to different forms of challenges in society: for
example, we were able to implement conferencing nationwide within one
or two years. This is conceived as a predominantly positive change for RJP
in Norway. The new state organization has the ability to develop strategies

and to implement them within a relatively short period of time. It is in short more efficient and hierarchical — which can also be described as a downside.

RJP and CJS

Implementations of RJP have to take into account the cultural, social and political context within which they operate. The Norwegian system for RJ can at this moment not be called a community-based system; or if it perhaps could be, it is one which plays only a modest role in society. What we still have is some sort of hybrid system. First we have a national state institution (Mediation Service, 85 staff members), geographically available for every citizen in the country, governed by the law of mediation. The General Director of Public Prosecution (GDPP) issues circulars on what kind of criminal cases we can handle (up to now this corresponds to the term 'diversion' as used in Anglo-Saxon jurisdictions). The decision to divert a case to mediation is made by the local prosecutor. If mediation fails, the case will be returned to the prosecutor and the case can be re-opened and treated as an ordinary criminal case.

On the other hand we emphasise the lay aspect of RJP. This is a heritage from Nils Christie's thinking. Between 600 and 700 lay mediators mediate (or facilitate conferences for) nearly all our cases. They are not experts in any form and are not formally qualified as mediators; they are equipped only with a short training. They are given support and coaching and participate in local mediator gatherings during their public duty as mediators. They learn to be a mediator through practice. They live in the same communities where the conflict or case has its starting point. The lay system is also flexible in a long and sparsely populated country, where travel costs are high and travelling time is quite extensive. It is also relatively easy to manage local ups and downs in the caseload.

Within the framework of what we can call the modern Norwegian society this system works and it also got an overall positive evaluation in December 2009 from the Nordland Research Institute.

To summarise; RJP is based on a governmental policy and is part of the CJS. This is a policy for promoting a more humane, cost-effective and presumably more effective way of responding to crime. Reducing harm and restoring relationships in society are in our setting considered as a positive side effect, even if the mediation service and its mediators see this as their main task.

RJP in our setting has to take into account the question of cost and effects. We have to take into consideration arguments and questions concerning recidivism and the effect of RJP on crime rates. Does RJP work better than other existing systems? If not, why should society put money in to it?

Maybe the question should be asked in a different way. How can RJP interact with other systems and perspectives to reduce the harmful effects of the punitive system or replace parts of it with more humane and workable methods? One traditional weakness in all public systems (and NGOs) is interaction and coordination.

Future Perspectives

RJP in Norway will in the future be a more complex service where we follow different strategies and methods within the same system. Restorative justice in Norway can develop in four main areas and constitute an alternative to punishment both in regard to less serious and serious crime and in addition a more important supplement in more serious crime:

(1) continued diversion of less serious crime;

(2) youth crime including serious crimes;

(3) domestic violence;

(4) civil cases.

Characteristics of the Criminal Justice System

Restorative justice in Norway has been — and is — a voluntary alternative to traditional punishment. This goes for less serious crimes, more serious crimes are only included if RJPs are used as a supplement. How can restorative justice play an even more important role in the CJS, not only in less serious crime but as a realistic alternative in more serious crime and thereby reducing the role of the pain-inflicting system?

One obvious reason why this is difficult follows from the dominant paradigm in the Norwegian legal system. Offending is understood to be a product of rational choice. The aim of intervention is to deter and to punish. Citizens will weigh up risks of possible punishment against the potential rewards of crime and then presumably choose desistance from crime. This is followed by the principle of proportionality between the deed and the punishment. What's being done is punishment and pain-infliction. The negative effects on the individuals, both victim and offender, have second priority.

The legal system (courts, prosecution authority and so on) will not accept RJP as a sufficient public deterrent, even if there is little evidence about the deterrent effect in general or in particular cases. So the leading dogma rests on the presumption that punishment (pain-infliction) works as a general deterrent, and that RJP does not. In Norway public deterrence is the most important argument for punishment by imprisonment. The argument of public security is not strong as most sentences are short.

The question of proportionality is even more difficult to meet. How can a RJ intervention give some hope of proportionality? I cannot go into this discussion here, only confirm the challenge. At the moment and in the near future it will be difficult to change the dominant public perceptions of deterrence and proportionality. The principle of proportionality between the deed and the punishment also has a positive side as it is relatively transparent and predictable.

1. Diversion

Looking into the future, RJPs have a potential to be a preferred way of handling conflicts or less serious crime. We believe we have the opportunity to expand the number of cases. In recent years the police and prosecutors have dealt with even more complex and serious cases within the framework of RJPs. Locally, prosecutors are challenging the limits set in the GDPP's circular, especially for young people and also in cases of domestic violence and families with children.

Case development 1999–2010

	1999	2008	2010
Shoplifting	28%	19%	14%
Vandalism	23%	18%	13%
Violence	9%	19%	21%
Threats/bullying	5%	11%	14%
Neighbour and other civil conflicts	9%	15%	17%

The total number of incoming cases is about 9,000 a year (in a population of around five million). About 7,000 cases are mediated including about 300 conferences. In total around 15,000–20,000 will meet in a restorative justice setting during one year.

Our numbers shows a shift from the most simple (shoplifting) to more complex and serious cases, i.e. cases with a personal victim, like violence and threats. Among the cases with violence involved there is a rising number of domestic violence and family conflicts. This is for the time being the fastest growing reported crime. These cases are referred both as an alternative and as a supplement to traditional punitive actions.

The number of people who meet in a RJP setting during one year is equivalent to the population of a small to medium-sized Norwegian city. We have also a growing number of civil cases. Still we have ups and downs in the caseload from one year to another and variation locally and there is still too much difference in practice between different police districts and different prosecutors. As pointed out before, the systems within (or between) which we operate is slow to change. There is not only a need to change laws, rules and circulars, but to change a predominantly punitive culture organized in a hierarchy of organizations: all this needs to take place within democratic discussions locally or nationally.

Fines are the most frequently used punishment for all age groups and especially for youths. There is reason to believe that they are used extensively because they provide an easy way out for prosecutors. To produce fines is a good way of keeping the throughput of cases high and time used low. This praxis is now finally being debated and there is a growing consciousness about the lack of rationality in the use of fines. At the same time there is a strong call for the use of RJP. It is too early to conclude in either direction, but it is obvious that there is a need to change the praxis of using fines.

2. Youth crime

The best way for RJP to challenge, go around or adapt to this basic understanding is to start with youth crime. Young people are considered as not yet fully developed, with all the implications for both the argument of public deterrence and proportionality. Punishment of young offenders conflicts with the need to help them to change, with the requirement to take account of their immaturity, and with the duty to promote their welfare.

This gives us a golden opportunity to mix different understandings of justice into new interventions, which could be less punitive and could work better. David Smith's book *A New Response to Youth Crime* points out the underlying tension between punishment and welfare and the contradictions between different objectives or rationalities within systems working to reduce crime (Smith, 2010: 1). This is interesting and corresponds to our experiences in Norway; the CJS works with its focus on the deed and the welfarist perspective with its focus on the individual affected. Different or incompatible objectives are unlikely to bring good results. A new youth intervention initiative in Norway, outlined below, has the ambition of bringing different perspectives together in what we can describe as reconciliation between objectives and perspectives—with the participation and contribution of RJP. It can be a painful process because compromises between different institutional and professional views have to be made.

Crime and the response to crime in Norway

Norway is a welfare state with relatively good distribution of society's surplus. Yet some citizens do not get their hands into the honeypot. When you meet Norwegian prisoners in lasting and deep conflicts with society they are not the average man in the street. From different surveys and research we have hard facts supporting the conclusion that the great majority of these prisoners belong to marginalised and poor groups. Every analysis of the criminal justice system has to take into account power imbalances, and questions of class, poverty and marginalisation.

On the other hand, Norwegian youth has never — in modern history — been so law-abiding as it is now. Most young people who are suspected of or charged with a crime never return to the criminal justice system. Most sentences for *all* age groups are short. There has been a stabilisation or even regression in the general crime statistics since the beginning of this century. Yet a small group of youths, not more than 2 to 4 per cent, have a life situation making such interventions (RJ-interventions) not sufficient as a single measure. Crime is often only one of many challenges these youths are dealing with, as they quite often have a drug problem, challenges at school, at home and so on. We have quite good knowledge about this group of youths and we also know a great deal of the shortcomings of today's efforts.

New youth intervention

Do we need to reject the presumption that punishment must be the infliction of pain? If so we need to develop interventions or responses to crime within the target group without the pain element. This is the central feature of new legislation. The law regulating the new youth intervention was sent to the Parliament in June 2011. The new youth intervention is built on experiences from a three-year long pilot project conducted in four cities in Norway. The project was initiated by the former government, prolonged and supported by the new left-centre government. The project was undergoing a process of evaluation ending-up in a final report in February 2009, by Øyvind Kvello and Christian Wendelborg of the Norwegian University of Science and Technology (NTNU) (Wendelborg and Kvello, 2009). The report's conclusions were quite clear: 'This project manages to get the attention of a high-risk group which normally falls outside all available welfare systems (and tend to end up in the criminal justice system)'. The project shows a clear drop in the rate of recidivism, few breaches in the action plan and there are indications of better psychological health. One other object of the project was to improve the cooperation and coordination between public services at local municipal level. The research's conclusions were also positive here. This was seen as a key to good results. One other important finding was the positive feedback from the youths who participated in the individual composed programmes.

Today's meaning of punishment is infliction of pain. The Norwegian system rests on this definition and the system works to inflict pain. At the same time welfarist perspectives have regained a relatively strong position after a certain setback in the 1970s and 1980s. So the two dominant perspectives for responding to crime are punishment and welfare (health included). As mentioned above these two perspectives, with their respective institutional systems, do not necessarily work in harmony. Since we know that young offenders in the target group need help not punishment, a new perspective opens up, namely RJPs. Society will not accept sending a young offender into an easy welfare programme (according to public opinion) without some kind of reaction. Some intervention is then needed and the intervention for children can be diversion (or referral by a court decision) into a youth conference followed up with a support-oriented action plan. The intervention is supposed to voluntary. The youth has to make a choice between traditional types of punishment (which could be prison or a long community sentence) or a youth conference followed by an action plan. To consent to this option means commitment to both a restorative intervention and the action plan lasting up to two years.

The new proposal is made possible through a newly released governmental report describing the initiative as 'Youth conferencing and young people plan'.[2] The intervention has a specific target group; young people from 15 and up to 18 years (with the ambition to include older youths later) who have committed serious crimes, with the exception of murder and rape.

We are now developing this intervention based on some basic principles. These are:

- focus on the child's best interest;

---

2. See www.stortinget.no/no/Saker-og-publikasjoner/Saker/Sak/?p=50940. This link is to Parliament; the proposition is called prp. 135L and has been confirmed by Parliament (Stortinget).

- strong participation by the young person and his or her family (if the young person has one) and a possibility to have a significant say in the content of the action plan;
- a restorative intervention (mediation, conferencing, family group conferencing) with the involvement of victims if they wish to participate;
- an intervention which can motivate change;
- an intervention which can reduce risk factors associated with recidivism (this can include support in school, work, housing, etc);
- an intervention which can strengthen the young people's own resources (empowerment, support, positive experiences);
- an intervention that can strengthen the network around each individual child or young person, both private and public;
- carried out in local communities;
- coordination between systems and institutions.

All elements should build on the ethics of RJPs even if RJPs are only a part of it. By this I mean an intervention that is in content demanding for the youth, but at the same time supporting and integrating—but not punitive. The intervention rejects the idea of crime as something that can be resolved within the CJS alone. It cannot, and it is essential to engage municipalities, local network as family and friends—and if possible—local sports clubs or other NGOs in the action plan.

Every good alternative to today's punitive system must be carried out in local communities where people live. Social control and support has to replace different punitive control mechanisms. However, local communities still do not exist as operative entities and they are sleeping (speaking of Norway). Talking about local communities we have to take into account municipalities and different locally based state and county services, and NGOs if available. It is however an important aim to support and empower a youth's family and—if existent—their network.

Bringing local welfare systems and different objectives together with the use of restorative justice practices and ethics

To bring young people out of the penal system we need to rethink the way the public sector (or NGOs) work. The key words are *co-ordination* and *cooperation*. What is a problem, at least in Norway, are the principles of organizing welfare. The welfare sector is divided between different ministries, public sector services are divided into different levels; state, counties and municipalities. There is no unified coordinated system working well together. A young offender meets a welfare system that is quite impossible to understand, even for adults, as researchers have pointed out; the target group of young offenders has a tendency to fall between all systems.

RJP, or as we define it more specifically here a conference, is a process that involves the victim or other persons affected by the crime, together with the most important professionals, the offender, family and guardians. One important element in such a conference is to establish a common and accepted narrative of the crime or crimes and its consequences. As pointed out; different institutions and professionals work with different types of goals and rationalities. This makes it difficult to agree on what a young offender actually needs in his or her action plan. Another challenge is the toolbox of the professionals; they have a tendency to impose a ready-made answer to a certain challenge without asking or involving the young offender. For these reasons the conference as a starting point of an action plan can build bridges between institutions and professionals. The common history shared in the conference and the involvement of the victim and the offender can be a good starting point for a more 'user-friendly' and 'involvement-friendly' action plan. The offender should not — or cannot — be fitted into some specific professional toolbox. One other important element in this intervention is the follow-up of the action plan by a dedicated coordinator, and the way in which meetings with the offender and his or her guardians are conducted in the period using restorative justice ethics and methods. Institutions and professionals have to sign an agreement committing them to follow up their part of the measures in the action plan. All measures in the action plan must be coordinated and conducted in some sort of understandable unity. The professionals will share all relevant information concerning the progress of the action plan after consent from the youth and guardians. The coordinator follows up the professional network (and the youth) and has the power to point at shortcomings in the commitment of the professionals in their responsibilities in the action plan.

Awareness of the dangers and challenges

The Norwegian criminologist Kjersti Ericsson wrote a book entitled *The Stepchildren of Society* (2009). The book is about how treatment historically has been used in a repressive way. The so-called treatment was actually worse than the punitive alternative. Through the history of the last century there is not one good example of success. An important lesson is to build in legal safeguards, e.g. predictability, legal aid and transparency in the interventions. The action plan should be adapted to specific individual need. It should not be more intense than needed for the youth involved. It is important to find a balance between the youth's needs and the ability to absorb or master the different measures. A lot of good helpers, with the best intentions for the youth, can often think that a lot of different measures at the same time are the best. To find this balance here is one of the most difficult parts of this work. Another problem is to convert a traditional time-oriented punishment into an action plan suited for individual needs! Even if we already have some experiences from the project period, this work is developing through practice and reflection. There is no easy way to good results.

3. Domestic violence

Domestic violence is the fastest growing recorded crime. There is reason to believe that this growth is due to raised awareness in society which is now less willing to accept domestic violence. This makes it easier for victims to come forward with their complaints. No more than five years ago, mediation (or other forms of RJP) in this complex of cases was quite politically incorrect.

From time-to-time we have discussions about the concept of mediation and its meaning. A lot of scepticism has been raised and it is claimed that mediation always has to include some kind of pragmatic solution from both sides; that mediation will give the strong party (read 'the man') the best outcome; and that mediation fails when it attempts to balance power in an uneven power relationship. To minimise the suspicion or critique of others we use the term 'meetings for dialogue', not mediation. This shift in terminology is not only because we fear being criticised, but it is actually a historical shift in the mediation service's understanding of its main task — from victim-offender mediation where we had a strong focus on the offender's needs — to a restorative approach, always keeping in mind the needs and best interests of the victim. Family group conferencing has also been used more and more as it seems to be a more powerful method in this type of cases. The privacy of the conflict is not necessarily good, and may not be good at all. At the same time there is a lot of shame involved in family conflicts and domestic violence. For this reason it is not an easy task to get the parties to accept other participants, such as friends or family, as participants in what is perceived as a 'private' conflict.

Three years ago the government launched an action plan against domestic violence. The action plan included three measures or projects with RJP as a central element. All three are now in the final year and the project that started up first has very recently been evaluated by NTNU and the findings are interesting. The target group was victims, offenders and others affected; this might include children, siblings, others from the family, neighbours, friends and public servants (MP, childcare and police). The project has a strong focus on children who experience, and are witnesses to, violence at home. As in youth intervention we try to involve other public services to a greater extent than before. This is due to the complexity and seriousness of these cases.

The project has an overall positive effect on victims and offenders and their life situation. The report points out that violence has been considerably reduced. Victims had greater positive outcomes than offenders. This was due, not to changes or remorse shown by the offender, but to awareness and focus from public institutions and other important stakeholders. The importance of being seen, heard and believed and taken seriously was the single most important positive finding in the research. The project has also contributed to awareness of and a focus on the problem of domestic violence. In the summary the researchers conclude positively and recommend the project as a permanent national measure. The report does not criticise the system of volunteer mediators, but points out the need for some specialised training in these kinds of cases.

4. Civil cases

The inclusion of civil cases in the service offered is regarded as a part of the service's identity. Civil cases are also considered as an interesting challenge for mediators. This gives parties an opportunity to solve conflicts in a cheap and informal manner. We will continue to develop our ability to offer mediation or conferencing in different types of cases, but as it seems likely that family cases, neighbour and community conflicts are in the core area. Civil conflicts can lead to a crime. Handling civil cases at an early stage is also considered as a supplement to other forms of crime prevention.

RJ Limitations or Dilemmas

One important discussion going on right now is the question of continued criminalisation of drug-related crime, or crime committed by drug addicts. Criminalisation of the use of drugs has some severe negative effects which are obvious even for those supporting the existing policy. At the same time there is no political will to change direction and to decriminalise the use of drugs (or some lighter drugs such as marihuana) or to give heavy users legal doses of heroin. Even those supporting the existing regime see drug addiction primarily as a health problem, not as a crime problem.

A governmental report[3] is in preparation and there is reason to believe the Government are looking for a way out of today's response system. What can be done without legalising? One probable answer is to use the same model as we are going to use in youth crime intervention as described in point 2 above. It looks now as it will be some kind of combination between RJP and an action plan.

This report will raise a number of critical issues for restorative justice. One of these is the question of the personal victim. RJ practices, at least in Norway, can only be used in cases where there is a personal victim (or for example a representative of a public institution or company). What then in cases where there are no personal victims, cases where the offended party is the state, as it is for example in drug cases? The new youth intervention opens the possibility to conduct a conference without a personal victim. Can RJ also be used as an alternative in drug cases?

Is restorative justice a universal good, available for all citizens, or is it only available for those whose victim happens to be willing to participate

---

3. The report, delayed because of the terror attack of 22 July 2011, has now been to a hearing (see www.regjeringen.no/nb/dep/jd/dok/hoeringer/hoeringsdok/2012/horing—-alternative-reaksjoner-for-mind.html?id=668950). It is expected that a draft law will be proposed to Parliament.

in a restorative justice setting, or for victims whose offender is willing, or for offenders who have committed a crime with a victim involved? Who are victims? Can we use the term 'affected by crime' and then see parents, family or other community members as part of a restorative process, even if we do not have a personalised victim? Who is the victim if people sit down in the street as a protest against the Government? What about people who are injured by the police in a demonstration?

We think it is possible to develop restorative methods for these cases. A future perspective is to have different restorative justice practices available and use different methods in different types of cases. Sometimes it is easy to choose the right kind of method but in most cases this can be decided after pre-meetings with the parties involved. We still believe that mediation (or dialogue meetings) has an important place here, supplemented with conferencing and circles with or without a victim but anyway with the participation of the affected parties (family, friends, community).

As pointed out before, to change the CJS is a slow process. We do not expect a revolution and from time-to-time we can even experience setbacks. Patience is needed. Our aim is to bring out to the public, to prosecutors and to politicians the good results and the need for RJP in Norwegian society. By doing this we will progress in the aim of civilising the CJS.

References

Christie, N. (1977), 'Conflicts as Property', *British Journal of Criminology*, 17(1), 1–15.

Christie, N. (2004), *A Suitable Amount of Crime*, London: Routledge.

Ericsson, K. (2009), *Samfunnets stebarn* (Society's stepchildren), Oslo: Universitetsforlaget.

Nordland Research Institute (2009), NF-Report nr. 14/2009, ISBN nr.978–82–7321–588–8.

Smith, D. J. (2010), *A New Response to Youth Crime*, Devon, Cullompton: Willan Publishing.

Valle, L. (1978), *Report on Criminal Justice*, Oslo: Ministry of Justice.

Wendelborg, C. and Kvello, Ø. (2009), *Prosessevaluering av det treårige prosjektet: 'Oppfølgingsteam for unge lovbrytere' i Kristiansand, Oslo, Stavanger og*

Trondheim, http://samforsk.no/Sider/Publikasjoner/Prosessevaluering-Oppf%C3%B8lgingsteam-for-unge-lovbrytere.aspx.

Wilkinson, R. and Pickett, K. (2009), *The Spirit Level: Why More Equal Societies Almost Always Do Better,* London: Allen Lane.

Civilising Criminal Justice

17

Downsizing the Use of Imprisonment in Finland

Tapio Lappi-Seppälä

Introduction

Finland is a small Nordic country with a population of 5.3 million. The Finnish juridical system is manifestly rooted in western, continental legal culture with strong influence from neighbouring Nordic countries. Today Finland profiles itself—together with the other Nordic countries, Denmark, Iceland, Norway and Sweden—as a country with an internationally high level of social security and equality, higher levels of social trust and political legitimacy, and lower levels of penal repression.[1] However, this has not always been the case. During the last century, Finland experienced three wars (the 1918 Civil War and the two wars against the Soviet Union between 1939 and 1944). These crises have left their marks on Finnish society and its criminal justice policy. The trends in prison rates have been more turbulent than in almost any other Western European country.

The harsh history of Finland can be read from her prison statistics. *Figure 1* displays the trends in prison rates (relative to 100,000 population) throughout the last century. The role of political and social and economic crises is highlighted by dividing prisoners into three categories: (1) prisoners serving their sentences for ordinary crimes, (2) prisoners placed in prisons for political crimes (treason-like activities) or those sentenced by the martial

---

1. The central social and political characteristics of the Nordic countries and their influence on national penal policies are discussed in more detail in Lappi-Seppälä and Tonry, 2011 and Lappi-Seppälä, 2007 and 2008.

courts during the war-times, and (3) prisoners placed in prisons for unpaid fines (fine defaulters).

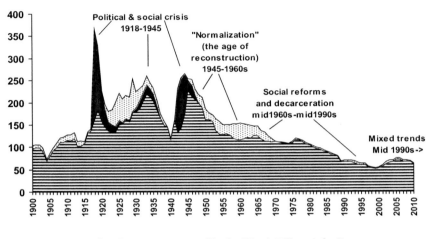

Source: National Statistics.

Figure 1 — Prisoner rates in Finland 1900–2010 (Annual averages).

Three main phases may be detected. The period from the Civil War 1918 until the end of the wars with the Soviet Union is characterised by recurring political, social and economic crises, and hugely varying incarceration rates. From the early 1950s there occurred a period of normalisation (known as the 'age of reconstruction'). Finland was recovering from the damages of war and paying war compensations; thus establishing also the industrial infra-structures which formed the foundations for a forthcoming welfare state.

The dire economic circumstances were reflected also in prison adminis-tration. In general terms, the criminal justice system of Finland in the 1950s and also in the 1960s was less resourceful, less flexible and more repressive than those of its Nordic neighbours. This was all about to change during the third phase of social reform, the 1960s onwards, which also forms the starting point of the following discussion.[2]

The Decline of Imprisonment in Finland

The reform-ideology of the 1960s and 1970s: against coercive care

In the 1960s, the Nordic countries experienced a heated social debate on the results and justifications of involuntary treatment in institutions, both penal and otherwise (such as in healthcare and in the treatment of alcoholics). In Finland the criticism of the treatment ideology was merged with another reform ideology that was directed against the overly severe Criminal Code and the excessive use of custodial sentences. The resulting criminal political ideology was labelled as 'humane neo-classicism'. It stressed both legal safeguards against coercive care and the goal of less repressive measures in general. In sentencing, the principles of proportionality and predictability became the central values. Individualised sentencing, as well as sentencing for general preventive reasons or perceived dangerousness was put in the background (see in more detail Anttila, 1971; Lahti, 2000; Lappi-Seppälä, 2007; and Törnudd, 1996).

Broadening the aims and means of criminal policy

Behind the shift in the strategies in criminal policy were more profound changes in the way the entire problem of crime was conceived. The theoretical criminal political framework and the conceptualisation of the aims and means of criminal policy underwent a change, as the social sciences and planning strategies merged with the criminal political analysis. The aims of criminal policy were defined in step with the overall aims of general social policy. Cost-benefit analysis was introduced into criminal political thinking. The result of all this was that the arsenal of possible means of criminal policy expanded to cover also general social welfare interventions, environmental planning and situational crime prevention. This new ideology was crystallised in slogans such as 'criminal policy is an inseparable part of general social development policy' and 'good social development policy is the best

---

2. For a broader view of penal changes in Finland see: Anttila, 1971, Lahti, 2000 and Lappi-Seppälä, 2008 and 2011b.

criminal policy'. The role of punishment came to be seen as relative. Once regarded as the primary means of criminal policy, it came to be regarded as only one option among many.

The function of criminal justice: indirect general prevention

After the fall of the rehabilitative ideal, the aim and the justification of punishment were also subjected to re-evaluation. The shift was once again towards general prevention. However, this concept came to be understood in a different manner. It was assumed that this effect could be reached not through fear (deterrence), but through the moral-creating and value-shaping effect of punishment. According to this idea, the disapproval expressed in punishment is assumed to influence the values and moral views of individuals. As a result of this process, the norms of criminal law and the values they reflect are internalised; people refrain from illegal behaviour not because such behaviour would be followed by unpleasant punishment, but because the behaviour itself is regarded as morally blameworthy (see Andenaes, 1974 and Lappi-Seppälä, 1995). This, too, had a number of policy implications. Indirect prevention is best served by a system of sanctions which maintain a moral character and demonstrate the blameworthiness of the act, and follow procedures perceived as fair and just by all parties. Instrumental compliance based on fear and sentence severity was reserved, but in a marginal role.

Sentencing: humane neo-classicism

In sentencing this all was condensed into a new sentencing ideology: 'humane neo-classicism'. The classical element in this theory was the revival of the old principle of proportionality. The humane elements were to be found in systematic efforts towards leniency. Minimisation of the suffering caused by the crime control system was among the generally accepted crime policy goals. The role and functions of the principle of proportionality were also seen in this spirit: it had its roots in the Rule of Law and the guarantees against the excessive use of force. The main function of the proportionality principle in Finland was to impose the upper limit which the punishment may not exceed. It is much less restrictive (but still relevant) when considering the possibilities of imposing sentences that are less severe than the offender's act would *prima facie* have deserved (see further: Lappi-Seppälä, 2001).

Legislative reforms and sentencing practices

Systematic legislative reforms started during the mid-1960s, and continued until the mid-1990s. They dealt with both the general sanction system as well as specific offences. The major law reforms affecting the number of prisoners are summarised in *Figure 2,* and commented upon briefly below.

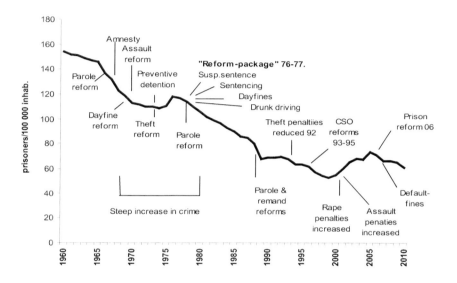

Source: Lappi-Seppälä, 2011b

Figure 2 — Prison rates and policy reforms in Finland 1960–2010

General structure of sanctions 1950–1990

The general structure of the sanctions system remained untouched in the 1950s to 1990s, consisting of fines, conditional sentence and imprisonment. The decrease in prisoner rates in 1950–1980 was technically a result of the general decline in the length of prison sentences and the expansion in the use of fines and conditional sentences. In 1950 the average length of all sentences of imprisonment imposed for theft was 12 months, in 1971 it was seven months and in 1991 three months. Similar changes occurred also in relation to other major crimes, such as robbery, assaults and drunken driving. Between 1950 and 1970 these reductions were court-initiated: from the 1970s onwards the trend was also supported by legislative reforms—see *Figure 3* below.

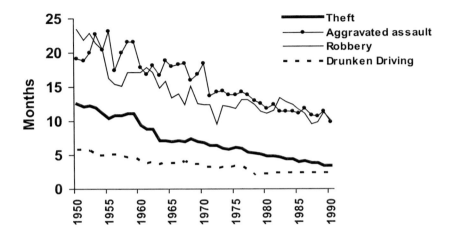

Source: Statistics Finland

Figure 3—Average sentence lengths for four different offences 1950–1990

From the late-1960s onwards all major offences started to increase, but the number of prison sentences remained more or less stable. The increased number of property and violent offences increased and they were punished either by conditional prison sentences or fines. The use of fines was expanded in order to substitute these for short-term imprisonment in 1977, and by raising the monetary value of day-fines (and thus making fines more severe). The scope of conditional imprisonment (suspended sentence) was extended by relaxing the prerequisites for the use of this sanction. The number of annually imposed conditional sentences rose from 4,000 (1960) to 18,000 (in 1990). Sentencing reform in 1976 restricted the role of prior record in sentencing by replacing old mechanical provisions with a regulation which allowed aggravation only when recidivism implies increased act-oriented culpability. This reduced the length of prison sentences especially among repetitive property offenders.

The expansion of petty traffic and property offences increased the use of fines, and this forced the legislators to adopt different forms of summary proceedings. The number of prosecutor's fines expanded from 80,000 in 1950 to over 300,000 in the 1990s. To ease these pressures an even more simplified fixed police fine was introduced in the 1980s. Today both the police and the prosecutor impose about half a million small fines, mainly for traffic and less serious property offences.

The adoption of summary proceedings has kept the annual number of court-imposed penalties at a fairly stable level (50,000–80,000). The absolute number of imposed prison sentences is today on the same level as over 50 years ago, and much lower than some 30 years ago. Increasing numbers of medium-rank offenders have been sentenced either to fines or to other community sanctions, and comparison between court-ordered sanctions other than fines, shows that the relative share of prison has reduced from 70 per cent to 25 per cent in 2008.

Reducing the penalty-scales for specific offences

In 1977 the law on drunken driving was changed in order to replace unconditional prison sentences with conditional sentences and fines. In a short period of time the proportion of prison sentences dropped from 90 per cent to 20 per cent. The introduction of community service in the mid-1990s brought another drop in the use of imprisonment to around 10 per cent.

In addition to drunk drivers, Finnish prisons in the 1950s to 1970s were also crowded with property offenders, especially thieves. Penalties for theft were reduced both in 1972 and 1991. These reforms decreased the share of unconditional imprisonment from 50 per cent to 25 per cent, while the share of fines increased from 20 per cent to 50 per cent. This 'depenalisation' of drunk-driving and property offences was reflected also in prison statistics. In the mid-1970s two out of three prisoners were sentenced either for drunk-driving of theft. Today the relative share of these offences has dropped to about one third. In 1975 there were 1,800 prisoners serving a sentence for theft, today their number is around 450. For drunk driving the corresponding figures are 1,000 and 300.

Specific offender groups

Targeted action was taken to reduce the size of the prison population within three groups of inmates. The use of default imprisonment for unpaid fines was approaching all-time record levels in the 1960s (almost 1,800 fine-defaulters on any given day). In 1969 the use of default imprisonment was restricted and the major source for these fines was removed by decriminalising public drunkenness. The daily number of fine-defaulters fell from over 1,000 to less than 50.

In the course of the 1960s the use of preventive (secure) detention for repeat offenders had also expanded to cover large numbers of property offenders. This lifted the number of prisoners held in prolonged custody to over 400 (5 per cent of the overall prisoner rate). In 1971 the use of preventive detention was restricted to serious violent recidivists only, and the number of people held in preventive detention fell overnight from 250 to less than 10.

Young offenders

During the 1970s the use on imprisonment for *young offenders* started to raise increasing criticism. This was reflected also in court sentencing practices, as the number of prison sentences imposed for juveniles started to decrease. Two law reforms contributed to this change during the 1990s. The Conditional Sentence Act was amended in 1989 by including a provision which allowed the use of unconditional sentences for young offenders only where there were extraordinary reasons calling for this. Also the reduction of minimum penalties for car-thefts (joy-riding) in 1991 had an impact on younger age groups as this offence is typically committed by young offenders (one third of prison sentences in the age group of 15–17 were imposed for this offence). In 1975 the courts imposed over 2,000 prison sentences for young adults (18–20 years) and more than 700 sentences for juveniles (15–17-year-olds). In the 2010 the corresponding figures were 500 and 50 respectively. By 2010 there were some 70 prisoners between the ages of 18 and 20, and only five in the 15 to 17 age group. In the mid-1970s the numbers were five to ten times higher.[3]

---

3. Here one needs to remember that in the age-group 15–17 child welfare bears the basic responsibility for rehabilitative actions including institutional care when necessary. The Finnish juvenile justice system is discussed in more detail in Lappi-Seppälä, 2011a.

Community service

The next major sanction reform was the introduction of community service in the mid-1990s. In order to ensure that community service would really be used in lieu of unconditional sentences of imprisonment (and not instead of other more lenient penalties), a specific two-step procedure was adopted. First, the court was required to make its sentencing decision without considering the possibility of community service. If the result was unconditional imprisonment, then the court was obliged to commute the sentence to one of community service under certain conditions prescribed in the law. The duration of community service varies between 20 and 200 hours. In commuting imprisonment to community service, one day in prison equates to one hour of community service. As a result, the number of prison sentences fell in tandem with the increase in the number of community service orders between 1992 and 1997. Within a short period of time, community service proved to be an important alternative to imprisonment. Today community service replaces around 35 per cent of short-term (maximum eight months) prison sentences.

Parole

The system of parole and early release has also proved to be a very powerful tool in controlling prisoner rates. In Finland practically all prisoners are released on parole on a routine basis. The minimum time to be served before the prisoner is eligible for parole is currently 14 days, and a series of reforms have brought it down to this. During the mid-1960s the minimum period was shortened from six to four months; during the mid-1970s from four to three months; and finally in the late-1980s from three months to 14 days. Also, the criteria for early release were relaxed and the conditions for the revocation of parole were made stricter. All this had a substantial effect on the overall scope of parole and early release. In the early 1960s less than 40 per cent of annually released prisoners were released on parole. In the late 1960s their share has increased into 50 per cent, and during the 1970s to 75 per cent. After the 1989 parole reform practically all prisoners are released on parole (see, in more detail, Lappi-Seppälä, 2011b).

Causes and Consequences: Explaining Penal Liberalisation

The long list of law reforms supports the conclusion that the decrease in the Finnish prison population was a result of a conscious, long-term and systematic criminal justice policy. In order to explain what made it possible to carry out these reforms, we must begin with certain features specific to Finnish society and the composition of Finnish political culture, and proceed from there to more general social, structural and cultural factors.

Political culture

Part of the answer can be found in the structure of our political culture. The Finnish criminologist Patrik Törnudd has stressed the importance of the *political will and consensus* in bringing the prison rate down. As he summarises: 'those experts who were in charge of planning the reforms and research shared an almost unanimous conviction that Finland's comparatively high prison rate was a disgrace and that it would be possible to significantly reduce the amount and length of prison sentences without serious repercussions on the crime situation' (Törnudd, 1993: 12). This conviction was shared by the civil servants, the judiciary, the prison authorities, and, as was equally important, by the politicians.[4]

Another and closely related way of characterising Finnish criminal justice policy would be to describe it as *exceptionally expert-oriented*: reforms have been prepared and conducted by a relatively small group of experts whose thinking on criminal policy, at least in its basic aspects, has followed similar lines. The impact of these professionals was, furthermore, reinforced by *close personal and professional contacts* with senior politicians and with academic research. Consequently, crime control has never been a central political issue in election campaigns in Finland, unlike in many other countries. At least the 'heavyweight' politicians have not relied on populist policies, such as 'three-strikes' or 'truth in sentencing'.

Media

This takes us to another element in the Finnish criminal justice policy composition — *media-market and the role of the media*. In Finland the media have

---

4.   At least to the extent that they did not oppose the reform proposals prepared by the Ministry of Justice.

retained a quite sober and reasonable attitude towards issues of criminal policy. The Finns have largely been saved from low-level populism. There is a striking difference between British and Finnish crime-reports in the media. The tone in the Finnish reports is less emotional, and reports — even when dealing with singular events — are usually accompanied with commented research-based data on the development of the crime situation.

In fact, the whole structure of the Finnish media market looks somewhat unusual. On the one hand, according to the information given by the World Association of Newspapers (World Press Trends, 2004), the most frequent newspaper-readers in Europe are to be found in Finland and Sweden where 90 per cent of the population read a newspaper every day, while on the other hand, in France, Italy and the UK the figures are 44, 41 and 33 per cent). Secondly, the clear market leader can be classified as a quality-paper; tabloids have a far less prominent role in Finland than in many other countries (including the UK). Thirdly, only a small fraction (12 per cent) of newspaper distribution is based on selling single copies. Almost 90 per cent of the newspapers are sold on the basis of subscription, which means that the papers do not have to rely on dramatic events in order to draw the reader's attention each day. In short, in Finland the newspapers reach a large segment of the population, and the market leaders are quality papers which do not have to sell themselves every day, since distribution is based on subscriptions. This all may have an effect both on the ways crime is reported, and the way people think about these matters.

Nordic co-operation

The early-1960s was a period of intensifying Nordic co-operation in legal matters. Crime and criminal justice were among the key issues in this agenda. In 1960 the Scandinavian Research Council was established with the support of the Ministries of Justice. This council became a central forum for the exchange of information between the Nordic countries. Interest in criminological research expanded and the status and resources of criminology were strengthened in the Nordic countries. The reform-work of the 1960s and 1970s in Finland was heavily influenced by this exchange of ideas, as well as by the legislative models offered by our Scandinavian neighbours (especially Sweden). In many instances liberal reforms could be defended with reference to positive experiences gained from other Nordic countries and the need for Inter-Nordic harmonization. This 'Nordic identity' was also strengthened by the fact that Finland was, in the 1960s, quickly reaching the levels of its other Scandinavian partners in economic and welfare resources.

A specific feature of this co-operation was that it was not founded on conventions but on non-binding agreements between the nations.[5] It was not led by politicians and governments, but by Ministries of Justice and their experts. It proved to be very effective and less bureaucratic. The results of this co-operation were manifested in legislative acts that have been adopted separately in each Nordic country, but with identical contents. These acts concern, for example, extradition from one Nordic country to another as well as the enforcement of sentences within these countries.

Judicial culture and sentencing structures

Furthermore, micro-level institutional arrangements and specific professional practices have contributed to this change. Co-operation with the judicial authorities — the judges and the prosecutors — and their 'attitudinal readiness' for liberal criminal policies have been of great importance in Finland. In many cases, legislators have been strongly supported by the judiciary and especially by the courts of first instance. Quite often the courts had changed their practice even before legislators had changed the law. In addition, the fact that judges and prosecutors are career officials with training in criminology and criminal policy in the law schools, contributes to this explanation. Moreover, different courses and seminars arranged for judges (and prosecutors) on a regular basis by judicial authorities — in co-operation with the universities — have also had an impact on sentencing and prosecutorial practices.

The Finnish sentencing structure, which treats sentencing as an area of normal judicial decision-making guided by valid sources of sentencing law, may also function as a shield against political pressures. Finland (and Sweden) has a highly structured system with detailed written provision on the general principles and specific sentencing criteria to be taken into account in

---

5. The foundation for the co-operation is based on the Helsinki Treaty (1962). The treaty obliged the contracting parties to 'strive to create uniform provisions concerning crime and sanctions of crime'. A general overview is to be found in Lahti, 2000.

deciding on both the type and the amount of punishment. Arguments that affect sentencing must be presented in a form that fits the accepted rules and standards. The specific structure of the decision-making process, as outlined in the general sentencing provisions (the 'notion of normal punishments') stresses the importance of uniformity in sentencing (i.e. avoiding unwarranted disparities). This places the existing sentencing patterns in a central position as starting points in sentencing. And this, in turn, gives sentencing strong inertia: rapid changes are unlikely to occur, unless or until these have been channelled through the valid sources of sentencing law (see in general Lappi-Seppälä, 2001).

Socio-economic and political factors

All of the factors mentioned above are more or less obvious to anyone familiar with Finnish society in general. However, a full account of the factors behind the 'humanisation of the Finns' should be able to explain it more fully. In the first place, it should explain the timing, why this process started when it did, and why the liberal policies have (more or less) prevailed ever since. Second, these explanations should be able to cover also the patterns to be found among different countries. This applies particularly to the other Scandinavian countries, as the policies adopted in Finland were strongly influenced by similar policies in the other Nordic countries. In short, the explanations for the Finnish 'exceptionalism' should also be able to be seen in common with the more general Scandinavian 'exceptionalism'.

This search for a more substantial explanation should start from the Nordic Welfare Model and the underlying social, political and cultural factors. Introducing these social and economic factors into the analyses (and the respective changes within them) helps to explain both the timing and the prevailing regional patterns. Liberal penal policies are associated with a strong welfare state. The years of penal liberation in Finland were also a period of radical social, economic and structural changes. From 1950 to 1970 the gross domestic product of Finland increased by 125 per cent, while the growth in OECD was on average 75 per cent, and in the UK and the USA 55 per cent. Between 1960 and 1998 the total public social expenditure as a percentage of GDP increased in Finland by 18 percentage points, in OECD countries by 13, in the UK by 11, and in the USA by 7. Between 1966 and 1990 the income difference, measured by the Gini-index, was reduced in Finland by 8.3 points (from 33.4–25.1). In short, Finland was joining the Scandinavian welfare family in terms of the level of economic prosperity, welfare provisions and income-equality, and this change was also reflected in our penal policies. By way of contrast, the prison expansion in the Anglo-Saxon world coincided with the concomitant general scaling down of welfare state provision (see Garland, 2001).

Nordic countries still represent a regional unity both in terms of their liberal penal model and their universalistic welfare model. This welfare model, in turn, has its own background, which also should be included in the analyses. Thus, giving a more complete explanation for those changes that occurred in Finland since the 1960s would require a wider perspective which encompasses also general social, economic, political and cultural factors.[6]

Imprisonment rates and crime rates

A profound change in the use of imprisonment naturally raises questions about its effects on crime rates. There are several well-known methodological difficulties in measuring causal relations between crime rates and prison rates. However, the possibility of comparing the Nordic countries, with strong social and structural similarities but with very different penal histories, provides an unusual opportunity to see how drastic changes in penal practices in one country have been reflected in the crime rates, compared with countries which have kept their penal systems more or less stable. *Figure 4* illustrates the incarceration and reported crime rates in Finland, Sweden, Denmark and Norway from 1950 to 2010.

There is a striking difference in the use of imprisonment (top), and a striking similarity in the trends in recorded criminality (bottom). That Finland has substantially reduced its incarceration rate has not disturbed the symmetry of Nordic crime rates. These figures, once again, support the general criminological conclusion that crime and incarceration rates are fairly independent of one another; each rises and falls according to its own laws and dynamics.

---

6. The role of macro-sociological factors in explaining penal differences is analysed in more detail in Lappi-Seppälä, 2008.

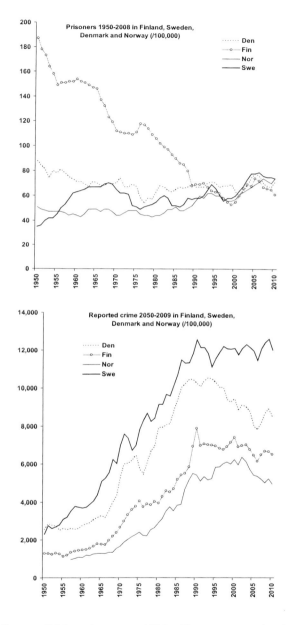

Sources: Falck et al., 2003, and Kristofferssen, 2010 updated.

Figure 4 — Scandinavian Prison Rates and Crime Rates 1950–2009

The Role of Restorative Justice — Mediation

Mediation has gained a substantial role in the handling of criminal cases in Finland; however, this has taken place outside the criminal law.[7] Mediation does not constitute a part of the criminal justice system but it has frequent interrelations with that system as far as referral of cases and their further processing is concerned. The criminal code mentions an agreement or settlement between the offender and the victim as a possible grounds for waiving of charges by the prosecutor, or waiving of punishment by the court and as a grounds of mitigating the sentence.

The first mediation experiment in Finland started in 1983 (see further: Grönfors, 1989 and Iivari, 2000). As was the case in other countries, the intention was to provide an alternative to the official criminal justice system in dealing with certain offences. By the early 2000s mediation services were available to about 80 per cent of the population. In order to secure equality before the law — and to expand the application of mediation schemes — mediation was extended to cover the whole country in 2006 by passing a national law on mediation. Provincial governments are obliged to arrange mediation services in their region, either in co-operation with municipal authorities or with other public or private partners. The overall organizational responsibility and supervision lies within the Ministry of Social Affairs. Mediators have no formal training requirements, but they must have proper 'skills and experience'. General preconditions for mediation include voluntariness and ability of the parties to understand the content and meaning of mediation. The parties have also always the right to withdraw from the process.

The 2006 legislation did not change this basic character of mediation, but gives closer instructions on how to handle mediation cases where minors are involved. Furthermore, there are general guidelines for the selection of cases suitable for mediation. In other respects, the law is quite flexible and much less formal that the corresponding Norwegian law, to take one example. In this context mediation was also given an official definition in the law, referring to '...a non-chargeable service in which a crime suspect and the victim of that crime are provided the opportunity to meet confidentially through

---

7. Other elements of restorative justice in the Finnish criminal justice system are discussed in more detail in Lappi-Seppälä, 1996.

an independent conciliator, to discuss the mental and material harm caused to the victim by the crime and, on their own initiative, to agree on measures to redress the harm' (*Law on Mediation,* 2006, Chapter 1, Section 1).

The process

Mediation can start at any time between the commission of the offence and execution of the sentence and by any of the involved parties. Once a case has been referred to the mediation office, the office contacts the parties in order to ascertain their willingness to participate in mediation. Where this is agreed, a first meeting is arranged. The mediation programme is managed by the municipal social welfare office. The initiative for submitting cases to mediation comes, as a rule, from the police or from the prosecutor. However, the consent of all parties is required before going into reconciliation. The sessions are often held in the evening, participants are addressed on first-name terms and the flow of discussion is relatively free. The mediator's principal role is only to mediate and act on a neutral basis. Once the process has started it normally leads to a written contract that contains the subject (what sort of offence), the content of a settlement (how the offender has consented to repair the damage), the place and date of the restitution as well as consequences for a breach of the contract.

What happens after a successful mediation depends largely on the category and seriousness of the offence. In complainant offences, successful mediation automatically means that the prosecutor drops the case. In non-complainant offences it is under the discretion of the prosecutor whether he/she is willing to drop the charge. This would be possible according to the law if prosecution seemed 'either unreasonable or pointless' due to successful reconciliation, and if non-prosecution did not violate 'an important public or private interest'. In mediation cases non-prosecution is, therefore, always discretionary. Unlike in some other countries, mediation does not automatically divert the case from the criminal justice system. This may narrow its diversionary effect, but on the other hand, it also prevents mediation from becoming restricted to trivial cases.

Aims and achievements

The roots of Finnish mediation initiatives are located in the abolitionist writings of Thomas Mathiesen and Nils Christie in Norway and Louk Hulsman in The Netherlands in the 1970s, as well as in the practices and experiments in New Zealand and North America (see Grönfors, 1989). The elements of informality, voluntariness, and community involvement were crucial from the very beginning. The forerunners of the mediation movement were careful not to integrate the system too closely into the criminal justice as there were healthy suspicions against 'institutionalisation'. Mediation had been presented as form of diversion and as an alternative to criminal justice. And this 'informal appeal' may partly explain its initial success and fast spreading in Finland. There were plenty of voluntary workers who wished to join a project that promised to do things differently and aimed to deliver services that the official criminal justice system was unable to deliver. In this respect mediation has retained its original promise: it has remained as a genuinely informal alternative.

Having said this, it is equally clear that its diversionary function is restricted only to minor offences, not to those punishable by imprisonment (at least in Finland). The diversionary role of mediation can be seen most notably in the expansion in the use of non-prosecution among juveniles. It is equally clear that for a substantial number of victims, mediation has provided a means to receive at least some compensation from the offender. One of the main goals of mediation is also to interrupt the criminal career of young offenders. The hope has been that the mediation process would enhance the offender's ability to realise the meaning of his or her offence and thereby enable a fuller accountability for the crime. Some studies, indeed, indicate that reoffending is more common in a control group than among those young offenders that have undergone the mediation process.[8]

The most heated debates have concerned the use of mediation in cases of domestic violence. During the enactment of the mediation act, feminist organizations expressed strong doubts of the suitability of mediation in these cases. Consequently, Parliament, when approving the bill, added

---

8. See Mielityinen, 1999. Re-offending was examined in a quasi-experimental setting, which still leaves open the question whether control group and mediation group were similar enough. For broader discussions on the experiences of mediation in Finland see: Elonheimo, 2010: Grönfors, 1989, Iivari, 2000 and 2010; and Lappi-Seppälä, 1996, all with references.

extra limitations for the use of mediation in these cases. According to the law domestic violence may be submitted to mediation only by the initiative of the police or prosecutor. Also the governmental programme for the year 2011–2015 obliges the authorities to evaluate the existing mediation practices in cases of intimate and domestic violence.

A recent evaluation study on mediation takes a critical view of some of these restrictions. According to Iivari (2010), interviews with police and prosecuting officials suggest that the heads of mediation offices and municipal social workers should have more discretion to decide which cases are referred. In overall terms, the key objectives of mediation — expertise, objectivity, confidentiality and justice were met in the majority of cases. Clients who had been involved in mediation of domestic discord had the most positive experiences of the objectivity, confidentiality and voluntary nature of mediation. On the other hand, in domestic violence mediation had not generally furthered the treatment of mental harm caused to the victim. The results suggest that mediation in domestic violence involves true challenges and careful preparation. There is also a risk of disappointment. There were striking differences between the experiences of those who had reached an agreement and those who had not. The latter group expressed deep disappointment over the mediation. All in all one out of three of those who did not reach agreement and answered the free-form questions (and five per cent of all respondents) reported having had very negative experiences with mediation, principally in terms of the quality of the services. According to the author of report, this warrants 'further intensive training for and supervision of mediators. It also warrants consideration of the introduction of a requirement for certification of voluntary mediators' (Iivari, 2010).

Practice

In terms of numbers mediation plays a substantial role in the Finnish justice system. After the introduction of mediation in the early 1980s, the total annual number of mediation cases had exceeded 5,000 by the mid-1990s. The enactment of the Mediation Act in 2006 extended mediation across the entire country and the latest statistics indicate about 12,000 referrals to mediation in 2010, double the number of annually imposed unconditional prison sentences. Detailed statistics for 2010 show the following profile. The clear majority of cases involve either minor forms of assault and battery (46 per cent) or minor property offences (30 per cent).

Most cases are sent to mediation by the police (81 per cent) or by the prosecutor (15 per cent). Only a small number of cases come directly from either the parties or the social welfare authorities (2 per cent each). In almost half of the cases the offender was under the age of 21. Fifteen per cent of the cases involved children below the age of criminal responsibility, and one fifth were attributable to the age group from 15–17. The majority of the victims were aged 30 and older.

Out of the 12,000 referrals mediation was started in 71 per cent (8459) of cases. Out of these 82 per cent (6,908) ended in an agreement. In all, 11,271 separate agreements were drafted. Out of these 40 per cent consisted of monetary compensations and 5 per cent compensation through work. The majority of agreements consisted of symbolic compensation. an apology (36 per cent), withdrawal from claims (11 per cent) and promise not to repeat the behaviour (7 per cent) and return of the property (1 per cent). Still, the total value of monetary compensations was 1.95 million euros.

Conclusion

Today, Finnish penal policy can be seen as an example of a pragmatic and non-moralistic Nordic approach, with a clear social policy orientation. It reflects the values of the Nordic welfare-state ideal and emphasises the fact that measures against social marginalisation and equality work also as measures against crime. Factors relating to all this have discussed within this essay. As has become evident, the 30-year period of decarceration would not have been possible without political consensus and agreements on principles. It was reached and upheld partly thanks to an active and influential group of penal reformers, working actively within political life, civil service, judiciary, universities and research institutes. The political system in general, however, showed little interest in crime policy. Also the media retained a fairly reasonable attitude on these issues, at least in comparison with many other countries. For Finland, the intensified Nordic co-operation in legal matters and the strengthening sense of a common Nordic identity provided extra elements in our effort to humanize the Finnish criminal justice system in the 1960s and 70s. Further developments were sustained and supported also by the effective spreading of criminological insight and knowledge among the criminal justice practitioners, often in co-operation with the Ministry of Justice, judiciary and universities.

A full account of the factors behind the humanisation of the Finnish penal system should, however, explain more. It should be able to address the question of timing: why did this all start when it did? The explanation should also be general enough to cover patterns across countries – and possibly even across regions. As the policies adopted in Finland were highly influenced by similar policies in the other Nordic countries, the explanations for the 'Finnish exceptionalism' should be able to cover also the more general 'Scandinavian exceptionalism'.[9]

The old slogan — 'Good Social Policy is the Best Criminal Policy' — tells the essential: societies do better by investing more money in schools, social work and families than in prisons. Historical and comparative analyses confirm that liberal penal policies are associated with strong welfare states.[10] The years of penal liberalisation in Finland were also the period when Finland was joining the Scandinavian welfare family in terms of economic prosperity, welfare provision and income equality. That change was reflected also in our penal policies, in the same way as the prison expansion in the Anglo-Saxon world coincides with the concomitant general dismantling of welfare states.

But also the Nordic welfare states — and Finland perhaps more than the others — have suffered from the economic crisis during the last 20 years. Nordic welfare states were not saved from the cutbacks in the public sector and the general scaling down of welfare provisions, increases in income differences and growing social distances. And also the Nordic criminal justice systems have received their share of the global 'punitive turn'. These changes may not be comparable in type and magnitude to those that have taken place elsewhere in Europe and overseas, but they are still real for the Nordic peoples (see, for instance: Tham, 2001 and Balvig, 2005).

---

9. At the other end of the scale we would find 'American exceptionalism' and the expansion of penal culture in the USA and many Anglo-Saxon countries (see Garland, 2001 and Tonry, 2004 and 2009).
10. On the relationships between macro-sociological factors and penal practices see Lappi-Seppälä, 2007 and 2008.

The question of whether Finland will also face similar growth in its prison population as is found in so many other countries would probably receive different answers from different observers. An optimist would point out that very few of the social, political, economic and cultural background conditions which explain the rise of mass imprisonment in the USA apply to Finland. The social and economic security granted by the Nordic welfare state model may still function as a social backup system for a tolerant criminal policy. Political culture still encourages negotiation and respects expert opinions. Social security, equality, trust and legitimacy granted by an affluent, universalistic welfare state will dampen public fears, punitive fervour and reactive populist posturing. The fact that Finland managed to reverse the steep increase in imprisonment rates at the turn of the millennium into almost as steep a decrease from 2005 onwards gives some support for this assertion.

For a pessimist, neo-liberalism has gained a firm footing in Finland from the early-1990s onwards, and will tighten its grip also in the coming years. Punitive and populist trends—more visible in Sweden and Denmark—will invade Finland also. An optimist might argue that the tone, still, is different compared with similar changes in many other countries. The Nordic Welfare Model may be under threat, but it certainly has not been abandoned or rejected. On the contrary, it has become a part of the common Nordic identity and is widely supported across the whole political field, at least at the level of political rhetoric. Uncontested as this model is, it may well prove to be one of the cornerstones of the argument for a more social and humane penal policy.

References

Andenaes, J. (1974), *Punishment and Deterrence,* Ann Arbor: University of Michigan Press.

Anttila, I. (1971), *Conservative and Radical Criminal Policy in the Nordic Countries,* Scandinavian Studies in Criminology, Vol.3. Oslo, pp. 9–21.

Balvig, F. (2005), 'When Law and Order Returned to Denmark', *Journal of Scandinavian Studies in Criminology,* Vol.5, pp.167–187.

Elonheimo, H. (2010), *Nuorisorikollisuuden esiintyvyys, taustatekijät ja sovittelu,* Turun Yliopiston Julkaisuja 2009/2010, Turku.

Falck, S., Von Hofer, H. and Storgaard; A. (2003), *Nordic Criminal Statistics 1950–2000*, Department of Criminology, Stockholm University, Report 2003:3.

Garland, D. (2001), *The Culture of Control: Crime and Social Order in Contemporary Society*, Chicago: University of Chicago Press.

Grönfors, M. (1989), 'Ideals and Reality in Community Mediation' in Wright, M. and Galaway, B. (eds.), *Mediation and Criminal Justice*, London: Sage, pp.140–151.

Iivari, J. (2000), 'Victim-offender Mediation in Finland' in European Forum for Victim-Offender Mediation and Restorative Justice, *Victim-offender Mediation in Europe: Making Restorative Justice Work*. Leuven: University Press.

Iivari, J. (2010), '*Oikeutta Oikeuden Varjossa. Rikossovittelulain Täytäntöönpanon Arviointitutkimus*' ('Justice in the Shadow of Justice'). An Evaluation Study of the Implementation of the Act on Mediation in Criminal Cases, National Institute for Health and Welfare (THL), Report 5/2010. Helsinki.

Kivivuori, J. and Lehti M. (2011), 'Homicide in the Nordic Area: Finland and Sweden Compared' in Tonry M. and Lappi-Seppälä, T. (eds.), *Crime and Justice: a Review of Research*, vol.40, Chicago: University of Chicago Press, 109–198.

Kristofferssen, R. (2010), *Correctional Statistics of Denmark, Finland, Iceland, Norway and Sweden 2004–2008,* Oslo: Correctional Service of Norway Staff Academy 1/2010.

Lahti, R. (2000), 'Towards a Rational and Humane Criminal Policy: Trends in Scandinavian Penal Thinking', *Journal of Scandinavian Studies and Crime Prevention*, vol. 1/2000, pp.141–155.

Lappi-Seppälä, T. (1995), 'General Prevention — Hypotheses and Empirical Evidence' in *Ideologi og Empiri i Kriminologien*, Reykjavik: Scandinavian Research Council for Criminology, pp. 136–159.

Lappi-Seppälä, T. (1996) 'Reparation in Criminal Law: Finnish National Report' in Eser, A. and Walther, S. (eds.), *Wiedergutmachung im Strafrecht*, Freiburg: Max-Planck-Institut, s.317–420.

Lappi-Seppälä, T. (2001), 'Sentencing and Punishment in Finland: The decline of the Repressive Ideal' in *Punishment and Penal Systems in Western Countries*, Tonry M. and Frase, R. (eds.) New York: Oxford University Press, pp. 92–150.

Lappi-Seppälä, T. (2008), 'Trust, Welfare, and Political Culture: Explaining Differences in National Penal Policies' in Tonry. M. (ed.), *Crime and Justice: A Review of Research,* vol. 37, Chicago: University of Chicago Press, pp.313–387.

Lappi-Seppälä,T. (2011a), 'Nordic Youth Justice: Juvenile Sanctions in Four Nordic Countries' in Tonry, M. and Lappi-Seppälä, T. (eds.), *Crime and Justice: A Review of Research,* vol.40, Chicago: University of Chicago Press, pp. 199–264.

Lappi-Seppälä, T. (2011b), 'Changes in Penal Policy in Finland' in Kury, H. and Shea, E. (eds.), *Punitivity: International Developments,* Vol.1, *Punitiveness: Global Phenomenon?* Bochum, Germany, Universitätäverlag Dr N. Brockmeyer, pp. 251–287.

Lappi-Seppälä, T. and Tonry M. (2011), 'Crime, Criminal Justice, and Criminology in the Nordic countries' in Tonry, M. and Lappi-Seppälä, T. (eds.), *Crime and Justice: A Review of Research,* vol. 40, Chicago: University of Chicago Press, pp. 1–32.

Mielityinen, I. (1999), *Rikos Ja Sovittelu,* Helsinki: National Research Institute of Legal Policy 167/1999.

Ministry of Justice (2006), *Criminal Policy in the Welfare State: Policy Plan for 2007–2011,* Helsinki: Ministry of Justice.

Tham, H. (2001), 'Law and Order as a Leftist Project?' in *Punishment & Society,* Vol.3, No.3, London and New York: Sage Publications, pp.409–426.

Tonry, M. and Lappi-Seppälä, T. (2011), *Crime and Justice: A Review of Research,* Vol. 40, Chicago: University of Chicago Press.

Törnudd, P. (1993), *Fifteen Years of Decreasing Prison Rates in Finland,* Helsinki: National Research Institute of Legal Policy, Research Communication 8.

Törnudd, P. (1996), *Facts, Values and Visions.* (Essays in criminology and crime policy), Anttila, I., Aromaa, K., Jaakkola, R., Lappi-Seppälä, T. and Takala, H. (eds.), Helsinki: National Research Institute of Legal Policy Publication No.138.

18

Conclusions

David Cornwell, John Blad and Martin Wright

How should human societies induce their members to behave well to each other? It can be done by peer pressure, which in turn can act through aspiration to be well-regarded by others, or by the threat, and on occasion imposition, of consequences for causing harm to another individual or the community. This requires a process for deciding whether the accused person was indeed responsible for the act (or confirming it if it is obvious or the person admits it), and then what the consequences should be.

There are two main traditions for selecting these consequences. One is that they should be punishments, which some people regard as synonymous with 'justice'. The other is to persuade and enable the offender to desist, and then to re-accept him or her. In the last half-century two further elements have been added, which also have ancient historical roots: reparation for the harm done, and involvement of those affected in the dialogue and decision-making. Punishment requires strong safeguards against wrongful conviction, and clear definitions of actions that are punishable: in effect, those acts that are so injurious to an individual or the community that the state must intervene.

But we may ask whether this has gone too far: the process, because it can be seen to induce the wish to minimise responsibility on the part of the offender, and safeguards against wrongful conviction may lead to the acquittal of the guilty; and the outcome, because punishment makes offenders less likely to admit responsibility, makes them think of themselves not their victims. Even with the recent improvements of the legal rights of victims in the criminal procedure (in some countries) one cannot conclude that a kind of justice is developing that serves the interests and needs of victims, offenders and society in a balanced, just and effective way. Should more types of wrongdoing therefore be dealt with under civil law or by informal processes? These are some of the issues which contributors to this volume have addressed. Our conclusions will inevitably only bring out a small selection of the complex and varied arguments they have presented.

An historical perspective has been provided by David Cornwell and Fred McElrea; Judge McElrea maintains that we are in the middle of a revolution, of the procedure as much as of the outcome of the justice process, and (with Serge Gutwirth and Paul De Hert) he proposes that courts and the criminal law should be the last resort. Like Claire Spivakovsky, he points to the ancient roots of a process which involved all those affected, and in which the process itself is a significant part of the outcome. The essence of this is that before imposing a solution by the authority of the state, applying complex definitions of what is 'criminal' and incurs punishment, it is based on dialogue, which is itself normative, in other words people set their own standards (Federico Reggio).

Gutwirth and De Hert propose a transfer of many offences to the civil law domain, reducing the scope of the penal law. In a similar vein, Lode Walgrave argues that not every immoral act should be prosecuted. However, he concedes that if the offence is a 'public event', people expect the authorities to respond. Someone's autonomy has been intruded upon and should be restored, but that is not enough: the public also needs to be reassured, by state intervention, but he presents arguments against using punishment, in the sense of inflicting pain, for this purpose. However, the conventional system is in place: any changes depend on the attitudes of those who administer them, and these are explored in Borbála Fellegi's study. It is likely that the revolution will be a gradual one, and meanwhile several authors consider the relationship of criminal justice to civil justice, which for some (such as Walgrave) is almost synonymous with restorative justice.

Under conventional criminal law Susan Easton and Christine Piper show some of the difficulties in the attempt to make punitive sentences proportionate to culpability. Sir Louis Blom-Cooper proposes that courts should limit themselves to deciding upon conviction and sentence, leaving responsibility for social measures, rehabilitation and reparation to other agencies.

He also suggests the use of civil law (and the civil standard of proof) as a prerequisite for a criminal trial in cases of rape and serious sexual assault. Even if the case did not proceed to the criminal court, more victims would be likely to gain the important satisfaction of having established their case in the courtroom. For Bas van Stokkom a restorative 'sanction-track' for those who show remorse and accept responsibility would operate in parallel with 'disciplining' sanctions for those who do not. Repentance would justify mitigating just deserts with mercy.

There are concerns, expressed by John Blad, that the criminal justice system is in fact becoming less civilised in both main senses of the word. It is often claimed that justice is there to control crime (for example by Lord Steyn, quoted by Blom-Cooper) and to prevent the Hobbesian war of all against all by monopolising the legitimate use of violence. The classical function of crime control should be limited and counterbalanced by the other classical aim of legal protection of the suspected offender by a more or less autonomous system of normative rules and principles, harnessing the power to punish. Besides the well-known flaws of the criminal justice system in controlling crime, its crucial function of protecting the suspected fellow-citizen against harsh and disproportionate punishments has begun to fade in recent decades. Incited by political meddling and mass media, the almost daily creation of new criminal offences, and the demonisation of minority groups such as immigrants, Roma, welfare claimants, and 'feral' young people, criminal justice seems to be becoming a theatre of stigmatisation and a celebration of the cruelty it was classically intended to control and limit. We need to reverse this trend, condemning the offence while respecting the offender's dignity, using less punishment and more restorative methods.

There has been a tendency to limit restorative justice to minor offences, for example in the 'neighbourhood justice panels' introduced as pilots in England and Wales in 2012, but Ann Skelton proposes that some cases could be removed from the criminal law altogether by using the civil law in a restorative way. Thomas Trenczek makes the case for using restorative justice in crimes arising from relationships including, controversially, violence within the family. It can also be used in the most serious cases of the abuse of power. Martin Wright cites a South African case of a heavy yet restorative sentence for rape which followed the principle of *primum non nocere* (above all, do not make things worse) by taking account of the victim's needs and wishes;[1] he also proposes the introduction of restorative meetings between delinquent leaders of big corporations (not their lawyers) and the victims of their mis-selling of pharmaceuticals, insurance and other products, or the environmental damage, injuries, illnesses and deaths resulting from their operations.

It remains to be seen how restorative justice can be implemented. Jean-Pierre Bonafé-Schmitt explains the difficulties encountered in France; in Norway it is used extensively and nationwide, and carried out by lay mediators, as Per Andersen describes. This is also the case in Finland, where Tapio Lappi-Seppälä shows how it has been accompanied by a massive reduction in the prison population, and is run by the Ministry of Social Affairs rather than the Ministry of Justice.

Is this, as Fred McElrea suggests, a revolution, or, using Howard Zehr's term (Zehr, 1995: *Chapter 6*), a paradigm shift? Thomas Kuhn, in his *The Structure of Scientific Revolutions* (re-published in 2012), suggests that paradigm shifts occur when the current paradigm is seen not to be working. A crisis provides an opportunity to re-examine the existing theory. For a while those working within the current paradigm resist the new one, or try to accommodate it within the familiar one, as the 16th-century astronomers tried to fit Copernicus' discovery into their geocentric view of the Cosmos. People see what their experience has taught them to see. In this volume are critiques of the conventional Western paradigm of social control. This is based on the idea that societies consist in the main of mostly law-abiding citizens. Over the centuries they have compiled lists of things which people are not allowed to do, which are constantly added to (and occasionally subtracted from) by their elected legislatures. The threat of punishment is intended to deter anyone from breaking these rules; a person who is convicted of (or admits to) having done so is brought before an authority figure (a judge) who imposes a punishment. The most severe punishment (in most Western democracies) is imprisonment, the duration of which is not determined by the time likely to be required to induce the offender to change his or her ways, but is supposed to reflect, quite arbitrarily, the heinousness of the offence.

---

1.   The sentence was later set aside by the Supreme Court of Appeal and replaced with an effective term of imprisonment of ten years.

This paradigm has major flaws, as contributors to this volume have pointed out. It relies on coercion (by force if necessary) and deterrence (i.e. fear of the consequences for oneself), imposed by authority, with little participation of those affected or even of the offender. The index of prohibited actions, i.e. the criminal code, grows ever longer but is never complete; many of them are also civil wrongs (torts) and could be dealt with as such. Punishment is only partly effective, or even counterproductive, and causes 'collateral damage' to innocent people. When a particular type of crime hits the headlines, politicians increase the maximum penalty (or even the minimum) and claim to have 'taken action'. These are familiar criticisms. The demand for punishment seems 'insatiable' (to use Braithwaite and Pettit's (1990) word) and prisons are chronically overcrowded. It is, as Blom-Cooper comments in this volume, not really a system.

This paradigm, in short, is in crisis. Some responses do not renounce it, but try to modify it, for example by compiling sentencing guidelines without acknowledging the fundamental inherent anomalies. But a new paradigm is being developed, based on different principles: to respond to harm by looking for ways to repair it and heal the victim. This volume shows how in some countries the process is facilitated by trained lay people (Andersen, Lappi-Seppälä) and non-governmental organizations (Trenczek). In psychological terms, the aim would not be to deter the offender on the behaviourist principle of fear of the consequences for himself, but to encourage empathy and hence remorse for the consequences for the victim (and this not infrequently also leads the victim to feel empathy for the offender). The person who caused the harm would be given the opportunity to overcome the stigma by 'earned redemption' (Bazemore's term, quoted in Bazemore and Schiff, 2005: 51). Various authors discuss whether this model could exist alongside conventional criminal justice or could aspire, eventually, to replace it.

These ideas have spread beyond criminal justice to a vision in which dialogue and consensus would be the preferred approach to maintaining justice (in the sense of fairness) and social order (the term preferred by Bonafé-Schmitt to 'social control'). Schoolchildren are being shown how to resolve conflicts restoratively, rather than by force or by appealing to higher authority. Community mediation centres are doing the same in neighbourhoods and workplaces. Paradoxically, the concept can resonate both with the communitarian Left and with the Right which believes in reducing the overreach of the state. Its advocates believe that the future of a civilised society will be restorative.

* * * * *

What would a restorative system be like? It would move away from the constant increase of state intervention towards use of civil law, and in particular mediation and conferencing; the tendency would be away from control by those in authority and towards increased civic participation, which we maintain would have a civilising influence both on the process and on the society in which it takes place. Without being too detailed or prescriptive we can begin by proposing that it should be based on coherent, stated principles. Secondly, rethinking of some traditional ideas will be needed. Thirdly, practicalities of putting it into effect need to be thought through, and developed in the light of experience. Lastly, it would extend into the rest of society as the means of maintaining social order. The principles may be summarised as:

1. The response to wrongdoing should be based on repairing the harm caused.

2. Persons affected should be able to take part in a dialogue about that response; the dialogue would itself be part of the response.

3. Individuals and community organizations would be involved in the process, and in providing the resources to assist in the repair of harm.

4. The state would oversee the process, with safeguards, to make sure that any reparation was fulfilled, but would intervene no more than necessary. It would also be parsimonious in defining 'crimes', that is, actions so damaging to individuals or the community that the state must control the process; other actions would remain in the 'civil' sphere.

5. Information about the circumstances in which the harm was caused would be collected and used to build social policy.

6. Interventions would be voluntary where possible; courts, coercion and ultimately detention would be regarded as the last resort.

Secondly, perhaps the greatest change would be from a social model based on coercion and a psychological one based on behaviourism ('carrot and stick') to a model based on relationships, respect, ethically positive example and the encouragement of empathy. The deterrence of externally imposed punishment and stigma (which set an ethically negative example) would be replaced by internally experienced remorse and the rebuilding of self-respect and the respect of others. This appears 'softer', and may well take more time and effort, but a social order based on consent should be more stable, and pleasanter, than one based on the use of force, even if force has to be held in reserve for general protection when the power of 'persuading and enabling' is not enough. To make this more credible, there needs to be more recognition of the ineffectiveness and even damaging effects of punishment, as Walgrave points out in this volume: big corporations can shrug off fines as 'operating expenses', criminals make their punishment a 'badge of honour', and it has been said that most hardened criminals are hardened in prison. They are motivated not to avoid their criminal behaviour but to avoid being caught, by the use of everything from clever lawyers to extreme violence. The effect of deterrent threats may be what Braithwaite calls 'reactance': 'intentions to control are reacted to as attempts to limit our freedom, which lead us to reassert that freedom by acting contrary to the direction of control' (Braithwaite, 2002: 106–7).

This would be linked to a reconsideration of sentencing. The principle of repairing harm would be the primary aim. The seriousness of the offence (the amount of harm) would be expressed by the amount of reparation. If additional measures were considered necessary for that purpose, this could be marked by a prison sentence; but it would be suspended unless detention was necessary for the protection of the public or the enforcement of the reparative measures. When possible the reparative actions would be agreed voluntarily by dialogue among those affected. Courts and coercion would be held in reserve as the last resort, but used parsimoniously.

Thirdly, how would it work? This can only be outlined here, but a framework could be on the following lines. When a person or persons are harmed by another, and know who he or she is, the first recourse could be to a mediation service. If the matter could not be resolved or was too serious, or the perpetrator was unknown, it could be reported to the police. They in turn, or the prosecutor, could refer the case to mediation, and if resolved it could be discontinued. Failing that, the case would go to court; before sentence a restorative meeting could be held, which the victim could attend and in most cases the agreement would form the basis of the sentence. Courts would also retain their function of determining cases where the accused denies the offence; but there is reason to believe that there would be less of what McElrea calls 'putting the prosecution to the proof', when the perpetrator denies the offence in the hope that there will be some gap in the prosecution's case.

The various possible contingencies would have to be provided for: the commonest would be support for the victim if the offender is not found, but also cases where the offender was willing and the victim refused, the victim was unwilling, a restorative meeting was considered likely to be harmful to either party (and means for determining that would be needed), cases of personality disorder, and so on.

The community would have to play its part, by providing a nationwide network of mediation services (either as NGOs or, as in Scandinavia, by municipalities), and by making available the resources needed to enable offenders to make their reparation, whether by work or by undergoing education, training, treatment or therapy. Another question is whether mediation is best conducted by members of other professions, such as police or probation, or by trained lay people, who have shown in Norway, Finland and elsewhere that they can provide a competent service to a professional standard, and it can be argued that for economic reasons alone, the state is unlikely to employ enough full-time mediators to provide a service to all who could benefit by it.

Lastly, for the response to be truly a system it should include feedback. It would be accepted that the prevention of wrongful behaviour belongs in the realm of social and educational policy rather than criminal justice, and information collected in restorative meetings about the pressures towards crime would be fed back to policy-makers

Restorative principles would not be confined to the criminal justice system. They could be, and already are being, applied in schools, so that children learn to use them, rather than violence, to resolve disputes. Where possible parents of schoolchildren could be involved, and could apply these principles in their own life and work; this would be reinforced in time as the children reach maturity. This would of course be a gradual process, but could point the way to the growth of a civil society.

References

Bazemore, G. and Schiff, M. (2005), *Juvenile Justice Reform and Restorative Justice: Building Theory and Policy from Practice,* Devon, Cullompton: Willan Publishing.

Braithwaite, J. (2002), *Restorative Justice and Responsive Regulation,* New York: Oxford University Press.

Braithwaite, J. and Pettit, P. (1990), *Not Just Deserts: A Republican Theory of Justice*, Oxford: Clarendon.

Kuhn, T. S. (2012), *The Structure of Scientific Revolutions,* Chicago: University of Chicago Press.

Zehr, H. (1995), *Changing Lenses: A New Focus for Crime and Justice.* (2nd edn.). Scottdate, PA: Herald Press.

Index

C

H

T

Restorative Justice
An International Journal

new in
2013

Editor in Chief
Ivo Aertsen, University of Leuven, Belgium

Managing Editor
Estelle Zinsstag, University of Leuven, Belgium

Book Review Editor
Gerry Johnstone, University of Hull, UK

Editors
Stephan Parmentier, University of Leuven, Belgium
Inge Vanfraechem, University of Leuven, Belgium
Lode Walgrave, University of Leuven, Belgium

Please visit the Hart Publishing website to see the Editorial Board and International Advisory Board

3 issues per year

Online ISSN
2050-473X

Print ISSN
2050-4721

**Contributors to
Volume 1. Issue 1**
(in alphabetical order)

Ivo Aertsen
John Braithwaite
Valerie Braithwaite
Nils Christie
Kathleen Daly
Jan Froestad
Hsiao-fen Huang
Shadd Maruna
Gabrielle Maxwell
Stephan Parmentier
Christa Pelikan
Monika Reinhart
Joanna Shapland
Clifford Shearing
Ann Skelton
Josep Tamarit Sumalla
Inge Vanfraechem
Lode Walgrave
Martin Wright
Estelle Zinsstag

Book reviews by
Gill McIvor
Susan Sharpe
Bas van Stokkom

● Seeks to facilitate the development and exchange of the best and most rigorously researched theoretical and practical scholarship within the domain of Restorative Justice (RJ).

● Aims to gather and present in a systematised way the fruits of academic research as well as practice and policy related information on RJ worldwide.

● Publishes original, ground-breaking and innovative articles about RJ and contains a vibrant book review section in which new books relevant to RJ are reviewed by leading scholars in the field.

● An invaluable source of information for those working in the field of RJ - academics, researchers, practitioners, policy-makers and interested citizens.

● Please visit the Hart Publishing website for information about subscription rates and reduced rates for members of Criminology / Restorative Justice associations and students.
www.hartjournals.co.uk/rj

Hart Publishing, 16C Worcester Place, Oxford, OXI 2JW, UK
Tel +44 (0)1865 517530   **Fax** +44 (0)1865 510710   **E-mail** mail@hartpub.co.uk
Hart Publishing Ltd. is registered in England No. 3307205

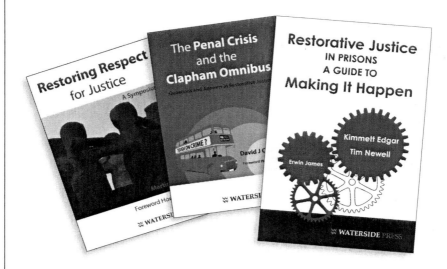